History
Magazine

October/November 2000

P9-APO-645

0 U.S
Cdn

Privateers of the Caribbean
Pirates Who Operated With Government Sanction

Bloodletting
A Once Universal, Now DiscreditedMedical Practice

Poor Richard's Almanac
The Book that Rivalled the Popularity of the Bible

Working Women in New York

The Panama Canal

The Knights Templar

11

0 56698

Cdn Publ. Mail Product
Sales Agreement No.

Contents of this issue of History Magazine

Bloodletting.
Page 15.

Panama Canal.
Page 29.

Privateers.
Page 36.

The Knights Templar.
Page 41.

VOLUME 2 NUMBER 1
EDITOR & PUBLISHER
Halvor Moorshead

EDITOR
Jeff Chapman

EDITORIAL ASSISTANTS
Jodi Avery
Roseanne Van Vierzen

SPECIAL PROJECTS MANAGER
Ron Wild

ADVERTISING SERVICES
Victoria Pratt

Published by Moorshead Magazines Ltd.
505 Consumers Road, Suite 500, Toronto,
ON, M2J 4V8 Canada
(416) 491-3699 Fax (416) 491-3996
E-Mail: magazine@moorshead.com

PRESIDENT
Halvor Moorshead

CIRCULATION MANAGER
Rick Cree

SUBSCRIPTION SERVICES
Jeannette Cox
Valerie Carmichael

History Magazine is published six times a year
(Feb/Mar, Apr/May, Jun/Jul, Aug/Sep,
Oct/Nov, Dec/Jan) by Moorshead Magazines.

POSTAL INFORMATION — CANADA
Canadian Publications Mail Product Sales
Agreement No. 1595695. Mailing address for
subscription orders, undeliverable copies and
change of address notice is:

History Magazine,
505 Consumers Road, Suite 500,
Toronto, Ontario, M2J 4V8 Canada

POSTAL INFORMATION — UNITED STATES
Periodical Postage Paid Lewiston, NY
USPS #018-154
Postmaster send address corrections to:
History Magazine,
PO Box 1201, Lewiston, NY, 14092-9934 USA
US Office of Publication
850 Cayuga St., Lewiston, NY, 14092

ISSN 1492-4307

© 2000 Moorshead Magazines Ltd.
Some illustrations copyright www.arttoday.com.

SUBSCRIPTIONS
Subscription rate for US (US funds):
1 year (6 issues) $24.00
2 years (12 issues) $40.00
3 years (18 issues) $55.00

Subscription rate for Canada (Cdn funds):
1 year (6 issues) $28.00 plus GST/HST
2 years (12 issues) $45.00 plus GST/HST
3 years (18 issues) $59.00 plus GST/HST
Quebec residents add 6.5% QST

GST # 139340186 RT
We welcome the submission of articles for publication. Please send a printed copy in addition to the
file in electronic format. Please do not send important documents with submissions. We will always
contact people who submit articles but the review
process may take several weeks. Authors' notes are
available on request.

Toll-Free Subscription Line:
1-877-731-4478

PRINTED IN CANADA
WEBSITE
www.history-magazine.com

Correction and Apology

In our last issue, the article "Poliomyelitis" by Dr. Peter A. Lawless was incorrectly attributed to another author. *History Magazine* sincerely apologizes for this serious error, and deeply regrets the inconvenience caused to Dr. Lawless.

CanCon

I am reading with interest *History Magazine*. In the first edition I was upset that Canada was not given much prominence, considering that many of your subscribers are Canadians. In the April edition there seemed to be a bit more of interest to Canadians. Nevertheless, it would be nice to read some stories on Canadian subjects with passing reference to the US, instead of vice versa.

Gordon Harris
Internet

The Wrong Words

As I read the article "The Blacksmith" by Nancy Hendrickson (April/May 2000), I stopped abruptly to see that she had listed the author of one of my favorite poems, *The Village Blacksmith*, incorrectly. The poem was written by Henry Wadsworth Longfellow. Perhaps Nancy was thinking of another great poet, William Wordsworth.

Charlene Homer
Nitro, WV

Stirring Up Controversy

In reference to Ron Wild's article on the stirrup (June/July 2000): Lynn White's theory that mounted combat is impossible without the stirrup gets passed from one non-horseman to another as gospel. I guess a bad idea never goes away.

It can be disproven on three grounds: first, modern reenactors have no trouble jousting without stirrups. Second, ancient historians who were eyewitnesses report on mounted combat without stirrups. Third, the US army required its trooper recruits and cadets to practice horse exercises without stirrups. If a soldier thought he needed the stirrups to fight, he would quit fighting when the stirrups broke.

If someone really wants to know what men and horses are capable of in combat, I suggest Ann Hyland's excellent work *The Medieval Warhorse* (Combined Books, Conshohocken, PA, 1994).

Ed Mills
Calvin, LA

Whose Slaves?

Beverly Downing's article "All Aboard" (August/September 2000) was informative and probably accurate. I found it good reading. I wish to comment, however, on a photographic caption that accompanies the piece, which refers to "African-American slaves". The picture is a depiction of slavers of the early 17th century. Were there "Americans" then? As this was long before the nation was formed, it would seem that English colonists would be a better description.

Sam T. Ferruzza
Laurel, MD

History Notes

Milk Chocolate: A Sweet Piece of History

The invention of milk chocolate only came about because of a love affair, a search for better baby food, and a failed candle business? History bears out that truth is often stranger than fiction.

Daniel Peter, originator of milk chocolate, began life as a Swiss butcher's son in 1836. Not content to follow in his father's footsteps, he began his working life as an assistant in a combination grocery store and candlemaking business. His employer, Madame Clement, seeing that Peter was intelligent and quick with his hands, soon promoted him to full time candlemaker. It seemed that his future was set, but it was not to be so. Shortly after Peter's entry into his career, the kerosene lamp arrived in Switzerland and replaced candles as the chief source of lighting. Almost overnight, Peter's profession became all but obsolete.

Luckily for Peter, and for all future chocolate lovers, he had been courting Miss Fanny Cailler, the eldest daughter of Master Chocolate Maker Francois Louis Cailler. Fanny introduced Peter to the world of chocolate and it was love at first sight, taste and smell.

Peter quickly became adept at working with the chocolate of the day which was bittersweet and slightly coarse. This chocolate was flavorful enough, but Peter dreamed of distinguishing his work by

Light or dark — take your pick!

creating a smoother, creamier version. Milk and sugar were plentiful, so he began experimenting by adding differing amounts of these ingredients to chocolate liquor. (Despite the implications of its name, chocolate liquor is the nonalcoholic sludge which remains after grinding roasted cocoa beans and extracting most of the cocoa butter produced.)

Try as he might, Peter could not coax the milk to mix smoothly with the chocolate liquor. What he did not yet realize was that milk has a high water content, and water causes chocolate to shrink and separate, which in turn caused each of his experiments to end in good-smelling but gloppy, unsaleable concoctions.

After eight long years of failure, Peter sought the aid of Swiss chemist Henri Nestlé. Nestlé had been busy developing a dairy-rich children's cereal and in

The easiest, most complete software for preserving your family history.

Generations is the most accurate and comprehensive genealogy software available today. It's also the easiest software to use. And, thanks to our partnership with Heritage Quest, you'll always have the newest and most up-to-date data available.

Generations Grande Suite 8.0 features 350 million names and resources, access to a professional genealogist, and the entire 1800 US Census. In addition, there's a new 3D Tree which allows you to "step inside" your family tree and view your roots with interactive animation.

Add video and audio clips to your files. Store old family movies, songs, pictures and keepsakes to enjoy anytime. These exciting new features, plus Generations' time-tested powerful tools and dynamic presentation software ensure your legacy will be strong for generations.

SIERRA Home™

For more information, please visit us at sierrahome.com

doing so had perfected a formula for removing over 60 percent of the water from milk. As a chemist, Nestlé saw that his new product, evaporated milk, might be just the cure for Peter's emulsion problems. He was correct and, in 1875 Daniel Peter and Henri Nestlé became the proud parents of the world's first milk chocolate.

Peter and Nestlé continued their association for the remainder of their lives. Their legacy lives on in the worldwide Nestlé Food Company and its specialized division of Peter's Chocolates. —KATHRYN CONRAD

Corsets

Corsets first came into fashion in the 1400s and were designed to make the female body more alluring. They were originally called a *cotte* from the French word *cote* meaning rib. These first corsets were made of linen stiffened with paste.

Iron corsets were introduced in the 1500s, but later more flexible whalebone stiffeners came into general

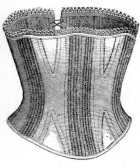

use. Whalebone and steel were the most popular stiffeners until elastic corsets took over in the 1930s following the invention of the process that turns latex into elastic thread.

The corset was thought of as a moral and medical necessity in the 1830s. Girls as young as four were laced-up in tight corsets. Tight lacing was thought of as virtuous and any woman whose corset was not properly laced was called a 'loose woman'. In the 1850s some resistance developed against tight corsetry with women adopting loose, flowing gowns but this did not last long and women continued to lace up.

Tight lacing was the rule for the upper classes, but working class women wore looser corsets and simpler clothes with less weight so they would be free to move around and do chores. It became a general rule that the tighter the corset, the higher the status in society. In the 1920s, corset sizes were standardized after a survey found that women were supposedly all made in five basic shapes regardless of height or weight. The corset changed again in the 1930s when cleavage in a corset was introduced.

Corsets remained widely used well into the 1900s. In 1950 people honored the corset by celebrating National Corset Week. A decade later, the corset went largely out of fashion with the realization that it was pulling the body into unnatural shapes and sizes.

Though the corset has been out of style for quite some time, they still enjoy a substantial mail order market. —ROSANNE VAN VIERZEN

The Plow

The plow ranks with the wheel as one of the greatest inventions of all time. It allowed the strength of an ox to be applied to agriculture.

The earliest plows were very different from those used today. The earliest was the "scratch plow" or "ard" made from a forked wooden branch. This formed a furrow for the seeds but did not turn the soil very effectively. This worked well enough on the light, dry soils of the middle east and southern Europe but

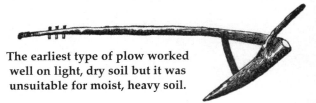

The earliest type of plow worked well on light, dry soil but it was unsuitable for moist, heavy soil.

was of no use on the heavy, wet (but rich) soils of northern Italy and northern Europe. The first improvement on this simple tool was to fit an iron tip to keep the end sharp.

The Roman Virgil (70-19BC) describes a plow in great detail in the *Georgics*, one of his poems describing husbandry. This had many of the elements of later plows including the beam (the framework which has the handles and is pulled by the ox or horse), the coulter (a vertical blade which cuts the earth), the share (which cuts the soil in a horizontal direction) and the moldboard (which turns the soil).

This type of plow however did not become common until a thousand years later when it was used to transform northern Europe. This type of plow, sometimes called the "heavy plow" greatly increased the fertility of the land as the whole of the top layer of soil was turned.

Numerous improvements were made to the plow during the early Industrial Revolution. Further modifications were necessary once the North American prairies were settled, as traditional designs could not cope with the hard, virgin soil.

The first plows were pulled by oxen and horses (and sometimes by people). Today tractors are almost universally the means of traction, but for a few decades stationary engines were used. These traction engines remained at the edge of the field and pulled the plow by a cable or chain.

Feather Quill Pens

Feathers were first used as writing instruments in Rome about 50BC. The word pen is derived from the Latin *penna* meaning feather. However, quill pens did not become popular until the 16th century.

The most commonly used feathers were from

geese. Swan feathers were considered premium grade but they were scarce and expensive. Fine lines were best made with crow feathers and occasionally eagle, owl, hawk and wild turkey feathers were used.

To get the strongest quill the feathers were removed from the third or fourth row of feathers while the bird was still alive. The left wing was preferred as it had the proper curl for right-handed writers. Tips were dipped in heated sand for greater strength. Still, quill pens only lasted about a week with regular use.

Thomas Jefferson is said to have specially bred geese to satisfy his great need for pens. Over 27 million quills a year were imported to Britain from St. Petersburg alone in the middle of the 19th century. At this time metal tips were made for quill pens as they rarely broke and did not need to be sharpened.

In 1884 feather quill pens became obsolete almost overnight with the invention of the fountain pen by insurance agent Lewis Waterman. —JODI AVERY

Matreshka

Matreshka, the popular Russian nesting dolls which are sized to fit inside one another, have two stories surrounding their origin.

One version suggests that the idea for the dolls originated on the Japanese island of Honshu and was brought to Russia at the end of the 19th century by the wife of Russian patron Savva I Mamontov.

The second version states that a Russian monk is responsible for bringing the idea of the special doll to Japan.

Whichever is true, the Chinese were said to have made something similar to nesting dolls as early 1000AD. However, their small carvings were in the form of buildings and palaces. It wasn't until the late 1800s that Russian doll-makers adopted the idea and started to make the matreshka.

The first sketches of the dolls were done by Serei Malyutib. The sketches illustrated a round-faced peasant girl with big, beaming eyes. The early dolls wore a *sarafan*, a floor-length garment held up by two straps, blouses that tied at the side or *kosovorotkas* and aprons. Each doll's hair was styled and

hidden under a bandanna of varying color. When dolls that depicted men were made they wore men's shirts, longs coats and were often painted with beards.

The name matreshka comes from Matrena, a popular Russian name for girls at the time. It originally comes from the Latin root *matrona*, which means mother or respected lady.

The popularity of the doll originally spread in the 1880s because of the renewed interest the Russians had in preserving their traditions while their culture and economy evolved. Eventually, the craft of making the dolls spread from Moscow to other Russian cities and towns, each developing its own style and way of decorating the dolls. It wasn't until the 1950s and 60s that nesting dolls became well known outside of Russia.

Now, the term matreshka applies to all dolls that have interrelated parts. Today they are produced in a variety of decorative themes including flowers, churches and even political leaders.
—ROSANNE VAN VIERZEN

A Piece of the Pie: A Timeline of a Favorite Dish

Taking the *Oxford American Dictionary*'s definition of pie, "a baked dish of fruit or meat or fish, etc. enclosed in or covered with pastry or another crust," the original pie likely occurred by mistake.

Pre-historic Pie: Early humans wrap food in clay, mud or leaves to protect meal from being burnt. This practice evolves into surrounding the food with an edible paste made from ground grain or nuts and water.

1000-1400AD: Recipes from medieval times refer to pie or "pasty", often in terms of theatrical presentations including one stuffed with live birds to be released from the crust upon serving.

1362: The *Oxford English Dictionary* reports pie was "a well known popular word."

1615: Spanish author Cervantes coins the phrase "a finger in every pie" in his novel *Don Quixote de la Mancha*.

1700s: Pie becomes a common breakfast food in Colonial America.

1800s: Hot pie shops offering a variety of meat-filled pastries are a common stop for Victorian consumers.

1935: National Biscuit Company (now known as Nabisco) prints a recipe for Mock Apple Pie on packages of their best-selling Ritz Crackers. The ad campaign is designed to provide a dessert option during food shortages while boosting sales.

1940s: Lattice-top pies that require less dough become popular, perhaps due to wartime rationing.

1950s: Deep Dish Pies take their place in the 50s-era notion that bigger is better.

1962: Pet Milk introduces frozen pie shells, ushering in a new era of pie making by providing a no-fail crust to go with the busy cook's canned pie filling. —KATHRYN CONRAD

HM

The 1800s

Jodi Avery describes some of the highlights of the decade.

THE FIRST DECADE of the 1800s was marked by struggles for political power and graced with intellectual and creative thought.

The European powers were trying to build their strength and influence over the rest of the world, both militarily and economically. The early 1800s saw many territorial battles as great empires scrambled to grab as large a chunk as possible of the developing world.

In the era immediately following the French Revolution, the French Republic was reborn as the Empire of the French, and Napoleon led his nation to war against most of France's aristocratic neighbors, who feared revolution and wished to depose Napoleon and replace him with a conventional Bourbon monarch. Instead, Napoleon sponsored republican sentiment in many of the countries of Europe, and spread his law code across the continent and beyond.

While France pursued military goals in Europe, other countries were exploring new uncharted regions around the world. The Lewis and Clark expedition explored a great deal of the land that is now the continental US as it charted territory acquired in the Louisiana

Napoleon, who crowned himself Emperor of the French in 1804, is the dominant European figure of the decade.

Purchase. Africa was being explored by both the Portuguese and the British.

Political strategy was not the only inventive concept of the early 1800s. The decade was also notable for many inventions and theories. Lamarck's animal adaptation theories examined the evolution of creatures through time and tried to explain the recent scientific evidence that showed snakes once had legs. He believed the legs were not passed down to other generations as the reptile did not use them.

Scientific discoveries included improvements in electricity, such as Volta's battery, and developments in chemistry, such as Dalton's atomic theory. Transportation was forever changed by the introduction of the steam locomotive (Trevithick) and the submarine (Fulton). William Young's shoe design made walking more comfortable; he created specific right and left shoes, instead of having the same design for both feet.

Creativity also spread through the arts. Beethoven's Third Symphony was released to the praise of some and the outrage of others; many felt his music was 'sinful'. The first section of Goethe's *Faust* was also released in this decade.

Beethoven's Third Symphony was originally dedicated to Napoleon, but Beethoven struck out this dedication after Napoleon assumed dictatorial power.

The Industrial Revolution

ALTHOUGH THE Industrial Revolution began before 1800, the first decade of the 19th-century saw several major discoveries.

New factories were being built to house the new machinery for growing industrial businesses. Factories were placed in the countryside and once completed, houses and even cities grew around the factories for workers to live in. The new industrial society was not perfect. Many of the new industrial workers were unused to city life and had to make adjustments; former farm workers were faced with little room to grow their own food and the conditions of urban homes were often poor.

Factories, such as this one which housed spinning machines, began to bring people into cities and away from farms.

The inventions of the early 1800s ranged from transportation to garment making. Each development influenced the factory boom and helped the revolution progress in its own way.

A French inventor revolutionized the way clothes and other textiles were made in 1805. Joseph Jacquard introduced the first weaving loom that allowed unskilled labor to produce patterns worthy of the most skilful weaver. This ability to create beautiful pieces soon changed traditional household chores. For thousands of years, weaving and spinning had been done in the home; the loom moved this into the factory, where fabrics and threads could be produced in greater quantity with less effort.

Perhaps the most important invention affecting transportation was the steam engine locomotive. The credit for this development goes to Richard Trevithick.

This English inventor built his first locomotive in 1801 and called it the "Puffing Devil". His second version, completed in 1803, improved on the original; however, it was still not able to ride in rough conditions. Trevithick designed the first locomotive which had the ability to run on rails in 1804, but it could only travel at about five miles per hour for about nine and half miles. The inventor soon realized that the problem was not with his locomotive but with the rails. He built his next locomotive in 1808 and called it the "Catch-Me-Who-Can". It became an entertainment ride called the "steam circus" which cost one shilling per ride for the public. Although Trevithick's locomotives all had problems, they were the starting point for an important form of transportation and communication in the coming decades.

The Industrial Revolution did not bring all positive changes to society. Working conditions for the factory workers and widespread use of child labor became major issues all over the industrialized world. Factories were often dirty and cramped and some impoverished parents even sold their children into the labor market. Governments attempted to make changes with new labor laws and civil codes. For example, British parliament enacted the Health and Morals of Apprentices Act in 1802 to regulate work days, factory conditions and workers' rights.

Although the early 1800s were in the middle of the Industrial Revolution, many social and economic changes greatly affected this decade.

The Ministry of All Talents

Upon the death of Prime Minister William Pitt, the British government needed to find a new leader in 1806. At the time of his death at the age of 42, Pitt he had been the Prime Minister of Britain for over 18 years. William Pitt's final words were, "Oh, my country! How I leave my country!"

Pitt's country was left to Lord Grenville, Pitt's cousin, whose task was to build a new government for Britain. Grenville created "the ministry of all talents": an alliance of politicians with special expertise. Charles James Fox was made Foreign Secretary, with his followers in other powerful positions. This group's responsibility was to make peace with France. The war office was headed by William Windham and

William Pitt.

the home office by Spencer Perceval. Lord Grenville was in charge of the money and had veto power over all the other leaders.

"The ministry of all talents" failed 14 months after its creation. The ministry fell apart over religious matters. At this time, Catholics could only hold lower ranks in the army and no positions were open to them in the navy. Ministers in the government wanted to unite their country in order to defeat Napoleon. Grenville demanded his ministers promise to not discuss Catholics in the military. His ministers all refused and resigned their posts.

King George III assigned the Duke of Portland to form a new British government in 1807.

1800

A referendum in France passed a new constitution, with Napoleon Bonaparte as first consul. His "coup de main" also made the army supreme in France.

Pope Pius VII was elected to succeed Pius VI, who died in 1799.

Austrians embarked on an offensive attack against France. However, they were defeated at Hohenlinden by the French, led by General Moreau.

A fierce undeclared naval war between France and America ended with the signing of the treaty of Morfontaine. The US returned captured warships and France lifted an embargo on American ships.

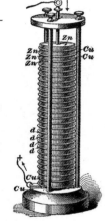

Roman inventor Alessandro Volta created the first method to produce a continuous flow of electricity. He called it an electric "battery". Using Volta's invention, two chemists, William Nicholson and Anthony Carlisle, discovered how to separate water into gases: oxygen and hydrogen.

1800: Alessandro Volta creates an electric "battery".

Tea, imported from China, became Britain's favorite drink. The average London household used seven percent of its income to purchase tea and the government collected 100 percent duties on tea imports.

On 24 December, an assassination attempt against Napoleon occurred. A bomb exploded as he was on his way to an opera in the Rue Saint-Nicaise. Napoleon was left unharmed and believed the Jacobin party made the attempt on his life. He had 130 known Jacobins arrested.

William Young designed the first shoes specifically for right and left feet.

1801

Thomas Jefferson and Aaron Burr were elected as the new American president and vice-president. The House of Representatives chose the pair after both received the same number of votes in the Electoral College. They were the first to be inaugu-

1804: Richard Trevithick built the first successful steam locomotive.

rated in Washington DC; at the time the city was still being built and most structures were still unfinished.

The Treaty of Lunéville ended the war between Austria and France with Napoleon victorious. This broke up the Holy Roman Empire and gave most of Italy to France.

Czar Paul of Russia, son of Catherine the Great, was strangled in his own bedroom by a group of drunken guard officers. His son, Alexander, replaced him as Czar.

Pasha (governor) Yusuf Karamanli of Tripoli (Libya), declared war on the US over a ship piracy issue. Immediately following, the US sent a fleet of ships to blockade Tripoli.

French troops left Egypt following the arrival of British troops.

Ireland and Great Britain created a legislative union, calling their joint nation the "United Kingdom of Great Britain and Ireland". This allowed Irish representatives to sit in British Parliament. However, the majority of Irish were Catholic and therefore not allowed to sit. This unity also modified the British flag; it added a thin, red diagonal cross to the existing diagonal white cross.

A "Concordat" between Napoleon and Pius VII reestablished the Catholic church in France. The deal was hard to negotiate, given Napoleon's anti-clergy attitude and the Pope's anti-Napoleon views. The two agreed to terms that made Catholicism the official majority religion in France, but made no mention of compensation for confiscated church property.

Alexander Hamilton and John Jay Post published the first *New York Evening Post* newspaper.

1802

Britain and France signed the Treaty of Amiens. This ended 10 years of war in Europe. Under the Treaty, Britain returned all its captured territories but two, which it gained from the Nether-

lands (Ceylon) and Spain (Trinidad).

Napoleon was voted "consul for life" with the right to designate a successor. Just over 8,000 people voted against the plebiscite, while over 3.5 million supported it.

Portuguese explorers began to travel across Africa from the west to east.

Dr. John Clinch inoculated more than 700 people for smallpox. He was the first person in British North America (Canada) to use vaccines.

1803

Napoleon angered Britain by continuing military activities in Italy, the Netherlands, Switzerland and Germany. Britain broke from the Treaty of Amiens and declared war, again, on France.

The US bought the Louisiana territory from France. France offered the land to the US to keep it away from Great Britain and create problems in the relationship between Great Britain and the US. It was sold for the bargain price of $15 million, about 4¢ an acre. This more than doubled the size of the US.

Ohio joined the American Union as the 17th state.

English chemist John Dalton proposed an atomic theory of matter that became the basis of modern chemistry. His theory included the first table of atomic weights and showed the atomic composition of molecules.

1804

Napoleon crowned himself as emperor of France (Napoleon I). He also passed the Code Napoleon, which reformed the French legal system to reduce injustice and confusion. This became the basis of law in much of Western Europe, South America, parts of Asia, modern France, Louisiana and the province of Quebec.

American explorers Meriwether Lewis and William Clark set out to explore the northwestern US. The two gathered a team of 40 men to explore new territory acquired in the Louisiana Purchase. The expedition started in St. Louis and moved up the Missouri River, across the Rocky Mountains and down the Columbia River to reach the Pacific.

English inventor Richard Trevithick built the first successful steam locomotive. It made its first run on 21 February on the Penydarren Railway in Wales.

Beethoven created his Third ("Eroica") Symphony. It was originally dedicated to Napoleon, but Beethoven removed this dedication after Napoleon's adoption of dictatorial powers.

1805

Britain, Russia, Austria and Sweden officially formed the Third Coalition against France. Britain and Russia initiated the alliance as they signed an agreement in St. Petersburg aimed at France.

The Sultan of Turkey, Selim III, appointed Mohammed Ali Pasha of Egypt.

Pasha of Tripoli Yusuf Karamanli was forced by a US naval fleet to surrender, thus ending the four year war between the two nations.

The Lewis and Clark Expedition reached the Pacific Ocean after 18 months and 4,000 miles.

Three important battles occurred in the Third Coalition fight: the Battle of Ulm, in which the French defeated the Austrians; the Battle of Trafalgar, where a Franco-Spanish fleet was defeated by the British navy; and the Battle of Austerlitz, which ended with the French victorious over Russia and Austria.

Joseph Jacquard invented the first weaving loom, allowing unskilled workers to produce intricate patterns.

1805: Joseph Jacquard invents the weaving loom.

1806

Napoleon attempted to isolate Britain with his Berlin Decree. Also known as "The Continental System", the decree called for the confiscation of all British merchandise, the imprisonment of all British subjects in France and the closure of all French ports to ships arriving from British territory.

Napoleon dissolved the Holy Roman Empire and replaced it with the Confederation of Rhine.

France defeated Prussia at the Battles of Jena and Auerstädt.

British Prime Minister William Pitt died and his government was taken over by Lord Grenville and Charles James Fox.

Emperor Jacques of Haiti was assassinated after he attempted to have almost all the entire white population of his nation murdered.

Turkey declared war against Russia and Britain.

1807

The slave trade was abolished in the British Empire. Parliament had been considering the issue since 1789.

US Congress placed a ban on all trading with other countries. Both imports from and exports to other nations carried economic sanctions. The US declared this after months of problems with British and French trade merchants.

Napoleon and Czar Alexander of Russia reached a peace agreement with the Treaty of Tilsit.

The British coalition of political parties collapsed. This coalition, also known as the "ministry of all talents", was formed after the death of William Pitt in 1806.

American inventor Robert Fulton designed the first submarine. However, most navies did not see the submersible vessel as practical.

The French invaded Portugal and captured Lisbon.

1808

British troops landed in Portugal and forced the French to surrender.

The French occupied Spain and Napoleon appointed his older brother Joseph as King against the wishes of the Spaniards.

The American presidential election replaced Thomas Jefferson with James Madison.

Napoleon had all American ships in French ports impounded. He claimed to be trying to help the US with its trade embargo against the entire world.

The law that banned the importation of slaves into America came into effect but was generally ignored. Importing African slaves carried a $500 fine for a single person and $20,000 for importing an entire shipload.

The British Royal Navy began its anti-slavery campaign. By patrolling along the West Coast of Africa, large numbers of slave ships were captured and slaves were released to the crown colony of Sierra Leone.

After accepting the Legion of Honor from Napoleon, Goethe published the first part of his acclaimed work, *Faust*.

Congress proclaimed that African Americans were to be credible witnesses in court cases. Before this time, the courts did not accept their testimony.

1809

The British army was defeated at a Spanish port in the Battle of Corunna.

Napoleon commanded General Radet to have Pope Pius VII arrested. The order came after years of opposition from the Pope towards Napoleon's self-crowning.

Jean Baptiste Lamarck perfected his theory, Zoological Philosophy, which explained his view on origins and adaptation of animal organs. Lamarck thought unused organs eventually decayed, and the traits were then not passed onto the next generation of animal.

After Austrian armies invaded the pro-French satellite of Bavaria, Napoleon marched on and seized the Austrian capital of Vienna. After several more engagements, Austria surrendered and agreed to join Napoleon in alliance against Britain.

Napoleon divorced his wife, Josephine. He was frustrated that she had not given birth to a son.

Czar Alexander broke the Continental System by allowing neutral countries to trade with Russia and by banning French imports.

According to a census study, the American population reached 7.2 million by the end of the year (up by 1.9 million from the previous decade).

Slavery in the Early 1800s

The early 1800s brought many changes in attitudes about slavery. Some countries still embraced the slave trade, while others saw it as an evil that needed to be abolished.

France had made the slave trade illegal in its colonies; however, Napoleon restored it on 20 May 1802.

Around the same time in the US many states were passing laws which gradually freed the slaves. In fact, New Jersey was the only state north of the Mason-Dixon Line with legal slavery. States south of the line were not willing to stop the slave trade. The issue was significant in the early 1800s and slowly began dividing the north and south regions of the nation. Slaves in the south heard stories of freedom elsewhere and revolts began. In 1802, 15 slaves in North Carolina plotted to kill their masters, but their plan was exposed and the state executed them.

In 1807, President Thomas Jefferson demanded that Congress pass a national anti-slavery importation act. He faced little opposition, and the bill passed on

Even in the cotton-dependent US, popular sentiment began to turn against the importation of slaves.

2 March of the same year. The terms of the act made the importing of slaves illegal. The purchase of a slave now carried a $500 fine and the equipping of a slave-trading ship was punishable by $20,000. Southern states had a large demand for slaves and this bill increased that need. Although people south of the Mason-Dixon Line largely ignored this bill, it showed the shifting of attitudes toward slavery in the US in the early 1800s.

Across the ocean in Britain,

Parliament first introduced an anti-slavery resolution in 1789. William Wilberforce, an independent MP, introduced the bill. Sugar producers fought to keep slave trade alive for their businesses and locals were fearful of revolutions. The British slave trade found a strong opponent in Wilberforce, however; he never gave up the struggle with his moral and ethical arguments. After much controversy, on 25 March 1807 British parliament passed an act to abolish the slave trade in all its colonies.

Britain created a new naval patrol in order to enforce the anti-slavery law in 1808. It inspected ships along 3,000 miles of the coast of Africa. Using six small ships, the patrol arrested slave traders and freed their prisoners. All freed slaves were taken to the colony of Sierra Leone, where the patrol was based, to begin their new lives.

With two out of three powerful nations of the early 1800s fighting against slave trade, the winds were truly changing.

The planning for a capital city for the US began in the late 1700s. Congress decided that it needed to find an area to establish a stable capital. In 1790, territory along the Potomac River was chosen as the permanent site.

Congress asked President George Washington to choose the exact area for the city. He decided upon 10 square-miles located in parts of Virginia and Maryland. Washington wanted to name the city "District of Columbia" after Christopher Columbus. Congress, however, wanted to name it after the President. A compromise was reached and "Washington, D.C." was born.

In 1791, Washington called upon Pierre Charles L'Enfant, a French engineer and army major he met during the Revolutionary War. L'Enfant produced his plan for the capital in 1792. It focused on the two main structures, "Congress House" and the "President

Washington, D.C.

House". The two were connected by a main road and all other streets began and ended at either of these two buildings.

The Washington city commissioners, who were also appointed by the President, were pleased with the plan at first but later became angry with L'Enfant as they felt he was not working fast enough.

In 1792, Washington dismissed L'Enfant as designer but still wanted to keep his original plan in tact. He appointed the city surveyor, Andrew Ellicott, to take over L'Enfant's position. However, after only a few months on the job, Ellicott quit over disagreements with the city commissioners.

As the government continued

to hire new designers, they remained very close to L'Enfant's original plans. President John Adams succeeded Washington and was the first president to move into the "President House" in 1800. At this time, Washington, D.C. was also made the official federal capital, housing congress and other federal bodies.

When President Adams and Congress moved into the city, it was still under development and some found it dreary. However, as the construction continued, many worries were laid to rest. Public buildings, such as museums and theaters, were scattered around the city and ceremonial spaces emphasized the natural beauty of the territory.

Today the Library of Congress holds the original plans of Pierre L'Enfant. Although he was not a part of the city planning for very long, L'Enfant is known as the original designer of Washington, D.C.

Napoleon at His Height

The peak of Napoleon Bonaparte's political and military career came in the early 1800s. His quick rise and powerful reign after the French Revolution lasted for the span of the decade.

Napoleon was born on 15 August 1769 to Carlo (Charles) Maria da Buonaparte and Letizia Ramolino at Ajaccio in Corsica. His ancestors were heavily involved in political matters and could be traced back to medieval Florence.

At the age of 10, Napoleon vowed to be a soldier. He played with drums and swords while other children played ordinary games. His father's political ties allowed him to send Napoleon to a military school in France in 1779. At the same time his older brother, Joseph, who his father saw as "dreamy", was sent to a religious school.

While at the military academy, Napoleon did not excel academically, but his instructors recognized his vigor and loyalty. Napoleon did not like the school and in 1784 transferred to a Paris military school. He enjoyed the strict discipline of his new school and made an even stronger impression on his superiors. This impression was so remarkable that after only a year of training he skipped over the intermediate level and was admitted into the army.

The death of his father in 1785 left him with family responsibilities and he took leave from the army. For the next decade he took up his family's fight to support the French republic in Corsica. The Bonapartes were faced with fierce opposition from Pasquale Paoli, a politician in Ajaccio who was against connections to France. The family eventually fled Corsica in 1793 to Toulon; at this time Napoleon returned to the army.

That same year, France was at war with England, Holland and Spain. Napoleon was quick to gain power in the military.

By 1799, he had achieved so

In 1804, Napoleon asked Pope Pius VII to perform the ceremony which officially made him the Emperor of France but in the end he crowned himself while Pius watched.

much power that he drew up a new French constitution that made him First Consul. A plebiscite in 1800 passed the document with only 1,562 out of three million people voting against it.

In 1801, Bonaparte's conquests were so successful that he had gained most of Italy by breaking up the Holy Roman Empire. The Second Coalition against France only had one survivor: Britain.

In 1802, following his military success, the people of France voted to make Bonaparte First Consul For Life, with the ability to name a successor.

In 1804, Napoleon crowned himself Emperor of France. The ceremony was to be led by Pope Pius VII, however, Napoleon took two golden laurels and crowned himself and his wife, Josephine. Many believed that Napoleon's 'self-crowning' symbolized his feelings towards organized religion.

This same year the new emperor produced one of his greatest achievements. Napoleon

reformed the French legal system with the introduction of the French Civil Code. The Code simplified and unified all the legal systems in France. Three years later, after gaining the acceptance of the French, Napoleon renamed it the Code Napoleon.

The year of 1805 brought France great opposition in the form of the Third Coalition. However, under Napoleon's military the country was, overall, victorious. Spain, Austria and Russia were each defeated.

In the following years, France attempted to gain more power with British blockades (the Continental System) and the creation of the Confederation of Rhine (formerly the Holy Roman Empire).

With his many countries to command, Napoleon began passing down territorial rule to others. He made his younger brother, Louis, the King of Holland in 1806 and his older brother, Joseph, the Spanish King in 1808. Many thought his choices for rulers were corrupt.

As the decade ended, Napoleon's reputation was under further speculation. In 1809, he angrily divorced Josephine, his wife of 13 years, as she had not yet produced a son. In the same year, he had Pope Pius VII arrested for his opposition towards Napoleon.

His first fall came in 1812 when he retreated after a major setback in the war with Russia. Two years later he was exiled to Elba after Austria and Prussia defeated him. Napoleon returned to France in 1815, overthrew King Louis XVIII, and was again in power. A Prussian Marshal and the Duke of Wellington quickly gathered an allied army to defeat Napoleon. Only three months after his return to France, the allies were victorious at Waterloo.

Napoleon was again exiled, this time to St. Helena in the South Atlantic. It was on this island that Napoleon Bonaparte died in 1821 at the age of 52.

The Lewis and Clark Expedition

The United States more than doubled its size on 30 April 1803 by means of the "Louisiana Purchase". The young nation now spanned from the Atlantic Ocean to the Rocky Mountains, though much of the new territory was uncharted. President Thomas Jefferson commissioned an expedition to survey the new lands. He appointed Meriwether Lewis and William Clark to take charge of this endeavor.

Meriwether Lewis and William Clark explored the northwestern United States from 1804 to 1806 with a team of 40 men.

Captain Lewis was Jefferson's secretary and had once fought in the Indian Wars. The other leader, Captain Clark, was also a veteran of the Indian Wars and once served as lieutenant of infantry in the US army. Lewis and Clark formed a group of about 40 men called the "Corps of Discovery". They set out on their journey from St. Louis on 14 May 1804.

With dangerous conditions across uncharted routes, the group made their way across the US. The explorers traveled up the Missouri River in longboats and canoes, through what is now the Dakotas and Montana. Their first big challenge was crossing the Rocky Mountains.

A young Native American woman, Sacajawea, became a helpful guide in the area west of the Rockies. Sacajawea was the daughter of a Shoshone tribe chief and was captured at the age of 10 by the Hidatsa. She was later purchased by Toussaint Charbonneau who married her and another captured Indian girl. Charbonneau was hired by Lewis and Clark as an interpreter for the expedition; he agreed to join the team on the condition that Sacajawea would also be allowed to go. Eight weeks before the expedition left, Sacajawea, who was now 16 years old, gave birth to her first son, Jean Baptiste Charbonneau. During the journey, the young woman saved Lewis from an angry Indian chief. On the other side of the Rocky Mountains, the expedition met with Sacajawea's tribe. The chief sold them horses to help finish climbing the mountains. Many believe that without Sacajawea's help, the expedition would have had more problems with the Indians.

Once past the mountains, the explorers traveled down the Columbia River. On 15 November 1805, they reached their destination: the Pacific Ocean. They had traveled across 4,000 miles of uncharted and difficult land and through 18 months of unpredictable weather. This made the group the first to cross the modern-day, continental US.

During their journey, they had sent back many plant, animal and mineral specimens. This helped scientists and the government understand more about the new American territory.

Upon their return to St. Louis on 23 September 1806, the US attempted to claim the land the expedition crossed, known as "Oregon Territory". However, Britain claimed much of the land at the same time.

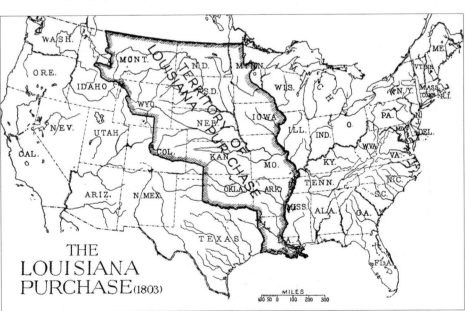

THE LOUISIANA PURCHASE (1803)

MILES
100 50 0   100   200   300

For the bargain price of about 4¢ an acre, the United States more than doubled its size with the Louisiana Purchase.

Bloodletting

Thomas Crowl looks at a now-discredited medical practice.

GEORGE WASHINGTON was the most prominent living American in 1799. When he contracted a severe throat infection on a raw day at Mount Vernon, his physicians applied the best medical therapy they knew: purging, blisters and bleeding. The first president was bled four times in two days until the blood was thick and flowed slowly. Thus weakened, further bleeding was prevented by the death of the patient. One of his physicians later admitted that perhaps the bleeding had been excessive.

By the medical standards of the 21st century, bloodletting, or venesection, is a discredited, barbaric practice. Yet it was widely employed before recorded history, and evolved into a highly ritualized therapy deeply ingrained in medical practice for centuries. In 1836, Marshall Hall, an English physician and researcher, proclaimed, "As long as bloodletting is required, it can be borne; and as long as it can be borne, it is required." In some forms it survived into the 20th century.

The origins of venesection are lost to antiquity, and yet it was practiced across the globe. As diverse a group of cultures as the Native Americans, Incas, ancient Greeks, Romans, Egyptians, Persians, Polynesians and African tribes all engaged in therapeutic bleeding in one form or another. Hippocrates, in the fifth century BC, was an advocate of bloodletting. To rationalize the perilous need to bleed a patient, Hippocrates developed the humoral theory to explain human physiology. In his essay "On the Nature of Man", Hippocrates postulated the existence of four humors within the human body: blood, phlegm, yellow bile and black

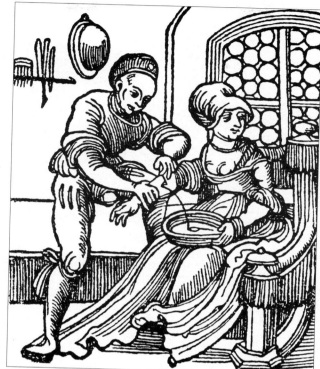

bile. When all the humors were in proper balance, good health was assured. However, a plethora, or overabundance, of one or more would cause disease. A cure would result if the excess humors were evacuated from the body.

A physician could return his patient to health by one of four methods: bleeding, starving, purging or inducing vomiting. Since the science of the time held that food was converted directly to blood, starvation and bleeding were viewed as equal. Bleeding was preferred because it was more quickly accomplished. So it was that bloodletting, combined with purgatives or emetics, together with laudanum for pain, constituted the physician's therapeutic arsenal in 1799.

As history progressed, the practice of bleeding became more ritualized, and complex in its application. In the second century AD, the great physician to Rome, Galen, refined the humoral theory and the practice of bloodletting. By the Middle Ages, the healing arts were well entrenched in the

guild system. Physicians reigned supreme, but usually limited themselves to diagnosis. The actual unpleasant work of bleeding and surgery was left to the barber-surgeon. From this association comes the most recognizable artifact of venesection, the striped barber pole. The red represented the blood being let; the white, the tourniquet and bandage used; and the pole represented the stick held by the patient to dilate the vein. As the medical profession evolved, the role of the barber decreased, and the surgeon merged with the physician.

Any medical practice requires certain decisions to be made regarding its application to the individual patient. Bloodletting was no different. The question of whether to bleed or not was rarely asked from the first to the 18th century, as bleeding was a universal treatment. In the first century AD, the Roman practitioner Celsus reflected current thinking when he wrote, "To let blood by incising a vein is no novelty. What is novel is that there should scarcely be any malady in which blood may not be let."

However, the decision of when to bleed in the course of a disease was a critical one. Hippocrates created an elaborate schedule to be followed. During the Middle Ages, complex astrological calendars were devised to precisely time the bleeding, and even to select the specific vein to be used. One of the earliest printed medical documents was *Calendar of Bloodletting* circulated in Germany in 1457. As the pseudo-science of medical astrology exerted greater influence over the practice of medicine, so precise were the calculations required of medical men that no treatment

Bloodletting in Veterinary Medicine

Bleeding wasn't just for humans. Given the almost total lack of medical knowledge which marked most of written history, it should not be surprising that bloodletting was a primary treatment for diseases of domestic animals. The veterinary profession did not appear as such until the late 18th century, and prior to that animals were treated by farmers, stockmen, or rarely, by medical practitioners. Those erroneous theories about human disease were simply transferred to animals for lack of any alternatives.

Often the bleeding of farm animals and horses was accomplished by the crudest of means. A tail or ear was amputated to cause bleeding. The resulting disfiguration was undesirable, so less stressful means were sought. As the anatomical knowledge of animals grew, useful veins were located. The typical straight blade lancets were employed, and larger, stronger spring lancets developed. Uniquely veterinary in use, however, was the fleam. The fleam was a pocket-knife-like device with single or multiple blades meant to be held against a dilated vein. Rapped sharply with a short stick, called a bloodstick, it would penetrate one wall of a vein. After bleeding, the wound was closed by suturing.

For animals, there was hardly a disease for which bleeding was not recommended: bloat, foot rot, founder, glanders, pneumonia, colic, milk fever and strangles to name a few. English veterinary surgeon Edward Mayhew wrote that for horses, "A pint now was better than a gallon later." Still, the bleeding of large domestic animals could be copious. One to three gallons from an adult horse or cow was not uncommon. Unfortunately, bleeding as a veterinary treatment lingered longer than its medical counterpart. It was advocated as a standard treatment for some maladies affecting horses as late as 1900. Fortunately, there were critics of the practice among those who wished to make veterinary medicine a scientific profession. One of the earliest was an English physician turned veterinary surgeon in Boston, George Dadd. He wrote of his concern in his 1850 book, *American Cattle Doctor*, "many thousands of our most valuable cattle die under treatment, which consists of little more than bloodletting..." Dadd's crusade against unscientific treatments for animals eventually bore fruit, and the fleam became an antique curiosity for veterinarians.

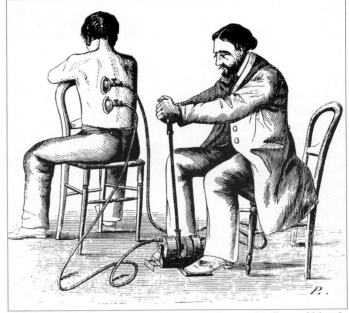

Cupping used vacuum-filled cups to enhance the flow of blood.

could be initiated without consulting the star charts. In an early effort to regulate the medical profession, the English parliament enacted laws requiring physicians to consult the charts before bleeding a patient.

The methods used to bleed a patient were relatively simple. In the beginning, any sharp flint or stick would do. Some South American natives would shoot small arrows at the patient, and hope their aim was true. Human ingenuity came to the rescue as more specialized devices were created. Lancets were sharp, short-bladed instruments designed to quickly open one wall of a vein. The vein would then be dilated by a tourniquet. When the treatment was completed, a bandage was applied to stem blood flow.

Thumb and scalpel lancets were simple instruments that were easily cleaned after use. The handles of scalpel lancets were of wood, bone or ivory. Thumb lancets folded into a handle of wood, horn, bone or ivory like a pocket knife. Digital pressure alone was employed to enter the vein.

Spring lancets were an advance of medical instrument technology. Small, delicate but nasty little devices not much larger than a man's thumb, they were an improvement over instruments needing digital pressure. Spring lancets were cocked like a pistol, and activated by releasing a catch mechanism. Spring lancets were quicker, and probably less stressful to the patient, but impossible to clean. They were popular in the US and Germany, where they undoubtedly contributed to the spread of disease.

Directly opening a vein was not the only means by which a patient could be bled. Leeches were a very popular alternative for centuries. The European species was favored, and could be procured at any well-stocked apothecary of the day. The small quantity of blood removed by a leech (which could be enhanced by cutting off the tail) made them popular for use around the eyes and mouth.

Another alternative, favored in the 17th and 18th

centuries, was cupping. Cupping was the application of a heavy glass or metallic vessel, shaped somewhat like a drinking cup, to an area of skin. The cup was secured to the skin by a vacuum created within it by burning a small fuel source such as lint or alcohol. The air was evacuated in later designs using a small hand pump. The exhaustion of air in the cup fixed it, and simultaneously drew blood to the skin. Frequently, multiple cups were applied. There were hundreds of designs for cups, some very elaborate.

Cupping could be performed *dry*, a method in which no blood was lost, or *wet*, in which case the skin was superficially lacerated so a small quantity of blood flowed. A medical device called a scarifier was developed which, when activated, produced multiple, small skin lacerations. Like spring lancets, scarifiers were spring loaded, but scarifiers contained several tiny retractable blades instead of a single large one. The vacuum within the cup naturally enhanced the flow of blood, but since veins were not opened, the amount of blood lost was small. Cupping was the last of the types of bloodletting to die out, lasting into the first half of the 20th century.

Deciding which vein to bleed was not a simple choice. Considerable controversy raged for centuries regarding the choice of a vein. Classical Greek medical doctrine dictated derivative bleeding, that is, as close to the problem as possible. Muslim protocols, popular during the Middle Ages, stressed revulsion, or bleeding from a vein far removed from the problem. The controversy was addressed by the French government which forbade derivative bleeding. However, after 1628, when William Harvey published his thesis on the circulation of blood, the debate became moot.

Most interesting, with our present understanding of physi-

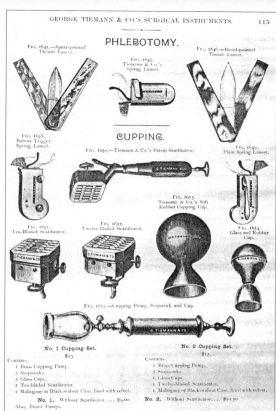

An 1889 advertisement for bloodletting instruments.

ology, is how it was decided how much blood needed to be let to effect a cure. In hindsight, the less blood lost, the better. However, the opposite was believed by the practitioners of the day. A complete lack of knowledge regarding true blood volume led to some very wild estimates. Avicenna (980-1037AD), the celebrated physician to the Persian court, believed each man contained 25 pounds of blood, double the actual amount, which is five to six quarts. The great Philadelphia physician and patriot Dr. Benjamin Rush (1746-1813) advocated bleeding a quart every 48 hours. Generally, experienced practitioners bled the patient to effect rather than remove a specific quantity. The desired effect was syncope, fainting caused by dangerously low blood pressure. This condition was determined by observing the patient's attitude, skin pallor and pulse. A degree of skill was necessary to avoid inducing irreversible hypovolemic shock. Thus the average patient was bled 16-30 ounces at

a sitting, and multiple bleedings were common.

In spite of its long and widespread acceptance, bloodletting always had its opponents. The ancient Greek author, Aeginious of Eris, questioned it. Philippe von Hokenheim, alias Paracelsus, a 16th-century Swiss observer attacked the humoral theory. In 1835, Pierre Charles Alexander Louis (1787-1872) published his "Researches on the Effects of Bloodletting". Louis' paper was the first to critically analyze the success of bleeding as a therapy. He confirmed what many suspected, that any benefits claimed were unsubstantiated.

Unfortunately, this knowledge did not save Hannah Green, who in 1848 was given the new anesthetic chloroform for a minor surgical operation. When he failed to revive her quickly, her surgeon, in a combination of the ancient and modern, bled her. Hannah Green's death thus ensured, she became the first to die of anesthesia inhalation.

As the era of modern medicine dawned, bloodletting, except for a few rare diseases, died out. At the end of the 19th century, Oliver Wendell Holmes wrote the epitaph for bloodletting when he commented, "The lancet was the magician's wand of the dark ages of medicine."

Further Reading
Bishop, W.J., *The Early History Of Surgery* (Barnes and Noble Books: New York, 1960).
Davis, Audrey and Appel, Toby. *Bloodletting Instruments* (The Printer's Devil: Arlington, MA 1983).
Lyons, Albert S. and Petrucelli, R. Joseph, *Medicine. An Illustrated History* (Abra Press: New York, 1978).
Wilbur, C. Keith, *Antique Medical Instruments.* (Schiffer Publishing: West Chester, PA, 1987).
Flexner, James Thomas, *George Washington, Anguish and Farewell* (Little, Brown and Co., Boston, 1972).

HM

INTRODUCTION TO GENEALOGY

Family Chronicle's
INTRODUCTION TO
GENEALOGY

Family Chronicle's Introduction to Genealogy has been written to answer the often heard question "I'm interested in starting my research — but where do I start?" It assumes no prior knowledge of genealogy and is designed to bring the reader rapidly "up to speed".

The presentation follows *Family Chronicle's* popular format. Features include how to find information about your ancestors in: Vital Records, City Directories, Census and Military Records, Naturalization Records, Social Security Records, Passenger Lists, Court Records, Obituaries and Church and Parish Records. This is followed by information on where to conduct your research: Family History Centers, Libraries and National Archives. There are also sections on keeping your data organized, manually or on a computer.

If you have traced your roots back across the Atlantic, we have a summary on conducting your research in a dozen European countries. When you have gathered enough information we show you how to start writing your family history.

We introduce you to computers, with advice on the type of computer to use, an overview of the software packages available and tips on getting online and making the most out the Internet. We explain how to find records on CDs or in the subscription services on the web.

There's a whole lot more including Heraldry, Tartans, Origins of Surnames, Societies, Preservation of Documents and Photos . . .

As with all our publications, if *Family Chronicle's Introduction to Genealogy* fails to meet your needs or expectations, we will gladly refund your money, for any reason or no reason. Any refund will be made promptly and cheerfully.
Halvor Moorshead, Editor and Publisher

The *Introduction* is designed to get you started on the right foot and to fill in any gaps if you are an experienced researcher.

$25 US
$30 Cdn
Prices include $5 shipping charge

Poor Richard's Almanac

Ron Wild examines a book that rivaled the popularity of the Bible.

THOUGH THEIR CONTENT was largely suspect, almanacs enjoyed tremendous popularity in the 18th century. Volumes filled with astrological prognostications and dire predictions of famines, deaths, plagues, wars, horrors and disasters proliferated.

To some, the popularity of these early almanacs and their influence on not only the general population but on leaders in society was alarming. The scandal of their excesses was growing to such an extent that satirist Jonathan Swift created his own almanac, *Predictions for 1708*, written to warn the people of England against being "further imposed upon by the vulgar Almanack-Makers". Publishing *Predictions for 1708* under the pseudonym Isaac Bickerstaff, Swift used ridicule, humor and pure fabrication to challenge the credibility of the offending almanacs.

Benjamin Franklin

Although he was only two years old when Swift undertook his campaign against the English almanac publishers, Benjamin Franklin decided to follow in Swift's footsteps in 1732. Almanacs had become so popular in the American colonies that Franklin could not resist the opportunity to publish his *Poor Richard's Almanack* under the pseudonym Richard Saunders.

In the introduction to the almanac, Franklin — posing as Saunders — explains that he has decided to write the volume not with a view to the public good, but rather because "I am excessive poor, and my Wife, good Woman, is, I tell her, excessive proud…. The Printer has offered me some considerable share of the Profits, and I have thus begun to comply with my Dame's desire." This rationale is quite contrived, as Franklin was the chief printer for Pennsylvania, owner of *The Pennsylvania Gazette*, chief clerk in the Philadelphia Conference and, while not yet rich, he was hardly poor.

Poor Richard, 1733.

AN

Almanack

For the Year of Chrift

1733,

Being the Firft after LEAP YEAR:

And makes fince the Creation — Years
By the Account of the Eastern *Greeks* — 7241
By the Latin Church, when ☉ ent. ♈ — 6932
By the Computation of *W. W.* — 5742
By the *Roman* Chronology — 5682
By the *Jewish* Rabbies — 5494

Wherein is contained

The Lunations, Eclipfes, Judgment of the Weather, Spring Tides, Planets Motions & mutual Afpects, Sun and Moon's Rifing and Setting, Length of Days, Time of High Water, Fairs, Courts, and obfervable Days.

Fitted to the Latitude of Forty Degrees, and a Meridian of Five Hours Weft from *London*, but may without fenfible Error, ferve all the adjacent Places, even from *Newfoundland* to *South-Carolina*.

By *RICHARD SAUNDERS*, Philom.

PHILADELPHIA:
Printed and fold by *B. FRANKLIN*, at the New Printing-Office near the Market.

To distinguish his almanac from the other seven being published in Philadelphia at the time, Franklin decided to create a controversy.

The Titan Leeds Hoax

In the introduction to his first edition, Franklin confided his reason for not having published an almanac earlier: "Indeed this motive would have had Force enough to have made me publish an Almanack many Years since, had it not been overpowered by my Regard for my good Friend and Fellow-Student, Mr. Titan Leeds, whose Interest I was extremely unwilling to hurt: But this Obstacle (I am far from speaking it with Pleasure) is soon to be removed, since inexorable Death, who was never known to respect Merit, has already prepared the mortal Dart, the fatal Sister has already extended her destroying Shears, and that ingenious Man must soon be taken from us. He

dies, by my Calculation made at his Request, on Oct. 17, 1733, 3:29 P.M. at the very instant of the conjunction of the Sun and Mercury: By his own Calculation he will survive till the 26th of the same Month. This small difference between us we have disputed whenever we have met these 9 Years past; but at length he is inclinable to agree with my Judgment; Which of us is most exact, a little Time will now determine."

Leeds did not cooperate in dying on either date, and, in his *American Almanack* of 1734, he had something to say about the prediction of his demise: "Kind reader, Perhaps it may be expected that I should say something concerning an Almanack printed for the year 1733, Said to be writ by Poor Richard or Richard Saunders, who for want of other matter was pleased to tell his Readers, that he had calculated my Nativity, and from thence predicts my Death to be the 17th of October, 1733 At 22 min past 3 o'clock in the Afternoon, and that these Provinces may not expect to see any more of his (Titan Leeds) Performances, and this precise Predicter, who predicts to a Minute, proposes to succeed me in Writing of Almanacks; but notwithstanding his false Prediction, I have by the Mercy of God lived to write a Diary for the year 1734, and to publish the Folly and Ignorance of this presumptious Author. Nay, he adds another gross Falsehood in his said Almanack, viz That by my own Calculation, I shall survive until the 26th of this said Month (October) which is as untrue as the former, for I do not pretend to that knowledge, although he has usurpt the knowledge of the Almighty herein and manifestd himself a Fool and a Lyar. And by the Mercy of God I have lived to survive this conceited Scriblers Day and Minute whereon he has predicted my Death; and as I have supplied my Country with Almanacks for three seven Years by

Poor Richard Improved

In 1758 Franklin published *Poor Richard Improved*. It included not only an expanded version of *Poor Richard's Almanack*, but also Franklin's famous essay *The Way to Wealth* (also known as *Father Abraham's Speech*). This 1758 almanac found its way into well-nigh every home in America. *Father Abraham's Speech* was translated into every European language and is probably Franklin's most widely-read work. It incorporated the system of virtues that Franklin conceived as the path to arriving at moral perfection. The virtues Franklin developed and applied are as follows:

Temperance. Eat not to dullness. Drink not to elevation

Silence. Speak not but what may benefit others or yourself. Avoid trifling conversation.

Order. Let all your things have their places. Let each part of your business have its time.

Resolution. Resolve to perform what you ought. Perform without fail what you resolve.

Frugality. Make no expense but to do good to others or yourself. Waste nothing.

Industry. Lose no time. Be always employed in something useful. Cut off all unnecessary actions.

Sincerity. Use no hurtful deceit. Think innocently and justly; and, if you speak, speak accordingly.

Justice. Wrong none, by doing injuries or omitting the benefits that are your duty.

Moderation. Avoid extremes. Forbear resenting injuries so much as you think they deserve.

Cleanliness. Tolerate no uncleanness in body, clothes or habitation.

Tranquility. Be not disturbed at trifles, or at accidents common or unavoidable.

Chastity. Rarely use venery but for health or offspring; never to dullness, weakness or the injury of your own or another's peace of reputation.

Humility. Imitate Jesus and Socrates.

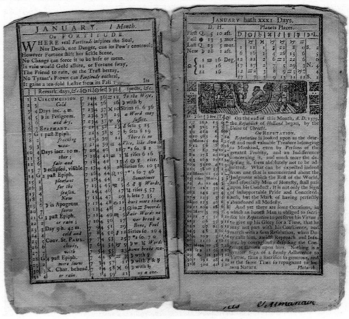

A calendar from the almanac.

past, to general Satisfaction, so perhaps I live to write when his Performances are Dead. This much from your annual Friend, Titan Leeds. October 18, 1733. 3 ho. 33 min P.M."

These kinds of exchanges continued for several years with Franklin stating that his prediction was accurate and that Leeds had died within minutes of the prediction, and that it was his friends and business associates who were continuing the publication of the late man's *American Almanack*. (Incidentally, Leeds appears to have been a friend and student of Franklin's and it seems possible that they acted in collusion to both of their benefits.)

The false controversy was successful in that the sale of *Poor Richard's Almanack* exceeded 10,000 copies annually at five pence each, which was a considerable sum in 1740.

Franklin's True Purpose

Having successfully established *Poor Richard's Almanack*, Franklin proceeded to share his brand of wit and wisdom with his readers with a view to establishing his strong beliefs in self-reliance and positive action to achieve desired results – a philosophy summarized by a quotation from an early edition of the almanac, "Energy and Persistence Conquers All Things".

Franklin began the task of educating the American public and *Poor Richard's Almanack* became a standard work that rivaled the presence of the Bible in the homesteads of colonial America. The yearly calendar included recipes, weather forecasts, jokes and numerous proverbs that are now so engrained in the American psyche they have become cliches.

Franklin kept publishing the almanac for 25 years, from 1733 to 1758. The content of the almanacs is now out of copyright and widely available on the Internet; a web search for "Poor Richard's Almanac" should produce results.

Though Franklin's almanac became a common fixture in the homes of colonial America, it was but one of his many accomplishments: in Philadelphia, he was instrumental in setting up the police force, the fire department, a library system and a learning academy that became the University of Pennsylvania. His scientific experiments earned him honorary degrees from Yale and Harvard and his diplomatic skills on behalf of the fledgling US are legendary. His signature is found appended to four great documents: *The Declaration of Independence,* the *Treaty of Alliance with France*, the *Treaty of Peace with England* and the *Constitution*. No other American can claim this distinction.

HM

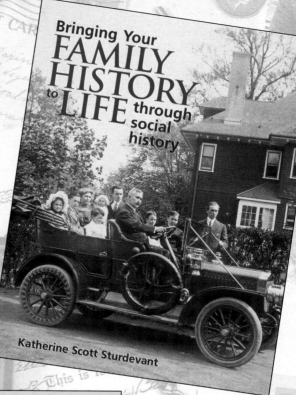

The Ever-Practical Paper

Barbara Krasner-Khait explores the development of modern paper.

WHEN THE PRINTING press came on the scene in the 15th century, books could finally be mass-produced. Earlier, books were laboriously copied by hand, usually by monks, and on parchment. An increase in literacy and newspapers added to the demand for reading material. Printing — and the industry that grew around it — could not have been possible without a practical writing surface — paper.

Throughout history, man searched for practical means to record stories, accounts and transactions. From about 2200BC, Egyptians used the abundant papyrus reed as their preferred writing surface. Tanners provided two relatively expensive competitors made from calf, goat and sheep hides: parchment, introduced about 1500BC in Asia Minor, and vellum. Fine quality parchment was quite valuable so it was treated with great care and was often used more than once. Parchment was used at Pergamum (from which the word "parchment" is derived) in present-day Turkey and gradually replaced papyrus in Mediterranean countries during the next few centuries.

A Brush With Paper

The development of paper began when one man in China revolutionized writing by inventing the camel's-hair brush in 250BC. The new brush popularized calligraphy and in turn required a cheaper and more practical writing material.

In 105AD, a courtier named T'sai Lun first reported the use of paper to the emperor. Accounts vary about whether he used a thin, felted material formed on flat,

Paper made from the papyrus reed was the preferred writing surface of the Egyptians.

porous moulds from macerated vegetable fiber or whether he used waste products — old rags, pieces of hemp rope

Eumenes, King of Pergamum, is sometimes credited with the invention of parchment.

and old fishing nets — to make his paper. Either way, the raw materials were boiled in water and wood ash. Then they were beaten so that the fibers broke apart to make a mushy pulp. The pulp passed through a flat, mesh strainer, draining the water and leaving fibers that became sheets of paper when dried.

For more than 500 years, the highly revered Chinese art of making paper remained a well-kept secret.

Buddhist Monks And Chinese Prisoners Reveal The Secrets

The secret spread when Buddhist monks from the part of China we now know as Korea brought manuscript books made of paper into Japan.

From China, paper made its way via established trade routes through central Asia and Persia. Captured by Arabs in what is now western Turkestan, Chinese papermakers were induced to continue their art and teach it to the Moors in the city of Samarkand, where flax and hemp were plentiful. From there, the once closely guarded craft spread to Baghdad in 795AD and then Damascus, Egypt and Morocco.

Europe Catches On

Parchment was used all over Europe from about 170BC on. But paper's practicality and relatively low cost signaled the demise of both parchment and vellum. The Crusades and the Moorish conquest of North Africa and Spain brought the art of making paper

By the 15th century, small-scale paper-making was becoming common in Europe.

to Europe. By the middle of the 12th century, the Spanish cities of Xativa, Valencia and Toledo served as the European headquarters of the paper industry. Accounts vary about when paper first appeared in Italy — some experts say it had an early debut, brought about through the Arab occupation of Sicily and that the oldest recorded document on paper was a deed of King Roger of Sicily in 1102. Others say paper reached Italy in the 15th century.

Industrial Growth
In 1276, mills began to spring up in Italy. A factory appeared in Padua in 1340 and then more in the city states of Florence, Bologna, Parma, Milan, Venice and other cities. Northern Italian factories supplied Germany's paper needs until the 15th century, though some German mills were established in the 14th century in Mainz and elsewhere. France and Burgundy supplied the Netherlands and England at first and Spain influenced France's first paper mills. By the

second half of the 14th century, western Europe used paper for all literary purposes, superseding vellum during the 15th century.

The first known British paper mill was built in Hertfordshire near the turn of the 15th century. These mills struggled to get enough linen to meet the demand for paper. Woven fibers from shredded, boiled rags were used for making pulp. It seems that no paper was made in England before the reign of the Tudors.

Until 1690, colonial Americans imported their paper from Europe. Philadelphia printer William Bradford and German paper maker William Rittenhouse opened their mill at Germantown, Pennsylvania. Others appeared in Pennsylvania starting in 1710, and in New Jersey and Massachusetts in 1728. William Parks, Virginia's first newspaper publisher built its first paper mill in 1744. New York's first mill debuted in 1768 in Hempstead, Long Island. A combination of the inability to get imports during the Revolutionary War and the increased need for newspapers, broadsides and pamphlets led to a serious paper shortage. By the time the war ended, about 80 or 90 new mills were in operation. By 1810 there were at least 185 mills or other establishments that manufactured paper, led by 60 in Pennsylvania and 40 in Massachusetts. Uses included school books, writing paper, wrapping paper, pasteboard, bonnets, hangings and cards and more.

Occidental Papermaking
Making paper required two men: one called a vatman, who dipped the mould into a vat of

Watermarks
Papermaking guru Dard Hunter wrote in his classic *Papermaking: The History and Technique of an Ancient Craft* (Dover Publications, 1978. Reprinted from the second edition by Alfred A. Knopf, 1947) that "In the entire craft of papermaking there is no part more interesting or fascinating than to couch a sheet of paper upon the felting and watch the impressed mark become clear and distinct as the water slowly evaporates." The first watermark appeared in Italy about 1282. Watermarking became common practice by the 15th century, featuring thousands of designs made by stitching wires onto the mesh of the mould. When the mould was filled with pulp, the paper fibers settled around the raised design.

According to Hunter, there were four groups or classes of watermark:
- Simple shapes — ovals, crosses, circles, knots, triangles
- Man and the works of man
- Flowers, trees, leaves, vegetables, grain, and fruits
- Wild, domesticated and legendary animals

Early marks included a pair of scissors (Italy, 1450), an elephant (France, 1500s) and a jester (France, 1570).

Watermarking increased in importance to protect the integrity of paper currency. In 1773, for instance, a British act forbade copying the watermark in English bank-note paper, punishable by death.

As machines took over the intricate manual processes, watermarking needed some help. John Marshall answered the call with his 1826 invention of a wire-covered roll — dubbed the dandy roll — that bore the design in wire.

pulp mixture, lifted it, threw off any excess pulp, and shook it from side to side to settle the fibers evenly and to drain the water. The other was the *coucher* (pronounced "coocher" from the French word *coucher* meaning "to lay down"), who put the mesh mould on a horn-shaped stand called an "ass" to drain out the water. Then he firmly pressed the contents onto a piece of wet felt — causing the sheet of paper to separate from the mould. The coucher laid the paper down on the felt, put another felt on top of the paper, and repeated this process until he built up a stack of felt and paper, called a post. Pressing then squeezed out the water and the resulting paper sheet dried in a room called the loft.

The Age Of Innovation

Though papermakers tried to speed up production, their processes were still too slow — until the 17th century when a new piece of equipment called the Hollander beater replaced the stamper. The stamper featured large wooden mallets that pounded wet rags into pulp using wind or water power, while the Hollander beater used metal bars on a revolving wheel. A German papermaker said in 1725 that "the Hollander in Freiburg furnishes in one day as much pulp as eight stamper-holes do in eight days." By 1760, one French mill eliminated its stampers altogether and used 12 Hollander beaters, giving it the capability to produce 75 reams of finished paper a day. Though there seemed to be widespread agreement that the older method made a more durable product, some monarchies, including Frederick the Great of Prussia and Maria Theresa of the Austro-Hungarian Empire, insisted on using the beaters. The French government, on the other hand, mandated use of stampers until

Modern papermills are highly automated and produce tremendous amounts of paper.

1861, to ensure production of higher quality paper.

About a century after the beater made its debut, Frenchman Nicholas-Louis Robert introduced another new machine to speed production even further, this time eliminating the need for the vatman and the coucher. Two Englishmen, Henry and Sealy Fourdrinier, adopted the machine for their mill at Frogmore, Two Rivers, Hertfordshire, in 1803. The machine was subsequently dubbed the Fourdrinier.

As paper came out of the Fourdrinier machine, it had to be cut in sheets and hung in a drying loft. Another production innovation appeared in 1821, when Thomas Bonsor Crompton invented heated cylinders to dry the paper as it emerged. The cylinders also enabled the paper to take a continuous or "web" form.

The continued use of rags and cloth made large-scale production impossible until 1800.

From Rags To Wood

The sharp rise in demand for books, newspapers and magazines during the first part of the 18th century depleted the supply of the cotton and linen rags that served as paper manufacturing mainstays. Desperately, paper-makers looked for less expensive and more practical raw materials while also seeking to build supply.

Ads in both European and American periodicals requested readers to save their rags. A Massachusetts paper mill went one step further: it used a watermark that read "Save Rags". To save linen and cotton for the paper industry, the British parliament decreed in 1666 that only wool could be used to bury the dead. In this way, about 200,000 pounds of linen and cotton were saved in one year. But ultimately, there was no question that more plentiful — and cheaper — materials had to be found. Though there was no question that woven material made for the best quality paper, the industry focused on quantity, speed and low cost.

Frenchman Rene Antoine Ferchault de Reaumur's 1719 treatise suggested a new raw material that might provide the practical alternative to cotton and linen. He described his observations of a group of wasps that produced very fine paper from wood filaments to build the walls of their nests. Reaumur recommended that the industry follow their example in using wood.

Reaumur's recommendation, advanced by pioneers like Jacob Christian Schaeffer and others, led to some experimentation of making pulp from wood. But it was not until the middle of the 19th century, with the invention of grinders and chemical digesters and discoveries using soda ash and sulphite treatments, that massive commercial use of wood became more practical.

Practicality characterized papermaking from its Chinese origins forward. The industry sought to constantly improve materials and processes in order to keep pace with the demand. If the secret had never been leaked, who knows, this magazine might have been handwritten on parchment. **HM**

Noble Learned Corporation

Jamie Pratt looks at the early history of the Royal Society.

"The noble learned Corporation
Not for itselfe is thus combyn'd
But for the publique good oth'Nation
And generall benefitt of Mankynd."

THE ABOVE LINES ARE taken from a poem entitled *The Ballad of Gresham Colledge* (*c.* 1663) which was addressed to "that choice Company of Witts and Philosophers who meet on Wednesdays weekly att Gresham Colledg." The poem both praises and lampoons the newly founded Royal Society of London for the Promotion of Natural Knowledge. Though a subject of satire, the "noble learned Corporation" was destined to become one of the most revered institutions of learning ever to exist. It is the oldest scientific society in the English-speaking world, and the second oldest anywhere (the oldest being France's Montmor Academy, founded in the 1650s, which became the better known Académie Royale des Sciences). The list of the Royal Society's early members rings out like a who's who of the scientific revolution. But as will be seen, in its formative years the survival of the Royal Society was by no means assured.

Predecessors
It can be said that the intellectual inspiration for the Royal Society and the new scientific outlook was the philosopher Francis Bacon (1561-1626). He reacted against the abstract reasoning of the medieval universities, asserting that the deductive logic taught since the time of Aristotle (the logic of syllogisms) was good for proving things we already know, but could not provide us with *new* knowledge. A syllogism is a three-sentence argument consisting of two premises followed by a conclusion. An example would be "All men are mortal (first premise). Socrates is a man (second premise). Therefore, Socrates is mortal (conclusion)."

A founding member of the Royal Society, Robert Boyle paved the way for the modern theory of chemical elements.

Bacon claimed it was best to assemble facts by observation and generalize from them — the *inductive* method of logic. More significantly, he believed in the importance of experiment in tying nature down and forcing it to yield up a yes or no answer to well-posed questions. In a work called *The New Atlantis*, he envisioned a utopian society which had an institution specially devoted to scientific research.

A precursor to the Royal Society was Gresham College. Sir Thomas Gresham (*c.* 1519-79) had been financial advisor to Queen Elizabeth I and is now primarily known for the economic principle which bears his name, Gresham's Law: "Bad money drives out good." Gresham left a will providing for his home in London to be turned over to the City in trust for its citizens, to become an institute for public lectures and assemblies. Thus, Gresham College was born in 1598. It was unusual for its time in being a school devoted to what we would now call "adult education". It consisted of seven unmarried professors who were provided with comfortable living quarters and paid £50 a year. Most importantly, scientific lectures were given in English as well as Latin, and regular citizens were welcome to attend. Gresham College would eventually house the new Royal Society and its collection of curiosities, the two institutions becoming so intertwined that Fellows of the Society would often be called "Greshamites".

Around 1645 a group of science-lovers began meeting as an informal luncheon club in a London tavern to discuss the latest scientific discoveries. They referred to themselves as the "invisible college", a college without buildings or professors and away from the turbulent Civil War politics of the period. Any talk of politics, religion or current affairs was expressly forbidden from the club. In this policy one can see the seeds of the Royal Society's reputation — and the reputation of scientists in general — for cool and detached observation and neutrality. Many members of the invisible college would go on to become founding Fellows of the Royal Society.

The Founding
On 28 November 1660 after hearing a lecture on astronomy at Gresham College by Christopher Wren (later to become famous for his architecture during the rebuilding of London after the Great Fire of 1666), some of those present met and decided to form a "College for the Promoting of Physico-Mathematicall Learning." They came up with a membership list of 40 names and agreed on a membership fee of 10 shillings (the membership limit was soon disregarded and fees proved difficult to collect). In September 1661 the group petitioned for royal

approval. Charles II granted them a Charter on 15 July 1662, and thus was born the Royal Society of London for the Promotion of Natural Knowledge.

Membership and Activities

In discussing the early members and activities of the Society it should be kept in mind that the words "science" and "scientist" did not necessarily mean what they do today. For instance, the official communications of the Society were classified as follows: mechanics and trade; weather; statics and hydraulics; architecture, ship-building, geography, navigation, voyages and travels; pharmacy and chemistry; monsters and longevity; and grammar, chronology, history and antiquities. Several of these classifications would not be listed among the sciences today. A little later, when the Society began publishing its journal, the *Philosophical Transactions* (which misses by three months the honor of being the world's oldest scientific publication), articles included whale-fishing in Bermuda, blood transfusion, making mulberry wine in Devonshire, tin-mining processes, and a description of a "very odd, monstrous calf" born in Lymington, Hampshire. A founding member, Joseph Glanvill, published a work entitled *Some Philosophical Considerations Touching Witchcraft and Witches* (1666). In short, whatever came to the interest and attention of the gentlemen of the Royal Society counted as science.

The members themselves were not scientists, but rather "virtuosi". A virtuoso was simply a gentleman with an interest in the new experimental learning. Thus, even a poet like John Dry-

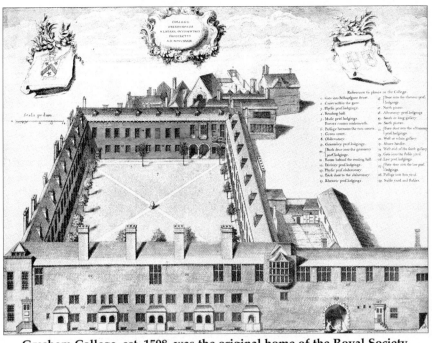

Gresham College, est. 1598, was the original home of the Royal Society.

den could be — and was — a Fellow. Some of the original Fellows of the Royal Society included Samuel Pepys (1633-1703), Secretary of the Admiralty and famous diarist; Christopher Wren (1632-1723), a scientist who later became more famous for his architecture; Robert Boyle (1627-91), founder of the theory of simple elements and of modern chemistry; Robert Hooke (1635-1703), Boyle's assistant, pioneer of microscopy, first to introduce the term "cell" to biology, and the Society's first curator of experiments; and John Graunt (1620-1674), pioneer of "political arithmetic" (statistics).

Besides meeting once a month to conduct experiments, a passion of these early virtuosi was collecting. Many members had large curio collections, which they bequeathed or donated to the Society. In the 18th century these collections were given away to form the basis of the British Museum. Also given to the Museum in 1830 was the Society's library, which by 1678 consisted of some 500 manuscripts and 3,000 printed books.

Crises of the Early Years

In 1667 Thomas Sprat, F.R.S. (Fellow of the Royal Society) wrote his *History of the Royal-Society of London*. Why would he write the history of an organization which was only five years old? There are two reasons. First, in the 17th century the word "history" had a similar meaning to what we now mean by "story". Thus, any discourse on a subject might be called a "history" of that subject. But more importantly, Sprat's *History* is a propaganda piece directed against various wits and enemies who were attacking the Society and its virtuosi. And the attacks were many.

Sprat probably had in mind Dr. Henry Stubbs, who thought the Society and its experimental bent was a breeding ground for atheism and popery. It was his opinion that the virtuosi were poking around in things that were not the concern of proper Christians. Fortunately for the Society, Stubbs died suddenly in 1676. However, it probably did not help matters that Henry Oldenburg, the Society's first Secretary and founder of the *Philosophical Transactions* had been imprisoned in the Tower in 1667 "for dangerous designs and practices", probably having to do with his vast correspondence with foreign intellectuals. There were some who were uncomfortable with the goings-on in the Society's meetings. There were various experiments, such as the infamous blood transfusions (from a sheep to a spaniel, and from a sheep to a "harmless lunatic"). Various animals were being asphyxiated in air-pumps and vivisections were performed.

The common person probably reacted to such practices much as today we might react to the genetic modification of food or the cloning of sheep. Others found in it much material for satire. A character in Thomas Shadwell's play *The Virtuoso* says, "I believe if the blood of an ass were transfus'd into a virtuoso, you would not know the emittent ass from the recipient philosopher." In *The Spectator* of 24 March 1711, Joseph Addison alluded to the disproportionate number of medical doctors ("Retainers to Physick") in the Society "who, for want of other Patients, amuse themselves with the stifling of Cats in an Air Pump, cutting up Dogs alive, or impaling of Insects upon the Point of a Needle for Microscopical Observations."

More serious threats to the Society were its declining membership and its financial troubles. Members numbered 119 in 1663, and 187 in 1671. But 20 years later membership dropped to 116 members and meetings were sparsely attended. The *Philosophical Transactions* were suspended from 1687 to 1691, the first and only time they were not published. From the beginning members seemed unable to pay their one-shilling in dues every week. In 1663 they owed £158 and £1,475 in 1670. Eventually members in arrears were struck from the rolls, and in 1728 lawsuits were undertaken against members negligent in paying their dues. Under the Presidency of Sir Isaac Newton and his successors in the 18th century, the Society's finances stabilized and its membership increased.

The frontispiece of the *History of the Royal-Society of London* depicts John Evelyn (left) and Francis Bason (right) humbling themselves alongside a bust of King Charles II.

Newton and Beyond

With the publication of Sir Isaac Newton's great *Mathematical Principles of Natural Philosophy* (1687) and his subsequent Presidency (1703-27) the Royal Society embarked on its journey to greatness, marred perhaps by the ugly feud between the followers of Newton and of the German philosopher G.W. Leibniz (1646-1716) over credit for the invention of the calculus.

Over the years the Society has sponsored much scientific research. In 1768 it backed James Cook's expedition to the Pacific.

It sent another expedition to the Gulf of Guinea to photograph the solar eclipse of 29 May 1919, verifying a prediction of Albert Einstein's new general theory of relativity. In addition, after its brief hiatus, the *Philosophical Transactions* continued to be published from 1691 to the present.

Every year the Society awards five medals (the Copley, the Davy, the Hughes, and two Royal medals) in addition to the Rumford and Darwin medals (every two years), the Sylvester medal (every three years) and the Buchanan medal (every five years). Of these, the oldest and most prestigious is the Copley Medal, dating from 1736. Eighteenth-century recipients include Benjamin Franklin, James Cook and Giuseppe Volta. Twentieth-century honorees include Ivan Pavlov, Albert Einstein and Niels Bohr. Today the Royal Society boasts over 9,000 Fellows and 90 foreign members.

Further Reading

Addison, Joseph and Steele, Richard. *The Spectator, Volume One*. London: Everyman Library, 1961. Sprat, Thomas. *The History of the Royal-Society of London, For the Improving of Natural Knowledge*. London: J. Martyn, 1667. Stimson, Dorothy. *Scientists and Amateurs: A History of the Royal Society*. New York: Henry Schuman, 1948. **HM**

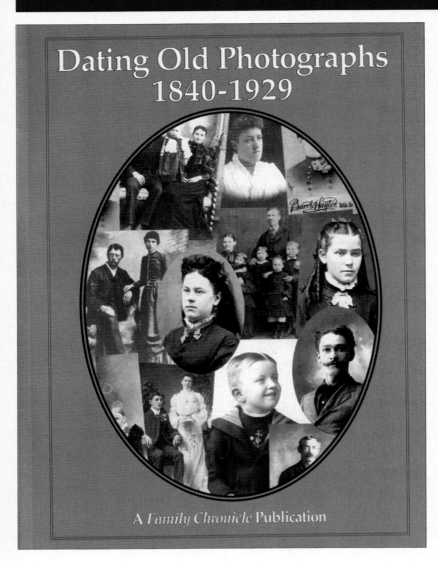

The Panama Canal

Jeff Chapman looks at the canal called "the gateway to the modern Atlantic-Pacific age".

VASCO NUÑEZ DE BALBOA'S 1513 discovery of the Pacific coast of Panama prompted the first dreams of a route that would enable ships to sail westward from the Atlantic to the Pacific across the Central American isthmus. In 1534, King Charles of Spain ordered the first survey of a proposed canal route through the Isthmus of Panama, but more than three centuries passed before the first construction was started. Following the US-financed construction of the Panama Railroad in the mid-19th century and the discovery of gold in California in 1848, interest in a canal was heightened.

The first attempt to build a canal across Panama was made in 1881. A French company led by Ferdinand de Lesseps, the diplomat who had overseen the construction of the Suez Canal, attempted to build a sea-level canal across the isthmus, which was at that time part of the nation of Colombia. The company collapsed in 1889 as a result of poor planning, manpower losses from yellow fever among the workers (up to 200 of whom were dying each month) and finally bankruptcy.

In the US, the 1902 Spooner Act authorized the purchase of de Lesseps' company and the building of a canal provided that a satisfactory treaty could be negotiated with Colombia. When treaty negotiations with Colombia broke down, the US saw the need for a country that would be more accommodating. In 1903,

A bird's eye view of the canal.

Panama declared its independence, and US warships and marines appeared suddenly to enforce Panama's right to secede. That same year, the Hay-Bunau-Varilla Treaty between Panama and the US granted the latter canal-building rights and sole control over a 10-mile-wide, ocean-to-ocean Canal Zone. The treaty granted the US the right to act "as if it were the sovereign" in the entire Canal Zone, effectively making the area a foreign colony in the middle of Panama.

As work on the canal began in the summer of 1904, the builders confronted the threat of tropical diseases such as yellow fever and malaria, which had proved devastating to the French canal crews. Armed with the knowledge that the diseases were spread by the tsetse fly and the mosquito, the Americans took radical steps to install mesh screens around all living quarters, to fumigate regularly, and to eliminate insect breeding grounds wherever possible. These steps, combined with careful quarantining of the sick, enabled the Americans to virtually eliminate yellow fever from the area. To guard against other potential hygiene problems, work on the canal was temporarily halted so the workers could construct proper sewers for the Panamanian cities they inhabited.

Having arrived at a solid, long-term solution to the manpower problem, the builders now faced the tremendous engineering hurdles associated with the project, the dominant problem being imposed by the different elevations of the Atlantic and Pacific Oceans. The engineers elected to utilize a high pass with locks, rather than a sea-level cut, to overcome the elevation

A cruise ship travels through the canal, which is a popular tourist attraction.

A map of the Panama Canal Zone, prior to the canal's official return to Panama at the beginning of 2000.

Panama Canal-related Websites

How the Panama Canal Works
www.ared.com/kora/java/pcc/ javaani.html

Official Panama Canal Site
www.pancanal.com

Panama Canal Cam
www.discovery.com/cams/pancan/ pancan.html

problem. The final plan was drafted in 1906 by John F. Stevens, chief engineer of the US Isthmian Canal Commission. Under the plan, workers dammed the torrential Chagres River on the Atlantic side of the isthmus and the Rio Grande on the Pacific side. This process created navigable lakes on either side of the continental divide, including Gatun Lake, which was at the time the world's largest artificial lake. At times more than 43,000 people were employed on the $350-million project, making it the largest and most expensive enterprise since the construction of the Pyramids.

In August 1914, the cement boat *Cristobal* made the first passage from the Atlantic to the Pacific through the canal, and the canal was officially opened to traffic shortly afterwards. Its length from deep water in the Atlantic to deep water in the

Pacific is about 51 miles. Using the canal, ships sailing between the east and west coasts of the US can shorten their voyage by about 8,000 nautical miles. The locks are duplicate, so that ships may pass in opposite directions simultaneously. With waiting time, ships require about 15 to 20 hours to negotiate the canal. The average transit time, once a vessel has been authorized to proceed, is about nine hours from deep water to deep water. Oil, grains and coal are the principal products transported through the canal.

Traffic through the Panama Canal is a barometer of world trade, rising in times of world economic prosperity and declining in times of recession. From a low of 807 transits in 1916, traffic rose to a high point of 15,523 transits in 1970 (more freight has traveled through the canal in subsequent years, but there have

been fewer transits because the size of shipping vessels has increased). Most freight passing through the canal travels between the east coast of the US and East Asia. All vessels passing through the canal pay tolls, with the exception of certain ships of the Panamanian and Colombian governments. (The lowest toll ever paid was 36 cents, which Richard Halliburton paid to swim the canal in 1928.)

Since 1903 the US has invested about $3 billion in the canal, approximately two-thirds of which has been recovered. Since its opening, the canal has been effectively controlled by the US, with varying degrees of directness. In 1977, however, a new treaty abolished the Canal Zone and control of the canal passed to the Panama Canal Commission, a joint agency of the US and the Republic of Panama. By mutual agreement, Panama gained complete control over the canal for the first time in its history at noon on 31 December 1999.

In a ceremony held two weeks prematurely to avoid potential difficulties related to the Y2K problem, former US president Jimmy Carter said, "It is yours," as he symbolically turned over the canal to Panama. Carter apologized that the original canal accords were unjust, and that the US "did not understand clearly enough that the arrangement defined a certain element of colonialism."

HM

Working Women in New York in 1880

Extracted from *Harpers New Monthly* by Nicole Brebner.

MODERN WOMEN tend to take for granted their ability to support themselves. Save for a few roadblocks like glass-ceilings and pay equity issues, women today are unlimited in their professional opportunities. While the effects of the Women's Movement remain fresh in our memories, it is only by looking further back into the past that we can recognize how far women, and society as a whole, have come.

A June 1880 article in *Harpers New Monthly* magazine provides fascinating insight into the plight of women and girls attempting to make a living in New York City as well as offering a glimpse of society's attitudes towards "the fairer sex". William H. Rideing wrote a passionate exposé of the dire situation facing the majority of women who needed to earn a decent living. Many of these women were unmarried or widowed and from very poor families. Their suffering seems to have been largely ignored by all but a few social agencies whose purpose was to seek justice and improved working conditions. Rideing's dramatic article paints a bleak portrait that was doubtless as shocking to the genteel society of 1880 as it is when we hear stories of sweatshops and dangerous working conditions today. Rideing's article is excerpted below:

There are many business men not wholly uncharitable in their way of looking at life who do not perceive anything out of the common, or calling for immediate alleviation, in the straits of a young

Room of a poor seamstress.

woman who has to live in the city upon four dollars a week. "If," they say, "she had any aptitude, she could earn more" and this, perhaps, is conclusive with them that nothing can be done, that nothing need be done. Not having aptitude is her misfortune; she is necessarily not worth much, and anyone who is inclined to look at the subject sentimentally is forced into a corner by the inexorable logic of political economy.

There are thousands of working-girls in New York who dress and live well, who have aptitude, dexterity, intelligence, and experience. It is they who combine the garniture of my lady's bonnet with an artistic sensibility to color, and give the muslin rose that is so soft and pinky its botanical realism; who, as designers and decorators, find positions of varied usefulness; and who, in retouching photographs, dress-making, and doing various work requiring facility and taste, command fair salaries. There is another class, poorer but still capable of earning a sum sufficient for decent board and clothing?— the workers on upholstery, fringes, feathers, and millinery goods. "Look at them!" says the commercial man to whom the subject of the condition of working women is broached — "look at them! my dear sir. They dress neatly? yes, very neatly; they are certainly not starving, nor overweighted by the sorrows of their circumstances, and I don't see that their faces show any tremendous defects in the ventilation of our factories." This dear good fellow has no other time for reaching into such matters than after dinner at his club, and there is no easier way of solving a social problem than through the medium of a mild and fragrant cigar and a pousse-café.

But there are many more thousands, in the city with no special ability and no special value, who toil, and blind themselves, and wear themselves to death, for an unimaginable, incredible pittance, who plod along for the sake of mere existence, enduring more than will be believed, filling every waking hour with labor, sacrificing themselves in every way, and willing to suffer so much to prolong it that the simple possession of life, though it is embittered to the extreme, seems to be sufficient compensation for a martyrdom.

Another plea for nonintervention with the privations of certain classes is that they are habituated to their condition, and that, not having a contrast to it, they do not feel its hardships as an observer perceives them. Nevertheless, there are some workingwomen in New York who, however inured they may be to hunger and the dismalness of tenement attics, however ignorant and unambitious, cannot help feeling the destitution and burdensomeness of their circumstances, who struggle without hope, and cling to life with a blind instinct, though the circulatory system is all that it yields them in the way of benefit. It is so easy to be partial in speaking of such a subject as this that, desiring the reader to weigh the evidence for himself, I feel that no other eloquence is necessary than that which the facts themselves possess, and perhaps there is no better introduction

Day nursery for children of working mothers on Mulberry Street, New York, in 1880.

for these than through the Working-women's Protective Union.

This society was established some 16 years ago, to promote the interests of women who obtain a livelihood by other employments than household service, and especially to provide them with legal protection from the frauds and impositions of unscrupulous employers.

In making shirts at fifty cents a dozen there may not seem to be scope for fraud; but little as some working women are paid, it is diminished by a variety of tricks of the trade, and sometimes it is withheld altogether. There are employers who are never able to make the exact amount of change on payday, and who deduct a few cents from week to week, until the total loss to the unfortunate employees is many dollars. There are other employers who find no little profit in exacting a deposit from the women to whom they give work, ostensibly as security, but practically as a premium, the depositor never obtaining her money again; and another way of still further impoverishing the worn-out women is to deduct something on the grounds that their work is not as good as the sample, or that it is delayed in delivery.

Who can say that it is a bleak, faithless, and merciless world when such men as these abound? It is against such mean swindles as these that the Protective Union exerts itself,

Women making fringes.

...a quiet read beside a brook
...a history or genealogy book
...from www.WillowBendBooks.com

and to prevent which it was founded. Left to themselves, the women imposed upon are often too ignorant to know how to seek the recovery of their [wages] or too poor to prosecute. They appeal in vain for consideration, scold the agent, and then subside in the sympathy of their neighbors unless they find the Union, which is an implacable litigant for them, carrying their cases from court to court, and employing the most capable counsel, if necessary, to secure justice. The mere fact of its existence represses much wrong, and it has contested its cases with such persistence that few defaulting employers are willing to defend a suit brought by it; but at the same time it should be said that it does not proceed to law until it is convinced of the validity of its cause, and it does not immediately take for granted all the ex parte testimony brought to it.

Sometimes the defendant is a woman moving in good society, or a fashionable milliner who has declined to pay her workwomen; and sometimes, too, a flourishing firm reveals how a part of its success at least has been obtained by cheating and oppression.

A few of the complainants are neatly dressed, and intelligent in face and manner. Among these are teachers and the higher grade of workers, who are also victims to some extent of the impositions which it is the object of the Union to put down; but what that is pleasing to look upon can be expected in most of them? Labor carried on far into the night, insufficient food, and perpetual distress wither and stupefy, and the faces that we see are sallow and

Cigar makers stripping tobacco.

lugubrious, the dresses are stained and torn, and the dispositions of the women are fretful or extremely subdued. Not a few of the clients of the Union taste meat only once a month, and their vegetarianism does not immediately prepossess one by its apparent effects.

There have been women

Women decorating candles.

among them who make shirts at thirty-six cents a dozen, and who could not collect even this pittance from their employers; others who make quilts, and toil eleven hours a day, for four dollars and fifty cents a week; others who make paper boxes ten hours a day for three dollars and eighty cents a week; and others who, as book-folders, have not been able to earn more than three dollars a week. When these women have appealed to the Union, it has not been to exact an increase of the amount, but to collect the amount itself, of which attempts have been made to defraud them.

"By beginning work at six o'clock in the morning and continuing it till dark, then finishing the buttonholes in the evening, a good worker can make three dozen shirts a day," a person well informed told me; and if, then, a woman had the extraordinary adeptness which the sewing of this number implies, she might make seven dollars a week, provided she had no objection to committing suicide in this deliberate and laborious way.

But very few succeed in making this much; most of them are to some extent distracted by family duties, and the average wages are probably less, if anything, than four dollars a week. Shirt-making is perhaps the poorest of all occupations, but there are many others little better.

It is a matter of curious interest how women who earn so little continue to eke out their existence. "How do they live?" we asked. "They don't live," said Mrs. Ferrer, the superintendent of the Union, and this seemed to be the only conclusion possible.

The majority of sewing-girls who work on such inferior articles as shirts which retail at forty or fifty cents apiece, toil from morning to night for little more than a loaf of bread, a cup of tea, and a bed in a tenement attic. The needle is the natural weapon of every woman who has to battle for herself in the world, and the occupations in which it is available are so over-crowded and underpaid that the benevolence strikes us as being misapplied which exerts itself in adding to the surplusage of seamstresses, as various industrial schools and sewing societies do exert themselves. Are there not other trades the reader may well ask, to which the young girls of the poor may be directed, and for which they may better be prepared than this precarious and at the best very unremunerative one? Is there, he may also inquire, any other occupation as hopeless, as hungry, as fatiguing as this? The answers of the two questions may be combined. The utility of teaching girls sewing, except for personal and family uses, in which it is obviously indispensable, does not appear very emphatic; but they demand so little? only enough to prolong a life however miserable, and to defer the uncertainty and horrors of death? that it seems a mercy to even put this resource before them.

Coming back to the question as to what other occupations besides sewing are open to women, the list is so long that a mere enumeration is impossible.

Shop girls in New York in 1880. Starting salaries were usually $1.50 for a 60 hour week rising to $10 after some years. The average pay was calculated at $6.

In the city or suburbs we find women employed in staining and enameling glass; in making glass signs; in cutting ivory, pearl, and tortoise-shell; working in gutta-percha, gum-elastic, and hair; making willow-ware and cane chairs; feeding printers' presses and setting type; making and packing candles; molding tablets of water-colors; assisting in the manufacture of chemicals and fire-works; making clocks, enameling dials, and painting the cases; finishing backgammon boards; making and dressing dolls and toys; stitching the cloths and making the pockets of billiard tables; painting the handles of brooms, and weaving twine into netting; making paper collars and twine; burnishing jewelry and making buttons. There are about five hundred millinery houses in the city, employing over two thousand milliners, and the manufacture of straw hats engages several thousand women in weaving the braid,

sewing, and bleaching. The artificial-flower trade employs about four thousand women, many of them French, and it is as lucrative to adept hands as any other. The manufacture of hoop-skirts is said to engage over ten thousand women, who spool the cotton, weave the tape, and cover the steel; and the cap trade gives employment to many more thousands; whose earnings vary from three to five dollars a week. Women also do the weaving of haircloth, the packing of confectionery, and the making of shoe "uppers".

Some of these occupations, and others to which we have not yet referred, are dangerous to the operatives, not merely from the long hours of toil, the insufficient food, and the lack of proper ventilation in the workshops, but from the nature of the materials and the manner of fabrication. "Behind our tinted Salviati glass, our painted Sevres china, our Minton majolica, and shining silver plate," a brilliant writer once said in this Magazine, "are long rows of pallid faces breathing death that they may live." The artificial-flower makers, the gold-leaf workers, the button-gilders, the cigar-makers, and the match makers also suffer from the nature of their occupation.

Should any woman who is seeking a means of livelihood, without previous experience, read these pages, she can not feel encouraged, and there is little, indeed, to be added that will stimulate her.

HM

Privateers of the Caribbean

Jeff Chapman looks at pirates who operated with government sanction.

WHEN ONE ENCOUNTERS the term "privateers", the first image that leaps to mind is of a pack of bloodthirsty, lawless pirates ruthlessly pillaging some poor seaside port. In reality, privateers were officially commissioned "special units" of national navies — but this isn't to say the first image that leaps to mind is in any way inaccurate.

Less than 150 years after Columbus' first landing in the New World, the great European sea powers of the day were scrambling for colonial outposts in and around the Caribbean. The Dutch, English and French governments were eager to get at some of the seemingly inexhaustible supplies of Aztec gold and Inca silver which the mainland Spanish colonies had tapped. Unfortunately, the Spanish had complete control of the mainland — as well as dominating the largest Caribbean islands, Cuba and Hispaniola. In the parlance of the time, the whole Caribbean region was frequently referred to as "the Spanish Main". It seemed there was little the other Europeans could do but occupy the leftover land in the Caribbean — the smaller islands, which were suitable for sugar cultivation and not much else — and be content to wave as the gold-and-silver-laden Spanish merchant ships sailed past on their way back to Spain.

Buccaneers

Of course, not everyone was content to play so nicely. In the later part of the 17th century, a class of roguish men — and a few roguish women — began successful raids on Spanish ships and settlements. These people, largely consisting of runaway slaves and deserters, were called buccaneers, a name derived from the French word *boucan,* a grill for the smoking of *viande boucanée,* or dried meat, for use in ships at sea.

By means of the *letter of marque,* men who had been mere bandits were able to reinvent themselves as brave patriots — without really behaving much differently.

While a 1676 English dictionary defines the term *buckaneers* as "the rude rabble in Jamaica", buccaneers speaking many different languages operated out of many ports — though Port Royal, Jamaica was certainly the main base for English buccaneers. The ruthless sea raiders kept the Spanish occupied at a time when the other western European powers were unable to spare fleets to protect their Caribbean holdings and, knowing that the Spanish were the primary victims of pirate attacks, the governors of Dutch, English and French colonies sometimes received orders to relax restrictions against buccaneers. In a few exceptional cases, buccaneers received formal expressions of gratitude from local or imperial governments — Henry Morgan received such a commendation after leading 1,500 buccaneers in successful raids against the Spanish towns of Santa Marta and Rio de la Hacha. (The following year, Morgan was briefly imprisoned in the Tower of London for appearances' sake, as England and Spain were not formally at war.)

Under the leadership of such famous men as Morgan, Edward Davis, John Eaton and Charles Swan, buccaneers achieved tremendous successes. Their free-booter victories against the Spanish caused the Dutch, English and French governments to become increasingly interested in their abilities. Starting with small raids against Spanish ships, the buccaneers graduated first to raids against settlements, and ultimately to complete conquests of Spanish cities. Buccaneers captured Puerto Bello in 1668, and in 1671 — by means of a surprise march across the Isthmus of Panama to New Spain's largely undefended Pacific Coast — sacked Panama, then the wealthiest city in the New World.

On the outbreak of the War of the Grand Alliance in 1689, in which France fought against all its neighbor states, the ship-hungry governments of Europe realized it was better to work *with* the buccaneers rather than against them. A system was formally introduced whereby captains who owned and operated their own ships could become unpaid but legally sanctioned raiders in the service of their nation. In such a manner, villainous buccaneers could become heroic privateers overnight.

Letters of Marque

Privateers were not entirely new to the New World, of course. As early as 1572, the independent captain Francis Drake had shown such promise in harassing England's enemies that he had been awarded what was essentially a license to plunder in the King of Spain's lands by Queen Elizabeth I.

While successful, independent captains such as Drake and John Hawkins had been exceptional in the late 16th century, by the middle of the 17th century such men were becoming increasingly common. Buccaneers in the New

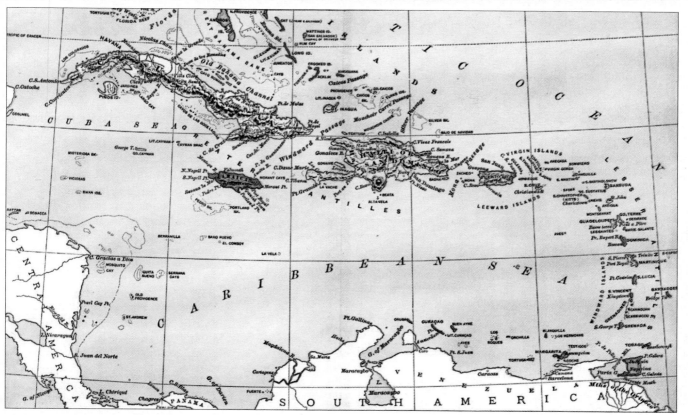

Buccaneers and privateers plied their trade in the Caribbean Sea, plundering the cities and ships of the Spanish Main.

World of the 17th century enjoyed a special position: they were rogues, but they were rogues with ships and guns, at a time when governments were desperate for ships and guns. It was truly a pirate's market.

When buccaneers traded in the Jolly Roger for a national flag, the document which formally recognized their changed status was the *letter of marque*. A *letter of marque* charged the privateer to disrupt enemy trade, sink enemy ships, destroy enemy settlements — and to defeat enemy privateers. In exchange for providing the privateer with a safe haven and license to attack, the issuer shared in the profits. The original function of a *letter of marque* (or letter of reprisal, as they were sometimes known) was to right a private wrong. For example, when a Dutch merchant had his goods stolen in Germany, and he could not gain satisfaction for his loss through legal or diplomatic means, he could be granted a *letter of marque* by the Dutch government. Such a letter would allow him to capture a German merchant ship to compensate him for his loss.

The function of the *letter of marque* changed over time, and the letters became used by governments to augment their navies. This gave the state a naval force which could attack the commerce of the enemy at no cost to public funds. The ships that privateers captured had to be brought before an Admiralty Court and tried to ensure they were a legal prize, and not the property of a neutral state.

Letters of marque did not completely safeguard a privateer from prosecution. When a privateer was captured by hostile nations he was often charged with being a pirate and executed. When countries made peace and a privateer failed to get the news about this in time he could be prosecuted for continuing to attack ships of the now-friendly nation.

Crews were not paid by the commissioning government but were entitled to cruise for their own profit, with crew members receiving portions of the value of any cargo or shipping that they could wrest from the original owners.

Consequences of Privateering

While no government got rich by sharing in the profits of its privateers, privateers were more than a mere annoyance to the enemy. As has been mentioned, even the largest and richest towns in the New World were vulnerable to a well-planned and large-scale pirate assault.

Though the French were not the most aggressive privateers and the English not the richest, between 1793 and 1814, French corsairs captured 10,871 English ships carrying more than £100,000,000 in cargo. During the War of 1812, the US privateer ship *Yankee* alone seized or destroyed $5,000,000 worth of English property.

The activities of privateers had an additional and more subtle effect on the balance of power between the great European empires: it was very difficult to conclude peace with a nation when special units of that nation's navy were continuing to disrupt your trade, capture your ships and raid your towns, even if that nation pretended to disapprove.

English Letter of Marque Against Spain

Imprimis, That all merchants and others who shall desire to have letters of reprizall for the takinge and detaininge of ships and goods of the Kinge of Spaine, or his subjects, shall first make proof or exhibitt such information before the Lord Admirall, or his leeftenant judge of the Admiraltye, or either of them respectively, as they shall thinke fitt and agreeable to his Majestye's intention, that their shipps and goods have bin taken out and detained from them, and that their losses and damages have bin such as they pretende to have susteined.

Item, That it shalbee lawfull for the merchants and others authorized by letters of Reprisall to sett uppon by force of armes, and to take and apprehende uppon the seas, or uppon any river, or in any porte or creeke, the shipps and goods of the Kinge of Spaine, or any his subjects whatsoever.

Item, That the said merchants, and others, shall give bond before the said Lord Admirall, or his leeftenant judge of the Admiraltye, that they and every of them shall bringe such shipps and goods, which they shall soe take and apprehende, to some such porte of his Majestye's realme as shalbee most convenent for them.

Item, That all shipps and merchandise taken by vertue of any commission aforesaide shalbee kepte in safetye, and noe parte of them solde, spoiled, wasted, diminished, or the bulke thereof broken, untill judgment hath firste passed in the highe courte of Admiralty that the said goods are lawfull prize; otherwise the said commission to bee voyed, as well to the taker, as to all others that shall buy or intermeddle with the said goods, or any parte of them.

Item, That yf, by reason of opposition in the adjudication of the shipps and goods taken for lawfull prize, there bee necessitye, before the adjudication, to sell them because they bee peritura, and servando sine damno servari non possunt, in this case the judge of the Admiralty shall graunte commission to take a true Inventory and Appraisement thereof by five honest and sufficient men, and sell the same plus offerenti, and to returne the proceed, together with the said Inventory and Appraisement into the courte of Admiralty, there to remaine to the use of them to whom of righte they shalbee adjudged to appertaine.

Item, That those merchants, and others, which shall have the said letters of Reprizall, shall not attempte any thinge against any of his Majestye's lovinge subjects, or the subjects of any other Prince or state in good league and amitye with his Majestye, but only against the Kinge of Spaine, and his subjects.

Item, That after adjudication passed in the highe courte of Admiraltye as aforesaid, it shalbee lawfull for the merchants and others to keepe such and soe many shippes, goods, and merchandise as aforesaid, as shalbee adjudged unto them, in their possession, and to make sale and dispose therof in open market, or howsoever ells, to their best advantage and benefitt, in as ample manner as at any tyme heretofore hath beene accustomed by way of Reprizall, and to have and injoye the same, as lawfull prizes, and as their own goods.

Item, That all and every of his Majestye's subjects, or any other person who shall, either in his owne person serve, or otherwise beare any chardge or adventure, or in any sorte further and sett forward the said enterprise, according to the Articles, shall not in any manner of wise bee reputed or challenged for any offender against anye of his Majestye's lawes, but shall stande and bee by vertue of the said commission from the said Lord Admirall free and freed, under his Majestye's protection, of and from all trouble and vexation that might in any wise growe thereby.

Item, That yt shalbee lawfull for all manner of persons, as well his Majestye's subjects, as any other, to buy of the said goods or merchandise soe taken and apprehended by the said merchants and others, and adjudged for lawfull prize, as is aforesaid, without any daunger, losse, hindrance, trouble, molestation, or incumbrance, to befall the said buyers, or any of them, and in as ample and lawfull manner as if the said goods had bin comen by through the lawfull trafficq of merchants, or as juste prizes in the tyme of open war.

Item, That the said merchants, and others, before the takinge of the said commission, shall give notice to the Lord Admirall or to his leeftenante judge of the Admiralty, of the name of the shipp, and her tonnage or burthen, and the name of the captaine or owner of the said shipp, with the number of mariners and men in her, and for what tyme they are victualled, and alsoe of their ordnaunce, furniture, and municon, to the intent that there may bee an accompte made therof at their returne.

At Hampton Court, the third of November 1625.

Honorable Rogues?

While buccaneer pirates like Edward Teach (Blackbeard) and François L'Olonnois are universally reviled, there is less consensus on the record of those pirates who operated under a national flag. Privateering, so long as it was commissioned and performed only during wartime, was fully legal — but could a mere piece of paper turn a scoundrel into a soldier?

Some pirates, it seemed, *did* quickly transform from bad to good. Henry Morgan escaped from a youth of indentured servitude on a Barbados plantation to become the leader of a large band of buccaneers operating out of Port Royal, Jamaica, the "wickedest city in the New World". Morgan was much feared by his enemies, as his brutal raids resulted in large-scale rape, torture and murder, but his ability as a leader and a strategist was unquestioned. After Morgan's sack of Panama and temporary show-imprisonment in the Tower of London, England's Charles II knighted Morgan and made him the lieutenant-governor of Jamaica. Morgan showed himself to be an able governor, and ironically functioned as a great pirate-buster. He prosecuted his former comrades until his death in 1688.

Another pirate turned pirate-buster was Woodes Rogers. Between 1708 and 1711, Rogers commanded a privateer-busting expedition sponsored by English merchants whose ships had been lost to foreign privateers. In 1717, Rogers was appointed royal governor of the Bahamas, which was estimated to be the home base of more than 2,000 pirates. From Nassau, Rogers managed to establish orderly government and bring many pirates to justice.

In most cases, however, pirates remained rogues in spite of their official sanction, and found it difficult to pass up a raiding opportunity simply because their nation wasn't at war with the right enemies. The notorious Captain William Kidd began sailing as a youth, and by 1689 was sailing as a legitimate privateer for England against the French. By 1695, Kidd

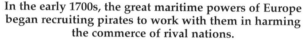

In the early 1700s, the great maritime powers of Europe began recruiting pirates to work with them in harming the commerce of rival nations.

To be a privateer instead of a pirate, one simply had to remember only to plunder and pillage towns and vessels flying the enemy flag.

had received a royal commission to apprehend pirates who molested the ships of the East India Company. While patrolling for pirates off the coast of East Africa, however, Kidd grew weary of waiting for ships he could attack legally, and began raiding and capturing neutral merchant ships. Sailing back to the New World in the captured Armenian ship *Quedagh Merchant*, Kidd made an unsuccessful attempt to persuade colonial officials of his innocence. He was shipped to London, and in 1701 he was convicted of murder and five counts of piracy and subsequently hanged.

American Privateers

No one supported privateering more enthusiastically than the American government, which, in the period following the Declaration of Independence, became quite dependent on privateers. The American navy was so small it was almost non-existent, so the US came to rely on privateers to provide assistance against the completely dominant English navy. During the War of Independence, the American colonists found it difficult to form a new navy because more than 1,000 privateers were already licensed. Among these was a man who had given up the slave trade, gone into hiding after murdering a man and, in the hope of avoiding trial, changed his name from John Paul to John Paul Jones. At the outbreak of war, Jones enlisted in the small American navy, and became as famed for his many victories against the English as for his response to an enemy challenge to surrender — "I have not yet begun to fight!"

The popularity of American privateering continued unabated after independence, and was in fact one of the causes of the War of 1812. Privateers also played an important role in this second major conflict between the US and England. The French privateer Jean Lafitte, who operated off the coast of New Orleans under a *letter of marque* from Cartagena, at that time fighting for its independence from Spain, somehow wound up in the middle of the American-English conflict. Though Lafitte knew the American governor of New Orleans had a price on his head, when the British navy requested his help in attacking New Orleans, Lafitte promptly sent warning to the Americans and offered his help in the conflict against the British. When American ships sailed to Lafitte's stronghold, presumably to show their gratitude, Lafitte bid them welcome. The American ships promptly destroyed his fleet. In spite of this abuse, Lafitte's pro-American sympathies persisted. He offered Andrew Jackson 7,500 guns and 1,000 men for use in the defense of New Orleans, an offer which Jackson reluctantly accepted. Without this assistance, it is likely that New Orleans would have fallen to the British, with an unknown effect on the already-concluded peace treaty. President Madison pardoned Lafitte and his men to reward their bravery.

In 1856, by the Declaration of Paris, England and the other major European countries (except Spain) declared privateering illegal. The US government refused to accede, arguing its small navy made reliance on privateering necessary in time of war. Both the US and Spain, however, had agreed to the terms of the declaration by 1908, and piracy has been all but unknown in the Western Hemisphere since that time. **HM**

Subscribe Now to

How did our ancestors live?

History Magazine is targeted at people who want to know about the lives their ancestors led: what did they eat, how much did they earn, what made them laugh or made them cry?

Here are just a few of the topics that are planned for upcoming issues:

THE SHOEMAKER. Shoemaking was one of the last industries to be automated. We present the history of the trade before machines.

CLOTHING FASHIONS IN THE 1850S. What was fashionable and what did ordinary people wear?

ROBERT GODDARD. A look at the first rocket scientist.

THE BICYCLE. The invention, rise and decline of the machine that provided most efficient method of converting human energy to propulsion.

OFFICE LIFE BEFORE 1920. What was the white-collar work world like in the days before air conditioning and no-smoking laws?

TEA. How a drink made of leaves and hot water caused the birth of empires, led to multiple wars and helped create the modern corporation.

HISTORY OF TAXATION. How the necessary evil of taxes — including the temporary measure known as income tax —crept into our lives.

The Knights Templar

John K. Dorriety looks at the rise and fall of a powerful economic and military force.

THEY EMERGED FROM the first crusade growing in strength across Europe and the Middle East vowing to protect pilgrims on the journey to the Holy Land. The order lasted only 188 years, but their legacy exists even today. Their formal title was the Poor Knights of Christ and of the Temple of Solomon, but perhaps they were better known as the Knights Templar.

Once loved and supported by the Catholic Church, the warrior-monk order grew in number and in power until it reached a point when it threatened the very fabric of the secular and religious authorities of Europe, thus bringing about its destruction.

In order to better understand the Templars, we must first look at the conditions under which the order was founded. The area of the world known as the Holy Land, and particularly Jerusalem, held a special place in the hearts of Christians of the Middle Ages. During this time, the land was held under occupation of the Muslim Turks. Captured in 638AD, Jerusalem had been cut off from Christendom and was under total control of Islamic rule. Following the call of Pope Urban II for Christians to "tear the land from the hands of these abominable people," Christian crusaders had retaken Jerusalem from the Turks.

The Birth of the Templars

Unfortunately for Christian pilgrims, the roads to the Holy Land were considered unsafe as the Muslims were now sworn enemies of the Christians. Out of it all a group of nine knights banded together with the goals of guarding those traveling to and from the Holy Land and to see to the safety of the Holy Sepulchre.

The knights traveled to Jerusalem, around 1119, and asked King Baldwin I to allow them to

The Templars combined piety with military prowess.

establish their headquarters on the site of the Temple Mount. King Baldwin had recently converted the al-Aqsa Mosque into his royal palace, but complied without question to the Templars' wishes. They were given large accommodations with several out buildings. These were all located next to the Dome of the Rock that marked the former site of Solomon's Temple.

In 1126, two of the Templar knights, André de Montbard and Gondemare, returned to their home to visit Montbard's nephew, Bernard of Clairvaux. Bernard was a man of great influence within the church, and the Templars delivered to him a letter from King Baldwin. This letter requested that the order be given "apostolic approval" and to have a "Rule of Life" set for them. It has been said, although not proven, that the Templars offered Bernard artifacts, relics or perhaps secret knowledge discovered during their archaeological digs at the Temple in ordered to receive his support.

Templar Privileges

At Bernard's request, Pope Honorius II granted an audience to the Templars. A council was convened at Troyes on 13 January 1128. A man named John Michael was chosen by Bernard to document the events of the meeting. The Templar knight Hugh de Payens traveled to Troyes to attend the meeting. There were three requests made of the council. First, that the order of the Templars should be given the blessing and recognition of the church. Second, that a rule should be written in order to govern every manifestation of their daily life. Finally, that practical aid should be granted to them which would consist of money and men in order to further their cause in the Holy Land.

After the Council of Troyes, Hugh de Payens traveled to Normandy where the English monarch, Henry I, received him with honors, bestowing gifts of gold and silver to the Temple of Jerusalem. He then traveled on to England and Scotland again receiving gifts. There is no proof that the order of the Templars was actually established in England at this time, but it is logical to assume that it was. Recruitment took place everywhere Hugh de Payens traveled. Other brothers who had attended at Troyes also traveled to their homelands and recruited members. There was an overwhelming acceptance of the order across Europe, especially in France.

During the growth of the order of the Temple, the Templars were granted many privileges from both secular and religious authorities. Through the document *Omne datum optimum*, issued by Pope Innocent II in 1139, they received the right to build their own churches and to appoint chaplains for themselves. Since the

Castle Kragin was one of the main Templar strongholds in the Holy Land.

Templars were defenders of the faith it was obvious that the church should support them. This led to the Templars being exempted from tithes to the church. The order could, however, collect tithes from others. These privileges gave them tremendous power and wealth.

Financial Growth

Although the Templars took a vow of poverty, the order itself was quite wealthy. However, no member owned any luxurious goods at all. Furniture used by the order was usually homemade; food was average with very little meat and a small amount of wine was allowed. Each member was regulated in the Rule precisely what property he could have in his personal possession although everything belonged to the order itself. The order, as a whole, was becoming a powerful financial institution.

Leaders of the order played political games quite well in order to further the order financially. This was seen to be true after the death of Henry I. The Templars profited immensely by playing King Stephen of England against his rivals by receiving gifts from both sides. Thus, the order grew in giant steps in monetary power across Europe. In England, as in other places, the

Templars were free from paying secular taxes. Many of their other privileges led to complaints. Among these were authorities who lost tax-paying land that had been given to the order or by merchants who had their prices undercut by the Templars.

Under the financial growth of the order, London became an "international money market," which contributed to the overall development of the English economy. Banks operated by the Templars rivaled those operated by the Jews, Genoese and the Lombards. In France, the Temple vault was the storehouse for King Philip's treasury. He even used the Temple in Paris as a sanctuary during riots. Even the Muslims were known to have banked with the Templars. Thomas W. Parker wrote, "Their power and accomplishments as feudal lords and bankers seem as great as, if not greater than, their achievements and contributions as soldiers of Christ and His Church..."

Military Strength

The Templars' military power came about after they acquired their great financial power. Their first military engagement was not their most successful adventure. It occurred in 1138 near a place named Teqoa. In an attempt to retake a city that the

Muslim forces had captured, the Templars made the terrible mistake of not pursuing the Muslims as they fled. This allowed the Muslims time to re-group and attack again. This time, it was written by Archbishop William of Tyre, a historian of the time, "the whole space from Hebron to Teqoa [10 miles] was strewn with Templar corpses."

One of the leading factors that contributed to the military strength of the Templars was the fierceness of their soldiers in battle. Templars vowed never to retreat unless the odds in combat were greater than three to one. Even under such conditions, if the men were ordered to fight until the last one was dead, they did so without question. Most of the members would expect to die in battle, as to pay ransom for a captured Templar was forbidden. Thus, those who were captured were executed.

Another factor that contributed to the military power of the Templars was the collaboration with the Order of the Hospitallers; another warrior-monk order also stationed in Jerusalem. The Templars fought at the side of the Hospitallers on many occasions. It was even written, in the *Rule of the Templars*, that if a Templar banner was not available to rally under, the members were to seek out the banner of the Hospitallers. This type of cooperation gave strength to the religious military orders.

The military might of the Templars was turned against the Christians themselves during the Fourth Crusade, which had Christian fighting against Christian. In an effort to reunite eastern and western Christendom, Pope Innocent III started a crusade of which he lost control. In a mockery of their religion, armies totaling over 33,000 soldiers sacked the Dalmatian port of Zara. From there the armies moved into Constantinople. The crusaders committed abominations against Christians similar to those the Muslims were accused of committing. In Europe, the crusade victory was celebrated. The Templars, along with

The Templar church in Luz, France was one of many Templar properties Philip IV wished to obtain from the order.

other military orders, joined in this crusade.

The Templar Threat

Financially powerful throughout Europe, the Templars held grips on the treasuries of individuals and states. Their name meant strength, not only in a military sense, but in a financial sense as well. People from all walks of life depended on them to safeguard their valuables, from private citizens to archbishops. Indeed, this in itself gave the Templars an ambiance of power that would threaten any kingdom of the time, but there was more. Not only could secular authorities be threatened by this, but also the papacy began to stand under their foreboding shadow. This was evident, as Sophia Menache wrote, that by 1223 Pope Honorius III claimed that the Templars had abused the privileges granted to them through interfering with secular activities and in behaviors that were not considered proper for Christians, especially monks.

Under the semblance of the *Omne datum optimum*, the Templars had every religious freedom imaginable to them. Their churches grew more and more numerous and their religious sovereignty intimidated many. Possession of many different religious relics influenced the power of the order as well and contributed to this

intimidation factor. One of the most powerful relics possessed by the Templars was believed to have been taken during the crusade against Constantinople.

Of the charges against the Templars during the Inquisition, the most noted was the supposed worship of an idol head. Speculation has arisen that this head may have been none other than the Mandylion, a cloth with the representation of the face of Christ on it. It has been further speculated that the Shroud of Turin and the Mandylion could have been one and the same, taken by the Templars during the raid of Constantinople. Although the Shroud is a full body length piece of cloth, its original display had it doubled in four. This means that it was folded in a manner that displayed the face only. Ian Wilson, an expert on the Shroud, states that the main body of evidence that points to the Templars possessing this relic is the Shroud's appearance in the 1350s with the knight Geoffrey de Charny. This name bears a striking resemblance to Geoffrey de Charney who was burnt at the stake along with the last Grant Master of the Temple, Jacques de Molay.

When Pope Clement V summoned the Grand Master to Paris in 1306 to meet with him, the Templar leader had no idea he was being called to his death.

King Philip IV had made a deal with Clement. This was the deal that initially put Clement on the papal throne. Part of the deal, it is said, was to support the destruction of the Templars. Because of their power and the fact that they were subservient only to the Holy See, Philip needed the pope to back his plan against the Order. This would allow the king to seize all of their wealth, which was considerable.

On Friday, 13 October 1307, Philip's master plan went into action. Every Templar in France was arrested under the authority of the Inquisition and their property seized. The charges were focused on three primary areas: denial of Christ and spitting on the Cross; homosexuality and obscene kissing; and idol worship. There were a total of 127 articles drawn against the Order.

Confessions were extracted by means of tortures so horrible that one would say anything or confess to anything in order to stop the pain. Even the Grand Master himself had confessed to the accusations placed upon him. On 18 March 1314, Jacques de Molay, the Master of the Temple; Geoffrey de Charney, Preceptor of Normandy; Geoffrey de Gonneville, Preceptor of Aquitaine; and Hugh de Pairaud, the Treasurer and Visitor of the Temple in France, were brought before a council of three cardinals to hear their final confessions. It was said that Pairaud had stated he would say anything to save himself and so he did. He and Gonneville affirmed their confessions and were taken away to prison. When the Grand Master finally spoke, he recanted his earlier confessions asserting the holiness of the Order. He refused to confess in this public forum to the charges laid upon them. The cardinals that were present took no action against the Grand Master, but placed the knights in the hands of the secular authorities. Philip dealt the final blow and sentenced them to death. They were burned at the stake on the same evening on a small island in the Seine near Notre-Dame, which lay opposite the royal gardens.

As the flames engulfed the Grand Master and the Preceptor of Normandy, Jacques de Molay shouted a curse to Pope Clement, King Philip and his family. Molay petitioned Christ to prove the Order's innocence and called Clement before God in judgement within 40 days and for King Philip within a year, for what they had done. Pope Clement died on the morning of 20 April 1314, 33 days after the execution, and King Philip followed that same year dying on 29 November. The Grand Master's curse had been fulfilled, whether by divine influence or at the hands of Templars. Perhaps the Grand Master's words were meant for Templars whom he knew were present in secret and hoping they might be eager to fulfill their Master's last wishes. Either way the price had been paid and the curse completed. Even in death they were men of honor, so much so that monks secretly retrieved their bones during the night.

To this day, no evidence has yet been presented which supports the accusations against the Templars. The facts are that they were granted many ecclesiastical and secular privileges and that they developed into a strong financial order with a powerful military backing. Perhaps the authorities of church and state felt as though they had created a monster they could no longer control or perhaps it was simply greed. Either way their memory should not be cast into the shadows of heretics and demon worshippers, for though their lives bore not the complete appearance of the saints, they were far from the countenance of devils.

The Templar symbol.

References

Barber, Malcom. *The Trial of the Templars* (London: Cambridge, 1978).

Curzon, Henri de. *The Rule of the Templars*. 1886. Trans. J.M. Upton-Ward (New York: Boydell, 1992).

Hamilton, Bernard. *The Medieval Inquisition* (New York: Holmes & Meier, 1981).

Hancock, Graham. *The Sign and the Seal* (New York: Crown, 1992).

Howarth, Stephen. *The Knights Templar* (New York: Dorset, 1982).

Menache, Sophia. "The Templar Order: A Failed Ideal?" *Catholic Historical Review* 79.1 (1993): 1-21.

Parker, Thomas W. *The Knights Templars in England* (Tucson: Univ. of Arizona Press, 1963).

Robinson, John J. *Born in Blood: The Lost Secrets of Freemasonry* (New York: M. Evans, 1989).

Sinclair, Andrew. *The Sword and the Grail* (New York: Crown, 1992).

Summers, Montague. *The History of Witchcraft & Demonology*. 1926 (Secaucus, N.J.: Castle, 1992).

Wilson, Ian. *The Shroud of Turin: the Burial Cloth of Jesus Christ?* (Garden City, N.Y.: Doubleday, 1978).

HM

Jonathan Sheppard Books

Box 2020, Plaza Station
Albany, New York 12220

www.jonathansheppardbooks.com
Serving Historians and Genealogists since 1977
Some Map Specials for Research

A WORD ABOUT OUR MAPS

All maps described below are black and white reprints of original maps in our collection. Unless otherwise indicated, maps are 18" X 24" and are printed on fine quality parchment stock. **Prices shown are in US dollars.**

IMPORTANT - PLEASE READ

SHIPPING: Map orders can be shipped either folded in a 9" X 12" envelope or unfolded and rolled in a sturdy shipping/storage tube. Please tell us your choice and add a shipping charge of either **$2.75 US** (folded) or **$4.50 US** (rolled in tube) to your total order. *Note that the shipping charge is per order, not per map. NYS & MA residents must add appropriate sales tax on total order, including shipping. For shipping to Canada, add an additional $1.50 US.*

SOME MAP SETS FOR RESEARCH:

[F 2] NEW YORK STATE SPECIAL: includes *New York - 1779*, C.J. Sauthier's famous failed Revolutionary War era map (2 sheets - h 23" X 29"); plus *New York Circa 1825* (11" X '); and also *New York - 1866*, showing towns, ny small villages, and other natural features. **All three maps: $20.95**

[20] PHILADELPHIA: 1872 & 1879. The ier map, issued by A. J. Johnson in 1872, shows city divided into wards, and identifies eteries, some suburban areas and ferries to New ey. It also includes an inset map of greater adelphia. The later map, issued by S. A. chell in 1879 and entitled *A Plan of the City of adelphia and Camden*, also shows wards and eteries, railway lines, ferries and identifies y public buildings in the downtown area. **The set: $11.95**

13] OHIO: 1885-87 (2 sheets). This double t set, first issued between 1885 and 1887, cts Ohio in extraordinary detail. Tiny munities - often with less than 25 people - are n, as are the county boundaries. In addition, ays, rivers and numerous small creeks and ms are shown and identified. Inset shows innati and Hamilton County. **$11.95**

[TF 14] ILLINOIS: 1885-87 (2 sheets). This double sheet set, first issued between 1885 and 1887, depicts Illinois in extraordinary detail. Tiny communities - often with less than 25 people - are shown, as are the county boundaries. In addition, railways, rivers and numerous small creeks and streams are shown and identified. Inset shows Chicago and Cook County. **$11.95**

[ZF 40] MISSOURI GROUP: This special set includes *Missouri Circa 1825* (11" X 17"); *Missouri and Part of Kansas - 1865*; *Missouri - 1873/74*; and *Missouri - 1880/81*. Illustrates the state's change and growth. **All four maps: $21.95**

[ZF 11] THE CAROLINAS: This pair of maps includes *North and South Carolina Circa 1825* (11" X 17") and *North and South Carolina - 1865*. Useful for locating early settlements and tracking migrations. **The pair: $9.95**

[XF 7] ENGLAND CIRCA 1875 (2 sheets): Counties, villages, and towns are identified in both England and Wales, as are the important railways and roads. Can be dissected and mounted to make a large 2' x 3' map. **The set: $11.95**

[ZF 86] WALES 1869: This set contains two 18" x 24" maps - **(R 1) North Wales - 1869** and **(R 24) South Wales - 1869** drawn by John Bartholomew and issued by A. & C. Black. Shows rail, cross and carriage roads, as well as towns and villages in all of Wales. **The pair: $11.95**

[XF 2] SCOTLAND (4 maps): Depicting all of Scotland in impressive detail from the Lowlands to the Hebrides, the 3-map set was first published in England in 1834 by the *Society for the Diffusion of Useful Knowledge*. Printed on three sheets, the maps represent Scotland in the early 19th century and include a table of place name changes. Towns, villages, shires and roads are clearly shown. We have also included a small 1805 map of Scotland in each set. **The set of 4 maps: $14.95**

[ZF 81] 19th CENTURY IRELAND: Includes our 2 popular sets of 19th century maps of Ireland, each printed on two 18" x 24" sheets. One set shows Ireland circa 1820; the other depicts Ireland circa 1875. Excellent detail. **The sets: $19.95**

[ZF 61A] EARLY GERMANY: This assortment contains 4 maps: **(M 1) Germany Circa 1760** was originally published in 1768 by

Thomas Kitchin and is a detailed representat of mid 18th century Germany, as well as mos Poland, Switzerland, Austria and the Netherlan Shows thousands of place names; set a includes **(X 5) Two Views of Germany** (two x 17" maps). The earlier map was made ab 1766 by the English engraver Bennet, and sho major cities and towns, as well as internal borde The second map, drawn in 1780 by Rigob Bonne, is an example of "scientific" mapmaki rich in detail; the fourth map, **(M 18) A N Map of Germany Divided into its Circl** (1805), is by the English mapmaker Thom Jeffreys and is useful for sorting out t numerous 19th century German states. **The group: $16.**

[ZF 67] SWITZERLAND: This speci contains two 18" x 24" maps: **(M 27) A Ne Map of Switzerland - 1794** by Laurie & Whitt shows cities, towns, large villages, castles, larg vineyards, Protestant & Catholic parishes, ca roads and footpaths. An inset shows the religiou and political affiliation of each canton. Als includes **(M 16) Switzerland Circa 1875** clearl identifying cantons and Alpine towns and rail an carriage roads. Mountain paths and some sma villages are also shown. **The pair: $11.9**

[ZF 68] DENMARK: This set includes: **(M 35) Denmark - 1799.** Entitled *A New Map o the Kingdom of Denmark,...*, this 1799 map b John Cary shows towns, villages, roads an internal subdivisions. The second map, **(M 13 Denmark, with Schleswig- Holstein and Lauenburg**, was engraved in 1846 by Adolph Stieler and has insets of Iceland, the area near Hamburg and a plan of Copenhagen. Coastal islands are identified, as well as the railway lines and roads. The southwestern tip of Sweden is also shown in some detail. **The pair: $11.95**

PAYMENT: *We accept checks (U.S. dollars/U.S. Banks), M.O.s, MasterCard and VISA. Please include your card number, expiration date and signature when ordering. Our 24 hour faxline for credit card orders is (518) 766- 9181.*

OUR SHOP: *Our bookshop - MARTLET BOOKS - is located on historic North Street in Pittsfield, MA. We stock thousands of out of print local histories and genealogies, along with our map reprints, original antique maps and a select assortment of unusual books in a variety of subject areas. If you plan to visit, send us a SASE and we'll send a descriptive flyer with directions and hours.*

CATALOGUE: *Can't visit our Pittsfield shop? Need maps for other geographic areas, different time periods? For complete descriptions of all of the hundreds of high-quality reprint maps in our collection, as well as a selection of our out of print books, please visit our website at:*

www.jonathansheppardbooks.com

Paper copies of our map catalogue are available for 66 cents in stamps.

Dr. Gatlin's Killing Machine

Brian Loosmore describes the invention of the first practical machine gun.

DURING THE DARK, bloody days of the American Civil War, a weapon was developed which would revolutionize warfare, a weapon so devastating, so superb, it would be used in almost every military action for the next 45 years.

This rapid fire gun was the invention of Dr. Richard Gatlin, who stands unique in the annals of medicine as the devisor of a means of mass killing. His motive, he claimed, was entirely humanitarian, the gun being a labor-saving device to reduce the number of troops required to fight a battle!

The Early Days

Gatlin was born in 1818, the fourth of seven children. He was brought up on his father's farm, went to the local school, did his farm chores, and hunted and fished in the stream like so many of his North Carolina neighbors. His father was descended from English immigrants who came to North America in 1700, was a relatively wealthy planter and owner of slaves. He taught young Richard carpentry and blacksmithing, and was something of an inventor himself, patenting a cotton planter and thinner. Son Richard Gatlin inherited this talent but it was not encouraged at his school, Buckhorn Academy, where he learned math, Greek, Latin, philosophy and science under strict discipline. After leaving school at 15, he heard of a reward for anyone who could develop an underwater device for propelling ships, this still being the age of sail. His imagination fired, Richard built a small boat with a screw propeller which worked well on a pond. Winter came on so he waited until spring to go to Washington to apply for a patent, and we can imagine his disappointment when John Ericsson claimed the patent the day before

Doctor Richard Gatlin.

Gatlin arrived. Delay had cost him dearly, a lesson he never forgot.

The Inventor

For several years he kept a store in the country, an occupation which gave him time to patent a seed-sowing machine for rice and wheat. By 1845, he was able to devote all his time to its promotion, which brought his first taste

> **Gatlin made several fortunes during his career and became a millionaire more than once.**

of fame. The success of his wheat drill brought many awards including a medal from the 1851 Great Palace exhibition in London. The British rights this time did bring a fortune.

Then a disaster struck which might have changed the direction of his life. In 1854, on a ship stuck in ice somewhere between Cincinnati and Pittsburgh, Gatlin contracted smallpox. For two weeks he languished near death before getting ashore suffering from pneumonia. He was left in a pest-house where neglect was probably

better than the primitive medical care of the time and only after three months did he manage to recover.

This experience together, shortly afterwards, with the deaths of two sisters aged 17 and 25 years, prompted Gatlin to study medicine. He soon attended lectures at Indiana Medical Collage and, later, at Ohio Medical College in Cincinnati. He graduated probably in 1859, the same year in which he patented a hemp breaking machine. It is not clear whether he then went into practice but he certainly became well known in medical circles and soon married Jemima Sanders.

Gatlin had not given up on agricultural inventions and patents kept rolling in, five by 1860, but, in 1861, the outbreak of the Civil War brought the invention which made his name famous.

War is a great spur for inventors who, genius or crackpot, focus their attention on more efficient methods of killing, patriotism being reinforced by avarice.

The First "Machine" Guns

Many attempts had been made to develop a repeating gun. As early as 1625 the "organ gun" was used in England, this being little more than about 10 muskets fixed side by side. In 1718 James Puckle patented the "Defense", a device which fired square bullets.

The first machine gun used in war was a Belgian design, the Montigny Mitrailleuse. This consisted of a bundle of 37 musket barrels held in a metal tube. Against the ends of these was placed a metal plate through which holes were drilled to mate with the barrels. A bullet was placed into each hole and this, a kind of magazine, was fitted to the ends of the barrels. A breech containing a firing mechanism was then closed over the plate and worked by turning a handle. The rounds could be fired one at a time or in quick succession. When all the rounds had been discharged, the breech was opened and a new plate and set of bullets inserted, so the firing was interrupted. The later Ager "Coffee Mill" gun and the Ripley machine gun were American designs which probably influenced Gatlin.

The Idea

Dr. Gatlin recounted the story of his invention in a letter he wrote in 1877:

"In 1861, during the opening events of the war (and residing in Indianapolis, Ind.), I witnessed almost daily the departure of troops to the front and return of the wounded, sick and dead. The most of the latter lost their lives, not in battle, but by sickness and exposure incident to the service. It occurred to me if I could invent a machine, a gun, which could by its rapidity of fire, enable one man to do as much battle duty as a hundred, that it would, to a great extent, supersede the necessity of large armies and consequently, exposure to battle and disease be greatly diminished."

He conceived the idea of the gun in the summer of 1861 and demonstrated the prototype early in 1862. The speed with which this one man project was accomplished was astounding.

The 1862 Gatlin gun had six rifled barrels arranged parallel to an axis and all revolving around it. Behind these was a revolving carrier breech block in which, behind each barrel, was an open trough. The barrels, block and strikers were revolved by a hand operated crank. As each open trough came uppermost, a round would fall into it from a hopper and as the block revolved a striker operated by a lug bearing on an inclined plane would be released suddenly to detonate a percussion

An early Gatlin Gun.

cap. The rounds consisted of metal cylinders with a closed end into which paper cartridges and .58 bullets were inserted. Each metal cylinder then fell out of the trough as its barrel became inverted and could be re-used. Each completed revolution of the barrel assembly

> **"If I could invent a machine, a gun, which could by its rapidity of fire, enable one man to do as much battle duty as a hundred, that it would supersede the necessity of large armies."**

resulted in loading, firing and ejection of six rounds. The gun was mounted on a two wheel carriage.

Incredibly, this instrument could fire 200 rounds a minute, an unimaginable performance in its day.

However, this 1862 model had problems and Gatlin was persuaded to modify it to use the recently invented self-contained metallic cartridge. At first the new cartridges were inserted into the old metal cylinders before loading but feed and flight problems recurred and Gatlin eventually devised a breech system which inserted and

withdrew each round from a chamber within each barrel, using a reciprocal motion for the breech mechanism. This was perfected by 1865 and was used in all later models.

Acceptance

The first Gatlin guns were made by Greenwood and Co. in Cincinnati, Ohio, though the original battery of six guns of proven ability were destroyed in a factory fire said to have been caused by Confederate saboteurs. Later McWhinney, Rindge & Co, were persuaded to finance the project and another 13 were built. Gatlin then approached Col. Ripley, at that time Chief of Army Ordinance, but he refused to buy them, citing the fact there was already too great a variety of guns in the service — 79 different models of musket alone. And how would they deploy such a weapon? Fortunately, in Baltimore, Gatlin's backer Rindge happened to meet Major General Benjamin Franklin Butler. Butler, totally lacking in military experience but fascinated by such a military curiosity, immediately bought 12 guns with 12,000 rounds of ammunition for $12,000, a huge price at the time. It is not clear from historical records but these guns, directed by the general, might have been used at Petersburg. Not until 1866 did the Gatlin gun become part of the official arm of the services, the navy following closely on the army.

The guns were now being made by Colt in Hertford, Connecticut, but factories were set up in Birmingham, England, and Vienna, Austria. As they became more sophisticated the firing rate increased from the original 200 rounds per minute to 1,000. A later model worked by an electric motor could discharge 500 shots in 15 seconds! The modern version, the Vulcan gun, developed for use on jet aircraft, can discharge 6,000 rounds a minute.

Gatlin promoted his invention vigorously and by October 1863, had interested the French army but could not arrive at a suitable contract with them.

The Civil War ended in April 1965, costing over 800,000 lives, but there is no hard evidence the Gatlin gun was used, in spite of rumors and anecdotes. It seems the military mind was not ready and not until 1898, at San Juan Hill, did the US army conceive its use as close support for infantry attack.

Dr. Gatlin made numerous improvements to his gun over the next 45 years and it saw effective action in many battles. The distress and slaughter produced soon secured for it a reputation around the globe and it was adopted worldwide. It was used effectively in the Franco-Prussian war of 1870-71, and against the Indians in the west.

Later Gatlin developed a new gun metal, an alloy of steel and aluminum, and from this made an eight-inch-calibre field gun for the US government. Gatlin received $40,000 from Congress for its development. The project ended in fiasco when the gun exploded at trials but Gatlin remained convinced it had been weakened maliciously during manufacture.

Other ideas flowed from his fertile imagination during this period, most concerning agricultural tools, but his interests ranged widely from early bicycles to a toilet flushing mechanism. As late as 1899 he patented a plow built like a car. He claimed this could do the work of eight men and 12 horses! It is strange that he did not apply his talents to the development of medical apparatus such as splints and artificial limbs and one wonders about his commitment to medicine.

Richard Gatlin was active as an inventor and in business to the very end. He was president of the

American Association of Inventors and Manufacturers from 1891 to 1897 and he died suddenly in New York in 1903, aged 84 years.

Gatlin made several fortunes during his career and had been a millionaire more than once. He spent and lost much on unsuccessful inventions and on investments in Western railroads.

In an obituary, *Scientific American* wrote: "Although best known as the inventor of a terrible death-dealing weapon, Dr Gatlin was the gentlest and kindliest of men...By making war more terrible it seemed to him nations would be less willing to resort to arms." Although this notion is now known to be misguided it "does demonstrate a compassion which, perhaps, led to the study of medicine, and gives the lie to the wag who commented that by giving up medicine Dr. Gatlin merely changed his method of killing!"

HM

The Complete History

The First Year of History Magazine

History Magazine Volume One is a reissue of almost all the editorial from the issues dated October 1999 to September 2000.

The colorful, bound volume includes all the editorial material from our first year of publication, including such features as: The Atlantic Cable, The Black Death, The National Road, Cleanliness, Bread, The Code Napoleon, The First Radio Station, The Longbow, 1000AD, The US Cavalry, Custer, Army Wives, Death Customs, Bellevue Hospital, The Impact of the Potato, An 1860s Dinner for Eight, The Rifle, The Oregon Trail, The Handcart Pioneers, Refrigeration, Games People Played, Contraception, The Suez Canal, Midwives, Longitude, The 1910s, Country Store, Connecting the World, Alchemy, Freemasonry, Early Newspapers, Influenza Pandemic, Chicago in 1880, The Privy, The Blacksmith, Saffron, Eli Whitney, Lunatic Asylums, Lighthouses, The 1900 House, Carpetbaggers, The Natchez Trace, Let's Eat!, How Brands Began, The Stirrup, The Shakers, Development of Photography, Insurance, Underground Railroad, Memsahibs of the Raj, California Gold Rush, Poliomyelitis, Wigs, decade profiles, historical trivia — and more!

History Magazine Volume One provides a full year of information about the lives our ancestors led.

Surviving Songs

Rosanne Van Vierzen looks at hymns throughout the ages.

HYMNS HAVE INFLUENCED music throughout history, and were the most common form of music for centuries. It has been said that hymns were the "most widely-known and memorized verbal structures of the 18th century". To understand why hymns became so ingrained in Western society, their history must be explored.

Although religious singing was known in earlier cultures in Egypt, India and China, the history of the hymn essentially begins in Greece. The word 'hymn' was used by the Greeks to mean a song or poem written in honor of the gods, heroes or famous men. Hymns were sung on happy, mournful or solemn occasions. Greek dramatists used the word 'hymn' to describe woeful songs and the word is mentioned in Homer's *The Odyssey*.

The first Greek hymns, which came from mythological poems, were written in the third century BC. These odes to Apollo, the god of music, bear little resemblance to modern hymns. At religious festivals, people listened quietly until the last refrains and then they all joined in reciting, singing or shouting their responses.

Hymns fell out of favor in the fourth and fifth century AD. Eastern monasteries only wanted to use the psalms and in Spain the use of hymns was completely forbidden.

The original Christian definition of 'hymn' was to praise God with song but the Catholic Church extended this definition to include praise for saints.

Christian hymns were confined to daily services, Mass and closed settings. Praising God with song was not a public affair.

In the Middle Ages, plainsong, which originated from Jewish synagogues, was used in most church services. It was a musical vehicle for prose, first Greek, then Latin prose of the Bible, and was best described as a 'chant'. But people wouldn't sing in public services. Even when church became a public

"Gregorian chants" are named after Pope Gregory I, though he probably had little do with their form.

institution, there was no singing in services until the late Middle Ages. Plainsong was only sung by members of a closed community, such as a nunnery or monastery. It wasn't written to be listened to, but to be sung. Hymns would not form a part of worship in normal churches until the Reformation.

Luther

The 16th century saw major changes in hymns.

At this time a system for writing down music was developed. This coincided with ability to print music scores which made distribution easier, rather than having to rely on oral traditions and hand-copied manuscripts.

More importantly, the 16th century was the time of the Reformation. This began in 1517 as an effort to reform the Catholic Church, but resulted in the separation of the Protestant churches. The Reformation led to new ideas for hymns and music in general.

While still a member of the Catholic Church in Germany, Martin Luther had noticed that the congregation wasn't participating in the music of the church — the

clergy dominated this aspect. The congregation just listened. Luther wanted more congregational participation and singing in the language of the people, so that everyone could join in. He envisioned a less formal service.

About six years after the start of the Reformation, Luther began to write his own hymns. In 1523, after he translated the New Testament into German and published *Concerning the Order of Public Worship and An Order of Mass and Communion* — a publication about the Mass which included a section mentioning hymns.

Luther created his own church, getting rid of the Mass, he substituted congregational songs for the regular choirs and chants in the Catholic services.

Although Luther was excited about his ideas on congregational singing, not all members of the church felt the same way. Many congregations still sang without accompaniment. The organ was used only for instrumental music, not for hymn singing.

Although Luther's ideas were slow to be adopted, more attention was being paid to harmony by the end of the 16th century. In 1586 a groundbreaking hymnal, *50 Spiritual Songs and Psalms*, was published in German. For the first time, a hymnal included different parts and notes for the congregation and the choir. Because of Luther's musical ideals, four-part harmony caused hymn singing in churches to grow in popularity and become an important part of the service.

Calvin's Psalters

Around the same time, John Calvin of Switzerland was less enthusiastic about congregational singing. Before hearing Luther's songs, he believed that sensual expression should be repressed during worship. He liked Luther's ideas but felt that the only lyrics fit for worship were those in the Psalms of

John Calvin, the founder of Calvinism, had less fondness for hymns than his contemporary, Martin Luther.

David. Calvin thought that psalms should be sung unaccompanied by choir or instrument. He established a tradition of lyrical psalm singing by publishing the *Genevan Psalter*, and people in Switzerland, Holland and Britain followed Calvin closely. They sang only biblical psalms until the 1700s when Isaac Watts appeared on the scene.

Watts

Known as the father of English hymnody, Isaac Watts totally changed the hymn. He disagreed with the strict Christian ideals in song and wrote his own praises using his own feelings and experiences. In doing so, he broke the tradition of basing hymns on Psalms. Watts thought that the song of the New Testament Church should express the gospel of the New Testament. His hymns were revolutionary compared to Calvin's and the inflexible Roman Catholic worship services.

Watts' most famous work is probably the popular Christmas choral *Joy to the World* which he published in his first hymnal in 1707. His hymns were based on scriptures (*Joy to the World* is Psalm 98, with Watts' own interpretation) and free expression. It was Watts who set the stage for the 18th-century explosion of hymnody in Europe and America.

Hymns in America

During the 1700s, hymns as we know them today began to be accepted everywhere and Watts' songs became popular. In North America, hymns flourished in New England where most of the religious institutions were Protestant. The earliest hymnal published in America was in 1640 out of Boston and was called the *Bay Psalm Book*. Most American churches continued singing these psalms until 1776 though some churches sang a limited amount of hymns brought over from Europe. The Presbyterians used the Scottish Psalter, the Congregationalists, or people who were for harmony and participation in church, used Watts' hymns, and Anglicans used Tate and Brady's hymnal which at the time was also popular.

The hymn gained popularity in America following the introduction of the Copyright Act of 1831. This Act was the first to copyright music. American hymns became legally protected and the led to more original music being written. One of America's great hymnists, Fanny Crosby, alone wrote over 8,000 hymns following the passing of the act.

A new form of hymn that originated in America became globally popular in the 19th century. Gospel songs became popular in the second half of the century with lively music and simple, catchy lyrics. Stemming from American folk hymns that emerged at the beginning of the 1800s, gospel brought life to noonday prayer meetings, camp music, regular Sunday

Gregorian Chant

In the 5th and 6th centuries, Gregorian chant, the predecessor to plainsong, appeared in the Catholic Church. It is named after Pope Gregory I (540-604) even though many believe he didn't influence the music greatly. It was a purely aural type of music, passed along only by ear and memorization. None of it was written down as notation of the music was not available before the 9th century.

The music had a powerful effect with incredibly simple words and unaccompanied melody and harmonies. It was originally composed of Latin words from Latin sacred texts; hence originally being called 'sung Bible'. This type of music became less popular in the Middle Ages and was eventually reworked into plainsong during the Renaissance and was used in this form for close to 200 years.

Gregorian chant experienced a huge revival in the early 1990s. Although the chants were changed slightly from their medieval form, they still produced a best-selling CD in 1994 performed by Benedictine monks.

church and Sunday School classes. The John Church Company printed the original collection, called *Gospel Songs*, in Cincinnati in 1874. The John Church Company was a name that became synonymous with gospel songs and was used to generally describe these songs for years afterwards.

When all the new forms of hymns came into use in North America, the surge towards church music slowed considerably. Following the growth in popularity that the 1800s brought, the 1900s saw a balance of the radical variations in church music with more conservative hymns.

Hymns are probably the oldest songs still in existence. Used by the ancient Greeks and still being used today, their style and meaning continues to change and is now also beginning to include prayer and spiritual meditation. **HM**

Hindsight

We believe the products included in Hindsight will be of interest to readers but *History Magazine* does not necessarily endorse these items.

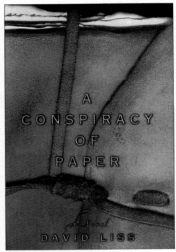

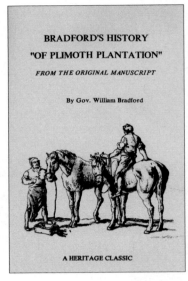

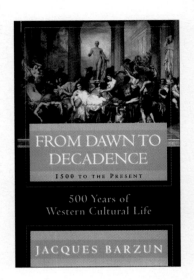

Although David Liss' **A Conspiracy Of Paper** is historical fiction, it offers rare insight into the world of early 18th-century London, with its coffee houses and carriages, dark alleys and lawlessness.

The main character, private detective Benjamin Weaver, takes on two outwardly unrelated cases; the circumstances surrounding a suicide and the theft of some papers. These cases in turn lead Weaver to examine his estranged father's mysterious death and his father's position as a stock jobber with the South Sea Company, which in reality would later be involved in the first stock market crash in the English-speaking world. Liss' choice of the central character allows the reader to understand the atmosphere and nuances of the era, as Weaver is depicted as an outsider due to his profession, his past and his Jewish background.

The author's attention to historical detail, plausible characters, well-written dialogue and intriguing situations throughout make for an enjoyable read and a praise-worthy debut. From Random House, hard-cover, 439 pages. Priced at about $25 US or $37 Cdn. Available in bookshops everywhere.

Originally begun in 1630 by the first elected governor of

Plymouth Colony, **Bradford's History "Of Plimoth Plantation"** is the history of the colony from its inception to 1647. This edition has been reprinted with the spelling and syntax of the era, along with the notes made by the author, Gov. William Bradford. Writing with firsthand experience, Bradford included important documents concerning the colony and correspondence throughout his book. An excellent reference source to learn about and understand life in earliest colonial America. 555 pages, soft-cover, with an index. This edition has two appendices: the original Mayflower passengers of 1620 and 'Commission for Regulating Plantations'. At about $40 US from Heritage Books, Inc., 1540E Pointer Ridge Place, Bowie MD 20716 or call 1-800-398-7709 or visit *www.heritagebooks.com*

At 877 pages, **From Dawn To Decadence - 500 Years of Western Cultural Life** is not to be approached by the mentally or physically weak. Though author Jacques Barzun had written some 30 books, this beautifully flowing narrative could well be called his magnum opus. Barzun draws upon his seven decades as a historian, his mind a vast storehouse of historical anecdotes and

details. The book is divided into four parts: the Reformation and Renaissance, the Enlightenment, the Romantic to the Modern Era, and the 20th Century and Beyond. Throughout, interesting quotes of the period by notable people are used to give insight and understanding to the culture and themes of the last 500 years. Hard-cover, with a full index from HarperCollins. At about $36 US or $55 Cdn. Available in bookshops everywhere.

The **History of Virginia** CD contains graphic images of essential works on the history of Virginia presented as they were originally published. Included is a history of the city of Fredericksburg, first settled by whites as early as 1622. This informative history covers many topics, including home industries, modes of punishment, the Revolutionary and Civil wars and the Freedman's Bureau. It also provides biographical sketches of some distinguished citizens buried in Fredericksburg. Includes an index of vital records for King George County and abstracts of wills presented in chronological order for Westmoreland County. CD# 1270 at around $30 from Heritage Books, Inc. 1540 E. Point Ridge Place, Bowie, MD 20716 or call 1-800-398-7709.

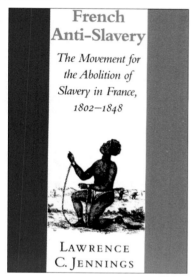

In 1794, France became the first great colonial power to abolish slavery, though this abolition was reversed under Napoleon in 1802. The French abolitionist movement began again in 1830, culminating in 1848 with the permanent abolition of French colonial slavery. **French Anti-Slavery: The Movement for the Abolition of Slavery in France, 1802-1848** examines the French anti-slavery lobby of the early 19th century. Author Lawrence Jennings studies the humanitarian group behind the anti-slavery movement and their struggle against the colonial lobby and an indifferent French government. The book also analyzes why the freeing of a quarter of a million slaves took place 15 years after Britain's decision to terminate slavery. From Cambridge University Press, hard-cover, 320 pages. With an index, several black and white engravings, and an extensive bibliography. Priced at about $55 US or $78 Cdn. Available in

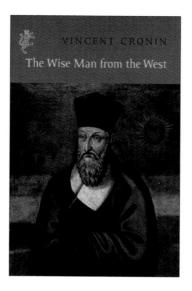

bookshops everywhere.
In 1582, Matteo Ricci, an Italian Jesuit, was the first missionary sent to China, which had been closed to foreigners for many years. **The Wise Man From The West** tells of Ricci's life, as a Westerner and a missionary, intent upon converting the Chinese Emperor and his people. While in China, Ricci learned the language and imparted the technological and philosophical knowledge of the West, which found him favor among the Mandarins, the men of learning who enjoyed high standing in the Imperial bureaucracy. Ricci did not succeed with his mission to convert the Chinese Emperor to Christianity, however, his life is worth examining for its uniqueness and importance in establishing Sino-European relations. Author Vincent Cronin's sources for the book are Ricci's correspondence, various reports, and Ricci's own history of the Chinese mission. From Harvill Press Editions, new edition of a 1955 publication. 300 pages, soft-cover, with an index. At about $15 US or $30 Cdn. Available in bookshops everywhere.

The Trail of the Huguenots by G. Elmore Reaman is the fascinating story of the great exodus of Huguenots from France at the end of the 17th century and their subsequent dispersal to the US, Canada, South Africa and other

countries in Europe. This book is primarily focused on those Huguenots who went to the US and Canada. By the second half of the 16th century, there were Huguenot settlements in South Carolina and in the next hundred years Huguenot families settled in North Carolina, Virginia, New York, Pennsylvania and New England. From 1534 until 1633 Canada was practically Huguenot controlled. The way in which these families enriched the life of the places to which they fled is preserved in this account of the Huguenot achievement. 318 pages, hardcover, indexed at around $25 from the Genealogical Publishing Co., Inc. 1001 N. Calvert St., Baltimore MD 21202 or call 1-800-548-1806.

The Game of Kings

Victoria King charts the evolution of the game of chess.

INDIA IS OFTEN credited with being the birthplace of chess, at some point in the 6th century. The game was known as *chaturanga* and played by four opponents with dice. Later only two opponents played the game and the use of dice was abandoned, eliminating the element of chance.

Chess spread eastward, undergoing variations along the way, and in the 8th century it reached China (also argued to be the birthplace of chess) and Japan, where it is known as *xiangqi* and *shogi* respectively. By the 10th century chess also had spread to the Middle East. The term "checkmate" is believed to have come from the Arabic *shah mat*, meaning "the king is dead".

Chess spread to Europe by the 11th century, brought there by Muslims and Byzantines. An archaeological dig in the Outer Hebrides on the Isle of Lewis discovered 78 walrus-ivory chess pieces dating from the 12th century.

Royalty and religious leaders periodically banned chess over the centuries. A church statute of Elna, in the *Council of Spain* stated "Clerks playing ... chess shall be ipso facto excommunicated." France's Louis IX banned the game in 1254.

However, chess found favor among royalty too. Ivan the Terrible of Russia, and several kings of England and Spain were supporters of the game. Chess was associated with wealth and knowledge and has been known as the royal game since the 15th century. The English court of Exchequer is believed to have taken its name from the board design of chess, which was used as a table covering on which taxes were reckoned, and some

Chess came to Europe from the East; the word "checkmate" is derived from the Arabic *shah mat*, "the king is dead".

20 English families feature chess rooks on their coat of arms. Peter I of Russia had a set made of leather, which he took on military campaigns.

Chess has been the subject of many manuscripts over its history. In 1474, William Caxton printed one of the first books called *The Game And Playe Of Chesse*. Interestingly, Shakespeare mentions the game of chess only once, in his second-last play, *The Tempest*.

The form of chess has only become standardized since the end of the medieval period. Previously there was a piece known as a counselor, which was the weakest piece on the board, limited to moving diagonally only one square

at a time. At the end of the 15th century, the counselor took on the movements of both the modern bishop and the rook and changed gender to become the present-day queen. Prior to the alteration, bishops had been limited to moving two squares diagonally, but under the new rules their range increased. Pawns that reached the other player's side had only been promoted to counselors; this changed too so pawns could be elevated to any piece (save kings).

The design of the pieces has changed over the years. The bishop was an elephant in India and Russia, and known as a fool in France. The rook was depicted as a ship in Russia. Early Muslim sets were made of simple clay or stone pieces in line with the Islamic ban on living beings' images.

By contrast European and Russian sets were quite opulent, depicting animals such as unicorns, warriors or kings enthroned, and some sets were studded with jewels. The Flemish created 'virtue versus vice'-themed sets, which pitted court officials and cherubs against satyrs and imps. Some chess sets produced in the 18th century featured such elaborate pieces that they took over neighboring squares. In the 1920s, Russian sets were produced featuring communists with joyful workers and harvesters on one side, and the other side with chained workers as pawns for the capitalists.

Today gameplay has been standardized to facilitate international competition. The standard design of chess pieces was developed in Britain and named after Howard Staunton, a master of the game in the 19th century. **HM**

Do *you* have New England ancestors?

No matter where you live, NEHGS is your best genealogical resource

NEW ENGLAND HISTORIC GENEALOGICAL SOCIETY

Since 1845, we've been building the nation's most comprehensive center for New England genealogical research. You don't need to live in New England to benefit from membership! NEHGS members enjoy:

- Borrowing privileges for the 25,000-volume Circulating Library, with books sent directly to members' homes

- Unlimited on-site use of the state-of-the-art research library with over 200,000 volumes

- Subscriptions to two Society publications: the renowned New England Historical and Genealogical Register and the informative news magazine, NEXUS

- Discounts on Society publications and educational programs and conferences held nationwide

- *AND MUCH MORE...*

"For anyone with New England ancestors, a membership in this organization is a must."
America's Best Genealogy Resource Centers, 1998

NEHGS

Yes! I want to become a member of the New England Historic Genealogical Society.

If you have questions about becoming a member of NEHGS, please call the Membership Department, toll-free, at 1-888-286-3447, or e-mail membership@nehgs.org.

Membership Categories

Individual $50
Family* $70
Student $20

*good for up to 3 persons in the same household

name _____

e-mail _____   phone _____

address _____

city, state, zip _____

payment information
__check enclosed, payable to NEHGS   __Mastercard __Visa

acct #_____   exp_____

signature _____

Mail to:
New England Historic Genealogical Society
101 Newbury Street
Boston, MA 02116-3007

1-888-286-3447 FAX: 617-536-7307
Join online at http://www.nehgs.org

History
Magazine

December/January 2001
$4.50 U.S.
$5.50 Cdn.

The History of
Whaling

Cdn Publ. Mail Product
Sales Agreement No.

Scrapbook for 1400-1424

Farming in the New World

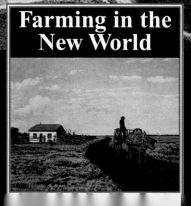

Christmas

LAUREN FAMILY HISTORY

Contents of this issue of History Magazine

The Early 1400s.
Page 8.

Roman Baths.
Page 25.

The Whaling Industry.
Page 37.

Old Ironsides.
Page 46.

OUR COVER: *Shooting the Harpoon* by J.H. Clarke.

VOLUME 2 NUMBER 2
EDITOR & PUBLISHER
Halvor Moorshead

EDITOR
Jeff Chapman

SPECIAL PROJECTS MANAGER
Ron Wild

ADVERTISING SERVICES
Victoria Pratt

Published by Moorshead Magazines Ltd.
505 Consumers Road, Suite 500, Toronto,
ON, M2J 4V8 Canada
(416) 491-3699 Fax (416) 491-3996
E-Mail: magazine@moorshead.com

PRESIDENT
Halvor Moorshead

CIRCULATION MANAGER
Rick Cree

SUBSCRIPTION SERVICES
Jeannette Cox
Valerie Carmichael

History Magazine is published six times a year
(Feb/Mar, Apr/May, Jun/Jul, Aug/Sep,
Oct/Nov, Dec/Jan) by Moorshead Magazines.
POSTAL INFORMATION — CANADA
Canadian Publications Mail Product Sales
Agreement No. 1595695. Mailing address for
subscription orders, undeliverable copies and
change of address notice is:

History Magazine,
505 Consumers Road, Suite 500,
Toronto, Ontario, M2J 4V8 Canada
POSTAL INFORMATION — UNITED STATES
Periodical Postage Paid Lewiston, NY
USPS #018-154
Postmaster send address corrections to:
History Magazine,
PO Box 1201, Lewiston, NY, 14092-9934 USA
US Office of Publication
850 Cayuga St., Lewiston, NY, 14092

ISSN 1492-4307

SUBSCRIPTIONS
Subscription rate for US (US funds):
1 year (6 issues) $24.00
2 years (12 issues) $40.00
3 years (18 issues) $55.00

Subscription rate for Canada (Cdn funds):
1 year (6 issues) $28.00 plus GST/HST
2 years (12 issues) $45.00 plus GST/HST
3 years (18 issues) $59.00 plus GST/HST
Quebec residents add 6.5% QST

GST # 139340186 RT
We welcome the submission of articles for publication. Please send a printed copy in addition to the
file in electronic format. Please do not send important documents with submissions. We will always
contact people who submit articles but the review
process may take several weeks. Authors' notes are
available on request.

Toll-Free Subscription Line:
1-877-731-4478
PRINTED IN CANADA
WEBSITE
www.history-magazine.com

The Real First World War

Regarding the claim that the Seven Years War was the first "world war" ("The First World War", October/November 1999), I'm sorry to say that I disagree with strong evidence with the great Winston Churchill. Churchill was Anglo-centric. I am Netherlandic-American-centric.

The Dutch War for Independence, from the 1500s to 1648, was the real first world war. It was fought on all continents except yet undiscovered Antarctica. In North America, Spanish trade from Cuba was interdicted and Caribbean Islands were seized from Spain. In South America, Brazil was captured after Portugal was gobbled up by Spain in 1580 and their overseas colonies became targets for the Dutch. In Africa, former Portuguese colonies in Angola, the Cape and Mozambique were seized. In Asia, Ceylon and Portuguese holdings (Formosa, Malaya, East Indies territories) were captured. In Australasia, Australia and New Zealand were discovered by the Dutch. The conflicts in Europe are obvious.

The Anglo-centric view of history usually does not mention that after the collapse of Spain, the United Provinces of the Netherlands became the dominant sea power for the next 100 years.

W. Aardsma
Westland, Mich.

History Written by the Losers?

Since my grandfather was Sioux, I read your article on the Battle of Little Big Horn (December/January 2000). This was not that battle that I know. This was not history. This was ONE side of a story through the government and the 7th Cavalry's eyes. I had intended to subscribe to your magazine for my grandchildren, but we teach the truth, not half-truths. I was looking for real history, not fiction.

MaryAnn Dark
Oglala Sioux

Lewis, Clark and Others

I realize your piece on the Lewis and Clark expedition article (from "The 1800s", October/November 2000) was meant to be just a short article on the expedition but still, a very male perspective. How about 40 people? Or 40 white men? Was Sacajawea the only female? I doubt it. See *http://users.erols.com/tdpedu/lectures/l&ccr.htm* for a list of the men. From what little I know, some of the men 'married' Indian women along the way.

Mary Arthur
Internet

Sacajawea is the only female who is said to have accompanied the party in the historical accounts of the expedition. To assume the presence of other women who were left out of the records would be a large speculative leap.

History Notes

Chewing Gum

The original base of modern chewing gum is called chicle. It comes from the sap of the sapodilla tree that grows in South America. Chicle first came to the US to be used in making synthetic rubber. After failing to prove the resin's elasticity, it was almost thrown

out when someone thought to use it as chewing gum.

A lot of bases other than chicle have been used for gum, namely candle wax in the 1850s and even asphalt in the 1920s.

After WWI the chewing gum industry really took off. Americans chewed three times as much after the war as they did before. Gum was even sent to soldiers in WWII while it was rationed at home, giving chewing gum a certain respectability that had never been associated with it before.

In major times of stress more gum is sold. In the Depression and during the Cuban Missile Crisis, the sale of chewing gum temporarily increased. Going into the 1990s, Americans chewed enough gum in a year to make a stick that stretches 5,000,000 miles long. Seventy-five per cent of that astounding figure was chewed by only 10 per cent of the population.
—ROSANNE VAN VIERZEN

Postage Stamps

The idea for adhesive postage stamps was first proposed in 1653 by the government inspector of finances in France, though it is believed that his mistress deserves the credit for the suggestion. When the inspector was fired from his position a few months later, the idea left with him.

By 1802, the British Revenue Department required stamps or labels to be gummed or pasted onto posted items that were to be taxed. But the idea of self-adhesive stamps didn't surface again until 1837, when Rowland Hill published a pamphlet named "Post Office Reform" which addressed the idea of uniform

The easiest, most complete software for preserving your family history.

Generations is the most accurate and comprehensive genealogy software available today. It's also the easiest software to use. And, thanks to our partnership with Heritage Quest, you'll always have the newest and most up-to-date data available.

Generations Grande Suite 8.0 features 350 million names and resources, access to a professional genealogist, and the entire 1800 US Census. In addition, there's a new 3D Tree which allows you to "step inside" your family tree and view your roots with interactive animation.

Add video and audio clips to your files. Store old family movies, songs, pictures and keepsakes to enjoy anytime. These exciting new features, plus Generations' time-tested powerful tools and dynamic presentation software ensure your legacy will be strong for generations.

Sierra Home™

For more information, please visit us at sierrahome.com

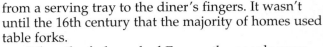

rates of postage combined with a system of prepayment. At that time the recipient usually paid for the postage, so if the item was refused, it was returned to the sender and no revenue was collected. Hill created a universal and inexpensive pre-paid postal unit for Britain — the postage stamp.

The first stamps issued in England were the "Penny Black" and the "Twopenny Blue" stamps issued in May 1840. The Penny Black featured a profiled head shot of Queen Victoria surrounded in black. Her profile was used as it was thought that a face would be difficult to forge due to the details. At that time, stamps were available for purchase only at the post office; just one penny sent a letter weighing half an ounce anywhere in the country.

In 1860 most countries had adopted the prepaid postage stamp system and by 1875 international standardization of postal procedures was achieved.

Stamp collecting became a popular hobby in Europe around 1861 and by 1890 some collections were known to be worth over 100,000 francs. Governments have been known to mass-produce errors on stamps to avoid stamp collectors making fortunes on a rare stamp. In 1962, a collector in the United States won an injunction from the Supreme Court to stop the post office from cheapening a rarity he owned.
—ROSANNE VAN VIERZEN

Forks

"Why use a fork when we have fingers?" This was the common objection to the use of the table fork when it was first introduced to Europe in the 11th century.

The fork can be traced back to the Ancient Greeks. A Greek kitchen fork was over four times the size of our modern table fork and had two long tines. It was used to hold meat still while carving.

Middle Eastern nobility were the first to use forks as a personal utensil. In the 7th century, the fork was made smaller, about half the size of modern forks, and using it was a sign of refinement.

The fork made its way to Europe through a Byzantine princess who married an Italian nobleman. Her mother gave her a set of utensils, including a table fork, as a present just before the couple moved to Italy.

Italians did not embrace this trend at first. Many began to use kitchen forks more often but they were only used to transfer food from a serving tray to the diner's fingers. It wasn't until the 16th century that the majority of homes used table forks.

When the fork reached France, the people were slow to adopt it as well. It is believed that the wife of King Henry II, Catherine de Medicis, brought the fork from Italy to France in 1533.

England first saw the fork in 1608 when an Englishman, Thomas Coryate, returned from a journey to Italy with a set of table forks. At first people thought forks were unnecessary and pretentious. However, soon forks were adopted by the wealthy in England. By the mid-1600s, it was sophisticated to carry your own utensil when dining out. Forks were often made from expensive metals, some even were accessorized with jeweled handles. By the 1700s table forks were used for large meals and special guests. At the end of the century, it was common practice to use a fork while eating.

Forks made their way to America through the expansion of the colonies of England. They were accepted almost immediately.

The number of tines on forks varies with date and geography. Original Italian forks were just smaller versions of kitchen forks, with two long tines. People often found it hard to keep food on this fork. The French used larger forks in the 16th century with three or four tines. By the early 19th century Germany, England and America used curved, four tine forks, to help scoop food and keep it under control.
—JODI AVERY

Vinegar

Vinegar was probably discovered more than 10,000 years ago, when some unsuspecting soul drank from a cask of wine that had gone sour. While the first person to consume vinegar may not have been overly impressed by the taste, the pleasant tanginess of the substance — which the French dubbed *vinaigre*, or sour wine — gradually caught on. The Babylonians first used it as a preservative and a condiment, and experimented with flavoring it with herbs.

Vinegar was once commonly used in drinks as well — in fact, Roman legionnaires would drink it straight. Probably the most famous vinegar-based drink was a creation of Cleopatra, when she was challenged to consume a fortune in a single meal: she drank pearls dissolved in vinegar. (Vinegar's ability to dissolve soft stone is also said to have aided Hannibal, who reportedly used vinegar to help dissolve limestone rocks that got in the way of his elephants crossing the Alps. When the rocks were heated and treated with vinegar, they crumbled easily.)

Vinegar has also been used as a medicine. Hippocrates extolled its medicinal qualities, and Biblical references show that vinegar was widely used for its healing properties. Vinegar was still being used to treat wounds as recently as WWI. Today it is recommended for treatment of rashes, bites and other minor ailments when camping, and some claim it is a "miracle substance" that cures a multitude of diseases and ends the pain of arthritis.

Though vinegar is traditionally made from grapes or apples, it can in fact be made from anything that contains sugar or starch. The natural sugars are fermented to alcohol and then undergo secondary fermentation that converts the alcohol into acetic acid. Through the centuries vinegar has been produced from such diverse materials as molasses, honey, rice, sorghum, fruits, berries, melons, coconuts, beer, maple syrup, potatoes, beets, malt, grains and whey.

While malt vinegar is preferred in England, white (clear) vinegar is favored in North America. These two vinegars are prepared by mashing milled, malted barley or oats in huge vats and processing the grain to convert the starch from the grain into sugar. The sugar is converted to alcohol through the addition of yeast to the sugar. The process of maturing takes about six months after which it is filtered and pasteurized. The clear distilled malt vinegar is produced from the vapors given off from the boiling of the brown malt vinegar. —JEFF CHAPMAN

Tulip Mania

In 17th-century Holland, a single tulip bulb could be exchanged as a bride's dowry or for a horse and carriage *and* 4,500 guilders ($2,250 US today).

Tulips are indigenous to the Caucasus and Black Sea regions, and first came to Europe through Turkey in the late 16th century. The tulip was prized for its striking shape and vibrant hues.

Early traders who planned to make a fortune packed their ships' hulls full of the tulip bulbs. When the cargo reached its destination, nearly all the bulbs were ruined and worthless. The shippers did not realize the tulip bulb needed to 'breathe' when shipped, and that importing only a few bulbs would meet with greater success than importing an entire shipload.

Demand for the brightly colored tulip soon drove the price of a bulb to astronomical heights. At first only growers and other specialists with wealthy patrons traded the flower, but their success led others to follow. Homes and businesses were mortgaged so that speculators could invest in the lucrative tulip market. Many of these transactions took place without the bulb ever leaving the ground.

In 1637, tulip mania ended when people began to realize that the price could not continue to climb as it had and speculators pulled out of the market. Many people lost their homes and livelihood, however, the love affair still continues. Today the Dutch still grow around three billion tulip bulbs a year, two billion for export. —VICTORIA KING

Mulled Wine

Mulled wine typically refers to red or white wine, with the occasional addition of brandy, warmed with sugar and spices. In medieval times mulled wines were called "Hipocras", a nod to the physician Hippocrates and the notion that warm, spiced wines promoted robust health. Glogg is a mulled wine of Scandinavian origin that often incorporated aquavit or brandy and a garnish of raisins and almonds, and was traditionally served during Advent.

Mulled Wine - yields four servings
2 whole cloves
1 stick cinnamon
1 fresh orange, cut in half
¼ cup sugar
2 cups Burgundy

a. Combine all ingredients in a heavy bottomed saucepan. Stir over medium heat until the sugar is dissolved. Turn off heat and cover for 20 minutes.
b. Strain into cups to serve or into a crock-pot for extended serving time. For a non-alcoholic version, replace the wine with apple cider.
—KATHRYN CONRAD

Hot Toddy

This drink of warm, spiced spirits belongs to a beverage group known as "toddies". The word origin is believed to come from British sailors' discovery of fermented palm tree sap, known by the Asian word "Tari", which the sailors thinned with water, flavored with lemon and spices and heated to ward off evening chills. The practice traveled to the American Colonies and became a standard, whether made with rum, whisky or brandy, for cold winter evenings.

Hot Toddy - yields four servings
4 tsp sugar
1 whole clove
1 stick cinnamon
4 oz rum, whisky, or brandy
4 slices lemon
Hot water

a. Combine the sugar, spices and liquor in a small saucepan and stir over low heat just until the sugar has dissolved. Cover and steep for 15 minutes.
b. Strain the mixture among four mugs. Squeeze a lemon slice into each mug, adding the squeezed slice to each serving.
c. Top each portion with very hot water. Stir well and serve. —KATHRYN CONRAD

HM

The Early 1400s

Victoria King describes some of the highlights of this quarter century.

THE WORLD changed dramatically during the tumultuous period between 1400 and 1424.

In England the period began with the deposed Richard II dying under mysterious circumstances. Conflicts along the borders with Wales and Scotland plagued first Henry IV and then his son Henry V. Internally the Lollards continued to cause social unrest.

England and France were pitted against one another in the Hundred Years War. The two nations had been foes for many years before as both had interests in Flanders, and France aided the Scots in their opposition to England. When Philip IV of France died in 1314, each of his sons reigned without producing a legitimate male heir and in 1328, the Capetian dynasty died out. Edward III of England could claim the French throne through his mother as she was a daughter of Philip IV, however, the French line passed through males only. The throne instead went to Phillip of Valois, who was a cousin of the last king through the male line. In 1340, Edward III formally claimed the French throne and the conflict began.

Over the next century, minor raids were made and three major battles were fought: Crécy in 1346, Poitiers 10 years later and Agincourt in 1415. Although English longbowmen won all these battles, the French won the war due to Joan of Arc's military prowess. In

Czech preacher Jan Hus led a popular movement in favor of a simplified and uncorrupted version of Christianity. As he became an increasing threat to the Church and the Holy Roman Empire, he was tried and condemned as a heretic.

1453, the French captured the fortress Castillon-sur-Dordogne in the south of France and the English retained only Calais in the north. The war was over.

In 1400, the papacy was at its lowest ebb up to that point. Two rivals, Benedict XIII of Avignon and Boniface XI of Rome, claimed to be the true pope and Europe was divided in its support of each pontiff. The Great Western Schism tore at the fabric of the Catholic religion and the Schism was only healed through the intervention of Sigismund, ruler of the Holy Roman Empire.

The Holy Roman Empire suffered from internal conflicts itself. Preacher and theologian Jan Hus, who appealed for a simplified church, found support among the Bohemian majority in Prague. A Czech, Hus began to be noticed as a preacher of the Bethlehem Chapel in Prague and theologian at the first university in the German world. He became a

spokesman for the non-Germans and fanned the nationalism of the Czech population. Hus had become a popular figure among the poor as he spoke out against the selling of indulgences by Pope John XXIII of Pisa in order to fill the papal coffers. Hus opposed the corruption in the church and its hierarchy, which also made him popular among the upper classes.

In 1415, Hus appeared before the Council of Constance, under safe-conduct guaranteed by Sigismund. Hus was asked to discuss his radical views before the council, in the hopes of resolving the decade of struggle between the Czechs and the Germans. When he appeared, however, the pledge of safe conduct was revoked and Hus was tried as a heretic. Hus refused to recant his beliefs and was burned at the stake on 6 July 1415. Instead of resolving the Bohemian issues, the council created a martyr of Hus. By 1419, Sigismund faced a religious civil war that lasted for the next generation.

Beyond Europe the Mongols under the leadership of Tamerlane were the terror of Asia and the Incas were building an empire that encompassed 12 million people. Both the Chinese and the Portuguese undertook great maritime exploration to new lands and new places previously not visited by either nation.

The End of the Great Western Schism

IN 1309, POPE Clement V (1305-14) moved the papal residence from Rome to Avignon under pressure from France's King Philip IV. Known as the 'Babylonian Captivity of the Church', the Avignon-based rule of Clement V and his successors was subservient to French interests.

In 1377, Pope Gregory XI (1370-78) yielded to demands to move the papal capital back to Rome, however, upon the election of his successor, the Schism began. While the Italian cardinals supported the election of the Italian Urban VI (1378-89), the French fraction of the Sacred College withdrew to Anagni, claiming that Urban VI's election was null because he had only been elected under pressure from the Roman mob.

The French cardinals then elected Robert of Geneva as Clement VII (1378-94), who was recognised by France, Scotland, Spain and Savoy. Meanwhile Urban VI of Rome, who was recognised by Italy, Germany, England and the northern European counties, excommunicated Clement VII, who responded in kind. Clement

Bishops argue about which of the three popes they serve.

VII and his supporters then moved to Avignon and established a rival College of Cardinals to the one in Rome. Both popes continued to appoint bishops, collect taxes and issue penances.

In 1409, the Council of Pisa was called to resolve the Schism. After meeting for four months, the bishops, lower churchmen and royal envoys decided to elect a new pope, Alexander V (1409-10), who made his court in Pisa. Unfortunately, when Alexander tried to depose Benedict XIII of Avignon (1394-1417) and Gregory XII of Rome (1406-15), they both refused,

and so there were three popes.

Holy Roman Emperor Sigismund called a general council at Constance, which began in November 1414. By this time the cardinals were united in working towards a resolution and set about to force all three popes to resign so Europe could begin anew with a new pope. All three popes were forced to take an oath that they would abdicate if their two rivals would do the same.

John XXIII (1410-15) of Pisa had 74 charges brought against him — including adultery, sodomy and incest — and was suspended as pope in May of the following year and deposed later that month. Gregory XII of Rome presented his resignation to the Council of Constance in July 1415. Benedict XIII refused to comply with the council and was deposed as a perjurer, a schismatic and a heretic in 1417. Scotland, the last loyal country to Benedict XIII, withdrew its support of him the following year.

In 1417, the Italian Cardinal Oddone Colonna was elected Pope Martin V, thus ending the Great Western Schism after nearly 40 years.

The Seven Voyages of Cheng Ho

WHEN THE PRINCE OF YEN came to power in 1402 and became the Ming Emperor Yung-lo of China, he wished to expand China's influence and trade throughout the Indian Ocean.

Chinese Admiral Cheng Ho was a eunuch and son of a Muslim who had risen through the army and had made influential friends at the Chinese court. Cheng was chosen to be in charge of a fleet of 300 ships and command over 27,000 men.

In 1405, Cheng set out on the first of his seven voyages, visiting Ceylon (present day Sri Lanka), Southeast Asia and Indonesia. He returned to China in 1407. In 1409, Cheng returned to Ceylon and defeated the forces of King Alagonakkara, whom Cheng took as a captive and brought to the Chinese capital of Nanking.

Cheng's third voyage in 1411 took him as far west as the Persian Gulf. In 1413 Cheng and his fleet set forth on another voyage. A detachment was dispatched south along the Arabian coast and a Chinese

A Chinese coin commemorating Cheng Ho.

mission was sent to visit Mecca and on to Egypt.

When Cheng returned from his fourth voyage he brought with him envoys from over 30 Asian states to pay homage to Emperor Yung-lo. On his fifth voyage in 1417 Cheng revisited the Persian Gulf and the coast of Africa. In 1421, Cheng returned the envoys from his fourth voyage to their homelands.

Yung-lo died in 1424 and his successor was not interested in naval expeditions. However, Cheng made one last voyage in 1431 to Southeast Asia, India, the Persian Gulf, the African coast and the Red Sea. He returned to China in 1433 and died shortly thereafter. Cheng had visited parts of Asia and Africa in his seven voyages that Europeans did not visit until decades later.

Unlike the European navigators of the same period, who merely established trade routes, the legacy of Cheng's voyages was Chinese emigration to Southeast Asia and the expansion of China's political interests throughout the area.

1400-1404

1400: Geoffrey Chaucer, English poet of the 1300s, dies. Chaucer left his last work, *The Canterbury Tales*, unfinished.

1400: The deposed Richard II of England dies under mysterious circumstances at Pontefract Castle.

1401: Tamerlane or 'Timur the Lame', leader of the Mongols, captures Baghdad for the second time.

1401: Welsh land rights are restricted in a new law.

1401: A law is passed in England that allows heretics to be handed over to the church and burnt. The first martyr, Lollard preacher William Sawtre, is burnt that year.

1402: Henry III of Castile sends an expedition to the Canary Islands.

1402: Bayezid I, the Turkish Sultan, is captured in the Battle of Angora by Tamerlane.

1402: Jan Hus, the religious reformer, begins to preach in Prague at the Bethlehem chapel. Hus called for a virtuous and simple church and was supported by the Bohemian people.

1402: The Scots invade England and are defeated at the Battle of Homildon Hill. The battle is won largely due to the use of the English longbow.

1403: Venice introduces a waiting period for visitors to the city to learn if they would develop the plague. The period was standardized at 40 days and it is from the French word for 'forty' that the word *quarantine* was developed.

1403: Henry IV of England marries Joan, the dowager duchess of Brittany and daughter of King Charles II of Navarre.

1401: Mongol leader Tamerlane leads his troops in the capture of the Persian city of Baghdad.

1403: The son of the earl of Northumberland, Henry 'Hotspur' Percy, victor of the Battle of Homildon Hill (1402), dies in battle at Shrewsbury. Percy and other northern noblemen revolted as they felt insufficiently rewarded for their assistance to Henry IV in asserting his claim to the throne of England.

1404: Japan begins to trade with Ming China.

1405-1409

1405: Tamerlane, ruler of the Mongols, dies in battle. He created an empire reaching from Tartary to India after defeating the Turks, Persians, Arabs and Mongols among others. Tamerlane was planning to take China at the time of his death.

1405: Konrad Kyeser writes *Bellifortis*, one of the earliest and most influential books about military warfare.

1405: Dutch fishermen are the first to use drift nets to catch fish.

1405: Cheng Ho of China sails with 300 ships and 27,000 men to Southeast Asia, Indonesia and Ceylon.

1406: Henry III of Castile dies and is succeeded by his one-year-old son, John II.

1406: Gregory XII becomes pope in Rome following the death of Innocent VII.

1406: A copy of Ptolemy's *Geography* is brought to Italy from Constantinople. Once translated into Latin, knowledge of geography throughout Europe increased.

1406: Scotland's King Robert III dies of starvation. Robert lost the will to live after his only son, James, was captured by English pirates that year as James was traveling to France. Robert was succeeded by James, who was held captive by the English until 1423.

1407: London's Bethlehem Hospital, nicknamed "Bedlam", becomes an institution for the insane.

1408: Tartars sack the Russian city of Serpuchov, near Moscow.

1409: Thomas Cusack is appointed as the first mayor of Dublin.

1409: The Council of Pisa consisting of bishops, lower churchmen and royal envoys, ends in failure. The Council met for months to attempt to resolve the Great Schism in the western church. Their solution was to elect a new pope, Alexander V — but both Benedict XIII of Avignon and Gregory XII of Rome refused to be deposed.

1409: Cheng Ho returns to Ceylon and captures the king, whom he brings back as a captive.

1410-1414

1410: John XXIII is elected pope after Alexander V dies at Bologna. Some say John poisoned Alexander to gain power.

1410: Sigismund becomes ruler of the Holy Roman Empire, although his half-brother Wenceslas retains the title until his death in 1419.

1410: The king of Kano, West Africa, Kanajejdi, dies. He is credited with introducing iron helmets and horse armor to the Hausa cavalry.

1411: After 30 years of war and truces, Aragon and Portugal make peace. With the war over, John of Portugal begins to concentrate on overseas expansion.

1411: The first Scottish university is founded by Bishop Henry Wardlaw at St. Andrews.

1411: Cheng Ho travels to the Persian Gulf.

1412: Joan of Arc is born.

1413: England's King Henry IV dies at the age of 45, after a 13-year reign, and is succeeded by his son Henry.

1413: Mehmed, son of Bayezid I, unites the fractured Ottoman Empire, broken by the Mongol attacks.

1413: The Brothers Limbourg, under the patronage of the Duc de Berry, began work on a Book of Hours now known as *Les Trés Riches Heures*. This work is acclaimed as the masterpiece of the International style of art. Books of Hours were created to help people follow their daily religious duties and were

1413: The Brothers Limbourg begin *Les Trés Riches Heures*.

used as symbols of status.

1414: The Council of Constance was called to attempt a solution to the Great Schism within the Catholic Church.

1415-1419

1415: Sigismund, ruler of the Holy Roman Empire, requested Jan Hus to speak at the Council of Constance, to discuss the latter's views. Hus refused until granted safe-conduct. Despite this, Hus was cross-examined about his views, imprisoned, convicted of heresy and burned at the stake that year.

1415: Even though greatly outnumbered, the English beat the French at the Battle of Agincourt.

1416: Alfonso V became King of Aragon, uniting the former with Sardinia, Sicily and the Balearic Islands.

1416: Owain Glyndwr dies. Glyndwr, a Welsh nationalist, proclaimed himself Prince of Wales in 1400 and began a rebellion against the English.

1417: The Council of Constance, after three years of deliberation over the Great Schism, decides to elect Martin V as pope. The Council gets rid of John XXIII, isolates Benedict XIII of Avignon and convinces Gregory XII of Rome to resign.

1417: John Oldcastle, leader of the Lollards and former friend of Henry V, is hanged and burned. Lollards were followers of John Wycliffe (d. 1384) who personally viewed the pope as the Antichrist and believed the 13th-century schism in the papacy heralded its end. Both Henry IV and Henry V sought to repress the religious movement that was responsible for social unrest, in particular the Peasants' Revolt of 1381.

1418: Scotland, the last country loyal to Benedict XIII, withdraws its support for him, thus finally ending the Great Western Schism within the Catholic Church.

1418: The queen of France orders that all the doorways in the royal castle be raised to a height of 8'4" to allow ladies with fashionably tall hair or hair ornaments passage without having to duck.

1419: The men of Charles, the French royal heir, murder John, the duke of Burgundy. John's son, Phillip II, becomes the new duke.

1419: The Hussite Wars begin between Bohemian followers of Hus and the Holy Roman Empire.

1419: Phillip II, Duke of Burgundy, and Henry V ally against Charles.

1420-1424

1420: Henry V, the victor of Agincourt, brings England and France together. He marries Catherine of Valois, Charles VI's daughter, to close the new agreement and bring peace to the two countries.

1420: A pack of wolves roams the streets of Paris, entering the city from the nearby forest.

1421: The Portuguese discover the island of Madeira in the Atlantic.

1421: Mehmed, Sultan of the Ottoman Empire dies and is succeeded by Murad II.

1421: English male doctors petition parliament to make the practice of medicine elite to men and university graduates.

1422: England's Henry V dies from dysentery. His eight-month-old son inherits the kingdom of England.

1423: The Venetians buy Thessalonica, in northwestern Greece, from the Byzantine Empire.

1423: England releases James I of Scotland from his 17-year captivity.

1424: England and Scotland agree to a seven-year truce.

1424: John Zizka, leader of the Hussites, dies of the plague.

The Battle of Agincourt

CASSELL'S *History of England* describes the reign of Henry V as being "like a chapter of romance," and says of the king: "Young, handsome, accomplished not only in arms but in learning, skilled in and fond of music, valorous, chivalrous, generous, and successful to the very height of human glory in arms, he lived beloved and died young, the pride of his native country, whose martial fame he raised above that of all others, and made it the wonder of the world."

Henry V had come to the throne in 1413 in his mid-20s. For over 70 years, England had been at war with France in what is now known as the Hundred Years War. Henry and his ancestors had long wished to add France to their domains.

European armies in the 15th century normally comprised a number of knights, who regarded warfare as almost sport, and as many peasants as the local feudal levy could raise.

In preparing to invade France, Henry adopted a surprisingly modern view: he preferred a small, professional army to a large untrained mob. His troops were well paid, well trained and disciplined. The largest part of his force consisted of expert archers using the English longbow. In the longbow, the English had perfected an extraordinary weapon. A trained archer could shoot six aimed arrows a minute, which could wound at 400 yards, kill at 200 and penetrate armor at 100. The English had special arrowheads for penetrating armor while others were designed to kill or maim horses.

The English army landed in France on 15 August 1415. Their plan was to take the fortress town of Harfleur quickly and then to march on Paris. The first part of Henry's plan did not go well. The French defenders of Harfleur put up a strong resistance and it was six weeks before they surrendered. During this time, the English army had been camped in a swamp and disease ravaged the camp. Of the 10,000 who had landed, almost half had died or had been returned to England, wounded or sick. Clearly the remaining force was too small to take Paris. Instead, Henry decided on a *cheveauege*, a march through enemy territory designed to annoy the enemy but avoid battle. The army would march 100 miles to the English enclave port of Calais at the narrowest point on the English Channel. They expected to reach it quickly and took provisions for only seven days.

The route taken by the English had to cross the River Somme. On reaching it, they found French troops guarding the crossings, forcing the army to march inland to find a safe crossing. Eventually they found an

A French painting of the battle done over a century later. It owes more to the artist's imagination than reality.

unguarded crossing but this had involved a 50-mile diversion, doubling the time of the planned march. Heavy rains that turned the roads to mud further slowed the journey. Once the Somme was safely crossed, the army continued its journey towards Calais.

The delay had been serious. The army was not only short of food but the French had had time to raise a huge army. The English found their route blocked near the village of Agincourt.

Agincourt

There is little agreement on the size of the French army: the lowest estimates (which are probably the closest to the truth) put it at 30,000; Cassell's *History of England* puts it at 100,000 and estimates go as high as 150,000. The French had the numbers and the confidence but they lacked organization. France's King Charles VI, weak and mentally ill, was quite unfit to lead an army, so this role fell to Charles D'Albert, Constable of France, and Boucicault, the Marshal. Both were experienced soldiers, but the French nobles did not consider their rank high enough to warrant respect and their commands were widely ignored.

The English army numbered about 5,700 of whom 5,000 were archers. The extended march meant they were hungry and tired. To add to their misery, there had been heavy rains which had saturated the ground.

Henry tried to avoid battle, offering to return Harfleur and the prisoners taken there, but the French replied that he must renounce his claim to the French

The order of battle. The English (red) archers are marked A, the men-at arms (lances) B. The French are shown in blue.

throne if they were to let him pass to Calais. Henry refused and battle became inevitable. The French, supremely confident of victory on the following day because of their enormous numerical superiority, spent the night carousing, taunting the English across the lines and dicing for the captives they were sure they would take.

The English did have a few points in their favor. Henry was a charismatic commander, popular with his men and able to motivate his troops. In addition, the English had defeated vastly greater French armies twice before, in 1346 at Crécy and in 1356 at Poitiers.

Some of the actual conversations prior to the battle were recorded. One of the English commanders, Sir Walter Hungerford, regretted that "they had not but one ten thousand of those men in England who do no work today." Henry replied, "Wot you not that the Lord with these few can overthrow the pride of the French?"

The Battlefield

The French had chosen an extraordinarily bad place to meet the English. The

road to Calais passed between two thick forests that were 1,300 yards apart at the French end but narrowing towards the English lines.

On the morning of 25 October 1415, Henry arranged his troops carefully. He placed his archers on the flanks and between the men-at-arms. Despite the French advantage in numbers, they refused to attack. At 11 o'clock, Henry, tired of waiting, gave the order to advance. With a cry of "Hurrah! Hurrah! Saint George and Merrie England" the English army advanced to within 300 yards of the French lines. There they placed sharpened stakes, angled towards the enemy to check any cavalry charge. When this was finished, they fired the first of their arrows.

Henry V was one of England's best loved monarchs.

The French had arranged themselves in three dense lines, one behind the other, between the forests. There were so many of them that they found it almost impossible to fire their crossbows and cannons effectively. Despite these problems, the French knights charged.

As they approached the English, the narrowing front formed by the two forests forced the knights into each other. The converging mass made movement very difficult. To add to this problem, the rain-saturated ground was turned into deep mud by the horses. All but the first ranks slipped and stumbled. The front ranks of the French cavalry who were able to advance received the full effect of English archers.

Even as the deadly hail of arrows decimated the front ranks, the French cavalry behind, unaware of what was happening up ahead, pressed forward through the mud, piling up on the dead and wounded at their front. Those who did reach the front had to climb a wall of dead and dying men and horses before they in turn were slain. Taking advantage of this confusion, the English slung their bows and laid into the confused mass with their swords.

To make matters worse, the French sent in a second wave, crushing their own men. The English grabbed some 1,700 prisoners from the mess — rich pickings in an age when noble prisoners could yield a substantial ransom — and sent them to the rear to be guarded with the baggage train.

The local French villagers, loath not to profit from the events of the day, took advantage of the poorly guarded baggage train to

There are no contemporary paintings of the Battle of Agincourt and many of those that do exist owe more to imagination than reality. This one by Spencer, depicting the scene after the battle, is probably accurate. Over half the archers were mounted and the exhaustion of the English soldiers is obvious.

help themselves to whatever they could find. When Henry learned of this disturbance, he believed it was an attack from the rear and ordered that the prisoners be killed to prevent their escape. At first the guards refused, not from any humanitarian principle but because of the loss of potential ransom. Henry even had to withdraw 200 archers from the battle to threaten his own men. The slaughter began and only ceased when the truth became known. But by this time most of the prisoners had been killed, only the most illustrious were spared.

As the battle progressed, the French became aware of the scale of the disaster. As the word spread, the French army started to slip away into the countryside and this quickly became a rout. One of the few consolations for the French was that the English were too tired and too few in numbers to make chase.

Aftermath

Estimates of the English losses vary greatly. Shakespeare gives the English dead as four nobles and 25 regular troops. Some historian's estimates go as high as 500 or even 1,000 but the most

widely accepted figure is 100-200 English dead. French losses are better known; the French themselves estimated these at between 8,000 and 11,000. A generation of French nobles had been destroyed: there was hardly a French noble family that did not lose someone.

The English troops collected so much loot on the battlefield that the army simply could not move. Henry ordered almost all of it to be placed in a local barn along with the English dead and this was then set ablaze.

Henry, a deeply religious man, refused to accept credit for the victory, ascribing it to God alone. Further expeditionary forces won battle after battle until 1420 when the French King Charles VI agreed that on his death Henry would become King of France, as well as being King of England. He gave his daughter Catherine in marriage to Henry.

But the glory did not last. Henry V died of dysentery in 1422. A few years later France produced her own hero, Joan of Arc, who began the reverse of English fortunes, eventually leading to the loss of all Henry's territories in France except Calais.

Shakespeare's play *Henry V* contains perhaps the best-known description of the battle, which forms a major part of the play. His version of Henry's pre-battle oration is one of the most stirring passages of English literature:

If we are marked to die, we are enough,
To do our country loss; and if to live,
The fewer men, the greater share of honor.

HM

The Development of Guilds

Barbara Krasner-Khait traces the rise and decline of merchant and artisan guilds.

BEFORE CORPORATIONS and labor unions, there was the guild — a brotherhood of friendship, mutual aid, religious celebration and economic control. Members shared common interests, lived in the same community, and supported each other as brothers would.

The guild had several points of origin. In ancient Rome, groups formed as *collegia* and focused on quality standards. Among the Germanic tribes, "fraternities of young warriors practicing the cult of heroes" and drinking clubs evolved into guilds, so called because group members were bound by rite, friendship, commitment to mutual support, and perhaps most importantly, payment of an entry fee — *geld*.

During the 6th century, guilds began to evolve under Byzantine rule. The state prefect governed what trades could do and not do, granting some professions special privileges, such as exempting bakers from religious worship to ensure continuous bread making. Notaries, jewelers, bankers, silk garment merchants, importers of Syrian silk, raw silk merchants, silk spinners, silk weavers, linen merchants, perfume dealers, candle makers, soap makers, grocers, leather cutters, butchers, pork dealers, fishmongers, bakers, innkeepers, joiners, plasterers, marble workers, locksmiths, and painters — all were noted in the Book of the Prefect that defined their work sites, rules, market practices, and production stan-

Rembrandt's painting *The Syndics of the Cloth Guild* shows Dutch merchants discussing financial matters while appearing to eye outsiders warily.

dards. The prefect kept lists of guild members and administered new ones.

The guilds formed to encourage cooperation among members and to discourage outside competition. Often the life force of a commune or town, they sprang up in the Low Countries, northern Italy, and southern France before spreading to the rest of Europe. As new trade routes established themselves throughout medieval Europe, new guilds emerged in the cities and towns along the routes.

Members of the guild tended to congregate in a particular part of the town, making it easier to keep an eye on each other. That also gave the guild the responsibility for civic life within its own district or quarter. It was not uncommon for the guild leaders to also become town leaders. The guilds relieved the town of the municipal burdens of social welfare, security and justice.

Guilds took on religious and social roles. They adopted patron saints, lead processions, and conducted festivals that also were

good for business. The guildhall, often the town's largest building besides the church, became a center of social activity.

When a member of the guild was ill, the guild gave food and medicine. If his home was robbed or burned, the guild came to his rescue. When he was dying, the guild made sure he received the last rites and if he was poor, saw that he had a decent burial. When a merchant lost his stock in a shipwreck or at the hands of a robber baron, the guild helped him get back on his feet. If a man in another town refused to pay a guildsman, the guild would seize the next inhabitant of the town who came its way.

The brotherly mutual support created a very tight circle around the town. The guild secured a monopoly for its members and sealed the economy of the town. A new merchant couldn't sell in the town if he didn't belong to the guild. If a foreign merchant came to town, he had to sell his goods to a guild member or at least pay a very heavy sales tax.

Guild statutes governed fair practice and leveled the playing field where the best performed alongside the mediocre. They also stipulated the number of hours a member could work. Some guilds, for instance, mandated that no work could be done in January as there was little daylight. To ensure that supply did not exceed demand, the guild regulated how

Guild houses, such as those seen in Belgium (left) and Germany (right), were designed to be impressive structures. The buildings demonstrated the guild's wealth and commitment to quality to potential customers.

many could enter the trade. The number of apprentices and the length of their service were determined by the guild.

For the consumer, the guild ensured a fair standard of work and punished those who didn't adhere to the standard.

Merchants and Craftsmen Split

At first most towns had one guild to which both merchants and artisans belonged. But the brotherhood was a little too close for comfort. Rivalry and jealousy reared their ugly heads. For one thing, the merchant could earn far more money. He wanted to sell goods at the highest price possible while his artisan brother wanted to buy the goods at the lowest price. The answer to this sibling rivalry was to separate the merchant from the artisan. Craftsmen formed their own guilds.

Craft guilds represented the more important industries of most towns by the end of the 12th century and they grew rapidly in the following century. Every conceivable occupation had its guild — even prostitutes. In a complex industry, a different guild corresponded to each step in the manufacturing process. So for cloth making, there were separate guilds for spinners, weavers,

fullers, and dyers. As a rule, members of the same guild lived on the same street.

The actions of the craft guilds were pretty much the same as those for merchants. The objective was to prevent competition. No member was allowed to make goods faster, cheaper or better.

Though split apart, dissent between merchant and artisan continued. The merchant guilds often sought political power and controlled many civic governments to the exclusion of the craft guilds. The craftsmen, seeking to also participate in the government, openly rebelled and rioted. According to several accounts of the English Peasants' Revolt of 1381, "disaffected and underprivileged artisans" were the major source of trouble.

The Master Recruiting System

On 7 April 1180 in Genoa, young Giovanni became an apprentice to turner Guglielmo Buscarono. Contracting himself for five years, Giovanni swore to stay in his master's service and to commit no fraud beyond 18 pennies a year. In return, Buscarono would give his apprentice food, clothing, and an annual salary of 12 solidi. And perhaps most importantly, the master promised to teach his

apprentice turning — the art of shaping wood or metal on a lathe — and to give him the tools of the trade at the end of the contract's term. Giovanni was of majority so he served as his own guarantor without the authority of his father or another relative.

Giovanni's story was fairly typical. Guild masters had the responsibility to recruit and train apprentices, usually from the families of members. Children of guild members were a captive talent pool, often destined to work a particular craft from the time of their birth. They were also granted special privileges such as small or no guild entry fees.

There were young apprentices under the age of 10 and their training period differed from the older apprentices who were contracted between the ages of 10-14. The younger ones got the short end of the stick. Both boys and girls received longer periods of training, and while serving in a craft or shop were little more than servants. The tailors of Bologna, for instance, maintained that apprentices younger than 10 would receive five years of training. Older apprentices would receive three. Older apprentices like Giovanni often received wages. They typically had a very

This is to Certify that ....
is enrolled a Member of the Women's Co-operative
Guild : a self-governing organization of ....
Women, who work through Co-operation for the
welfare of the people, seeking Freedom for their
own progress, and the Equal Fellowship of men
and women in the Home, the Store, the Workshop
and the State.   A Honora Rufield.

Date.   General Secretary.

A guild membership card from a women's guild in the US.

The Seven Great Guilds Of Florence

Not all guilds were created equal. These *arti maggiori* were held in higher esteem and had more wealth than the *arti minori* that included butchers and shoemakers.

Finishers and dealers of foreign cloth
Importers of wool and manufacturers of local cloth
Money changers and bankers
Judges and notaries
Physicians and apothecaries
Furriers
Big retailers and silk entrepreneurs

different type of relationship with their masters. In either case, master status was not guaranteed.

Many notarial records exist of master-apprentice contracts, typically between unrelated parties since guild members didn't see the need to write down agreements with their own children. Steven Epstein wrote of several contractual agreements in *Wage Labor and Guilds in Medieval Europe*:

• One blacksmith promised to teach his apprentice how to care for the health of the horse and how to prepare ointments for it, in addition to the blacksmith craft. In return, the apprentice agreed never to practice in the same spot or land where the master worked.

• The smiths of Bologna required apprentices to supply rations of wine, grain and meat every year, while the masters provided shoes and clothing.

• The makers of belts and straps in Paris stipulated that if an apprentice married during his term of service, he could no longer dine at the master's table three times a day. He would, though, receive a per diem wage that would probably cover the cost of the meals.

In many cases, the master needed to provide for the apprentice's emotional needs as well as food and shelter. Master and apprentice often lived as a family unit. Conditions were not great, so to protect the brotherhood contracts often dealt specifically with

repercussions for runaway apprentices.

The Downfall

Guilds were the mainstay of medieval towns from the 12th to the 15th centuries. But their days of owning the town were waning. Discord continued to exist between guilds and within them.

For one thing, apprentices and journeymen — a sort of middle step between apprentice and master for former apprentices who worked by the day — were finding it harder to achieve master status. Entrance fees rose steeply and many guilds demanded a kind of masterpiece to demonstrate master skills that few journeymen had time to make. Only the sons and sons-in-law of existing masters could hope to become masters, since their entrance fees were often waived.

Guild statutes of fair play inhibited innovation. One example of this took place in England in the 13th century: a water mill could far more effectively perform a fulling (thickening of cloth) operation than a manual method. But because water power was not available to all the fullers' guilds, the potential for increased efficiency fell to the wayside. The fullers' guild even coerced other guilds to refuse goods fulled in mills.

In 1335, King Edward III of England passed a law that allowed foreign merchants to trade freely in English towns. This was a blow to the English mer-

chant guilds and ended the monopoly they had enjoyed for so long. Their power had begun to decline.

By the end of the 14th century, the merchant guild in its old form had almost disappeared from most countries of western Europe. Yet it had served a great purpose. It had regulated trade and brought order and government to towns when there was no one else to do so. It had paved the roads and erected mills and bridges. The merchants themselves continued to play major roles in their towns and cities.

Craft guilds continued past the 14th century and some still exist today. While we most often think of them operating throughout Europe, guilds also appeared in Asian and Middle Eastern cultures. But as capitalism developed and infighting abounded, the brotherhood of the medieval guild necessarily changed to meet the needs of the Renaissance and Reformation.

Further Reading

Black, Antony. *Guilds and Civil Society in European Political Thought from the Twelfth Century to the Present* (Cornell University Press, 1984).
Epstein, Steven A. *Wage Labor and Guilds in Medieval Europe* (University of North Carolina Press, 1991).
Renard, George. *Guilds in the Middle Ages* (Augustus M. Kelley Publishers, 1968).

HM

INTRODUCTION TO GENEALOGY

Family Chronicle's **INTRODUCTION TO GENEALOGY**

Family Chronicle's Introduction to Genealogy has been written to answer the often heard question "I'm interested in starting my research — but where do I start?" It assumes no prior knowledge of genealogy and is designed to bring the reader rapidly "up to speed".

The presentation follows *Family Chronicle's* popular format. Features include how to find information about your ancestors in: Vital Records, City Directories, Census and Military Records, Naturalization Records, Social Security Records, Passenger Lists, Court Records, Obituaries and Church and Parish Records. This is followed by information on where to conduct your research: Family History Centers, Libraries and National Archives. There are also sections on keeping your data organized, manually or on a computer.

If you have traced your roots back across the Atlantic, we have a summary on conducting your research in a dozen European countries. When you have gathered enough information we show you how to start writing your family history.

We introduce you to computers, with advice on the type of computer to use, an overview of the software packages available and tips on getting online and making the most out the Internet. We explain how to find records on CDs or in the subscription services on the web.

There's a whole lot more including Heraldry, Tartans, Origins of Surnames, Societies, Preservation of Documents and Photos . . .

As with all our publications, if *Family Chronicle's Introduction to Genealogy* fails to meet your needs or expectations, we will gladly refund your money, for any reason or no reason. Any refund will be made promptly and cheerfully.
Halvor Moorshead, Editor and Publisher

The *Introduction* is designed to get you started on the right foot and to fill in any gaps if you are an experienced researcher.

Christmas in America

Beverly Smith Vorpahl describes the evolution of the celebration of Christmas.

NORTH AMERICA'S POPULATION is comprised of those whose ancestors migrated here from every corner of the globe and, as they melded into one citizenry, they brought with them the traditions of their homeland holidays. So, just as we are a melting pot of ethnicity, so is the manner of our Christmas celebrations.

Our diverse holiday traditions as they're observed today evolved slowly, as first one country's tradition merged with another and another to become a truly blended celebration.

If our forefathers had had their way, we wouldn't celebrate the birth of Christ and certainly not the arrival of Santa in any form. What follows is a summary of how we arrived at the 21st-century Christmas season.

Puritans and Christmas

And you thought Scrooge was a grump about Christmas! Compared to the 17th-century Pilgrims and Puritans, the 19th-century Charles Dickens character that will be forever associated with Christmas was an angel about the holidays. America's Founding Fathers not only disapproved of Christmas, they outlawed it! It was, they reasoned, a pagan festival and had nothing to do with the birth of Jesus. There's no biblical or historical support that 25 December is the birth date of Jesus. "If God had intended for the anniversary of the Nativity to be observed, he would surely have given

some indication as to when that anniversary occurred," Stephen

---

Compared to the 17th-century Puritans, Scrooge was an angel about the holidays!

Nissenbaum quoted Puritans in *The Battle for Christmas: A Cultural History of America's Cherished Holiday*. An attempt to suppress the celebration of Christmas in this country was immediate with the Pilgrim's first 25 December in the New World. Governor Bradford reprimanded Christmas-keepers among the Pilgrims when they

tried to take the day off, rather than follow his edict of working as though it were just any other day. In *Plymouth Plantation 1620-1647* by William Bradford, editor Samuel Eliot Morison wrote: "On the day called Christmas Day," Bradford called the *Mayflower* men to work that day as he did every day, but some "excused themselves and said it went against their consciences to work on that day." The governor reluctantly granted their wish — but only until they could better inform themselves about the day's true identity.

However, when Bradford and the others returned for their noon meal, the "conscientious objectors" were openly playing in the street: "some pitching the bar, and some at stool-ball (a game resembling cricket) and such like sports. So (Bradford) went to them and took away their implements and told them that it was against his conscience that they should play (while) others work. If they made the keeping of (Christmas a) matter of devotion, let them keep (it in) their houses; but there should be no gaming or reveling in the streets."

Most northern European cultures in the 17th century lit candles and brought greenery inside their homes during December's darkest days. Those who could afford candles lit them for a bit of extra light through the winter solstice when sun and light would slowly begin to brighten the days again, Nissenbaum wrote.

The Pilgrims found no biblical support for celebrating Christmas. To them it was another working day, trying to scratch a living for their families or defending themselves against Indians.

Staunch, conservative Christians disapproved of any "Feast of Lights," with its excessive eating, the Yule log, candles, holly, mistletoe… A little frivolity might lead to outrageous conduct as had happened in England. In the 16th century, Anglican Bishop Hugh Latimer wrote, "Men dishonor Christ more in the 12 days of Christmas than in all the 12 months besides."

Cotton Mather scolded his Boston parishioners during his Christmas Day sermon in 1712: "Can you, in your Conscience think that our holy Savior is honored by Mirth, by long Eating, by hard Drinking, by lewd Gaming, by rude Reveling, by a Mass fit for none but a Bacchus or Saturn?" Such actions, Mather said, were more of hell than heaven. So, evidently some Colonists were having a very good time, or the Puritan minister wouldn't have been so agitated.

Origins

"Christmas came by its godless reputation with mid-winter pagan festivals of Norsemen and Celts; and with the Romans, who debauched during a midwinter feast called Saturnalia," according to *A Victorian Christmas, Joy To the World,* by Cynthia Hart, John Grossman and Priscilla Dunhill.

A case in point might be the tradition of "mumming," which crossed over from the Romans to the English in which men, dressed in women's clothes and women in men's, set about the town begging. Poor wassailers extorted food and drink from the wealthy, who hosted open house, like it or not. It was legal for scalawags to walk into a lord's home and help themselves to liquor and food.

Puritans vowed such barbaric ways would not be tolerated in New England, where they intend-

It was the Victorians who began to include children in the Christmas celebrations.

ed to revel in religious freedom. In 1659, the Massachusetts Bay Colony enacted a fine to deter those who insisted on commemorating the holiday:

"Whosoever shall be found observing any such days as Christmas and the like, either by forbearing labor, feasting or any other way upon such account as aforesaid, every such person so offending shall pay for each offense five shillings as a fine to the country." Those of our forefathers who chose to settle in the continent's warmer climes, however, were more relaxed about enjoying themselves. In fact, they balanced Christmas as both a time to worship and a time to play, according to Robert Ostermann in Proclamations of Christmas, a chapter in *The Great American Christmas Almanac A Complete Compendium of Facts, Fancies and Tradition,* by Irena Chalmers and

Friends.

Cats fared well on Christmas Day in the hill country between the North and South, according to the almanac. Their saucers brimmed with milk to keep them quiet, because a meowing cat that day portended bad luck.

In Appalachia, "Old Christmas" was celebrated on 6 January, "when there was a feast in even the poorest houses, and bonfires at night with much gunplay and fireworks," wrote David Hackett Fischer in *Albion's Seed, Four British Folkways in America.* "Stanging," was a rough ceremony celebrated during Old Christmas "in which a victim was hoisted on a long pole and made to dangle in the air until he bought himself free."

That's a far cry from the date's more civilized observation of the feast of the Epiphany.

Post-Puritan Christmas

The holiday began to mantle a new shape as the rigid Puritan religion and way of life gradually assumed a more tolerant Congregationalist appearance. Still, it would be generations before Christmas would come anywhere near familiar to our senses of sight, smell, sound and taste. Benjamin Franklin did his part to further the celebration of Christmas. Actually, he and other almanac writers urged New Englanders to do away with periodic binges and commemorate Christmas as a time of cheer. In moderation, that is. The year 1730 seems to have been a Christmas watershed.

"Almanacks," according to Samuel Johnson's period dictionary, were calendars; books "in which the revolutions of the seasons, with the return of feasts and facts, is noted." Before 1730, almanac writers seldom mentioned Christmas, but after that year they seldom *failed* to mention the holiday, Nissenbaum wrote in *Battle for Christmas.*

In 1734, Franklin wrote in his *Poor Richard's Almanac,* that "If you would have Guests merry with

STEP INTO HISTORY.
THEN GET OUT OF THE WAY.

Relive an era with Mississippi's Civil War battle re-enactments

and magnificent antebellum homes.

Or catch a casino show, stroll along the beach and trace the origin

of the blues. Call 1-888-669-7662

for your free Mississippi *Travel Planner*.

THE SOUTH'S WARMEST WELCOME

www.visitmississippi.org

your Cheer,/Be so yourself or so at least appear."

Christmas Carols

Although Christmas carols were first sung in the Middle Ages, according to *The Great American Christmas Almanac*, they didn't come into their own until the 18th and 19th centuries, when they helped serve as a bridge of acknowledging Christmas from one form to another. The carols were written as poetry making them adaptable to already existing hymns. In England's early days of observing Christmas, caroling was a disgrace, since it was most often done "in the midst of Rioting and Chambering and Wantonness," Nissenbaum wrote.

The 1800s

Christmas in America hit its stride beginning with the last half of the 1800s. Until the mid-1800s, it was a hit-and-miss holiday, observed by some and ignored by others, according to Nissenbaum. For some, it was a time of pious devotion or one of mirthful joy. It was a time of feasting with or without libations but mostly with.

The evangelical denomination of Universalists openly celebrated Christmas in the late 1700s with church services. In the early 1800s, they furthered the caused of Christmas more than any other denomination. By 1800, Unitarians called for public observance of Christmas, knowing full well that 25 December was most likely not the date of Christ's birth. They simply wanted to celebrate His birth, and not because God had directed them, Nissenbaum said. The Unitarians also hoped their more genteel method of celebration might purge the holiday's history of excess and disorder.

"In the 19th century, Christmas came tiptoeing into churches through the back door so to speak, when the American Sunday School Society began advocating

Christmas tree candles were lit only twice during the holidays, once on Christmas morning and again on New Year's Eve.

Christmas programs for children," according to *Joy to the World*.

During the 1800s, Christmas began to become associated with children. Before then, children were delegated to the bottom rung of society's hierarchy, along with servants and apprentices. Before the Victorian age, there would have been no thought at all given to have a holiday revolve around mere children.

St. Nick, St. Nicholas, Santa Claus

Washington Irving, of *Sleepy Hollow* fame, gave Americans their first detailed information of Santa, based on the Dutch version of St. Nicholas. Under the pseudonym Diedrich Knickerbocker, Irving told of Santa's arriving horseback each "Eve of St. Nicholas."

But Clement Moore, with his 1822 poem "A Visit from St. Nicholas," is the hero of Christmas as we have come to celebrate it. But there's more to the creation of his well-loved poem than the simple legend of his writing it for a sick daughter. Moore didn't actually invent Santa Claus. Instead, he created him from the writings of poets and historians who had already made reference to Santa's sleigh and reindeer, Santa as an elf, Santa smoking his pipe and Santa's rotund figure. Even the

meter of his poem can be found elsewhere. In fact, Moore's phrase, "lays his finger aside of his nose," was drawn directly from Irving's 1809 description. But it was Moore who put them all together in one everlasting poem.

The American image of Santa Claus came more into a 21st-century focus by illustrator Thomas Nast, who depicted a rotund Santa for Christmas issues of *Harper's Magazine* from the 1860s to the 1880s. It was Nast who added Santa's workshop at the North Pole and the list of good and bad children all over the world.

Santa was introduced to America just in time to rival the figure of Belsnickle, a German man dressed in high buckskins, a white robe and an enormous flax wig, who was known to visit Pennsylvania families in the 1820s.

Belsnickle wasn't nearly as jovial as Santa. True, Santa does maintain a list of children's names throughout the world, which he does check twice, but he's inclined to look the other way at naughty children. Not so, Belsnickle. To parents of good children, Belsnickle would present gifts as though they came out of heaven, directly from Jesus Christ, Nissenbaum wrote. But Belsnickle would give a rod to parents of ill-behaved imps, and recommend they put it to good use.

If Moore gave us Santa Claus, it was Charles Dickens who illustrated a Victorian Christmas for us with his descriptive images in *A Christmas Carol* and other period books.

The Crèche

On the religious front, it was in Victorian America that the crèche came to be a symbol of the Christ Child's birth. According to *Joy to the World*, it was derived from "the touching story of an adolescent Mary, great with child, and her gently middle-aged husband Joseph." After a 90-mile journey from Nazareth to Bethlehem, the couple couldn't find any rooms anywhere in town, and finally settled for a stable, where Christ was born.

"The crèche itself, like the Christmas tree in America, was of German extraction, come by way of Italy," according to *Joy to the World*. By the 1870s, most churches welcomed the light and greenery of the season. Christmas hymns were sung and candles chased away shadows.

Christmas in the 1800s was a time for music lovers. Solos, duets, choruses were sung in church or anywhere humming Americans might find themselves.

Although "The First Noel" was written 400 years earlier, it was the Victorians who rediscovered it.

Christmas Cards
Christmas cards are especially popular in America, according to *The Great American Christmas Almanac*, and their popularity continues to grow since their 1874 beginnings, when Louis Prang, a Boston lithographer, printed cards in 20 colors. The English preferred Prang's delicate reproductions of flowers, while Americans bought cards featuring tranquil Madonnas, floating golden cherubs and quaint children in nightgowns anxiously awaiting St. Nick.

Christmas Trees
Christmas trees in America assume as many "personalities" as there are those who adorn them. The festive decoration began appearing in American homes during the 19th century, brought here first by Germans who settled in Pennsylvania. Trees were also promoted by mercantile New York City, says *Joy to the World*.

Trees increased tremendously in popularity following an 1848

The traditions associated with Santa Claus developed throughout the 19th century.

etching of England's Royal Family that appeared in *The Illustrated London News*. Gathered around the elaborate tree in Windsor Castle were Queen Victoria and Prince Albert (her German-born consort) and their children. It wasn't long before the ultimate Christmas decoration traveled across the Atlantic and set up its stands in America.

When conservationist President Teddy Roosevelt refused to have a Christmas tree in the White House, the first Christmas tree farm was planted the next year near Trenton, New Jersey. Trees were then grown for the sole purpose of decorating homes. No more depleting a natural resource.

Wealthy Victorian families often decorated 10-foot or taller trees, anchoring them in a heavy stone crock filled with sand and water. "The candles were lit only twice during the holidays once on Christmas morning and again on New Year's Eve, for 20 minutes each time," say the authors of *Joy to the World*.

In the early 1800s trees were decorated with home-baked cook-

ies and cakes, and handmade ornaments, such as cotton-batting Santas and cornucopias fashioned from silver paper.

Christmas Stockings
There's a delightful legend behind hanging Christmas stockings, according to *The Great American Christmas Almanac*: "St. Nick, so the story goes, tossed gold coins down the chimney of three sisters, doomed to spinsterhood for want of a dowry." When the tossed coins hit the fireplace grate, they were "netted by the maidens' stockings hung to dry by the fire."

Christmas in the South
Victorian Christmas in the South included firing cannons and muskets on Christmas morning; revelers parading in the streets, beating on drums, pots and kettles; blowing tin horns and penny whistles, drinking free eggnog and rum at local taverns.

Christmas Today
It seems as though the 21st century America still emulates the Victorian period. But today's families have refined their individual traditions that they honor year after year. As children grow into adulthood and marry, they start their own holiday traditions with touches of Christmases past from both the bride's family, and the groom's. Their merged traditions are handed down to another generation, and so on.

Christmas Recipes

Kathryn Conrad describes the origins of some favorite seasonal beverages

*"Here we come a-wassailing among
the leaves so green,
Here we come a wand'ring,
so fair to be seen"*

WAIT A MINUTE, here we come a-what? While some may be familiar with the original words to that 17th-century carol, many have learned the more modern wording where "a-wassailing" is replaced with "a-caroling". Much is lost in the newer rendition as wassailing and caroling are as different as Glogg and Grog, and of course everyone knows that distinction! Or perhaps not.

In the interest of historical appreciation, and making the most of holiday entertaining, here is a quick look at the origins of some favorite seasonal beverages and their accompanying recipes.

Wassail

The word itself stems from the Norse expression "Ves Heill", meaning "to your health". The practice of wassailing was a boisterous ceremony where friends and neighbors shared large bowls of spiced ale or wine floating with roasted apples in a toast to each other's health and the hopes for a prosperous New Year. The wassailing tradition was also shared with farm animals whereupon they would be toasted and fed special treats. The carol "Here we come a-wassailing" refers to the tradition of going door to door to wish neighbors the best of the season with a holiday toast.

Wassail

1 dozen apples, cored and peeled
1 cup water
4 cups sugar
5 whole cloves
5 allspice berries
1 stick of cinnamon
1 tsp each grated nutmeg, ground
    ginger, ground mace
1 bottle Madeira
2 bottles semi-dry red wine

a. Pre-heat oven to 375°.
b. Place the cored, peeled apples in the bottom of a very lightly greased roasting pan and bake until tender, approximately 25 minutes.
c. Combine the water, sugar and spices in a saucepan and heat until the sugar dissolves. Add the wine and heat, stirring over medium heat, until the mixture is hot. Turn the heat to warm and add the roasted apples. Allow the mixture to sit at low heat for 15 minutes.
d. Remove the apples and strain the wine mixture into a large punch bowl. Add the apples back to the bowl and serve in mugs or cups.
Note: For extended serving times, a crock pot is perfect for keeping the wassail warm without boiling the wine. For a non-alcoholic Wassail, replace the wine with apple cider.

Eggnog

There are various explanations for the name "eggnog" as referring to the mixture of eggs, cream, spices and alcohol. One story relates that European wine and egg punches were made in the colonies with rum, then called "Grog", which resulted in "Egg n' Grog", later shortened to "Eggnog". Another version attributes the name to wooden tavern mugs called "noggins". A measure of liquid served in a "noggin" was a "nog", therefore and egg punch in such a mug would be an "Egg Nog".

George Washington was known to adore eggnog, and even wrote his own recipe that included rum, sherry and rye. The following recipe is authentic, but not quite so extreme as that founding father's.

It should be noted that many eggnog recipes call for raw eggs. To avoid health hazards associated with raw eggs, heat any egg products used over a pan of hot water until a kitchen thermometer reads 160°.

Eggnog — yields eight servings

6 large eggs
¾ cup sugar
1 cup brandy
½ cup rum
4 cups milk
4 cups cream
½ cup powdered sugar
Nutmeg for garnish

a. Separate the egg yolks from the whites. If using non-pasteurized eggs, stir the yolks with the granulated sugar, retaining one tablespoon for later use, and 4 tablespoons of the milk over simmering water to 160°. Stir the egg whites with the remaining tablespoon of sugar and three tablespoons of water over simmering water to 160°.
b. Beat the yolks with the sugar until the mixture is thick and light yellow in color.
c. Gradually beat the brandy and rum into the yolk mixture. Whisk in the milk and half of the cream. Transfer the mixture to a large bowl and chill well.
d. In a large bowl, whip the egg whites and half of the powdered sugar to stiff peak.
e. In a separate bowl whip the remaining cream and remaining powdered sugar to medium peak.
f. Fold the whipped egg whites into the yolk mixture, then fold in the whipped cream.
g. Serve in individual glasses with a garnish of freshly grated nutmeg.

For a quick, non-alcoholic version, whip one cup of cream and one teaspoon of vanilla extract to soft peak and fold into fi gallon of purchased eggnog. Ladle into serving glasses and top with freshly grated nutmeg.

Welcoming your friends and neighbors with a warm treat and a toast to their health is an ancient tradition well worth continuing. A simple wish for all things good conveyed in the original Wassail Song is relevant and heartfelt today. To your health, happiness, and the best of this season of joy.

*"Love and joy come to you,
and to you a-wassail too,
And God bless you and send you a
happy new year,
And God send you a happy new year."*

HM

Bathe as the Romans Do

Jodi Avery looks at the institution of Roman public baths.

THE INSCRIPTION *LAVARE VIVERE* ("to bathe is to live"), found in the ruins of a small town outside of Rome, illustrates the importance of public bathhouses to the ancient Romans. No other aspect of social life was as popular and significant in ancient Rome as communal bathing.

There were two types of bathhouses in the Roman Empire: *Balnea* (Latin for bath) and *thermae* (Latin for warm bath). The *balnea*, first introduced in 250BC, was simply a large pool enclosed in stone walls with air heated by a furnace. For a small fee, Roman men could enjoy a quick dip in the bath. At this time it was only customary to bathe once a week. The *balnea* quickly became the fashionable place for the meeting of friends and businessmen. Although many Romans had their own private baths at home, they still enjoyed the indulgence of the *balnea* and the opportunity to socialize.

It was not until 25BC that Marcus Agrippa, a Roman general, decided to improve upon this social arena by designing and sponsoring the first *thermae*. The *thermae* were more elaborate and luxurious than *balnea*. Agrippa's original building began the boom in bathhouses. In less than 10 years there were 170 baths, both *thermae* and *balnea*, in Rome alone. By the fall of the Roman Empire, there were almost 950 bathhouses in Rome.

Thermae Design

Designers wanted their complexes to be different from others but still hold true to the beloved original bathhouse of Agrippa. *Thermae* were elaborate complexes with two basic sections: entertainment and, of course, the baths. The order of rooms and the layout of

While bathing was primarily a social activity for the Romans, private bathing rooms were also available.

the bathhouses differed slightly, but any that veered too far from the traditional *thermae* were not popular.

The bathing areas could have anywhere from two to 15 rooms. The primary room was like a modern-day locker room, the *apodyteria* (dressing room). Here, Romans would leave their towels, massage oils and other bathhouse necessities on shelves in the wall. Most would also leave a slave behind to guard their property, as theft was common.

The next room could be the *tepidarium* (lukewarm room), a room with a slightly warm temperature with water basins for washing and marble benches for slaves to rub perfumed oils into their masters' skin. These oils

would open the pores and prepare them for deep cleansing in the next room, the *caldarium*. This was the main bathing area and the hottest of all the rooms. With at least one communal heated pool and often other smaller hot baths, this room also acted as a sauna. *Labrum* (tubs) were placed around the outside of the caldarium baths. These were cold water basins used for a quick cooling off in this steamy room.

Beside the *caldarium* were two entrances, one leading back to the *tepidarium* and another leading to the *frigidarium*. The *frigidarium* was the coldest of the rooms. Most bathers would first return to the *tepidarium*, to cool down slowly then they would head to the *frigidarium*; however, some enjoyed the chilly rush of cold immersion pools while still sweating from the *caldarium*. Normally, the *frigidarium* had two communal pools: the *piscinae* (fish pond) was a slightly chilled pool and the *natatio* (swimming pool) was a pool placed underneath a skylight, with the sun making it slightly warmer than the *piscinae*. The *frigidarium* was also used by people returning from the sports area of the *thermae*.

The bathhouse's entertainment complex was just as important as the baths themselves. A central courtyard with an open roof, the *palaestra* (gymnasium), was used for lifting weights and other exercises. There was also a garden for bathers to enjoy. Often this area was adorned with magnificent sculptures and marble pedestals.

An important room in the *palaestra* was the *unctorium* (from *unctor*, "anointing"). In this massage-parlor-like room, bathers had their slaves rub oils and perfumes into their skin. Afterwards, a banana-shaped, metal strigil could be used to scrape the oil and dead skin cells off the body.

Other rooms branching off from the courtyard could include libraries, private meeting rooms, restaurants, boxing circles, board gaming rooms and halls for ball games. This area of the *thermae* would not be complete without some sort of bath; shallow footbaths could be placed around the exercise area or like a moat around the paths of the garden.

These lavish bathing buildings can be compared to modern day country clubs. The smallest ones held 300 people while the largest could accommodate over 3,000. For a fee of one quadrand a Roman could bathe, get a massage, play sports, eat, lift weights, wrestle, shop, read, socialize and everything in between.

Technology

Two major advances in ancient technology allowed for the lush atmosphere of bathhouses: aqueducts and hypocaust heating.

The main necessity of the bathhouse was, of course, water. When Agrippa finished designing the first *thermae*, he did not have to worry about water supply as he built his complex close to the Tiber River. However, as bathhouses' popularity began to increase at huge rates, cities away from natural water supplies tried to find ways to build their own thermae. The answer was found in aqueducts. Stone pipes lined with concrete were run at ground level or just below from a water source into cities. Their initial use was for bathhouses but they soon became used for public fountains and private baths. The Romans used gravity to their advantage and ran water from the highest point of the city making deposits at various distribution tanks all over the city. Some aqueducts

This drawing of the interior of a large *thermae* demonstrates how luxurious imperial bathhouses were.

were large enough to run horses through. In 100AD, Rome had eight aqueducts, delivering almost 300 gallons of water a day per Roman to 11 *thermae*, 836 *balnea* and 1,352 fountains.

Once a thermae had water, it then needed heat. The hypocaust system, invented in the first century BC, was universally used in Roman baths. The rooms were situated in order, from very hot to warm then to cold. This allowed the same air to heat or cool the rooms as needed. The floors were supported by brick landings and air passed underneath the pools. The fire furnaces that heated the air were located closest to the *caldarium* and the hot air traveled here first. It passed under the rooms, then through channels in the walls to the next rooms. As the air slowly cooled it passed to the cooler rooms, efficiently keeping the rooms at their desired temperatures. The air in the *frigi-*

darium escaped through the open roof above the *piscinae*. The baths themselves could be heated further with water boiled on top of the furnace. In the *caldarium*, where the hottest air circulated, bathers had to wear special shoes in order protect their feet from the scorching floors.

Social Hygiene

The bathhouses of ancient Rome were seen as the center of social life. People met daily to discuss business, the arts, politics and the latest community gossip. The bathhouses were also sources for entertainment, food and of course bathing.

Romans would visit the daily baths and high time would be about one or two in the afternoon. Most bathhouses opened at 10:30am and closed at dusk. They did not stay open in the evening because the staff needed time to re-fill and clean the baths, as fresh water was used each day. Additionally, Roman streets were not safe at night. No one ventured far from their homes after dark, not even to their favorite bathhouse.

The discussion of the news of the day could occur in one of the communal baths or in a private bathing room adjacent to the *caldarium*. Many historians have speculated that the plot to kill Julius Caesar may have been hatched in a *thermae*.

Surprisingly, Romans only washed their entire bodies once a week. This illustrates how much importance was place on the social purpose the bathhouse served; hygiene was only a secondary consideration. This is not to say that Romans were not clean people. They washed more often than most societies in history; in fact, after the fall of Rome washing more than three times a year was commonly thought to be harmful.

Gender Issues

When *balnea* became popular, and before *thermae* were introduced, women were not allowed into the baths. It was unthinkable for them to bathe with the men and they were seen as unable to understand the conversations that took place. Men believed that women did not need to hear of business and political talk, as their thoughts were mostly domestic. As women's stature advanced in society so did the size of bathhouses.

Agrippa allowed women into his *thermae*, but at separate times from the men. The men's hours were longer than women's were, so it took careful planning for a woman to take full advantage of the facilities. Dawn to noon was ordinarily for women bathers, with the men receiving the rest of the daylight hours. As time passed women were more accepted in the bathhouses. Larger *thermae* even accommodated both men and women at the same time by building separate areas for the two.

Mixed bathing first occurred late in the third century. It was not accepted by all Romans. However, by the last few decades of the Roman Empire, almost all large *thermae* without separate quarters had communal gender bathing. This changed the atmosphere of the baths greatly. It was now more erotic at times. Prostitution even began to spread through the smaller bathhouses. This enraged groups of Romans who were already opposed to *thermae*.

Opposition

Not everyone in Rome was enthusiastic about bathhouses. Long before mixed bathing came into practice, there were those who opposed *thermae*. Before the birth of Christianity, the Pagan culture held opposition to bathhouses. They felt that they were breeding grounds for sinful acts and thoughts.

As Christianity spread after the first century AD, the Christians voiced their opinions concerning bathhouses. Christians nicknamed the buildings "Cathedrals of Flesh". Like the Pagans, they believed *thermae* were off-limits to

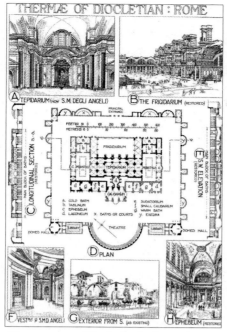

The emperor Diocletian's *thermae* was one of the largest bathhouses in Rome.

the law, and the gambling, nudity and barbaric wrestling that occurred inside was sinful. They did not agree with the amount of time Romans spent in baths as well as communal bathing. Christians believed that the sort of cleanliness offered by bathhouses was not next to Godliness.

Philosopher and statesman Seneca (4BC–62AD) was particularly opposed to bathhouses. He had many reasons for his distaste of the most popular social arena and he voiced all of them repeatedly in his public speeches and writings. Seneca once said that sweating should result from physical labor and not relaxation in a steam room. He felt the bathhouses were too lavish and Romans were not pleased unless they were surrounded by marble. Seneca's home was located near a *thermae* and he was disgusted by the grunts and moans heard through the open roof of the *palaestra*. He also wished for the return to days of "men smelling like farm and army life".

Imperial Baths

Most large *thermae* were designed by and built for emperors.

There were seven notable baths built by emperors: Nero (65AD),

Titus (81AD), Domitian (95AD), Comodus (185AD), Caracalla (217AD), Diocletian (305AD) and Constantine (315AD). Each emperor tried to surpass his predecessors in the size, popularity and splendor of their bathhouses. The Baths of Caracalla were over 27,000 square feet. Over 3,000 bathers could be accommodated in the Baths of Diocletian, which is almost double the amount Caracalla's baths could hold. Entrance fees for imperial baths were usually low or totally free.

Emperors used their own baths to gain popularity or relax with their citizens; some say that Diocletian bathed seven or eight times a day in order to keep in touch with his public. Nero is said to have enjoyed a soak in his bathhouse after a day of prosecuting Jews and Christians.

Wars, disease, greed and barbarians have been blamed for the demise of the Roman Empire. It declined quickly and as it fell so did its bathhouses. *Balnea* and *thermae* were deserted as people fought for their cities and lives. By the middle of the 5th century, bathhouses were empty shells, no longer spirited and lively.

The best preserved bath is located in Pompeii, a city buried by a volcanic eruption in 79AD that has now been excavated. An engraving announcing the *thermae*'s opening is still intact: "There will be a dedication of the baths and the public is promised a slaughter of wild beasts, athletics, awnings to shade the sun and perfumed sprinklings." The ruins of the Baths of Nero, Titus, Caracalla, Diocletian and Constantine remain today as well.

HM

Farming in the New World

Beverly Downing charts the evolution of farming practices in North America.

THE FIRST SETTLERS in the New World hoped to find wealth from a variety of ventures, but they didn't seem to expect any reward from farming except sustenance. Little did they realize that the settlement of North America would alter the status of the farmer and bring about revolutionary changes in the practice of agriculture.

The first settlers at Jamestown had little experience at farming. Two Indian captives tried to show them how to grow corn but they paid little attention and as a result almost starved to death.

Jamestown

Thirteen years before the *Mayflower* arrived, the settlers of Jamestown had spent more time exploring ways to make their fortunes than in planting a few seeds for survival. History reports that their winter food supply was meager at best. Two Indian captives tried to give some minimal instruction on growing crops, and a little nourishment was produced, but the settlers didn't pay a lot of attention and persisted in focusing on the pursuit of gold and glory. By 1610, new arrivals at Jamestown found a half-starved group of colonists existing on oysters, snakes, roots, acorns and wild fruit.

Most of the colonists wanted to own, and perhaps farm, the land. Plenty of land was available, but many of the Europeans that entered the New World in the 17th century had very little agricultural experience. As Jared Eliot writes in his *Essays Upon Field Husbandry*, "When we consider the small number of the first settlers coming from an old culti-vated country, to thick woods, rough unimproved lands, where all their former experience and knowledge was now of very little service to them...It may be said, that in sort, they began the World anew."

Beginning the "world anew" meant beginning with the first step of farming — clearing the land for cultivation. The settlers learned how to do this from those who were there already — the Indians. When the Indians, who had no metal tools, no wheeled carts and no draft animals, wanted to clear a space in the forest, they began by "girdling" the trees. Using their stone hatchets, they cut a ring through the bark and around the trunks of the designated tree. Over a period of time, the tree would die due to the interrupted flow of water and nutrients.

The Indian version of "cutting down" the dead trees was a long and tedious process. First, fires were built around the base of the tree. After the tree trunk was burned a little, the men chipped away the charred wood with their hatchets. The burning and chipping continued, day after day, until the trees fell. To prevent the flames from spreading too high and jumping to other trees, the Indian women would apply wide bands of wet clay around the tree a few feet from the ground. The tree stumps still remained when the land was "cleared", but it was considered suitable for cultivation.

Planting

After showing them how to clear the land, the Indians taught the colonists how to grow corn. They believed that to ensure a good crop, the corn must be planted when the new leaves on the oak tree reached the size of a mouse's ear. Around 10 May, seeds were sown in small dirt hills located about three feet apart in the sunlit areas under dying

trees. A dead herring, which served as fertilizer, was placed inside this mound next to the seeds. When the corn stalks were two to three feet high, bean, pumpkin and squash seeds were planted around them. This allowed the vines to use the corn stalks as a pole. As the vegetables grew, large clam shells were used for weeding.

The colonists observed, and then followed, the Indians' methods of clearing and planting. The work was slow, tedious and discouraging. In a year, the average settler cleared no more than an acre or two of land. A lifetime of work produced fewer than 100 new acres for the next generation.

When the farmer was ready to plant, he turned the dirt by using a shovel, or hoe. To ready it for cultivation, he pulverized the earth with heavy logs, or harrows. He planted the corn seeds by walking along the furrowed rows, opening a hole in the mounded dirt with a stick, or hoe, and placing the corn seed (and the herring) in the hole. According to Rhys Isaac's *The Transformation of Virginia*, this produced a scene of "men and women moving through the mire, bending over about six thousand times a day, making holes in the crowns of the hills with their fingers or a small stick for the reception of the corn seeds."

Corn, Corn, Corn
Even though the farmers followed the Indian methods for planting corn, and gladly accepted the Indian recipes, along with their Indian names — pone, hominy, samp and succotash — they refused to call corn by the Indian word, *maize*. Instead, they insisted on using the term "corn", which was their generic term for cereal grains. Corn was considered a miracle plant, since it was equally nourishing for man and beast, immune to most diseases and easy to raise. The yield per acre was high — seven times that of wheat or barley.

No part of the corn plant went unused: the stalk served as winter

This shows a somewhat idealized home for pigs. Generally, pigs were left on their own to forage in the woods. They would become independent and aggressive, eating roots, acorns, rattlesnakes, or any other snake passing by, for dinner. If they became too wild to journey back to civilization for butchering, the farmer's rifle took care of the reluctant animal on the spot!

fodder for the cattle, the husks stuffed mattresses, and the cobs were used as jug stoppers, tool handles and bowls of corncob pipes. Of course, the availability of corn limited the colonist's diet to corn mush, corn bread, corn pone, or corn pudding — served three times a day! Meat did not always accompany the corn, although the New World was rich in game. Hunting in Europe was a sport available only to the gentry so few of the colonists were skilled in the use of the clumsy rifles of the period.

Plowing
The passage of time did not make farming easier. Agricultural accomplishments were limited by the farmer's lack of manpower and tools. His work force usually consisted of himself, his children,

and probably his wife. For the first 12 years in the New World, the pilgrims faced another setback — no plows! Once a few plows had arrived, the farmers still had to wait for the arrival of oxen and horses to pull them.

The colonists found the plows difficult to use in between the burned out stumps. Early models were cumbersome implements — huge wooden objects made up of heavy beams, and a moldboard (the rotating piece behind the point of the plow which turns the earth). To use the plow required the efforts of several men; one to hold the plow, one to remove the soil that stuck to the moldboard and one, or two, to guide the oxen. Sometimes, four, six, or even eight oxen were needed to drag the plow through the soil at a depth of about three inches.

By 1700, some of plows were manufactured with metal tips on the cutting surfaces. This enabled the farmer to plow a little more land, perhaps an average of one acre a day. As more plows became available, and more metal was added to the blade, a few towns paid a bonus to any resident that owned the improved model and who would be willing to sell his services to others. Even with these scattered improvements, farming methods, and equipment, would change very little over the next hundred years.

Isolation
Besides being ill equipped to farm the land, the settlers were not used to the loneliness of farm life. Those who migrated from the Old World had lived their lives within the sound of their own church bell. Their village friends were only a short walk away, as were the services of the blacksmith, the cooper, the carpenter and the candlestick maker. But, in North America, the great distances between individual properties left the farm family in a state of semi-seclusion. Services that were provided by others were too far away to access on a regular basis.

Men, women and children expected farm life in the New World to be harsh. Men did the

Corn was originally planted by hand but in the 19th century machinery made this easier. By the middle of the century, machinery was available to do this with very little manual labor.

By the 1860s 10,000 reapers were in use, lightening the workload of the average farmer.

The sheaves of wheat had to be carted back to the farm for threshing.

heavy labor, but since the agricultural economy divided the chores among every member of the household, many jobs took on a unisex status. It wasn't unusual for the woman on a farm to help with chores usually done by men. The butchering of smaller animals — like pigs — was considered well within her domain. Holding the squealing swine tightly against her legs, the farmer's wife would plunge a long-bladed knife through the animal's heart. When the bleeding stopped, the swine would be placed in boiling water for a few minutes, then pulled out and rubbed with rosin. The hairs would be scraped from the skin and it would be disemboweled. Organ meats were used immediately, intestines were cleaned and saved for sausage casings and the rest stood in salt water for a few weeks and was then hung in the chimney for "smoking". When butchering a pig, the thrifty farmer's wife used "everything but the squeal!"

Besides helping with the butchering, the planting and the harvesting, tasks related to the dairy were also under the wife's charge — from managing the cows to overseeing the final production of cream and butter. Cows ran wild and foraged as best they could, but when the farm wife had to milk them, they were driven into a fence corner by the children of the family and distracted until the job was completed. The milk was stored in springs, or dugout cellars, located near the house. Here it was cooled, the cream was skimmed and the butter was stored. The farm wife churned butter at least twice a week — "working the butter" with wooden paddles in a large wooden bowl. Molding it into fancy shapes, cleaning the pails and utensils was as much a part of women's work as washing the dishes.

A Woman's Work is Never Done

With all of these chores demanding her attention, you might come to understand how the old adage "a woman's work is never done" came into use!

"*6 Thursday*. Up late making wine. *7 Friday* Hot as yesterday. I am dirty and distressed. Almost weared to death, Dear Lord, deliver me…. *11 Tuesday*. Clear and very hot, O, I am very unwell, tiered almost to death cooking for so many people. *12 Wednesday* Fine clear weather. Much fretting about dinner. *13 July 1769, Thursday* This day is forty years sinc I left my father's house and came here, and here…. I seene little els but hard labor and sorrow, crosses of every kind. I think in every respect the state of my affairs is more than forty times worse then when I came here first, except that I am nearer the desiered haven. A fine, clear cool day. I am unwell." (*The Diary of Mary Cooper; Life On a Long Island Farm*)

Along with backbreaking labor, the farm family had to deal with the perils of nature. In 1635, the first recorded hurricane in New England knocked down hundreds of trees and toppled houses. In 1660, "wheat blast" ruined a succession of harvests, while farmers in the South hoped their cattle (and their families) would avoid jimsonweed. Ingesting the plant could drive cattle crazy and turn a man into a "natural fool".

Pests

Tobacco was a profitable crop, but since three to five acres was about all an individual could harvest in a year, it took a lot of manpower to produce enough of the leaf for a profit. Children were given the tedious job of keeping the leaves free of the large caterpillars — "cutworms" and "tobacco hawks" — that ate the leaves. Walking down the cultivated rows, they would pick these insects off the plant and crush them between their fingers.

Besides the tobacco-eating caterpillar, there were pests galore just waiting to turn the farmer's success into despair. Rats and mice were a continual menace to grain farmers, so farmers used both cats and snakes to keep them in check. Certain types of larvae ate fields of barley and wheat, raccoons delighted in feasting on newly ripened corn and a single deer could ravage a whole crop. Worst of all, flocks of migrating passenger pigeons — "maize thieves" — could strip a cornfield in minutes! It is recorded that the migratory flights of these birds (which might continue for hours) almost shut out the light of the sun. They settled into trees in such large numbers that thick branches broke under their weight. Men and boys slaughtered them, clubbing them as they slept. Millions were cooked and eaten; the surpluses were fed to the hogs. The destruction of these birds was so complete that they became extinct in 1914.

The Animals
Pigs, like cows, were left on their own to forage in the woods. They would become independent and aggressive, eating roots, acorns, rattlesnakes, or any other snake passing by, for dinner. If they became too wild to journey back to civilization for butchering, the farmer's rifle took care of the reluctant animal on the spot!

Since they let most of their domesticated animals run wild, farmers soon discovered that the wolves, wildcats, black bears, and even the occasional hungry Indian, wanted their livestock for dinner. After some deliberation, they found that an ideal place for a pasture (and where the livestock couldn't roam too far) was an island free of predators. An ear, or nose, notch showed ownership of each animal. Each farmer had his own pattern of notches and the design was recorded at the courthouse.

By the middle of the 18th century, the average northern farm was around 50 acres of cleared, tillable land. The farm-

houses were small and unpainted, since paint was expensive and had to be imported. By the house there was a kitchen garden, and not too far away, an orchard. Most farmers had a plow and a few oxen to pull it, plus a horse or two for travel. Behind the house was the barn. Here the farmer housed the animals in winter, stored the fodder, kept his tools and threshed the grain.

Threshing and Winnowing
Threshing began when the grain was ripe. It was cut with sickles, or scythes, and either bound into shocks or stacked and cured. Then, the bundles of grain were placed on the barn floor and threshed with wooden flails. (A flail is a heavy piece of wood about three feet long with a hole bored in one end. A leather thong was passed through the hole so the board could be fastened to a handle.) After threshing the bundles with the flail, the farmer forked off the straw and swept the grain into piles.

Some farmers found that having oxen, and later horses, "trample it out", was a faster way to release larger amounts of grain. To "trample it out", the farmer would spread several bundles of grain in a circle on the barn floor and walk the horses over and around it. When the grain had been knocked out of the straw, the harvesters forked the straw to one side, swept up the grain, and stored it, or bagged it. Two men and six horses could thresh around 100 bushels a day, or the yield of around six acres of wheat.

Winnowing was the process that separated the chaff from the grain. The grain would be placed on a wooden tray, tossed gently in the air, or dropped from one tray to another. This process continued until the chaff was removed and the grain was clean. Corn was still shucked and shelled by hand. Mechanical "shellers" were available, but they usually

Horses on treadmills provided the power to thresh the wheat.

Farmers would save the best corn for the following year's seed.

A woman's work was never done. Here a farmer's wife and her child are shredding cabbage to store for the winter.

Clearing the land was an enormous task.

Many farms had maple trees which could be tapped in the spring to provide sap which in turn could be boiled down to make syrup.

Farmers' wives grew their own vegetables and herbs.

missed the end kernels, so someone still had to clean those by hand.

Barter

Corn could be eaten, or used as a type of payment for other services. By the measure of the day, colonists ate well, but few had currency readily available. A majority of the people conducted business by barter. In most towns, lists were drawn up showing what amount of barley, corn, oats, fish or butter could pay for a minister's salary, a blacksmith's fee or a child's tuition. As the population of North America increased, and towns became established, farmers looked for ways to sell their surplus in order to earn money for the items they did not make themselves.

To earn the coveted currency, farmers had to get their surplus produce to market. Since there were few accessible roads, and a workable freighting system hadn't been established, transporting goods was a major problem. To alleviate the situation, the rural store became an important distribution point for the community. Storekeepers became commodity traders, buying hides, tobacco, wool and other items.

To Market

In colonial America, settlements followed the network of rivers and transportation was mostly by water. If a farmer did decide to venture beyond his community, he would probably transport his marketable produce on a raft. Reaching his destination, he sold his produce, plus the lumber from the raft, and then returned home on foot. The entire trip might take over a month, during which time the farm was run by the rest of the family. On the few decent roads that did exist, farmers might drive herds of cattle, sheep, or pigs to market. During the 18th and 19th century, some of these "drives" began at South Carolina and ended in Pennsylvania, or New York.

Moving West

After the Revolutionary War, the population began to push inland from the coast of the Atlantic, across the Appalachian Mountains into the interior of North America. Here was the ideal setting for anyone with little capital to carve out an existence. The process of making "the World anew" began… again!

As the population moved westward, farmers kept the agricultural practices of their ancestors and changed their farming methods only when necessary. Along with their knowledge (and muscle), they brought the basics to start a new life — an ax, a hoe, a sack or two of corn for food and seed, an iron pot, a skillet, a few animals and some extra clothing.

Clearing the Land

The first order of business was to find land, ideally near a spring. When they found something suitable, they constructed a flimsy three-sided shelter called a "half-camp", and began to clear some land for a corn crop. Depending on the time of year, or what tools and manpower were available, the settler might "cut smack smooth" and clear the land he needed all at once, or he might clear part of his land, start his crops and then finish the clearing job later.

Many trees in the virgin forest were five and six feet in diameter. Generally, trees and underbrush less than 20 inches thick were cleared immediately, while the larger trees were cleared by the age old practice of "girdling". As the girdled trees died, farmers would clear the acreage with a "deadnin" — setting fire to several acres of dead trees at once. If not burned out by a "deadnin", lifeless beech and sugar maples would begin to fall about the third year after being girdled; oak, poplar and walnut might stand for several more years. Stump-pulling was a springtime chore. After winter, the ground had settled, the roots were looser, and the big tree stumps were easier to pull out. Usually, one man and an ox could do the job. The tough roots were almost impossible to burn, so farmers used to push them into a row in a fence formation. This "fence" wasn't pretty to look at, but it lasted many years.

Since wooden plows were still used, some of the large tree roots near the surface were cut off with an axe to make plowing a little easier. Metal was so expensive that it was used as sparingly as possible on the plow blades. As iron technology and production increased, metal plows became more widely available. When Charles Newbold of Burlington, New Jersey, secured the first American patent for a cast iron plow in 1797, he had some trouble persuading farmers to use it. They believed that the iron blades "poisoned the land" and encouraged the growth of weeds!

Always Something to Do
The grinding of wheat into flour was one of the first operations to leave the farm. If the mill wasn't nearby, a round trip of 20 or more miles could take three or four days. The miller would take his payment for grinding the wheat "in kind" — keeping an eighth or a quarter of the product for himself. The amount kept depended upon the location of the mill, the competition and local regulations.

Most fresh meat was used immediately, or dried, but some of the pork was placed in brine, or "smoked" in the smokehouse. Behind the smokehouse, the farmer's wife kept an ash hopper where she collected a winter's worth of wood ashes. In the spring, the lye was leached from the ashes to make the family's soap. It was mixed with any kind of fat and boiled until it was strong enough to float a potato or an egg. To make sure the soap would "come", it was stirred in one direction only. The end product was a smelly, slimy mess that

could be hardened with salt, but seldom was.

Most farm families owned an almanac. The almanac was based on the study of astronomy and was a bestseller in the early 19th century. Farm men and women felt much in tune with the natural cycles of growth, procreation and death. They felt that the moon governed the cycles of life, and consulted the almanac for advice on when to wean the baby, plant the crops or slaughter the pig. In the case of slaughtering the pigs the almanac suggested that you not butcher hogs during a waning moon in December, "otherwise the pork would shrink and wither away in the barrel" (of brine).

The seasons were divided into monthly chores and became the farmer's work guide. January was the time to clean the icehouse and get it ready for a new batch of ice. February 2, Candlemas Day in England, was a checkpoint for the farmer's mid-winter inventory of tasks — "The provident farmer on Candlemas Day/Has half of his fires and half of his hay." In March, the almanacs advised farmers to "look to your fences". In May, the farmer was encouraged to plow his fields and look for "pole" wood. Poles, an important part of early farm equipment, were used as slides and rollers for moving heavy loads, hay stack supports, or for hanging tobacco. June was the season of long daylight and the shearing of sheep and was followed by the season of weeds and the month for haying — July.

The time for "haying" wasn't an exact date, just a combination of man's instinct and the weather — "the best time for haying is haying time". During haying season, workers remained in the field for at least a 12-hour day. Sometimes the hot chore of haying was done during a full moon to take advantage of the moon's illumination and the cool summer evening. Harvesting the hay by

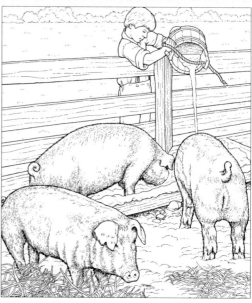

The children had their own chores which might include feeding the pigs.

Until the coming of refrigeration, most farms would keep a cow for milking.

Both oxen and horses were used for plowing.

hand was more than just cutting and piling grass. First it was cut with a scythe and then repeatedly turned to make sure it was dry. If it was stored in the barn while it was damp, it could mold, or, even worse, take heat, start a fire and burn down the barn.

Technology Comes to the Farm

New inventions made life a little easier for farmers. Obed Hussey patented his reaper in 1833; Cyrus McCormick followed with his version of the reaper in 1834. McCormick proved to be the better businessman and, by the 1860s, 10,000 of McCormick's reapers were lightening the workload of the average farmer. Close on the heels of McCormick and his reaper followed Hiram and John Pitts with their threshing machine. The machine's output was astounding! Whereas a single man using a flail could thresh between eight and 16 bushels of wheat in one day, the man with the threshing machine could deliver 20 bushels of wheat in an hour!

The drudgery of planting corn lessened with the invention of a mechanical corn planter. As in the past, the seeds were still planted in hills about three feet apart, but as Wheeler McMillan describes in his book *Ohio Farm*, "a wire was unrolled across the field. At predetermined intervals, the wire had a small knot, and, as it passed through a small V-shaped device at the side of the planter, tripped the seed plate and dropped the grains. Metal stakes at each end of the field held the wire taunt and after each crossing had to be moved to a new position. If the wire was always kept at the same tension, the cross rows would be just as regular and straight as the long rows…. This made it possible to drive the cultivators both ways and reach all the weeds."

New inventions, like the corn

planter, helped the North to prosper during the Civil War. Cultivated acreage had increased, prices were up and even with the men away and focused on battle, the women and children could take their places and produce a bountiful crop. After the war, between 1870 and 1900, more land was cultivated than at any other period in American history.

Hired Help

To work the additional land, and make a better profit, some farmers were forced to use hired hands. In the mid-19th century, Thomas Atkeson remembers that "the question of hours never was considered in all the years of my growing up. There was just one time for quitting and that was when the sun disappeared behind the range of hills on the western side of the Kanawha River…. Everybody was expected to be ready for the daily occupation at 6 o'clock (a.m.)…. According to my father's account book, he hired men the year round at from seven to twelve dollars a month. A day's work was thirty-seven cents for most jobs, fifty cents for clearing land, or rolling logs, and one dollar for pulling flax." (*How My Father Farmed — Thomas Atkeson*)

Even with hired hands, most farmers continued to use the same seasonal schedule and the same farming methods as those who had

worked the land before them. The big difference for the farmer was the availability of the new farm machinery and the big difference for the farmer's wife was that she didn't have to spin or weave the cloth for the family's clothing. She could buy her fabric, flour, eggs and butter at the local store. But along with these conveniences came the expectation for better housekeeping practices.

Taking Pride

Before 1820, trash was tossed out the door for the pigs and chickens to fight over, and no one cared much about the outward appearance of their house or out buildings. A dwelling was viewed as a place to provide shelter, not serenity or ambience. By the mid-1800s, appearances became important. Inside the house, oil lamps began to replace candles and beds were moved from the hearth into separate rooms. Outside, trash was buried, houses and outbuildings were painted, trees were planted, and flowers and shrubs were strategically placed to hide the privy.

Food was plentiful, and the excess was often taken to town to sell. But since a large number of the people in town kept cows, no dairy products except butter had any market value. Gallons of extra milk went to feed the pigs and calves on the farm. Melons were often eaten in the patch where they grew and a watermelon might be kept cool in a corn shock for just the right moment of consumption. Apples were harvested in the fall, then preserved through winter by burying them in a pit and covering them with straw. During the winter, the apples were dug up as needed, the farmer often chopping through the frozen earth to get them.

By the late 19th century, many changes had taken place in farm technology, processing and transportation. In a paper for the *Western Reserve Historical Society*, retired

United States judge Martin Welker compared the farm life of 60 years ago to "modern" times of 1892: "the sickle, scythe and cradle have given place to the reaper, the binder and the mower and the flail and sheet to the thrasher and separator; the old Barshear to the sulky plow; hand sowing and planting to the seeder and the check-row planter; and the hay-loader and fork and railway for loading and moving hay have taken the place of the hay fork and muscle to do the work. The hoe is superseded by the sulky cultivator in the raising of corn…the potato planter and digger compete with the old hoe and the stump puller with the mattock and spade. The incubator is crowding the business of the old setting hen…. Thus in many ways have ingenuity and inventions relieved farm labor of its hard toil."

The Tractor
Ingenuity and invention continued with the development of the internal combustion engine, which paved the way for the tractor. By 1892, the first gasoline-powered tractor was developed but by 1907 there were only 600 gas-powered tractors in the country; 13 years later, in 1920, there were 264,000! The tractor would dramatically alter the farmer's existence. It not only lightened the farmer's workload, but it required less maintenance than the animals. Since fewer animals meant less fodder was needed to feed them, the tractor increased the land available for growing human food.

Bigger Farms, Fewer People
The history of agriculture showed first an increase of farmers as they settled a vast and nearly empty land. The trend was reversed by the 20th century. The number of farmers decreased as farm size increased and farm people moved to the cities. During Thomas Jefferson's time, nine out of 10 people were farmers. By 1890, urbanization had begun to take its toll and the number of farmers had dropped to 65 percent of the population. By 1920, only 49 percent of the population farmed the land, and in the year 2000, farmers represented a mere two percent of the population.

Today, farming is big business and modern farmers do not make decisions to meet family, or community, needs — they make decisions for business reasons, or to increase efficiency. Generally, those decisions are not dictated by the seasons and the weather. Scientific breeding and genetic engineering that produce bigger and faster growing livestock and crops make those decisions. The results are shown in improved production: chickens lay twice as many eggs as 80 years ago and we harvest a wheat crop that has tripled in the last 40 years.

Though farming is now more of a business, individual farmers of today still know the spiritual connection between time and life, and feel the intrinsic satisfaction of a job well done. They possess our forefather's fundamental understanding that there is "a time to every purpose" and "to everything a season."

HM

Thar She Blows!

Nancy Hendrickson profiles a huge industry of the past that has all but disappeared.

*"So be cheery, my lads,
let your hearts never fail,
While the bold harpooner
is striking the whale."*
                    Old Nantucket song

GEORGE DODGE WAS BORN with saltwater in his veins. Growing up in Salem, Massachusetts, he wandered the wharves, captivated by seamen's tales of faraway lands. In 1831, he left home and headed for Nantucket, center of the New England whaling trade. On his arrival, he signed onto the whaler *Baltic*. He would not see home again for nearly four years.

On the first night at sea, the *Baltic*'s greenhorn hands could only wonder at what foolishness possessed them to sign on for a long voyage. Wretchedly seasick, they writhed in their cramped bunks, praying for home. As the next days and weeks passed, the seasickness disappeared but the reality of life onboard a whaler hit home. The mate used a cat-o'-nine tails on the crew's backs, and every day was spent in the constant practice of lowering and raising the boats and learning to handle the long oars. Soon, they settled into the tedium of the long voyage or what old salts called the "sailor's horror".

A month into the voyage, a cry was heard from the masthead. "There she blooooooows! There she breaches!" Dodge wrote, "The boats were made ready to lower and everything prepared for the chase." George Dodge was about to begin the adventure of his young life.

The Hunt

"There she blows!" shouted the lookout. "There she rises!" As the call was shouted down from the mainmast, excitement raced through the ship as the crew clambered on deck and lowered the boats.

---

*The Skipper's on the quarter-deck a-squinting at the sails,
    When up aloft the lookout sights a school of whales.
    Now clear away the boats, my boys, and after him we'll travel,
    But if you get too near his fluke, he'll kick you to the devil!!*
                    J.C. Colcord

Goaded to superhuman effort by the mate, the men rowed hard and fast to catch up with the fleeing whale. Rowing for all they were worth, the men faced the boatheader, not the whale, and were forbidden to look over their shoulders for fear they would panic at the sight of the great beast.

When the boat drew close to its prey, the harpooner left his position at the oar and braced himself at the bow, his long harpoon at the ready. When mere feet away, the harpooner struck his lance hard and deep.

George Dodge wrote that when the whale was first harpooned he took a violent plunge and threw his massive tail or flukes high in the air and lashed the sea. This moment of initial agony was one of the most dangerous of the hunt. Would the whale smash the boat or dive to the bottom, taking them with him?

As soon as the harpoon was set, the harpooner tossed out slack line and changed places with the mate. The crew pulled as hard as they could, backing away from the wounded whale, as line from the harpoon was given a turn around the loggerhead and doused with salt water to keep it from burning. Next, the men braced themselves for a high speed chase across the open sea — the Nantucket sleigh ride. "After a whale is speared," wrote Dodge, "he races through the water with the whaleboat in tow. A sleigh-ride is no comparison. A fast whale hits about 25 miles an hour."

At times, instead of running, a whale would dive deep. All eyes were on the line, for fear the whale would breach directly below them. Dodge relates a time when the harpoon so enraged the whale that it came straight for the boat. The officer shouted "Stern all, boys, for dear life, or he will knock us all into the briny deep to make food for the sharks!"

With the men rowing for their lives, they barely missed the huge open mouth of the harpooned whale.

In due time, the whale tired of the chase, and the crew took up the line until they were alongside him. The mate then sunk a lance deep into the whale's lungs, thrusting it up and down to hasten death. The crew then backed off as the whale thrashed and the sea turned to bloody foam. In the end, it rolled onto its side, "fin out".

Today most of us would prefer to watch whales play and hunting has virtually been eliminated but 150 years ago it was a huge industry which dominated the economy of much of New England.

Blubber to Oil

After the whale's death, the mate cut a

hole in its head and attached a line. The crew then towed their prize back to the ship and the men went to work removing the blubber. Great "blankets" of fat were cut from the body and thrown onto the deck. After all of the blubber was removed, and the stomach searched for ambergris — an ingredient in perfume — the carcass was abandoned to the waiting sharks.

On a deck covered with "gurry" — blood and blubber — the crew began the "trying out" process. Blubber was cut into large wide pieces that were then cut into smaller "books". The books were tossed into the try pots and boiled. Finally, the oil was bailed out into a large copper cooling tank set next to the brick tryworks. Once the oil was cool it was bailed into casks which were secured to the bulwarks. The men then turned towards butchering the next prize.

The Whaling Trade

Whales have been hunted since ancient times. The Basques of Spain are credited as being Europe's first whalemen, although the Vikings hunted whales long before recorded history.

When the *Mayflower* sailed the coastal waters of New England, one of the passengers wrote: "and every day we saw whales playing hard by us." Indeed, it was the presence of whales that that kept the *Mayflower* from heading further south. They knew that the whale could provide an importance source of income to the settlers.

The coast of colonial New England was alive with whales.

The normal whaleboat was 28 feet long, sharp and clean cut as a dolphin, bow and stern swelling amidships to six feet, with a bottom round and buoyant. It could make 10 miles an hour in the chase using the oars alone.

When the Pilgrims arrived, the Indians were already adept at chasing the leviathans.

According to a 1605 account in *Waymouth's Journal*, "one especial thing is their manner of killing the whale which they call a Powdawe; and will describe his form; how he bloweth up the water; and that he is twelve fathoms long: that they go in company of their kind with a multitude of their boats; and strike him with a bone made in fashion of a harping iron fastened to a rope, which they made great and strong of the bark of trees, which they veer out after him; then all their boats come about him as he riseth above water, with their arrows they shoot him to death; when they have killed him and dragged him to shore, they call all their chief lords together, and sing a song of joy."

At first there were so many whales, the whaling ships never ventured far from the coast. However, in 1712, Christopher Hussey was blown out to sea where he ran across a sperm whale which he killed and brought home. The oil was superior to that of other whales, so whalers began to pursue the giants into deeper water.

Whaling towns like Nantucket and New Bedford sprang to life, their lively economy based on the booming whale trade.

Whale oil provided fuel for lamps and lubrication for machinery. Everyone needed it and the whalers had it.

The economy wasn't the only part of New England life based around whaling. The girls of Nantucket formed a secret society, vowing not to marry a man until he had struck a whale. George Dodge wrote, "To get a wife in Nantucket you had to double Cape Horn three times, fasten to a whale, and do everything else appertaining to a whaling voyage."

The whaling industry thrived in America, especially during the years between the War of 1812 and the Civil War. During the "Golden Years", Yankee whalers sailed the oceans of the world in search of the great whales. They were some of the first to round Cape Horn and enter the South Pacific. They were the first to enter Japanese waters and explore the Arctic Ocean. The ports they visited were remote and exotic. They stopped in Honolulu and Lahaina for refitting and crew liberty, in the Galapagos for turtles and fresh water, and in the Azores for supplies. San Francisco was a favorite port for refitting and liberty until crews deserted en masse during the California gold rush. New grounds were located in the Arctic and millions of dollars flowed through towns like Nantucket, Provincetown, New Bedford and Bristol. By 1857, New Bedford alone had 329 whalers in its fleet. However,

Life for the men who went whaling was plagued with more leisure time than they could fill. Once the whales were sighted, everything changed. Killing the whale was very dangerous work.
Once killed, the blubber was removed in great "blankets" (shown below) which were moved onto the deck where they were cut into smaller pieces before being put in the boiler pots. Larger whales could yield hundreds of barrels of oil, mostly used for lighting and lubrication.

the first rings of the death knell sounded in 1859, with the discovery of petroleum.

The Whales

Who were the leviathans hunted almost to extinction?

A favorite target for whalers was the Right whale, so-called because it was just right to capture. Slow, and heavy with oil, it was easy prey for the hunters. And, once killed, its body didn't sink to the bottom of the sea. Right whales were almost 50 feet in length and yielded over 200 barrels of oil.

Herman Melville's Moby Dick was a sperm whale, the largest whale with teeth. Males grew to over 60 feet in length and yielded 160 barrels of oil. Sperm whales were notorious for attacking boats and ships. In 1819, a sperm whale was responsible for ramming and sinking the *Essex* in less than 10 minutes, and in 1850 the *Alexander*. The sperm whale could dive to a depth of 3,000 feet and when he sounded whalers prayed their boat was clear of his path.

Other targets were the massive blue whale and

the small humpback. Growing over 100 feet long and weighing over 100 tons, the blue whale was and is the largest whale on earth. Whalers knew the much smaller humpback as the "dancing whale", because of its ability to leap clear of the water, and to stand on its nose and beat the water into foam with its flukes. Found in all the oceans of the world, the humpback is difficult to capture because it sinks when killed. To prevent loss of their prey, whalers tried to drive the humpbacks into shallow water where their carcasses could be retrieved.

Whaling Ships and Their Men

Whalers were built for service and durability, not speed. Among the gear they carried were pots, cooling tanks, housing to boil blubber, whaleboats, gear for the boats, spare boats, supplies for a three- or four-year voyage, and casks for oil.

The spacious officers' quarters were in the stern, the crew were packed up forward in the forecastle, and the specialists like the harpooners, coopers, carpenter, blacksmith and cooks slept amidships.

The whaleboats themselves — the small boats used to chase down the whales — were sleek and fast. Captain William M. Davis wrote in 1874, "The whaleboat is simply as perfect as the combined skill of the million men who have risked life and limb in service could make it . . . it is 28 feet long, sharp and clean cut as a dolphin, bow and stern swelling amidships to 6 feet, with a bottom round and buoyant . . . . Here we have a boat which two men may lift and which will make ten miles an hour in dead chase by the oars alone."

In addition to carrying six men to paddle, the small whaleboats carried 18,000 feet of line, a hatchet, a sharp knife, water keg, candles, lantern, compass, bandages, and a dragging float.

Whaling men like George Dodge actually spent very little time in pursuit of whales. Ships took months to get to and from the whaling grounds, with no guarantee of finding whales once there.

The men were plagued with more leisure time than they could fill. To help fight boredom, they carved and engraved the teeth and jaw bone of the sperm whale into scrimshaw. First, the rough teeth were rubbed smooth, then original designs or designs taken from newspapers or magazines were engraved on the surface. Next, paint, tar or soot were rubbed into the etchings to bring out the design.

Crewmen lived in crowded and filthy quarters, often shared with bugs and rats. Their only ventilation was a small hatch in the ceiling, which was closed during rain or heavy seas. The ceiling was so low that a man of average height couldn't stand up straight. In whaling's heyday, profits were huge and owners paid shares to the officers and crew. However, seamen were docked for various items they charged at the ship's

store, including clothing, tobacco, needles and thread. Mary Lawrence, wife of the captain of a New Bedford whaler, wrote that the ship charged double what items cost, with a 25-cent sheath knife being sold for 74 cents, and a $1.60 pair of pants going for $3. Seamen were also charged a share of outfitting the ship's medicine chest. In some instances, they actually returned to port in debt.

Once back home, the crew members with money in their pockets were set upon by "land sharks" who enticed them to spend their money and sign up for another voyage.

An 1860 issue of *Harper's Magazine* reported, "A cart rattles by, loaded with recently discharged whalemen — a motley and a savage-looking crew, unkempt and unshaven, capped with the headgear of various foreign climes and peoples — under the friendly guidance of a land shark — hastening to the sign of the "Mermade", the "Whale," or the "Grampus," where, in drunkenness and debauchery, they may soonest get rid of their hard-earned wages, and in the shortest space of time arrive at that condition of poverty and disgust of shore life that must induce them to ship for another four years' cruise."

Going Home

George Dodge returned to Nantucket in 1835, after nearly four years out on the *Baltic*. His share of the profits was $125.

He had learned all there was to know about whaling, survived life onboard ship, seen faraway places and discovered something about courage. In his mind, he had made a good voyage. It was his last.

HM

Lying-In

Rosanne Van Vierzen explains how childbirth has changed since Roman times.

TODAY, CHILDBIRTH BRINGS to mind images of maternity wards and nurseries, but these are both relatively new parts of the childbearing process. While giving birth has remained fundamentally the same for thousands of years, some of the conditions and practices surrounding the actual delivery have changed. Obstetrics, the study and care of women during pregnancy and birth, has gone through an interesting evolution since ancient times.

The practice of birthing in classical Rome was heavily influenced by Soranus of Ephesus (98-138AD). Soranus' textbook of obstetrics was the first work to dispel superstitions and include instructions on how to care for a newborn. His textbook also taught women how to use the least painful, easiest way to deliver a baby at that time — the obstetric, or birthing, chair.

The birthing chair, or birthing stool, had a horseshoe-shaped seat. The laboring woman sat on it and delivered the baby through the opening cut into the seat and into the midwife's arms. On the side of the armrests were handles for the mother to grasp during delivery. If no birthing chair or stool was available, the woman would sit on someone's lap. The chair fell into disuse for centuries, but was reintroduced in Italy in the 1400s. It became popular again throughout Europe and was used in the ensuing centuries.

There are few maternity records from medieval times. Soranus' works were lost, and nothing replaced his knowledge. No advances were made in obstetrics for hundreds of years. Instead of bringing progress to obstetrics, the Middle Ages brought superstitions into the lying-in, or birthing, room and locked men out.

During medieval times, pregnant women had many superstitions surrounding them before, during and after the birth. Some superstitions were treated with

The birthing chair, invented by Soranus of Ephesus, had a horseshoe-shaped seat.

skepticism, while others were commonly thought to influence the unborn child. For instance, if the mother looked at the moon while she was pregnant, she was supposed to give birth to a lunatic or sleepwalker. Placing the right foot of a hyena on the pregnant woman was believed to cause an easy delivery, while the left foot resulted in the death of the baby. A vulture's feather underneath the woman's feet apparently helped the delivery go smoothly. It was also common to encourage the birthing mother to sneeze as that was thought to relieve a difficult labor. 'Magic' girdles were worn by the woman in labor because they supposedly had the power to 'push' the child out. In fact, the girdles were often passed down in families to help other generations. Some were still exchanging hands in the 1800s.

The most popular superstition was that men were not allowed in the room when the woman was giving birth. This belief lasted for centuries — throughout medieval times and into modern times — and was taken very seriously.

Female midwives delivered all the babies born in this period. In fact, for a man to be present while a woman was in labor was considered a serious offense. In 1522, Dr. Wertt of Hamburg dressed as a woman in order to get into a lying-in room to study a case of labor. He was caught and burned at the stake! While the Enlightenment dispelled the majority of the other superstitions surrounding childbirth, this one remained and female midwives were still used throughout the next few centuries.

During the Renaissance, attention to obstetrics was renewed. Schools began to teach courses on anatomy and the field of obstetrics. Methods that had gone unused since the 7th century were restored and improved. New medical knowledge was spread by the newly invented printing press. The first book on obstetrics in English, *The Birth of Mankynde*, was published in 1544. After making no advances for hundreds of years, the study of obstetrics was opening up again.

Birthing Positions

Until the mid-1800s, women were made to walk around during the first stages of labor, and keep moving to speed up delivery. But when the birth began, women were free to choose the position in which they had their child.

The mother generally chose which way she felt most comfortable. Before the 18th century, women delivered babies squatting, kneeling, leaning over or standing and using a rope of sheet flung over the rafters for support. It was said that French women at the time preferred to lie on their backs supported by pillows. Many women also relied on the birthing stool, but by the 1840s it was no longer used because of its strong association with the pain involved in childbirth and lack of comfort.

British upper-class women were the first to use the bed for

In the "borning room", mothers-to-be were attended to by midwives. Superstition forbade any men from being present during a woman's labor.

childbirth. The practice rapidly caught on in the other classes and countries because it was the most comfortable position for the birthing mother. By the early 1700s it was considered fashionable to deliver in bed. British and North American women in particular were said to favor lying on their left side with their legs drawn up during birth. This was deemed the 'English Position', but not all classes adopted this position as readily as using the bed.

Only in the past century has the woman giving birth been encouraged to use the 'lithotomy' position in which she lies on her back with her feet up.

In the 'Borning Room'

Before the 1900s, women gave birth in the home, no matter what their social standing. However, the type of room in which the baby was born was determined by status. In larger European houses, the woman would give birth in the main bedroom. The midwife might come days before the birth to tend to the expectant mother.

The woman's female relatives would also come to help the baby to be born.

Similarly in colonial America, the woman's mother and female friends would all come and support her by helping with the household duties. Colonial women of this period also usually gave birth in a borning room. The borning room was small and located behind the chimney in most houses, and also separated from other living areas so as not to let drafts in.

Because of the high mortality rate of women giving birth, heat was important in the birthing chamber. Any hint of fresh air would send terror flying around the room. The fire was kept at a roaring temperature and was considered essential in all birthing rooms until the 20th century.

Those who were poor did not have enough rooms in their homes to dedicate one solely to having babies. Internationally, in peasant communities, the baby was born on hay or on the bare floor. The woman would also have her

mother and friends helping her, but her visitors actually attended the birth. There are reports of up to 30 women being present to help one woman give birth! The midwife and friends would give the mother massages and strong drinks, help her move around before the pain worsened and apply hot cloths to her body.

New Help in the Lying-In Room

The last 400 years have seen major improvements to childbirth. The main advances that have made childbirth more successful and safer include the invention of the obstetric forceps, the invention and use of anesthesia and the use of antiseptics.

The obstetric forceps, used to grasp the baby's head in an obstructed labor, were invented in England by Dr. Peter Chamberlen in the 1650s and kept a family secret for years. No one knows why the forceps were kept concealed, but by 1747 the secret was leaked and forceps were in general use. William Smellie is credited with being the true pioneer of the forceps. Smellie made his forceps out of wood or steel padded with leather. He was also the first to realize that the fetal head rotated during birth and the first to revive a suffocating baby by using a silver catheter to inflate the lungs.

Using any form of anesthesia to relieve the pain of childbirth was frowned upon over the centuries. Even though there were options in plant and natural form to quell the pain, no attempts at relief were made. Christians strongly believed that the pain experienced during childbirth was punishment for Eve's sins. In turn, if anyone tried to relieve the mother's pain, they were punished. Agnes Simpson used opium in 1591 to suppress birth pains and was burned at the stake for her actions.

Attitudes changed as time went on, but as recently as 150 years ago women were still using just poppy mandragora and henbane to relieve the pain. No artificial drugs were used until J. Y. Simpson introduced first ether anesthesia and then chloroform in 1847. Chloroform proved to be the best cure for pain, as it was a simple sedative that still allowed operations to be performed, and it quickly became the favored remedy for the greatly feared pain of childbirth.

By the 1800s, male doctors were attending to women in labor and many women were going to the hospital to deliver their babies. Male physicians had begun to attend births in the 1700s, but it still cost more to have a doctor help deliver. Midwives continued to deliver many babies, both the doctors and the trained physicians now helping with hospital births were male. Even with women beginning to visit the hospital to have children, no thought had been given to the relationship between cleanliness and disease before the mid-1800s. Although there had been many

Wealthier families could afford a greater number of midwives.

advances that made childbirth safer since the Renaissance, many women still became infected with diseases and viruses spread easily in labor, particularly puerperal fever.

Puerperal fever was responsible for many deaths. In 1722, the fever reached epidemic levels in Paris, Vienna and other large European cities — 20 percent of new mothers died of puerperal fever in these cities. Sadly, the mortality rate of women in childbirth did not dramatically decrease until the mid-1800s when Ignaz Philip Semmelweiss connected puerperal fever with dirty, infected hands of the medical examiners. Semmelweiss told the students at the Vienna Lying-In Hospital to wash their hands with chloride of lime before each surgery and any other contact with the patient. The clinic reported a huge decrease in death from puerperal fever: from 11 percent in 1846 to one percent in 1848. By 1870 hospitals had adopted the rule of seriously cleaning maternity wards with antiseptics and the mortality rates were reduced dramatically.

From Home to Hospital
The medical advances made by the 1900s resulted in a great shift in the Western world from having babies at home to childbearing in hospitals. During the first half of the century, people strayed from midwives as hospitals and anesthetics grew in popularity. In the 1960s, midwife training programs were emphasized as midwifery became a field that required a certificate to practice. Midwives became popular again as they promised natural methods and personalized care.

Birth practices are still changing today. In the last hundred years, the focus of childbirth has changed from the survival of mother and baby, to the event of the birth holding an almost spiritual attachment. HM

Would someone you know like a subscription to History Magazine?

Differing Points of View

Edwin M. Knights presents three different accounts of a classic naval battle.

HISTORIANS ARE FACED WITH the formidable task of sorting out the truth from conflicting descriptions. This predicament peaks when the subject matter concerns a war or a famous battle in a particular war. Probably most confused about the events are those who were intimately involved, having had no opportunity to get a broad overview of what actually transpired. Often misleading are accounts provided by the leaders on either side, each attempting to justify his own actions and portray himself in the best possible light. Add to this the possibility of inaccurate, biased news reports and we end up with a potpourri of perceptions, or a montage of misconceptions, often so contrasting that it's difficult to realize that everyone is describing the same event!

Recreating the engagements between armies has been somewhat easier than between navies, as military strategies were often dictated by the terrain. Naval battles are far more difficult to visualize, especially those which took place in the days of sailing ships. We have been forced to rely upon the biased accounts provided us by the combatants, usually limited to poorly documented descriptions provided by the winners. Often the losers either didn't survive to tell their tales or they were incarcerated where their experiences could not become public knowledge.

Interpreting Naval Warfare
There are many factors to consider other than bare statistical comparisons, and this was especially true with confrontations at sea. Wind velocity and direction were of great concern to sailing ship captains. In a stout breeze, the ship to windward had a great advantage, being better able to maneuver, plan its attack, perhaps remain at long range or even flee from an adversary. Weather, too, played a major role in the outcome.

When a naval battle ends, the

"Old Ironsides" under full sail.

roar of the cannon fades into silence, the wind carries away the smoke, and the sea once again prevails, washing away the evidence of man's follies. The horror of the recent events only remains etched into the minds of the survivors. Each carries away his own unique souvenirs of the event — perhaps painful burns, the loss of a limb, lasting tinnitus or perhaps other disfiguration, but always a haunting, lifelong vision of the shocking events.

We intend to take a look, or more accurately, several looks at such a naval battle. It was fought in the North Atlantic Ocean off of Halifax on 19 August 1812 and it involved two ships known as "frigates." But before plunging into the fray, it would be well to see what events led up to this dramatic confrontation.

Paying Ransom To Rogues
Merchant ships of the US faced some major problems in 1790. *Alliance*, the last ship of the Continental Navy, had been sold at auction in 1785. Neither privateers nor naval vessels were now available to America's merchant marine.

Particularly threatening were hostile ships encountered along the North African coast. Although commonly referred to as "Barbary

pirates," they were actually controlled by the regional leaders of naval powers like Tripoli, Tunis and Algiers. Their sailing vessels were speedy xebecs, two or three-masted ships with shallow draft and an overhanging bow and stern. They used lateen rigs — triangular sails at a 45 degree angle to the hull, sometimes with head sails or a square rigged sail on the foremast. As the largest xebecs could carry several hundred armed men and mount up to 24 guns, they were formidable opponents and terrorized the merchantmen. American seamen captured by the Moroccan marauders and their ilk faced enslavement and hard labor in African ports. The US Government was forced to pay ransom for their release, and to pay dearly. In 1795 a treaty was signed with Algiers which committed the US to pay $642,500 to free captive Americans, make further payments for "free trade" in the Mediterranean and send an annual tribute of $21,600 in naval stores. The US even agreed to build a 32-gun frigate for the dey, their political leader.

If this weren't enough, American ships were being routinely boarded by naval forces from European countries and American sailors were being "impressed" into serving aboard the foreign ships. This small nation had no means of escorting or defending its merchant vessels, leaving them easy prey at sea.

Gestation Of Federal Frigates
In 1794 Congress had finally decided it was time for a new navy, authorizing the construction of six frigates: *Chesapeake*, *Congress* and *Constellation*, each with 36 guns, and the slightly larger *President*, *Constitution* and *United States*, each carrying 44 guns. Several cities also began building warships to contribute to America's new naval force. Joshua Humphreys, a Quaker shipbuilder from Philadelphia, was appointed to supervise the building

of the federal frigates. Humphrey's concept was to equip the tiny navy with sturdy, powerful frigates having superior cruising ability, enabling them to outgun foreign frigates but also out-sail and escape massive ships of the line.

The hulls were constructed of sturdy white oak, basked by an even stronger, closely-spaced framework of live oak and an inner "spirketing" layer of interlocking timbers, reaching a maximum thickness of over 21 inches near the waterline. Hulls were further strengthened by a unique series of diagonal braces to help distribute the weight. An inward slope above the waterline provided a "tumblehome," so that an enemy cannon ball might strike only a glancing blow. Their masts were taller and sturdier. One of these ships was to have a date with destiny in 1812.

The Frigate *Constitution*
Constitution was to be built in Boston, at the Hartt brothers' shipyard, following plans outlined by Joshua Humphreys, naval architect Josiah Fox and draftsman William Doughty. The slightly smaller *Constellation* was already taking shape in Baltimore. Except for political delays, construction proceeded much on schedule. Paul Revere provided the hull's copper sheathing and rivets, which he imported from England, as British hostilities at that time were directed toward France. Launching this heavy a ship was a new experience for the shipyard, and it was flubbed on the first attempt. It failed again on the second. On 21 October 1797 the ship finally slid down the ways into Boston Harbor. Captain Samuel Nicholson was assigned to be its first commanding officer.

At this point the ship was far from complete, and it would be months more before construction of the interior bulkheads was finished, the masts stepped and the rigging assembled. Armament not only included all the correct can-

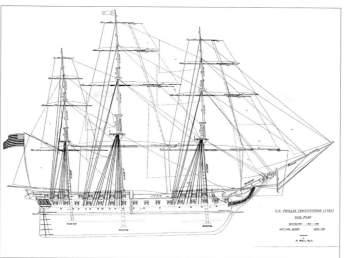
The sail plan of the USS *Constitution*, a fairly typical frigate.

non and their shot, but pistols, boarding axes, cutlasses and 60 muskets for the Marines. Lastly, provisions had to be stowed in the holds. Meanwhile, recruitment proceeded slowly, perhaps because the blustering nature of the captain convinced sailors to sign aboard other vessels looking for crews. In fact, in July, Captain Nicholson even anchored far out in the harbor to discourage desertion by members of his new crew.

It was nearly four years after the laying of her keel that *Constitution* finally set to sea. Her construction had established a new tradition in Boston — one that continues to this day in the "Big Dig" — known as "cost overrun". *Constitution*'s was 260 percent, based upon the anticipated cost for a frigate in those days of about $100,000. The ship's accomplishments early in her career are well documented in numerous accounts by talented authors who have described her colorful captains and their capable crews. Following her shakedown cruises, *Constitution* saw service in the West Indies and action at Puerto Plata, Hispaniola. After being commanded by several able captains, *Constitution* was placed under the command of Captain Isaac Hull.

The British Navy
Early in the 19th century, the Royal Navy was the largest in the world. They categorized their fighting ships of the line by a rating system

of one to five. The navy had 10 first rate ships, 37 second rates, 94 third rates and 19 fourth rates.

Lastly, there were the frigates, mounting fewer than 50 guns which were located on one enclosed gun deck and also on the open spar deck overhead. There were 63 36-gun and 16 38-gun frigates in 1812, plus a few mounting 44 guns. There were also many frigates which had been captured from foreign navies, especially the French. French ships handled better than the British but were constructed of less durable pine, rather than oak. HMS *Guerriere* was one of these.

Joshua Humphreys had carefully planned the new American frigates to outperform those which met the Royal Navy specifications; it remained to be seen whether the captains and their crews were up to this task. The US was pitting 16 ships, none larger than *Constitution*, against the huge British Royal Navy. Every author reports a different total of British warships at that time. Anne Grimes Rand places it over 600 ships; Thomas C. Gillmer states that in 1811 there were 219 ships of the line and 296 frigates, but this figure doesn't include large numbers of captured foreign vessels.

The *Chesapeake-Leopard* Encounter
The young US Navy did not get off to an auspicious start. In May 1807, while the US and Great Britain were still at peace, *Chesapeake* was ordered to relieve *Constitution* as flagship of the Mediterranean squadron. She was in Norfolk, where she hastily took on supplies and sailed forth, her decks laden with items which were yet to be stowed away. Upon leaving Chesapeake Bay, the ship encountered the HMS *Leopard*, a 50-gun British frigate, which produced a Royal Navy order to "stop and inspect" the American ship for suspected deserters. This order being refused, *Leopard* opened fire, resulting in numerous casualties and forcing

Capt. Barron to strike his flag. Four sailors were seized and taken aboard the British ship; two Americans were later returned, an Englishman was hanged and another died of his injuries. British ships were the worst offenders at stopping and searching American merchant ships at the time, finding a ready source for new crew members whom they impressed into service, and the American public was becoming enraged. By 1811, Congress resolved to build 12 ships-of-the-line and numerous frigates, although such a construction project would require several years to complete. By June 1812, because of "Free Trade and Sailors' Rights" and the attempted annexation of Canada, it became apparent that US and Britain would soon be at war. *Constitution* had just been overhauled in the Washington Navy Yard and Captain Hull was taking on stores in the Potomac River, at the same time recruiting and interviewing experienced seamen for his command.

War With Britain

The famous encounter between USS *Constitution* and HMS *Guerriere* might never have occurred if Hull had not left port before receiving orders and soon thereafter succeeded in escaping from a squadron of British warships in July 1812. Brilliant seamanship, aided by "Lady Luck" and a light breeze, enabled Hull to outdistance his pursuers and avoid almost certain capture or destruction. On 18 August, Hull intercepted an American privateer and learned that a British man-of-war was lurking nearby. The hunt began, and on the afternoon of 19 August, a sail appeared on the horizon.

It proved to be one of the frigates from the squadron of Commodore Philip Broke from which *Constitution* had only recently escaped. It was HMS *Guerriere*, under Captain James Dacres, now backing her mainsail and eager to fight. Dacres had commanded this ship over a year and had recently challenged Captain Rodgers of USS *President* "or any other American frigate" to a duel. He was now to have his wish fulfilled.

"Old Ironsides" berthing at Charlestown Navy Yard after a "turn-around" service.

Comparing The Combatants

As noted earlier, unbiased reporting is a rare commodity when it comes to accounts of warfare, and this famous sea battle was no exception. Americans were so thrilled when an American frigate bloodied the nose of the British lion that superlatives drowned any efforts toward objectivity. The British press was in a profound state of shock. *The London Times* wrote: "It is not merely that an English frigate has been taken, after, what we are free to confess, may be called a brave resistance, but that it has been taken by a new enemy, an enemy unaccustomed to such triumphs, and likely to be rendered insolent and confident by them. He must be a weak politician who does not see how important the first triumph is in giving a tone and character to the war. Never before in the history of the world did an English frigate strike to an American."

While in the Boston pubs, they sang: "*The Constitution long shall be/The glory of our Navy,/For when she grapples with a foe,/She sends him to old Davey./Yankee doodle, keep it up/Yankee doodle, dandy/We'll let the British know that we/At fighting are quite handy.*"

British historians have pointed out that *Guerriere* was a smaller ship than *Constitution*, and in need of repair. HMS *Guerriere* was also short several of its crew who had been left aboard a French prize, plus 10 impressed American seamen whom Captain Dacres gallant-

ly permitted to go below during the battle. It had the advantage of a battle-experienced crew. The large 460-man American crew had benefited from almost daily training in aiming and firing their guns. Also, lead foil powder cylinders enabled faster firing of the Americans' guns.

The Brawl

The battle that ensued could not be categorized as one of the classic examples of brilliant seamanship which have become legends from the golden age of sail. It was more like a street brawl, and the bigger and tougher opponent prevailed. Hull withheld most of his fire until *Guerriere* was "half a pistol shot to larboard," then raked his opponent with blast after powerful blast. Soon the British ship's mizzen mast toppled to starboard and the main yard was shot away. The Americans cheered, "We've made a brig of her — now make her a sloop!"

Meanwhile, the British frigate's fire was high, causing damage to the Americans' rigging. The sturdy oak hull and its "tumble-home" design above water caused British cannonballs to glance off into the sea, giving birth to the now-famous nickname of "Old Ironsides."

The wreckage dragging from *Guerriere* made her almost impossible to steer, and "Old Ironsides" began to pull ahead. At this point *Guerriere* swerved to starboard, snagged its bowsprit in

The Complete History

History Magazine

Volume One

October 1999 - September 2000

The First Year of History Magazine

History Magazine Volume One is a reissue of almost all the editorial from the issues dated October 1999 to September 2000.

The colorful, bound volume includes all the editorial material from our first year of publication, including such features as: The Atlantic Cable, The Black Death, The National Road, Cleanliness, Bread, The Code Napoleon, The First Radio Station, The Longbow, 1000AD, The US Cavalry, Custer, Army Wives, Death Customs, Bellevue Hospital, The Impact of the Potato, An 1860s Dinner for Eight, The Rifle, The Oregon Trail, The Handcart Pioneers, Refrigeration, Games People Played, Contraception, The Suez Canal, Midwives, Longitude, The 1910s, Country Store, Connecting the World, Alchemy, Freemasonry, Early Newspapers, Influenza Pandemic, Chicago in 1880, The Privy, The Blacksmith, Saffron, Eli Whitney, Lunatic Asylums, Lighthouses, The 1900 House, Carpetbaggers, The Natchez Trace, Let's Eat!, How Brands Began, The Stirrup, The Shakers, Development of Photography, Insurance, Underground Railroad, Memsahibs of the Raj, California Gold Rush, Poliomyelitis, Wigs, decade profiles, historical trivia — and more!

History Magazine Volume One provides a full year of information about the lives our ancestors led.

Guarantee

There is no risk. If **any** *History Magazine* **product** fails to meet your needs, or live up to the promises we have made, you are entitled to a refund for any reason or no reason. Any refund will be made promptly and cheerfully.

Halvor Moorshead
Editor & Publisher

Constitution's rigging and smashed the captain's gig. At close range, accurate musket fire from both sides began to take its toll, especially that from the US Marines, who killed the British second lieutenant and wounded Captain Dacres, his first lieutenant and the sailing master. *Constitution*'s momentum separated the ships, but the Briton's foremast and mainmast now crashed down, leaving it totally dismasted. The battle was over. The severely damaged *Guerriere* couldn't be saved and had to be blown up.

Another View
A long-lost account of this battle can be found in *Our First Century*, by R. M. Devens in 1878. When *Guerriere* had taken her French prize, a Frenchman carrying dispatches to the US Government had been brought on board, relieved of his books and papers and ordered below. The man was quite overwhelmed by the loss of these documents, aggravated still more by the haughty bearing of Dacres. Once or twice, addressing him with his blandest manner and best English, he said, "Captain Dacre, I tank you sare, for my government deespatch and my law books."

The captain replied with some rude comments referring to a common amphibious creature and sent him back below.

A while later, however, a sail was spotted on the horizon. The tall masts and graceful trim soon convinced the lookout it was a Yankee vessel. Dacres, spyglass in hand, had observed her from a mere speck. When satisfied that she was American, he gave vent to wild expressions of joy. Pacing the deck with exulting step, he swore he would "take that craft in fifteen minutes." To crown his anticipated triumph, he directed that a hogshead of molasses be hoisted upon deck, "to treat the —— Yankees" (probably with switchel, a drink made from rum and molasses). The order was obeyed, but by chance, one of the first shots from *Constitution* shattered the hogshead, spewing its viscid contents all over the deck.

Now the Frenchman reappeared, and with his most winning smile, requested permission of Captain Dacres to stay above and see the fight. Dacres was too busy to reply with more than a few expletives, so the little man soon ensconced himself up in the rigging while the two vessels drew ever closer. The author quotes the lively French prisoner's account: "Captain Dacre, he sail dis way, and den he sail dat way, and again he go — boom! De Yankee man, he say nothing — but still keep comin'. Again, Captain Dacre sail dis way, and den he sail dat way, and again he go — boom! Enfin, de Yankee man go 'pop, pop, pop, — pop, pop, pop!' I say to Captain Dacre, 'Sare, wid your permission I go below — 'tis too hot here!'"

He later appeared again, with some final remarks to the wounded captain, just before the ship was surrendered: "You tell me, sare, you take dis ship in fifteen minutes; by gar, he take, you! Now, sare," he added with a low and bitter emphasis, "I tank you for my gernment deespatch and law books."

Of course we can't swear to the accuracy of this account, which appears in the 1878 book by R. M. Devens, but it was a vivid description! And molasses was found spilled over the spar deck of the ill-fated HMS *Guerriere*.

The American Version
According to Commander Tyrone Martin's lengthy review, published by the US Naval Institute, "Captain Hull, hungry himself for glory and public recognition, did all he could to ensure full mileage out of this success. He wrote two reports of the engagement to Secretary Hamilton; neither said anything about the relative positions of the antagonists as they began their slugfest or of the two collisions. The second one was shorter and more ambiguous than the first, and Hull appended a note... suggesting that the less said about 'a brilliant victory such as this' the better." It was this report that was publicized and became the basis of most historic descriptions of the famous battle.

Hull also commissioned Michel Felice Corne to paint a series of four illustrations depicting events in the battle. In these the ships' relative positions were reversed, in order to avoid any criticism of his having taken a slightly downwind position. This had resulted in the collision of the two ships and the possibility of a successful boarding of *Constitution* by the crew of *Guerriere*.

Here we have three views of the same battle — take your choice! Some facts seem to prevail. A more powerful warship manned by a larger, well-trained and motivated crew but led by a captain inexperienced in battle, soundly defeated a smaller, undermanned frigate which was due for an overhaul. The British vessel's experienced captain could not overcome the relative difference in strength of the two combatants. The unexpected naval victory greatly boosted morale among Americans while sending enormous shockwaves through the British establishment. As a result of wild, uncritical enthusiasm of Americans and the wounded pride of the arrogant Royal Navy, the psychological impact of the battle of *Constitution* vs. *Guerriere* lingers to this day. And in spite of sophisticated technology, little has changed — there is nothing more elusive than objectivity when it comes to describing military engagements.

References
Devens, R. M. *Our First Century* (Springfield, Mass., Nichols & Co., 1878).
Frost, John. *An Illuminated History of North America* (New York, Henry Bill, 1857).
Gillmer, Thomas C. *Old Ironsides: The Rise, Decline and Resurrection of the U.S.S. Constitution* (Camden, Maine, International Marine, 1993).
James, William. *A Full and Correct Account of the Chief Naval Occurrences of the Late War between Great Britain and The US of America* (London, T. Egerton, Whitehall, 1817).
Magoun, F. Alexander. *The Frigate Constitution and Other Historic Ships* (New York, Dover Publications, 1987).

HM

STEPPING STONES

English Street & Trade Directories on CD £11.99 each + £2.00 P/P

Available Now—detailed contents on our web page

Northumberland 1822 Trade Directory (Pigot's)
Northumberland 1848 Trade Directory (Slater's)
Durham 1834 Trade Directory & Surrounding Villages (Pigot's)
Newcastle & Gateshead 13th & 14th Century Journal
Cumberland 1834 Trade Directory (Pigot's)
Scarborough 1902 Street & Trade Directory including Whitby, Filey & surrounding villages
East Riding of Yorkshire 1872 Post Office Directory (Kelly's)
East Riding of Yorkshire 1897 Residents Directory (Kelly's)
East Riding of Yorkshire 1822 Trade Directory (White's)
North & East Riding of Yorkshire 1872 (Kelly's)
North Yorkshire 1897 Street & Trade Directory (Kelly's)
North & East Riding of Yorkshire 1897 Court & Profession Directory (Kelly's)
North Riding of Yorkshire 1822 Trade Directory (Whites)
Hull & surrounding Villages 1897 Trade Directory (Kelly's)
York 1897 Street & Trade Directory including York Inns, & now with added Photo's
York 1822 Trade Directory (White's)
West Riding of Yorkshire 1822 Trade Directory (Bain's)
Leeds 1853 Street & Trade Directory
Lancashire 1848 Trade Directory (Slater's)
Sheffield 1822 Town Centre Trade Directory (Bain's)
Liverpool 1848 Trade Directory (Slater's)
Manchester 1848 Trade Directory (Slater's)
Cheshire 1828-29 Trade Directory (Pigot's)
Devonshire 1830 Trade Directory (Pigot's)
Wiltshire 1851 Trade Directory (Slater's)
Shropshire 1858-59 Trade Directory (Slater's)
Essex 1832-33 Trade Directory (Pigot's)
Cornwall 1919 Trade Directory (Kelly's)
Principal Cities 1822 Trade Directory (Bain's)
North Wales 1828-29 & South Wales 1830 (Pigot's)
London 1865 Trade Directory Part 1
London 1865 Trade Directory Part 2
London 1865 Commercial Directory Part 1
London 1865 Commercial Directory Part 2
Somersetshire 1851 Trade Directory (Slater's)
Middlesex 1837 Trade Directory (Pigot's)
Bristol 1852-53 Trade Directory (Pigot's)
Worcestershire 1828-29 Trade Directory (Pigot's)
Edinburgh & Leigh 1848-49 Post Office Directory
Staffordshire 1828-29 Trade Directory
Cambridgeshire 1830 Trade Directory
Norfolk 1830 Trade Directory (Pigot's)
Kent 1832-34 Trade Directory (Pigot's)
Sussex 1832-34 Trade Directory (Pigot's)
Suffolk 1840 Trade Directory (Pigot's)
Surrey 1840 Trade Directory (Pigot's)
Illustrated Yorkshire Churches

Contact us at
Stepping Stones
PO Box 295
YORK
YO31 1YS
England
Tel :- 01904 424131
Fax :- 01904 422351
Email :- judd@mjudson.freeserve.co.uk
Order on line at Web Page www.stepping-stones.co.uk

Coming soon
Suffolk 1883
Leeds 1907 Street & Trade
Lincolnshire 1876 Post Office Directory
Glasgow 1838 Annual Directory
Nottingham Street Directory
Hampshire 1830
Derbyshire 1842
Herefordshire 1835
Northamptonshire 1841
London Street Directory Part 1
London Street Directory Part 2

New Directories arriving all the time check our Web page for updates

Trade Enquiries Welcome

Hindsight

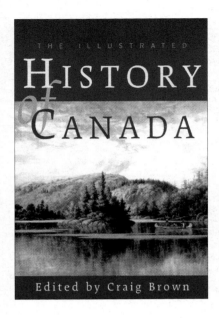

If your knowledge of Canadian history is shamefully inadequate, then **The Illustrated History Of Canada** is for you! Beginning with Jacques Cartier's first visit to Newfoundland in 1534 through to the devastating ice storm of 1998, this richly-illustrated book covers Canada's fascinating cultural and political history. Edited by Craig Brown, this book is filled with illustrations, maps and photographs. Canada's history is revealed in all its glorious details from the playing card money of New France to the last spike of the Canadian Pacific Railway and the Group of Seven to the rise of the Reform Party. This is an excellent resource for the eternal student of Canadian knowledge. Third edition, 600 pages, with an index. From Key Porter Books, distributed by Firefly in the US. Available in paperback at $25 Cdn or $20 US. Available in bookshops everywhere.

With 60 illustrations serving as examples, **Dress In The Middle Ages** is an excellent introduction to the subject. Written by Françoise Piponnier and Perrine Mane, and translated by Caroline Beamish, the book examines the materials used, how clothing was acquired, the different clothing of the social classes (from prostitutes to knights) and how fashion was regulated. Research is based on paintings, sculptures, literature of the period and surviving samples of clothing and jewelry. Clothing of the Middle Ages reflected society's attitudes and concepts about its wearers; today this allows the historian to understand the people and society of the period in greater depth and meaning. From Yale University Press, soft cover, 168 pages. With a glossary and bibliography. Priced at about $15 US or $24 Cdn. Available in bookshops everywhere.

As only one document survives from Richard Pierpoint's life, a petition for relief from 1821, much of **A Stolen Life: Searching for Richard Pierpoint** is surmised from his involvement in the African slave trade, the Seven Years War, the American War for Independence and the War of 1812 as an African man in North America. Tracing Pierpoint from his enslavement in 1760 at the age of 16 through to his death in 1837 in rural Ontario, the authors Peter and David Meyler use Pierpoint's life as insight into black military regiments and black settlements, and the early days of Upper Canada. From Natural Heritage (natherbooks@idi-rect.com), soft cover, 144 pages. With illustrations and an index. Priced at about $20. Available in bookshops everywhere.

If only my university texts had been as worthy of note as **The Crisis Of Reason: European Thought, 1848-1914**, I might have managed higher marks. Part of

Yale University Press' series on the Intellectual History of the West, J.W. Burrow's book, covering the second half of the 19th century up to the outbreak of WWI, documents the fascinations and obsessions of the period: racial biology, decadence and degeneracy, class and criminality. *The Crisis Of Reason* is a broad cultural survey of a time of revolutionary change and great anxiety. From Yale University Press, hard cover, 271 pages, 16 black and white plates, with an index and a selected bibliography. Priced at about $30 US or $47 Cdn. Available in bookshops everywhere.

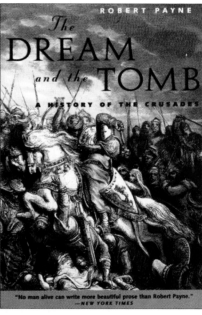

With such personalities as Saladin, St. Louis and Richard the Lion Heart, and the desire for a testament of faith, we should see the Crusades as more than a series of wars fought centuries ago. **The Dream And The Tomb** examines the eight holy wars that took place between 1095 and 1270, exploring both the political desires of princes and the suffering of the ordinary people. With the understanding and depth of the author, Robert Payne, these rich and memorable details bring the past to life. 421 pages, with maps and many black and white illustrations, notes, bibliography and an index. Available in paper-

back from Cooper Square Press in the US and Madison Books in Canada. Priced at about $20. Available in bookshops everywhere.

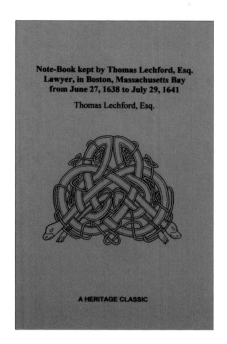

Bringing him into close contact with all classes in early Boston as New England's first lawyer, **Note-Book kept by Thomas Lechford, Esq. Lawyer, in Boston, Massachusetts Bay from June 27, 1638 to July 29, 1641** is engrossing in its details of early colonial life. In truth, the note-book is dry and professional in its outlook, but it is full of information about the colonists in their new home and their need for order and law through the creation of wills, contracts, deeds, settlements, letters, legal petitions and other legal documents. At about $35 US from Heritage Books, Inc., 1540E Pointer Ridge Place, Bowie MD 20716 or call 1-800-398-7709 or visit *www.heritagebooks.com*

Written with sympathy and depth, **Marie d'Agoult: The Rebel Countess** by Richard Bolster is enthralling to read. Known in her time as the writer Daniel Stern and the lover of Franz Liszt, d'Agoult was a daring woman who lived her life on her own terms in a time of change. A

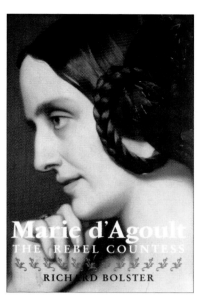

member of the court of Charles X of France, d'Agoult left her marriage and lived with Liszt in Italy for five years, bearing him three children. After the relationship failed, d'Agoult returned to Paris and formed a salon where she moved in the social circles of Sand, Chopin and Dumas. Based upon her memoirs, letters and other published writings, the book also discusses her support for democracy and women's rights in the mid-18th century. From Yale University Press, hard cover, 278 pages, with illustrations, notes, index and bibliography. Priced at about $25 US or $39 Cdn. Available in bookshops everywhere.

Trial by Ordeal

Ron Wild looks at the justice system once favored by the church.

IN THE MEDIEVAL PERIOD, many trials were handled by the church rather than the state. The root idea behind the church-favored concept of "trial by ordeal" was that an appeal was being made for Divine Assistance in settling difficult questions of innocence and guilt. Before undergoing trial by ordeal, the accused would fast for three days and then attend church where there was a form of service proper for the occasion. The medieval mind was firm about justice. The world was meant to be a peaceful place free from sin and wrong-doing and it was the duty of all medieval people to make it so. Wrong-doing required both reparation and punishment. Reparation was usually a payment of money to victims, their families or to the king. Punishment was designed to deter others but to leave the sinner alive and able to repent.

The Ordeals

The most common forms of trial by ordeal were by means of hot iron, cold water or by battle. When the ordeal was hot iron, the accused person had to grasp a red-hot iron rod and carry it nine paces. The burn was then bound and inspected three days later. If it was healing, God had shown that the person was innocent. If it had begun to fester, then they were guilty.

If the ordeal was cold water, the accused was tied up and lowered into a river or village pond on a rope. If the accused sank he was innocent. If he floated he was guilty and was sent for punishment.

Trial by battle was more rare and usually reserved for when two people accused each other of crimes or wrong-doing. It was a no-holds-barred battle to the death. This form of ordeal lin-

Being forced to carry a hot rod for nine paces was one form of "trial by fire"; if the wounds began to heal after three days, the accused was found innocent.

gered on until the 19th century in the form of the duel, to which men subjected themselves as a way of righting an injured honor or libel.

Rigging the Trial

Members of the clergy who administered the trials occasionally faced awkward situations where the law had been broken, but no real sin had been committed, and they empathized with their congregations. So many laws had come into force principally as generators of revenue to the landed gentry that it was virtually impossible for the ordinary citizen to escape them. Simple acts such as gathering wood for winter fires and picking flowers for garlands and gathering nuts and berries for sustenance, under the Forest Laws, became acts against the king and required fines and trial by ordeal. Accordingly, churchmen learned how to conduct trials in a fashion that ensured that only the most serious of crimes resulted in guilty decisions.

It had been observed by the clergy that if the iron rod

employed in the trial by fire was heated to a white hot condition then the resulting deep burn was cauterized and began to heal during the three day inspection period. If the iron rod was merely very hot it invariably caused serious blisters which within days became infected and resulted in a guilty decision. Similarly the clergy had noticed that the natural reaction to being lowered into cold water was for the person being tried to take deep, strong breaths before going below the surface. This resulted in the person being more disposed to float to the surface to face a guilty verdict. If breath was dispelled on entering the water then the person was more likely to sink and could then be pulled out to face the celebrations associated with a not guilty result. The clergy had developed many techniques to control the outcome of these trials by ordeal and this no doubt allowed them to consolidate their control and influence on the people at the expense of their medieval lords and masters who caused the unjust laws to be enforced.

An End of Trial by Ordeal

Orthodox theologians began to seriously question the morality of trial by ordeal in the 13th century on the grounds that it was wrong for anyone to demand a service from God under conditions of a trial. Appeals were made to the Pope, who in 1215 forbade the use of trials by fire and water and recommended that judgment by one's peers become the norm. Trial by battle, much favored by the aristocracy in the form of dueling, continued on for centuries until it too was outlawed in most countries.

HM

..a quiet read beside a brook
...a history or genealogy book
...from www.WillowBendBooks.com

How the Subway Transformed Cities

History
Magazine

February/March 2001
$4.50 U.S.
$5.50 Cdn.

Scrapbook
of 1770-79

The History of Tea

Early Office Life

The Scourge of Typhoid

BUTCHER'S HALL

Feb/Mar 2001

dn Publ. Mail Product
ales Agreement No.

0 56698 94944 2

03

Contents of this issue of History Magazine

The 1770s.
Page 9.

Unraveling the Stars.
Page 24.

Tea: The Brew of Empires.
Page 36.

Winged Messengers.
Page 42.

OUR COVER: A depiction of the Boston Massacre, as engraved by
Paul Revere.

VOLUME 2 NUMBER 3
EDITOR & PUBLISHER
Halvor Moorshead
EDITOR
Jeff Chapman
EDITORIAL ASSISTANTS
Nicole Brebner
Victoria L. King
SPECIAL PROJECTS MANAGER
Ron Wild
ADVERTISING SERVICES
Victoria Pratt
Published by Moorshead Magazines Ltd.
505 Consumers Road, Suite 500, Toronto,
ON, M2J 4V8 Canada
(416) 491-3699 Fax (416) 491-3996
E-Mail: magazine@moorshead.com
PRESIDENT
Halvor Moorshead
CIRCULATION MANAGER
Rick Cree
SUBSCRIPTION SERVICES
Jeannette Cox
Valerie Carmichael

History Magazine is published six times a year
(Feb/Mar, Apr/May, Jun/Jul, Aug/Sep,
Oct/Nov, Dec/Jan) by Moorshead Magazines.
POSTAL INFORMATION — CANADA
Canadian Publications Mail Product Sales
Agreement No. 1595695. Mailing address for
subscription orders, undeliverable copies and
change of address notice is:
History Magazine,
505 Consumers Road, Suite 500,
Toronto, Ontario, M2J 4V8 Canada
POSTAL INFORMATION — UNITED STATES
Periodical Postage Paid Lewiston, NY
USPS #018-154
Postmaster send address corrections to:
History Magazine,
PO Box 1201, Lewiston, NY, 14092-9934 USA
US Office of Publication
850 Cayuga St., Lewiston, NY, 14092

ISSN 1492-4307

SUBSCRIPTIONS
Subscription rate for US (US funds):
1 year (6 issues) $24.00
2 years (12 issues) $40.00
3 years (18 issues) $55.00
Subscription rate for Canada (Cdn funds):
1 year (6 issues) $28.00 plus GST/HST
2 years (12 issues) $45.00 plus GST/HST
3 years (18 issues) $59.00 plus GST/HST
Quebec residents add 7.5% QST
GST # 139340186 RT
We welcome the submission of articles for publication. Please send a printed copy in addition to the
file in electronic format. Please do not send important documents with submissions. We will always
contact people who submit articles but the review
process may take several weeks. Authors' notes are
available on request.
Toll-Free Subscription Line:
1-877-731-4478
PRINTED IN CANADA
WEBSITE
www.history-magazine.com

History Notes

Zippers

It is hard to imagine a world without zippers. The versatile fasteners are used to close everything from clothing and footwear to surgical incisions. However, when zippers were first introduced to the world, they were largely ignored.

The zipper was patented on 29 August 1893 by a Chicago mechanical engineer named Whitcomb Judson. Judson was already a successful inventor with a dozen patents to his credit. He invented the zipper as an alternative to the lengthy shoelaces used to close both men's and women's boots. His creation was called the "clasp-locker" and was an arrangement of hooks and eyes with a slide clasp for opening and closing. Judson's device was clumsy and frequently jammed but it did work.

Judson's invention was displayed at the Chicago World's Fair in 1893 to an audience of up to 20 million people. The response was underwhelming. Judson sold 20 clasp-lockers to the US Postal Service to be used to close mailbags. Judson and his business partner Lewis Walker sewed the device into their own boots but their company, Universal Fastener, despite further refinements, never succeeded in marketing it.

In 1913, a Swedish-American engineer, Gideon Sundbach, remodeled the fastener into a more streamlined and reliable form and sold an order to the US Army. The Army used the zippers in the clothing and gear supplied to its WWI troops. The only drawback was that the zipper would rust closed after repeated washings.

The term "zipper" was coined by B.F. Goodrich. Goodrich ordered 150,000 for his new product — rubber galoshes. He named the zipper after the zipping sound they made as they were fastened. By the late 1920s zippers were in common use and by the mid-1930s they had been embraced by the fashion industry.

Unfortunately, Judson died in 1909 and never knew of the success of his invention. —NICOLE BREBNER

Confetti

The word "confetti" comes from an Italian word referring to small bits of candy. In Italy, it was traditional to throw candy-coated nuts at newlyweds, as a way of wishing them a fruitful union. Later, it became popular to throw confetti during any celebration, such as Carnival. Gentler participants would wrap their candies up in small bits of paper so as to minimize the sting the candies would cause. In an article in *Harper's Magazine*, Constance Fenimore Woolson describes the use of confetti during the Roman Carnival: "In watching some of the more dexterous throws about me, I was amused to see what a test of organization and temperament confetti-throwing could resolve itself into.... There were laughter and mirth, and quick return charges of confetti fire; there were young French art students filling their bags with shot, and young German officers bringing Von Moltke's tactics to bear."

Perhaps being stingier with their bonbons, when the French adopted the Italian custom they dropped the candy, applying the name confetti to little bits of colored paper thrown during celebrations such as Mi-Careme and Mardi Gras. Near the turn of the previous century, a French newspaper estimated that 1.5 million pounds of confetti were sold in the days leading up to Lent. In an 1896 article in the *Louisville Courier-Journal*, a correspondent described the French tradition to the folks back home: "Confetti are thrown on you to make you beautiful, and before a fete is over you are very beautiful indeed, both inside and out, as confetti get down your back, and when you disrobe at night there is a shower of confetti.... From the beginning to the end of a fete the children and the confetti are so mixed that when a mother wants her child she feels around in the confetti until her hand rests on a head. If the head is that of her own child and not that of her neighbor's child, she leads the young one home." At the height of confetti's popularity in France, confetti would pile up to five inches deep on the main streets of Paris, and the government had to forbid those who couldn't afford their own confetti from gathering up and throwing handfuls of confetti off the ground, as the used confetti was mixed with the dirt and dust of the street.

Confetti is thrown at New York's Times Square on New Year's Eve.

In modern times, confetti-mania has cooled off considerably, but its offspring can clearly be seen in many modern traditions, such as dropping tickertape at parades, throwing rice or birdseed at weddings or dispensing doubloons at Mardi Gras. —JEFF CHAPMAN

Jonathan Sheppard Books

Box 2020, Plaza Station
Albany, New York 12220

www.jonathansheppardbooks.com
Serving Historians and Genealogists since 1977

Maps: Eastern States & European Areas

Visit our website for a listing of all available maps and for special prices on featured reprint maps, original antique maps, and out-of-print books.

Check back often! See what's on special!

◆◆◆◆◆◆◆◆◆◆◆

IMPORTANT - PLEASE READ

ABOUT OUR MAPS: All maps described below are black and white reprints of original maps in our collection. Unless otherwise indicated, maps are 18" x 24" and are printed on fine quality parchment stock. **Prices shown are in US dollars.**

SHIPPING: Map orders can be shipped either folded in a 9" x 12" envelope or unfolded and rolled in a sturdy shipping/storage tube. Please tell us your choice and add a shipping charge of either **$2.75** US (folded) or **$4.50** US (rolled in tube) to your total order. *Note that the shipping charge is per order, not per map. NYS & MA residents must add appropriate sales tax on total order, including shipping. For shipping to Canada, add an additional $1.50 US.*

MAPS FOR THE SOUTH & EAST...

[PNF25] Special Map Group for North and South Carolina. Includes maps: **(S 4) North and South Carolina Circa 1825**, shows county lines, roads, towns, rivers and creeks, coastal islands, and many lakes (11" x 17"); **(S 27) North and South Carolina: 1865**, shows rivers and swamps, towns, settlements, roads, railway lines, and county boundaries; **(S 50) North and South Carolina: 1889**, shows counties, county seats, villages, rivers, creeks, and railroads; **(F 21) North Carolina 1850** and **(F 25) South Carolina 1850** show counties (8 ½" x 11"). **All 5 maps: $17.95**

[PNF33] Special Map Group for Kentucky and Tennessee. Includes maps: **(S 2) Kentucky and Tennessee Circa 1825**, shows county lines, roads, settlements, creeks, river forks, and mountain ranges (11" x 17"); **(S 25) Kentucky and Tennessee: 1865**, shows towns, settlements, rivers, creeks, county lines, roads, and railways; **(S 49) Kentucky and Tennessee: 1890**, shows county divisions, towns, villages, rail lines, and small settlements; **(F 10) Kentucky 1850** and **(F 26) Tennessee 1850** (each 8 ½" x 11") show counties. **All 5 maps: $17.95**

[PNF 21] Special Map Group for Virginia and

West Virginia. Includes maps: **(S 1) Virginia and Maryland Circa 1825**, shows towns, roads, county lines, rivers, creeks, and mountain ranges (11" x 17"); **(S 24) Virginia with Delaware, Maryland and West Virginia: 1864**, shows newly created West Virginia, counties, roads, towns, railways, rivers and creeks; **(S 43) Virginia and West Virginia Circa 1884**, (17.5" x 27.5") shows rivers, creeks, small villages, settlements, railway lines, and insets of Norfolk Harbor, Hampton Roads and Harper's Ferry; **(F 29) Virginia 1850** (8 ½" x 11") shows counties. **All 4 maps: $16.95**

[PNF23] Special Map Group for Maryland and Delaware. Includes maps: **(T 16) Maryland and Delaware: 1885-87**, shows settlements, creeks, railways, rivers, streams and county boundaries; **(F 4) Delaware 1850** and **(F 13) Maryland 1850** (each 8 ½' x 11") show counties. **All 3 maps: $ 8.95**

[PNF29] Special Map Group for Georgia. Includes maps: **(S 8) Alabama and Georgia Circa 1825**, shows county lines, roads, principal towns, Creek and Cherokee boundary lines, major rivers, and creeks (11" x 17") ; **(S 28) Georgia and Alabama: 1863**, shows county lines, towns, villages, creeks, railroads, and ranges; **(S 48) Georgia: 1895**, shows county divisions, rivers, creeks, small towns, settlements, 63 railroad lines and their stations; **(F 6) Georgia 1850** (8 ½" x 11") shows counties. **All 4 maps: $16.95**

[PNF27] Special Map Group for Alabama. Includes maps: **(S 8)** *(see PNF29 above)*, **(S 28)** *(see PNF29 above)*, **(S 44) Alabama 1878**, shows counties, railroads, rivers, creeks, many small villages, and towns; **(F 1) Alabama 1850** (8½" x 11") shows counties. **All 4 maps: $16.95**

[PNF35] Special Map Group for Arkansas and Louisiana. Includes maps: **(S 6) Mississippi, Louisiana, & the Arkansas Territory Circa 1825** shows Indian lands, county lines, settlements, rivers, creeks and roads (11" x 17"); **(S 29) Arkansas, Mississippi and Louisiana: 1866**, shows county boundaries, railway lines, small towns, settlements, small rivers, branches, and creeks; **(F 2) Arkansas 1860** and **(F 11) Louisiana 1850** (each 8 ½" x 11") show counties. **All 4 maps: $11.95**

[PNF31] Special Map Group for Mississippi. Includes maps: **(S 6) Mississippi, Louisiana, & the Arkansas Territory Circa 1825** *(see PNF35 above)*; **(S 29) Arkansas, Mississippi and Louisiana: 1866** *(see PNF35 above)*; **(S 45) Mississippi: 1878**, locates counties, railway lines, rivers, creeks, small villages, and towns; **(F 16)**

Mississippi 1850 shows counties (8 ½" x 11").
All 4 maps: $16.95

[PNF37] Special Map Group for Texas. Includes maps: **(S 21) Texas: 1866**, shows counties and settlements, railway lines, creeks, forks, table lands, military forts, and an inset map of Galveston Bay; **(F 27) Texas 1850** shows counties (8 ½" x 11"). **Both maps: $ 7.95**

... AND EUROPEAN AREAS

[PEF21] Special Map Group for Switzerland. Includes maps: **(M 16) Switzerland Circa 1875**, shows Cantons, Alpine towns, rail and carriage roads, mountain paths, and some villages: **(M 27) Switzerland: 1794** shows towns, large villages, castles, vineyards, Protestant & Catholic parishes, cart roads, footpaths, the religious and political affiliation of each canton. **Both maps: $11.95**

[PEF39] Special Map Group for Southern Italy. Includes maps: **(R 21) Calabria 1890**, shows the region south of the Gulfs of Taranto and Policastro. (11" x 17"; **(R 22) Sicily 1890** (11" x 17") is useful for locating the many small Sicilian villages. Includes a small inset map of the Islands of Lipari; **(R 27) Southern Italy: 1842**, shows Italy south of Rome, the *Mezzogiorno* area divided into provinces, villages, towns, railway lines, roads, and regional subdivisions in Sicily. **All 3 maps: $12.95**

[PEF37] Special Map Group for Austria/Hungary. Includes maps: **(M 8) The East-Central Provinces: Bohemia, Moravia and Silesia 1844**, shows areas east of modern day Bavaria and Saxony and west of the city of Crackow, mountain ranges, roads, internal boundaries, railways, small towns, and villages; **(M10) Hungary and Part of Siebenburgen 1845**, details the area east of Vienna and north of Belgrade, shows provinces, roads, and hundreds of villages; **(M 21) The Austrian Empire 1875**, shows the area from Tyrol on the Swiss border east to Transylvania and as far south as the province of Sclavonia, provinces, major towns, and railroads. **All 3 maps: $17.95**

PAYMENT: We accept checks (U.S. dollars/U.S. Banks), M.O.s, MasterCard and VISA. Please include your card number, expiration date and signature when ordering. Our 24 hour faxline for credit card orders is (518) 766- 9181.

OUR SHOP: Our bookshop - MARTLET BOOKS - is located on historic North Street in Pittsfield, MA. We stock thousands of out of print local histories and genealogies, along with our map reprints, original antique maps and a select assortment of unusual books in a variety of subject areas. If you plan to visit, check our website for directions and hours or send us a SASE.

CATALOGUE: Can't visit our Pittsfield shop? Don't have Internet access? Complete descriptions of all of the hundreds of high-quality reprint maps in our collection are included in our catalogue. Paper copies are available for 66 cents in stamps.

www.jonathansheppardbooks.com
CHECK BACK OFTEN!

Male Vanity

Much has been made of the lengths to which women will go in an effort to make themselves more attractive to men. However, men are no less vain nor are they above employing artificial enhancements in the pursuit of female attention. One interesting example of this is the artificial calf.

In late 1700s England, stylish young men were referred to as macaronis. These dandies affected the latest in Continental fashions and influenced trends. They were very concerned with appearing desirable to women. Those who felt inadequate looked for cosmetic assistance.

The male calf was considered to be an area of sexual attractiveness and the size and shape were important. One accessory introduced by the macaronis was the calf pad. Strapped around the lower leg and covered by a stocking, its purpose was to enhance and accentuate the shapeliness of the male calf, which was exposed below the tight, knee-length breeches of the time. Calf pads remained popular until the introduction of long pants in the mid-1800s made them unnecessary. —NICOLE BREBNER

Tarot Cards

Tarot cards were originally used as playing cards when they appeared in France and Italy in the later 14th century. Early tarot decks had varied numbers of cards, and one could commission a set with certain cards missing such as the Tower card, symbolizing adjustment to catastrophe, the

Devil card, which stands for a person's shortcomings, or the Death card, representing a major turning point or challenge.

The church condemned tarot cards as it was thought that all playing cards were an invention of the devil, since cards were used for gambling.

The first people to use tarot cards for fortune telling were the Romany. The trend spread in the 18th century under the influence of writers who wrote of the mystic properties of the tarot cards, claiming their creation in Egypt.

The standardized tarot deck of today has 78 cards: 22 cards in the Major Arcana and 56 in the Minor Arcana. The cards of the Major Arcana each have pictures and names. The Major Arcana also have a numeric value for each card, except the Fool, which is unnumbered or a value of zero. The numeric value is likely a holdover from their playing card past. —VICTORIA KING

Medieval Shoes

Throughout much of history, shoes indicated the rank or the wealth of the wearer. Long, pointed toes with different kinds of decorations showed high rank in the middle ages. In the 1300s, a shoe called "la Poulaine" in France and the "crackowe" in England had pointed toes that became so long that a chain, usually fastened to the knee, had to be used to hold the tip up so the wearer could walk. The styles became so ridiculous that the English Parliament legislated against them in 1463, banning shoes with toes or "beaks," more than two inches beyond the toe.

After the long toe went out of style, the square toe came in. In 1545, shoe toes became more rounded and the cut approached the natural form of the foot. In the mid-17th century a new style arrived: the shoe with a long square toe. One practical joker, it was said, crept up to a gentleman unobserved and nailed the toe of his shoe to the floor. During the reign of Queen Mary of England, the "duckbill" or "bear's paw" shoe was so wide that another law was passed limiting the width of a shoe's toe to six inches.

Some time about 1570, the women of Venice revived the idea of the old stilt-like "chopine" and played it up as a new fashion item. This style, a sort of pedestal-shaped sole, was originally designed for overstepping sand, mud and general filth in the streets in days long before plumbing. Versions of it were unearthed in Egyptian tombs, and the style had once been popular throughout the Orient. When returning traders described the style back in Europe, it struck the fancy of Italian women while the ladies of France and England copied it as fast as they could. The chopines rose as high as 13 to 18 inches. Concealed by a woman's flowing skirts, they made her appear extremely tall. Many women were incapable of tottering about without the help of a servant. This was not as serious as it sounds as ladies of fashion traveled mostly by gondola on the Venetian canals. Shakespeare's Hamlet remarked that milady "is nearer to Heaven by the altitude of a

chopine." Records show that Queen Elizabeth I heightened the heels of her slippers to add to her stature. Diamond studded heels were considered smart by those who were well informed and could afford them.

Although we find these fashions slightly ridiculous, we should be reminded that the idea of the modern high heel is a direct descendant of the chopine.
—Reproduced courtesy of the *Daughters of the American Revolution Magazine*, from an idea by Donna Potter Phillips.

Political Mascots

The Democratic donkey and the Republican elephant have been associated with the political parties as early as 1828 in the case of the donkey and 1860 with the elephant.

When Andrew Jackson ran for president in 1828 with the slogan "Let the people rule" his opponents tried to label him a "jackass". Jackson turned this to his own advantage by using the donkey on his campaign posters. During his presidency, the donkey was used to represent Jackson's stubbornness when he vetoed the re-chartering of the National Bank.

In 1860 and again in 1872 cartoons in national publications connected the Republican party with the elephant but it wasn't until the presidential campaign to elect Ulysses Grant to a third term that cartoonist Thomas Nast's donkey and elephant symbols were used to great effect. The Republicans were defeated and the donkey and elephant as symbols of the two great parties became firmly established.

The Democrats think of the donkey as humble, smart, courageous and loveable whereas the Republicans think of it as stubborn, silly and ridiculous. The Republicans think of the elephant as dignified, strong and intelligent whereas the Democrats think of it as bungling, stupid, pompous and conservative. The symbolism is still with us even if the donkey and elephant have become highly stylized, complete with red, white and blue coloring and stars. —RON WILD

Buttons and Buttonholes

Why do women's outfits have buttons on the left side of the garment and men have it on the opposite side?

It is believed the buttons and buttonholes were sewn in this manner so that a right-handed man could reach for his sword without catching his cuff on the placket as he withdrew his sword, and a right-handed woman could breast-feed her child with greater ease, as the baby was typically held in the left arm as the right hand dexterously unbuttoned the outfit.

Also, women needed assistance with their restrictive clothing, so maids, the majority of whom were right-handed, could button the clothing easily as they faced the buttons differently to the wearer, whereas a man usually dressed himself.
—VICTORIA KING

HM

STEP INTO HISTORY.
THEN GET OUT OF THE WAY.

Relive an era with Mississippi's Civil War battle re-enactments

and magnificent antebellum homes.

Or catch a casino show, stroll along the beach and trace the origin

of the blues. Call 1-888-669-7662

for your free Mississippi *Travel Planner*.

THE SOUTH'S WARMEST WELCOME

www.visitmississippi.org

The 1770s

Victoria King describes some of the highlights of this turbulent decade.

THE 1770S WERE A watershed decade. Although there had been conflict between Britain and her American colonies in previous years, at the beginning of the decade Britain and her colonies were on good terms. By the end of the decade, the colonies had declared their independence, while France and Spain had joined the American side against Britain.

The map of the world changed considerably in the 1770s, both in terms of political boundaries and geographic discoveries. Russia was engaged in war with the Ottoman Empire (1768-74) and won control of Azov, the Crimea, Bessarabia and Moldavia. The Russians also defeated the Turks in Bulgaria. Russia was involved with Prussia and Austria in the partitioning of Poland, which would eventually lead to the country disappearing from the map. In the south Atlantic, Britain regained control of the Falkland Islands from Spain.

Captain James Cook changed the map of the Pacific with his three voyages to the region. He had discovered new lands, charted

The Declaration of Independence was adopted on 4 July 1776 in Philadelphia. The United Colonies, as they were then known, renounced allegiance to the British crown.

the area and increased Britain's domain. Samuel Hearne became the first European to reach the north coast of North America and H.J. Wikar explored the Orange River in Africa.

The period was also dominated by great personalities, "enlightened" monarchs who worked towards social reforms, religious toleration and political changes. Frederick the Great of Prussia dominated the politics of the continent, while in Russia, Catharine the Great proved to be the country's most brilliant leader since Peter the Great. Maria Theresa of

Austria strove to reform her empire, granting religious tolerance to Hungarian non-Catholics.

Although Louis XVI of France freed the last remaining serfs on royal land, a number of reforms in this period alienated the government and the people and civil unrest occurred due to food shortages. Louis XVI's support of the American struggle for independence was to show his people that rebellion against their monarch was acceptable.

Other figures of the Enlightenment who were influential in this decade were Voltaire, correspondent of monarchs, and Thomas Paine, whose pamphlet *Common Sense* assisted with the drive towards American independence. Adam Smith published his *An Inquiry into the Nature and Causes of the Wealth of Nations*, which has shaped economic thought to the present.

At the end of the 1770s, the course of history had changed because of the recent events and the stage was set for revolt and reform throughout western civilization.

Iron Bridge

IN 1779 a cast-iron bridge was erected over the River Severn in Shropshire, England. It was the first of its kind in the world.

The Severn was a shallow river in the summer, but in winter racing waters made it difficult to pass, and the local mining of coal and limestone and the iron smelting industry made the river a busy thoroughfare.

The span of the cast-iron bridge was 100 feet, six inches. The bridge was constructed of 378 tons of iron, which was smelted in the nearby Coalbrookdale valley. The arch of the bridge, which rose over 45 feet above the river, was constructed of five huge cast-iron ribs, each part cast in two halves. The bridge and its surrounding area both became known as Ironbridge.

The bridge was admired in its day. Thomas Jefferson is said to have purchased drawings of the bridge while Minister to France. Today the cast-iron bridge is a British national monument and a World Heritage Site, and is still in use by pedestrians.

1770
Marie Antoinette of Austria marries the French Dauphin, Louis.

James Cook claims Australia for the British Crown.

In New York, a group calling themselves the Sons of Liberty attacks British troops.

Famine hits Bengal; approximately 10 million people starve to death.

Lord North becomes Prime Minister of England.

The Russians destroy the entire Ottoman fleet at the battle of Cesme in the Aegean Sea.

The Boston Massacre takes place. British soldiers kill five people. The soldiers are later acquitted of the murder charges.

Louis XV of France issues a disciplinary edict and all members of the Paris parliament resign, along with several provincial members.

Thomas Gainsborough paints *The Blue Boy*, and Benjamin West paints *The Death of General Wolfe*.

The first public restaurant is established in Paris.

1771
On his third Arctic expedition, Samuel Hearne becomes the first European to reach the north coast of North America. Hearne had been sent north to look for the fabled Northwest Passage and large copper deposits, but found neither.

Nicolas Maupeou, Chancellor of France abolishes the parliaments and establishes new courts. This action is unpopular with the people.

Adolphus Frederick of Sweden dies and is succeeded by his son Gustavus III.

The Falkland Islands are restored to the British after the Spanish seized the islands a year before.

The Russians drive the Turks from the Crimea.

Coining copper in London is made a felony due to the increase of forged coins.

Glasgow imports 46 million pounds (20 million kilograms) of tobacco from the southern American colonies, reaching a new annual record.

Scotsman John Hunter publishes *The Natural History of Human Teeth*, the first study of dental anatomy.

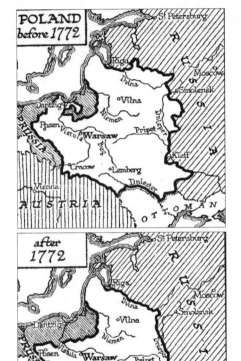

1772
Prussia, Russia and Austria sign a treaty partitioning Poland to satisfy their territorial ambitions. Over the next 23 years, the three countries wore down Poland, until it ceased to exist. In the first partition, Prussia takes West Prussia. Russia seizes the eastern part consisting of Belarus, Ukraine and Lithuania. Austria takes Galicia.

James Cook sets sail on his second voyage, returning to the Pacific.

Lord Mansfield presides over the case of James Somersett, an escaped slave, and declares that slavery is illegal on English soil.

Under the Royal Marriages Act, George III of England is allowed the right to veto marriages of royal family members under the age of 25.

Catherine II of Russia abolishes the privileges of the Cossacks.

Pressing, the laying of weights upon a person lying on their front as a form of punishment to those refusing to stand trial, is abolished in British prisons.

1773
The Pugachev rebellion in Russia takes place. The peasants call for the abolition of serfdom.

The British government passes the Tea Act. The act was created to aid the failing East India Company by allowing the direct export of tea to the American colonies.

A congress held at Bucharest concerning the Russo-Turkish war ends in failure.

Benjamin Franklin publishes *Rules by which a great empire may be reduced to a small one* in several English newspapers. The work was written as a reaction to the proposal of taxing all tea imported into the colonies.

The Boston Tea Party takes place. Angry colonists, many dressed as Indians, boarded three ships in the harbor and dumped the tea cargo overboard.

Mustafa III, sultan of the Ottomans dies, and is succeeded by his son Abdulhamid.

Twenty-year-old Phillis Wheatley, an African slave residing in Boston, Massachusetts, publishes in Britain her *Poems on Various Subjects, Religious and Moral*. American publishers had refused Wheatley's book.

1774

Louis XV of France dies and is succeeded by his grandson, Louis XVI.

Maria Theresa, Empress of Austria, grants religious tolerance to the Hungarian non-Catholics.

British parliament repeals the Tea Act and passes the Coercive Acts, also known as the Intolerable Acts, which close the port of Boston and reduce the power of the Massachusetts assembly. The Quartering Act is also restored; this act requires all colonies to provide housing for British troops.

The treaty of Kuchuk-Kainardji is signed by the Russians and the Turks, ending their six-year war. Russia gains control over most of the northern Black Sea coast, Moldavia and Wallachia are returned to Turkey and the Crimea is made independent.

The Quebec Act is passed, increasing the boundaries of Quebec to include other North American French-speaking settlements and allowing religious freedom to Roman Catholics.

English scientist Joseph Priestley discovers that plants release a gas (oxygen).

Robert Clive, victor of many wars in India, takes his life while in London. A year previously, charges brought against Clive by a parliamentary inquiry were dropped. The charges were concerning his involvement in oppression and tyranny in India.

Goethe publishes *The Sorrows of Young Werther*. Many of its readers commit suicide in imitation of the title character.

Architect John Wood completes the Royal Crescent in Bath, England. The Royal Crescent is a majestic row of 30 connected houses, the building is considered to be the height of opulence. The Duke of York made one of the houses his home.

1773: The Boston Tea Party. American colonials dressed as Indians boarded ships in Boston harbor and dumped the tea cargo overboard.

1775

George Washington becomes commander-in-chief of the American rebels.

Austrian Empress Maria Theresa abolishes the *corvee*, the obligation of tenants to work for landlords for a certain number of days per year, in Austria and Bohemia.

In Lexington, shots are traded between the British army and the American colonists. The British lose 73 soldiers and the Americans 49. The Americans were forewarned by Paul Revere of the British mission to destroy the Americans' supplies and armaments.

In Paris, and the Champagne and Brie regions, there is civil unrest due to a poor harvest and bread shortages.

Despite huge losses, the British are victorious over the Americans at Bunker Hill.

George III rejects the Olive Branch Petition, the offer of peace from the colonies.

Abul-Dhahab of Egypt invades Palestine.

Mecklenburg County in North Carolina declares its independence from Britain.

Benjamin Franklin and Benjamin Rush form the first colonial anti-slavery group, called the Society for the Relief of Free Negroes Unlawfully Held in Bondage.

1776

Adam Smith publishes *An Inquiry into the Nature and Causes of the Wealth of Nations*. The influential work declares that state intervention should be minimal in economies.

British and Canadian forces defend the city of Trois-Rivières against an American attack.

Thomas Paine publishes the pamphlet *Common Sense*. Paine sells over 500,000 copies of the work, which calls for the independence of the American colonies.

Ben Franklin travels to Montreal to invite Canadians into the union. Franklin's mission fails.

The British parliament issues an embargo on Irish exports to secure additional provisions for the British forces in North America.

The Declaration of Independence is signed in Philadelphia, thereby renouncing allegiance to the British crown and dissolving all political ties between the former colonies and Britain.

France secures a supply of slaves from the Kilwa sultanate to work in Île de France (present-day Mauritius) and the Reunion Islands.

David Hume, philosopher and historian, dies. Hume was very influential in his time, his writings spread to economics and he was the first person to write a history of England.

The Turtle, a one-man submarine, is used in war for the first time in the Battle of New York Harbor.

Edward Gibbon publishes the first volume of *Decline And Fall of the Roman Empire*.

Cook returns to the Pacific on his third voyage.

1777

Louis XVI of France recognizes the independence of the American colonies.

Emperor Joseph of Portugal dies and is succeeded by his daughter, Maria of Braganza.

George Washington is twice defeated by General Sir William Howe, once at Philadelphia and then at Germantown, Pennsylvania. Washington defeats the British at Princeton and General John Burgoyne surrenders at Saratoga. The British hope of recapturing New England is lost.

The first French daily newspaper, *Journal de Paris*, is printed.

The earl of Buckinghamshire, John Hobart, becomes the lord lieutenant of Ireland.

British prison reformer John Howard publishes *The State of Prisons*, which reveals the terrible conditions faced in jail. People were held in prison without being tried before court and were not released upon being found innocent as the unsalaried jailors hoped to collect money from the prisoners.

Richard Brinsley Sheridan's *School For Scandal* is first performed at the Theatre Royal in Drury Lane.

1778

France enters into the war between Britain and the United States by signing a trade agree-

British tax collectors were the unfortunate victims of colonial hostility.

ment with the latter and then declaring war on Britain.

William Pitt, the elder and first earl of Chatham, dies after collapsing in the House of Lords. The statesman is laid to rest in Westminster Abbey.

The political theorist Jean-Jacques Rousseau dies. Rousseau was the author of the significant *Social Contract*, which advocated direct democracy and the idea of 'general will' of the citizens to be followed by the government

Joseph Bramah patents the ballcock for use in water closets.

James Cook's expedition reaches the Sandwich Islands (present-day Hawaii).

Philosopher and man of letters Voltaire dies. Voltaire was famous for his works *Philosophical Letters*, *Candide* and his *Philosophical Dictionary*, and was a correspondent of European roy-

alty. However, Voltaire was unpopular in his native France, he was twice imprisoned and lived a large part of his life in exile.

John Montagu, the earl of Sandwich hungry while playing cards, asks for a meal between two slices of bread, thus creating the sandwich.

1779

After signing a secret treaty with the French, Spain declares war on Britain and attacks Gibraltar and later seizes control of Baton Rouge in Louisiana.

James Cook is stabbed to death upon his return to the Sandwich Islands. Cook had left the islands in search of the Northwest Passage, but returned upon finding impregnable frozen waters.

Quebec City has the first circulating public library in Canada. The library was opened to inform its patrons of English law and customs.

Swedish explorer H.J. Wikar explores the Orange River from its mouth on the Atlantic into the interior of Africa.

Louis XVI of France frees the last remaining serfs on royal land.

Under George Rogers Clark, American troops recapture the fort at Vincennes in Illinois after Henry Hamilton, the British governor, surrenders.

The regent of Persia, Karim Kand, dies.

The first iron bridge in the world is completed at Coalbrookdale in Shropshire over the river Severn.

The British Royal Navy orders that fruit juices be supplied to sailors to prevent scurvy, a disease caused by lack of vitamin C.

The Complete History

History
Magazine

Volume One
October 1999 - September 2000

The First Year of History Magazine

History Magazine Volume One is a reissue of almost all the editorial from the issues dated October 1999 to September 2000.

The colorful, bound volume includes all the editorial material from our first year of publication, including such features as: The Atlantic Cable, The Black Death, The National Road, Cleanliness, Bread, The Code Napoleon, The First Radio Station, The Longbow, 1000AD, The US Cavalry, Custer, Army Wives, Death Customs, Bellevue Hospital, The Impact of the Potato, An 1860s Dinner for Eight, The Rifle, The Oregon Trail, The Handcart Pioneers, Refrigeration, Games People Played, Contraception, The Suez Canal, Midwives, Longitude, The 1910s, Country Store, Connecting the World, Alchemy, Freemasonry, Early Newspapers, Influenza Pandemic, Chicago in 1880, The Privy, The Blacksmith, Saffron, Eli Whitney, Lunatic Asylums, Lighthouses, The 1900 House, Carpetbaggers, The Natchez Trace, Let's Eat!, How Brands Began, The Stirrup, The Shakers, Development of Photography, Insurance, Underground Railroad, Memsahibs of the Raj, California Gold Rush, Poliomyelitis, Wigs, decade profiles, historical trivia — and more!

History Magazine Volume One provides a full year of information about the lives our ancestors led.

Captain James Cook

By the time of his death in 1779, James Cook had changed the map of the world.

When Cook's naval career began in 1755, he already had experience with the North Sea trade as a mate. One of Cook's first tasks in the Royal Navy was to survey and sound the St. Lawrence River. Cook also participated in the Seven Years' War (1756-63), playing a role in the siege of Louisbourg in Nova Scotia and the assault on Quebec.

In 1766, Cook witnessed a solar eclipse off the coast of Newfoundland and sent his observations to the Royal Society in London. This proved to be fateful as two years later the Royal Society with the Admiralty organized a scientific expedition to the Pacific and selected Cook as commander. The goals of the three-year expedition were to observe the transit of the planet Venus across the sun and conduct further geographic research in the Pacific.

On board HMS *Endeavour*, Cook and his crew, along with the scientists, journeyed to Tahiti to observe the transit of Venus. Cook then proceeded to New Zealand, which had first been charted in the 1640s by the Dutchman Abel Janszoon Tasman. There, Cook spent six months charting and surveying the coast, but remained on board due to the hostility of the indigenous peoples. Then Cook sailed to New Holland (present-day Australia), which had also been discovered by Tasman, where Cook surveyed the eastern coast. The name New South Wales was given to the southern region as it held a resemblance to Glamorganshire. Botany Bay was named as such due to its lush vegetation. Cook then successfully navigated the Great Barrier Reef. Next Cook voyaged to New Guinea and confirmed that the island was not an outlying part of a large land mass. Cook returned to England in 1771.

Based on the success of Cook's first expedition, a second was organized in 1772. This expedition was undertaken to finish mapping Terra Australia.

After passing the Cape of Good Hope, Cook traveled south further than anyone had journeyed before and became the first to cross the Antarctic Circle. After discovering no land, Cook journeyed to New Zealand. From there he struck out towards the east and combed the sea for evidence of the continent. After visiting several islands, Cook established that no land mass existed beyond that of New Holland and New Zealand and the small islands. Cook then ventured to Tahiti to refit the ships.

From Tahiti, Cook crossed the Pacific to the New Hebrides, previously discovered by Quiros. Cook then discovered New Caledonia, Norfolk Island and the Isle of Pines. Cook returned to New Zealand and once more traveling eastward crossed the southern Pacific to Cape Horn. Once in the Atlantic, Cook discovered the South Sandwich Islands and South Georgia Island. Then the ships journeyed north to St. Helena, Ascension and the

Azores, then on to Plymouth, which was reached in July 1775.

By the end of Cook's second voyage, the ships had traveled more than 20,000 leagues, more than three times the circumference of the globe. Cook had also managed to keep his crew well and free of scurvy, a rare ability on long sea voyages in the 18th century. Cook fed his crew a diet of oranges, cress and sauerkraut. While Cook was in England he submitted a paper on scurvy to the Royal Society, which won the gold Copley Medal, one of its highest honors.

Cook volunteered for his third Pacific expedition and set sail on the *Discovery* in 1776 in search of the Northwest Passage. Cook returned once more to New Zealand, then on to Tahiti. North of Tahiti, Cook found the Sandwich Islands (present-day Hawaii). From there Cook journeyed west to the North American coast. Turning north, Cook surveyed the coast up to the Bering Straits. Once at the Bering Straits he met a wall of ice that rose 12 feet out of the water and stretched as far as the eye could see. Cook turned around and made his way to the Asian side of the Bering Straits and then returned to North America.

In early 1779, the great explorer returned to the Sandwich Islands. On 13 February 1779, the Hawaiians stole a cutter from one of the ships. The next day Cook sailed to shore with a party to retrieve the boat; while on shore, a scuffle broke out between the crew and the Hawaiians. The crew withdrew to their boats. Cook was the last to retreat and as he neared the boat, he was hit from behind. Cook fell and was killed by the Hawaiians. The great explorer was buried at sea and his crew returned to England in 1780.

Due to Cook's thoroughness, he left a lasting legacy by altering the map of the world, introducing science to navigation and conquering scurvy.

Chemical Discoveries

DURING THE 1770s, several great discoveries were made in chemistry. Previously only three gases were thought to exist: air, hydrogen and carbon dioxide. In 1772, Carl Wilhelm Scheele discovered oxygen. However, Joseph Priestley of England is usually credited with this as he independently discovered oxygen two years later, but managed to publish his findings three years earlier.

Priestley was one of the most prolific scientists of the decade. He was able to isolate several other gases: ammonia, sulphur dioxide, nitrous oxide and nitrogen dioxide.

Priestley called his discovery of oxygen 'dephlogisticated air' as it was believed then that all combustible bodies contained the substance 'phlogiston', which was released in combustion. Other gases discovered during this period were also known as 'phlogisticated' gases.

French chemist Lavoisier and his wife. Lavoisier is known as the father of modern chemistry.

Also in 1772, Scotsman Daniel Rutherford confirmed there was a distinction between 'noxious air' (nitrogen), considered to be another phlogisticated gas and carbon dioxide.

Antoine Laurent Lavoisier of France was also active during the 1770s. He is known as the father of modern chemistry. In 1774, Lavoisier met Priestley in France. The meeting was pivotal to chemistry, as Priestly discussed how he obtained his dephlogisticated air. Lavoisier repeated the experiments and from these was able to deduce that oxygen was an element and to determine its role in the atmosphere. Lavoisier also gave oxygen its name and discovered its function in combustion, which led Lavoisier to discredit the phlogistic theory. Lavoisier's attack on the phlogistic theory gathered a great amount of support over the last years of the century. However, Priestley could not accept the evidence for oxygen, and upheld the phlogistic theory until his death in 1804.

The First Partition of Poland

WHEN THE Prussian-endorsed and favourite of Catherine II of Russia, Stanislaus Augustus Poniatowski, was elected king of Poland in 1764, he became the ruler of an extremely weak and vulnerable country. Poland was surrounded by powerful nations: Prussia to the west, Russia in the east, and Austria to the south. The country was also plagued by internal religious problems between Protestants and Catholics.

In 1768, the Ottoman Empire demanded that Catherine II cease interfering in Polish internal affairs. War broke out, and Russia won several battles over the Ottomans at Azov, the Crimea, Bessarabia, Moldavia and Bulgaria, moving westward toward the Austrian border. These military

A cartoon showing the partition of Poland as suggested by Frederick the Great, depicted second from the right.

successes worried Austria, who threatened to join the Ottoman Empire against Russia.

The same year, civil war broke out in Poland. Frederick II of Prussia did not want conflict in the region, so the suggestion of the partition of Poland was made. All three neighboring nations saw the

politically unstable Poland as a possible threat and its instability made its domination easy.

On 5 August 1772, Prussia, Russia and Austria signed a treaty partitioning Poland to satisfy their territorial ambitions. The weak Polish government ratified the agreement, unable to resist takeover due to its weak state. Prussia took West Prussia. Russia seized the eastern part consisting of Belarus, Ukraine and Lithuania. Austria took Galicia. The partition robbed Poland of one-half of its population and almost one-third of its land. Over the next 23 years, the three countries wore down Poland until it ceased to exist. Poland would not exist again until the end of WWI.

The Struggle for American Independence

AT THE END OF THE Seven Years' War, Britain was victorious but financially weak. Britain turned her gaze to her American colonies.

To replenish the Empire's coffers, Parliament passed a series of four acts in 1767 known as the Townshend Acts. Together these four acts were designed to assert British authority in her colonies by way of banning representative assembly, as the colonies had traditionally been self-governing, and to raise revenue for Britain by taxation of imported goods such as glass, paint, paper and tea.

The American colonists resented these acts, as well as their predecessors, the Sugar Act (1764) and the Stamp Act (1765). The colonists resisted these measures with wars of words, acts of violence and dodging of duties. The British responded to this insubordination by landing troops at Boston in 1768, to quell the colonists who were "teetering on the brink of anarchy". The colonists saw this deployment of British troops as further provocation.

In 1770, parts of the Townshend Acts were repealed. All duties save that on tea were lifted, and the British troops were removed from Boston. However, in 1773, the Tea Act was passed, which reignited the hostility between Britain and the American colonies. The Tea Act was created by Lord North's Parliament to aid the ailing British East India Company by allowing the company to charge the Townshend duty (a duty of three pence per pound) and export directly to the colonies.

On 16 December 1773 hundreds of colonials, many dressed as Indians, boarded three British ships in the Boston harbor. On board the *Beaver*, the *Dartmouth* and the *Eleanor* were several hundred tea chests, which the disguised colonials dumped into the

In the 5 March 1770 "Boston Massacre", British troops opened fire on demonstrators, killing five. The troops were later acquitted of murder charges.

harbor. Although many colonials were armed, no members of the ships' crews were harmed, and no other cargo was damaged. Writing of the Boston Tea Party, John Adams said, "This destruction of the tea is so bold…it must have important consequences."

The British Parliament reacted by repealing the Tea Act and passing the Coercive Acts in May 1774. The Acts closed the port of Boston, reduced the power of the Massachusetts legislature and required that all colonies provide housing for British troops. The last act, known as the Quartering Act, caused further hostility toward the British.

The colonies reacted to the Coercive Acts by calling a Continental Congress in December of that year. The Congress, attended by delegates from each American colony, affirmed the rights to life, liberty, property, assembly and trial by jury. Taxation without representation was condemned.

In April 1775, fighting broke out at Lexington and Concord between the British and the colonials. In the months leading up to

the conflict, the colonies had trained independent companies of militiamen and the committee of public safety in Massachusetts decided to purchase military equipment for 15,000 colonists. This became known as the Continental Army. General Thomas Gage of the British army set out from Boston to seize the military store of the colonists, which was kept at Concord. The colonists were forewarned of the British arrival by Paul Revere and the two armies met at Lexington. Although the colonists did not win at Lexington, they won at Concord, with the British retreating to Boston. A second continental congress was called in May 1775 and there George Washington was appointed as commander-in-chief of the Continental Army.

The fighting continued in Boston with a yearlong siege (April 1775-March 1776) of the city, where 6,500 British troops were quartered. In June 1775, the battle at Bunker Hill was fought. Both armies wanted command of a strategic hill that overlooked Boston. Although the British won control of the hill, it was with significant losses and the British army did not continue its offensive.

In July 1775, the Olive Branch Petition was sent to King George III. This document, signed by many of the Founding Fathers of America, was an attempt at reconciliation between the colonies and Britain. George III rejected the petition. The colonists next turned to the north and invaded Canada in the autumn of 1775. They captured Montreal, but failed to take Quebec. The colonists retreated to Fort Ticonderoga in the spring as British enforcements arrived in the area.

In March 1776, the siege of Boston ended. General Washington captured Dorchester Heights, which was another strategic outlook over Boston, and the British withdrew from the city.

A Continental Congress met and adopted the Declaration of Independence in Philadelphia on 4 July 1776. The United Colonies, as they were then known, renounced allegiance to the British crown and dissolved all political ties between the former colonies and Britain. Of the 13 colonies, 12 voted for the declaration. New York abstained only as it lacked permission to act; New York later approved the declaration.

Several battles were fought later in 1776. General Howe, Gage's replacement, defeated Washington's troops on Long Island. Washington retreated to Manhattan, and then fought Howe again at Chatterton Hill. Lord Cornwallis pushed the American forces to the bank of the Delaware, and then stationed his army in New Jersey for the coming winter. On the night of 25 December, Washington's forces crossed the Delaware and attacked Cornwallis' forces at Trenton, capturing 900 soldiers.

Under General John Burgoyne, a British force of 8,000 moved south from Canada in 1777. The British forces were victorious at Fort Ticonderoga, but were defeated and finally forced to surrender to General Gates at Saratoga. Burgoyne had expected to meet other British armies at Fort Ticonderoga, but due to poor communication, he faced a larger American army alone.

This was considered the watershed moment for the war: from this point onward, events favored the Americans. General Howe's forces moved from New York and defeated Washington at Brandywine Creek and occupied the capital city of Philadelphia. Washington attacked Germantown, Pennsylvania, which was held by the British, in October 1777. The victories at Saratoga and Germantown influenced the French to support the American side.

Over the winter of 1777-78, Washington and his troops were stationed at Valley Forge. Despite the initial setbacks of inadequate

The decisive victory for the Americans came at the siege of Yorktown, Virginia in 1781. The British troops of Cornwallis surrendered to the victorious George Washington.

supplies, the army was reorganized and with the assistance of Prussian officer Baron von Steuben, the army became a well-trained organization.

In 1778, France entered the conflict officially by declaring war upon Britain. France sent troops to the southern States where victories were achieved over the British at Savannah, Kings Mountain and Cowpens. A peace commission was sent from Britain in 1778 to the United States, the official name of the former colonies since September 1776. Under the Earl of Carlisle, the commission hoped to have the Americans reconciled with the British under a type of self-rule within the empire. The commission was destined to fail even before it left, as news of France's support for the Americans became known. After signing a secret treaty with the French, Spain declared war on Britain in 1779 and won control of Baton Rouge that year. The following year, the Netherlands joined the war against the British.

The British under Cornwallis were successful at Camden in South Carolina (1780), which destroyed Gates' reputation, and

at Guilford House in North Carolina (1781), but success came at a heavy price. The conclusive victory for the Americans was the siege of Yorktown, Virginia in 1781. Cornwallis' forces surrendered to the victorious George Washington. Fighting between the Americans and the British ended on land, however, naval warfare continued between Britain and America's allies in Europe for several years.

The Peace of Paris, which ended the American War of Independence, was signed in 1783. Britain recognized the independence of the United States, and Florida was ceded to Spain. France received Senegal and Tobago from Britain. The Netherlands ceded Nagappattinam in India to the British.

There are many reasons the Americans won the war for independence. The British lacked coordination and were unable to provide sufficient armies, and the distant government was economically weak. The American army became highly trained, used guerrilla tactics, and had international support, and they understood the war was for freedom, life and liberty. **HM**

INTRODUCTION TO GENEALOGY

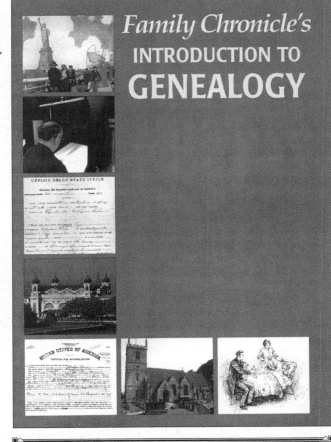

Family Chronicle's Introduction to Genealogy has been written to answer the often heard question "I'm interested in starting my research — but where do I start?" It assumes no prior knowledge of genealogy and is designed to bring the reader rapidly "up to speed".

The presentation follows *Family Chronicle*'s popular format. Features include how to find information about your ancestors in: Vital Records, City Directories, Census and Military Records, Naturalization Records, Social Security Records, Passenger Lists, Court Records, Obituaries and Church and Parish Records. This is followed by information on where to conduct your research: Family History Centers, Libraries and National Archives. There are also sections on keeping your data organized, manually or on a computer.

If you have traced your roots back across the Atlantic, we have a summary on conducting your research in a dozen European countries. When you have gathered enough information we show you how to start writing your family history.

We introduce you to computers, with advice on the type of computer to use, an overview of the software packages available and tips on getting online and making the most out the Internet. We explain how to find records on CDs or in the subscription services on the web.

There's a whole lot more including Heraldry, Tartans, Origins of Surnames, Societies, Preservation of Documents and Photos . . .

As with all our publications, if *Family Chronicle's Introduction to Genealogy* fails to meet your needs or expectations, we will gladly refund your money, for any reason or no reason. Any refund will be made promptly and cheerfully.
Halvor Moorshead, Editor and Publisher

The *Introduction* is designed to get you started on the right foot and to fill in any gaps if you are an experienced researcher.

The First Subways

Jeff Chapman looks at the earliest major subway systems.

THE IDEA OF BUILDING a railway under a city was radical as recently as 150 years ago. When engineers and city planners in the great cities of London, Paris and New York first started considering the idea in the mid-19th century, the notion was denounced and ridiculed by the public. At that time, the most popular conception of the underground was that found in Dante's *Inferno*: the general public was afraid of the subterranean world, and clergymen denounced the idea of extending civilization underground as being no less than Satanic. The idea was also widely thought to be foolish — members of the general public might not have an engineering degree, but it was plainly apparent to them that hollowing out the ground beneath the city streets would cause the city itself to be swallowed up by the earth.

Combating these widespread fears, however, was the increasingly obvious problem of urban congestion. Most major cities had evolved roads that followed pre-industrial traffic patterns developed in a time when few people left their own neighborhood. Cities rarely spread more than a mile from their town halls and walking from one end of a city to the other was a viable option. From the beginning of the 19th century onward, however, cities spread miles away from their core and ever-increasing numbers of people needed to move all over their sprawling cities, traveling between islands and crossing great rivers. Horse-drawn omnibuses were not up to the task of solving major metropolitan traffic crises, and the commerce of large, dense cities was being smothered by traffic congestion.

London

In the middle of the 19th century, London was the seat of the world's

A cut-away diagram of the Underground below London's Piccadilly Circus shows the complexity of the system.

most powerful empire and the world's most populous city. London's rapid population growth caused problems for the city, however. Two and a half million people were crammed into 60 square miles, and traffic was so congested that it was choking the profitability of business.

The solution Charles Pearson, solicitor to the City of London, came up with was completely unheard of: the city would construct a railway beneath the streets, becoming the first city in the world to have an underground railway.

In 1863, the Metropolitan Railway opened the first stretch of underground track of what the *London Times* called "the greatest engineering triumph of the day." The line measured nearly four miles and ran between Paddington (Bishop's Road) and Farringdon Street. The line was constructed using what was called the "cut and cover" method: streets along the route were dug up, tracks were laid into deep trenches, then the tracks were roofed over and the

road surface replaced. Though this method caused considerable disruption to surface traffic, it proved quick and effective in the early days of subway construction. The first trains to run beneath London's streets were steam-powered locomotives that burned coke or coal and emitted sulfurous fumes. In spite of this, the line was a success from its opening, carrying 26,500 passengers a day for its first six months and 9,500,000 passengers in the first year of its existence.

While other routes, such as the Great Western line and the Hammersmith and City line, appeared to serve passengers on the north side of the River Thames, the engineers of the underground railway understood that if the network was to provide a solution to transport problems across the city, the lines also had to cross deep under the river to south London. The problem of dealing with unstable, waterlogged soil was solved by Marc Isambard Brunel, father of the great engineer Isambard Kingdom Brunel. Marc Brunel's tunneling machine involved using a subway-tunnel shaped shield to protect workers at the cutting face, and was the prototype for all subsequent machines. The next crucial development was devised by the engineer James Henry Greathead. Greathead's shield was smaller, lighter and circular, providing optimum strength. The tunnel boring method had been invented, and with it, the tube.

It wasn't until 1890 that electricity was introduced to the London subway system, when the first deep-level electric railway line was opened. Twenty-five-horsepower electric locomotives traveled between King William Street in the City of London under the River Thames to Stockwell at speeds of up to 25 miles per hour. The new 3.6-mile line under the Thames

The Beach Subway

Though New York's real subway system didn't open until 1904, the city can lay claim to having an underground railway of a sort as early as 1870.

The experimental subway was the independently conceived and financed creation of Alfred Ely Beach, the publisher of *Scientific American* and the inventor of the pneumatic tube. When Beach was unable to obtain the necessary construction permits due to opposition from Boss Tweed, he obtained a charter for a small tunnel to demonstrate the pneumatic tube's usefulness in mail delivery, and then instead excavated a full eight-foot-diameter subway tunnel. Beach's men dug out the subway tunnel in secrecy, working in the dead of night and smuggling the excavated dirt out through the basement of Devlin's clothing store.

When finished, the tunnel ran a mere 312 feet under Broadway between Warren Street and Park Place. The experimental line was powered not by steam or electricity but by pneumatic pressure. A 100-horsepower blower/exhauster pushed and pulled the single 22-passenger car back and forth through the tunnel. The car was effectively shot from one end of the tunnel to the other, using the same principle which powers the delivery of mail through pneumatic tubes.

Beach was convinced pneumatic technology was superior to the alternatives, and after seeing his experimental line fully functional, he began to conceive plans for an entire city-wide network. Beach prepared to unveil his secret project to the public by decorating his subway's subterranean "waiting room" in grand style — even going so far as to furnish it with a grand piano!

The demonstration of the line was a success, but adoption of the pneumatic system was blocked partly by Tweed's opposition, partly by the financial panic of 1873, and finally by the arrival of electric traction.

The "UndergrounD" lettering was adopted in 1907, and the Roundel symbol was introduced in 1909. The two were combined in 1913.

took four years to excavate using Greathead's tube tunneling method, and the subway's common name of "The Tube" dates from this time. The now-official name of "The Underground" did not come into use until 1908. "Underground" was short for "The Underground Electric Railway Company of London Limited", the group which gradually absorbed most of the other companies building underground lines.

The original steam-powered lines were converted to electrical power, and electric traction lines proved even more popular than the original steam-powered lines. The popular subway system began to make healthy profits for the private companies that controlled it. Until 1907, the normal fare for riding the subway was a mere two pennies, hence the nickname "Twopenny Tube". With the addition of each new interconnected line, the effectiveness and popularity of London's subway system grew. Before long, the London subway began to touch the lives of almost everyone in the capital region. The shape of the city itself was altered drastically as the system pushed beyond the greenbelt and enabled the existence of com-

muter suburbs. The subway also affected the social patterns of the city. Aside from a special car on each train set aside for smokers, there was no special seating, so gentlemen and ladies rode alongside factory workers — a mingling of classes that was all but unheard of in the regular course of above-ground life.

On 1 September 1939, WWII broke out and the British government assumed control of the private company called London Transport under the provisions of the Emergency Powers (Defence) Act. As most surface buses were converted to use as ambulances, London's subway began to assume even greater importance. From September 1940 until May 1945, Underground station platforms were used as air raid shelters during German air raids on London. Seventy-nine stations were equipped with bunks, clinics and sanitary facilities, and subway trains began to deliver food, to accommodate the almost 200,000 Londoners who sheltered in stations each night. The Piccadilly Line's Holborn-Aldwych branch was closed and used to store treasures of the British Museum. Other parts of the system were used as underground factories for the military.

The British government kept control of London Transport after the war concluded, gradually paying off the private interests that had controlled the transit company previously. Under government control, the London Underground has continued to expand massively. Today, London's subway serves 275 stations over 253 miles of railway. In the past year, 927 million passenger journeys were made, and this number is expected to rise to more than one billion in 2001.

Paris
Paris began to construct its *Chemin de Fer Métropolitain de Paris* subway line — known as the Metro because the people of Paris borrowed and shortened the original name of London's subway, the Metropolitan — in 1898, more than 25 years after the opening of the first line under London. The main

motivation behind the construction of the Metro was the need for France to impress the other industrial nations of the world at the upcoming 1900 World's Fair, to be held in Paris.

The construction of the Paris Metro was more complex than the construction of the London Underground. The earth under Paris was not firm clay as in London, but wet mud laced with debris from abandoned stone quarries and other uncharted underground obstacles. These included archaeological discoveries ranging from ancient Roman coins to the remains of the Bastille Prison, all of which had to be excavated and shipped to museums. The tunneling crews had to reroute any water, gas, or sewer lines or electric cables they found under the streets, while excavating more than 35,000 cubic feet of dirt every 24 hours in order to meet their deadline. Under the direction of head engineer Fulgence Bienvenue, thousands of men worked on the line in shifts that went around the clock. After 17 months, Bienvenue reported to the city authorities that tunnel construction on the first line of the Paris Metro had been completed on schedule. The Metro opened for business with eight stations on 19 July 1900, and began shuttling throngs of Parisians to and from the World's Fair. In its first two weeks of operation, more than half a million passengers had used the Metro.

Construction of subsequent lines of the Metro proved to be more challenging, as the lines had to be dug further underground, often into areas for which the city owned no maps. As well as the city's extensive and much-beloved sewer system, underground Paris was filled with catacombs and limestone and gypsum quarries up to 10 storeys deep. The city was also filled with buried rivers and underground springs, and the digging crews had to deal with sudden flooding of the tunnels. Paris itself was flooded by torrential rains during the winter of 1910, and all but one line of the Metro was flooded as well. Despite this,

After their introduction in the early 1900s, Hector Guimard's *art nouveau* entrances became the distinguishing mark of the Paris Metro.

the system expanded steadily, with construction slowing only during and immediately following WWI.

In the era following WWI, the development of the Metro system both affected and was affected by shifts in housing patterns around Paris. The high cost of living in the city prompted the population of the suburbs surrounding the capital to swell from under one million to more than two. Suburban workers relied on public transport to get to their jobs in Paris, and the government met this need by expanding Metro service beyond the city limits. In this manner, what had traditionally been a small, dense city blossomed into a vast populous region known as *le Grand Paris*, or Greater Paris.

Whereas Londoners used their subway system to defend themselves from Nazi Germany during WWII, in occupied Paris the Nazis took over the Metro system. Some lines were closed and stations

were converted into subterranean factories for the production of airplane parts. On the lines that remained operational, Jews were only allowed to ride in the last car of the train, which was dubbed "the synagogue". Towards the end of the war, Parisians took refuge in deep Metro stations during Allied air-raids on the capital, and the French resistance used unoccupied tunnels to assist in sabotaging and spying upon Nazi operations.

New York

Strangely, considering the progressive and ambitious character of the city, New York followed both London and Paris in constructing a subway system. Part of the reason for this was that metropolitan New York City was a relatively new creation: only in 1898 had the boroughs of Manhattan and the Bronx been joined by the previously independent boroughs of Brooklyn, Queens and Richmond (as Staten Island was officially known). This new and more rational political organization strengthened the case for efficient systems of interborough transportation, as well as swelling the population of New York.

As was generally understood, public transit systems worked most efficiently in densely populated areas. Though New York was not yet the largest city in the world, it was the most densely populated. At the time that New York first began to seriously consider the construction of a subway, it was home to four million people. In the area of the city known as the Lower East Side, population density averaged 9,000 residents per acre — the most dense concentration of people that the world has ever known, even exceeding the current densities of Calcutta's slums or downtown Tokyo.

Manhattan had been served by elevated ("el") railways since 1870, but the steam-powered locomotives used on the elevated lines were dirty, noisy and tended to cause fires. Even after the el lines were electrified in the early 1900s, they continued to be a noisy eyesore along their routes through Manhattan and Brooklyn, and they were never embraced by the public.

Construction of the first line of the New York subway system — to be owned by the city and leased by a private interest called the Interborough Transit Company (IRT) — began in 1900. The IRT engineers elected to employ the awkward and costly construction method of shallow excavation directly under the streets, using the cut-and-cover system. Their reasoning was that deep stations served by elevators, as were common in London, would not be able to handle the demands of a New York rush hour, and that building near the surface would enable the system to save money on elevators.

Over the course of four years, tunnels were dug and tracks were laid in a route traveling much of the length of the island of Manhattan. Mayor George B. McClellan opened the first section of the New York system on 27 October 1904, announcing, "Now I, as Mayor, in the name of the people, declare the subway open." After the opening ceremony, the mayor drove the train on its initial public run. According to the *New York Times*, "all along the way crowds of excited New Yorkers were collected around the little entrances talking about the unheard trains that they knew were dashing by below, and waiting eagerly for the first passengers to emerge from the underground passageways at their feet." When the train reached Harlem, the account continues, "it broke up a ball game. It was a hotly contested game, too, and one of the players had just made a home run; yet as the olive green train shot past, the players dropped bat, ball and the business of the hour, the spectators forgot that there was such a thing as baseball, and the whole crowd surged up to the fence waving bats and handkerchiefs and yelling like mad at this beginning of fraternity between Harlem and City Hall Park." It was widely

The construction of the New York subway enabled the city to largely abandon elevated ("el") trains.

accepted that the IRT had successfully met the terms of its contract, which stipulated, "all parts of the structure where exposed to public sight shall... be designed, constructed, and maintained with a view to the beauty of their appearance, as well as to their efficiency."

A few initial problems, such as large gaps between the platform and the subway cars in curved stations and excessive crowding during rush hours, were solved through the introduction of mechanized platforms and automatic subway doors. With these minor fixes, the subway quickly proved itself to be an astounding success. The subway was extended north to the Bronx in 1905, and east to Brooklyn in 1908. The IRT was making considerable profits within a year of its opening, and these profits caught the attention of competitors. After a highly political bidding war, the city launched what were called the Dual Contracts lines, which shared the responsibilities for new subway lines between the IRT and the Brooklyn Rapid Transit Company (BRT, later known as the Brooklyn-Manhattan Transit Company or BMT). These new lines in Manhattan, Brooklyn and Queens were mostly finished by 1920, and had some trains that were operated by both companies. The Independent

subway (IND) was built by the city in the late 1920s as an independent system that was not connected to the IRT or BMT lines. The IND subway featured lines in Manhattan, Brooklyn, the Bronx and Queens. After the city assumed control of the bankrupt IRT and BMT lines in 1940, the three systems were gradually unified through the introduction of various free transfer points. The city compensated for this greater ease of use by doubling the subway fare to 10 cents in 1947.

Today, the New York subway's 20,000 employees and 6,500 cars serve four million passengers a day. Though New Yorkers are quite convinced that their system is the greatest in the world, there are few areas in which the New York subway system ranks first. The New York subway was not the first underground railway in the New World, Boston having claimed that honor in 1897. It is not the longest system in the world, that honor going to London. It is not the busiest system in the world, as both the Tokyo and Moscow systems serve more passengers each day, nor is it the most efficient, most sanitary or most easy-on-the-eye system. In terms of superlatives, New York must be content to hold the title as the system with the most cars. It is also, of course, the most famous system in the world.

Further Reading

Benson Bobrick. *Labyrinths of Iron: A History of the World's Subways* (New York: Newsweek Books, 1981).
Michael W. Brooks. *Subway City* (New Brunswick, NJ: Rutgers University Press, 1997).
Brian J. Cudahy. *Under the Sidewalks of New York: The Story of the Greatest Subway System in the World* (New York: Fordham University Press, 1995).
Tamara Hovey. *Paris Underground* (New York: Orchard Books, 1991).
John R. Day. *The Story of London's Underground* (London: London Transport).

HM

Unraveling the Stars

Nancy Hendrickson looks at the quest to understand the universe.

A THOUSAND YEARS ago, a Zuni Sun Priest stood high on a mesa, waiting for the first rays of the sun to pierce the pre-dawn darkness. As the sun appeared behind a distant rock formation, the Priest made a mark on his pinewood calendar. He would announce to his people that soon the sun would be nearing its winter home — the solstice was almost at hand.

Like the Sun Priest, humanity has followed the course of the sun and the stars for as long as recorded memory. Ancient cultures defined their lives by the passing of the seasons. When they traveled, their map was the sun during the day and the stars at night. The movement of the sun was a signal for sowing, reaping, hunting and storing. When the sun reached its southernmost point in the winter sky, ritual races were held to give it enough strength to return to its northern home, and bring summer with it.

Ancient cultures had a complex relationship with the sun and the stars that was both scientific and religious. The Blackfoot believed meteors signaled sickness; the Chumash saw them as a soul on its way to the after-life. Egyptian farmers realized the bright star Sirius appeared before dawn just a few days before the waters of the Nile began to rise. The Anasazi, who populated the Four Corners area of the American Southwest from 900AD to 1300AD, laid out east-west walls in direct alignment with sunrise or sunset at the solstices or equinoxes. The heavens and their fiery phenomena were loved and feared and those who could pre-

Stonehenge, first used long before the time of the Druids in 3100BC, is now believed to have been an astronomical observatory for the ancient Britons.

dict their movement held great power.

Today, urban dwellers who live under a canopy of streetlights instead of starlight rarely experience the night sky of the past. In our time, the Milky Way has become a rural experience.

The Hubble Space Telescope has opened the door to our own celestial past, its photos reaching back close to the beginning of time. With orbiting observatories and giant Earth-based telescopes answering questions that have puzzled astronomers for centuries, it's hard to understand that it wasn't very long ago that Greek philosophers like Aristotle believed the sun and the stars traveled across the sky on crystal celestial spheres.

How did astronomy make its long journey to the present?

Prehistoric Skywatchers

We know ancient people watched the stars with great interest, thanks to the picture records scratched into layers of desert varnish. At Fajada Butte, in Chaco Canyon, three sandstone slabs were placed high on a rock panel and carefully decorated

with a pair of spiral petroglyphs. At noon on the summer solstice, the sun shines between the slabs, throwing a bright sliver of light onto the center of the larger spiral.

At another Anasazi site at Chaco Canyon the sun's rays enter a window and strike a niche in the Northwest wall to mark the summer solstice. Evidence has even been found of petroglyphs that scientists believe represent the great supernova (exploding star) seen in 1054AD.

The study of the sun and stars grew more sophisticated in the hands of Mayan astronomers. At Chichen Itza, once the center of Mayan civilization, a pyramid called El Caracol was built as an observatory. Nearby, another pyramid known as El Castillo was designed so that at the spring equinox, a stream of light appeared to slither down the steps onto the pyramid's north face, eventually striking the stone serpent heads below.

The Mayans also studied the Milky Way; for them it represented the World Tree and the star clouds that form the Milky Way's center were seen as the tree of life from which all life began.

Not all observatories, however, were as complex as that of the Mayans. Half a world away, and a thousand years earlier, Britons built a stone circle whose bluestone menhirs and approach avenue were aligned toward the sunrise on the day of the summer solstice. Although no one knows for sure exactly how Stonehenge was originally used, it is certain it served as a prehistoric observatory.

Stone circles like Stonehenge

have also been found in the United States and Canada. High in the Montana mountains, the Big Horn Medicine Wheel is 27 meters in diameter and was designed with a central cairn of stone from which radiate 28 individual spokes. Certain features of the wheel align with the solstice and the brightest stars of midsummer dawn. At the time of its 1880 discovery, the nearby Crow Indians said the wheel was placed there "before the first light came".

One of the oldest sites linked to the sun's movements is in Ireland. Recent studies indicate that the Newgrange Tomb, built north of Dublin 5,150 years ago, was used to track the sun. Thousands of years ago the first sunlight of the winter solstice flowed down the tomb's long central corridor and illuminated a carving made up of three spirals.

Ancient people may not have known why the sun and the stars moved, but they did understand that celestial bodies followed a distinct pattern. They knew that the sun rose every morning in one direction, moved westward across the sky and disappeared in the west. Each night, more than 1,000 bright stars followed the same course. They knew that in the summer the sun rose north of east and in the winter, south of east, and they also knew that distinct seasonal changes came with the movement of the sun during the course of a year. Of all the ancient skygazers, the Egyptians were the first to believe that the sun moved around a sphere of fixed stars in 365 days and nights.

Babylonian and Greek Astronomers

The Egyptians, Chinese and Mayans drew maps of star patterns — constellations — but the Babylonians were experts at plotting star movements and translating them to a calendar. Babylon-

Nicholas Copernicus was more a philosopher than an astronomer, but his heliocentric view of planetary motion was revolutionary.

ian astronomers were the first to calculate in advance the appearance of a new moon (when the lunar crescent first appeared after sunset). Archaeologists have found hundreds of cuneiform tablets that show the precise mathematical calculations used to determine the phases of the moon.

The ancient seafaring Greeks described how the constellations such as Orion the Hunter, The Great Bear (Big Dipper) and the Pleiades (Seven Sisters) could be used in navigation. A poem composed by Hesiod described to farmers which constellations rose before dawn at different seasons of the year, as an aid to determining the proper times for plowing, sowing and harvesting.

Even though the Chinese were the first to record a solar eclipse, the Greeks were the first to understand why they occur. Like other ancient civilizations, the Greeks personalized the sun. Early on, they viewed the sun in much the same way as the Egyptians did, but from about the fifth century BC, the sun became associated with the god Phoebus Apollo. It was about this time that a few Greek philosophers began to question the true nature of the sun. Some of the beliefs they held were that of a small sun, a sun very close to Earth, and a flat sun supported by air.

Philolaus, a follower of Pythagoras, believed that the earth, sun, moon and planets revolved around a central fire hidden from view by a "counter-Earth". About 370BC, Eudoxus of Cnidus wrote that a giant sphere bearing the stars moved around the earth daily. Aristarchus was one of the first to believe that Earth turns around on its axis once every 24 hours and revolves around the sun. Most Greek philosophers scorned his ideas, because they believed Earth was a motionless globe. The popular theory, known as "geocentric" (Earth-centered) remained the scientific standard for almost 2,000 years.

Plato, who was well aware of the patterns of the sun, moon and planets across the sky, suggested that their paths were a combination of simple circular motions. Eudoxus, a student at Plato's academy, placed all the fixed stars on a huge starry sphere that rotated above a smaller sphere, Earth, once every 24 hours. Eudoxus went on to state that the sun was attached to yet another sphere within the large sphere. Aristotle wrote a narrative which accounted for all the observed planetary motion—his work stated there were 55 concentric transparent spheres!

A Timeline in Astronomy

813AD Al Mamon founds the Baghdad school of astronomy. *Mathematike Syntaxis* by Ptolemy is translated into Arabic as *al-Majisti* (Great Work).

903 Al-Sufi draws up his star catalogue.

1054 Chinese astronomers observe supernova in Taurus.

1543 Copernicus publishes *De Revolutionibus* in which he provides mathematical evidence for the heliocentric theory of the Universe.

1576 Tycho Brahe founds the observatory at Uraniborg.

1600 Giordano Bruno is charged with blasphemy, immoral conduct and heresy for challenging the official church doctrine on the origin and structure of the universe. He is burned at the stake.

1609 Galileo first uses the telescope for astronomical purposes.

1631 Kepler predicts the Transit of Mercury which is observed by Gassendi.

1633 Galileo is forced by the Inquisition to recant his theories.

1666 Cassini observes the polar caps on Mars.

1668 Isaac Newton builds the first reflecting telescope.

1687 Newton publishes his revolutionary *Philosophiae Naturalis Principia Mathematica*, considered to be a turning point in the history of science.

1705 Halley predicts the return of the comet later named after him in 1758.

1750 Thomas Wright speculates about the origin of the solar system.

1781 Charles Messier, searching for the comets, discovers galaxies, nebulae, and star clusters which he compiles in his catalogue.

1814 Fraunhofer provides a detailed description of the solar spectrum.

1837 Beer and Madler publish the first accurate map of the moon.

1851 Foucault provides evidence for the rotation of the Earth.

1897 The Yerkes Observatory is founded.

Beginning in 1781, Charles Messier discovered and catalogued over 100 galaxies, nebulae, and star clusters.

Renaissance Astronomy

From our modern perspective, it's difficult to imagine being born into a world where no one realized stars were suns, and where the Church controlled the state of scientific thought. In the 15th century, it was still believed that Earth was the center of the universe, and that the sun was a pure, unblemished body. This was the world of the Polish scholar, Nicholas Copernicus.

Born in 1473, Copernicus studied both medicine and law and became a skilled physician. Around 1510, he became interested in the solar system — not so much as a full-fledged astronomer but more of a philosopher who thought the geocentric system was too complex and inaccurate.

Copernicus favored a heliocentric — or sun-centered — theory. He wrote: "And so, as if seated upon a royal throne, the Sun rules the family of the planets as they circle round him." He successfully plotted planetary orbits, understood that Earth and its moon orbited the sun between Venus and Mars, and that Mercury was the planet closest to the sun. However, Copernicus was a political pragmatist. When he published his scientific findings in *De Revolutionibus* (1543) he was shrewd enough to dedicate it to Pope Paul III.

What made Copernicus' work so controversial? Perhaps the Church felt that if the heavens were truly infinite and Earth just one of many planets, human status would lose its uniqueness and the power of the Church would decline. However, in a geocentric world — the world dictated by the Church — the universe was created to serve man and revolve around him.

Because the Aristotelian philosophy of an Earth-centered universe coincided with religious beliefs, the Medieval Church declared that other schools of thought were heretical. One of the more outspoken proponents of a Sun-centered universe, Giordano Bruno, was burned at the stake as a religious heretic. Little wonder that Copernicus dedicated his work to the Pope.

The influence of the planets themselves was a popular subject in mid-15th-century Europe. Early "block books" — books created from wood block carvings — contained depictions of the planets in anthropomorphic form, along with the condition of their "children" — the people influenced at birth by the planet. The text described Jupiter as:

"Great Jupiter is now my name,
The second planet, strong in fame.
I am moist and truly warm,
By nature I can do no harm.
Two signs I have, their houses mine-
Archer and fishes, which golden shine.
Seek and prove me there, I pray:
Much good will surely come your
way.
When in the Crab, I'm lifted high.
Weaker, in the Goat I sigh.
My passage round the twelve signs is
In twelve long years accomplished."

For block book readers in the Middle Ages, the entire solar system was set up and put in motion by God, and it was by His will that the planets influenced life on Earth in a regular way. In addition, the planets were thought to have an influence on people's health. Wise men of the day used astronomically-based tables which recommended the correct days or zodiacal position of the moon for bleeding or purgation.

A scientist named Galileo Galilei, working with the newly invented telescope, discovered the phases of Venus which indicated to him that the planet revolved around the sun. He also discovered four moons revolving around Jupiter, as well as the rings of Saturn. Galileo also turned his telescope to the Sun and reported the imperfections which dotted its surface —

Galileo Galilei discovered Jupiter's four large moons and the rings of Saturn. He also supported a heliocentric view of the solar system, until the Church forced him to recant.

sunspots. Although he wasn't the first to report sunspots — Aristotle's pupil Theophratus made the first sunspot report in the fourth century BC — he was the first to study them through a telescope. Beginning in 1608, Galileo began three years of sunspot observations and concluded that they were part of the sun's surface, not high-flying birds!

Galileo began to speak in favor of the Copernican theory, however his attempts to publicize these beliefs caused his arrest and subsequent trial, at which he was forced to recant his beliefs.

While Galileo's sunspot observations laid the foundation for the next century of solar studies, he didn't stray too far out on an astronomical limb when speculating about the Cosmos. For example, Galileo didn't believe that stars were other suns, although French astronomer Rene Descartes (1596-1650) did. Descartes even moved from France to Holland where he felt it would be safer to explore his ideas. But even Descartes didn't go so far as to suggest planetary systems around stars other than our own. He knew what *that* theory had earned Giordano Bruno.

Emergence of the Modern Astronomers

From 1580 to 1597, Danish astronomer Tycho Brahe observed the sun, moon and planets, keeping a meticulous record of their movement. Convinced that advances in astronomy could only take place through accurate observation, he strove to keep a consistent record of the work done at his observatory on an island near Copenhagen. In total, Brahe catalogued over 1,000 stars.

Based on Brahe's data, his German assistant, Johannes Kepler, formulated the laws of planetary motion, stating that the planets revolve around the sun in elliptical orbits at varying speeds, and that their distances from the sun can be determined from the observed periods of revolution.

Using Kepler's work, Sir Isaac Newton argued that a force exists between the sun and each of the planets. This force, which depends on the masses of the sun and planets, and on the distances between them, provides the basis for the physical interpretation of Kepler's laws. Newton's mathematical discovery is called the law of universal gravitation.

After Newton's time, astronomy branched out in several directions, as scientists used the telescope and newly emerging theories to better understand celestial mechanics. Discoveries came fast and furious.

In 1705, Edmond Halley correctly predicted the return of the comet that now bears his name. Charles Messier, another comet-seeker, catalogued over 100 galaxies, nebulae and star clusters. The planet Uranus was discovered by William Herschel in 1781, Fraunhofer split the light in the solar spectrum, and Foucault provided evidence for Earth's rotational movements.

Although more sophisticated instruments would be designed, the basic tools of the astronomer were now in place and the era of modern astronomy had begun.

HM

"If you haven't discovered Family Chronicle, you are in for a treat... [it is] beautifully produced and informative."

Myra Vanderpool Gormley, C.G. Los Angeles Times Syndicate

"One of the most informative magazines I have ever seen." — Carole Kiernan, *Family Heirlooms*

"Without a doubt the best journalistically and genealogically printed magazine." — Al and Margaret Spiry, *Madison Courier*

"It belongs on every researcher's bookshelf to be used again and again." — Carllene Marek, *Ancestree-Seekers*

"[*Family Chronicle*] has matured into the acknowledged finest genealogical magazine available today." — Bob Meeker, *Legacy of America*

"[*Family Chronicle*] has been one of the brightest new publications, with articles which [are] both easy to read and written by authorities." — Kenneth H. Thomas Jr., *Atlanta Journal Constitution*

FOR INFORMATION ON BULK SALES CALL
(416) 491-3699

How Good Are Internet Subscription Databases?

Family Chronicle
The Magazine for Families Researching their Roots

January/February 2001

$4.50 U.S.
$5.50 Cdn

French-Canadian Roots

Fraudulent Genealogies

The Lost City of Henricus

Websites Worth Surfing

How to Research Fraternal Society Records

What Counts as Evidence?

Champlain Street, Quebec City

Legacy Family Tree 3.0 Review

Now Available FREE See Page 28

Visit Our Website:
www.familychronicle.com

Family Chronicle
The Magazine for Families Researching their Roots

Use any of these three convenient ways to subscribe:

- Phone Toll-Free **1-888-326-2476**. Please have your Credit Card ready.
- Fax this order form to (416) 491-3996.
- Mail to: *See US and Canadian addresses on page 3.*

Please use this form when ordering at this special rate.

I want to subscribe for:

❑ One year (6 issues) at $24 US / $28 Cdn ❑ Two years (12 issues) at $40 US / $45 Cdn
Payment by: ❑ Check (enclosed) Charge my Credit Card: ❑ Visa ❑ MasterCard
Canadian orders add 7% GST or 15% HST as applicable. Quebec residents add 7.5% QST.

Card Number_____ Expiry Date_____ / _____

Signature_____

Last Name_____ First Name_____

Address_____

City_____ State/Prov. _____ Zip/ Postal Code _____

Phone Number_____ GST# 139340186 RT

Family Chronicle does not rent or sell subscriber names.

HM9

The All-American Spirit

Edwin M. Knights, Jr. immerses himself in the story of bourbon.

WHEN THE VIKINGS began to explore the strange new land they'd found by sailing westward across the sea, a few of them came far enough south to find nuts and grapes, but they probably didn't have the opportunity to make wine. Some time later this feat was accomplished by the English settlers, who found abundant wild grapes co-existing with the poison ivy of New England. The development of sea trade with the West Indies brought supplies of molasses, from which the settlers could distill rum. The 18th century brought Scotch-Irish and Prussian immigrants whose talents included making whiskey. All they needed was some barley. Alas, barley proved to be a reluctant immigrant — difficult to grow in American soil. But rye did just fine, and by mid-century rye whiskey was abundant and popular. Too popular, perhaps, because when Washington desperately needed money to pay off the war debts in 1791, he turned to an old British custom — the excise tax.

Washington didn't expect an enthusiastic reception, and he didn't get one. Many had fought in the Revolutionary War in protest of British taxation. Now their own government was doing the same thing to them, taxing the very citizens who'd risked their lives to serve their country. The distillers rebelled, the veterans rebelled, and they had lots of support from the whiskey-drinking public. They tarred and feathered the unfortunate tax collectors, even burning their homes. The "Whiskey Rebellion" had to be quelled by Federal troops.

Westward Ho!

Large numbers of settlers were already moving westward from Virginia's coastal areas. The state's economy was heavily dependent upon growing tobacco, but the tobacco fields had to be rotated in

Bourbon can be enjoyed in Manhattans and mint juleps. Harry Truman and Sam Rayburn proclaimed "bourbon and branch water" as their favorite drink.

order to produce the best crops. The best land was already in the hands of a few wealthy, aristocratic families. News came of fertile land just to the west. At that time the area was still part of Virginia, but it would later become Kentucky. Patrick Henry promoted and succeeded in passing the "corn patch and cabin rights" law, giving settlers land rights if they built a cabin and grew corn. The corn grew well, and soon there was a surplus — enough to distill. By the late 1700s there was enough "corn likker" to roll the barrels onto flat boats and ship them down the Ohio and Mississippi Rivers from piers at Limestone, in Bourbon County. Thus the tradition of bourbon in oak barrels was born. The bourbon they drank then in New Orleans was aged only by the length of time it took to make its way down the mighty Mississippi.

Aging Perfects The Product

Any sailor who drank "torpedo juice" during WWII can attest that whiskey can be much improved by aging. Although some folks credit the Baptist minister Elijah Craig with creating bourbon, it was a Scotsman, Dr. James Crow, who first aged the liquor in charred oak casks to produce a product much like the bourbon we know today. By 1850, sour mash bourbon was a reality — a distinctly American product. Many years later Congress even appropriated exclusive use of the old French name. Although bourbon does not have to be made in Kentucky, as some purists insist, it must be made in one of the United States to be labeled bourbon.

What's In A Name?

Just as other spirits, such as rum, rye or single malt scotch have unique characteristics, bourbons vary according to their ingredients and methods of distillation. Each manufacturer has tried to leave its own imprint on its products. But there are strict guidelines that they must follow if their product is to be "straight" or "blended". Rye whiskey, which was the most popular spirit prior to bourbon, already came in straight or blended varieties.

To qualify as a straight whiskey, it must be distilled entirely from grains. Only water can be added to achieve the desired alcohol concentration or proof. Straight bourbon must contain at least 51 percent corn; the other grains are not specified and give much of the character that defines the various manufacturers' products. Blended whiskeys are fortified with neutral grain spirits and usually have added flavorings or colorings. Straight whiskey must end up with less than 80 percent alcohol by volume. It must be aged at least two years in new charred oak barrels, but now nearly all bourbon is aged four or more years. It can contain no added coloring or flavoring.

Heating the barrel staves helps to bend them into shape to make the bourbon barrels. This results in an inner red layer which both colors and flavors the product. The insides of the assembled barrels are also charred with open flames, further contributing to the distinct flavor.

Sour Mash Whiskey

It was Dr. James Crow who developed the sour mash method of distilling bourbon. Following the first distillation, he drained the liquid from the leftover mash of grain and added it to the mash of cooked grains and yeast of the next batch. This tends to reproduce the features of the bourbon in each succeeding batch, at the same time controlling the acidity of the mash. Most straight bourbons are made by this method.

The grains that control bourbon's flavor are known as the mashbill. As noted, the law requires at least 51 percent corn in bourbon, but most have over 70 percent. Among other grains, rye is the most popular. Adding rye gives bourbon a spicier taste, while wheat seems to add smoothness. Malted barley is present to start fermentation. But there other factors which contribute to the flavor of the final product. The water is extremely important.

Distilling and redistilling is done in a variety of stills with such intriguing names as thumpers and doublers. Some brewers are returning to the use of pot-stills of copper construction. Aging is also critical, but so are factors such as temperature, the thickness of char on barrel linings and even the practice, by some distillers, of barrel rotation. Yeast strains differ, and distillers guard and pamper their yeast strains, even adding hops or lactic acid-producing bacteria to the yeast mashes.

It is apparent that there are many ways bourbon can be coaxed into providing a distinct

CAPT. POE (1807-88), like other old salts, often lashed a keg of whiskey beneath his rocker and rocked it mellow. He recaptured the rolling motion of his ships at sea on which he'd mellowed many casks of whiskey.

The Old Custom of "Rocking the Keg" led to Smooth, Mellow Rocking Chair!

THESE "KEG-ROCKED" whiskeys taught Old Mr. Boston how rocking mellows whiskey. So in Rocking Chair he recaptures that flavor by *controlled agitation* in his special blending process.

GET ROCKING CHAIR today! Treat yourself to that rich, mellow flavor that won such widespread fame for whiskeys "rocked in the keg." Treat your purse to a surprisingly low price!

95 Proof (86 Proof in some States), 75% Grain Neutral Spirits
Ben-Burk, Inc., Boston, Mass.

OLD MR. BOSTON
BRAND
ROCKING CHAIR
BLENDED WHISKEY

In the post-war period, many distilleries merged and appeared under new ownership. Some brands disappeared.

taste to combine with a unique bottle, a witty slogan and clever marketing. Surprisingly, the ingredient that is never mentioned is the grain that is the foundation for the whole bourbon industry: corn. Thanks to breeding techniques which are now blessed (or cursed) with the description of "genetic engineering", recent years have seen the introduction of remarkably improved corn, especially that which ends up in the supermarket. Hybrid varieties, having kernels with high sugar content, give grocery store corn features that only could be found in corn "picked with the morning dew still on its husk." It is hard to believe that the industry has been blind to this development, but they are strangely silent about it.

The Cocktail

Although many prefer to savor

their favorite bourbon neat or on the rocks, drinkers love to experiment with mixed drinks and bourbon ended up in many of them. Some mixed drinks seem to have been created by grabbing a fistful of bottles that were nearby on the shelf, but a few have qualities which have given them enthusiastic devotees world wide.

At a banquet given in the 1870s by Lady Jenny Churchill honoring Samuel J. Tilden in New York's Manhattan Club, the Manhattan made its debut. Its combination of straight bourbon and sweet vermouth (in about a 2:1 ratio), plus a couple of dashes of bitters, is still popular today. Of course the traditional Kentucky drink is the mint julep, especially appropriate if imbibed from a silver stirrup on the day of the Kentucky Derby. Some connoisseurs love to debate whether or not the mint leaves should be crushed, while others would rather just gaze cross-eyed at the leaves on top of the drink, as they taste the sweetened bourbon through a straw. After a few juleps the eyes remain crossed even if the mint leaves have fallen to the floor. And, "By the way, who won the Derby?"

The sweet bourbon old-fashioned and its tart cousin, the whiskey sour, offer contrasting but refreshing solutions for quenching one's thirst on a hot summer's day (or, if you prefer, a cold winter's night).

Bourbon On The Rocks

Bourbon has had a rocky road to travel in the more than two centuries it has been on the scene, even if it was a cottage industry before America had cottages. Back when drugs were not a major social problem, alcohol was already taking its toll. Not without some justification, it was deplored by the abolitionists. Temperance tracts were widely distributed early in the 19th century. The crusade against demon rum and the evils of alcohol inspired many a Sunday sermon. Bourbon had hardly made its presence known when T. S.

Arthur wrote his famous book which, in the words of the publisher, came "just at the right time, when the subject of restrictive laws is agitating the whole country, and good and true men everywhere are gathering up their strength for a prolonged and unflinching contest." Arthur's book was entitled *Ten Nights in a Bar-Room and What I Saw There*. Published in 1854, it "traces the downward course of the tempting vender and his infatuated victims, until both are involved in hopeless ruin."

It was mainly women who carried the temperance torch. The Women's Christian Temperance Union, founded in 1874, was but one of many temperance groups organized by ladies fiercely dedicated to their cause. One of the most devout and determined crusaders was Mrs. Carry A. Nation, whose husband's drinking had ruined their marriage. Carry stalked into saloons wielding her hatchet and when she emerged, often in the custody of the law, the beer barrels couldn't even be used as planters. By 1916 saloons were banned in 21 states, largely through the efforts of the Anti-Saloon League.

The Noble Experiment
On 16 January 1919, Nebraska became the last state needed to ban the manufacture, sale or transportation of intoxicating liquors, by passing the 18th Amendment to the US Constitution. The resulting Volstead Act was aimed at the entire liquor business and all-male saloons which were threatening the quality of family life across the nation.

Prohibition's "noble experiment" resulted in the proliferation of organized crime, demoralization of countless police departments forced to serve under corrupt public officials and more flagrant disregard for the

Temperance movement member Mrs. Carry A. Nation was known to enter saloons with a hatchet. When Nation was escorted out in the custody of the law, the barrels couldn't even be used as planters.

law than America had ever previously experienced. Known criminals drove defiantly through the cities in their armored cars, more concerned about confrontations with rival gangsters than with law enforcement officials. Bribed city employees, confronted with exposure of their newly-acquired wealth, would plead their innocence — the standard excuse involved the surprise appearance of a cash-filled "little tin box" inherited from some kindly relative.

Prevarication prospered under Prohibition, which also encouraged ingenuity and talent for improvisation. Two-thirds of the liquor came from Canada; most of the rest arrived by sea. High-speed launches churned across Lake St. Clair and the Detroit River. A "rum-row" of whiskey-laden freighters lay anchored off New York City, just outside federal jurisdiction limits. Following the enactment of Prohibition, the federal government took over all the warehouses of

the distilleries, padlocking them and placing them under surveillance. In spite of elaborate attempts at federal protection, legal liquor destined for "medicinal use" mysteriously disappeared from numerous distilleries. According to Sam Cecil, some of this was replaced by moonshine that was left to age after which it was also stolen. Many other warehouses were merely torched to conceal the theft of whiskey.

Prohibition proved a boon to winery owners. Under the new law, private individuals were allowed to make 200 gallons of wine at home "for personal consumption." Anyone in the wine business became a grape grower and shipper. In addition, bootlegging was profitable and quite safe. Over 300,000 acres of vineyards were planted during Prohibition. A dealer in Chicago could sell 25 freight-car loads of grapes a day. Many customers bought far more boxes than needed to make their allotted 200 gallons. Mobsters under Al Capone controlled most of the distributors in the Chicago area, enforced by at least 400 gangland killings.

Meanwhile, while individual citizens across the country experimented with bathtub gin, the distillers of Kentucky, West Virginia and Tennessee proved equal to the challenge. Not wanting their skills to become rusty, they blanketed the mountaintops with the fragrance of wood smoke and distilling whiskey. As the old song goes:
*"My Uncle Will's got a still
  on the hill
Where he brews up a gallon
  or two.
The birds in the sky get so
  drunk they can't fly
Just from sniffin' that good
  ol' mountain dew."*
Call it mountain dew, moon-

shine or white lightnin', it found its way into many jugs during Prohibition, while the distillers impatiently waited for better times to return. Or did they? Perhaps some of them never had it so good. We'll never know! We note that federal regulations still have a category called corn whiskey. If it is aged, and aging is not required, it can be in either new or used uncharred oak barrels. Probably little prohibition booze even met those standards.

Despite elaborate attempts at federal protection, legal liquor destined for "medicinal use" disappeared during Prohibition.

Rebirth Of Bourbon: Prolonged And Painful

Prohibition ended in December 1933 — the first constitutional amendment ever to be repealed. It wasn't a total failure, as public drunkenness decreased and alcohol-related illnesses declined. Effects of its repeal were slow to be felt by the bourbon industry, as public alcohol consumption didn't return to pre-Prohibition levels until 1975. Prominent politicians, such as Harry Truman and Sam Rayburn proclaimed "bourbon and branch water" as their favorite drinks, but whiskey now faced serious competition from sophisticated scotch and widespread use of vodka, gin and rum in mixed drinks. Even in the economy market, Thunderbird, at 60 cents per quart, soared far above Old Crow in the Battle of the Birds. Wine became more popular, and production of inexpensive domestic wines matching the quality of costly imports added further competition in the liquor industry.

Even prior to Prohibition, bourbon distilleries were struggling to stay in existence. The Distillers and Cattle Feeders Trust, established in 1887 to control the production of industrial alcohol, managed to circumvent antitrust laws and buy or close more than 40 Kentucky distilleries at the end of the 19th cen-

tury. By the time Prohibition was law, half of the acquired facilities had disappeared, with only the most popular brand names surviving. Some were produced in Canada. After repeal, the bourbon industry faced competition from Canadian and Scottish whiskeys. This continued right on through WWII, when Joe Kennedy, America's Ambassador to Great Britain, was able to fill supply ships returning to the US with scotch.

In the post-war years, as the public was became increasingly concerned with quality, the bourbon industry was self-destructing. Distilleries kept merging and appearing under new ownership. Many attracted foreign investors. More attention was being paid to marketing than to product excellence and individuality. Aging of bourbon was reduced to the minimum and distillation was modified to increase productivity rather than improving product standards.

The Sweet Fragrance Of Success

Eventually, nine Kentucky distillers survived, although you will find several old familiar brand names associated with each. The bourbon distillers have found the key to success is making quality a

top priority for all their products. Master distillers, talented and skillful, direct the surviving facilities. They use their abilities to create superior, individually recognizable bourbons for each of their brand names. Their efforts have resulted in a new appreciation of this uniquely American product — an appreciation which has become global. Some of their most loyal customers are the Japanese, many of whom enjoy American whiskey and can afford the top-of-the-line brands. Another factor which contributes to their continuing success is that it takes a lot of land to grow corn. So far, corn-laden container ships haven't been seen shuttling back across the Pacific to Japanese distillers and there doesn't seem to be a rush to produce hydroponic maize. Meanwhile, Japanese distributors and others involved in liquor sales enjoy their annual pilgrimage to Bardstown, Kentucky.

Further Reading

Apple, R. W., Jr., "Born-Again Bourbon" in *Civilization* (Library of Congress; Dec. 1999/Jan. 2000).

Dabney, Joseph Earl, *Mountain Spirits: A Chronicle of Corn Whiskey from King James's Ulster Plantation to America's Appalachians and the Moonshine Life* (New York; Charles Scribner's Sons, 1974).

Dabney, Joseph Earl, *More Mountain Spirits* (Asheville, NC; Bright Mountain Books, 1980).

Kroll, Harry H., *Bluegrass, Belles and Bourbon: A Pictorial History of Whiskey in Kentucky* (New Jersey; A.S. Barnes, 1967).

Cecil, Sam K., *The Evolution of the Bourbon Whiskey Industry in Kentucky* (Paducah, KT; Turner Publishing Co., 1999).

Regan, Gary and Mardee Haidin Regan, *The Bourbon Companion: A Connoisseur's Guide* (Philadelphia; Running Press, 1998).

HM

Office Life Before 1920

Barbara Krasner-Khait examines how offices worked before 1920.

PRIOR TO 1870, business was dominated by simple partnerships and small offices, entirely staffed by men. Most employees began their careers as office boys, eventually becoming copyists, clerks or bookkeepers, with the thought of one day running their own business. Division of labor was pretty rudimentary and workers performed a variety of tasks, learning about the business along the way. Until the end of the 19th century, many clerks were working as apprentices as a means of learning the business. The one exception to this was the copyist, who was hired specifically to perform a single task — to transcribe letters and other documents.

Office employees had close contact with their employers, worked fairly autonomously and accepted the responsibilities they were given. Often the relationship between employer and worker took on a paternal nature. Loyalty to the employer was the name of the game.

After 1870, dramatic changes occurred in North American business. National corporations formed, downtown offices expanded, businesses consolidated, and as offices grew, so did their need for workers. By 1900 women made up more than one-third of all clerical workers, and by 1920, more than half. These working women tended to be white, young and living on their own. Clerical jobs paid better than factory work, domestic service or retail, and offered economic and social mobility. Bureaucracy, hierarchy and need for re-organization grew. Larger companies required efficient operation and order.

Clerks lost control over their work as specific tasks were defined. Instead of being responsible for an entire transaction, the clerk became a "process worker". With specialization in a depart-

Typewriters helped pave the way for women to enter the office.

ment like accounting, purchasing, auditing, credit, personnel, marketing or filing, taking responsibility for a piece of the entire process became the accepted way to conduct business. The office began to operate like an assembly line.

Efficiency in the office was introduced for greater output and greater profits. William Henry Leffingwell introduced "scientific management" to the office. The foundation of this belief system was the assumption that anyone's work could be reduced to a single task.

Clocking — And Docking — Time

Many employers had trouble getting their employees to work every single minute they were paid. Leffingwell talked of how one company went about dealing with the problem. It made its hours nine to five and instituted time sheets with a 15-minute grace period until 9:15 a.m. Any employee arriving later would have his or her pay docked. To help matters, the time clock entered the business office in 1910.

Efficiency did, of course, improve. A clerk who could only handle some 20 letters before and with some difficulty, could now handle 60 with ease. Like behavior modification systems used today, there were contests, rewards and recognition in the office to congratulate the efficient worker. Says Adrian Forty in *Objects of Desire: Design and Society from Wedgwood to IBM*, "Managers were advised to cultivate friendly relations with their staff, to drop casual hints about how much more work one was managing to do than another, to chart the production of each worker and offer gold stars to those who exceeded the weekly norms, and to set up, in a spirit of healthy fun, office competitions to see who could achieve most in a week."

Desk Set

The desk became a tool "for making the quickest possible turnover of business papers." Gone was the standard 19th century senior clerk's desk, such as the famous Wooton Rotary Desk, with a high back with cubbies and drawers, where the worker could squirrel away papers in all the nooks and crannies. This was an enemy of efficiency and obstructed the flow of paper. Instead, the clerk would work at a flat-top desk, like the Modern Efficiency Desk, designed for the Equitable Assurance Company in 1915 — a flat-top desk with shallow drawers and no privacy. In fact, managers sometimes checked the drawers to monitor the clerk's

ny was not without its problems. It found itself with a temporary glut of tea and financial burden. In May 1773, British Parliament passed the Tea Act of 1773, authorizing the company to export a half million pounds of tea to the American colonies without the usual export duties and tariffs in an effort to save "the corrupt and mismanaged company" from bankruptcy. This move would enable the company to undercut any competitors, including smugglers, in the American market. In New York, Philadelphia and Charleston, colonists were successful in forcing tea shipments to return or be warehoused. In late 1773, three ships landed at Boston Harbor. Company agents refused to resign as their counterparts had in the other colonies and they were supported by the local governor. In retaliation and to prevent the heavily-taxed tea from selling on the open market, Samuel Adams, Paul Revere and others disguised themselves as Mohawks, broke open the more than 300 tea chests, and threw them into the harbor.

But there was more to the story than met the eye. One Boston Tea Party-er, George Hewes, recalled: "During the time we were throwing the tea overboard, there were several attempts made by some of the citizens of Boston and its vicinity to carry off small quantities of it for their family use.... One Captain O'Connor, whom I well knew, came on board for that purpose, and when he supposed he was not noticed, filled his pockets, and also the lining of his coat.... The next morning, after we had cleared the ships of the tea, it was discovered that very considerable quantities of it were floating upon the surface of

The Japanese have elevated the making of tea into an elaborate ceremony.

the water; and to prevent the possibility of any of it being saved for use, a number of small boats were manned by sailors and citizens, who rowed them into those parts of the harbor wherever the tea was visible, and by beating it with oars and paddles so thoroughly drenched it as to render its entire destruction inevitable."

Despite the loss of the American market, tea continued to be a major revenue source for Britain and taxes continued. By the 1830s, the British East India Company

A Russian samovar kept as many as 40 cups of tea ready to enjoy.

was importing an average of 29 million pounds of tea each year into the United Kingdom from Canton. It hired a fleet of more than 20 large vessels to carry it. It had a fix on pricing.

But the British East India Company was still in financial trouble. The Manchus of China demanded that the company pay for the tea in silver bullion. To deal with this, the company found a way for India-grown opium into Chinese markets.

The End of One Monopoly Begins Another
The charter of the financially troubled East India Company was up for renewal in 1834. Opposing merchants from Glasgow, Liverpool and Bristol took advantage of this. A case had been growing against the company for some time, arguing unfair pricing and deals. A committee conducted studies, asking for reports and samples from all over Europe and America. A bill providing that the company should cease to trade was introduced into Parliament, received the Royal Assent in the summer of 1833, and went into effect in April 1834. Thus ended the monopoly on China tea.

In 1834, the British East India Company, its wings clipped, decided to move its trade to India and therefore within the borders of the British Empire. There had been many attempts to introduce the Chinese tea plant into India but without success. A fortuitous discovery of indigenous tea in India's Assam region meant that the British Empire could grow its own supply and monopolize production, sale and distribution.

Ceylon, which became a British crown colony in 1798, suffered the loss of its coffee estates to a fungus. It, too, became a major site of tea production.

By 1888, tea exports from India surpassed those of China

The Art Of Tea In Europe

Afternoon tea became a custom in Britain and the Netherlands in the 17th century, in an effort to ward off hunger pangs between lunch and dinner. Unlike coffee consumed in the coffee house, tea was a part of home life, probably because its expense limited consumption to the well-to-do. Tea was considered a meal and involved the family. If guests were part of the meal, they became, in turn, temporary members of the family. Servants and other members of household staff typically took their tea separately from the family. And there was a ritual. Woodruff D. Smith writes in *Consuming Habits* (Routledge, 1995), "Tea was intended to manifest family solidarity. It was the duty of the presiding woman to make sure it did so, and the duty of the other participants to defer to her leadership... it was part of what it meant to be a family, a ritual that gave a family as a whole a psychological meaning apart from the dual relationships among individuals in it."

Tea gardens and "high tea" customs developed as well. By 1732, an evening spent dancing or watching fireworks in the gardens would be rounded off by serving tea. More and more tea gardens opened in Britain. Afternoon tea became high tea for the masses, where hot tea, meats, bread and cakes were served.

American colonists dumping tea into Boston Harbor.

and the China tea trade began to decline. Aiding the decline was the demand shift toward Empire-grown black teas. Eventually, British East Africa — Nyasaland, Kenya and Tanganyika — joined in the tea production. All around, the tea trade within the Empire was a well-run machine.

A Glass of Chai in Russia

In Russia, the Imperial court began favoring the drink as early as the 17th century. Tea was introduced to Russia by the Khan of Mongolia, who had presented 100 pounds of it to a Russian embassy. Several 19th century developments led to tea's widespread use in Russia: the opening of the Treaty Ports, the cutting of the Suez Canal, the founding of Russia's merchant marine, and the opening of the Trans-Siberian Railway. Tea was so cheap that nearly everyone could afford to drink it. Russian literature is filled with examples of huddling around the samovar, which always kept tea — about 40 cups of it — ready.

The American Contribution

Daniel Vernon and Benjamin Harris were granted a license to sell tea "in publique" in Boston in 1760. Though not yet taxed, it was too expensive for most colonists to buy. When taxed, of course, it became enormously expensive and was dumped into Boston Harbor in 1773.

The American tea trade began in 1784 when the first American ship sailed to China to pick up a cargo of tea. By 1787, more than one million pounds of tea constituted the trade. Soon tea merchants and shipbuilders worked together to launch fast clipper ships, leading to the famous Yankee clippers.

Tea outsold coffee throughout most of the 19th century. The Volstead Act of 1919, which ushered in Prohibition, led to a dramatic rise in coffee as a substitute for alcohol, ultimately stripping tea of its first-place rank.

Americans provided the tea industry with two innovations. Richard Blechynden, a tea plantation owner, served the first "iced tea" at the 1904 St. Louis World Fair. Four years later, tea wholesaler Thomas Sullivan sent silk-wrapped samples of his tea blends to restaurant customers, marking the debut of the tea bag.

The Brew of Empires

Aside from water, tea is most popular drink in the world. It has had more historical impact on the shape of the world than any other beverage. It's been a source of colonial and national development and a source of revenue. British Prime Minister William Gladstone once said, "Thank God for tea! What would the world do without tea! How did it exist? I am glad I was not born before tea."

Further Reading

Arkin, Marcus. *Storm in a Teacup*. Cape Town, South Africa: C. Struik (Pty) Ltd., 1973.
Forrest, Denys. *Tea for the British: The Social and Economic History of a Famous Trade*. London: Chatto & Windus, 1973.
Okakura, Kakuzo. *The Book of Tea*. Tokyo and New York: Kodansha International, 1989.
Yü, Lu. *The Classic of Tea*. Boston: Little, Brown and Company, 1974.

HM

Subscribe Now to

How did our ancestors live?

History Magazine is targeted at people who want to know about the lives their ancestors led: what did they eat, how much did they earn, what made them laugh or made them cry?

Here are just a few of the topics that are planned for upcoming issues:

THE SHOEMAKER. Shoemaking was one of the last industries to be automated. We present the history of the trade before machines.

CLOTHING FASHIONS IN THE 1850S. What was fashionable and what did ordinary people wear?

ROBERT GODDARD. A look at the first rocket scientist.

THE BICYCLE. The invention, rise and decline of the machine that provided the most efficient method of converting human energy to propulsion.

THE RISE OF UNIVERSITIES. This article traces the development of advanced education from the 12th century.

THE KOREAN WAR. Fifty years ago saw the Korean peninsula in major conflict. Edwin M. Knights Jr. (who was there) describes this "police action".

HISTORY OF TAXATION. How the necessary evil of taxes — including the temporary measure known as income tax — crept into our lives.

Guarantee

There is no risk. If *History Magazine* fails to meet your needs, or live up to the promises we have made, you are entitled to a refund on all unmailed copies for any reason or no reason. Any refund will be made promptly and cheerfully.

Halvor Moorshead
Editor & Publisher

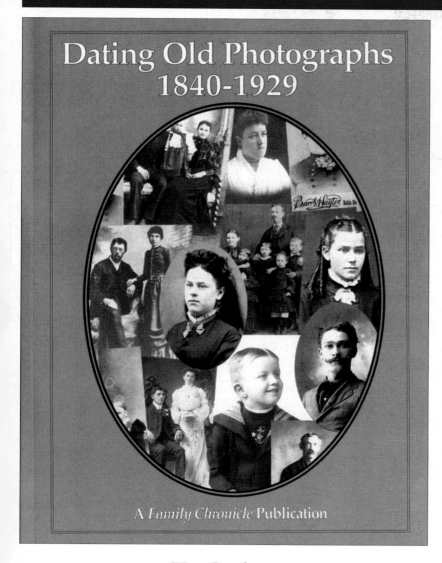

Winged Messengers

Thomas Crowl reveals how pigeons became the humble heroes of wartime.

THEY HAD NICKNAMES like G.I. Joe, Yank, The Mocker and Cher Ami. They were duly enrolled members of the armed services. They experienced combat, suffered wounds and some died. A few won praise from generals, and medals for valor. But they weren't soldiers; they were humble pigeons.

Books, movies and television have documented the role of animals, especially dogs and horses, in the armed forces. Less acknowledged is the part played by homing pigeons. Since the Biblical return of Noah's dove, man has employed winged messengers. Legendary commanders like Julius Caesar and the Duke of Wellington, who kept homing pigeons with their armies, valued the bird's speed and reliability.

The first well-documented use of pigeons in the modern era occurred during the siege of Paris (1870-71) in the Franco-Prussian War. After provoking conflict with the German states, the French were forced into wholesale retreat, and the Germans besieged Paris. Trapped in the city, French government officials made a desperate, but successful, escape by hot air balloon.

Other balloons followed bringing not only aeronauts, but also homing pigeons provided by the bird fanciers of Paris. The pigeons' release and eventual return to their Paris lofts offered a tenuous, but invaluable, link with the outside world. Advances in photography, which allowed for the miniaturization of images, made it possible for a single bird to carry up to 40,000 cryptic messages rolled, waxed and attached to a tail feather. Although only 302 birds participated in this early air mail (57 successfully) their exploits sparked worldwide interest far beyond the actual impact of their contributions. The French soon surrendered, but by 1880 the major military powers of

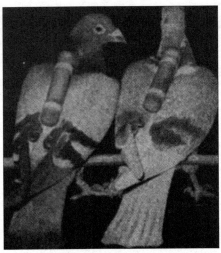

Invaluable when all other means of communication failed, a single pigeon could carry up to 40,000 messages.

continental Europe had established pigeon-messaging services.

Military Value

Pigeons were, at the end of the 19th century, a logical choice for military communications. Telegraph, telephone and wireless communications were in their infancy. A strong tradition of pigeon propagation and fancy in Europe ensured a ready supply of quality birds. Husbandry and training methods were well understood, and lightweight leg bands for identification had been perfected. Pigeons reproduced rapidly making them inexpensive and expendable, and young birds could be up and flying at four months of age.

At first, pigeons were deployed from permanent lofts strategically located along national frontiers or in major cities. It was believed that a trained bird would only return to its fixed home loft, and no other. This required an anticipation of future communication needs in locating the lofts, and lacked flexibility. In 1905, Japanese naval officers, observing pigeons flying from moving Chinese fishing junks, realized that the birds would return to a moving home loft.

This discovery led to the concept of the mobile pigeon loft to which the birds would return, even if the loft was relocated a short distance. This mobility was of great military value since it meant that pigeons could be deployed much closer to the front line, and move with it, reducing message delivery time. The mobile pigeon loft would become the standard means of deploying pigeons on the battlefield.

When war broke out in 1914, most European armies had well-established pigeon services. The Belgians, with a strong tradition of pigeon husbandry, had perhaps the best service in the world. Unfortunately, when Antwerp fell to the advancing Germans, the retreating Belgians destroyed most of their lofts and birds. The remaining Belgian birds were confiscated by the Germans.

The British were an exception. Although they had utilized homing pigeons with some success in the Boer War, by 1908 the British military establishment saw pigeons as obsolete and favored the use of telephone and wireless. However, the obvious value of the birds, as demonstrated by allies and enemies alike, sent the British scrambling to build a pigeon service of their own. In late 1914, A.H. Osman, a well-known racing-pigeon fancier in England, was offered an officer's commission to assemble a top quality pigeon service.

Beginning with donated birds, including his own, Osman first assisted the Royal Navy in establishing a messenger service for coastal patrol vessels, mine sweepers and trawlers, which were not equipped with wireless sets. Thousands of ship-to-shore communications were delivered by these birds during the war, including news of the first Zeppelin attacks on Royal Navy ships.

One of the first dramatic

flights that captured public attention occurred when a German submarine attacked a British trawler, the *Nelson*. The mortally wounded skipper, whose name was Crisp, his boat sinking beneath him, sent a bird off with his location and a plea for assistance. A destroyer arrived to rescue the crew, thanks to the pigeon that, although wounded, completed its mission. Captain Crisp, who went down with his ship, was awarded the Victoria Cross for gallantry. The bird was thereafter recognized as "Crisp, V.C." in honor of the bravery both exhibited.

The British also placed homing pigeons aboard patrol aircraft to relay intelligence, and to assist in locating downed machines. A pigeon named Pilot's Luck flew 200 miles to report the location of two downed seaplanes. Over 700 such urgent messages were delivered by pigeon during the war at average distances of 50 to 150 miles.

Ingenious Intelligence Work
As they came to appreciate the highly organized German mobile loft system, the potential of homing pigeons became obvious to the British Army. Under the command of Major Alec Waley in France, the British pigeon service was in place in time for the disastrous 1916 Somme offensive, and over 400 messages were delivered on the first day of the battle. In the new tank units, pigeons were often the only means of communication available, although strong exhaust fumes tended to disorient the birds. So useful did Osman's creation prove, that the Germans attempted, unsuccessfully, to bomb his London headquarters on Doughty Street more than once.

Recognizing the potential of homing pigeons for intelligence work, the Allies designed vests and overcoats in which agents could hide pigeons. Parachute baskets, containing pigeons suspended in corsets, were dropped to agents behind the lines. Unusually ingenious was a small balloon with multiple single bird

The mobile pigeon loft, able to relocate as the front lines shifted, became the standard means of deploying pigeons on the battlefield.

baskets attached by a ring to a timer. Released into favorable winds, the balloons were designed to periodically release a basket over occupied territory, where it parachuted to the ground. It was hoped that patriotic civilians would follow the instructions to place any information they felt important in the bird's message capsule, and release it. Civilians who failed to turn birds they found over to the German occupiers faced harsh penalties. The Germans occasionally replaced Allied pigeons with their own in the baskets to entrap civilians passing intelligence.

Among the Allies, the Italians deployed a very large pigeon service, which by 1917 had as many as 30,000 pigeons. The French found homing pigeons invaluable during battles like Verdun when all other communications failed. The employment of mobile lofts, usually only a few miles from the front, ensured that 98 percent of these messages were delivered, often in minutes, due to the bird's 40 mph air speed.

America Plays Catch-Up
The Americans, latecomers to the Great War, lacked almost every military necessity, including homing pigeons. The US Army's

flirtation with pigeons began modestly under Nelson Miles' command in Dakota Territory in the 1870s. Although General Miles later wrote that he felt the birds could be "quite useful," those in the Dakotas were mishandled and plagued by predatory hawks. Thereafter, periodic experiments by the Army and Navy, which included flights from Havana to Key West, and forays into Mexico with the Punitive Expedition in 1916, failed to impress the War Department. On the eve of America's entry into WWI, there was no pigeon service.

However, in July 1917, when American Expeditionary Force commander General John J. Pershing and his staff inspected Allied armies in France, and saw first hand the success of pigeon messaging, he requested an American version. The War Department authorized the US Army Signal Corps to proceed. It was the beginning of a 40-year relationship between pigeons and the US Army.

Selected to create the new pigeon service for the Signal Corps was an infantry lieutenant, Wendell Levi, who had extensive prewar pigeon racing and breeding experience. He was directed to study the employment of

Soldiers with prior experience handling pigeons in civilian life were selected for the pigeon units and became known as pigeoneers.

mobile lofts. Beginning with just 60 donated birds and 65 men, Levi laid the foundation for a pigeon service. Levi himself, however, preferred the infantry and left the pigeons to sail with his division to France in 1918.

Chosen to command the Signal Corps pigeon units in France were two lieutenants, J.L. Carney and D.C. Buscall. Together they selected soldiers with prior experience handling pigeons in civilian life, who would be known thereafter as pigeoneers. Their first lofts were constructed in the shadow of the Statue of Liberty to acclimate the birds for the ocean voyage to France.

It was during this time that Lt. Buscall designed an American version of a combat mobile pigeon loft. Constructed by a Cincinnati wagon maker, it contained perches and nest boxes for a minimum of 70 birds. There were removable observation cages, a bird-bathing pan and an insulated water tank. The trapping mechanism for returning pigeons could signal arrivals electrically. Each loft was to be manned by a sergeant, corporal and private, frequently assisted by a motorcycle dispatch rider.

During the August-September 1918 St. Mihiel offensive, the first major American action, almost 400 pigeons went "over the top" with American troops, most with infantry, but some

with tanks. Although poor flying weather predominated, 90 important messages were delivered. Ironically, as was often the case in WWI, many of the birds were acquired from the French.

Decorated Heroes
The hard fought Meuse-Argonne offensive saw another 400 birds deployed, and produced America's most famous war bird, Cher Ami. During the first week of October 1918, Cher Ami was one of eight birds accompanying a battalion of the 77th Division as it took the offensive in the Argonne. The battalion, commanded by Major Charles Whittlesay, was inadequately supported in its advance and cut off by German counterattacks. Known for posterity as the "Lost Battalion," the men were more out of communication than lost, but still pinned down and surrounded. Those eight pigeons became Whittlesay's only connection to headquarters.

After two days, with casualties mounting and his men suffering from friendly artillery fire, the Major called for his last pigeon, his bird handler having allowed the seventh bird to escape. Cher Ami was a small, black checked bird, a British donation from Colonel Osman, with a dozen successful flights to its credit.

Thirty minutes and 25 miles

away, Cher Ami appeared at her loft missing a leg, an eye and with a bullet wound in the breast. Nevertheless, Whittlesay's frantic message to stop the misdirected artillery barrage was still attached to her leg, its last line reading, "For heaven's sake, stop it!" Cher Ami survived to receive the French *Croix de Guerre*, and a send off for home by no less than General Pershing.

Cher Ami was a worldwide sensation, but not unique. A bird named The Mocker carried a message spotting German artillery, which was silenced by counter-battery fire. This flight cost The Mocker an eye and a head wound, but also won him the *Croix de Guerre*. Unlike Cher Ami who died in 1919, The Mocker went on to live for over 20 years. Spike, another 77th Division pigeon, delivered a record 52 messages during the war. Truly unique was The Kaiser, a German military pigeon captured in the trenches and shipped to the US, where he lived a record 30 years as a prisoner of war siring pigeons for the Signal Corps.

By the Armistice, the British Army counted over 20,000 pigeons, 400 men and 150 mobile lofts on the Western Front. In addition, there was an extensive internal and coastal network in the British Isles including rebellious Ireland. The commander of the British Department of Signals said, "If it became necessary... for me to select (only one method of communication), I should unhesitatingly choose the pigeons."

By November 1918, the American Expeditionary Force had over 8,000 birds, 333 men and 60 stationary and mobile pigeon lofts. Over 90 percent of the messages sent by homing pigeon were delivered. A postwar Signal Corps report declared the work of the birds "highly satisfactory," considering the Army's lack of experience with pigeons.

However, it wasn't all praise. A post-war examination by the Army's Chief Signal Officer labeled the indiscriminate use of pigeons by lower echelon combat units "tactically unsound". One doughboy, pressed into service as a handler, expressed his sentiments when he released his bird with the following message, "Take it away. I'm tired of carrying this damned bird!"

Overall, the reliable little birds captured the hearts of soldiers and the folks back home. Books and poems were written about Cher Ami, and when she died in 1919, she was mounted and sent to the Smithsonian Institution. One humorist said that the Signal Corps bred pigeons with parrots so they could speak, with angels so they could sing, and with Western Union boys so they could speak and sing. Both the French and Belgians erected monuments to their *Au Pigeon Soldat* (pigeon soldiers) at Lille and Brussels.

The rapid demobilization in 1919 that followed the Armistice resulted in many surplus pigeons. The best were saved for breeding at facilities like the US Army's Pigeon Breeding and Training Facility at Fort Monmouth, New Jersey and the naval air station at Lakehurst, New Jersey. The rest were sold, given away or, in Britain, returned to their donors with certificates of appreciation.

The inactivity of the interwar years was briefly interrupted when an argument arose in the San Francisco press over whether a homing pigeon or airplane could carry a message faster; such was the state of aviation in 1922. The famous Air Corps pilot Henry "Hap" Arnold accepted the challenge on behalf of the airplane to be pitted against Army pigeons.

The race took place from Portland, Oregon to San Francisco, a distance of over 500 miles, with the governor of Oregon as Arnold's passenger. After mechanical problems, delays and sightings of pigeons far ahead of him, Arnold arrived at the finish 7.5 hours later, ready to concede defeat. However, the real Signal Corps pigeons did not arrive for another 48 hours. The earlier

The British placed pigeons aboard aircraft and used them to assist in locating downed planes. The birds averaged flights of 50 to 150 miles and successfully delivered over 700 such urgent messages during WWI.

sightings were possibly inspired by bookies who handled the heavy betting that accompanied the race.

Volunteer Efforts

On the eve of WWII in 1938, the British military establishment, now well aware of the value of homing pigeons, established a volunteer civilian organization, the National Pigeon Service, to provide birds to the government. Thousands of young birds were sent to all British armed forces as the "only munition of war which was provided free of charge." When war came, the birds provided battlefield communications for the British Army, were dropped in occupied territory by intelligence services, went to sea with the Royal Navy and went aloft as standard equipment aboard Royal Air Force bombers and reconnaissance aircraft. During the Blitz in 1940, homing pigeons also carried civilian messages when bombing disrupted telephone and telegraph communications.

Anticipating war, the US Army also sought pigeons from civilian fanciers. In addition, civilians were sought who had experience racing pigeons to serve in the Signal Corps pigeon companies. These specialists, pigeoneers, brought needed experience in avian husbandry to the Army. Also, for the first time, veterinarians were assigned to the pigeon units to ensure the birds' health.

The first combat experience for American pigeons came with the North African Pigeon Platoon, which arrived in Morocco in late 1942 following the American invasion of North Africa. The military campaign in North Africa against the Germans and their Italian allies was highly mobile with fluid battle lines. The harsh climate was hard on equipment, and homing pigeons were frequently the only means of communication available to the British and Americans. Even General George S. Patton, in command of an American Army Corps, relied on pigeons to communicate.

It was in North Africa in March 1943 that a bird named Yank achieved fame by flying 90 miles in under two hours in heavy rain to report the American capture of the Tunisian city of Gafsa. The dispatch Yank carried gave the first news of the Italian retreat, making headlines around the world.

Continuing on the offensive, the Allies launched the Italian Campaign in 1943. The rugged, mountainous terrain disrupted radio transmissions, and forced a reliance on homing pigeons not seen since WWI. By late 1944, some advanced Allied headquarters were receiving 300 messages a week by pigeon courier.

One of the most famous American pigeons of WWII was G.I. Joe. In October 1943 G.I. Joe, temporarily attached to British forces, flew 20 miles in 20 minutes to deliver the report that the Italian town of Colvi Veccia had fallen unexpectedly to British troops. This message prevented Allied bombers from mistakenly bombing the British, and saved an estimated 300 lives.

As the Allies pressed their attack in Italy, preparations for the invasion of France were underway in England. Fearing the introduction of disease, especially typhoid fever, which the birds could carry, the British refused to allow the importation of pigeons from America after a single small initial shipment. American Armies in northern Europe would be using British-bred pigeons instead.

Prior to the invasion, civilian lofts in Plymouth on the English coast were acquired for military

Pigeons were employed by both sides during both WWI and WWII.

use. Allied intelligence services began regularly parachuting homing pigeons into northern France seeking military information from sympathetic civilians. Using the information received, several German radar and radio sites were located and destroyed. Across the English Channel, the German occupiers were hastily confiscating shotguns from the French, lest they interrupt communications by shooting German pigeons.

On the eve of the 6 June 1944 invasion, several hundred Plymouth birds were assigned to the assault forces. Very few of those dropped with paratroops ever returned. However, pigeons that accompanied troops ashore in Normandy delivered the film

with the first photographs of the battle on the beaches.

As the Allied armies spread out across France from their Normandy beachhead, combat mobile pigeon lofts accompanied them. The combat pigeon lofts of WWII were smaller than their predecessors of WWI. Generally mounted on trailers to be towed by jeeps or small trucks, they were more mobile and easier to conceal. Courier pigeons were used primarily to deliver lower priority communications such as photographic film, war correspondents' dispatches and supply reports. Continued improvements in the range and reliability of radio transmissions made the need for live couriers less urgent.

Homing pigeons were deployed in the Pacific theater also, but due to the island-hopping nature of the fighting and vast geographic distances in the Far East, their utility was diminished. Only on large islands like New Guinea and Luzon in the Philippines were company-sized pigeon units in action. More commonly they were deployed in small units of a few men and birds. One two-man detachment was sent on an 18,000-mile odyssey to train Nationalist Chinese guerillas in the use of pigeons.

Some deliveries made by pigeons in the Pacific were more valuable than others. One group of American servicemen on an isolated island received their pay by pigeon when paymasters were unable to reach them.

It was in Southeast Asia that pigeons received the most recognition. Burma Queen, a hen, was air dropped to an isolated Allied unit trapped by the Japanese. Although only five months old, she flew over 300 miles with information that facilitated the unit's relief. Jungle Joe, a cock, was only four months old when, after being held for eight days in a shipping basket, he flew 225 miles to deliver valuable intelligence gathered by Allied scouts.

The US Navy maintained a small pigeon service at naval air stations on both coasts of North America. The birds were used in conjunction with airships on anti-submarine patrol over coastal waters when radio silence was necessary. At some stations female naval personnel were assigned to care for the birds and were nicknamed pigeonettes.

Medals of Honor
In England in 1943, the People's Dispensary for Sick Animals, a charitable humane organization, inaugurated the Dickin medal (named for the organization's founder, Mrs. M.E. Dickin) for animals that performed heroic deeds. Forty WWII pigeons were honored. Examples include Beachcomber, a pigeon who accompanied the Dieppe com-

mando raid in 1942, Gustaf, who accompanied a Reuter's war correspondent on D-Day, and William of Orange, who parachuted with troops into Arnhem, Holland and returned 260 miles to England in 4.5 hours. Only one American bird, G.I. Joe, was so honored. In 1946, the Lord Mayor of London presented him with the medal.

The conclusion of WWII marked the end of the last major military deployment of homing pigeons. Significant and ongoing improvements in electronics made messenger pigeons obsolete. Although attempts were made to train pigeons to fly at night, and to multiple home lofts to increase their utility, these efforts met with limited success. The US Army deactivated the last of its pigeons in 1957, donating the surviving heroes to zoos in cities across the US, and selling the rest. Only a monument remained at Fort Monmouth to mark the homing pigeons'

accomplishments. Poorly executed experiments with pigeons in Korea and Vietnam were failures. Smaller nations including Switzerland, India and Iraq continued their military pigeon services into the 1990s. Now gone from the scene, the military pigeons were a unique chapter in the history of warfare.

Further Reading
Bonner, Mary Graham. *Couriers of the Sky* (Alfred A. Knopf, 1964).
Home, Allister. *The Fall of Paris: The Siege and The Commune, 1870-1871* (St. Martin's Press, 1965).
Levi, Wendell M. *The Pigeon* (Levi Publishing Co., 1957).
Osman, A.H. *Pigeons in the Great War* (Racing Pigeon Publishing Co., 1926).
Pratt, Jerome J. *Courageous Couriers* (American Pigeon Journal Co., 1977).

HM

Typhoid

Beverly Downing describes a disease that devastated our ancestors.

IF YOU HAD BEEN alive in 1850, you probably wouldn't have considered cleanliness "next to Godliness"! As cities multiplied and the population expanded, lack of knowledge and lack of sanitation opened the floodgates of vulnerability and invited the spread of contagious diseases. High on the list of "visitors" was typhoid fever. Spread by unsanitary handling of food or by contaminated milk or water, typhoid fever's symptoms included fever, headache, loss of appetite, spots on the trunk of the body and constipation. Left untreated, the disease could weaken the wall of the intestines, causing perforation, internal hemorrhaging... and possibly death.

In 1861, typhoid fever killed at least 50,000 people in England. In 1900, the US reported 350,000 cases of typhoid fever resulting in 35,000 deaths. In 1906, in New York alone, there were 3,467 reported cases of typhoid fever with 639 deaths.

Science was hard at work looking for ways to stop the disease. By the early 20th century, it was well-known that human beings could be carriers of typhoid fever; what was not known was that the carriers could be healthy human beings.

Mary Mallon, "Typhoid Mary", was the first healthy typhoid carrier to be identified by public health officials in the US and it took some "detective" work to find her!

In 1906, during a summer vacation at Oyster Bay on Long Island, New York, six out of the 11 people in the family of wealthy New York banker, General Henry Warren,

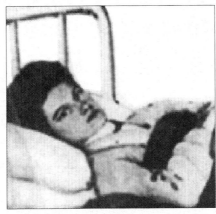

"Typhoid Mary" (Mary Mallon) spent a total of 26 years in hospital to prevent her from spreading the disease.

came down with typhoid fever. Since there had been outbreaks the summer before, the General hired health investigator George Soper to track down the cause of the disease.

"Typhoid Mary"

Soper started with tests on the property's cesspool and bathing facilities but they proved negative for the typhoid fever bacillus. He doggedly followed other leads and soon established a link with the disease and an Irish immigrant cook who had been hired for part of the summer: Mary Mallon. On 4 August 1906, Mallon had been hired as the Warren family cook and on 27 August, the fever had claimed its first victim. Five other members of the household were stricken within the next seven days. By the time the investigation was completed, and suspicions were aroused, Mallon had moved on to another job.

Soper knew he was on to something, but he needed more proof before he could accuse Mallon of being a carrier. He spent hours combing through Mallon's past employment records and soon discovered that seven other households where she had been employed as a cook had been hit with typhoid fever during, or soon after, her employment. With the evidence in hand, he was ready to confront Mallon and hoped to gain her cooperation in helping to stop the spread of the disease. But when confronted at her current place of employment, Mallon — "five feet six inches tall, a blonde with clear blue eyes, a healthy color and somewhat determined mouth and jaw" a woman "who prided herself on her strength and endurance" — refused to cooperate. When Soper suggested gallbladder

Considerable effort was put into discovering a suitable vaccine against typhoid. This painting commemorates the work conducted in this area.

surgery (one known way to rid the body of the tenacious bacteria), Mallon vehemently declined. Frustrated, he asked for a sample of Mallon's blood, feces and urine to prove his theory. In response to his query, Mallon "seized a carving fork and advanced in [Soper's] direction!" (*Silent Travelers*; Alan Kraut).

Even as she voiced her refusal, Mallon had already infected another affluent family. Her current employer's daughter was near death and a laundress in the same household had been taken to the hospital — both had been diagnosed with typhoid fever.

Since George Soper could not get Mallon to cooperate, he sent a colleague, Dr. S. Josephine Baker to see her. Again, Mallon refused to comply with their requests. Frustrated, and frightened by the potential disaster harbored inside Mallon's intestines, Dr. Baker returned with the police. Mallon answered the door, armed with another kitchen fork for her defense. When the police began to force their way inside, Mallon ran and hid in an outdoor shed. Once found, she was dragged kicking and screaming to a waiting ambulance and then transported to Willard Packer Hospital. (To prevent her from escaping, Dr. Baker had to sit on top of Mallon's body the entire way.)

For the next several months, Mallon was kept in isolation at the hospital. She was tested, again and again, for the bacteria that causes typhoid fever: *bacillus typhosus*. Every test was positive. She continued to refuse gallbladder surgery, and no other "cures" seemed to work, so she was placed in isolation at Riverside Hospital on North Brother Island, New York. Eventually, she

A Leavenworth, Kansas, ice cream factory found to be contaminated with typhoid in 1919.

was allowed to live by herself in a small bungalow on the property. But, thanks to newspaper magnate William Randolph Hearst (who was always on the lookout for a controversial story), Mallon was to be given another chance to infect more people. As her case gained notoriety through Hearst's publications, free advice and legal counsel came flooding her way. Finally, bowing to the many impassioned pleas from the public, Judge Ernest Lederle decided to trust Mallon. He released her, saying that he felt that she had learned how to take care of herself and not infect others. But that trust was short-lived.

After her release, Mallon lived under several aliases, and, since cooking was the only trade she knew, she found employment in the kitchens of several hotels, restaurants and hospitals. In 1915, when 20 cases of typhoid were traced to the kitchen at New York's Sloane Hospital for Women, it was discovered that cook Mary Brown was really Mary Mallon. But Mallon knew how to handle the public health system — she ran — and when the authorities came looking for her, she was long gone. Eventually, Mallon was captured and, again, she was isolated on North Brother Island.

As the years passed, a mutual trust was established between Mallon and her jailers and she was given permission to leave the island for short visits with friends. On Christmas Day, 1932, Mallon was found paralyzed on the floor of her cottage. After living as a paralytic for six years (and typhoid carrier for 24 years), she died on 11 November 1938.

Mary Mallon was the most notorious of the typhoid carriers who were relegated to isolation in prisons and hospitals, but unlike Mallon, most people who were diagnosed with the disease cooperated with health officials. They submitted to an isolated, sanitized existence, living out their days in the company of other chronic carriers. Since early antibiotics couldn't kill the typhoid bacteria, gallbladder surgery was the treatment of choice as late as the early 1960s.

The History
Typhoid fever is no stranger to history. Along with typhus (a deadly disease spread by lice and fleas), it was the scourge of the old world, striking crowded populations made vulnerable by famine and war. In fact, complications from typhoid fever may have killed 32-year-old Alexander the Great.

On 10 June 323BC, after a night of heavy drinking, Alexander developed severe abdominal pain (of such severity that he supposedly cried out in anguish), a fever and eventual paralysis. Records suggests that his demise was due to a gastrointestinal infection that led to an intestinal perforation, which in turn led to peritonitis. In comparison, an analysis of 500 untreated cases of typhoid fever in 1907 reported symptoms of ".... intestinal perforation which characteristically resulted in the sudden onset of severe abdominal pain.... and then a generalized peritonitis ensued.... the course was almost always fatal" ("A Mysterious Death"; *The New England Journal of Medicine*, June 1998).

During the Middle Ages, intestinal diseases, like typhoid fever, were rampant throughout Europe. Typhoid fever was present in every town, because as cities grew, vast amounts of human and animal waste accumulated in the streets and alleys, and the bacteria from the waste seeped into the town water supply.

Typhoid fever remained a killer until it was realized that it resulted from unsanitary conditions. Up until the beginning of the 20th century, typhoid, along with dysentery, had the power to paralyze entire communities, army garrisons and naval establishments throughout the world.

Typhoid fever was one of the diseases that plagued soldiers in the Thirty Years' War (1618-48). With the continual troop movements across Germany, the influx of fresh soldiers from foreign countries, and the cities teeming with refugees, the scene was ripe for the spread of the bacteria that caused the disease.

When European settlers came to the New World, they brought a new way of life, and new diseases. These diseases, including typhoid fever, could efficiently wipe out entire Indian tribes. For the "white man", fevers, cholera and other seasonal maladies usually made the months of late summer and early autumn a period of terror. Typhoid epidemics came and went and took their toll, but little was known concerning the cause, or spread, of this disease. It is found listed as "typhus" fever, "nervous" fever, or "brain" fever. Causes were generally supposed to be the night air, fear, unripe fruit and lack of sleep. Bloodletting was the recommended cure.

How Typhoid Fever may be Propagated.

In a recent number of the *Popular Science Monthly*, Ely Van De Warker, M.D., of Syracuse, N. Y., under the title "Typhoid Fever Poison," reports seventeen cases of the fever in an isolated suburb of the city in which there were but fourteen houses. The first case was imported; thence through the overflow of the privy in which all the excrement of the patient had been thrown, a well became contaminated. All the persons who were taken ill used this well. It was the constant or occasional source of supply of seven of the fourteen families. No cases occurred in households where the inmates did not use this well. Some cases were developed in every family who drew water from it. The families who escaped were exposed to every other influence but that of this particular well; their own water supply was the same, less the privy contamination. It is not unlikely that their own wells received some of the overflow from their own vaults, but as these were free from typhoid poison, no ill results ensued.

About eight years since, Dr. Flint, who has studied and written a great deal on the subject, became satisfied that a source of typhoid fever existed which was little dreamed of, and which at first thought would seem impossible. This source, as he then enunciated it to his home medical society (and not to his knowledge having been before suggested), is found in ice. If this idea is thoroughly investigated, it will not appear to be very problematical. In the first place, the poison is not destroyed or impaired by freezing (some one long ago remarked that ice often masks or conceals what it does not kill). Now, whence comes our ice supply? Often from shallow reservoirs in the midst of neighborhoods of large towns purposely made to receive surface drainage from all around, under the erroneous idea that no harm will ensue, as freezing is supposed to purify and render harmless what might otherwise be objectionable. Great quantities of ice are taken from canals, from creeks, from stagnant ponds, and from streams that are either the natural or artificial recipients of surface drainage, of the outpourings of sewers, and of uncleanliness from various sources. The danger from ice taken from improper places is not only from that which is drunk, but from its use in refrigerators and preservatories, where milk, butter, fruits vegetables and meats are subjected to its saturating influences as it vaporizes. Several instances have fallen under the doctor's observation where the disease, by the most careful investigation, could not be traced to any other source; and if we accept as a fact the statement positively made by Budd in the London *Lancet*, in July, 1859, that it never originates *de novo*, but proceeds from a special and specific poison which is capable of diffusion to a great extent, and which preserves its noxious qualities for a long period, even if buried for many months, we cannot reject the hypothesis of ice infection; and it is hoped that it will be made the subject of very thorough and careful investigation.

The link between poor sanitation and typhoid was suspected long before the proof. This is demonstrated by this report from a magazine of August 1879.

Throughout the American Civil War (1861-65), typhoid fever was common among the troops. During 1862-63, among a force of some 460,000 men in the eastern US, there were 29,666 cases of

typhoid and 7,092 of those cases were fatal. In the central region of the US, in a force of 403,000 men, there were 23,530 cases of typhoid fever, 8,970 of them fatal.

Typhoid fever wasn't class conscious. In 1861, Prince Albert, beloved consort of Queen Victoria, succumbed to the disease. He was 42 years old and left behind nine children and a widow who grieved his death until her last breath.

During the Spanish American War (1898), poor hygiene paved the way for typhoid fever, yellow fever and malaria. Even though the basic principles of troop deployment had been to spread soldiers out to minimize the danger of infection, the scarcity of proper housing upon arrival in Florida meant that the troops were stacked on top of each other. Camp kitchens and hospitals were situated near the latrines and garbage pits. The crowded conditions, coupled with the lack of shovels to dig latrines, disinfectants to control germs and kettles to boil water, promoted the spread of disease and every regiment developed typhoid fever within eight weeks of assembling. Because of these conditions, 2,500 American officers and men died of typhoid, yellow fever, malaria and dysentery, 10 times the number that died in battle!

During the Boer War (1899-1902), the British Army, "with an average strength of just over 208,000 men, had 57,684 cases of typhoid fever, with 8,022 deaths. Between February 1900 and the end of 1901 some 6,425 men died in battle, or from wounds; but 11,327 died of disease, while the total number of typhoid patients in the period amounted to 42,741" (*Insects and History*, J.L. Cloudsley-Thompson). By WWII, typhoid fever had ceased to be of military significance, because inoculations of typhoid vaccine were routine in all armies.

Today

But even today typhoid fever still hasn't been eradicated. Although powerful antibiotics are now available, making the exile of the

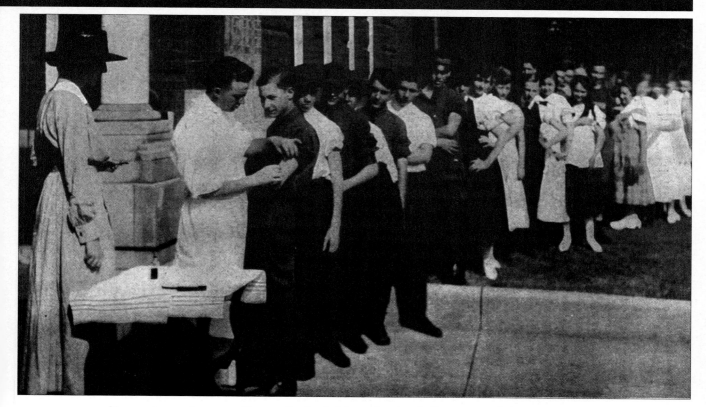

Young men and women line up for typhoid vaccination in Leavenworth, Kansas, in 1919.

typhoid carrier a thing of the past, there are still those who carry the disease in many parts of the Third World today. A recent survey in Indonesia found that typhoid fever afflicts between 800,000 and 1.6 million people in that country every year, killing one to five percent of them. Children are the main victims; 80 to 90 percent of those stricken with this disease are between the ages of two and 19.

Narain H. Punjabi, a medical research scientist for a US Navy laboratory, said that children are more vulnerable than adults because a child's immune system has not fully developed. "Most children also don't realize the importance of good hygiene and sanitation, so they merely depend on adults to provide them with food," he said. "What people consume is the key to typhoid fever… *salmonella typhi bacteria*, the disease's causative agent, is transmitted by the ingestion of contaminated food or water. The bacteria then travels to the digestive system where it multiplies, causing bleeding and perforation of the small intestine. If it stays there long enough, it will get in the bloodstream and move to the liver and the rest of the body, causing other complications. The bacteria, which is discharged in feces, will survive and become contagious to other human beings." (*The Jakarta Post*; 31 July 2000).

Typhoid fever is not a major threat to us today, since the food in our environment generally is sterile, refrigerated and processed. Additionally, because our ancestors often dined on rotten meat and contaminated fare, our digestive tracks have evolved to defend us against a huge range of bacteria and viruses.

Although clones of "Typhoid Mary" are alive and well in some underdeveloped countries around the world, modern medicine has replaced bloodletting, isolation, and gallbladder surgery, with Chloramphenicol, or a cortisone derivative, to combat the effects of typhoid fever.

HM

Hindsight

We believe the products included in Hindsight will be of interest to readers but *History Magazine* does not necessarily endorse these items.

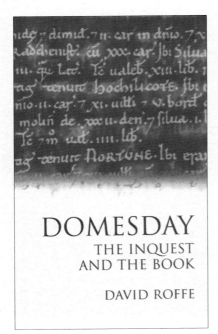

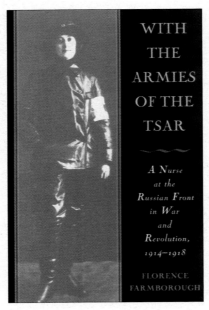

As its title suggests, **Domesday: The Inquest And The Book** addresses Domesday as two separate parts that were not meant to be combined as most scholars have done in the past. The inquest of 1085 was to address England's system of taxation and defence, sparked by Denmark's threat of invasion, while Domesday Book was a land register for administration purposes brought about by a revolt during the reign of William II in 1088. Author David Roffe argues in this scholarly work for the separation of the two events, leading the reader to a deeper understanding of Norman England. From Oxford University Press, hard cover, 282 pages, with an index and bibliography. Priced at about $45 US or $73 Cdn. Available in bookshops everywhere.

In 1914, young English diarist Florence Farmborough returned to Russia to visit a family she had been governess to a few years before. While Farmborough was there, WWI broke out and she was accepted as a Voluntary Aid with the Red Cross. Florence worked in Poland, Austria and Rumania over the next four years on the front lines, tending to wounded sol-

diers, and seeing firsthand both war and the beginnings of the Soviet empire. Her diary **With The Armies Of The Tsar** is a testimony to the honor of duty and the horrors of war. 422 pages, with maps, black and white photographs (taken by the author) and an index. Available in paperback from Cooper Square Press. Priced at about $20 US or $30 Cdn. Available in bookshops everywhere.

In an age when wearing a sword was functional and not just fashionable, martial arts were taught by professional masters-of-arms

and their schools were found across Europe. **The Martial Arts of Renaissance Europe** discusses one-to-one combat, duels fought with swords, bare hand fighting and jousting with horses. Author Sydney Anglo also examines the armor and weapons of the period, such as staffs, daggers and lances to name a few. From Yale University Press, hard cover, 384 pages, numerous black and white illustrations, plus 32 color plates, with an index, notes and bibliography. Priced at about $45 US or $70 Cdn. Available in bookshops everywhere.

In the early 1800s, the abuse of the Irish taxation system based on tithes and 'country cess' was rampant; landowners and tenants sought a countrywide uniform system. In 1825, Richard Griffith began the first of his three valuations of Ireland, which were to end the misappropriation. **Richard Griffith And His Valuations Of Ireland** by James R. Reilly looks at the history and the methods used by Griffith and his team for this project and the genealogical information available. 108 pages, soft cover with many illustrations and several appendices, at about $22 from the Genealogical Publishing Co., Inc., 1001 N. Calvert St., Baltimore MD 21202, 1-800-548-1806 or www.GenealogyBookShop.com

Drawn from the Peiresc archive of more than 100,000 pieces of paper, **Peiresc's Europe: Learning And Virtue in the Seventeenth Century** examines the life of one of Europe's most famous people in his age. Nicolas-Claude Fabri de Peiresc (1580-1637) was a friend of Pope Urban VIII, Galileo and Rubens to name a few, and a lead-

MAIL ✈ POSTE

Canada Post Corporation
Société canadienne des postes

Postage paid   Port payé
if mailed in Canada   si posté au Canada
Business Reply   Réponse d'affaires

0077712999   01

0077712999-M2J4V8-BR01

HISTORY MAGAZINE
500-505 CONSUMERS RD
PO BOX 45371 STN BRN B
TORONTO ON   M7Y 7V1

ing member of the intellectual culture of his period. Author Peter Miller brings light to the scholarly world of the early 17th century: the personalities, the aspirations and the ideas. From Yale University Press, hard cover, 234 pages, 20 black and white plates, with extensive notes and index. Priced at about $40 US or $62 Cdn. Available in bookshops everywhere.

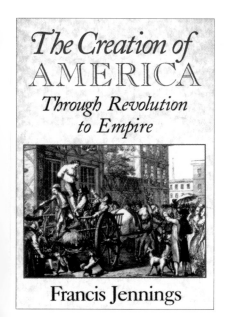

Controversial in its criticism of the great figures and the aims of the American Revolution, **The Creation of America: Through Revolution to Empire** argues that the revolution was not supposed to be the birth of a democracy, but the birth of new empires for a privileged few. Author Francis Jennings details many revolutionary-era events that had little to do with liberty, such as seizure of property, persecution of Quakers and Mennonites and the betrayal of American Indians. Jennings re-evaluates the achievements of the American Revolution in the context of the period showing forgotten facts, contradictions and iniquities. From Cambridge University Press. 340 pages, soft cover with an index and bibliography. At about $20 US or $31 Cdn. Available in bookshops everywhere.

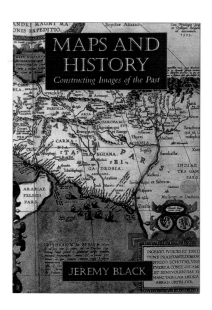

The evolution of the historical atlas is explored in **Maps And History: Constructing Images of the Past**, beginning with Abraham Ortelius' historical atlas of 1570 to maps of today showing non-traditional perspectives and the impact of technology. Historical atlases allow us to understand our predecessors' geographic worlds and their concepts of space and area. Examining what was included and what was omitted reveals many details of the past. From Yale University Press, soft cover, 278 pages, 53 colour and black and white illustrations, with notes and index. Priced at about $20 US or $49 Cdn. Available in bookshops everywhere.

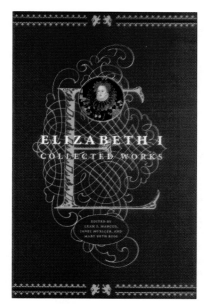

Elizabeth I of England was a mighty and shrewd monarch; she was also a great writer. Her speeches, letters, prayers and poems have now been gathered together as **Elizabeth I: Collected Works**, edited by Leah S. Marcus, Janel Mueller and Mary Beth Rose. Beginning with Elizabeth's childhood letters, the book shows the intelligence, insight and wit that would be the hallmarks of Elizabeth's style. This collection also has new translations of Elizabeth's Greek, Latin, Italian, Spanish and French works, and modernized spelling, however, this does not temper the impact of the prose. From University of Chicago Press. 446 pages, hard cover with copious footnotes, an index of names and several black and white illustrations. At about $40 US or $62 Cdn. Available in bookshops everywhere.

Saved By The Bell

Nicole Brebner unearths the truth about premature burial.

There was a young man at Nunhead
Who awoke in his coffin of lead;
"It is cosy enough"
He remarked in a huff,
"But I wasn't aware I was dead."
(a popular limerick in 1900)

THE FEAR OF BEING buried alive would be considered by most to be quite irrational. However, in Europe and North America from the 1600s to the early 1900s, the fear of premature burial was not only rampant, it was somewhat warranted. Physicians of that time were limited in their knowledge of medicine, often lacking a degree. As a result, comatose or unconscious patients were occasionally incorrectly pronounced dead. The shocking and miraculous revival of the deceased at their own funerals was always widely and sensationally reported in local papers, leading to a growing public paranoia.

Between 1700 and 1900 several hundred articles, books and essays were published describing the fallibility of the diagnosis of death, including Edgar Allan Poe's *Premature Burial*. Collapse and apparent death were not uncommon during epidemics of plague, cholera and smallpox. Poe's macabre stories were extremely popular and were often passed on as truth. As sensational as some of the fictitious stories may have been, there were plenty of well-documented cases of the dead suddenly reviving. As a result, in the 1800s, the fear of premature burial became all-consuming and elaborate measures were devised to prevent it. The formation of the Society for the Prevention of People Being Buried Alive led to changes in the way the dead were treated. The supposedly deceased were left lying in their caskets for days or weeks before being declared sufficiently dead to bury. In an extreme example of the practice, when the Duke of Wellington died in 1852 his burial was postponed for two months after his death.

Other preventative measures included placing crowbars and shovels in caskets so that, in the event the deceased were to revive, they could dig themselves out. Or, pipes were placed through the ground into the casket to allow post-burial emergency communications. Wealthy families sometimes hired servants to wait by the pipe to listen for cries for help.

There were also options to ensure the dead and buried stayed that way. Coffins were fitted with special nails which, when hammered in to seal the coffin, would puncture capsules and release poison gas inside the casket. Less elaborate measures included placing guns, knives or poison in the casket so that if the buried person awoke they had a means to quickly rejoin the deceased.

The most popular preventative measure was the Bateson Revival Device, invented and patented by George Bateson. It was advertised as "a most economical, ingenious, and trustworthy mechanism, superior to any other method, and promoting peace of mind amongst the bereaved at all stations of life. A device of proven efficacy, in countless instances in this country and abroad." Popularly known as Bateson's Belfry, the device consist-ed of an iron bell mounted on the lid of the coffin just above the deceased person's head. The bell was connected to a cord that ran through the coffin lid and was placed in the hand "such that the least tremor shall directly sound the alarm."

The ringing of the bell was quite common and not at all upsetting to the ever-present mortuary caretakers. Due to the build-up of gases within the coffin, the corpse would distend and the resulting movement would sound the alarm. According to an account by William Tebb, "This frequently happens; the warning bell is so sensitive that the least shade of the corpse sets it in motion. But the guardian is not at all flustered; various causes may agitate the bell, and the waking of a corpse is a very rare occurrence. Nevertheless, the caretaker goes to ascertain the cause of the alarm, and, having assured himself that the corpse preserves all the signs of death, he readjusts the cord, and returns to continue his sleep."

Although there is no record of the Bateson Belfry having saved anyone from premature burial, it did leave its impact by originating the saying "saved by the bell". The obvious value of Bateson's invention was the peace of mind it offered. The device was popular for many years and Bateson became a rich man. Unfortunately, Bateson's own fear of being buried alive is thought to be the root of his eventual madness. In 1866 he committed suicide by dousing himself with linseed oil and setting himself on fire.

In the late 1800s the introduction of arterial embalming, which includes removing the blood and injecting lethal chemicals into the deceased, helped to quell the fears of premature burial. If death hadn't killed you, embalming surely would. The fear of premature burial contributed to the rapid acceptance of embalming as a common burial practice. **HM**

Scrapbook for 1520-1529: Reformation

History
Magazine

April/May 2001
$4.50 US
$5.50 Cdn.

The Tower of London
and some of
her "guests"

The First Crusade

The Hanseatic League

The Rise of Universities

05

0 56698 94944 2

Apr/May 2001

Publ. Mail Product
es Agreement No.

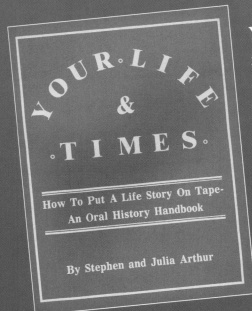

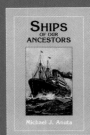

Contents of this issue of History Magazine

The 1520s.
Page 7.

The Hanseatic League.
Page 23.

The First Crusade.
Page 29.

The Tower of London.
Page 43.

OUR COVER: *The Tower of London From Tower Hill* by Thomas Homser Shepherd.

VOLUME 2 NUMBER 4
EDITOR & PUBLISHER
Halvor Moorshead
EDITOR
Jeff Chapman
EDITORIAL ASSISTANTS
Nicole Brebner
Victoria L. King
SPECIAL PROJECTS MANAGER
Ron Wild
ADVERTISING SERVICES
Victoria Pratt
Published by Moorshead Magazines Ltd.
505 Consumers Road, Suite 500, Toronto,
ON, M2J 4V8 Canada
(416) 491-3699 Fax (416) 491-3996
E-Mail: magazine@moorshead.com
PRESIDENT
Halvor Moorshead
CIRCULATION MANAGER
Rick Cree
SUBSCRIPTION SERVICES
Jeannette Cox
Valerie Carmichael

History Magazine is published six times a year
(Feb/Mar, Apr/May, Jun/Jul, Aug/Sep,
Oct/Nov, Dec/Jan) by Moorshead Magazines.
POSTAL INFORMATION — CANADA
Canadian Publications Mail Product Sales
Agreement No. 1595695. Mailing address for
subscription orders, undeliverable copies and
change of address notice is:
History Magazine,
505 Consumers Road, Suite 500,
Toronto, Ontario, M2J 4V8 Canada
POSTAL INFORMATION — UNITED STATES
Periodical Postage Paid Lewiston, NY
USPS #018-154
Postmaster send address corrections to:
History Magazine,
PO Box 1201, Lewiston, NY, 14092-9934 USA
US Office of Publication
850 Cayuga St., Lewiston, NY, 14092
ISSN 1492-4307

© 2001 Moorshead Magazines Ltd.
Some illustrations copyright www.arttoday.com.

SUBSCRIPTIONS
Subscription rate for US (US funds):
1 year (6 issues) $24.00
2 years (12 issues) $40.00
3 years (18 issues) $55.00

Subscription rate for Canada (Cdn funds):
1 year (6 issues) $28.00 plus GST/HST
2 years (12 issues) $45.00 plus GST/HST
3 years (18 issues) $59.00 plus GST/HST
Quebec residents add 7.5% QST

GST # 139340186 RT
We welcome the submission of articles for publication. Please send a printed copy in addition to the
file in electronic format. Please do not send important documents with submissions. We will always
contact people who submit articles but the review
process may take several weeks. Authors' notes are
available on request.
Toll-Free Subscription Line:
1-877-731-4478
PRINTED IN CANADA
WEBSITE
www.history-magazine.com

History Notes

Gunpowder and Saltpeter

Few chemicals have had a greater impact on history than potassium nitrate — popularly called saltpeter (sometimes spelled saltpetre).

Saltpeter is the key ingredient used in making gunpowder, the other components being carbon and sulfur. Gunpowder is not a chemical compound but a simple mixture of these three ingredients. Carbon (from charcoal) and sulfur (called brimstone in the past) were widely available. Naturally occurring saltpeter was found in caves, the result of bat droppings. It was also found naturally as a white crust on top of manure piles (either from animal or human waste), as it is formed wherever there are organic materials containing nitrogen. Bacteria in the soil or waste oxidize the nitrogen compounds to form nitrates. These are highly soluble in water which wicks to the top of the pile where the water evaporates, leaving a crust.

Before modern sewers, most outhouses were fitted with a drawer under the seat that would be emptied by the neighborhood night-soil collector. There was a market for this manure: it was emptied into concrete tanks where bacteria did their work. The liquid was then drained into shallow trays where the water was allowed to evaporate leaving the saltpeter.

During the Revolutionary War, the Continental Army was desperately short of gunpowder — and especially the key ingredient saltpeter. General Washington urged ladies to "save the contents of their chamber pails". Wandering tinkers collected the contents which were poured onto beds of straw; this was known as a niter bed. The nitrates were leached out of this to supply the army with desperately-needed saltpeter. —HALVOR MOORSHEAD

Mirrors

The first evidence of human-fashioned mirrors is found in Ancient Egypt, where very small sheets of mirrored glass were as valuable as gems. The Ancient Egyptians believed mirrors held the power to capture souls, and thus turned mirrors to the wall during an illness and following a death.

The Greeks and Romans learned the art of mirror making from the Egyptians and, like the Egyptians, used slightly convex disks of metal, either bronze, tin or silver, that reflected light off their highly polished surfaces. In his *Natural History*, Pliny the Elder records that during the time of Pompey the Great (106-48BC), mirrors were more commonly fashioned from polished silver than polished bronze.

Throughout Europe, the use of a flat plate of glass with a reflective metallic backing became popular during the early Middle Ages. By the time of the Renaissance, Venice had established a reputation for high quality glass and mirror production. Venetian craftsmen employed a well-guarded secret technique to bond clear glass to a wafer-thin reflective backing made from an amalgam of tin and mercury. By the 1700s, Venetian craftsmen were producing the first large mirrors and selling them for astronomical sums. To protect their large mirrors during transport, the Venetians developed mirror frames, which were usually crafted out of ivory, silver, ebony or tortoiseshell. The science of mirror making was not widely understood outside of Venice; in the 1600s, Dutch housewives covered their mirrors with curtains to prevent the mirrors from losing their reflectiveness through overuse.

Unfortunately for Venice, the city's profitable monopoly on mirror production ended as Venetian trade secrets gradually leaked to the rest of Europe. By the mid-1800s both London and Paris had established successful mirror industries. Despite the end of the Venetian monopoly, large mirrors were still extremely expensive. Wishing to astound the nobility of Europe with French wealth, Louis XIV of France planned for one of the most opulent rooms at his new Palace of Versailles to be a Hall of Mirrors.

The Hall of Mirrors in the Palace of Versailles.

BUSINESS REPLY MAIL
FIRST-CLASS MAIL   PERMIT NO. 72   LEWISTON, NY

POSTAGE WILL BE PAID BY ADDRESSEE

History Magazine

P.O. Box 1201
Lewiston NY 14092-9923

The era of modern mirror making commenced after Justus von Liebig discovered a chemical process for coating a glass surface with metallic silver in 1835. This new and cheaper technique of mirror production led to a proliferation in the use of mirrors by the late 1800s. Today, mirrors are made by applying a thin layer of molten aluminum or silver onto the back of a plate of glass in a vacuum, and are both commonplace in homes and an essential tool in many modern industries. —JEFF CHAPMAN

Sideburns

The fashion of men growing long side whiskers came to prominence in North America in the early 1800s. Ambrose Everett Burnside, a Union general in the American Civil War popularized the new trend when he cultivated a fabulous example of the style. While we now know them as sideburns, they were originally labeled "burnsides" in

General Ambrose Everett Burnside

honor of the general. Over time, the general faded from memory and the words were reversed to their current form. —NICOLE BREBNER

The Jerkers

The early years of the 1800s saw Christian revivalist groups sweep across the US, particularly in the frontier states. Though the Mormons and the Shakers are perhaps better known, the "Jerkers" were also a significant group.

The eastern Tennessee Jerkers were principally an offshoot from the Presbyterians and Methodists and the Hardshell Baptists. Descriptions of the practices of the Jerkers are few and obviously biased, referring to the practice as a malady and the participants as victims.

"Its victims in times of religious excitement would be instantaneously seized with spasms or convulsions in every muscle nerve or tendon. Heads were jerked or thrown from side to side with such rapidity that it was impossible to recognize the visage and fears were entertained lest necks be dislocated or brains dashed out. Arms and legs followed similar rapid convulsions and it was a miracle that serious bruising or breakages of arms or legs on pews and beams did not take place. Women with long hair soon shook their hair loose from combs and ribbons and their head movements were so violent that their hair would strike the floor in front and behind them with a crack like a wagoneer's whip."

It had a contagious effect on observers who if they did not quickly run from the building became themselves afflicted. Some outraged members of the ministry and high society attended a meeting to put an end to such nonsense but themselves became afflicted, to their great distress. A minister of a large Protestant congregation went to a Jerkers' meeting to see and protest against the practice only to become afflicted himself and on demonstrating to his congregation afflicted all of them to their great consternation.

It is not surprising that on the frontier more liberal attitudes towards religious observance were being practiced. This same liberalness was being experienced in other aspects of social behavior such as courting, marriage customs, health practices and economic relationships as a mobile and expanding population shook off the restraints and traditions of past generations.

Ultimately the practices of the Jerkers were discontinued although they still exist today in some born-again Christian congregations and at revivalist meetings around the US and Canada. —RON WILD

Chatelaines

Named for the lady in charge of a castle, a chatelaine was a loop with a set of chains hanging from it. Chatelaines were worn by both genders, though mainly by women, and attached to belts, girdles or pockets. At the end of the chains were clips or hooks from which hung various small items necessary in the day-to-day running of a household.

Items one might have had on a chatelaine included keys, a watch, scissors (usually in a protective case), a small pen knife, a mirror, a writing tablet or covered notebook, a pencil, a seal, a needle case or a money purse. Some women had several chatelaines; the additional chatelaines would have carried other items, such as gardening tools or full sewing sets with pincushions and thimbles.

Medieval in origin, chatelaines peaked in popularity in the 1700s and were often given as wedding gifts from the groom to his new bride and mistress of his home. Chatelaines were made of steel, silver, brass, bronze or even gold. Some had biblical or mythological themes, or were decorated with engraving, filigree or precious and semi-precious stones.

Chatelaines declined in popularity at the beginning of the 20th century as large households disappeared. —VICTORIA KING

The 1520s

Victoria King describes some of the highlights of this pivotal decade.

THE 1520S WERE dominated by the personalities of kings and members of the clergy. The most dominant personality in Europe in the period was Charles V, Holy Roman Emperor and King of Spain. He was the axis about which most of the events within Europe and beyond turned as a direct or indirect result of Charles' vast power and wide interests.

Charles V inherited his many domains due to dynastic alliances made decades before his birth. Charles' maternal grandparents were Isabella of Castile and Ferdinand of Aragon; their marriage created Spain, one of the most powerful countries in Europe. Charles' paternal grandmother was Maria of Burgundy and his grandfather was Maximilian, the Holy Roman Emperor. Charles became king of Spain in 1516 and, three years later, elected Holy Roman Emperor and Archduke of Austria (he gave Austria to his younger brother, Ferdinand in 1521).

It was a decade of warfare. The Holy Roman Empire and France fought over the control of Italy. The conflict, known as the Italian Wars, which began at the end of the previous century, was over a distant dynastic claim that the French house of Valois had to the kingdom of Naples. In 1521, France was surrounded by the territories of Charles V and war resumed between the two nations after a peace of five years. This stage of the war continued throughout Italy until the peace of Cambrai was signed in 1529. Under the treaty, France relinquished its claims in Italy, Flanders and Artois, in addition to a ransom of two million crowns. Charles, the victor, agreed to renounce his claims to Burgundy.

Beyond Europe, Suleiman the Magnificent, sultan of the Ottoman empire, was the greatest threat to Christians. Like Charles, Suleiman ruled over a vast area, encompassing over 20 million subjects. In the

Charles V, Holy Roman Emperor and King of Spain, was the most powerful monarch in Europe in the 1520s.

1520s, Suleiman had military successes, first against the Hungarians in Belgrade in 1521. In 1522, Suleiman drove the Knights of St. John from the island of Rhodes. At the battle of Mohacs in 1526, the Ottomans defeated Louis II, king of Hungary, who was killed in battle. In 1529, Suleiman's siege of Vienna was unsuccessful. A truce would be reached in the following decade between Suleiman and Ferdinand, the successor of Louis of Hungary.

The decade saw the end of the Italian Renaissance with the fall of Rome in 1527 to Charles' imperial troops. The death of the Renaissance was also heralded by the end of knightly conduct in battle, with the end of hand-to-hand combat due to the increased use of firearms in warfare. Success no longer depended on training in battle, but in the superiority of weapons and numbers.

It was also a decade of diplomacy. Henry VIII's Lord Chancellor Thomas Wolsey was instrumental in asserting England's role in continental affairs. Wolsey organized a meeting in June 1520

between Henry VIII of England and Francis I of France, known as the Field of Cloth of Gold, to address the shift in the European balance of power due to Charles' election as Holy Roman Emperor.

It was also a decade of discovery, with further investigation of the Americas. Magellan discovered the strait at the southern tip of South America, and his crew went on to circumnavigate the globe. Francisco Pizarro explored the Pacific coast of South America, setting the stage for the conquest of the Incas in the next decade. Charles' influence was also felt in the new world with the fall of the mighty and wealthy Aztec empire to the Spanish conquistador, Hernán Cortés.

In the sphere of religion there was great change. The Protestant Reformation was able to spread through Germany because of Charles' preoccupation with international matters. Charles needed the support of Frederick the Wise (who was Martin Luther's protector) and, as Charles could not afford to alienate Frederick, and the latter continued to wield power over the matter of the disobedient monk until his own death in 1525.

The printing press, invented in the previous century, played a major role in the spread of the Reformation throughout Europe as Luther's 95 theses circulated the continent. In 1525, William Tyndale published an English translation of the New Testament, an act which would later cost him his life.

The seeds of the English reformation were sown at the end of the decade. Pope Clement VII, a puppet of Charles refused to annul Henry VIII's marriage to Catherine of Aragon.

All events within Europe and her sphere of influence in the 1520s were influenced by Charles, Holy Roman Emperor and King of Spain, the most powerful monarch of the age.

STEP INTO HISTORY.
THEN GET OUT OF THE WAY.

Relive an era with Mississippi's Civil War battle re-enactments

and magnificent antebellum homes.

Or catch a casino show, stroll along the beach and trace the origin

of the blues. Call 1-888-669-7662

for your free Mississippi *Travel Planner*.

THE SOUTH'S WARMEST WELCOME

www.visitmississippi.org

The Conquest of the Aztecs

BEFORE THE ARRIVAL of the Europeans in the new world, the Aztec empire was one of the mightiest that had existed. The Aztec empire encompassed about 400 small states with a total population of six million people. Its capital was Tenochtitlán, with a population of over 100,000 inhabitants. However, the Aztec empire under its emperor Montezuma II was unstable as the burden of tribute it placed on subject tribes and the demand for religious sacrifices of humans made the empire hated.

In 1504, Hernán Cortés, the Spanish conquistador arrived in Hispaniola where Diego Velázquez was governor. With Velázquez, Cortés sailed to Cuba and began to be known as a man of leadership.

Velázquez ordered Cortés to travel to and colonize the mainland. By February 1519, Cortés secured 11 ships with approximately 700 men. At this point Velázquez regretted empowering the charismatic Spaniard and rescinded the orders. Cortés left for the mainland with his men and ships, also taking with him firearms and 16 horses. Once on the mainland, Cortés assessed the situation, learning of the resentful subject tribes of the Aztecs and began to take advantage of the unstable situation. The Spaniard won over local tribes, eventually amassing an alliance of over 200,000 Indians. Cortés also trained his men into a strong, disciplined army. Cortés then set fire to the ships; he and his men would win by conquest or die — retreat was not an option.

Through the summer of 1519, Cortés and his army moved towards Tenochtitlán. During his

Cortés forced Montezuma to appear before his people to ask them not to resist the Spanish. The Aztecs, angry with their weak emperor, pelted him with rocks.

travels, Cortés was presented with 20 women by a chieftain. One, known as Marina, proved instrumental in Cortés' success, as she was fluent in the language of the Aztecs. On his way to the Aztec capital, Cortés made an alliance with the Tlaxcala nation, enemies of the Aztecs.

Cortés with his army and 1,000 Tlaxcaltecs entered the island city of Tenochtitlán on 8 November 1519. Tenochtitlán was situated on an island in the salt-water Lake Texcoco. A system of aqueducts brought fresh water from the surrounding mountains into the city and several causeways were the only way into the city. Upon his arrival in Tenochtitlán, Cortés was greeted by the Emperor. Cortés, fearing ulterior motives, quickly made Montezuma his prisoner and began to take control of the Aztec empire.

Then, in June 1520, Panfilo de Narvaez, under orders from Velázquez, arrived at Tenochtitlán. Having regretted his original orders, Velázquez sent Narvaez to capture Cortés and head the expedition instead. When Narvaez arrived, Cortés left a garrison to hold Tenochtitlán. Cortés defeated Narvaez, made

him prisoner, and then took Narvaez's army and added it to his own. Cortés returned to Tenochtitlán to find his garrison under siege from the Aztecs, angry with the Spanish for massacring Aztecs.

Cortés made the captive Montezuma appear on a rooftop before his people and ask them not to resist the Spanish. Angry with their submissive emperor, the Aztecs responded to the plea by pelting Montezuma with rocks. Within a few days, Montezuma was dead; the Spanish said he died from the wounds of the rocks, but the Aztecs claimed that the Spanish took advantage of the situation and killed the Emperor.

The Spanish were driven from the island capital later that month suffering huge losses. Cortés fled to Tlaxcala territory and regrouped his army, making more allies of the surrounding tribes of Tenochtitlán. The new emperor Cuitláhuac tried to gather a single force against the Spanish, but died of smallpox in October of that year. Cuitláhuac was succeeded by his nephew Cuauhtémoc who was to be the last emperor of the Aztecs.

In December 1520, Cortés and his army marched on Tenochtitlán. Cortés and his men destroyed the aqueducts of Tenochtitlán cutting off the supply of fresh water. Cortés also had several boats built to sail in the lake from which to attack the Aztecs. Thirst, famine and disease struck the Aztecs.

The city was destroyed and most of its inhabitants died. The siege lasted until 13 August 1521 when Tenochtitlán, and with it the Aztec Empire, fell to the Spanish.

1520

Pope Leo X issues a papal bull, known as *Exsurge Domine*, condemning Martin Luther's 95 "heretical and scandalous" theses. The 95 theses protest the sale of indulgences by the Church.

Suleiman the Magnificent becomes Sultan of the Ottomans.

The Field of Cloth of Gold is held near Calais. Francis I of France and Henry VIII of England meet; Henry VIII asserts his desire to be a member of European politics by offering support to Francis I against the latter's enemy, Charles V, Holy Roman Emperor and King of Spain.

Sailing for the Spanish, Portuguese navigator Ferdinand Magellan enters the Pacific by way of a strait (later named after the explorer) at the southern tip of South America.

Christian II, king of Denmark and Norway, defeats the Swedes at Lake Asunden. Christian II is crowned king of Sweden in Stockholm.

Henry VIII of England signs a secret treaty with Charles V, Holy Roman Emperor. The treaty makes the two allies in the event of war with France.

Aztec Emperor Montezuma II dies while a captive of the Spaniards.

Raphael, Italian painter and architect, dies.

Plague breaks out in Dublin.

1521

Hernan Cortés, the Spanish conquistador, conquers Tenochtitlàn, capital of the Aztec Empire. Upon the ruins of Tenochtitlàn, the Spanish found Mexico City. The city is intended to become the capital of New Spain.

1520: The diplomatic meeting known as the Field of Cloth of Gold is held near Calais.

Luther appears before the Diet of Worms and is excommunicated and condemned.

The Ottomans, under Suleiman the Magnificent, capture Belgrade after a three-week siege.

The Holy Roman Empire and France fight for control of Italy.

Pope Leo X names Henry VIII of England 'Defender of the Faith' for defending the seven sacraments against Luther in the work *Assertio Septem Sacramentorum*.

Explorer Magellan dies in present-day Philippines, killed in an altercation with natives.

1522

Adrian of Utrecht, Regent of Spain, is elected Pope Adrian VI. Adrian VI is the last non-Italian pope for the next 450 years.

James V of Scotland and Henry VIII of England agree to a truce.

Charles V, Holy Roman Emperor and King of Spain, defeats the French at the battle of Biocca, driving the French from Milan.

Fifteen crew members on board the *Vittoria*, sole surviving ship of Magellan's expedition, return to Spain completing the first circumnavigation of the globe.

Rhodes, home of the Knights of St. John, falls to the Ottomans under Suleiman at the end of a five-month siege. Suleiman allows the Knights to leave the island unharmed and Charles V, Holy Roman Emperor and King of Spain, resettles the Knights of St. John on Malta.

In China, Chia Ching becomes the 11th Emperor of the Ming dynasty.

1523

Swiss Protestant reformer Ulrich Zwingli publishes his 67 Articles. This work attacks the papacy and the doctrine of transubstantiation.

Pope Adrian VI dies. Clement VII, a member of the powerful Florentine Medici family, is elected pope.

Gustavus Vasa becomes king of Sweden after leading a revolt against Christian II.

The Spanish found the town of Saint Jago de la Vega on Jamaica.

Followers of Zwingli found the Anabaptist movement, a Protestant sect that opposes infant baptism and advocates withdrawal from society.

Christian II of Denmark leaves the country after rebellion breaks out.

In Brussels, two of Luther's followers, Augustine monks, are burnt at the stake.

Anthony Fitzherbert writes the *Boke of Husbandrie*, the first manual in the English language for agriculture and home management.

The first marine insurance policies are issued in Florence.

1524

Florentine explorer Giovanni de Verrazzano, sailing for the French, explores the eastern coast of North America. Verrazzano sailed to the present-day Carolinas and then north to present-day Cape Breton, discovering "600 leagues and more of new land".

France invades Italy and recaptures Milan from the Spanish.

Inspired in part by the teachings of Luther, German peasants demand the abolition of serfdom, the reduction of tithes and the right to choose their own pastors.

The treaty of Malmo is signed; Sweden under Gustavus I becomes independent from Denmark.

Tahmasp I succeeds to the Persian throne upon the death of his father, Ismail.

Portuguese navigator Vasco da Gama, the first European to round the Cape of Good Hope, dies.

Luther abandons monastic life and vows.

1525
After losing 6,000 soldiers, Francis I of France is captured at the Battle of Pavia, south of Milan, and made a prisoner. Charles V, Holy Roman Emperor and King of Spain, controls Italy. This victory was the first major battle that infantry armed with firearms won; firearms from this point on were standard in warfare as the technology spread.

Cardinal Thomas Wosley presents Hampton Court to Henry VIII.

In Spain, the Moors, who had worked on the estates of the Valencian plains, are expelled.

The German Peasants War is put down by German princes, resulting in the beheading of one of the leaders, Thomas Munzer.

Zwingli abolishes the Catholic masses in Zürich.

A peace agreement is signed between England and France.

Frederick the Wise, elector of Sax-

1521: Luther appears before the newly-crowned Charles V at the Diet of Worms.

ony and protector of Luther after the latter was placed under an imperial ban in 1521, dies. While under Frederick's protection, Luther translated the Bible into German.

Babar, King of Kabul, invades the Punjab.

Hops are introduced to England from Artois.

1526
While a captive of Charles V, Holy Roman Emperor and King of Spain, Francis I of France is forced to sign the treaty of Madrid, renouncing claims to Naples, Milan and Genoa.

The Holy League of Cognac is formed. The released Francis I, Pope Clement VII and Francesco Sforza of Milan, Venice and Florence unite against Charles V, Holy Roman Emperor and King of Spain.

The Ottomans defeat Louis II, King of Bohemia and Hungary, at the battle of Mohacs. Louis II and 20,000 of his soldiers are killed in battle.

Copies of William Tyndale's Eng-

lish translation of the New Testament reach England. Tyndale went to Germany to have the translation printed at Cologne and Worms as English authorities prevented its printing in his native land.

Ferdinand of Austria, younger brother of Charles V, Holy Roman Emperor and King of Spain, is elected to the united Bohemian and Hungarian thrones. Ferdinand was brother-in-law to Louis II and had a strong claim to the thrones.

After his release from Spain, Francis I of France declares the treaty of Madrid null and void and forms an alliance with Suleiman, the Ottoman Sultan, against Charles V, Holy Roman Emperor and King of Spain.

Babar, King of Kabul, defeats the last Sultan of Delhi, Inbrahim Lodi, at the battle of Panipat in India and founds the Mughal Empire. Babar used modern weapons against the traditional arms, war elephants and archers of Muslim India.

The succession to the Hungarian throne is disputed between the Ottomans and Ferdinand of Austria.

Hans Holbein the Younger, the German painter, visits England for the first time. The English court later patronizes Holbein.

1527
Spanish and German troops sack Rome, killing 4,000 inhabitants and capturing Pope Clement VII. The city is sacked due to the wish of Charles V to punish and defeat the League of Cognac.

Ferdinand of Austria is crowned King of Bohemia in Prague.

France and England become allies against the Holy Roman Empire after signing the treaty of Westminster.

Henry VIII of England asks Pope Clement VII to grant him an annulment from his wife, Catherine of Aragon. Clement refuses as he is under the influence of Charles V, who is Catherine's nephew, and a papal bull had already been issued to allow the marriage to take place as Catherine was the widow of Henry's brother.

Niccolò Machiavelli, author of *The Prince*, dies. Dedicated to Lorenzo de Medici, *The Prince* was condemned for its uncompromising tenets and ruthlessness and the principle that the end justifies the means.

1528
Giovanni de Verrazzano dies in the Caribbean. Verrazzano was searching for spices from the Indies when captured by natives of the islands who killed and ate the seasoned explorer.

German painter and wood engraver Albrecht Durer dies.

Weavers in Kent, England riot over Wolsey's plan to move Eng-

land's principle source for wool from Antwerp to Calais.

Francis I of France signs a trade treaty with the Ottomans.

Henry VIII of England explains to his nobles his motives for seeking an annulment of his marriage to his wife, Catherine of Aragon.

Paris becomes the capital of France.

1529
The Ottomans lay siege to Vienna, which successfully repels the invaders.

Disappointed with his inability to secure the annulment of Henry VIII's marriage to Catherine of Aragon, Lord Chancellor Wolsey is dismissed by Henry. Thomas More is appointed as Wolsey's replacement.

Charles V, Holy Roman Emperor and King of Spain, and Pope Clement VII agree to the Treaty of Barcelona.

The second Diet of Speyer is held. Those who protest against Rome are given the name Protestants.

Francisco Pizarro sails down the western coast of South America to the frontier of the Inca Empire.

Henry VIII of England summons the Reformation Parliament and begins to sever ties with the Church of Rome.

Baldassare Castiglione dies. Castiglione had published, a year before his death, *The Book of the Courtier*, a book about manners for courtiers instructing them to be graceful, courteous and to do good acts when observed by one's lord. The work embodied the ideals of the Italian Renaissance and was translated into many languages and widely read in its day.

After France renounces claims to Italy, Flanders and Artois, the Peace of Cambrai is made between France and Spain.

Ulrich Zwingli

A CONTEMPORARY OF Martin Luther, Ulrich Zwingli was a church reformer in Switzerland. Zwingli, a former Swiss army chaplain, began to preach against the secularizing of the Church in 1516, a year before Luther wrote his 95 theses.

In 1518, Zwingli became a secular preacher in Zürich, where the clergy and the people supported his views of reform. In 1520, the governing council of Zürich granted Zwingli permission to preach the "true divine scriptures". Zwingli preached against clerical celibacy and fasting during Lent, which led to civil unrest in the following years.

In 1523, Zwingli presented his 67 theses as an agenda of reform. These were approved by the council and followed by the canton's priests. The use of organs in church services was abandoned, images were taken down from churches and monasticism was ended. Priests were allowed to

marry and baptism of infants was rejected. In 1525, Zwingli banned the Mass and began to hold a simple form of Holy Communion.

The cantons of Basel and Bern began to follow the reforms of the Zürich Reformation, which led to an alliance, while the cantons of Luzern, Schwyx, Unterwalden, Uri and Zug rejected the alliance.

Tension was released when fighting broke out at the monastery of Kappel, on the borders of the Roman Catholic canton of Zug and the Protestant canton of Zürich in 1529. An uneasy peace was reached later that year, but tension continued, which resulted in the outbreak of conflict again in October 1531. On 11 October 1531, Zwingli died in battle. Peace was reached the following month.

Like Luther, Zwingli drew from his humanistic background of learning, finding his convictions in the Scriptures, but Zwingli was more radical in his approach. Unlike Luther's reform in the Holy Roman Empire and beyond, Zwingli's reforms did not survive his death. Anabaptists followed Zwingli's belief that infant baptism was unnecessary and that baptism was to be administered to adults. Today Mennonite and several Baptist sects are the ideological heirs of Zwingli and the Anabaptist movement.

Thomas Wolsey

In the 1520s, Thomas Wolsey dominated English politics. Wolsey became Lord Chancellor of England in 1515 under Henry VIII and began to shape England's political policies, both domestically and internationally.

Wolsey was also a man of the Church, twice a candidate for the papacy. He was made archbishop of York in 1514 and cardinal a year later. Wolsey was a capable administrator and his secular and spiritual offices made him a wealthy and powerful man, second only to his monarch.

In 1518, Wolsey succeeded in having the major European states agree to peace, with England as the mediator. Before the union of the Holy Roman Empire and Spain in 1519 under Charles V, England had played France, the Holy Roman Empire and Spain against each other, offering or withdrawing support as fortunes waxed and waned. However, once the Holy Roman Empire and Spain were united, Wolsey opted for neutrality as the situation was politically unstable, given that England had been at war with France in 1515.

In June 1520, Wolsey organized

a meeting, known as the Field of Cloth of Gold, between Henry VIII and Francis I of France. The two kings discussed the new balance of power in Europe under Charles' election as leader of the Holy Roman Empire. Little was accomplished politically at the meeting and Henry subsequently offered his support to Charles a month later at a meeting in Bruges, where they signed a secret treaty to be allies in the event of war with France.

In 1521, war broke out between the Holy Roman Empire and France. Two years later Wolsey sent English troops to fight on the side of

the Holy Roman Empire. In order to finance the support, Wolsey raised taxes, which was unpopular.

Wolsey changed sides to support the French after the capture of Francis at the battle of Pavia in 1525, as he was concerned that the balance of power favored Charles. But in 1529, Francis and Charles made peace and England was isolated.

By this time, Henry VIII had initiated annulment proceedings against his wife, Catherine of Aragon, aunt of Charles V. Henry entrusted the arrangement of the annulment to Wolsey. Pope Clement VII, under the control of Charles, refused to grant the annulment. When Wolsey failed to secure the annulment in July 1529, Henry turned on Wolsey and this led to Wolsey's dismissal as Lord Chancellor in 1529.

The unpopular Wolsey left for York, the only archbishopric he retained. Wolsey was arrested on charges of treason in 1530 and was to appear before Henry, however, the former Lord Chancellor died in November 1530 while on his journey south to appear before his sovereign.

THE SACK OF ROME

Italy was the battleground for Spain and France for much of the beginning of the 16th century. In 1494, Charles VIII of France claimed the kingdom of Naples and this first Italian war ended in 1516 with the peace of Noyon. The kingdom of Naples was retained by Spain, while France took Milan.

The uneasy peace that existed after the first Italian war broke down in 1521 when Charles V of the Holy Roman Empire refused to recognize the terms of the peace of Noyon. In 1522, Charles' Spanish troops took Milan from the French.

The 1525 Battle of Pavia was the most important engagement of the second Italian war. Spain with her imperial troops and hired mercenaries defeated the French and took Francis I, king of France, captive. Francis was released after

signing the Treaty of Madrid, which rescinded his claims to Italy. Upon Francis' release he declared the treaty null and void, and proceeded to form the Holy League of Cognac with the Papacy, Venice, Florence and the Sforza of Milan.

The imperial response to the formation of the Holy League of Cognac was the May 1527 sack of Rome. The leader of the Spanish forces, Charles de Bourbon, was

killed in the initial attack on Rome. The imperial troops and mercenaries, many of whom were Protestant, were left leaderless and unpaid, and pillaged the Eternal City. Four thousand people were killed; homes were sacked and churches were destroyed. The uncontrolled plunder of the city lasted little more than a week, but the majority of the city was destroyed and Christians throughout Europe were appalled.

Pope Clement VII took refuge in the Roman castle of Sant'Angelo, but later surrendered. He was discovered in a storeroom with 12 cardinals and forced to sign a notice of surrender.

The Imperial troops held the Eternal City until February 1528. The sack of Rome is considered by many historians to be the end of the Italian Renaissance.

The Beginning of the Protestant Reformation

"...not with sword or target...but with printing, reading and writing..."
—John Foxe (Protestant author of *The Book of Martyrs*)

IN THE EARLY 16TH century, the Church was seen to abuse its powers by serfs and princes alike. Popes Innocent VIII (1484-92) and Alexander VI (1492-1503), both fathers of illegitimate children, were paragons of vice, while their immediate successors were more interested in the glory of the arts than the salvation of souls. As the Church moved further away from being a spiritual leader, it grew wealthier and more powerful, maintaining a hold over secular affairs that was resented by political leaders, members of the clergy and its flock.

The Church had been attacked throughout its history by reformers. Two of the more recent groups of reformers were the English Lollards of the late 14th century and the Bohemian Hussites of the early 15th century. Both criticized the Church for its hierarchy and its wealth. The Church had also come under attack for the Great Western Schism (1378-1417), which had greatly weakened the Church's prestige.

In October 1517, a German monk who was a theology professor at the University of Wittenberg made public his arguments against the selling of indulgences. Martin Luther, the Augustinian monk and professor, is believed to have nailed the 95 theses to the Wittenberg church's door on the last day of the month, the eve of All Saints' Day. Notices of this type were usually posted on the church's door for theological debate.

At that time indulgences — the remission of penalties owed for sins — were sold to raise funds for the Church and its projects, especially the rebuilding of St. Peter's in Rome. Johann Tetzel, a Dominican friar who preached and sold indulgences around Saxony, but was not allowed in Wittenberg by Elector Frederick the Wise of Saxony, is said to have been instrumental in

Martin Luther's dissention with the Church was theological.

provoking Luther to write his 95 theses. Luther argued that indulgences and acts of piety were unnecessary as salvation was independent of humans' earthly actions, Christ's sacrifice making the salvation of all faithful Christians assured.

The 95 theses were translated from Latin into German and printed and distributed throughout Germany. Peasants agreed with Luther and sales of indulgences declined. Within a few weeks, Luther had become a voice for the Germans.

What made Luther's attack different from that of the Lollards and Hussites was that his predecessors opposed the corruption of the Church, while his dissension was theological. Another important difference to Luther's struggle was the role of the printing press. Invented in the middle of the 15th century, the printing press allowed the spread of reading materials to more people. This elevated the publication of the 95 theses from a minor incident in Wittenberg to one of international importance.

Luther's attack was successful because of its wide appeal to people from all backgrounds. The movements of the Lollards and the Hussites appealed mainly to peasants and had roots in nationalism.

With its worldliness and secularization, Rome was highly unpopular in the early 16th century with many believing that reform of the Church was necessary.

Luther sent two copies of the 95 theses to the Archbishop of Mainz and the Bishop of Brandenburg. The 95 theses were submitted to Rome with a report stating that the theses were of a heretical nature. Pope Leo X, dismissing the matter as a local affair, asked the local authorities to deal with the disobedient monk. The matter was mulled over and, under pressure from Dominicans, heresy charges were leisurely begun against Luther. This "quarrel between monks" provoked a slow, almost casual response, which was to prove fateful as the issues raised by Luther spread unchecked.

In 1518, Luther was summoned before Cardinal Cajetan at Augsburg where the matter of indulgences, among others, was debated between the papal legate and the monk. Under normal circumstances, Luther would have appeared in Rome. However, as Elector Frederick's support was needed in the election of a new Holy Roman Emperor, the Church authorities did not want to provoke a dangerous situation. After the discussion turned into an argument, which spread to many points of disagreement beyond the selling of indulgences, the Cardinal dismissed Luther. Luther wrote of his interview with the Cardinal for publication for the German people.

The next confrontation between Luther and the Church occurred when Luther agreed to publicly debate with Johann Eck, a scholar from Ingolstadt and former friend of Luther's, who condemned the heretical 95 theses. Eck declared himself the victor of the debate, managing to get Luther to admit that several of his views were similar to those of Jan Hus, the heretical leader of the Hussites. However, Luther's views continued to gain popularity throughout Germany. Luther lost the debate because he was a poor debater: rough, unrefined, plodding and peasant-like; these characteristics lost the debate, but won the support of the Germans.

In June 1520, Leo X issued a papal bull condemning Martin Luther's 95 "heretical and scandalous" theses. This was given to Eck (then in Rome) to take back to Germany. Instead of achieving the desired effect, Luther became more radical; he posted a notice inviting people to witness him burn the bull on 20 December 1520. Luther spent his time writing *An den chrislichen Adel deutscher Nation* (Address to the Christian Nobility of the German Nation) which argued for secular leaders to intervene in the reformation of the Church as the clergy was unable to reform itself. Luther wrote two other works in that period which attacked not only papal authority, but also the Mass and the sacraments, especially the doctrine of transubstantiation.

The papal bull of excommunication for Luther was issued in January of 1521. Frederick the Wise urged that Luther should be allowed to defend his actions, so on 17 April 1521, under safe conduct from Frederick and with a large group of supporters escorting him to the meeting, Luther appeared before the assembly of the Holy Roman Empire at Worms. Charles V, newly-crowned Holy Roman Emperor, nobles and members of the Church attended. When asked if the writings attributed to him were indeed his, Luther requested time to think, which caused the assembly to break and gather the following day. A larger crowd gathered the next day to hear Luther speak, which he did at some length. Luther refused to recant his beliefs, and explained that he would only do so if reason or the Scripture proved him wrong. It is said that Luther summarized his speech and his thoughts with "Here I stand, I can do no other." Confusion broke out in the assembly and Charles V ended the meeting when Luther and Eck began arguing.

The result of the Diet of Worms was an edict branding Luther as a heretic and outlaw, and his works were banned. Frederick the Wise

At the Diet of Worms in April 1521, Luther defended himself. He summarized his thoughts by saying, "Here I stand, I can do no other."

'kidnapped' the monk and took Luther to Wartburg. There Luther began to translate the New Testament into German, which was to have a deep impact on the German language as it was widely read. After a year in hiding, Luther returned to Wittenberg and began to preach again. In this period, Luther made plain his views against the Catholics and against the radicals (Schwäwer) who took his reforms to an extreme, protesting against the latter's violence.

Tension in Germany broke with the Peasants' War in 1524; peasants revolted against taxes and repression by their lords and the Church. Luther's writings were, in part, responsible for the uprising. Although Luther supported the revolt for its aims, he condemned the revolt for its violence, penning *Wider die räuberischen und mörderischen Rotter der andern Bauern* (Against the Murdering and Thieving Hordes of Peasants). The Peasants' War ended the following year with the massacre of thousands of peasants and the beheading of peasant leader Thomas Munzer at Frankenhausen. By this time, Luther had abandoned monastic life and married Katherina von Bora, a former nun.

The Edict of Worms was suspended at the first Diet of Speyer,

held in 1526. Although Holy Roman Emperor Charles V opposed Luther, the external threats of the Ottomans and the formation of the Holy League of Cognac were greater to Charles and his many possessions throughout Europe. It was agreed that religious autonomy was to be allowed within each state, Catholic or Protestant "its subjects, act, live, and govern in matters touching the Worms edict in a way each can justify before God and his Imperial Majesty." This assembly legitimized the reform of the Church for many people within Germany.

Having defeated his adversaries by 1529, Charles V, at the second Diet of Speyer, reenacted the Edict of Worms of 1521, which was to haunt Luther for the rest of his life, and the religious changes of the last decade were to be abolished. Luther's supporters protested against the overturning of the first Diet of Speyer, hence their name Protestant.

The question of the legitimacy of the Protestant faith within the Holy Roman Empire remained unanswered until the Religious Peace of Augsburg in 1555. The Peace of Augsburg acknowledged *cuius regio, eius religio* (whose territory, his religion), legalizing the Protestant religion throughout the land.

HM

The Complete History

Volume One

October 1999 - September 2000

The First Year of History Magazine

History Magazine Volume One is a reissue of almost all the editorial from the issues dated October 1999 to September 2000.

The colorful, bound volume includes all the editorial material from our first year of publication, including such features as: The Atlantic Cable, The Black Death, The National Road, Cleanliness, Bread, The Code Napoleon, The First Radio Station, The Longbow, 1000AD, The US Cavalry, Custer, Army Wives, Death Customs, Bellevue Hospital, The Impact of the Potato, An 1860s Dinner for Eight, The Rifle, The Oregon Trail, The Handcart Pioneers, Refrigeration, Games People Played, Contraception, The Suez Canal, Midwives, Longitude, The 1910s, Country Store, Connecting the World, Alchemy, Freemasonry, Early Newspapers, Influenza Pandemic, Chicago in 1880, The Privy, The Blacksmith, Saffron, Eli Whitney, Lunatic Asylums, Lighthouses, The 1900 House, Carpetbaggers, The Natchez Trace, Let's Eat!, How Brands Began, The Stirrup, The Shakers, Development of Photography, Insurance, Underground Railroad, Memsahibs of the Raj, California Gold Rush, Poliomyelitis, Wigs, decade profiles, historical trivia — and more!

History Magazine Volume One provides a full year of information about the lives our ancestors led.

History Volume One
Magazine

Use any of these three convenient ways to order:

- Phone Toll-Free **1-877-731-4478**. Please have your Credit Card ready.
- Fax this order form to (416) 491-3996
- Mail this order form to History Magazine, PO Box 1201, Lewiston, NY, 14092-9934 or in Canada to History Magazine, 505 Consumers Rd., Suite 500, Toronto, ON M2J 4V8
- ❑ Please send me a copy of *History Magazine Volume One*. The cost is **$25 (US)** incl. shipping or in Canada **$30 (Cdn)** incl. shipping

Canadian orders please add GST/HST. Ontario residents add 8% PST.

Payment by: ❑ Check (enclosed) Charge my Credit Card: ❑ Visa ❑ MasterCard

Card Number_____ Expiry Date_____ /_____

Signature_____

Last Name_____ First Name_____

Address_____

City_____ State/Prov_____ Zip/Post Code_____

Phone Number_____

HM10

Coffee Conquers the World

Edwin M. Knights chronicles the emergence of the coffee culture.

ACCORDING TO ANCIENT Abyssinian folklore, a young goat herder named Kaldi used to make up tunes on his pipe, following his hungry charges as they scoured the mountainsides for food. Late each afternoon he would call them with a loud musical blast which they recognized as a signal that it was time for them to return home.

One afternoon Kaldi blew on his pipe, but no goats appeared. He repeated the call again and again, but there was no response. What had become of his precious herd? He became ever more frantic as he climbed the winding mountain trails, pausing frequently to beckon them again with his pipe. At last, hearing a distant bleating, he scurried in that direction, scrambling through the bushes that flourished under the canopy of tall trees.

And there were his goats, but what had gotten into them? They were leaping around, prancing on their hind legs, butting each other playfully and bleating excitedly. They'd gone crazy! Were they bewitched?

Then Kaldi noticed they were eagerly munching bright berries and green leaves of some shrubs he'd never seen before. He prayed that the goats wouldn't die, for he feared he'd meet the same fate when he had to face his father! He waited and waited — the goats showed no signs of dying but obviously they were in great spirits and in no rush to return home. Hours later he coaxed his tired but happy flock back down the tortuous trails.

The next day Kaldi's goats made a bee line to the same grove and were enjoying a repeat performance when he caught up with them. Kaldi soon decided that he wasn't going to let the goats have

Coffee berries.

all the fun! First he nibbled on a few leaves. They were bitter, but a tingling sensation began to spread through his body. The berries were slightly sweet, especially the gummy coating of the paired seeds inside. Soon Kaldi was dancing around with his goats, composing new tunes on his pipe and becoming convinced that a goat herder's life could be far more enjoyable than he'd ever imagined.

The legend relates how Kaldi told his father about the magical shrubs. He probably introduced his girlfriends to them, too, although this has been omitted from the traditional rendition of the tale. Many years later, in the 10th century, an Arabian physician named Rhazes wrote about coffee, but by that time coffee consumption had progressed from chewing to brewing. Roasting and grinding appeared around the 16th century.

The preparation of coffee remains to this day an elaborate ceremony in Ethiopia, where the sun-dried beans are roasted over a bed of glowing charcoal. The invigorating effects of coffee beans soon captivated the Arab world, as word spread that a coffee drinker could "unhorse forty men and possess forty women." Several Arab rulers found it necessary to close the rowdy coffee houses. Punishment for drinking coffee varied: first offenders received a harsh beating; coffee addicts were sewn into leather bags and thrown into the Bosporus.

Turkish Delight

Soon the Turks were enthusiastically cultivating coffee in Yemen and exporting it from the port of Mocha. In Turkey, coffee became so important that, as a part of the wedding ceremony, a man promised never to let his wife be without coffee. Doing so was grounds for divorce. After arriving in Suez and being toted by camel to Alexandria, coffee was acquired by Venetian and French merchants. Although the Turks tried to protect their coffee monopoly, it was not long before seeds were smuggled to the mountains of Mysore in India and the Dutch carried a coffee tree to Ceylon and others to Java, Sumatra and many of the islands of the Dutch East Indies. In Java and Sumatra, Thurber reported in 1881 that each native family was responsible for the care of 650 coffee trees, harvesting and processing the coffee for Dutch masters who gave them no opportunity to earn more than basic subsistence. Arnold described no better conditions in India, where the entire family worked and was forced to pay homage to the great white sahib. The powerful Dutch fleet would control the coffee market throughout the 18th century.

Coffee use spread across Europe faster than the Black Plague. By 1650 coffee was being sold by Italian street vendors and it soon became popular in the Vatican and Venice. It reached Vienna in 1683 via a most improbable route, thanks to the Turkish Army, which had besieged the city. The Ottoman Empire had already

When Coffee came to England

COFFEE HOUSES were the haunts of men of wit and fashion, and from these gatherings comes the proverb—"a good talker is a connoisseur of coffee."

The popularity of really fine coffee is unquestioned. That it promotes good fellowship and inspires to mental and physical effort, there is no question. But —we are speaking about "really fine" coffee such as is our splendid **"WHITE HOUSE" COFFEE** and if YOU would glean from coffee drinking not only the pleasurable satisfaction to the palate but the invigorating effects which promote energetic action, don't, we beg of you, allow your grocer to substitute something else. Be sure and ask for "White House" coffee and GET it.
Sold only in 1, 2 & 3-lb Sealed Tin Cans
DWINELL-WRIGHT CO.
PRINCIPAL COFFEE ROASTERS
BOSTON & CHICAGO GUARANTEE IT

An advertisement for coffee extols its mental and physical benefits.

spread in all directions from Constantinople, conquering Serbia and Bosnia, Walachia, Syria, Mesopotamia, Hejaz and Egypt. A Polish army, rushing to the rescue, was contacted through the brave efforts of Georg Kolshitsky, a Pole who had been a Turkish interpreter. Slipping through the Turkish lines, he carried a message to the Duke of Lorraine, who led a relieving army. After a fierce and bloody battle, the defenders of Vienna jointly routed the Turks and forced them into such a hasty,

disorganized retreat that they had to abandon their camels, their military equipment, and stores of food. Also left behind were 500 sacks filled with strange looking beans, thought to be camel fodder. The Viennese soldiers weren't particularly overjoyed with eating camel burgers, and probably decided they'd better burn these bean-bags before someone suggested a more balanced diet. The crafty Kolshitsky, who'd lived in Arabia, took just one sniff of the smoke and realized his fortune was made. He'd received a thousand gulden from the mayor of Vienna, plus a charter to pursue any occupation he wished. He promptly rescued the remaining beans and soon thereafter opened Vienna's first coffeehouse, the Blue Bottle Café, which soon became the Starbucks of Vienna. Kolshitsky's timing couldn't have been better, as Vienna's vineyards were beyond repair. The sturdy branches had been cut to help make palisades, and the fertile soil soaked with the urine of thousands of quadrupeds and bipeds. The Viennese loved their wine, but now it had to be imported at great expense. Still they detested the strong Turkish coffee, filled with grounds. Kolshitsky was resourceful — he strained out the grounds, doctored it with honey and diluted it with milk. Within 20 years Vienna was bubbling over with coffeehouses catering to the intellectual classes.

French Disconnection

In France, coffee was introduced by a Turkish Ambassador in 1669; reaction was predictable. Its popularity was especially disturbing to many physicians, who apparently felt this new wonder drug should be available only by prescription. And, of course, it was a distinct threat to the economy of influential French wine-growers. About 20 years later the first coffeehouse, Café de Procope, was successfully introduced into the theater district by an Italian immigrant. Before long the actors, authors and musicians were joined by theater patrons and visiting notables. Even the local for-

tune-tellers deftly switched from tea leaves to coffee grounds. Intellectual discussions, previously dulled by alcohol, now blossomed under the stimulus of caffeine.

Like the Viennese, the French weren't happy with the strong Turkish brew and by early in the 18th century they were pouring boiling water over bags of powdered coffee. They also added milk to sweetened coffee to create the popular *café au lait*. But writers such as Balzac found that black coffee enhanced their literary creativity, and coffee consumption is credited with playing a significant role in the French Revolution.

All of the French contributions were not salutary. Battling with Britain in 1806, Napoleon decreed that France should become self-sufficient and no longer rely heavily on foreign products. The French succeeded admirably with the propagation of sugar beets, but alas, they could not find a substitute for the coffee bean. They turned to using the root of an herb known as chicory; roasting, grinding and brewing it to produce a dark bitter brew that neither smelled nor tasted like coffee. They resumed using coffee beans in 1814, but chicory-adulterated coffee is still commonly served by the French, including French Creoles in Louisiana.

Deutschland Trincken

The Germans also embraced and imbibed the coffee beans, although at first it involved only the more affluent citizens. With typical German precision, Herr Beethoven ground exactly 60 beans to the cup. As in France, coffee soon became a threat to the established beverage, in this case beer, causing coffee bean roasting to be banned by Frederick the Great in 1777. His subjects soon tried roasting various grains and even chicory, hoping it would mask the tell-tale scent of coffee from his "coffee smeller" spies. Eventually coffee prevailed and the *Kaffeeklatch* became an enduring German tradition.

From Germany it was but a short hop to Scandinavia. Although the Scandinavians were late to climb aboard the coffee express, they eventually surpassed all other Europeans in coffee consumption.

Coffee Makes Olde England Merrie
The first coffeehouse in England is reported to have been at Oxford University in 1650, followed by one in London two years later. The Greek owner of the London establishment optimistically claimed that coffee cured headaches, cough, consumption, gout and scurvy, but he does deserve credit for warning customers not to drink it after supper, for it would "hinder sleep for three or four hours." The London coffeehouses multiplied to over 2,000 sites. Loquacious Londoners were highly selective in choosing their coffeehouse companions, gravitating to those patronized by persons having similar religious, political, professional or occupational backgrounds. Coffeehouses became choice hunting grounds for bankers, lawyers and insurance salesmen stalking new clients and for journalists bending an ear for the latest news. Alcohol consumption probably decreased in London, although sobriety never reached epidemic proportions. Tobacco more than held its own in this new, smoke-filled environment.

Exasperated women battled coffee houses as fiercely as they did pubs, and lively debates ensued over the negative or positive effects of coffee on sexual prowess. The women's efforts were briefly rewarded when King Charles II issued his Proclamation for the Suppression of Coffee Houses late in 1675. Although Charles rescinded the proclamation shortly before it was to take effect, tea was to become the more popular drink in Britain, partly because it was more available, more profitable and much easier to brew. Coffee did not disappear from the scene, though, because the next century brought the Industrial Revolution. Home-based crafts were soon being replaced by mills producing everything from

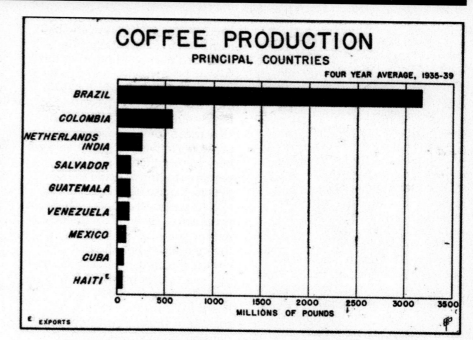

In the first half of the 20th century, Brazil's dominance of coffee production was even more pronounced than it is today.

iron to textiles. Many of the employees were women and children. Factory workers, struggling to exist on paltry wages, lived on a diet consisting mostly of coffee and bread. Morning coffee replaced beer soup for breakfast, and as Mark Pendergrast observes in *Uncommon Grounds*, the chosen beverage of aristocracy had also become the preferred drug of the masses.

Coffee in the New World
Coffee arrived in Brazil as the result of a border disagreement between Dutch and French Guiana. A supposedly neutral Portuguese Brazilian was asked to mediate the dispute. He took advantage of the opportunity to bed with the wife of the French governor. Whether the governors were pleased with his arbitration is not recorded, but the governor's wife was obviously satisfied, as she gave the mediator a floral bouquet when he departed for Brazil. Ripe coffee berries, concealed by the flowers, were planted in Para and seeded the world's largest coffee exporting trade.

The Portuguese had exploited and subjugated Brazil — importing huge numbers of African slaves to work in enormous sugar cane plantations under conditions so deplorable that the workers seldom

lived more than seven years. It was less expensive to replace the slaves than pay for medical care. As sugar prices declined in the 1820s, attention turned to growing coffee, mostly in the mountains near Rio de Janeiro. Importation of African slaves increased from about 26,000 in 1825 to nearly 44,000 annually within the next three years. When international outrage resulted in the importation of slaves being banned by the Queiroz Law in 1850, there were an estimated two million slaves in Brazil. Seventeen-hour work days were common and slaves were reduced to a subhuman existence. It was not until 1871 that all the babies born to slaves were declared free. Coffee production on vast *fazendas* provided a royal lifestyle to the plantation owners but it prolonged slavery in Brazil, which was the last country in the Western Hemisphere to exploit slaves. Even then the lives of black workers barely improved, for coffee was an ever more important cash crop and foreign competition was fierce. Five-hundred million coffee trees in the state of Sao Paulo enriched the planters but did nothing to improve the food supplies for the neglected majority of the population.

San Domingo (Haiti) was supplying half of the world's coffee by 1785, grown and picked by African

Coffee Additives

"Bonus" ingredients in coffee included almonds, arrowhead, asparagus seeds and stalks, baked horse liver, barberries, barley, beechmast, beetroot, box seeds, bracken, bran, bread crusts, brewery waste, brick dust, burnt rags, burrs, carob beans, carrot, chickpeas, chicory, chrysanthemum seeds, coal ashes, cocoa shells, comfrey roots, cranberries, currants, dahlia tubers, dandelion roots, date seeds, dirt, dog biscuits, elderberries, figs, Jerusalem artichokes, juniper berries, kola nuts, lentils, linseed, lupine, malt, mesquite, monkey nuts, mulberries, parsnips, pea hulls, pumpkin seeds, quaker-grass roots, rice, rowan berries, sand, sassafras, sawdust, sloes, sunflower seeds, swedes, turnips, vetch, wheat, whey, wood chips, etc. Not included in this list were poisonous dyes containing arsenic and lead which were used to color the beans. (From *Uncommon Grounds*, by Mark Pedergrast.)

slaves who were managed by French masters. Overworked and underfed, the workers lived in windowless huts. In 1791 the slaves started a revolution which would take 12 years to succeed, only to find the government replaced by a black Haitian leader who made them slaves of the state. By then other entrepreneurs, such as the Dutch, had seized much of the coffee market. It was now the Javanese who became slaves. Other countries began to compete in the world coffee markets: Jamaica, Mexico, the Antilles. Production spread through much of India, Ceylon, Venezuela and most of Central America. Coffee's greatest impact was on Brazil.

A Coast-To-Coast Roast

In America, thanks to the British Stamp Act of 1765, drinking tea was not only unpopular but also unpatriotic, as colonists gathered in taverns, quaffing coffee and various alcoholic beverages while they plotted the American Revolution. American consumption of

good and bad coffee (mostly bad) increased by leaps and grounds. It reached a new height during the War of 1812 when Americans had no access to British tea. By 1830, the average American consumed three pounds of coffee a year; by 1859 the figure was up to eight pounds. Native Americans also got hooked on coffee — retaliation, perhaps, for introducing the settlers to the use of tobacco.

As Americans moved westward across the vast continent, coffee and tobacco were staples in their existence, helping them endure the hardships, dangers and privations of frontier life. It was brewed over campfires, in the hearths of primitive cabins, or roasted in sizzling cast-iron frying pans on wood stoves.

Brewing coffee at home merely meant boiling the grounds in water and letting them settle to the bottom of the container. Some added an egg, others a cod, to expedite the process. In contrast, European coffee processing was now becoming more sophisticated. Count Rumford, an ex-American who is better remembered for his efficient fireplace designs, devised a drip method for coffee. The bitter American coffee was treated with milk and sugar to make it drinkable.

The early American armies received an allowance of "spruce beer, cider or molasses," but as a result of a continuing debate over the wisdom of these rations, President Andrew Jackson finally decreed that coffee and sugar must replace the "spiritous liquors". By 1860, every 100 men received 10 pounds of coffee and 15 pounds of sugar weekly. When the Civil War broke out, the Union blockaded southern ports and deprived Southerners, including Confederate troops, of coffee. Historians have failed to give full credit to the role this played in the eventual Union victory. While Union soldiers gathered around campfires and enjoyed their evening repast of hardtack and coffee, Confederate troops could only mutter expletives as the breezes wafted the aroma of roasting coffee over the darkened hillsides. They gagged over drinks concocted from such unlikely

sources as okra, peanuts, cotton seeds, acorns, chicory and nearly anything else that was handy. The daily ration for Union soldiers was one-tenth of a pound of green coffee beans — three pounds of coffee a month! Union soldiers also learned that boiling coffee poured over their hardtack helped to rid it of weevils, and Union sentries relied upon coffee to stay alert. Ironically, coffee helped to free slaves in one part of the world yet prolonged slavery in others.

The Arbuckle Era

The Arbuckle brothers, John and Charles, along with uncle Duncan McDonald and William Roseburg, were to expand a Pittsburgh grocery business into a 19th-century success story in the processing and marketing of coffee. Starting with an ingenuous roaster invented by Jabez Burns, they combined efficient mechanized processing with brilliant marketing of a distinctive brand of coffee which they dubbed "Ariosa". John Arbuckle devised numerous methods for improving coffee processing, first patenting a system for glazing coffee beans to prolong their fresh taste and aroma. Then he perfected the roasting. Coffee could now be sold in one-pound packages, already roasted, sparing the consumer the chore of grinding the beans. By 1871, Arbuckle Brothers Coffee was popular from the Atlantic to the frontier. Over the next 10 years, they developed branches in Kansas City and Chicago, plus multiple offices in Brazil and Mexico. They occupied 12 blocks of the Brooklyn waterfront. The Arbuckles controlled every phase of their business, harvesting timber, assembling barrels, growing sugar cane and even printing the labels. Later, John Arbuckle gave generous support to many charities, including the Riverside Home for Crippled Children and numerous charities for the support of the homeless.

Chase and Sanborn

Two New Englanders, Caleb Chase and James Sanborn, also established a rapidly growing business in coffee and tea. Starting in Boston, they sealed their products

in tin cans and by 1882 they were selling 100,000 pounds of coffee a month and had outlets in Chicago and Montreal. They were adept at marketing and advertising, introducing the use of premiums and other novelties. The Chase and Sanborn Seal Brand was accompanied by other cleverly-named coffee brands of lesser quality. The company pioneered the use of tasters to help with quality control.

The Folgers Harpoon A Winner

The Nantucket Folger whaling family, lured to San Francisco by the Gold Rush, really struck gold when they turned to coffee roasting. With the help of a cash infusion by wealthy Otto Schoemann, J.A. Folger and Co. recovered from the post-Civil War recession and bankruptcy to create a coffee business which soon reached from coast to coast across America.

Similar successes awaited others who abandoned wholesale grocery businesses to specialize in the selling of coffee. The field was not without its charlatans, who adulterated coffee with an array of substances and devised protective glazes for coffee beans, some of which did little more than add to the weight and mask defective beans. Even "coffee essence" was widely produced from black-strap molasses, chicory and a bit of coffee extract. As might be expected, survival of a coffee firm boiled down to public approval and purchase of their products.

Coffee beans were also colored to satisfy preferences for black, olive green or yellow. This was done so that beans from Brazil and elsewhere in the western hemisphere could be disguised as highly regarded Mocha from Arabia and Java from the Dutch East Indies. Unfortunately some of the colors applied contained deadly poisons. Rio coffee beans could be transformed into an attractive green color when covered with arsenic and lead.

In spite of setbacks, coffee popularity continued to grow and by 1876 US coffee consumption had reached 340 millions pounds per year. Coffee demand had major impacts worldwide on social

Coffee was one of many items rationed during WWII; domestic supplies were rerouted overseas to troops.

practices and human rights, creating and then devastating national economies in a manner never before experienced. While consumers around the world enjoyed the pleasures of drinking coffee and adopted coffee as a part of their cultures, relatively few profited immensely, while huge numbers of people endured abject poverty as a result of the burgeoning coffee economy.

The Coffee Conundrum

Probably no other natural crop has had the global impact of coffee. Its presence has become daily entwined with human lives almost everywhere since its rapid spread from Ethiopia. Its effects on those who drank it must be weighed against its sociological and environmental ramifications. The enormous demand it created for cheap labor doomed millions to lives of abject poverty, while creating fortunes for a select few. It definitely prolonged the existence of slavery in the Western Hemisphere. It has resulted in the decimation of vast rain forests, pollution of waterways and loss of avian habitats.

It has encouraged free speech and independence, caused political upheavals, pushed human endurance beyond its natural limits and played a significant role in military confrontations. Its effects are attributable to caffeine, a habit-

forming drug which has been used medically for many years to enhance the effectiveness of other drugs, but efforts to regulate or restrict its use have all ended in failure. Overdosage with caffeine causes nervousness, irritability, sleeplessness and rapid heart beat.

Coffee has helped spark revolutions, caused cartels to rise and fall, and rewarded entire nations with fleeting financial successes which ended abruptly in economic despair. It has inspired inventions, rewarded innovative marketing with sensational sales, energized the elite while simultaneously renewing the resolve and strengthening the spirits of the sleep-deprived stalwarts of society.

Coffee's popularity has expanded in North America so that now we have espresso culture, regular or decaf, and Starbucks franchises have begun to outnumber places for religious worship. To North Americans, coffee ranks in importance beside gasoline for their vehicle. The coffee break has become a firmly entrenched corporate perk. And all this because Kaldi's goats got a little high on the mountain!

Suggested Reading

Baxter, Jacki. *The Book of Coffee: The Connoisseurs Handbook* (Edison, N.J., Chartwell Books, 1995).
Fugate, Francis L. *Arbuckles: The Coffee that Won the West* (El Paso, Tex. Texas Western Press, 1994).
Jacob, Heinrich Eduard. *Coffee: The Epic of a Commodity* (Short Hills, N.J., Burford Books, Viking Press, 1962).
Pendergrast, Mark. *Uncommon Grounds: The History of Coffee and How It Transformed Our World* (New York, N.Y., Basic Books, 1999).
Rolnick, Harry. *The Complete Book of Coffee* (Hong Kong, Mellita, 1982).
Schoenholt, Donald N. "A Myth is as Good as a Mile: The Mocha and Java History Mystery" (*In Good Taste*, pp. 7-8, March, 1994).
Strain, Eric; Mumford, G. K. et al. "Caffeine Dependence Syndrome" (*Jour. Amer. Med. Assoc.*, pp. 1043-48, 5 Oct. 1994).
Vogel, Jason. "Carriage Trade Coffee" (*Financial World*, pp. 62-65, 25 April 1995).

HM

The Hanseatic League

Jeff Chapman reveals the trade secrets of the group that once dominated Northern Europe.

IN THE MEDIEVAL ERA, trading ventures in northern Europe were a dangerous business. A lack of powerful nations, armies or navies in the region allowed outlaws to operate freely outside city walls. Marauding pirates ruled the seas, and brigandage was simply a fact of life for those who traveled or shipped goods by road. As a consequence, commerce was stagnant, and social and economic progress was slow, until a loose community of towns called the Hanseatic League emerged.

The emergence of the League began with the construction of a canal between the large north German cities of Hamburg and Lübeck in the early 1200s. Shipping by canal was much cheaper than transportation by road, and the canal allowed the two towns to take control of the profitable north German salt trade, which had previously been dominated by the city of Kiel and the "Kiel salt road". Furthermore, as the two cities were situated on opposite sides of the base of the Danish peninsula, any sea traders that wished to avoid the long and potentially dangerous journey around the Danish peninsula had to pass through both ports.

Working together to divert an ever-greater share of the north German and Baltic trade through their shared canal, the merchants of Hamburg and Lübeck began to prosper. In 1241, the merchant associations of the two cities agreed to a treaty providing for joint control of the canal route between the Baltic and North seas. In 1259, the merchants of Rostock and Wismar concluded an alliance with Lübeck for common action against bandits and pirates. The confederacy that would become the Hanseatic League was born.

The increased wealth and prestige that confederation brought to the Lübeck-centered association allowed it to acquire

The Baltic cog was a new type of ship that was slow but held a large amount of cargo.

trading privileges in Flanders and England, at that time the two main manufacturing centers of northern Europe. Envious of these privileges, a previously-rival trading association based in the wealthy city of Cologne and smaller towns on the banks of the Rhine joined the Lübeck-centered association. Less than a decade later, this enlarged confederation of western German merchants was joined by yet another association of German traders operating in the Baltic, inducting Danzig and many important Baltic port cities into the confederation.

With these two mergers, the Lübeck-centered association became the largest merchant organization in Europe, and its size radiated stability in a time when merchants wanted nothing more than stability. Attracted by the mounting influence and prosperity of the association, other northern German towns, notably Bremen, became affiliated with the organization. Other German mercantile leagues soon accepted the hegemony of Lübeck and its partners. Towns in Westphalia, the Rhineland, the Low Countries, the duchy of Saxony, the mark of Brandenburg, Prussia and Livonia

all flocked to join, and the association was soon dominant throughout northern Germany.

The predominant town in all dealings was Lübeck, which occupied a key position on both the Hamburg-Lübeck canal and on the Baltic side of the Danish peninsula. As one of northern Germany's few Imperial Free Cities, Lübeck owed its allegiance to the Holy Roman Emperor alone, which kept taxes low and allowed the city greater freedom of action. Its easy access to rich herring fisheries and its secure hold on all trade coming into or leaving the Baltic Sea ensured Lübeck's dominant position.

A League Without Ideology

The confederation included more than 85 towns when it officially assumed the name of the Hanseatic League in 1343. The German word "hansa" simply means a community or league, which makes the term "Hanseatic League" somewhat redundant. Perhaps the insignificance of the League's name offers some insight into what was important to members of the League: the lack of any reference to ethnic, linguistic or regional affiliation, or to any religious or political ideology, suggests that it was simply the idea of being part of a large and influential association which attracted members.

The requirements for entrance into the League were not difficult to meet: any town whose merchants took part in the Hanseatic trade was eligible. From about 1350 onward, League representatives voted on formal applications, and cities were only permitted to join when it was determined that their admission was advantageous to the League. In one notable case, the Dutch city of Utrecht was refused membership in 1451 when the League ruled that its admission would not strengthen the League, but normally most appli-

hand, the production of each book was a laborious process. From the seventh to the ninth century the illuminated manuscript prevailed. Monks in monasteries throughout Europe produced these elaborately illustrated works. Monasteries were also the repositories of Greek and Roman texts, painstakingly copied and preserved. However, no one outside the monasteries would have access to these books or the ideas within. Education was dominated by the Church and during this time, the production of bibles flourished.

During the 1200s the rise of the merchant class along with the establishment of many universities created the first real market for secular books. For the first time, formal education was not focused on the church. Lacking access to the manuscripts locked away in monasteries, students and other readers had to look elsewhere for their books. Stationers and book copiers set up shop near each university. The stationers provided paper and supplies to students who needed to copy texts and the book copiers performed the copying for those students who could afford to pay. Unfortunately, there was a real problem inherent in this form of book production — human error. Copiers would inadvertently omit information, introduce errors or pass on errors from earlier versions, and some scribes took it upon themselves to correct perceived errors in order to create a "better" text. The result was that no one knew for certain that the books they studied were accurate.

The Beginning of a Revolution
Errors notwithstanding, the demand for books began to grow. Religious texts gave way to political and scientific manuscripts and even a few how-to books that addressed ordinary issues of everyday life, but booksellers had difficulty meeting the demand. In the 1440s everything changed

In 1474 William Caxton became the first to print a book in the English language. This page is from one of his popular illustrated books. Over the course of 14 years, he printed more than 70 books, 20 of them his own translations from the originals in Latin, French, and Dutch.

when a goldsmith from Germany named Johann Gutenberg invented a method of printing using moveable type. Inspired by wine presses, Gutenberg created a press for printing on paper. He realized that cutting individual letters in a form of reusable type could achieve speed and efficiency. Gutenberg spent years perfecting his press and in 1455 he presented a bible with 42 lines per page — the first book ever printed from type — at the Frankfurt Trade Fair. A letter written by Enea Silvio Piccolomini to the Cardinal of Carvajal, dated 12 March 1455 describes Gutenberg's bible at the fair:

"I did not see any complete Bibles, but I did see a certain number of five-page booklets of several of the books of the Bible, with very clear and very proper lettering, and without any faults, which Your Eminence would have been able to read effortlessly with no glasses. Various witnesses told me that 158 copies had been completed, while others say there were 180. I am not certain of the quantity, but about the books' completion, if people can be trusted, I have no doubts whatsoever. Had I known your wishes, I would certainly have bought a copy. Several of these five-page booklets were sent to the Emperor himself. I shall try, as far as possible, to have one of these Bibles delivered for sale and I will purchase one copy for you. But I am afraid that this may not be possible, both because of the distance and because, so they say, even before the books were finished, there were customers ready to buy them."

Gutenberg's invention had an immediate and far-reaching impact. Suddenly, books could be created quickly, cheaply and consistently. By 1490 printing presses had been set up in Italy, France, Spain, Holland, England and Denmark. The first printing press in the New World was established in Mexico City in 1533 followed in 1638 by Cambridge, Massachusetts. The Gutenberg printing press was so effective it remained virtually unchanged until the 20th century and the advent of the computer.

Spreading the Word
One result of the Gutenberg press was the availability of inexpensive books. Originally the domain of clerics and scholars, books were made available for a wider audience. In 1460, Albrecht Pfister of Bamberg began printing books on the press he purchased from Gutenberg. Pfister added illustrations to help explain the text, making the books comprehensible to far more people. He was the first printer to abandon Latin and Greek and print in the vernacular. By providing people with books printed in their own language, Pfister created a demand for literacy from a public that could barely read. Printers in other countries immediately followed suit. Religious reformers took full advantage of the printing press. For the first time ever it was possible to reproduce reading material quickly and in vast quantities. Martin Luther was able to spread his ideas

A Brand New Special from Family Chronicle

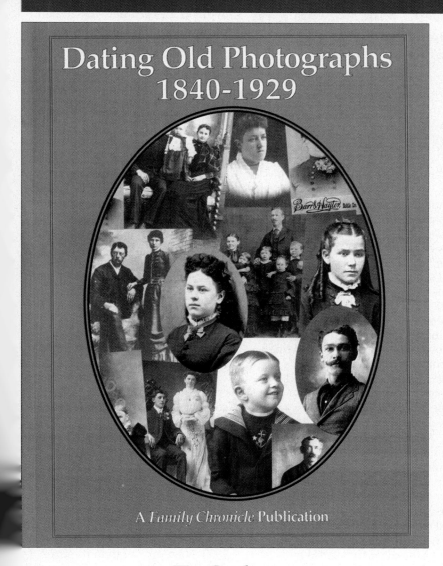

YOU'VE ALMOST CERTAINLY faced the problem: you've got an album or box of old photographs but almost all of them lack any identification. *Family Chronicle's* new special can't help you to identify the subject but it probably can help you with dating when the picture was taken — often within a couple of years.

A number of books have already been published that describe how to date old photographs but they rely almost entirely on descriptions: *Family Chronicle's* book is almost all reproductions of old photographs of known date. There are over 650 pictures covering the period from 1840 to the 1920s. By comparing your undated pictures to those in our book, you will be able to compare clothing and hair fashions, the poses adopted by the subject and the background settings. The book provides convincing evidence that our ancestors were at least as fashion conscious as we are today and that their fashions changed just as frequently.

Some of *Family Chronicle's* most popular issues have been those that have included supplements featuring old photographs of known date.

Our *Dating Old Photographs* book has been compiled from a number of sources but the majority of them are photographs submitted by readers of our magazine.

To Order:

US orders: Send $12 (includes shipping) check, money order, Visa or MasterCard (including expiry date) to Family Chronicle, P.O. Box 1201, Lewiston, NY, 14092.

Canadian orders: Send $15 (includes shipping) plus GST/HST as applicable. Send cheque, money order, Visa or MasterCard (incl. expiry date) to Family Chronicle, 505 Consumers Rd., Suite 500, Toronto, ON, M2J 4V8.

Or call Toll-Free (888) 326-2476 during office hours EST with your credit card. Or order online at
www.familychronicle.com

$12 (US) including shipping
$15 (Cdn)

Since their creation books have been burned in an attempt to stop the spread of ideas.

for the reformation of the church in the language of the people.

In 1474, Englishman William Caxton produced the first book ever printed in English. *The Recuyell of the Histories of Troy* was printed in Bruges, Belgium and proved to be very popular. In 1476, Caxton returned to England and set up his press near Westminster Abbey. He printed many famous books including Geoffrey Chaucer's *Canterbury Tales* and Thomas Malory's *Le Morte D'Arthur*.

While the printing press led to a revolution in book production and the spread of information, Europe had a very low literacy rate. Most people did not know how to read at all. However, the elites who controlled society were very interested in books. Non-literates were still able to access the book culture because traveling raconteurs would stand in the marketplaces and read from books as a way to make a living entertaining people. As a result, by 1501 there were 1,000 printing shops in Europe, which had produced 35,000 titles and 20 million copies.

Dangerous Books

In 1525, William Tyndale printed his historic English translation of the New Testament. It was immediately denounced by English bishops. Sir Thomas More — famous for his publication, in Latin, of *Utopia* — challenged Tyndale's work with the 1528 publication of his *Dialogue*.

Tyndale responded in 1530 with *An Answere unto Sir Thomas Mores Dialoge*. The lively, printed debate was cut short when More was executed in 1535 for opposing Henry VIII's Act of Supremacy. Tyndale himself, who had escaped England under threat of death, was branded a heretic and in 1536 he was arrested in Antwerp. Tyndale was executed by strangulation followed by burning at the stake. Tyndale's work, however, eventually led to the official English translation of the Bible, known as the *King James Bible*, which was first printed in 1611.

As printing in English became more acceptable, the number of readers increased, affecting the demand for writers. The 16th century saw the rise of dramatists. The most famous of these was William Shakespeare. However, other writers had popular publications as well: Miguel de Cervantes with *Don Quixote* and Edmund Spenser's *The Faerie Queene* to name but two. Reading books was developing into a form of entertainment as well as enlightenment and London became the capital of the book-publishing world. Works of fiction began to capture the public's imagination. Daniel Defoe's *Robinson Crusoe*, published in 1719, was written in plain prose to immediate and lasting success. Henry Fielding's *Joseph Andrews* sold 6,500 copies in 1742 and his *Tom Jones*, published in 1749, was received even more enthusiastically by the

reading public. By the end of the century every town in England had its own printer and bookshop.

Enterprising publishers began to print books serially (in parts) in order to spread out the cost of printing. In the case of successful books, this also served to heighten demand for each new installment. Charles Dickens' novels were an excellent example of this phenomenon. His popularity crossed the ocean and had crowds at the New York docks shouting "Is Little Nell dead?" as the ship arrived with the next installment of *The Old Curiosity Shop*. Harry Potter is in good company.

Prior to the 19th century most books were sold unbound. During the 1800s books came to be considered status symbols and were bound in elaborate leather covers. Having a private library in the home was a sign of refinement. Unfortunately, the cost of these books was out of the reach of many people. Circulating libraries existed where people could borrow books for a small fee. In 1850 free public libraries were created for the use of the general public and led to the decline of the fee-based libraries.

To this day, some people view certain books and the ideas they contain as threats to governments, to morality, to the status quo. Writers around the world have been imprisoned and executed since books were first created. Books have been banned and burned from their very beginnings. In 213BC, Chinese Emporer Shih Huang-ti ordered that all the books in his realm be burned. On 10 May 1933, Nazi propaganda minister Joseph Goebbels presided over the burning of over 20,000 books in front of a cheering crowd in Berlin. In the year 2000 several school boards in North America banned the wildly popular Harry Potter children's books.

Literacy rates have vastly improved over the last 200 years and the general public today takes the ability to read for granted. But reading is a pleasure that many still cannot experience. According to UNESCO, in 1985 28 percent of the world's population could not read. HM

The Tower of London

Nancy Hendrickson investigates one of England's most famed landmarks.

IN SHAKESPEARE'S *Richard III*, a young Edward V asked about the origin of the Tower of London. "Did Julius Caesar build that place, my lord?" The Duke of Buckingham replied, "He did, my gracious lord, begin that place; which, since, succeeding ages have re-edified."

Although the thought of a Roman Emperor helping build one of London's most famous landmarks must have appealed to the Bard of Avon, his poetic license was far off the mark.

Construction of the Tower of London was begun by William the Conqueror in 1066. Almost immediately following his coronation, William ordered the construction of a fort to be strategically located to command the River Thames. Ten years later, William began transforming this fort into a great stone tower which would serve as a fortress for his center of power — London.

Work began on the White Tower around 1078, under the supervision of a Norman monk. It is believed the tower was completed about 1097, 10 years after William's death. The White Tower rises 90 feet to its battlements, and is 118 feet long from east to west, and 107 feet from north to south. Its walls are 15 feet thick at the base and 11 feet at the top. The walls were built of Kentish ragstone, a sandy, rough blue to green-gray limestone. Over time, Caen stone, a fine grained yellow or yellow-white limestone imported from France was used around door and window openings. At regular intervals the limestone was whitewashed, giving the White Tower its name.

Turrets stand at each of the White Tower's corners, three are rectangular and one is rounded. The rounded turret contains the main spiral staircase. At different periods in the Tower's history, the White Tower served as a royal residence, with the king occupying

Plan of the Tower of London. The Crown Jewels are held in the Waterloo Barracks (#12).

the upper floors and the Constable of the Tower occupying the ground floor. At one time, the only way up to the royal residence was the turret staircase which the builders had wisely placed the furthest possible distance from the Tower entrance. It was thought if an enemy gained entrance to the Tower, they might be prevented from harming the king if they could not access the staircase.

To the east and south, the White Tower was protected by old Roman walls; ditches as large as 25 feet wide and 11 feet deep pro-

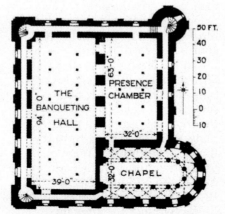

Plan of the White Tower's third floor. The chapel was used as a storeroom for state records in the 19th century.

tected the Tower on the north and west. Although William constructed the Tower as a fortification, its primary function was to serve as a power base in London, and a royal refuge during times of turmoil.

The stone tower rose at the southeast corner of an old Roman wall and immediately became known as the Tower of London. As the royal fortress enlarged over the centuries, the central tower was named the White Tower, and the entire fortress including its 20 towers became known as the Tower of London.

The Medieval Tower

In 1189, Chancellor William Longchamp began an expansion of the Tower, in the absence of crusading Richard I. Longchamp recognized the need for a stronger fortification because of the political instability in Richard's kingdom.

Longchamp doubled the area covered by the Tower, first by digging new and deeper ditches and then building new sections of wall. Longchamp had the opportunity to test the strength of his fortifications when John, Richard's younger brother, set siege on the Tower. Although the fortress was immune to attack, Longchamp was forced to surrender due to lack of provisions. When John was crowned upon the death of Richard I in 1199, he made virtually no changes to Longchamp's Tower.

John's son, Henry III, made major changes to the fortress, creating royal chambers, and adding a royal menagerie (zoo). Once again, the area covered by the Tower was increased, the walls enlarged and guard towers placed at regular intervals on the walls.

In recent years, the remains of Henry's menagerie have been uncovered beneath the Tower ramparts, including bones of rhinoceroses, tigers, antelopes, snakes and alligators. It is believed that most of the early animals came from monarchs of Europe exchanging gifts with England's royalty, such as the gift of a polar bear from the King of Norway.

Because rebellious barons threatened the security of the throne for Henry III, the reinforcement of royal castles was a priority, including extensive changes to the Tower of London. Two towers were added on the waterfront side, and a new wall enclosed the west side of the fortress. When Henry realized his major defenses consisted of an empty moat, the wall built by Longchamp a century earlier and old Roman walls, he ordered construction of a new wall around the east, north and west sides of the Tower. The new wall was so extensive it included the church of St. Peter ad Vincula. In addition, nine new towers were added to the complex. London citizens saw the expansion as a threat to their own security and an affirmation of the absolutism of royal power.

When Henry's son, Edward I, came to the throne, the Tower once again underwent an expansion, with Edward spending twice as much on the Tower as his father. Edward ordered another wall built, encompassing the earlier fortifications. At this point in time, the Tower of London encompassed 18 acres. Not only did it serve as a royal residence, it also became the storehouse of official documents, a royal mint which struck gold and silver coins, a treasure house, armory and a prison. In 1303, the Crown Jewels were moved to the Tower from Westminster Abbey. At the conclusion of Edward's work, the Tower became the strongest and largest concentric castle in England — that is, a castle with one line of defense within another.

Although Edward was an

The Tower of London in the late 15th century, during Edward IV's reign.

infrequent visitor to the Tower, his son, Edward II, used it as a refuge during ongoing battles with his barons. The conflicts arose because the barons were incensed at Edward's lavishing of money and other expensive gifts on his male companions.

The Garden Tower, built under Henry III in the 13th century, is now known as the Bloody Tower because it is believed to be the place where the 'Young Princes' were murdered. The princes, 12-year-old Edward and his younger brother Richard, the sons of Edward IV, had been living in the Tower since their father's death in 1483. When preparation began for Edward's coronation, it was discovered that the children were illegitimate and thus barred from the throne. The children were placed under the guardianship of their uncle who became King Richard III, last of the Plantagenet kings. In the two months after their father's death and the commencement of Henry VII's reign, the

young princes disappeared. It is not known if the children disappeared while under their uncle's care or after Henry's seizure of the throne. In the reign of Charles II, bones of two children were found buried near the White Tower and were officially interred in Westminster Abbey as the remains of the young brothers.

The Tudor Tower
Henry VII, the first Tudor king, extended the royal residence in the Tower, added a new private chamber, a long gallery, and a formal garden. These lodgings were further expanded by his son Henry VIII, even though he rarely used the Tower as a residence. During this time, the Tower was frequently used as a prison for political and religious dissenters. Although Henry faced fewer challenges than his predecessors, a major conflict arose from Henry's 1534 Act of Supremacy, in which he declared himself head of the Church of England.

One of the first Tudor prisoners to be executed was Sir Thomas More, who refused to recognize Henry VIII as the head of the Church of England. Anne Boleyn, the King's second wife, was executed a year later, and in July 1540, Thomas Cromwell was executed. Two years later, Henry's fifth wife, Catherine Howard, was beheaded just outside the Chapel Royal of St. Peter ad Vincula. During the reign of Victoria, the Chapel Royal was restored and hundreds of graves were found, most of which were parishioners who were buried within the church. However, several coffins contained the remains of beheaded people who were reinterred within the church.

The Restoration Tower

During the English Civil War of 1642-49, the Tower of London was seized from the monarchy and held by the parliamentary government until the monarchy was restored in 1660. During the reign of Charles II, the Tower became more of a military supply center than a prison. It was during this period that the Crown Jewels were put on public display at the Tower. A permanent garrison of soldiers were housed in the Tower, guns were set around the walls and the arsenal expanded.

In 1675, the round turret in the White Tower was used by astronomer John Flamsteed to make celestial observations.

The Modern Tower

Nineteenth-century visitors to the Tower of London would see a large fortress almost identical to what today's visitors see. In 1812, the Royal Mint moved outside the castle, and in 1834 what was left of the Royal Menagerie became the nucleus of the London Zoo. By the mid-19th century, the Tower was regarded as a national monument rather than a military compound.

During WWI and WWII, the Tower returned to use as a prison and 11 spies were held and executed between 1914 and 1916. During WWII, the Crown Jewels were moved to a secret location which, to this day, has never been revealed. The Tower's last execution was in 1941, and its last prisoner was Rudolf Hess, Deputy Fuhrer of Nazi Germany. Hess was held during WWII and then transferred to Spandau prison in Berlin.

Today the Tower of London is one of London's most popular tourist attractions and visited by over two million people annually.

Crown Jewels

The Crown Jewels are a favorite of visitors to the Tower. Housed at various times in the Martin Tower and the Wakefield Tower, today they are kept in the Jewel House.

The White Tower and its surroundings in the early 20th century.

The Coronation Regalia (those items used at a coronation) was originally kept at Westminster Abbey, and included the relics of St. Edward, who was King Edward the Confessor. Following the execution of Charles I in 1649, Cromwell, through his Parliament, ordered the ornaments be "totally broken" as being symbolic of the "detestable rule of kings". The metal was melted down for coinage and the gems sold. However, in 1661, pieces of the original regalia reappeared and were used for the coronation of Charles II.

The Crown Jewels include the Jeweled State Sword which was made for the coronation of George IV in 1821, and the Imperial State Crown. The major gemstones set in the crown include a sapphire taken from a ring buried with Edward the Confessor in 1066 and a ruby presented to the Black Prince in 1367.

The crown of Queen Elizabeth, the Queen Mother, holds the 108-carat Koh-i-Noor ("mountain of light") diamond discovered in southern India. The Koh-i-Noor was presented to Queen Victoria in 1850 to mark the 250th anniversary of the founding of the East India Company. The Scepter with the Cross, made for Charles II, contains the Star of Africa, at 530 carats, the largest top-quality cut diamond in the world. The Sovereign's Orb and Scepter have been used at every coronation since Charles II.

Tower Ravens

It is believed that there have been ravens at the Tower of London since its earliest days, with the large birds attracted by the piles of castle refuse. The ravens have had their wings clipped and are protected from harm, thanks to the legend that without them, the Tower will fall and with it the kingdom. Six ravens and two auxiliary ravens are kept at the Tower at all times and are cared for by the Raven Master, one of the Yeoman Warders.

The Ceremony of the Keys

The ceremony of the keys is the nightly tradition of locking the Tower of London. Every night at dusk, the Chief Yeoman Warder and an armed escort lock all the gates and doors leading into the Tower. The keys are then turned over to the Tower Governor for safe keeping.

In 1826, when the Duke of Wellington was Constable of the Tower, he ordered the time for the ceremony be fixed at 10 p.m., to make sure all his soldiers were inside the tower before the gates were locked. Since then, every night at seven minutes to 10, the Chief Warder begins the ceremony, carrying a lantern lighted with a candle in one hand and the keys in the other. After locking the Tower gates, the Chief Warder takes the keys to the house of the Resident Governor. It is believed the Ceremony of the Keys, which began nearly 700 years ago, is the oldest surviving military ceremony in the world.

HM

Notable Prisoners of the Tower

**William Wallace
(c. 1270-1305)**

**John II
(1319-64)**

**Henry VI
(1421-71)**

**Thomas More
(c. 1478-1535)**

**Anne Boleyn
(c. 1507-36)**

Gryffydd ap Llywlyn (died 1244): While trying to escape the Tower of London using a rope of sheets, Welsh prince ap Llywlyn fell to his death as the knots unraveled.

Sir William Wallace (hanged, disemboweled, beheaded, and quartered 1305): Scottish hero who led resistance to Edward I, Wallace was victorious at Stirling in 1297, but defeated and captured at the battle of Falkirk.

John II, King of France (imprisoned 1357-60): Defeated by the Black Prince at Poitiers during the Hundred Years' War, John was taken to the Tower to be ransomed back to the French for three million florins. After three years, other prisoners took John's place so the king could raise the funds. John returned to England after three years of freedom as his son (a replacement) escaped and John felt dishonored. John, while a captive, died in London in 1364.

Charles, Duke of Orleans (imprisoned 1415-40): Captured at the Battle of Agincourt, Charles was held for ransom for 25 years in the Tower. Charles spent his time composing poetry.

Henry VI, King of England (murdered 1471): King during the War of the Roses, Henry was deposed in 1461 by Edward IV of the house of York, but regained the throne in 1470 after a Lancastrian uprising. Henry was deposed again by Edward in 1471 and was murdered in the Tower.

Sir Thomas More (beheaded 1535): Lord Chancellor to Henry VIII, More was imprisoned after refusing to take the oath on the Act of Succession which sanctioned Henry's marriage to Anne Boleyn. More's fate was sealed when he opposed the Act of Supremacy.

Queen Anne Boleyn (beheaded 1536): The second wife of Henry VIII and mother of Elizabeth I, Boleyn was beheaded by a French swordsman for alleged infidelities.

Queen Catherine Howard (beheaded 1542): The fifth wife of Henry VIII, Howard was accused of infidelity. She confessed and was executed.

Lady Jane Grey (beheaded 1554): Protestant great niece of Henry VIII, she was placed on the throne by her ambitious relatives on Edward VI's death. Forces loyal to the Catholic Mary ousted Grey, who was beheaded the following year.

Princess Elizabeth, later Elizabeth I (imprisoned 1554): The Protestant Elizabeth was imprisoned on the orders of her Catholic half-sister Mary I after the failed rebellion of Thomas Wyatt. Elizabeth was released after assuring Mary of her loyalty.

Robert Devereux, Earl of Essex (beheaded 1601): Courtier and soldier, Devereux was a favourite of Elizabeth I; he consistently provoked the Queen's anger, but was forgiven until he raised an army against Elizabeth in 1601. He surrendered after it failed.

Guy Fawkes (hanged, disemboweled, beheaded and quartered 1606): An English Catholic who planned to blow up Westminster Palace where Parliament sat. The Gunpowder Plot was discovered and Fawkes was caught in the cellar where the gunpowder had been stored.

Sir Walter Raleigh (beheaded 1618): Accused of treason against James I, Raleigh was imprisoned and then released to find El Dorado. Raleigh returned from his voyage unsuccessful and was imprisoned again and then executed. While in the Tower for the first time, Raleigh wrote *The History of the World, Part I*.

Samuel Pepys (imprisoned 1679): As Secretary of the Admiralty, Pepys was accused of treason and practicing Catholicism. Charles II dissolved Parliament shortly after Pepys' imprisonment, and this gave the famed diarist time to gather together a case which led to his release within six weeks.

Simon Fraser, 11th Lord Lovat (beheaded 1747): The last person to be beheaded in Britain, Fraser was a Scottish Jacobite who took part in the failed rebellion of 1745. Fraser was captured and beheaded at the age of 80.

**Jane Grey
(1537-54)**

**Robert Devereux
(1567-1601)**

**Walter Raleigh
(c. 1552-1618)**

**Samuel Pepys
(1633-1703)**

**Simon Fraser
(c. 1667-1747)**

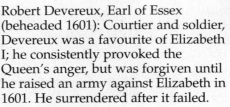
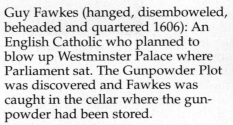
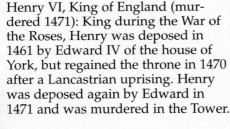

STEPPING STONES

English Street & Trade Directories on CD £11.99 each + £2.00 P/P

Available Now—detailed contents on our web page

Northumberland 1822 Trade Directory (Pigot's)
Northumberland 1848 Trade Directory (Slater's)
Durham 1834 Trade Directory & Surrounding Villages (Pigot's)
Newcastle & Gateshead 13th & 14th Century Journal
Cumberland 1834 Trade Directory (Pigot's)
Scarborough 1902 Street & Trade Directory including Whitby, Filey & surrounding villages
East Riding of Yorkshire 1872 Post Office Directory (Kelly's)
East Riding of Yorkshire 1897 Residents Directory (Kelly's)
East Riding of Yorkshire 1822 Trade Directory (White's)
North & East Riding of Yorkshire 1872 (Kelly's)
North Yorkshire 1897 Street & Trade Directory (Kelly's)
North & East Riding of Yorkshire 1897 Court & Profession Directory (Kelly's)
North Riding of Yorkshire 1822 Trade Directory (Whites)
Hull & surrounding Villages 1897 Trade Directory (Kelly's)
York 1897 Street & Trade Directory including York Inns, & now with added Photo's
York 1822 Trade Directory (White's)
West Riding of Yorkshire 1822 Trade Directory (Bain's)
Leeds 1853 Street & Trade Directory
Lancashire 1848 Trade Directory (Slater's)
Sheffield 1822 Town Centre Trade Directory (Bain's)
Liverpool 1848 Trade Directory (Slater's)
Manchester 1848 Trade Directory (Slater's)
Cheshire 1828-29 Trade Directory (Pigot's)
Devonshire 1830 Trade Directory (Pigot's)
Wiltshire 1851 Trade Directory (Slater's)
Shropshire 1858-59 Trade Directory (Slater's)
Essex 1832-33 Trade Directory (Pigot's)
Cornwall 1919 Trade Directory (Kelly's)
Principal Cities 1822 Trade Directory (Bain's)
North Wales 1828-29 & South Wales 1830 (Pigot's)
London 1865 Trade Directory Part 1
London 1865 Trade Directory Part 2
London 1865 Commercial Directory Part 1
London 1865 Commercial Directory Part 2
Somersetshire 1851 Trade Directory (Slater's)
Middlesex 1837 Trade Directory (Pigot's)
Bristol 1852-53 Trade Directory (Pigot's)
Worcestershire 1828-29 Trade Directory (Pigot's)
Edinburgh & Leigh 1848-49 Post Office Directory
Staffordshire 1828-29 Trade Directory
Cambridgeshire 1830 Trade Directory
Norfolk 1830 Trade Directory (Pigot's)
Kent 1832-34 Trade Directory (Pigot's)
Sussex 1832-34 Trade Directory (Pigot's)
Suffolk 1840 Trade Directory (Pigot's)
Surrey 1840 Trade Directory (Pigot's)
Illustrated Yorkshire Churches

Contact us at
Stepping Stones
PO Box 295
YORK
YO31 1YS
England
Tel :- 01904 424131
Fax :- 01904 422351
Email :- judd@mjudson.freeserve.co.uk
Order on line at Web Page www.stepping-stones.co.uk

Coming soon
Suffolk 1883
Leeds 1907 Street & Trade
Lincolnshire 1876 Post Office Directory
Glasgow 1838 Annual Directory
Nottingham Street Directory
Hampshire 1830
Derbyshire 1842
Herefordshire 1835
Northamptonshire 1841
London Street Directory Part 1
London Street Directory Part 2

New Directories arriving all the time check our Web page for updates

Trade Enquiries Welcome

History Magazine and Mississippi Tourism

Explore the Natchez Trace... Discover America.

Tupelo

Kosciusko

Ridgeland
Jackson

Natchez

Natchez Trace Parkway

Win a Tour Worth $2000!

History Magazine, in conjunction with the Mississippi Division of Tourism, wants to give you the chance to travel the Natchez Trace and experience true Mississippi hospitality. You could win an all expense paid 7-day vacation for two exploring this famous parkway.

Your trip will began in Tupelo where you will learn the history of the Trace, enjoy a visit to a Chickasaw Indian village site, Elvis Presley's birth-place and two Civil War Battlefields. Highlights of the trip will include tours of historic Kosciusko homes and sites; shopping, fine dining and the MS Craft Center in Ridgeland; and historic state buildings and museums in downtown Jackson the capital city of Mississippi. Your trip will end in Natchez, overlooking the mighty Mississippi River, with tours to the famous antebellum mansions that this historic town is so famous for.

The extensive itinerary, which includes far more than we can mention here, is given in detail on the website: *www.nps.gov/napr*

All meals, accommodations and tours are included for you and a companion (based on double occupancy and availability). The winner will be responsible for transportation to Tupelo and for the return from Natchez.

After the closing date (30 June 2001) a random draw will be held to select the winner. The winner will be advised by telephone or mail.

History Magazine

• Please enter my name into your contest to Explore the Natchez Trace. I understand that I will be responsible for transportation to Tupelo and that any prize must be taken by 30 November 2002.

• The winner will be selected at random from all entries in a draw held shortly after the closing date. Entries must be received by 30 June 2001.

• Mail this entry form (or a photocopy) to **History Magazine**, PO Box 1201, Lewiston, NY, 14092 (from the US) or **History Magazine**, 500-505 Consumers Rd, Toronto, ON, M2J 4V8 (from Canada). Only one ballot permitted per entrant.

Last Name_____ First Name_____

Address_____

City_____ State/Prov. _____ Zip/Postal Code _____

Phone Number_____ (only to be used to advise winner)

The Scholarly Guild

Barbara Krasner-Khait traces the rise of universities.

Sing unto the Lord a new song, praise him with stringed instruments and organs, rejoice upon the high-sounding cymbals, for your son has held a glorious disputation, which was attended by a great multitude of teachers and scholars. He answered all questions without a mistake and no one could prevail against his arguments. Moreover, he celebrated a famous banquet, at which rich and poor were honored as never before, and he has duly begun to give lectures that are already so popular, that others' classrooms are deserted and his own are filled.

If you had received a letter with these words in the Middle Ages, it could only have meant one thing: your son graduated. If he had attended the University of Bologna, he probably now had a law degree, since that is what Bologna was known for. Had he gone to the University of Paris, he would have studied theology. It did not matter what language he actually spoke, since Latin was the universal language of books and lectures. And he was a member of the guild — the scholarly guild of masters and students.

Universitas and the Guild

Universities as we know them today got their start around 1100, an outgrowth of Europe's cathedral and monastery schools. New sources of knowledge had made their way to Europe through the Arab scholars of Spain and included works of the great Greeks and Romans that had been hidden during the Dark Ages. Said historian Charles Homer Raskins in *The Rise of Universities*, "This new knowledge burst the bonds of the cathedral and monastery schools and created the learned professions; it drew over mountains and across the narrow seas eager youths…to form in Paris and Bologna those academic guilds which have given us our first and our best definition

The first universities did not have buildings. Lectures would take place wherever students and masters could gather.

of a university, a society of masters and scholars."

The name university derives from *universitas* — a group of people organized for a common purpose, a corporation, a guild of masters and students. Some of the oldest universities are believed to be the University of Bologna, the University of Paris and Oxford University, all of which were established during the 1100s. *Universitas* took on different meanings: in Bologna, it stood for the whole body of students. In Paris, it stood for the group of masters.

Through the 1200s, the great majority of the productive thinkers were Dominican and Franciscan friars, who had been educated at their own schools and then went on to study theology at university. They became thought leaders at the University of Paris and Oxford University.

Former Oxford students founded Cambridge University in 1209. Though initially overshadowed by Oxford, Cambridge soon

developed its own unique approach to theological and philosophical problems and its reputation grew.

In southern Europe, a number of universities emerged in the early 13th century. Bologna continued to shine in Italy, marked by three dramatic differences: lay participation, primacy of legal studies and the subordination of the teaching masters to their student "nations" and their rectors. The universities of Vicenza (1204) and Padua (1222) were products of Bologna student migrations. Naples followed in 1224 (founded by Frederick II), while Palencia (around 1208), Salamanca (around 1220) and Valladolid (around 1250) were established in Spain. New French universities included Angers (1229), Toulouse (1229) and Orleans (1235) — which provided technical training in canon and civil law. Montpellier, a celebrated medical school in existence by 1137, rapidly eclipsed its Italian counterpart at Salerno.

By 1300, there were 23 universities, with a heavy concentration in Italy and Spain, five in France plus Oxford and Cambridge in England. By 1500, there were 75 universities, including three in Scotland and 16 in areas east of the Rhine.

The University of Heidelberg, founded in 1386, was openly modeled on the University of Paris. The founding of universities like Prague (1348), Vienna (1365) and St. Andrews (1411) was a reaction against the likes of Paris, Oxford and Bologna, aimed at promoting regional needs of Bohemia, Austria and Scotland. These regional centers attracted local aristocratic interest and patronage. Rulers like Friedrich Barbarossa of Germany in 1158 and Philip Augustus of France in 1200 gave scholars privileges that separated them from their secular authorities. Pope Innocent III formally recognized the University of Paris around the

A College or a University?

In the Middle Ages, there was a distinct difference between a college and a university. The former originated as an endowed hospice or residence hall and became a staple of university life. Often, a college simply secured room and board for scholars who could not afford that for themselves. Over time, the college expanded to become centers that absorbed much of the university's activities. Unlike the university, the college had walls, buildings and endowments.

There was a college at Paris as early as 1180 and 68 colleges by 1500. The system continued until the French Revolution. Only fragments remain, such as the Sorbonne.

Perhaps the most renowned homes of the college are Oxford and Cambridge, where the college became a distinctive feature of university life, encompassing teaching and social activities. This left the university's role to serve merely as an examining and degree-conferring body.

Latin was the universal language of all lectures. This allowed students from all over Europe to attend any university regardless of their native tongue.

year 1210, followed by other grants of authority to the guild of masters and students.

The Curriculum

The beginning of the university also marked the beginning of formal degrees and exams. While schools of higher learning had been around since antiquity, degrees were not previously conferred nor exams administered.

Entering freshmen or "yellow beaks" were about 16 years old. Students usually underwent some sort of hazing administered by senior classmen. They typically attended three lectures each day. They became well versed in the art of disputation — argumentation and debate. Lectures were read from a text, augmented by the lecturer's commentary. As historian Daniel Boorstin explains, "For a formal disputation, the master offered a thesis. Objections would then be raised by the master, by students, or by anyone else present. A younger teacher (baccalar-

ius) would uphold the thesis and answer the question. At the next lecture the master would resume the subject, restate the thesis, select the arguments against it, and offer his own decision, while refuting objections."

Not only were disputations held by each master, there were also public disputations during the second week of Advent and the third or fourth week of Lent — anybody could submit a question on any subject. This art of questions and answers became the trademark style of Peter Abelard and later St. Thomas Aquinas and formed the basis of scholasticism.

The Bachelor of Arts degree required study of the trivium: grammar, rhetoric and logic. The Master of Arts degree required completion of the quadrivium: arithmetic, geometry, astronomy and music. At Paris, becoming a master typically required completion of six years of study and 21 years of age for liberal arts and eight years and 34 years for theology.

The university claimed the right to grant licenses for teaching in any part of the world.

Tools of the Trade

Before the invention of the printing press, text had to be laboriously copied. Therefore, universities relied on just a few great volumes

— Gratian's *Concordian* and Peter the Lombard's *Four Books of the Sentences*. This latter compilation of opinions dealing with God, the Redemption and the nature of the Sacraments did more than any other single work to determine the aims and principles of scholastic thought for two centuries. Revised Latin translations of Aristotle were used — for the first time, medieval philosophers had in their hands a detailed analysis of a universe in which God played no part. As early as the 1220s, Pope Gregory IX warned the University of Paris against the use of Aristotle's texts until they had been "examined and purified."

Peddlers were a source of textbooks, even if unreliable. Renting books became a profitable trade. At Bologna and at other universities, every professor was required to provide the university "stationer" with a copy of his lectures so they could be transcribed and rented or sold. The stationer was so called because he stayed in one place versus the traveling peddler. The stationer long remained the authorized source of textbooks and writing materials; he also operated a circulating library.

By the mid-15th century, the making or transcribing of books became a prosperous industry, centered in university towns. Universities began to acquire their own libraries, mostly as a result of

The University of Salamanca, founded around 1220, is one of the world's oldest.

bequests. For instance, by the mid-14th century, the library of the Sorbonne listed nearly 2,000 volumes.

Latin was the language of the university, creating a kind of single university system: teachers and students could move from Bologna to Heidelberg, Heidelberg to Prague, Prague to Paris and still feel at home in the classroom. For instance, Nicolas Copernicus studied at the University of Cracow, Bologna, Padua and Ferrara; lectured in Rome, and settled at Frauenburg on the Rhine.

All lectures were delivered in Latin and students were required to speak only Latin outside the classroom; a rule enforced by penalties and by informers called "wolves". This system might also have been designed to limit conversation. University of Paris entering students were greeted with lists of colloquial phrases to help them exchange money, and buy candles, writing materials and different foods. In 1480, Heidelberg offered a conversation manual that provided students with phrases to use during hazing, when buying dinner for an upperclassman or for writing home for money.

Hands-on laboratory training was not yet in use at medical universities. Instead, students relied on translations of Hippocrates, though some advances were made in anatomy and surgery at Bologna and Montpellier.

A League of Nations
At Paris, students and administration belonged to one of four groups or "nations," depending on where they came from: the French, the Normans, the Picards and the English. The Picards included all the Low Countries, the French included all Latin countries, and the English included the Germans and countries north and east. Teachers had to be Masters of Arts in order to be members of their nation, headed by proctors. The four nations represented a dramatic departure from the inwardly focused approaches of the monks. Universities that followed the Paris model, most notably Heidelberg, also instituted this practice.

Loose but Tight Control
There was no administration of the university, as we know it today. Control was held either by the students or the masters, depending on the opportunity. In the early years of the university, there were no ivy-covered, stately buildings to house classrooms. This left students free to move away en masse, threatening to disturb the local economy. It led to fixed pricing for books and lodging. Even the masters, like the local merchants, depended on students for their fees. And while the students regarded their professors as the enemy, they also wanted to make sure they got their money's worth. In fact, early Bolognese statutes in 1317 forbade professors to be absent without leave, and required that a master who departed the city should give a deposit to ensure his return.

Armed with their degrees at inception, the medieval event we would know as commencement, students — when wrenched away from their academic pursuits and often bawdy student life — moved on to the vocation they came to study.

Further Reading
Compayre, Gabriel. *Abelard and the Origin and Early History of the Universities.* (Scholarly Press, 1967).
De Ridder-Symoens, Hilde (editor). *A History of the University in Europe: Universities in the Middle Ages (History of the University in Europe Series, Volume 1)* (Cambridge University Press, 1991).
Haskins, Charles Homer. *The Rise of Universities* (Cornell University Press, 1965).
Rashdall, Hastings. *Universities of Europe in the Middle Ages* (Oxford University Press, 1997).
Rudy, Willis. *Universities of Europe, 1100-1914: A History* (Fairleigh Dickinson University Press, 1984).
Van Engen, John (editor). *Learning Institutionalized: Teaching in the Medieval University (Notre Dame Conferences in Medieval Studies, 9)* (University of Notre Dame Press, 2000).

HM

Hindsight

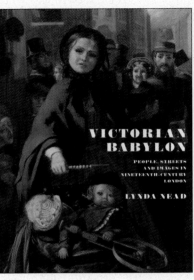

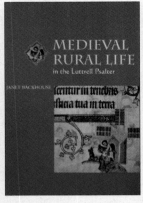

Immigration to America in the 19th century was no small undertaking. People from every walk of life left their homes and all they had known, faced the long and difficult ocean voyage, the possible quarantine and problems at customs and the harsh realities of a different society at the end. Told with compassion, **Going To America** by Terry Coleman chronicles the stories of the immigrants hoping for a better life for themselves and their children. 317 pages, soft cover with notes and an index. At about $20 US from the Genealogical Publishing Co., Inc., 1001 N. Calvert St., Baltimore MD 21202, 1-800-548-1806 or www.GenealogyBookShop.com.

Focusing on the public places of 19th-century London, **Victorian Babylon: People, Streets and Images in Nineteenth-Century London** investigates beyond the parlors and kitchens of the city. In the reign of Victoria, London became a modern city, its streets, parks and many entertainments transformed the city. Author Lynda Nead addresses the images of construction and change in the landscape, gas lighting and its impact, along with the rise of

pleasure seeking. Beyond the pleasure seeking, there was the growth of obscenity, as pedestrians were tempted with suggestive wares along Holywell Street and that which existed beyond the streets of London. From Yale University Press, hard cover, 252 pages, color and black and white illustrations, with an index and notes. Priced at about $35 US or $47 Cdn. Available in bookshops everywhere.

As few first-hand sources remain, medieval manuscripts are prized for their beauty and the rare glimpses they offer into the everyday life of the Middle Ages. **Medieval Warfare in Manuscripts** by Pamela Porter, part of the Medieval World in Manuscripts series, looks at the art of war. Examples in manuscripts of castles under siege and the blood-soaked battle grounds of Europe are shown with descriptions of the technology and the

armor of the period. Another book in the Medieval World in Manuscripts series is **Medieval Rural Life in the Luttrell Psalter**. Author Janet Blackhouse examines the treasure known as the Luttrell Psalter, explaining the manuscript in great detail, drawing attention to the marginal illustrations and the details that show everyday scenes of the Middle Ages such as knife sharpening and the dressing of hair. Each book is 64 pages, soft-cover, with numerous color illustrations and an index. At about $20 Cdn. each from University of Toronto Press, 5201 Dufferin St., Toronto ON M3H 5T8 Canada. Tel: (800) 565-9523, fax: (800) 221-9985.

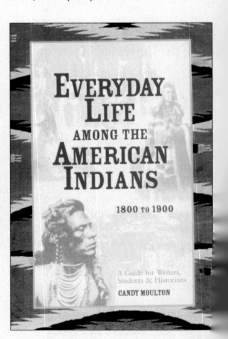

Full of interesting facts, **Everyday Life Among The American Indians** covers the period from 1800 to 1900. The first section of the book

MAIL ⇒ POSTE
Canada Post Corporation
Société canadienne des postes

Postage paid	Port payé
if mailed in Canada	si posté au Canada
Business Reply	Réponse d'affaires

0077712999   01

0077712999-M2J4V8-BR01

HISTORY MAGAZINE
500-505 CONSUMERS RD
PO BOX 45371 STN BRN B
TORONTO ON   M7Y 7V1

covers how the Indian people traded among themselves and examines wars of the period. The second section covers everyday life and deals with subjects such as birth, puberty, marriage, death, food and clothing. Moulton also divides certain subjects by geographic regions. The final section covers entertainment, language, customs and religion of the Indian people. Author Candy Moulton writes about the world of the 19th-century Indian with understanding. 304 pages, hard cover, with illustrations and indexed at about $16 US or $27 Cdn. Available in bookstores and from Writer's Digest Books, 1507 Dana Ave., Cincinnati OH 45207 Tel: 800-289-0396

Perfect for philatelists and historians, **Special Delivery: Canada's Postal Heritage** is a beautiful book detailing the history of Canada's postal system. The book covers 'tools of the trade' such as ink pots, early cards and the stamps themselves. The narrative is full of rich details, such as a story that letters were left under stones along Cape Hope by sailors in the 17th century hoping that ships returning to Europe would pick up the letters.

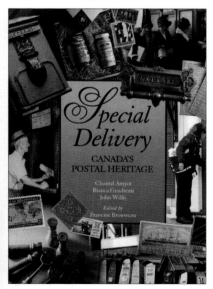

The book also discusses the importance of the post office in the past as a link to the outside world. By the time you're done with this book, you will want to write a letter. From Goose Lane Editions, hard cover, 150 pages, full color

with an index. Priced at about $45 Cdn. Distributed by General Distribution Services (800) 805-1083 or directly from Goose Lane Editions (888) 926-8377 or through *www.chapters.ca.*

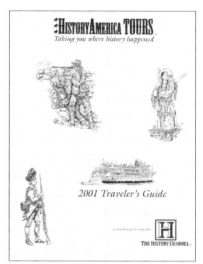

2001 Traveler's Guide from History America Tours is a catalog of 25 of the most memorable guided history tours and cruises of North America. Tours such as The Apache Wars of Indian Chiefs Cochise and Geronimo take travelers to remote historic sites in Arizona and New Mexico where clashes for survival took place. Colorado Splendor takes travelers aboard modern streamliners and historic steam trains. The Assassination of JFK is a detailed examination of that historic weekend in Dallas that changed American history and left a legacy of controversy that exists to this day. Maya Equinox and the Return of the Sun Serpent cruise allows travelers to discover the ancient culture of the Mayas and visit Mayan ruins. A team of renowned authorities presents lectures, seminars and roundtable discussions with nights on deck with astronomers, witnessing the starry grandeur. Tour departures are year round. Call for the free 2001 catalog to History America Tours 1-800-628-8542 or request online at *www.historyamerica.com.*

History of Middle Tennessee Baptists by J.H. Grime is a reprint memorial by Willow Bend Books to

those pioneer heroes who, through many trials and hardships, planted the standard of truth and established a church among the vine-clad hills of Cumberland Valley, Tennessee. The descendants of those early Tennessee Baptist pioneers must now number in the tens of thousands and this book would be a great find for them. It deals extensively with the pioneer leaders of many Tennessee Baptist congregations with brief biographies and often photographs and genealogies. In the early 1800s, when these leaders were establishing congregations, a religious revival was sweeping America. The stories of their courageous determination to establish their congregations, often traveling miles barefoot with little food in what was then frontier land, are inspirational. 564 pages, softcover, illustrated and indexed at about $37 US from Willow Bend Bend Books, 65 East Main St., Maryland 21157-5026. Call 1-800-876-6103 or order online at *www.WillowBendBooks.com.*

Bundling

Ron Wild exposes the courting custom known as bundling.

READERS OF FINANCIAL columns of newspapers will by now have become very familiar with the modern business technique of "bundling", which essentially involves tying the sale or availability of one product or service to the sale of a less popular one to limit competition.

From the late 1700s to the late 1800s bundling was the name given to an entirely different human activity having nothing to do with business.

Bundling was a courtship custom that allowed an unmarried couple to sleep together, with certain restrictions, in the bed of the young woman with the approval of parents and other family members. The young couple would lie together in bed, partly clothed and would kiss and fondle and engage in other courtship activities short of intercourse. The restrictions would vary in different parts of the world depending on local tradition and mores but could vary from very restrictive requirements to almost none. Bundling as a social custom spread throughout Europe and came to North America in the late 1700s along with the old country immigrants.

In Holland, where bundling first became very popular in the 1700s, it was necessary for a special bundling blanket to be made. The entire family might be involved in the cutting and sewing of the bundling blanket; it was a fun family event during which many sly comments were made amid much snickering and laughter from younger siblings. It resembled two sleeping bags sewn together with special double and triple stitching down the center to prevent rupture of the separating seal. The young man and woman then got into their separate compartments. The bundling blanket had string draws around the top and these were pulled

In Europe and America in the 1700s, courtship often involved the practice of bundling.

snugly around the neck so that only heads were left outside.

A German variation saw a bundling board attached down the middle of the bed in much the way that a headboard is attached to top and bottom and this was firmly fixed in place to keep the young couple on their respective sides.

An English variation was a padded bolster that ran from the top of the bed to the bottom and which was really a very long and narrow pillow that ran between the young couple to separate them from too intimate contact. The English bolster also required that the couple be fully dressed and frequently the young maiden's legs were tied at the ankles with a special bundling knot that only the father knew how to untie so that no unwarranted intrusion could take place.

In Protestant America, a simpler bundling blanket was contrived that consisted of two sacks sewn firmly together with holes at the bottom for feet to stick out and ties around the top with pull

draws. One of father's jobs was to diligently examine the bundling sacks to make sure that no surreptitious holes appeared that might jeopardize the courting.

The young man usually arrived at his sweetheart's home around six or seven in the evening and often had an evening meal with the family. The young couple then went to the woman's bedroom to get the bundling underway. The suitor was expected to leave around 10 or 11 p.m.

It was not uncommon for a young lady during her courtship years to have many bundling partners. As may be expected, who was bundling who was a major topic in the local taverns and around the hot stove in the local store with many bawdy comments aimed at young men who might venture by.

Strong opposition from ministers and pastors of the church brought bundling into disrepute by the early 1900s and it is no longer practiced openly, although some religious communities are reputed to allow their young couples to try it as an alternative to supervised courtship.

No doubt many modern parents with teenage sons and daughters would gladly consider bundling as an alternative to the nightly consternation caused by the warning from many North American TV stations: "It's 11:00 o'clock. Do you know where your children are?" **HM**

...a quiet read beside a brook
...a history or genealogy book
...from www.WillowBendBooks.com

The Letter That Triggered the Opium Wars

History
Magazine

June/July 2001
$4.50 US
$5.50 Cdn.

Good For What Ales You
A Sober Look at the History of Beer

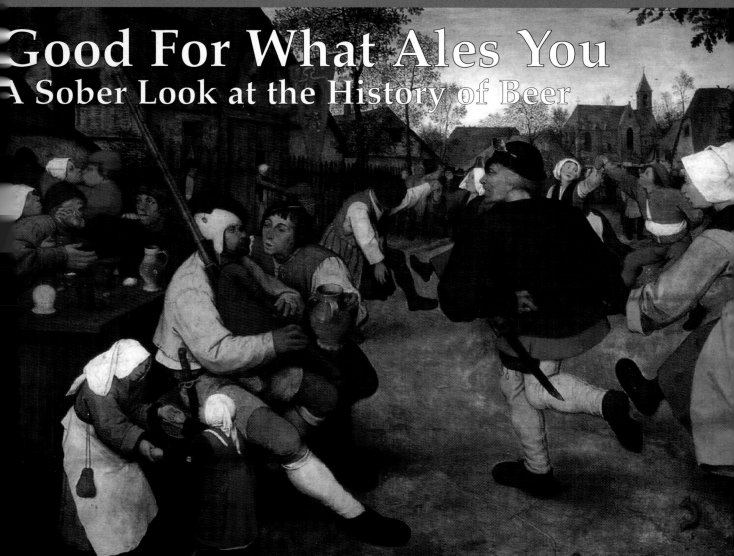

07

56698 94944   2

June/July 2001

In Publ. Mail Product
ales Agreement No.

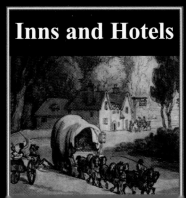

Inns and Hotels

The Kitchen:
Heart of the Home

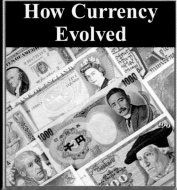

How Currency
Evolved

Contents of this issue of History Magazine

The 1860s.
Page 7.

Inns and Hotels.
Page 29.

Money.
Page 34.

Beer.
Page 43.

OUR COVER: *Peasant Dance* by Pieter Bruegel the Elder.

VOLUME 2 NUMBER 5
EDITOR & PUBLISHER
Halvor Moorshead
EDITOR
Jeff Chapman
EDITORIAL ASSISTANTS
Nicole Brebner
Victoria L. King
SPECIAL PROJECTS MANAGER
Ron Wild
ADVERTISING SERVICES
Victoria Pratt
Published by Moorshead Magazines Ltd.
505 Consumers Road, Suite 500, Toronto,
ON, M2J 4V8 Canada
(416) 491-3699 Fax (416) 491-3996
E-Mail: magazine@moorshead.com
PRESIDENT
Halvor Moorshead
CIRCULATION MANAGER
Rick Cree
SUBSCRIPTION SERVICES
Jeannette Cox
Valerie Carmichael

History Magazine is published six times a year
(Feb/Mar, Apr/May, Jun/Jul, Aug/Sep,
Oct/Nov, Dec/Jan) by Moorshead Magazines.
POSTAL INFORMATION — CANADA
Canadian Publications Mail Product Sales
Agreement No. 1595695. Mailing address for
subscription orders, undeliverable copies and
change of address notice is:
History Magazine,
505 Consumers Road, Suite 500,
Toronto, Ontario, M2J 4V8 Canada
POSTAL INFORMATION — UNITED STATES
Periodical Postage Paid Lewiston, NY
USPS #018-154
Postmaster send address corrections to:
History Magazine,
PO Box 1201, Lewiston, NY, 14092-9934 USA
US Office of Publication
850 Cayuga St., Lewiston, NY, 14092
ISSN 1492-4307

© 2001 Moorshead Magazines Ltd.
Some illustrations copyright www.arttoday.com.

SUBSCRIPTIONS
Subscription rate for US (US funds):
1 year (6 issues) $24.00
2 years (12 issues) $40.00
3 years (18 issues) $55.00

Subscription rate for Canada (Cdn funds):
1 year (6 issues) $28.00 plus GST/HST
2 years (12 issues) $45.00 plus GST/HST
3 years (18 issues) $59.00 plus GST/HST
Quebec residents add 7.5% QST

GST # 139340186 RT
We welcome the submission of articles for publication. Please send a printed copy in addition to the
file in electronic format. Please do not send important documents with submissions. We will always
contact people who submit articles but the review
process may take several weeks. Authors' notes are
available on request.
Toll-Free Subscription Line:
1-877-731-4478
PRINTED IN CANADA
WEBSITE
www.history-magazine.com

History Notes

Trenchers

Prior to the late 14th century, a meal in medieval England would not have included any fine china. In fact, there wouldn't have been any plates at all.

Meals at that time were brought to the table on large serving platters or in large bowls, to be shared by many.

Individual portions of food would be eaten from each diner's trencher. Trenchers were made from heavy bread and were either flat and square — to be used like a plate — or hollowed out rounds — to be used as a bowl.

In wealthy homes, fresh bread was used to make the trenchers. Following a banquet, the trenchers, soaked with the juices of the meal, were collected and distributed to the poor. In peasant homes, stale bread was used and it was not frowned upon for hungry diners to eat their trenchers.

By the end of the 14th century, square or circular plates were fashioned out of wood but were still referred to as trenchers. By the beginning of the 17th century, trenchers were replaced by pewter ware, followed by earthenware and porcelain. —NICOLE BREBNER

Flowerpots

Some historians note that potted plants were depicted in art 770 years before the recognized invention: an altar decoration found in the Maltese Temple of Hagar Quim depicts what appears to be a potted plant.

The more common date given for the invention of the flowerpot is 1230BC, with credit given to the pharaoh Ramses III, a great inventor who is remembered for his elaborate temple and palace designs. Ramses III used flowerpots in the 514 public gardens he designed throughout Egypt. He used earthenware pots containing flowers, shrubs and papyrus to decorate the garden pathways.

In the 6th century BC, the Greeks adopted the Egyptian technique. Women began using pots during the festival of Adonis. Seedlings were planted in pots and left to die at the statue of Adonis, symbolizing the god's early death.

Romans used terracotta flowerpots for gardening and decoration. Many homes in the empire had gardens on their roofs using different sizes and styles of flowerpots. Homes with balconies often had windowsill pots. Large potted plants often lined city streets in order to remind Romans of their agricultural roots.

Flowerpots in the home did not sprout up in Europe until the 1600s. A book on growing plants indoors, *The Garden of Eden*, was published by Sir Hugh Platt in 1653.

It was not until the 1800s that the decorative potted plant, *jardinières*, became highly popular in England. —JODI AVERY

Bowling for Dollars

The common North American game of 10-pin bowling was invented as a sneaky means of playing an outlawed game. The origins of bowling are ancient — a small set of pins and "bowls"

were discovered in the tomb of an Egyptian child and date back to 3200BC. In the 3rd and 4th centuries, German monks used clubs called *kegels* (which they usually carried for self defence) to represent sins or temptations. They would throw rocks at the "sins" in the attempt to knock them down. In a variation of this, the *kegel* represented the devil and those who hit it were judged to be free of sin.

In England, the game of skittles saw participants propelling a ball or "cheese" at nine large pins in order to knock them down. There are many variations to the scoring and method of throwing the cheeses. In some versions it was flung at the pins while in others it was rolled down an alley or required to bounce once before striking the pins. As skittles was commonly played in pubs, miniaturization began to occur as a space-saving device. Versions of skittles were played in many parts of Europe for centuries and the tabletop game is still played today.

Dutch and English settlers introduced skittles to North America where it became wildly popular. Unfortunately nine-pin bowling was so popular that it attracted crowds of gamblers. The game was subsequently banned in some areas. However, the ban referred only to "nine-pin bowling". By adding an extra pin, bowlers avoided a costly fine and 10-pin bowling was born.—NICOLE BREBNER

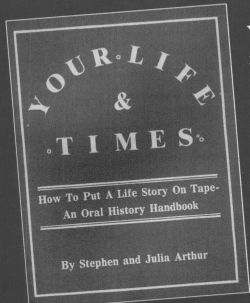

Batteries

While it is possible some form of battery may have been used by the Parthians as early as 300BC, the first well-documented uses of chemical batteries occurred in Italy in the late 18th century.

While doing some unusual experiments with frogs' legs in 1780, physician and physicist Luigi Galvani discovered that when he stuck a brass hook and a steel hook into a frog's leg and connected them by wire, the frog's leg would twitch. In 1791, he published an essay titled *De Viribus Electricitatis in Motu Musculari Commentarius* (Commentary on the Effect of Electricity on Muscular Motion). He concluded that animal tissue contained an innate force — an "electrical fluid" produced in the brain which activated nerves and muscles touched by metal probes.

Galvani's friend Alessandro Volta recognized that Galvani had generated an electric current, but he was less certain about his colleague's conclusions. In 1794, Volta began experimenting with metals alone and found that placing two metals in an acid solution generated a current, and that animal tissue was unnecessary. Volta used his findings to devise the first modern voltaic cell or battery. In 1801 in Paris, he gave a demonstration of his battery's generation of electrical current before Napoleon, who made Volta a count of the Italian kingdom of Lombardy.

The generation of a continous electric current through a chemical reaction was an important scientific breakthrough, and others quickly built upon Volta's foundations. In 1836, English chemist John Daniell developed the standard form of the dry-cell battery, with the active parts encased in a cover to keep air outside and the electrolyte solvent inside. The rechargable battery — which can be recharged by DC voltage and current to almost its original state — was invented by French physicist Gaston Planté in 1859. An improved form of Planté's battery is used in most automobiles today.

The volt, the basic unit used to measure the electromotive force that drives current, was named in honor of Alessandro Volta in 1881. —JEFF CHAPMAN

The King's Evil

The custom of scrofula sufferers being healed by the touch of the reigning sovereign came into practice in England under Edward the Confessor (1042-66). Edward imported the custom from France where he had lived in exile for several years. Known then as the king's evil, scrofula was a disease that caused hard swellings of the lymph glands.

In the reign of Henry VII (1485–1509), a ceremony evolved around the custom. After being touched for the king's evil, people were presented with a coin, called a touch piece or angel gold, for the figure of an angel engraving upon it, which could be worn as an amulet.

James I (1603-25), a staunch believer in the divine rights of kings, was reported to be very pleased with his healing of the king's evil.

During the reign of James' grandson, Charles II, the custom reached its peak. During his 25-year reign, Charles was said to have touched over 90,000 subjects.

Charles II touched many thousands of sufferers from the King's Evil.

The chronicler John Evelyn reported that "his Majesty sitting under his state in the Banqueting-house, the chirurgeons cause the sick to be brought, or led, up to the throne, where they kneeling, the king strokes their faces, or cheek with both his hands at once, at which instant a chaplain in his formalities says, 'He put his hands upon them and he healed them'…. When they have been all touched, they come up again in the same order, and the other chaplain kneeling, and have angel gold strung on white ribbon on his arm delivers them one by one to his Majesty, who puts them about the necks of the touched as they pass, whilst the first chaplain repeats, 'This is the true light who came into the world.'"

The service was printed in some prayer books from the reign of Charles I (1625-49) to 1719. Queen Anne was the last English monarch to practice the custom. The queen touched the famed writer Samuel Johnson "without effect" when he was a child.

In France, Louis XIV (1638-1715) touched 1,600 subjects during one ceremony with the words "*Le roi te touche, Dieu te guerrisse*" (the king touches you, God heals you). The custom continued in France until the reign of Charles X (1824-30).

The king's evil is known today as cervical tuberculous lymphadenopathy. —VICTORIA KING **HM**

The 1860s

Victoria King describes some of the highlights of this salient decade.

THE 1860S WERE A fascinating period. The decade saw changes in every part of society, from international relations to the books that people read.

The period was marred by conflicts throughout the globe. The US was torn apart by the Civil War. Prussia, under Bismarck, began to dominate the German Confederation with the expulsion of Austria in the aftermath of the Austro-Prussian War. China was involved in international and internal conflicts, suffering defeat in the Opium Wars, and the bloody Taiping rebellion ended after 14 years and the loss of an estimated 20 million lives. In Central Africa, a holy war was waged by forces loyal to Al-Hajj 'Umar Ibn Sa'id Tal Peul.

The map of the world changed drastically in this decade. In Europe, the Italian states united under King Victor Emmanuel of Sardinia–Piedmont and the Austro-Hungarian Empire was created. In North America, the dominion of Canada was created and the US bought Alaska from Russia. In Central America, several colonies declared independence.

Social changes included the emancipation of slaves in the US and the freeing of 20 million serfs in Russia.

The great writers of the period published some of their greatest works. One in 10 readers claimed to be a Charles Dickens fan and Dickens created one of his most memorable characters, Pip, in *Great Expectations,* in the 1860s. Victor Hugo breathed life into the character of Jean Valjean in *Les Miserables.* A shy Oxford university lecturer and deacon writing under the pen name of Lewis Carroll immortalized the story of a little girl who fell down a rabbit hole in *Alice's Adventures in Wonderland* and Louisa May Alcott gave us the story of the March sisters, Meg, Jo, Beth and Amy, in *Little Women*.

Technological advances included the linking of Europe and North America through the Transatlantic Cable and the opening of the Suez Canal. The building of railways changed both cities and their countries and strategies of war. Progress in science ranged from the creation of the periodic table of elements to the invention of dynamite. Cro-Magnon Man was discovered and Gregor Johann Mendel established laws of heredity.

The 1860s were a pivotal era and many of the decisions, changes and conflicts of the period echo to our age.

The Pony Express

THE FIRST PONY EXPRESS rider left St. Joseph, Missouri on 3 April 1860. After a journey of 1,966 miles (3,164 km), the first delivery arrived in Sacramento, California on 13 April consisting of 49 letters and three newspapers.

The Pony Express was developed by William H. Russell, William B. Waddell and Alexander Majors who founded the Central Overland California and Pikes Peak Express Company. Previously mail took about three weeks to be delivered from the midwest to California.

The company advertised for riders with the following: "Wanted - Young, skinny, wiry fellows, not over 18. Must be expert riders, willing to risk death daily. Orphans preferred. Wages $25 a week." The youngest rider was 11 and the company's most famous rider was Buffalo Bill Cody.

The mail was carried in a specially designed apron called a mochila, which had four pockets, one

at each corner. Three pockets were locked at the beginning of the journey and were not opened until arrival. The fourth was for mail collected along the route. The first deliveries cost $5 per ½ ounce. This rate was later dropped to $1.

Beginning in Missouri, the Pony Express passed through Kansas, Nebraska, Colorado, Wyoming, Utah, Nevada and ended in California. Pony Express riders traveled through Indian areas, across rivers, night and day

in all weather conditions. The runs usually took 10 days; the fastest was 7 days and 17 hours for the inaugural address of President Lincoln. The announcement of the outbreak of the US Civil War was also delivered by Pony Express.

Departures from the east and west occurred once a week; in mid-June 1860, this was changed to twice a week. Riders changed horses every 10 to 15 miles, and traveled 75 to 100 miles before passing along the delivery to a new rider at one of the stations along the route. The Pony Express only lasted 18 months; its last run was in late October 1861. Only one delivery was lost during its existence. The mail service was discontinued when the transcontinental telegraph system was completed on 24 October 1861. The mail system was a financial failure, owing $200,000 when it ended. Today the Pony Express National Historical Trail is designated part of the US National Trails System.

STEP INTO HISTORY.
THEN GET OUT OF THE WAY.

Relive an era with Mississippi's Civil War battle re-enactments

and magnificent antebellum homes.

Or catch a casino show, stroll along the beach and trace the origin

of the blues. Call 1-888-669-7662

for your free Mississippi *Travel Planner*.

THE SOUTH'S WARMEST WELCOME

www.visitmississippi.org

1860

Abraham Lincoln is elected as 16th president of the US.

The slave state South Carolina secedes from the US.

The Prince of Wales becomes the first member of the British royal family to make an official visit to British North America (present-day Canada) and the US.

The Opium Wars end between China and the victorious British and French, with the signing of the Beijing treaty.

Former Crimean War nurse Florence Nightingale establishes a school for nurses, known as the Nightingale School for Nurses, at St. Thomas's Hospital in London.

German philosopher Arthur Schopenhauer dies.

George Eliot publishes *The Mill On The Floss* and Wilkie Collins publishes *The Woman In White*.

1861

Other slave states of the US (Alabama, Arkansas, Florida, Georgia, Louisiana, Mississippi, North Carolina, Tennessee, Texas and Virginia) secede from the union to become the Confederate States of America. The US Civil War begins.

Alexander II of Russia emancipates 20 million serfs.

Britain, France and Spain send an expedition to Mexico to collect outstanding debts. The US protests against the invasion and after several months, Britain and Spain withdraw after reconsideration.

Frederick William IV of Prussia dies and is succeeded by William I.

Union forces in the US mount an offensive attack at Richmond, Virginia, capital of the Confederacy. The Union forces are repulsed at Bull Run.

Designer William Morris and an association of "fine art workmen" found Morris, Marshall, Faulkner & Company. Disappointed in the lack of quality and craftsmanship

THE UNIFICATION OF ITALY

FROM THE TIME OF THE FALL of the western Roman Empire, Italy had been more a geographical concept than a nation. For centuries, the Italian peninsula had existed as a haphazard collection of minor kingdoms, duchies and republics used as playing pieces in the military and diplomatic struggles between the empires of the Spanish, French and Austrians.

Italians yearned to be free of outsider control, and many saw national union as the best means to achieve this goal. In the mid-19th century, conditions for Italian unity were favorable. The coming of railroads had strengthened the region considerably, and the northern cities of Turin, Milan and Genoa were becoming important and well-linked financial and industrial centers. The power of the Spanish was in rapid decline, and ongoing conflict between the French Republic and the Austrian monarchy offered opportunities to play the two against one another.

Diplomatically, the key player in bringing about Italian union was the moderate aristocrat Camillo Benso di Cavour. As head of the cabinet of the dominant northern Italian Kingdom of Piedmont-Sardinia, Cavour wanted unification on Piedmont's terms. Cavour first sought to score important diplomatic points by

Prior to unification, Italy existed as an idea rather than a nation.

supporting the French and British in the Crimean War. After the allied victory in 1856, Cavour negotiated a treaty with Napoleon III whereby the Piedmontese would surrender Nice and Savoy to France and, in return, France would declare war against Austria in the event of Austrian aggression against Piedmont. Cavour then set about provoking Austria into declaring war against Piedmont. The Austrians obliged him in early 1859, and the French and Piedmontese alliance succeeded in driving the Austrians back. Piedmont added the important king-

dom of Lombardy to its domains. Eager to follow Piedmont's lead, northern Italian regions of Modena, Tuscany and the Papal Legations held plebiscites and voted to join the new Piedmont-led Italian confederation.

Meanwhile, radical revolutionary Guiseppe Garibaldi was leading a volunteer force known as the Thousand in the liberation of southern Italy. Assisted by republican sentiment among Sicilian peasants, Garibaldi captured the entire island of Sicily in less than three months. With Sicily secure, Garibaldi crossed the straits of Messina and made a triumphant entry into Naples. In October and November 1860, a plebiscite in the former Kingdom of the Two Sicilies endorsed annexation into the new Kingdom of Italy.

Victor Emmanuel II of Piedmont was officially proclaimed king of the new Kingdom of Italy on 17 March 1861. Venice remained under Austrian rule until 1866, at which time Venetia was annexed while Austria was distracted by war with Prussia. Rome remained under Papal control, supported by French troops, until 1870. After the withdrawal of the French garrison, Italian troops entered the city in September 1870. After a plebiscite in October 1870, Rome was made the capital of a united Italy.

in mass-produced items of the era, the company becomes a leader in the Arts and Crafts Movement, which sought the standards of the Middle Ages.

Prince Albert, consort of Queen Victoria of Great Britain, dies of typhoid at the age of 42.

William Lyon Mackenzie, a leader of the Upper Canada rebellions of 1837-38 and former mayor of Toronto, dies.

Victor Emmanuel II of Sardinia–Piedmont is named king of Italy after forces under Giuseppe Garibaldi, an Italian patriot, conquer Sicily and Naples in southern Italy.

Isabella Beeton publishes *Beeton's Book of Household Management*. The tome covers every aspect of household management from the "general observations on the common hog" to "rearing and management of children, and diseases of infancy and childhood".

Charles Dickens publishes the first episodes of *Great Expectations* in the periodical *All The Year Round*.

1862
Confederate General Robert E. Lee assumes command of the armies of North Virginia.

France annexes Cochinchina (present-day southern Vietnam), under the treaty of Saigon signed between France and Annam (present-day central Vietnam).

Otto von Bismarck, former Prussian ambassador to Russia and the court of Napoleon III, is made prime minister and foreign minister of Prussia.

After ill treatment from King Victor Emmanuel, Garibaldi's army marches on Rome, capital of the Papal States. Italian forces at the battle of Aspromonte defeat Garibaldi's volunteer army.

Japan expels all foreigners.

American doctor Robert Gatlin

patents a gun that fires 200 rounds per minute. The new "machine" gun was not used in the US until after the Civil War.

Frenchman-in-exile Victor Hugo publishes *Les Miserables* while living in the Channel Isles.

1863
US President Abraham Lincoln signs the Emancipation Act, which proclaims slaves in the Confederate States to be free.

The International Committee for the Relief of the Wounded is created due in part to the efforts of Henri Dunant, a Swiss humanitarian. Today the organization is known as the Red Cross in predominantly Christian countries, and as the Red Crescent in predominantly Islamic countries.

The first underground railway opens in London. A four-mile train line is opened, between Farringdon Street and Paddington (Bishop's Road).

The African city of Timbuktu is captured by the forces of Al-Hajj 'Umar Ibn Sa'id Tal Peul, who wages a *jihad* or holy war throughout central Africa.

Confederate General Thomas Jonathan "Stonewall" Jackson, defending commander at the first battle of Bull Run, dies from wounds received in battle at Chancellorsville.

In Taranaki, New Zealand, fighting erupts between British settlers and Maoris.

J. Grant and J.H. Speke establish that Lake Victoria is the source of the Nile River.

William Thackeray, popular author of *Vanity Fair*, dies.

1864
British North America's Maritime colonies organize a conference at Charlottetown to discuss union. Canada West (present-day Ontario) and Canada East (present-day Quebec), learning of the confer-

ence, request to attend and suggest a union of all British North American colonies. Newfoundland is also invited to attend the conference and join the proposed union. A second conference is held that year at Quebec City where 72 resolutions are adopted for the proposed union of the colonies.

General William Tecumseh Sherman and his Union forces plough through the Confederate cities of Atlanta and Savannah.

Austrian Archduke Maximilian is appointed emperor of Mexico.

The Republicans nominate incumbent President Lincoln as their candidate for the US presidential election, which Lincoln wins later in the year.

Karl Marx establishes the First International Workingmen's Association in London. Its charter members include British trade union leaders and foreign exiles.

The Taiping rebellion in China ends. An estimated 20 million people lose their lives during the 14-year rebellion.

London pubs are closed between one and four in the afternoon in an attempt to lower incidents of public drunkenness.

Nathaniel Hawthorne, American author of *The Scarlet Letter* and *The House of the Seven Gables*, dies.

1865
Confederate General Robert E. Lee surrenders unconditionally at Appomattox, Virginia to the Union General Ulysses S Grant, thereby ending the US Civil War.

President Lincoln is assassinated by John Wilkes Booth while attending a play at Ford's Theatre in Washington.

After defeating Denmark in the Danish War, Prussia takes control of the Duchy of Schleswig and Austria takes the Duchy of Holstein.

A climbing party conquers the Matterhorn, part of the Swiss Alps, a peak previously thought insurmountable.

Peru and the Dominican Republic both declare their independence from Spain.

Leopold I of Belguim dies and is succeeded by his son, Leopold II.

Austria incorporates the east-European region of Transylvania into Hungary.

Charles Lutwidge Dodgson, under his pen name of Lewis Carroll, publishes *Alice's Adventures in Wonderland*.

Wellington is made the capital of New Zealand.

1866
The Transatlantic Cable is brought to shore at Heart's Content in Newfoundland. The ship *Great Eastern* averaged 120 miles a day while paying out the cable from its departure in Valentia, Ireland and covered a distance of 1686 miles. Customers paid $1 per letter to send messages across the Atlantic.

The Austro-Prussian War erupts over the former Danish territories of Schleswig and Holstein. The war, also known as the Seven Weeks' War, is won by Prussia, which acquires both territories, in addition to the German state of Hesse-Kassel, the Duchy of Nassau, the Kingdom of Hanover and the free city of Frankfurt. Although outnumbered, the Prussian forces under General Helmuth von Moltke were victorious, largely due to the use of the new technologies of the telegraph and railroads.

Italy, allied with Prussia in the Seven Weeks' War, occupies the former Austrian holding of Venice.

The 14th Amendment is passed by the US Congress, despite its rejection by most Southern states. The amendment expanded the definition of national citizenship to include blacks.

1868: Louisa May Alcott's *Little Women* is published.

Swedish chemist and engineer Alfred Nobel invents dynamite. After amassing a large fortune from this invention, Nobel goes on to endow the annual prizes named after him.

Austrian monk Gregor Johann Mendel presents his paper *Versuche über Pflanzenhybriden* (Experiments in Plant Hybridization) to the Brünn Society for the Study of Natural Science. Mendel had established certain heredity laws that govern all species. These laws became the building blocks of genetics.

Russian Fyodor Dostoyevsky publishes *Crime And Punishment*.

1867
The Dominion of Canada is created under the British North America Act from the four former colonies of New Brunswick, Nova Scotia, Canada East and Canada West. Canada East and Canada West are renamed Quebec and Ontario, respectively.

The Austro-Hungarian Empire is formed after Austria's expulsion from the German Confederation. Under the *Ausgleich* (German for compromise), Austria and Hungary were ruled as a dual monarchy under Austrian Emperor Franz Joseph. Each country had its own parliament and constitution.

Japanese Emperor Komei dies, and is succeeded by his son Mutsuhito.

The US purchases Alaska from Russia for $7.2 million, approximately two cents an acre.

Tokygawa Keiki, the 15th shogun or top military commander of Japan, resigns his position, ending a dynasty that began in 1192.

Diamonds are discovered in South Africa, in territory disputed between the British and the Boers.

Former president of the Confederate States Jefferson Davis is released from prison after serving two years.

Mexican Emperor Maximilian is executed under the orders of his republican president, Benito Juarez. Maximilan was installed due to Napoleon III's desire to establish a Catholic empire in Mexico.

Karl Marx publishes the first volume of *Das Kapital*.

Johann Strauss composes the *Blue Danube* waltz.

1868
Queen Isabella of Spain flees to France after being deposed by Francisco Serrano y Domínguez and Juan Prim.

William Gladstone becomes prime minister of Britain for the first time.

Republican Andrew Johnson, US president, escapes impeachment. Johnson had dismissed his secretary of war, contrary to the Tenure of Office Act, which states that Congress must agree to removals from office. In turn the House of Representatives voted articles of impeachment against Johnson. However, the vote fell one vote short of the two-thirds needed for Johnson's impeachment.

Ulysses S Grant, former general of the Union armies, is elected president of the US.

Flogging in the British army is banned in times of peace.

Canadian politician Thomas D'Arcy McGee, a former Irish Fenian, is assassinated in Ottawa by a Fenian angered by the politician's public condemnation of his former colleagues.

The skeleton of Cro-Magnon Man is discovered in France by Louis Lartet.

Louisa May Alcott publishes *Little Women*.

1869
Pope Pius XI opens the Vatican Council, the first general council of the Catholic Church since the Council of Trent 300 years before.

The Suez Canal opens, linking the Mediterranean and the Red Sea.

King Ludwig II of Bavaria orders work to begin on his castle, Neuschwanstein, perched in the

1869: Work begins on Ludwig II's Neuschwanstein, perched in the Bavarian Alps.

Bavarian Alps. When completed the medieval-styled castle was

decorated with scenes from Wagner's operas and today Neuschwanstein is a popular tourist attraction.

Russian chemist Dmitri Mendeleyev creates the periodic table of elements.

The *Cutty Sark* is built at Dumbarton, Scotland. The tea clipper served in the English-Chinese tea trade and the Australian wool trade. Today the vessel is berthed on the River Thames at Greenwich as a maritime museum.

Russian Leo Tolstoy publishes *War and Peace*, his *magnum opus* about the Napoleonic wars in Russia.

John Stuart Mill, the British political philosopher, publishes *On The Subjection of Women*, which calls for the enfranchisement of women.

The Discovery of Heredity Laws

GREGOR JOHANN MENDEL (1822-84) was an Austrian monk who lived a relatively obscure life. Mendel was a natural science teacher in Brünn, Moravia (present-day Brno, Czech Republic) who spent many hours in the monastery's garden.

Taking garden peas that exhibited different characteristics in height, color and shape, Mendel controlled their pollination. The offspring of the crossed garden peas in turn had their pollination controlled. Mendel discovered that the breeding of a tall and a short garden pea produced tall descendant plants, however, when the second generation plants were cross pollinated, approximately one quarter of the third generation plants were short.

Mendel established that the first generation's tall plant had the dominant heredity units or genes (AA) and the short plant had the recessive genes (aa). The second generation had both the dominant tall trait and recessive short trait (Aa), one from each parent, which in turn were passed to the next generation. When the

second generation garden peas were cross-pollinated, half of the third generation carried the tall (dominant) trait and the short gene (Aa or aA). The combined traits of recessive shortness and dominant tallness resulted in tallness, with one quarter having both of the tall genes (AA) and the other quarter had both of the short genes (aa) that had been carried recessively from the first generation. The monk, with his

background in science and mathematics had established certain heredity laws that govern all species. These laws became the building blocks of genetics.

In 1865, Mendel appeared before the Brünn Society for the Study of Natural Science to report the findings of his experiments on the monastery's garden peas. Mendel's works were published the following year as *Versuche über Pflanzenhybriden* (Experiments in Plant Hybridization). The scientific community largely ignored his paper.

In 1868, Mendel was elected abbot of his monastery. Failing eyesight and the extensive duties of the new position left the monk little time for his garden experiments. Mendel died in 1884, well loved by his fellow monks and others, but unknown beyond. Mendel's works were rediscovered by three separate botanical investigators (Tschermak, De Vries and Correns) at the beginning of the 20th century when their importance was finally acknowledged.

THE ROAD TO CANADIAN CONFEDERATION

ON THE FIRST DAY of July 1867, the Dominion of Canada was created from the three colonies of New Brunswick, Nova Scotia and Canada (the united colonies of Canada East and Canada West). The nation-wide holiday that marked the day celebrated the long history towards the unification of the colonies of British North America.

At the end of the 18th century, Britain held several possessions in North America. The largest colony was Quebec, which the British had won from France at the Battle of the Plains of Abraham, fought in 1759. On the Atlantic coast, Britain also held the possessions of New Brunswick, Nova Scotia, Île Saint-Jean (renamed Prince Edward Island in 1799) and Newfoundland.

In 1791, Britain decided to divide Quebec in two parts to settle Anglo-French tensions in the region caused by the Quebec Act of 1774. The British Parliament passed the Quebec Act to increase the boundaries of Quebec to include other North American French-speaking settlements, and allowed religious freedom to Roman Catholics. One of the aims of the Quebec Act was to foster loyalty among the French of British North America to the British crown. British settlers did not welcome the Quebec Act as it gave the French important concessions and revived tensions. Ethnic tensions continued to mount as immigration from Britain increased and loyalists to the British crown fled to British

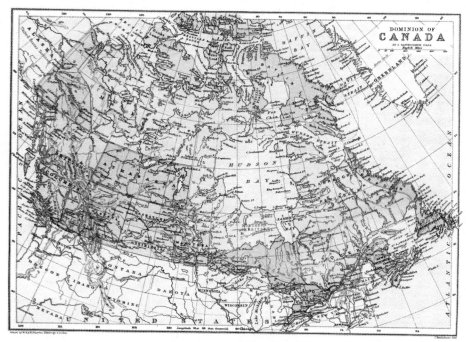

Since 1895, Canada's boundaries have changed dramatically. Manitoba, Ontario and Quebec have grown northwards. Alberta and Saskatchewan became provinces, while many other territories have disappeared from modern maps.

North America from the Revolutionary War in the American colonies.

To solve the Anglo-French tension in Quebec, the British Parliament passed the Constitutional Act of 1791, dividing Quebec into the colonies of Upper Canada (present-day Ontario) and Lower Canada (present-day Quebec). Upper Canada was the area to the west of the Ottawa River, above the Great Lakes, and its population was largely English-speaking and Protestant. Lower Canada stretched from the Ottawa River along the St. Lawrence to the Atlantic, and the majority of its population was French-speaking and Roman Catholic. Although united, each colony was to have its own institutions and legislature.

War between Britain and the United States broke out on 18 June 1812. The powerful British navy had been interfering with neutral ships during the Napoleonic Wars (1792 to 1815). French ports were blockaded and the British inspected American ships and required duties to be paid on cargo. The British navy

also boarded American vessels and removed sailors of British birth to serve on British vessels. The Americans objected to this treatment and war was declared. Although declared largely due to naval conflicts, the war was mainly fought on North American soil. The US mounted several invasions against British North America from different locations, and each was eventually successfully repelled. When the War of 1812 ended with the Treaty of Ghent (1815), both nations signed due to the stalemate conditions of the unpopular war. To this day, both sides claim victory in the war. A result of the War of 1812 was the establishment of the border between British North America and the US.

In the following decades, internal tensions continued in British North America with political revolts in Nova Scotia, Canada East and Canada West. In Nova Scotia, Joseph Howe, a politician and journalist, was elected to the House of Assembly in 1836, where he fought for responsible government for the colony. The political revolts of Quebec were aimed at each of the ruling elites who controlled the governments. In Lower Canada, Louis-Joseph Papineau led a revolt against the Château Clique, a powerful English-speaking group. Papineau's revolt failed and he fled to the US. Newspaper publisher William Lyon Mackenzie of Upper Canada led a revolt in York (present-day Toronto). After being repelled by soldiers on the outskirts of York, Mackenzie also fled to the US. These two revolts were known collectively as the Rebellions of 1837.

In the aftermath of the abortive revolt in Lower Canada, Britain sent Lord Durham, appointed as Governor General and commissioner of British North America, to inquire into the Rebellions of 1837. Lord Durham submitted a detailed report, known as the *Report on the Affairs of British North America,* calling for responsible government in the colonies and the union of British North America.

Britain responded to Lord Durham's report by uniting Upper and Lower Canada into Canada by the Act of Union (1841). Upper Canada was renamed Canada West, and Lower Canada was renamed Canada East. However, the British government was slow to act on responsible government for British North America. Nova Scotia was the first colony to be granted responsible government in 1848, with the Canadas following the next year.

In the united Canadas, responsible government was created by equal representation from Canada East and Canada West, although in the 1840s, French Canada East had a larger population. By the 1860s, English Canada West's population had surpassed Canada East's. Imbalance between the English and French factions of the government caused several parliaments to fall.

In September 1864, the colonies of New Brunswick, Nova Scotia and Prince Edward Island organized a conference at Charlottetown, Prince Edward Island to discuss union. The Canadas, learning of the conference, suggested union of all British North American colonies. Twenty-seven delegates from the Maritime colonies, Newfoundland and the united Canadas attended the conference. A second conference was

The old Parliament Centre Block that housed Canada's first government. The building burnt down on 3 February 1916 and only the Victoria Library remains. The present Centre Block was built where the old building stood.

held in October of that year at Quebec City where 72 resolutions, known as the Quebec Resolutions, were adopted for the proposed union of the colonies.

Support for confederation was strongest in the united Canadas. Voters in Prince Edward Island and in New Brunswick rejected the proposal, while Nova Scotia and Newfoundland also held reservations about the union. Britain supported the proposed union as the dominion could better defend itself, and Britian hoped the union would lead to economic growth and an end to the ethnic tensions between the English and the French.

Both New Brunswick and Nova Scotia reversed their opposition to confederation as the colonies realized Britain's support for the union. In late 1866, representatives from the Canadas, New Brunswick and Nova Scotia traveled to London to have the Quebec Resolutions approved. The Quebec Resolutions, with minor changes, were adopted and Queen Victoria consented on 29 March 1867.

The date of 1 July 1867 was set for the implementation of the Constitution Act of 1867 (formerly known as the British North America Act) creating the Dominion of

Canada. The Dominion of Canada was created from the three former colonies of New Brunswick, Nova Scotia and the united Canadas. Canada East and Canada West were renamed Quebec and Ontario, respectively. Ottawa, the capital of the united Canadas, was named as the Dominion's capital.

In 1870, Rupert's Land, the vast area owned by the Hudson's Bay Company, was sold to the Dominion of Canada for £300,000. The Hudson's Bay Company retained one-20th of the land with mineral rights. Rupert's Land became known as the North-West Territories (present-day Northwest Territories).

Carved in part from the North-West Territories, Manitoba joined the Dominion of Canada in 1870. In 1871, British Columbia on the west coast joined confederation. Prince Edward Island reversed its earlier position and joined confederation in 1873. The Yukon Territory was created in 1898 and the provinces of Alberta and Saskatchewan joined Canada in 1905. Newfoundland and Labrador was the last province to join confederation in 1949 after voters chose to join confederation. The Northwest Territories was further divided in 1999 with the creation of the Nunavut Territory.

The Causes of the US Civil War

FROM 1861 TO 1865, the US was torn apart by the Civil War. Seen by many as the most important event in the nation's history, much has been written about the Civil War: the causes, its heroes and their battles and the aftermath of the war. Entire books are devoted to single battles and the war has become the subject of countless movies and many periodicals.

The direct causes of the Civil War can be traced to the Missouri Compromise of 1820. Missouri applied for statehood in 1817, when steps were taken to admit the territory as a free state. Congress, divided equally between free and slave states, could not agree on Missouri's status. Maine then applied for statehood as a free state in 1819 and a compromise was worked out. Maine was admitted as a free state, Missouri as a slave state and the remaining western territories north of Missouri's southern border (36° 30′) were made free.

When California applied for statehood in 1849, the slavery question returned to the forefront, as California's constitution prohibited slavery. Henry Clay of Kentucky, known as the 'Great Compromiser', suggested admitting California with its stand against slavery, and the territories of Utah and New Mexico were to adopt the doctrine of Popular Sovereignty, a belief that the territory should decide for itself if it wished to enter the union as a slave state or free. The slave states of the union were appeased with the Fugitive Slave Act, which addressed the return of runaway slaves in free states. The Compromise of 1850 is believed to have postponed the Civil War for another decade.

When Kansas and Nebraska were organized as territories under the Kansas-Nebraska Act, they were deemed free under the Missouri Compromise. However, supporters of the Compromise of 1850 and Popular Sovereignty believed the territories should be governed under its terms. Abolitionists and proponents of slavery poured into Kansas to establish

General Sherman surveys the destruction of Savannah in 1864.

control of the territory, resulting in a minor civil war known as Bleeding Kansas. By 1857, the abolitionists were victorious in Kansas and the delicate balance of power between the free and slave states was upset. During this period, the southern states began to refer to themselves as a separate national group.

The Dred Scott decision propelled the US closer to war. Dred Scott was a slave in Missouri who was taken to the free state of Illinois, then to Wisconsin, a free territory and then returned to Missouri. Upon being sold to a citizen of New York, Scott sued for his freedom. The St. Louis Circuit Court in Missouri ruled that Scott was free, as he had resided in a free state and territory. The Missouri Supreme Court overturned the decision, and then the case was brought to the US Supreme Court. The court in 1857 ruled that a slave could not sue his owner, as he was not entitled to the rights of a US citizen. The Supreme Court went on to declare the Missouri Compromise to be unconstitutional, as Congress had no power to prohibit slavery in the US territories. This decision pulled the North and South further apart.

Civil war drew closer in 1859 with the raid on Harpers Ferry in Virginia (present-day West Virginia). Abolitionist John Brown seized the arsenal at Harpers Ferry, intending to raise an armed slave rebellion. US Marines under the command of Robert E. Lee captured Brown within days of the attack; after a trial, Brown was hanged. The North saw Brown as a martyr, while the South saw him as part of an organized movement to end slavery.

The division between North and South grew with the 1860 presidential election. The Republican Party, created by opponents of the Kansas-Nebraska Act in 1854, nominated Abraham Lincoln as its candidate for the presidency. Lincoln was elected, despite his name not appearing on many ballots in the South.

Between Lincoln's election and his inauguration, South Carolina withdrew from the union. Mississippi, Florida, Alabama, Georgia, Louisiana and Texas followed. Together the states formed the Confederate States of America, and chose Jefferson Davis as their president. Within weeks of Lincoln's inauguration, the Civil War erupted.

The Civil War began on 12 April 1861 with Confederate shells falling on Fort Sumter, a federal military post in Charleston Harbor in South Carolina. The Civil War would continue until the unconditional surrender of the Confederacy by General Robert E. Lee nearly four years later on 9 April 1865 at the Appomattox Court House in Virginia.

The Union forces won the war for many reasons. The South had one-third of the population of the North (nine million, which included 3.5 million slaves, versus 22 million), and the North also had a steady flow of immigrants. The North was more industrialized and had a vast network of railways compared to the agrarian society of the South. The navy also remained loyal to the union.

By the end of the Civil War, over 600,000 Americans had lost their lives. These deaths total more than the combined losses suffered by US personnel in WWI, WWII, the Korean War and the Vietnam War.

HM

A Tale of Two Benjamins

Edwin M. Knights presents the story of two irrepressible geniuses from Massachusetts.

THEY WERE BOTH BORN in Massachusetts in the 18th century, into families of modest means. These gifted children were both extremely ambitious and persevering. They lived in a time which rewarded self-reliance and courageous decisions. Both met the challenges and achieved success, but the swirling tides of revolution propelled them on contrasting courses. Franklin Roosevelt rated them, along with Thomas Jefferson, the greatest minds America had produced.

Both were named Benjamin. The first was born in Boston in 1706, the eighth of 10 children. Ben left school at age 12 after struggling with mathematics, becoming an indentured servant in an older brother's printing shop.

The other Benjamin was born in 1753 in Woburn, a town north of Boston. His father, a farmer, died when Ben was but 20 months old and an uncle took over the farm. His mother remarried and had four more children. He attended school in Woburn and nearby towns.

Both were precocious children. Later they'd exhibit astounding creativity, strength of character, tenacity, persuasiveness, passion and generosity, excelling in both science and politics. They would publish extensively. They had musical talent. In spite of similarities, they had sharply differing traits. As a result, one Benjamin is firmly ensconced among the greats in history, while the other, though knighted by Britain and later a count in Bavaria, is far less famous.

Slipping Away In A Sloop

Ben Franklin's apprenticeship in brother James's print shop was to last nine years. Soon he was avidly reading borrowed books by John Locke, Cotton Mather and Daniel Defoe, and using Addison's works in the *Spectator* to hone his writing skills. At age 16 he composed 14 anonymous letters from "Silence

Benjamin Franklin, in a portrait by David Martin.

Dogood" which were published in his brother's *New England Courant*, launching a lifetime literary career. When some provocative publications of the newspaper landed brother James in jail, Benjamin Franklin became the new publish-

Though he was many things, Franklin foremost considered himself to be a printer.

er. Although this was in name only, it terminated Ben's certificate of indenture, enabling him to escape from Boston.

Ben slipped his moorings, boarding a sloop heading down the coast, boarded another in New York and arrived in the Quaker city of Philadelphia in October 1723. Here he found work in the printing business but some bitter experiences which he later included among the "great errata" of his life made him less trustful of strangers. Unprepared for the abrupt transition from boyhood to manhood, he soon experienced another major disappointment, this time resulting from broken promises by Pennsylvania Governor Sir William Keith which left him stranded in London. Although Ben soon found a job, he was happy to join a Quaker merchant as his clerk and return to America. On 11 October 1726, he again stepped ashore in Philadelphia.

Seeking His Fortune In Philly

The Benjamin Franklin who returned to Philadelphia was in debt but now a capable, ambitious and resourceful young man. He found friends with whom he shared experiences and, inspired by British coffee houses, founded a club named Junto. He also edited and published a newspaper and began to print pamphlets on diverse subjects.

Now thinking of marriage, he focused on Debby Read, a young lady with whom he'd been emotionally involved prior to his London adventure. That Debby had since married complicated matters a bit, but Debby's husband had abandoned her for two years. The new marriage was of the common law type that is a nightmare to genealogists. Three children arrived during their marriage, but the stork's itinerary for the first remains a mystery. Many attribute this son to a servant named Barbara.

Ben established a small library for his friends which evolved into a lending library, supported by subscriptions. The printing business grew, aided by public contracts for stationery. Ben set a personal goal of moral perfection based upon standards he defined for temperance, silence, order, resolution, frugality, industry, sincerity, justice, moderation, cleanliness, tranquility, chastity and humility. He later admitted difficulty in attaining all these lofty goals. A major triumph was his *Poor Richard's Almanak*. If he couldn't achieve all his personal objectives, he successfully promoted them to others.

He loved music and devised improvements for the glass harmonica. He championed the establishment of well equipped volunteer and paid fire departments, promoted good nutrition and medical care, became the Philadelphia postmaster, studied architecture and entered politics as clerk of the Provincial Assembly. Meanwhile he devised the cast-iron Franklin stove.

Ever-Widening Horizons

As people turned to Franklin to solve community problems, the postal appointment and Assembly clerkship became springboards for greater public service. As his business ventures grew and prospered, Ben found capable partners to manage his expanding printing empire. When he saw a need for change, he usually led the way, as he'd done with the Union Fire Company. Soon he found a way to provide the public with fire insurance. Ben briefly served as a colonel in military action during the French and Indian War. Fortunately he didn't consider a military career, for the pacifist Quaker philosophy that pervaded Pennsylvania even made it difficult to protect outlying colonists from hostile Indian tribes. He astutely declined when Governor Denny offered him a general's commission to lead militia against Fort Duquesne, probably realizing

One of Benjamin Franklin's earliest publishing endeavors was the *American Weekly Mercury.*

that Denny's real objective was to absent him from the Assembly, either temporarily or permanently.

Franklin was alert to making the postal system more user-friendly. He knew good communication could bind and strengthen the colonies. Business and politics left little time for science, but he was especially fascinated with electricity. His contributions to understanding electricity and its relationship with lightning (and lightning rods) were original and significant, but because they didn't arise from a recognized academic institution, they failed to spark recognition by the natural philosophers of England's Royal Society. This unenlightened response proved to be a blessing to America, as Franklin immediately addressed the need for more colleges by founding an academy that would become the University of Pennsylvania. As always, he pursued the pragmatic, if provocative, approach. In contrast to the few existing colleges, which excelled in matriculating ministers, he advocated teaching such radical subjects as business management, political science, agriculture and even athletics. Fortunate-

ly he didn't electrocute himself during his experiments. And eventually the Royal Society awarded him the Copley Medal.

Life In London

In the next seven years Benjamin Franklin provided unmatched foreign service for fellow colonists. Political turmoil prevailed, as colonists became increasingly resentful of their treatment by Britain. Life became a series of crises, marked by both successes and failures. But he thrived in London, which offered amenities sadly lacking in Philadelphia. He enjoyed the theater, concerts and interaction with famous scientists. His travels with his son William would be exhausting even today, but he still found energy for an active social life, attended London clubs with scientists, philanthropists and explorers, and continued some scientific investigations. Appointed to the Council of the Royal Society, he served several terms and received the honorary Doctor of Laws from the University of St. Andrews.

Pennsylvania had petitioned for royal colony status, but widespread colonial opposition to the Stamp Act forced Franklin to devote all his efforts to getting it rescinded. Facing hostile cross-examination by the House of Commons, he coolly argued successfully for its repeal, temporarily making him a hero in America. But shortly thereafter came the despised Quartering Acts, inflicting regiments of British soldiers upon the colonies, supported by local taxation.

Franklin's fertile mind continued to ponder such diverse subjects as silkworm culture, fireproofing and transatlantic postal service. Franklin's suggestion that ships make use of the Atlantic Gulf Stream to speed up postal deliveries was stubbornly ignored by British postal authorities and ship captains.

The Boston Massacre, a minor incident blown out of proportion, further worsened British-American relations. Franklin's mail was now routinely scanned by the British secret service. Many prominent Londoners resented his outspoken advocacy of the colonists. Yet back in Philadelphia, some considered him a despicable agent of British domination.

Franklin was now 65, hoping for peace along with continued association of America with the British Empire. This attitude was much resented by the patriots of Massachusetts. Ben Franklin had been asked to represent Massachusetts and three other states in England but the British considered him too hostile to their government, while many in Massachusetts regarded him as too conciliatory to represent their cause. The storm clouds had gathered and before long even the inventor of the lightning rod would admit the futility of his cause, predicting in 1775, "more Mischief than Benefit from a closer Union". By now all 13 colonies were "insubordinate" in the eyes of the British as they joined to restore their basic liberties. Benjamin Franklin returned home, but wasn't put out to pasture. He became the senior deputy at the second session of the Continental Congress. And at age 75 he rendered invaluable service as ambassador to France. When Benjamin Franklin died in April 1790, every religious leader in Philadelphia led the funeral cortege and half the city's population joined in mourning this remarkable man.

Benjamin Thompson
Many Americans sided with Britain — United Empire Loyalists who'd prospered and preferred the colonial system to risky revolution. They received little sympathy from their neighbors, who forced some to go back to England. One of these was Benjamin Thompson. Better suited to the classroom than the farm, Ben learned mathematics from Rev. Barnard and became a medical apprentice to a Woburn physician. He attended philosophy lectures at Harvard College, stud-

Benjamin Franklin wrote extensively on many subjects, including scientific matters, morality, economy and statecraft. His writing was witty and popular.

ied French and fencing, played the violin and became a fine draftsman. By age 14 he could track a solar eclipse. He tried building a perpetual motion machine, devised a crude generator and almost ended his career while making fireworks. He devised a daily timetable to improve his efficiency. When he and a friend repeated Franklin's experiment of kite flying during a thunderstorm, they were suddenly engulfed by flames, which caused a "general weakness in their joints and limbs and a kind of lifeless feeling".

Talented Ben's tutoring children of rich families led to the opportunity to run a small school in Concord, New Hampshire. At age 19 he was tall and handsome, with blue eyes and powdered hair. Not long afterward he married Rev. Walker's recently widowed 30-year-old daughter. He now transformed into a country gentleman, festooned in a Hussar cloak with a flamboyant scarlet lining. The cloak proved a great investment, because when Governor John Wentworth was reviewing the Second Provincial Regiment of New Hampshire in 1772, he was so impressed by Benjamin astride his white charger, that he offered him a major's commission at age 20. This propelled Ben undeservedly into a military career, much to the disgust of fellow offi-

cers. When the Thompsons had a daughter, Sarah, two years later, British-Colonial relations were near rupture.

Unfriendly To Liberty?
The Boston Massacre was followed by the Boston Tea Party, and the British closed the Port of Boston. The colonists organized militia, "minutemen", and the names of Lexington, Concord (Massachusetts) and Bunker Hill became engraved in history. At a time for fervent patriotism, Benjamin Thompson failed the test. The Peoples' Committee of Concord charged him with "being unfriendly to the cause of liberty". The verdict was "not proven" rather than "not guilty", a poor endorsement for the young major.

Benjamin Thompson sold his land, hurried to Narragansett Bay, and was picked up by the British frigate *Scarborough*, which returned him to Boston. There he reported to General William Howe. He left for England with the British when they evacuated Boston on 17 March 1776. He didn't see his daughter again for 20 years and never inquired about his wife until 30 years later, after she had died. A letter by him found only 50 years ago proves he'd been "unfriendly to liberty". It was partly inscribed in India ink, but 700 words were in invisible ink, using gallanotannic acid. Soaking in iron sulfate revealed a detailed document of espionage. Another 11-page document provided details of military equipment, stores, ordnance and military preparations, plus a highly critical description of the Rebel Army. Benjamin Thompson had made his choice and, as would be his life-long pattern, acted decisively.

Ben Builds Fort Golgotha
Thompson quickly established himself in London, presenting Lord George Germain with references from Governor Wentworth and General Howe. Germain was

Benjamin Thompson, like Benjamin Franklin, was an inventor, writer and statesman. He is best remembered as the inventor of the efficient Rumford fireplace.

much impressed and they became fast friends. Ben became Secretary of the Province of Georgia, but also worked evaluating refugees' claims for the government. His main interest, though, was experimenting with gunpowder, proving the common practice of moistening gunpowder decreased its explosive force. He was placed in charge of providing clothing and stores for troops serving overseas. Buying silk for uniforms by weight and reselling it in America, he profited from its 10-percent weight increase from absorbing moisture during shipment. This new wealth bought him a lieutenant colonel's commission and command of the King's American Dragoons.

The war was almost over when Thompson reached America. Cornwallis had surrendered and the British were seeking an honorable conclusion to hostilities. Thompson and his Dragoons were assigned to Huntington, Long Island, where the Dragoons soon became "Goons" to the local populace. Thompson crassly built barracks for his men in a burial ground. Gravestones were used to construct baking ovens, resulting in local residents receiving loaves of bread having the names of their deceased relatives baked into the crusts. They christened his camp "Fort Golgotha".

When the war ended, Thompson sought new challenges. He used his contacts to get promoted to full colonel at only 30 years of age so he could eventually retire on half pay. And like Ben Franklin, he published many papers. His first scientific one, on the force of gunpowder, earned him membership in the Royal Society of London. He also wrote on the art of cookery, recipes for cheap food, the importance of water in nutrition, fireplace improvements and employment of the poor. Although appearing utterly without compassion, his writings were oddly humanitarian. His scientific expertise centered on the properties of heat, which he considered a type of motion. Prior to his experiments measuring heat produced by boring the barrel of a cannon, physicists embraced the caloric theory of heat as a fluid. They still remained unconvinced until others confirmed his observations.

Having the knack of being in the right place at the right time with all the right connections, he became colonel for the Elector of Bavaria. This required permission from King George III, but the king valued this new Bavarian contact so much that he knighted Ben and hustled him off to Munich.

Thompson's triumphs in Munich were numerous. He became Minister of War, with the rank of major general, Minister of

Police and Chamberlain to the Court. He also sired a new illegitimate daughter named Sophia. He completely reorganized the army, of which 25 percent were officers, with a sprinkling of field marshals. The soldiers were unwilling conscripts or convicted criminals, so badly underpaid they took on other jobs to survive. Discipline was harsh, morale poor. Thompson established a military academy and offered education for soldiers and their families. Enlisted men received plots of land and were encouraged to plant gardens. He studied the efficiency and conductivity of materials, selecting cotton for summer and wool for winter, and personally supervised the selection and manufacture of uniforms.

Banishing Beggars From Bavaria

Bavaria was overrun with beggars. Entire families specialized in begging, staking out their territories in Munich. With the blessing of the elector, Thompson attacked the problem with military precision. He renovated an old factory, installing workshops, a refectory, kitchen and bake house. On New Year's Day, a popular day for begging, the army and local police arrested every beggar they found; Thompson himself arrested the first one. After they were "booked" they were sent home with orders to report the next day to his "House of Industry". They were promised dinner, medical care and training so they could receive wages for their labors. Most jobs consisted of spinning, weaving, sewing and knitting for 12 hours a day. His social experiment was a huge success; before long some workers were even taking work home. Many became self-supporting citizens and in a few years Thompson's House of Industry even showed a profit. Bavaria made him a Knight of the White Eagle. Sir Benjamin Thompson chose the title of Count Rumford, after the original name for Concord, New Hampshire.

In 1796 he returned to Munich from London. Munich was trying to remain neutral during the French and Austrian War but was awkwardly situated between the opposing armies. The authorities fled to Saxony, entrusting Rumford with Munich's defense. The wily Count managed to maneuver the two armies into battling just outside the city, sparing the city from invasion and not losing a single soldier.

Harnessing Radiant Heat

Count Rumford continually applied his scientific knowledge for practical use. Best known is his Rumford fireplace, still considered state of the art. Utilizing radiant heat, he designed a tall, wide, shallow fireplace with widely splayed covings to maximize heat. Other inventions included central heating, kitchen ranges, thermal underwear, the double boiler, a drip coffee pot and a pressure cooker, a folding bed and an improved lamp design. Meanwhile, he played a major role in founding and financing the Royal Institution, which still exists in London today, hiring Humphrey Davey as a lecturer.

Another Experiment

The *Literary Tablet* in London carried the following brief notice in October 1805: "Married; in Paris, Count Rumford to the widow of Lavoisier; by which nuptial experiment he obtains a fortune of 8,000 pounds per annum — the most effective of all the Rumfordizing projects for keeping a house warm." Count Rumford had wooed the charming widow of the famous Antoine Lavoisier, the father of modern chemistry who'd lost his head to the guillotine in a senseless act of the French Revolution. The prospects of a successful union between these two strong-willed persons were slim, and a letter from Ben to daughter Sarah a year later, describing his spouse as a "female Dragon" confirmed the heated state of their marital bliss. He had few good friends and even his favorite mistresses were now deceased. His last illegitimate son was born 3 October 1813. He died suddenly in 1814 at age 61 and was buried at Auteuil. Only a few people attended his funeral.

Ben Vs. Ben: A Comparison

The two Bens shared a common brilliance, scientific curiosity and political talents. Yet they could be very abrasive. Here Count Rumford excelled, but Ben Franklin lost an election partly because he'd referred to German immigrants as "Palatine boors". They both had musical talent, or more accurately, enjoyed wine, women and song. So much, in fact, that they each produced illegitimate offspring.

Neither man's curiosity was limited to pure science, but both sought practical applications. Both published extensively on nutrition and health. Both played roles in founding educational institutions — Franklin with his academy in Philadelphia and Rumford's Royal Institution in London. Both received honorary degrees from colleges, the Copley medal from the Royal Society and showed particular fondness for Harvard. Harvard awarded Benjamin Franklin a M.A. degree in 1753. He later sent them electrical equipment and art for the college library. Rumford made Harvard chief beneficiary of his estate for a Rumford professorship "to teach... the utility of the physical and mathematical sciences for the improvement of the useful arts...."

Their personality contrasts are striking. Benjamin Franklin had a warmth that interacted well with others. He loved children and they adored him. Count Rumford liked the concept of humanity but hated people to his dying day. Franklin moved freely between Europe and America, acquiring more friends than enemies. Rumford was "a man without a country".

Ben Franklin's most significant advantage was his marvelous sense of wit and humor. If Ben Thompson had any at all, he successfully concealed it from his biographers. Franklin's writings are cogent and sparkling, while Rumford's read like the directions for assembling a bookcase. They were both coffee lovers, but it percolates down to:
*"If you would not be forgotten
As soon as you are dead and rotten,
Either write things worth reading,
Or do things worth the writing."*
—Ben Franklin

HM

Taxes: Maker and Breaker of Empires

Barbara Krasner-Khait looks at the evolution of the institution of taxation.

"IN THIS WORLD NOTHING is certain but death and taxes," said Benjamin Franklin. Six thousand years of history bear out his statement. Good taxation systems created major empires. Poor systems destroyed them. Taxation caused shifts in the world's balance of power and it was a balancing act to create and execute a system that actually worked well.

Taxation has been a frustrating but inevitable fact of life since ancient times.

Early Tax Systems

Taxes have always enabled governments to bring in revenue. The ancient Egyptians taxed exports, imports, business, foreigners, sales and slaves. Not even cooking oil was exempt. The temples owned one-third of Egypt's lands, and because the priests were tax exempt, there was no revenue coming from these lands. In the 12th century BC, the pharaoh Akhenaten focused on his religious reform to monotheism and lost sight of his empire's financial health. His subject territories lost faith and stopped paying tribute, another financial blow. Eventually, the empire's tax base was cut in half and his downfall was inevitable.

In the city-states of ancient Greece, a voluntary contribution — the liturgy — was devised among the wealthy, based on the premise that they should carry the burden of their city's expenses. Heavy taxation, then, was not necessary. The Greeks also established a new way of raising revenues — tax farming. A tax farmer was a contractor who bid at public auctions for the right to collect a certain tax. The practice started out innocently enough but gained a poor reputation by the time the Macedonians ruled the Middle

East in the third to first centuries BC. In Ptolemaic Egypt, tax farmers checked on not only taxpayers but on tax collectors. Tax farming in Egypt was big business, and tax farmers became bankers, loaning the necessary funds so taxpayers could meet their obligations. Tax evasion was not an option.

The Roman Empire was notorious for its taxes. Every five years, a census assessed the wealth tax to pay for wars. Each citizen was obliged to declare his wealth. Foreigners were exempt, but the poor were not. Failure to come forth resulted in enslavement or other penalties. Roman citizens paid tribute, which originated as a head tax, but was later extended to real estate. The Roman provinces relied on head and land taxes for their revenues. Roman land taxes were initially independent of yields from the land. Later, this land tax was modified to correlate to the land's fertility, or as an alternative, one-tenth of the produce was collected as a tax or tithe. Some historians contend that the fall of Rome was largely due to heavy taxation: the wealthy citizens who could afford the taxes were able to evade them, while the poor farmers who could

not meet the obligation fled, leaving the state's war chest empty. Roman taxes disappeared by the eighth century AD.

No Unified System, But Taxes Remain

Charles Adams, author of *For Good and Evil: The Impact of Taxes on the Course of Civilization* (Madison Books, 1993), writes: "The early kingdoms of medieval Europe did not have the expertise to operate the revenue systems of the Romans. The old Roman land tax did have some usefulness if a king wanted to exterminate someone. The undesired person would be appointed land tax collector and sent out to collect delinquent land taxes, and the unfortunate fellow seldom returned." One such person, Berthold, while under the orders of his Frankish queen, did return — he was smart enough to surround himself with 300 armed men. The Edict of Paris in 614, agreed to by the kings of the Frankish empire, forbade any new taxation. The Magna Carta in 1215 protected trade from internal tolls and duties and prohibited excessive tolls at seaports.

Russian Taxation Swells The Ranks Of The Serfs

Each winter, the princes of Kiev, Novgorod and Pskov journeyed to the small villages to collect taxes. About 950AD Princess Olga divided Russia into tax districts with their own local tax director, responsible for all revenue. The improved system helped elevate Kiev to dominant status until the Mongol Golden Horde took over. The Mongols introduced taxation in three phases. In the first phase, the Mongols contracted Moslems as tax farmers, leaving the distasteful duty to the Moslems. In the second phase, the khan divided Russia into military financial districts, governed by a warrior-supported Mongol tax director. In the third phase, the khan relinquished tax collection to the local Russian princes. One of these local princes was Ivan, known by the nickname Moneybags, with a reputation for tax collection prowess. Full tax collection duties were assigned to Ivan, who lived in an obscure place called Moscow.

Overtaxed peasants sought refuge in bondage to landowners. They believed that paying taxes as free men was worse than bondage. Landlords devised their own tax schemes to keep the tax collector away and to keep the serf financially bound to them. Poll taxes were based on a census taken every five years, not often enough to capture everyone.

When Peter the Great came to power in the 17th century, Russia was in decline. Peter reformed the tax system to stimulate economic growth. He abolished the plow tax and household tax that had crippled his country and replaced them with a single poll tax on all males. When that did not produce significant revenue, he re-instituted the census. The unemployed had few choices: serfdom, slavery or government service. Landowners were forced to accept anyone seeking serfdom and that meant paying the serfs' taxes as well. Tax collectors visited these landowners three times a year to audit

Among the lower classes, only serfs did not have to pay taxes. Some overtaxed peasants sought refuge from the taxman by becoming serfs.

their affairs and count the number of souls for the poll tax.

Taxing Revolts In Spain
Bad taxation and bad taxpayers spelled the end of the great Spanish empire. A 10-percent excise tax on real and personal property called the alcabala was a very productive, very unpopular revenue-producer. The Moslems introduced this tax in Spain in the Middle Ages. Though several rulers wished to abolish the tax, it was so successful that it eventually expanded to food. To avoid paying taxes many times over on the same goods, smuggling developed and gold and silver were moved out of the country. After a revolt in Castile, Charles V instituted a no-new-tax policy. But tax

revolts in the provinces continued and devastated the empire's coffers. Civil wars ensued. The tax problems at home invited other countries to seize Spanish holdings abroad.

Prussian Tax Rolls Roll Back
In the 18th century, Frederick the Great of Prussia inherited great wealth from his predecessors, but his military pursuits soon emptied the treasury. That forced him to reverse his policy of "no new taxes", which he had tried to institute to position himself as a benevolent ruler. Since there was no statute of limitations and because towns and not individuals were taxed, the tax rolls were opened back to the year 1221. Current inhabitants had to pay. Prussian taxes fell into three basic categories: land taxes in rural areas, occupation tax to carry on business and trade in the cities, and excise and custom taxes. To carry out tax collection, Frederick replaced his army collectors with French tax farmers.

Taxing Burdens Fall On French Peasants
In France, a land and wealth tax called the *taille* was hated but productive. It provided more than 80 percent of the country's revenue. Peasant uprisings catalyzed by massive taxation occurred repeatedly throughout the 14th to 16th centuries. The peasants were not represented in the Estates General, but they were forced to bear most of the burden. Violence became their voice. Says Adams, "The revenue system that finally

THE TAXMAN COMETH

"You can have a Lord, you can have a King, but the man to fear is the tax collector," read ancient Sumerian clay tablets. No matter what historic period or geographic region, the coming of the tax collector instilled fear in the taxpayer. And with good reason. Here's what one Roman wrote around 35AD:

"The rulers of the cities must stop breaking the necks of the cities by continuous and heavy taxes. . . . They choose on purpose the most merciless of tax collectors, full of inhumanity.

"Recently, a man was appointed tax collector among us. When some of those who were supposed to owe taxes fled . . . he carried off by force their wives and children, their parents and the rest of their families. The tax collector did not release them until he had tortured their bodies with racks and wheels and had killed them with newly invented devices of death."

evolved out of the taxing powers granted to the French monarch in the Hundred Years' War was everything a good tax system should not be." The taille became an annual assessment, depending on the country's military needs. By the 18th century, it was called the "peasant's tax", because peasants were the only ones left to pay it. Louis XIV introduced a poll tax, with 22 classifications that designated a distinctive rate based on wealth. When he died, the tax was repealed. An excise tax was placed on seemingly everything, including food and wine. Wine alone was subject to five taxes. The stamp tax, an excise tax placed on special papers for commercial use and seals, made its debut.

French tax farmers became very powerful. They created national corporations. They generated money and extended credit to the government.

By the time Louis XVI came to power in 1774, many believed that the only route to effective tax reform was revolution.

The English Miracle Of No New Taxes

In the 15th century, each tax district in England paid a fixed amount to the treasury in a system of "fifteenths," "tenths," and subsidies. "Fifteenth" meant 1/15 of the assessed value of the taxpayer's property, "tenth" mean 1/10

By the terms of the Magna Carta, King John bowed to pressure from his nobles to end tolls on internal trade and to reduce port duties.

of real property rentals, and the subsidy was fixed at £80,000. There were no audits or appraisals and everybody knew, and accepted, what they were supposed to pay. Amounts stayed the same for generations.

When Queen Elizabeth inherited the throne in 1558, the coffers were empty and the country was in debt. Rather than focus on new tax systems, she focused on gaining the loyalty of her subjects and increasing goodwill. She accepted meager revenues and lived within her means. She relied heavily on the patriotism of her subjects. When she traveled she relied on them for lodging. When she needed money, they contributed without being incrementally taxed. Perhaps wisely she knew that heavy taxation would only result in revolt. During her reign, England rose to a super-power, without a burden of increased taxation. In the opinion of some historians, this was a miracle.

Under Oliver Cromwell (ruled 1653-58), fifteenths, tenths and subsidies were deemed too slow to collect. Instead, Cromwell introduced heavy excise taxes, including a new wealth tax and a weekly fast tax, equal to the value of one meal. Parliament was in charge of the treasury and taxation. Consent to taxation was no longer the issue. It was replaced by trying to figure out the most effective way to tax. New taxes, including a hearth tax, were adopted. Tax farmers, known as chimney men, entered each home to record just how many hearths there were to tax. The hearth tax was repealed and replaced by a poll tax in 1641. And the poll tax was replaced by a window, house and land tax. Now tax collectors could make their assessments without entering the home. They simply counted the number of windows and if there

THE CELTIC QUEEN WHO WOULD NOT BE TAXED

She was quite a vision. According to Roman historian Dio Cassius, "she was huge of frame, terrifying of aspect, and with a harsh voice. A great mass of bright red hair fell to her knees.... She wore a great twisted golden necklace, and a tunic of many colors, over which was a thick mantle, fastened by a brooch."

Queen of the Celtic Iceni tribe, the widowed Boudicca stood flanked by her daughters on the chariot that carried them into battle against the Romans. Born around 30AD, she married Prasutagus, King of the Iceni tribe. When he died in 61AD, his will named his two daughters and the Roman emperor, then Nero, as his co-heirs. But the Romans wanted all of his former possessions and refused to acknowledge Boudicca as the queen. She gathered some 230,000 people and attacked three towns, including Londinium (London), to fight for freedom from Roman oppression.

According to Dio Cassius, she stood ready to do battle with spear in hand and spoke the following words: "For what treatment is there of the most shameful or grievous sort that we have not suffered since these men made their appearance in Britain? Have we not been robbed entirely of most of our greatest possessions, while for those that remain we pay taxes? Besides pasturing and tilling for them all our other possessions, do we not pay yearly tribute for our very bodies? How much better it would be to have been sold to masters once and for all than possessing empty titles of freedom, to have to ransom ourselves every year? How much better to have been slain than to go about with taxes on our heads?"

The revolt did not succeed and Boudicca died by poisoning herself.

were more than seven, the inhabitant would have to pay the tax. Taxpayers used all sorts of methods to hide their windows into the 19th century. Unlike taxation systems in other countries, this tax excluded peasantry — they did not generally have homes with more than seven windows.

In the 18th century, uprisings against excise taxes and their surveillance systems occurred, often violently.

The world's first income tax was introduced in England in 1798.

Taxation Without Representation

In 1637, British orator John Hampden coined the slogan "Taxation without Representation" against Charles I. In 1761, the words were picked up in the American colonies and extended to "Taxation without Representation is tyranny" in reaction to a series of tax measures inflicted by the British. At the core of adverse reaction was the concept that such taxation was illegal, because a 1724 decision said only Parliament or representative bod-

Georgii III. Regis.

CAP XII.

An Act for granting and applying certain Stamp Duties, and other Duties, in the British Colonies and Plantations in America, towards further defraying the Expences of defending, protecting, and securing the same, and for amending such Parts of the several Acts of Parliament relating to the Trade and Revenues of the said Colonies and Plantations, as direct the Manner of determining and recovering the Penalties and Forfeitures therein mentioned

WHEREAS by an Act made in the last Session of Parliament, several Duties were granted, continued, and appropriated, towards defraying the Expences of defending, protecting, and securing, the British Colonies and Plantations in America And whereas it is just and necessary, that Provision be made for raising a further Revenue within Your Majesty's Dominions in America, towards defraying the said Expences We, Your Majesty's most dutiful and loyal Subjects, the Commons of Great Britain in Parliament assembled,

The Stamp Act introduced one of several new taxes that turned American colonists against Britain.

ies could raise taxes, and the colonials had no representation. Opposition was strong against 1764's Sugar Act and 1765's Stamp Act, both of which were repealed under pressure. Continuing taxes on tea

resulted in boycott and the 1773 Boston Tea Party.

Within the colonies, taxation — combinations of property, poll, commercial and mean taxes and import and export tariffs — varied widely. With one or two exceptions, this taxation was still very light compared to that imposed by the British government within Britain itself.

The Price For A Civilized Society

Throughout history, taxpayers paid with their property, personal possessions, meager earnings, and sometimes with their lives. The ability to know when to tax, what to tax, and whom to tax was a risky game in which governments and rulers engaged. Sometimes their systems worked and empires grew. Sometimes their systems failed and empires fell apart. The words of Oliver Wendell Holmes, inscribed over the entrance of the Internal Revenue Service building in Washington, DC, remind us: "Taxes are the price we pay for a civilized society." **HM**

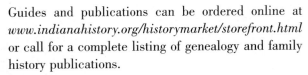

INTRODUCTION TO GENEALOGY

Family Chronicle's **INTRODUCTION TO GENEALOGY**

Family Chronicle's Introduction to Genealogy has been written to answer the often heard question "I'm interested in starting my research — but where do I start?" It assumes no prior knowledge of genealogy and is designed to bring the reader rapidly "up to speed".

The presentation follows *Family Chronicle*'s popular format. Features include how to find infomation about your ancestors in: Vital Records, City Directories, Census and Military Records, Naturalization Records, Social Security Records, Passenger Lists, Court Records, Obituaries and Church and Parish Records. This is followed by information on where to conduct your research: Family History Centers, Libraries and National Archives. There are also sections on keeping your data organized, manually or on a computer.

If you have traced your roots back across the Atlantic, we have a summary on conducting your research in a dozen European countries. When you have gathered enough information we show you how to start writing your family history.

We introduce you to computers, with advice on the type of computer to use, an overview of the software packages available and tips on getting online and making the most out the Internet. We explain how to find records on CDs or in the subscription services on the web.

There's a whole lot more including Heraldry, Tartans, Origins of Surnames, Societies, Preservation of Documents and Photos . . .

As with all our publications, if *Family Chronicle's Introduction to Genealogy* fails to meet your needs or expectations, we will gladly refund your money, for any reason or no reason. Any refund will be made promptly and cheerfully.
Halvor Moorshead, Editor and Publisher

Subscribe Now to

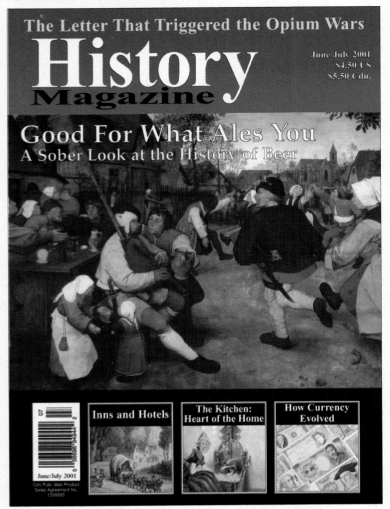

How did our ancestors live?

There is no magazine that covers history like *History Magazine*. We cover military history *only* as it impacted people's lives and we rarely cover personalities or histories of an area. **But** we carry features about the lives of ordinary people that you will find nowhere else like:

The Atlantic Cable, The Black Death, The National Road, Cleanliness, Bread, The Code Napoleon, The First Radio Station, The Longbow, 1000AD, The US Cavalry, Custer, Army Wives, Death Customs, Bellevue Hospital, The Impact of the Potato, An 1860s Dinner for Eight, The Rifle, The Oregon Trail, The Handcart Pioneers, Refrigeration, Games People Played, Contraception, The Suez Canal, Midwives, Longitude, The Country Store, Connecting the World, Alchemy, Freemasonry, Early Newspapers, Influenza Pandemic, Chicago in 1880, The Privy, The Blacksmith, Saffron, Eli Whitney, Lunatic Asylums, Lighthouses, The 1900 House, Carpetbaggers, The Natchez Trace, Let's Eat!, How Brands Began, The Stirrup, The Shakers, Development of Photography, Insurance, The Underground Railroad, Memsahibs of the Raj, California Gold Rush, Poliomyelitis, Wigs, period profiles, historical trivia — and more!

Guarantee

There is no risk. If *History Magazine* fails to meet your needs, or live up to the promises we have made, you are entitled to a refund on all unmailed copies for any reason or no reason. Any refund will be made promptly and cheerfully.

Halvor Moorshead
Editor & Publisher

History
Magazine

Use any of these three convenient ways to subscribe:

- Phone Toll-Free **1-877-731-4478**. Please have your redit Card ready.
- Order online using our secure server: www.history-magazine.com
- Mail to **History Magazine**, PO Box 1201, Lewiston, NY, 14092 (from the US) or
  History Magazine, 500-505 Consumers Rd, Toronto, ON, M2J 4V8 (from Canada)

Please use this form when ordering at this special rate.

I want to subscribe for:

☐ One year (6 issues) at $24 US / $28 Cdn ☐ Two years (12 issues) at $40 US / $45 Cdn
Payment by: ☐ Check (enclosed) Charge my Credit Card: ☐ Visa ☐ MasterCard
Canadian orders add 7% GST or 15% HST as applicable. Quebec residents add 7.5% QST.

Card Number_____ Expiry Date_____ /_____

Signature_____

Last Name_____ First Name_____

Address_____

City_____ State/Prov. _____ Zip/ Postal Code _____

Phone Number_____

History Magazine does not rent or sell subscriber names.   GST# 139340186 RT   **HM11**

Inns and Hotels

Jeff Chapman looks at the development of inns and hotels.

WHILE TRANSIENT lodgings of a sort have existed since the time of the early Roman Empire, the inn did not really become a significant institution until the modern age. Inns and hotels exist to serve the traveling public and, prior to the late medieval period, Europe didn't really have a traveling public to speak of. Travel between towns was expensive and rare, and the few who did travel, such as pilgrims, merchants and government officials, were accommodated by churches or by their hosts.

European inns supported, and were supported by, stagecoach routes. It was good business for inns to have a steady stream of travelers passing through.

Coach Inns

As the medieval era came to a close and trade expanded, people began to travel more widely and frequently. The gradual development of improved roads and the development of stagecoach travel fed, and was fed by, inns. The inns provided clean beds, decent meals and stabling services to merchants and other travelers. Roadside innkeepers established and expanded an increasing number of coach services, and it was rumored that the coaches run by some inns tended to run a little slower than was strictly necessary, to ensure that travelers would have to take rooms on more nights than they might have wished.

Seventeenth-century traveler William Harrison observed, "Those townes that we call thorowfaires have great and sumptuous innes builded in them for the receiving of such travellers and strangers as pass to and fro.... Our inns are

In the age before railways, English inns achieved an international reputation for cleanliness and hospitality.

also verie well furnished with napery… for beside the linen used at the tables, which is commonly washed dailie… each commoner is sure to lie in cleane sheets, wherein no man hath beene lodged since they came from the laundresse."

It was in about 1820 that more exclusive British inns began to adopt the French name "hotel" (a term derived from the same Latin root as "hospitality"). The first railways came to Britain a few years later.

Railway Hotels

The birth of the railways in the early 19th century drastically changed the world of hotelkeeping. Often under the initiative of the railways themselves, many large hotels were built close to rail stations. "Terminal hotels" were built at either end of the major rail lines, as well as any number of hotels at destinations along the route. The railways that controlled the majority of the new railway hotels profited doubly by this measure: not only did they collect substantial rent from the guests at their new hotels, but the existence of large, quality hotels at all the key destinations for commerce and vacationing encouraged people to travel by rail more often.

As cheap and quick rail travel began to replace travel by stagecoach, many inns serving the old coach routes were forced out of business. An 1844 letter written by Majorie St. Aubyn to her cousin demonstrates the rapid decline of the roadside inns: "We drew up at The Golden Lion, which ten years since was one of the busiest inns on the road. The inn looked deserted — no ostler, no horses ready saddled as in the times when we were children and landlords took a real pride in their stables.... I followed the landlady into the guest room. I looked around at the desolate room while the woman went off for chairs, and noted the old bell pulls which seemed to have become melancholy since the Bristol mail stopped."

A Stay at the White Hart Inn

AN ANONYMOUS DUTCH traveler offered this account of his 1815 stay at England's White Hart inn:

"I have just landed and have been shown into The White Hart inn. The boatswain has returned to the packet for my luggage, which is to get to the Customs House. First, I will breakfast, and then view the town. I ring the bell and a person dressed like a gentleman comes in. He is of enormous bulk — a typical John Bull. I make this man a bow, taking him for the host, and dismiss him to send a waiter to me. "I am the waiter, sir," he replies. He then disappeared, and within five minutes served up a most elegant breakfast... I felt very comfortable, such was the elegance of the fireplaces, the polished steel grate, the fender of polished steel and the poker, shovel and tongs, with vase tops, with which it was such a delight to stir the fire.

"I had leisure to inspect the private room. It was spread with a pretty carpet worked to a uniform pattern, with a large White Hart at the centre. Breakfast over, I asked to be shown to my bedchamber. There I found comfort and elegance. A carpet covered the centre of the floor, on which stood a mahogany bed with a painted cornice and dimity curtains, and a most wholesome counterpane as white as snow, with a beautiful design of flowers. On the right was a bow-fronted mahogany chest of drawers with a stand glass of the finest workmanship upon it; on the left, a closed-up wash-stand with blue Staffordshire jug and bason; at the side was a towel-horse with two towels neatly folded. The sash windows were hung with dimity, and besides, had white blinds to let up or down at will. There were

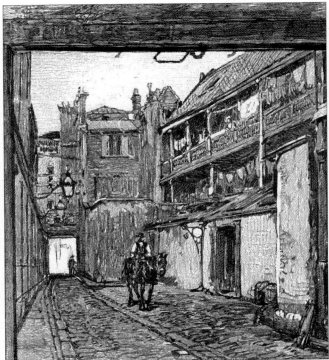

The White Hart Inn, Sussex, England.

two light chairs with cane bottoms, a night-stool and a small table for writing. The fireplace had a hob grate with two figures, one on either side, cast with the metal. What a contrast to the hotels of my own country, where everything is so antique! Oh, I thought, if the rooms of the public inns are like this, what must the apartments of the nobility be like!

"Well satisfied, I gave notice of my intention of spending the rest of the day in seeing the town. Dinner was on the table when I came back, but soup and table napkins I did not see. The waiter, the fat one, did stare when I asked for these, but it appears that the White Hart did not understand my wants, so I was forced to use my handkerchief. But the table was crowded with things. It had a cotton cloth, quite clean, and many utensils which looked like silver, including an epergne with glass dishes in which were grapes, apples and sweetmeats. There was an immense joint of roast beef at the head of the table, and a leg of mutton of equal bulk at the bot-

tom, both awaiting and defying the guests. The table was set for ten persons, and each set of knives and forks was flanked with two different sorts of fruit pies. There were two large dishes of potatoes, and French beans, and wedged among these was a mahogany waggon in which rode an enormous Cheshire cheese. With the potatoes was butter sauce, and in glass jars I did notice some pickled onions and source walnuts, which give a particular relish to the beef. The company being seated, we fell to. For drink, there was London porter, and for wine, some port, which I found to be mixed with brandy. The meal over, three waiters appeared and whipped the cloth from over our heads. It was done so dexterously that no one seemed to mind. Then they brought on the dessert — grapes, walnuts, apples — and crackers with a special service of highly decorative plates, as well as napkins of checked pattern, evidently of wool, which were of no use, and so with eating, drinking and talking, the time did pass till tea was ready, and there was no great difference between this meal and my breakfast. Then at nine o'clock, being tired, I retired to my bed-chamber with a plated candlestick I had seen outside on a table in the corridor, awaking next morning to find my boots jet black with some polish, and so again I took my breakfast in the private room and prepared for my journey to London. The bill was most reasonable, amounting to some twenty-six shillings per day, including the service, but I was perturbed at the number of persons who came with me to the door — the cook, the chambermaid, the under-waiter, the head-waiter, the boots — all claiming a fee. I got rid of this legion for ten shillings."

Luxury Hotels

It was in this era of the railway hotels that English lodgings began to acquire their reputation for being the cleanest and most comfortable in the world. In the mid-19th century, London's older first-class hotels, such as Claridge's, the Albemarle Hotel and Pulteney's, were geared towards serving a clientele of royalty and nobility. At some of the more exclusive London hotels, guests who were not members of the nobility had to have a formal invitation in order to acquire a room. While hotels such as these were considered to be among the most palatial in the world, they were actually rather lacking in some respects. Prior to the 1880s, proper baths, elevators, electricity and telephones were all but unheard of in hotels, where guests made do with candles, lamps and hip baths. When London's world-famous Savoy Hotel opened in 1890, many thought the owners had gone too far in providing their hundreds of guests with an astounding 70 bathrooms. The second-most highly-regarded hotel in London, the Victoria, provided only four bathrooms for its 500 guests.

While English hoteliers were famous for their impeccable taste and perfect hospitality, the hoteliers of continental Europe were more famed for their exquisite food and renowned opulence. As travel for pleasure became increasingly popular during the 19th century, a number of new luxury hotels debuted across Europe, particularly in France, Monaco, Italy, Switzerland and Austria. Some of the more famous European hotels of this period include the Grand Hotel National at Lucerne, Switzerland, the Grand Hotel at Monte Carlo, the Hotel Splendide in Paris and the Hotel de Paris. Such establishments prided themselves on providing succulent meals and a tremendous array of services for their guests, which included both high royalty and American millionaires such as Cornelius Vanderbilt and J.P. Morgan.

While British and European hotels were competing to be the best, North American hotels competed to be the biggest. In New York, the early trend was towards skyscraper hotels like the Waldorf-Astoria.

In the late 19th century, Swiss national César Ritz elevated the standards of hotels across Europe to such an extent that his name has become synonymous with elegance. Serving as the *maitre d'hôtel* in great cities and resort areas across Europe and Britain, Ritz learned the craft of providing spectacular service to the wealthy. For example, at a party for South African millionaire Alfred Beit, Ritz arranged to have a ballroom flooded and decorated to look like Venice. The guests were seated at dinner tables on gondolas and entertained by the songs of genuine gondoliers while they ate.

Together with his famed chef Auguste Escoffier, Ritz opened his first hotel in Baden Baden in 1887, and established many of the conventions of the modern luxury hotel, such as the proper attire for hotel staff and the organization of the kitchen into departments under separate chefs. Ritz was persuaded to become the manager of England's new Savoy Hotel for a time before opening his own Ritz Hotel in London. Ritz and Escoffier introduced London society to *haute cuisine*, and also to the practice of dining out in opulence. While English dining rooms had traditionally been silent, Ritz introduced the practice of having music play during a meal when he hired Johann Strauss to give a series of private concerts at the Savoy. Ritz's crowning achievement was the Ritz Paris, which opened in 1898. This was the first hotel to feature electric lighting throughout and to equip each guest room with its own private bath and telephone.

Grand Hotels and Chains

Though the US had not yet caught up to Old World standards of hospitality, American hoteliers were breaking new records for size. By 1800, the hotels of the US were the largest in the world. San Francisco's The Palace had 800 rooms sprawled over 2.5 acres when it opened in 1875. During the 1920s, such famous grand hotels as New York's Waldorf-Astoria and Hotel Pennsylvania opened their doors. It was also at this time that Chicago's Stevens Hotel opened with 3,000 rooms, becoming the largest hotel in the world. The trend soon spread beyond the US; in Canada, Toronto's Royal York Hotel was able to claim the distinction of being the largest hotel in the British Empire when it opened in 1929.

Another new turn in the history of the hotel industry began with the 1908 opening of the Statler Hotel in Buffalo, NY. Owner Ellsworth Milton Statler introduced many new amenities for the benefit of the growing class of business travelers, such as providing a free morning newspaper to his guests. He applied his successful innovations to other hotels in what was to become the first great hotel chain. Statler found that running a chain of hotels increased efficiency in such areas as purchasing, marketing and reservations. Other chains, such as Westin, Sheraton, Hyatt and Hilton, became the dominant force in the hotel industry after WWII. Many

Under the management of César Ritz, London's Savoy hotel achieved a reputation for unparalleled elegance.

LAS VEGAS

WHILE THE SUCCESS of Las Vegas is founded on the gambling industry, hotels have also played a very important role in the city's history. Often acting in partnership with casinos and nightclubs, Vegas hotels have traditionally vied with one another for the business of tourists by offering top-name entertainment and excellent restaurants.

The state of Nevada legalized gambling in 1931, and some people were quick to realize that the small town had great potential for attracting Californian tourists — even if it was in the middle of the desert.

Beginning with construction of the El Rancho Vegas Hotel-Casino, Las Vegas experienced a small building boom in the late 1940s along what later became known as the Las Vegas Strip. Early hotels included the Last Frontier, Thunderbird and Club Bingo. By far the most celebrated of the early resorts was the Flamingo Hotel, which mobster Benjamin "Bugsy" Siegel opened under a giant pink neon sign on New Year's Eve 1946.

Las Vegas's "Strip" soon became famous for its bright neon signage, colorful electronic billboards and extravagant facades on casinos and hotels. The city quickly acquired a reputation as "Sin City" — which wasn't an entirely bad thing for the tourist trade. More and more hotels sprung up all the time. Las Vegas hoteliers worked hard to establish the city as an ideal location for conferences and conventions so they could fill the thousands of hotel rooms that might otherwise sit empty during slower periods.

Las Vegas restyled itself as a family vacation destination during the 1980s and 90s, launching a new building boom during which extravagant hotels like the Luxor, Excalibur, Treasure Island, the MGM Grand, the Bellagio and Mandalay Bay were constructed. These new hotels have taken César Ritz's concept of providing the spectacular to new heights: the wave pool at Mandalay Beach can generate waves as high as six feet for surfing, and the hotel's Shark Reef has five of only 12 golden saltwater crocodiles in existence. The salt is shipped in from the Red Sea.

Today, Las Vegas boasts more than 90,000 hotel and motel rooms, and is home to most of the 20 largest resort hotels in the world.

of the large chains were able to establish hotels in virtually every sizable North American city; often, the same chain established two hotels in a city, one serving the downtown area and one serving the airport.

Today, while some hotels are growing larger and more spectacular than ever, others are returning to their roots. As railways opened the way for an entirely new variety of hotel, air travel has also spurred a tremendous growth of hotels in the vicinity of airports. Highways and cars have both spawned that poor cousin of the hotel, the motel, and to some extent revived the more old-fashioned concept of the roadside inn. The popularity of modern bed and breakfast hotels seems to indicate that bigger isn't necessarily better.

Further Reading
• *The British Hotel Through the Ages* by Mary Irene Cathcart Borer (Lutterworth Press: London, 1972).
• *British Railway Hotels* by Oliver Carter Riba (Silver Link Publishing: St. Michael's, Lancashire, 1990)
• *A Different World* by Christopher Matthew (Paddington Press: London, 1976).

HM

A strange recent trend among Las Vegas hotels has been to imitate other cities, such as New York, Paris and Venice.

Jonathan Sheppard Books

Box 2020,   Plaza Station
Albany, New York 12220

www.jonathansheppardbooks.com
Serving Historians and Genealogists since 1977
Maps: Midwestern States & European Areas

Visit our website for a listing of all available maps and for special prices on featured reprint maps, original antique maps, and out-of-print books.

Check back often! See what's on special!

◆◆◆◆◆◆◆◆◆◆◆◆

IMPORTANT - PLEASE READ

ABOUT OUR MAPS: All maps described below are black and white reprints of original maps in our collection. Unless otherwise indicated, maps are 18" x 24" and are printed on fine quality parchment stock. **Prices shown are in US dollars.**

SHIPPING: Map orders can be shipped either folded in a 9" x 12" envelope or unfolded and rolled in a sturdy shipping/storage tube. Please tell us your choice and add a shipping charge of either **$2.75 US** (folded) or **$4.50 US** (rolled in tube) to your total order. *Note that the shipping charge is per order, not per map. NYS & MA residents must add appropriate sales tax on total order, including shipping. For shipping to Canada, add an additional $1.50 US.*

MAPS FOR THE MIDWEST...

[PNF39] Special Map Group for Ohio. Includes maps: **(S 5) Indiana and Ohio Circa 1825**, shows towns, county lines, roads, inset plan of Cincinnati, Indian areas in NW corner of Indiana, and lower part of Michigan Territory. (11" x 17"); **(S 16) Indiana and Ohio 1873/74**, shows railway lines, cities, towns, and county lines; **(T 6) Ohio 1864**, shows both county and township boundaries, towns, and railway lines; **(T13)Ohio 1885-87 (2 sheets)**, shows tiny communities, county boundaries, railways, rivers, creeks, streams, and insets of Cincinnati and Hamilton Co.; **(F 22) Ohio 1850** shows counties (8½" x 11"). **All 5 maps: $23.95**

[PNF41] Special Map Group for Indiana. Includes maps: **(S 5)** *(see PNF39 above)*; **(S 16)** *(see PNF39 above)*, **(S 31) Indiana 1880/81**, shows railroad lines, villages, and post office towns; **(T 7) Indiana 1864**, shows county and township boundaries, rivers, creeks, towns,

settlements, roads, and rail lines; **(F 8) Indiana 1850** shows counties (8 ½" x 11").
All 5 maps: $22.95

[PNF43] Special Map Group for Illinois. Includes maps: **(S 15) Illinois 1873/74**, shows railway lines, cities, towns, and county lines; **(S 32) Illinois 1880/81**, shows villages, post office towns, and railroad lines; **(T 8) Illinois 1864**, shows both county and township boundaries; **(T 14) Illinois 1885-87 (2 sheets)**, shows tiny communities, county boundaries, railways, rivers, creeks, and insets of Chicago and Cook County; **(F 7) Illinois 1850** shows counties (8 ½" x 11"). **All 5 maps: $24.95**

[PNF44] Special Map Group for Chicago. Includes maps: **(B 15) Chicago 1873**, shows a mostly rebuilt Chicago after the devastating fire of 1871, wards, ward boundaries, railway lines, public parks, canal system, and branches of the Chicago River; **(F 35) Chicago 1850** (8½" x 11"). **Both maps: $ 7.95**

[PNF55] Special Map Group for Iowa. Includes maps: **(S 18) Iowa 1873/74**, shows railway lines, cities, towns, and county lines; **(S 35) Iowa 1880/81**, shows an inset view of Des Moines, locates counties, numbered townships, small towns, villages, and railways; **(T 10) Iowa and Eastern Nebraska 1864**, shows both counties and townships in Iowa, the 32 easternmost counties in Nebraska, as well as Indian reservations, roads, trails, and small settlements in both areas; **(F 9) Iowa 1850** shows counties (8 ½" x 11"). **All 4 maps: $18.95**

[PNF51] Special Map Group for Missouri. Includes maps: **(S 7) Missouri Circa 1825**, shows Indian and Bounty lands, the Potosi Lead mines, county lines, roads, villages, settlements, rivers and their tributaries (11" x 17"); **(S 20) Missouri 1873/74**, shows railway lines, cities, towns, and county lines; **(S 30) Missouri and Part of Kansas 1865**, includes Kansas east of the 6th Principal Meridian, shows county boundaries, forts, railroads, important routes such as the Pony Express route and the Osage Road, and the New York Indian Lands; **(S 42) Missouri 1880/81**, shows an inset plan of the St. Louis area, counties, towns, villages, small settlements, railroads, and eastern Kansas; **(F 17) Missouri 1850** shows counties (8 ½" x 11"). **All 5 maps: $22.95**

[PNF53] Special Map Group for Kansas. Includes maps: **(S 19) Kansas 1873/74**, shows railway lines, small towns, rivers, and county

boundaries; **(S 30)** *(see PNF51 above)*; **(S 41) Kansas 1880/81**, shows railway lines, counties, small towns and villages, rivers, creeks, and military forts. **All 3 maps: $17.95**

... AND EUROPEAN AREAS

[PEF27] Special Map Group for Holland. Includes maps: **(M 31) Holland 1814**, shows the provinces of Groeningen, Friesland, Overyssel, Drent, Gelders, West Friesland, Delft, Zealand, Utrecht and Dutch Flanders and Brabant; **(M 32) The Netherlands 1814**, shows the area between the France - Germany border south of Dutch Flanders and Brabant, including modern day Belgium. Includes the area west of the Rhine from Cleves to Speyer; **(X 4) Holland/Belgium (3 maps) 1860, 1783, 1772**, the 1860 map shows provinces, railways, towns and villages; a small 1783 map depicts what is now Belgium and Luxembourg; another small 1772 map depicts The Seven United Provinces, and the Austrian, French, and Dutch Netherlands. **All 5 maps: $21.95**

[PEF23] Special Map Group for Denmark. Includes maps: **(M 13) Denmark, with Schleswig- Holstein and Lauenburg 1846**, shows coastal islands, railway lines, and roads, insets of Iceland, the area near Hamburg, and a plan of Copenhagen. The southwestern tip of Sweden is also shown in some detail; **(M 35) Denmark 1799**, shows towns, villages, roads and internal divisions. **Both maps: $11.95**

[PEF25] Special Map Group for Sweden & Norway. Includes maps: **(M 11) The Northern States 1772**, shows provinces, governments, and Governmental districts in neighboring parts of Russia, Poland and present-day Baltic states; **(M 39) Sweden & Norway 1875**, shows the internal provincial subdivisions, railroad lines, principal rivers, cities, towns and many villages. **Both maps: $11.95**

PAYMENT: We accept checks (U.S. dollars/U.S. Banks), M.O.s, MasterCard and VISA. Please include your card number, expiration date and signature when ordering. Our 24 hour faxline for credit card orders is (518) 766- 9181.

OUR SHOP: Our bookshop - MARTLET BOOKS - is located on historic North Street in Pittsfield, MA. We stock thousands of out of print local histories and genealogies, along with our map reprints, original antique maps and a select assortment of unusual books in a variety of subject areas. If you plan to visit, check our website for directions and hours or send us a SASE.

CATALOGUE: Can't visit our Pittsfield shop? Don't have Internet access? Complete descriptions of all of the hundreds of high-quality reprint maps in our collection are included in our catalogue. Paper copies are available for 66 cents in stamps.

www.jonathansheppardbooks.com

CHECK BACK OFTEN!

Money, Money, Money!

Beverly Downing tells how modern currency evolved from shells and animal skins.

HUMANS FIRST BEGAN to use money when their transactions became too complex to be accommodated by the barter system. Overall the barter system worked well enough, but sometimes it was difficult to agree about the different values of the exchange. For example, if a farmer raised cows and needed a tool, and a blacksmith needed a cow, an even trade could be made. But, what if the blacksmith wanted a cow, but the farmer didn't need new tools? The blacksmith would have to search for someone who wanted tools, or had something that the farmer would take for a cow.

To make exchanges of merchandise and services easier, people began to designate specified objects as common mediums of exchange, or money. Generally speaking, anything could be used as money if it was accepted in trade for goods or services; if the value of the goods or services could be measured; and if it was a way to store or accumulate wealth.

For thousands of years, the people of India, China and parts of Africa used the cowrie shell as currency. When archaeologists excavated Chinese tomb sites of the Shang period (16th to 11th centuries BC), they dug up large quantities of money cowries. In late 18th-century Uganda, the price of a woman was two cowrie shells and, if you wanted to brag about the size of your fortune, you could wear your accumulation of shells like a necklace. According to David Standish in *The Art of Money*, "cowries were so significant for so long that the written character for 'money' in Chinese today is a stylized pictographic representation of the shell".

Cultures that didn't use cowrie shells as currency might use feathers, eggs, amber, drums, ivory, jade, leather or vodka, just

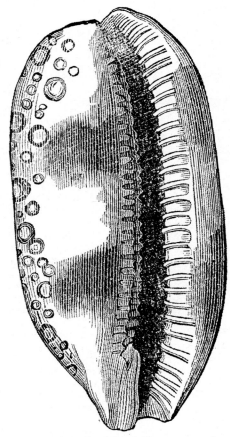

Cowries and other shells were used as units of currency until problems with counterfeiting emerged.

to name a few possibilities. The people of New Guinea paid their debts with boars' teeth and, until the 1940s, people on the island of Yap used *fei* — a stone currency. *Fei* currency was not small — in fact, the larger the stone, the more it was worth. Some of these stone discs (a number of them were 20 feet in diameter!) had holes drilled through the center so they could be carried from place to place on poles. Since the large stones were rather inconvenient for smaller negotiations, "change" monies such as beads and coconuts were in circulation, too.

It was hard to "make change" when trading with livestock, but in many cultures cattle became one of the best means of measuring price and evaluating a trade of goods or services. Cattle were

considered the "measure" of a man's worth and even today, some major transactions in East Africa are still calculated in cows and bulls. The word *pecuniary* ("related to money") is derived from the Latin word *pecuniarius*, meaning "wealth in cattle". The value of the Roman coin, the *as*, was one-hundredth of a cow.

In ancient Rome, a measure of salt was used to pay the Roman soldiers (in fact, the word *salary* is derived from the Latin word for salt — *salarium)*. But while salt, rocks, cattle, and feathers were considered valuable, they were not always durable or convenient to use.

Although the exact time when metallic coins were adopted as a means of completing transactions is lost in the uncertainty of ancient records, the earliest known coins were made about 700BC in the nation of Lydia (now Turkey). The Lydians, seagoing traders who wanted to have a more universal trading currency, made their coins out of electrum — a natural mixture of gold and silver. They ensured the value of each nugget by stamping it with a lion's head, signifying that the coin's value had the backing of the king. The stamping flattened the metal, resulting in a small, flat coin.

Other Mediterranean societies picked up on the idea and developed their own coins. Most coins were round, some were shaped like shells and animals; others were ring-like with holes in the middle. By the 13th century, coins were being traded for goods and services in most of Europe, Asia and the Middle East.

New coins were probably not on the mind of Columbus when he stumbled upon the New World, but his discovery led to the plundering of the Aztec and Inca empires and helped to send a glut of gold and silver to Europe. Since Spain was the

When the Continental Congress printed far more "Continental" paper bills than the American colonial treasury could support, the currency was devalued and Americans lost their faith in paper money.

most powerful nation in the world, the Spaniards commandeered an abundance of the gold. Most of the gold and silver was used to make coins. Spanish "dollars" — *pieces of eight* — became the most sought-after and widely circulated coin in the world. The coins were known as *pieces of eight* because each was worth eight small Spanish coins called *reales*.

Even with the British pound and shilling, money in the British colonies was in short supply. In 1652, to alleviate the cash situation, the Massachusetts Bay Colony opened a mint in Boston. It produced the "Oak" and "Pine" tree shilling, as well as a sixpence and threepence piece. In 1686, the British Crown ordered American coin production to cease, but the colonists tried to circumvent prosecution by continuously printing the 1652 date.

Even before the British Crown ordered the American mints closed, counterfeiting ran rampant, not only in the colonies, but in England and continental Europe. One of the punishments for counterfeiting in England was to send the guilty party to the colonies, but during the 1700s when illegal tender was abundant, the punishment for counterfeiting escalated to death.

In 1775, freedom, not death, was on the minds of the Continen-tal Congress when they issued the first American paper money known as Continental Currency. Made in numerous denominations, the currency increased in five-dollar increments up to 80 dollars. The value of the currency was supposedly backed up by an equal supply of gold, but unfortunately, Congress did not have enough gold to substantiate all the bills it printed and the currency lost its designated value. By 1778, a "Continental" had depreciated to 33½ percent of its face value; by 1779 its worth had plummeted to 2½ percent of its face value. Add the huge decrease in value to the fact that the "Continentals" could not be redeemed until the colonies became independent (a risky bet in the late 18th century) and you can see why the Continental Congress became a little panicked; they made it treasonous for anyone to refuse to accept the provisional money, or discourage its use.

As Abraham Resnick observes in *Money*, George Washington commented on the purchasing power of continentals when he remarked, "A wagon load of money will scarcely purchase a wagon-load of provisions." The government stopped making Continental Currency in 1781. The failure of the currency left Americans suspicious of paper money, and these concerns lasted for many years.

WAMPUM

There was another form of currency available in the American colonies — wampum.

Wampum (meaning "a string of white shell beads") was made from the small beads of quahog shells. Its value varied and depended on the size, workmanship, design and proportion of white shells used to purple, or black shells. The purple and black shells were twice as valuable as the white ones. Making payments for things with wampum is where the phrase *shelling out* originates.

Shelling out in Connecticut, or Dutch New York, meant trading with three black shells, or six white shells — the equivalent of an English penny. The beads were usually assembled in strings of 360, called *fathoms*. A *fathom* was worth about two dollars. According to Carl Moore in *Money*, "One of the reasons wampum was used as money was that it was largely imperishable, easily divided and not very bulky. It was accepted in payment for both large and small items and for some time it was a general rule in the North American colonies that unless some other means was specified, it was assumed it would be in wampum."

As usual, some were not satisfied with what they had and wanted more, and counterfeiters soon appeared on the scene. One family of immigrants began producing ceramic wampum and other enterprising settlers discovered that the white shells could be dyed purple. A number of homemade tints were devised, one of the most popular being blackberry juice. The "new and improved" beads were quickly spent before the tint rubbed off!

Inevitably, with the expanded harvesting of shells (and counterfeiting!) the monetary value of wampum began to decline.

MONEY TALKS!

Money terms from the past are still used freely in our conversations today:

"Paying through the nose" was a phrase derived from the punishment inflicted by the Danes on the population of Ireland during the 9th century; they slit the noses of those unable, or unwilling, to pay the Danish poll tax!

A *buck* is a one-dollar bill; the term probably came from the custom of using buckskins as money.

A *fin* is a five-dollar bill. Fin is short for *finf*, the Yiddish word for five.

Hard money refers to coins.

Lettuce or *cabbage* is paper money; it alludes to the green color.

Pin Money means extra cash. It came from the allowance given to women in colonial times to spend on pins. Pins were scarce and expensive, but as they became more plentiful, the money was spent on other things.

A *sawbuck* is a 10-dollar bill and related to the use of buckskins as money — probably meaning a group of skins, or exceptionally fine skins.

Exceptionally fine old coins can be *"worth a mint"* today! If you're lucky enough to come across one of the first coins authorized by the new government of the US — a silver half-dollar in relatively good condition — you could be $20,000 richer! A mistake in stamping also increases the price of individual coins. In 1937, the US mint made a mistake and a three-legged buffalo nickel was circulated. That mistake could be worth as much as $1,500 in today's market.

Paper money has gradually become an acceptable substitute for precious metals.

Following the American Declaration of Independence, a number of state legislatures authorized the issuance of coins and paper bills. Between 1793 and 1861, approximately 1,600 private banks were permitted to print and circulate their own paper currency. With over 7,000 state bank notes available, plus the foreign money already in circulation, trading became confusing and difficult.

The new republic knew that to gain credibility it had to develop a national currency system that was respected throughout the world. In 1787, the first national coin was produced — a copper one-cent piece decorated with a chain of 13 links representing the original 13 colonies. The links circled the words, "We Are One".

The Constitution, passed in 1788, declared that "no State shall coin money, omit bills of credit, make anything but gold and silver coin a tender in payment of debts." On 2 April 1792, George Washington signed the Coinage Act. This legislation adopted the dollar as the standard monetary unit and established the country's first mint to produce the coins. It also authorized the death of any employee of the mint who "debased the coin for profit, or fraudulent use".

Although devaluation occurred again during the US Civil War, afterwards the treasury adopted a firm policy whereby paper money was "backed up" by gold — for every dollar in paper money, the US owned an equal amount of gold bullion (bars). Beginning in 1865, the government began printing pieces of paper money known as gold certificates that could be exchanged for gold bullion. These certificates continued to circulate until 1933. These certificates were later replaced with silver certificates (first issued in 1878). By the late 1960s, there was a worldwide shortage of silver, so the government stopped circulating silver certificates. Silver certificates were replaced with Federal Reserve notes that are still in use today.

Even with mistakes, wars, inflation and depression, what began thousands of years ago with simple pieces of shells, beans, silver and gold, has evolved into the complex monetary system that we know today. The most remarkable feature of this system is its extraordinary flexibility, blending new technology and traditional currency together to meet modern demands for speed and convenience. Although the use of checks, credit cards, and computerized banking has made a major impact on the world in which we live, perceptions about money are still pretty much the same all over the world — people trade their labor for the money they need to buy the goods and services that make their lives more pleasurable.

HM

A Diplomatic Blunder

Ron Wild looks at the letter that triggered the Opium Wars of the 19th century.

IN 1839, THE CHINESE HAD repeatedly appealed to the British government to stop the importation of opium that was rapidly beginning to enslave many Chinese people to this highly addictive narcotic. The powerful British East India Company had managed to obtain a monopoly on the poppy trade in Britain's Indian Empire. Although China had a flourishing poppy industry at home, the quality of the Indian poppy was far superior and much in demand for its potency and superior hallucinatory properties. Lin, the Chinese Imperial High Commissioner, was assigned the task of ending the importation of opium and began his campaign by destroying 20,000 chests of British-imported opium held in Chinese warehouses. In addition, Lin sent the following high-toned letter to Queen Victoria:

Lin, high imperial commissioner, a president of the Board of War, viceroy of the two Keäng provinces, &c., Tang, a president of the Board of War, viceroy of the two Kwang provinces, &c., and E., a vice-president of the Board of War, lieut.-governor of Kwangtung, hereby conjointly address this public dispatch to the queen of England for the purpose of giving her clear and distinct information (on the state of affairs) &c....

During the commercial intercourse which has existed so long, among the numerous foreign merchants resorting hither, are wheat and tares, good and bad; and of these latter are some, who, by means of introducing opium by stealth, have seduced our Chinese people, and caused every province of the land to overflow with that poison. These then know merely to advantage themselves, they care not about injuring others! This is a principle which heaven's Providence repugnates; and which mankind conjointly look upon with abhorrence! Moreover, the great emperor hearing of it, actually quivered with indignation, and especially dispatched me, the commissioner, to Canton, that in conjunction

In India and China, land traditionally for food production was instead used to cultivate opium poppies.

with the viceroy and lieut.-governor of the province, means might be taken for its suppression!....

We find that your country is distant from us about sixty or seventy thousand miles, that your foreign ships come hither striving the one with the other for our trade, and for the simple reason of their strong desire to reap a profit....

Every native of the Inner Land who sells opium, as also all who smoke it, are alike adjudged to death. Were we then to go back and take up the crimes of the foreigners, who, by selling it for many years have induced dreadful calamity and robbed us of enormous wealth, and punish them with equal severity, our laws could not but award to them absolute annihilation!....

We have heard that in your own country opium is prohibited with the utmost strictness and severity — this is a strong proof that you know full well how hurtful it is to mankind. Since then you do not permit it to injure your own country, you ought not to have the injurious drug transferred to another country, and above all others, how much less to the Inner Land! Of the products which China exports to your foreign countries, there is not one which is not beneficial to mankind in some shape or other....

Your honorable nation takes away the products of our central land, and

not only do you thereby obtain food and support for yourselves, but moreover, by re-selling these products to other countries you reap a threefold profit. Now if you would only not sell opium, this threefold profit would be secured to you....

Moreover, we have heard that in London the metropolis where you dwell, as also in Scotland, Ireland, and other such places, no opium whatever is produced. It is only in sundry parts of your colonial kingdom of Hindostan, such as Bengal, Madras, Bombay, Patna, Malwa, Benares, Malacca, and other places were the very hills are covered with the opium plant....

Suppose the subject of another country were to come to England to trade, he would certainly be required to comply with the laws of England, then how much more does this apply to us of the celestial empire! Therefore it is that those foreigners who now import opium into the Central Land are condemned to be beheaded and strangled by the new statute, and this explains what we said at the beginning about plucking up the tree of evil, wherever it takes root, for the benefit of all nations....

Our celestial empire rules over ten thousand kingdoms! Most surely do we possess a measure of godlike majesty which ye cannot fathom!....

Let your highness immediately, upon the receipt of this communication, inform us promptly of the state of matters, and of the measure you are pursuing utterly to put a stop to the opium evil. Please let your reply be speedy. Do not on any account make excuses or procrastinate. A most important communication.

P.S. We annex an abstract of the new law, now about to be put in force. "Any foreigner or foreigners bringing opium to the Central Land, with design to sell the same, the principals shall most assuredly be decapitated, and the accessories strangled; and all property (found on board the same ship) shall be confiscated. The space of a year and a half is granted, within the which, if any one bringing opium by mistake, shall voluntarily step forward

He contended that many small fires were more efficient than one large one. He designed four types of cooking apparatus: the roaster — a metal cylinder set into a brick enclosure connected to a flue, the enclosed fireplace — a forerunner of the modern kitchen stove, the register stove — a forerunner of the modern range, and the family boiler — an improvement on the steam kitchen. He published the designs in *On the Construction of Kitchen Fire-places and Kitchen Utensils* in 1799 and many notable homes and institutions in North America and Europe relied on them.

By the late 18th century, the cellar kitchen was commonplace in society homes, separating the living area from the heat and smell of cooking. The house staff operated it; the mistress of the house rarely saw it. Here also was the cook's room and the pastry room. The scullery was also sometimes the birthplace of homemade beer.

In the Chesapeake region, kitchens eventually became separate from the house itself.

Economics Drive Change
By 1820, the time was ripe for change, catalyzed by improved stove design, a burgeoning need for improved heating, and a continuous rise in firewood cost in northern cities caused by 150

If the kitchen was the cosiest place in the home, it was also one of the most dangerous: while cooking in their long dresses, many women were injured by open flames.

years or so of land clearing and deforestation. Stoves burned about one-third less wood than the open fireplace. Says Jack Larkin, Director of Research and Collections at Old Sturbridge Village, Sturbridge, Massachusetts and author of *The Reshaping of Everyday Life 1790-1840* (Harper-Collins, 1988), "Northern Americans living in cities and villages began to install cookstoves to replace their kitchen fireplaces, and accepted the most significant change in the technology, and the experience, of domestic heat since the fireplace itself had come into common use in the late Middle Ages."

The need to economize spread quickly in the north and more slowly through the south and west.

"The cookstove became the first major domestic appliance in American history," says social historian Merritt Ierley. The James stove debuted in 1815. Though expensive, it came in eight sizes, and its height was suited for the standing cook. The Stanley stove, patented in 1832, introduced burners.

The new stoves, together with their lighter accoutrements and waist height saved "much female strength, which over a fireplace has to be exerted over heavy pots and kettles," according to the *New England Farmer* in 1837. The stove's heat was generally more comfortable to cook over than a blazing fire.

Economics and convenience, though, could not easily replace tradition. Women still resorted to the fireplace for baking. Harriet Connor Brown of Athens, Ohio wrote, "When we went to keeping house in 1845, Dan'l and I, he bought me a little iron stove, a new thing in those days. It was no good, and would only bake things

THE KITCHEN APOTHECARY

In colonial days, the kitchen was used not only to prepare and cook food, but to create a wide assortment of medicines, salves, poultices, astringents, liniments, herb teas, syrups, lozenges and more. The kitchen apothecary, otherwise known as the woman of the house, had all the tools she needed — mortar and pestle, bowls, crocks, bottles, jugs, pots, saucepans, cauldrons, sieves, ladles, spatulas, skimming spoons, knives, hatchets, homespun cloth for bandages, needles and flax thread for sutures. She more than likely relied on medicinal recipes recommended in the popular Nicholas Culpepper's *English Herbals* or *The English Physician Enlarged*, which appeared in 23 editions from 1653 to 1824. Native American remedies were also widely used.

A Brand New Special from Family Chronicle

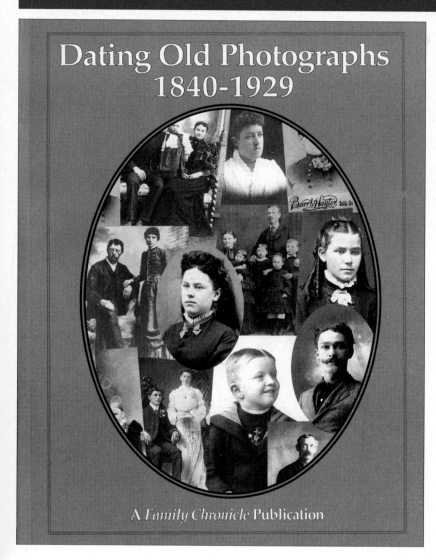

Dating Old Photographs 1840-1929

Barr & Hayter

A *Family Chronicle* Publication

YOU'VE ALMOST CERTAINLY faced the problem: you've got an album or box of old photographs but almost all of them lack any identification. *Family Chronicle's* new special can't help you to identify the subject but it probably can help you with dating when the picture was taken — often within a couple of years.

A number of books have already been published that describe how to date old photographs but they rely almost entirely on descriptions: *Family Chronicle's* book is almost all reproductions of old photographs of known date. There are over 650 pictures covering the period from 1840 to the 1920s. By comparing your undated pictures to those in our book, you will be able to compare clothing and hair fashions, the poses adopted by the subject and the background settings. The book provides convincing evidence that our ancestors were at least as fashion conscious as we are today and that their fashions changed just as frequently.

Some of *Family Chronicle's* most popular issues have been those that have included supplements featuring old photographs of known date.

Our *Dating Old Photographs* book has been compiled from a number of sources but the majority of them are photographs submitted by readers of our magazine.

To Order:

US orders: Send $12 (includes shipping) check, money order, Visa or MasterCard (including expiry date) to Family Chronicle, P.O. Box 1201, Lewiston, NY, 14092.

Canadian orders: Send $15 (includes shipping) plus GST/HST as applicable. Send cheque, money order, Visa or MasterCard (incl. expiry date) to Family Chronicle, 505 Consumers Rd., Suite 500, Toronto, ON, M2J 4V8.

Or call Toll-Free (888) 326-2476 during office hours EST with your credit card. Or order online at *www.familychronicle.com*

$12 (US) including shipping **$15** (Cdn)

BOARD AND DRESSER

Food was prepared or "dressed" on a board prior to cooking as early as the 17th century. By the 18th century, the dresser included one or more drawers to hold spices, knives and other small utensils. It could be folded or stacked away.

The board table — literally a long board or pair of boards nailed together — was the forerunner of the dining room table, located fairly close to the fireplace. The family sat at benches, stools or chests pulled up to the table to eat. If there was a chair, it was reserved for the head of the household, who served as "chairman of the board".

Iron cooking stoves using wood, charcoal or coal tended to radiate large amounts of heat that made the kitchen unpleasantly hot.

on one side. I soon went back to cooking at an open fireplace."

More improvements came in 1845, larger stoves with larger ovens. By 1850, a typical unit had four-to-six boiling holes and an oven that was the full length of the stove. The range was expensive. It got larger and offered multiple fireboxes that allowed different types of cooking at the same time. This helped in the summer because the entire cookstove did not need to be heated, only the part being used. Of course, the huge cast iron or steel range used up a lot of space, generated a lot of heat, and needed to be fairly isolated from other kitchen appliances, such as the ice box.

Despite all the convenience, even by 1860, many women still preferred to roast meats over the open fireplace.

Everything But The Kitchen Sink
For centuries, the system of using buckets to bring in and dispose of water seemed to work just fine. Washing was done within the bucket. Kitchen sinks as we know them today did not appear readily until 1805 and even they were merely slabs of stone that drained through a pipe in the wall. There was no running water. By the 19th

century, metal became a popular surface. For instance, the Hayden, Gere & Company catalog in 1866 offered copper sinks in nine sizes, ranging from 12x20" to 18x30". Sinks were also made of cast iron and faucets came from the wall over the basin rather than being part of the sink itself.

The Kitchen Becomes A System
The efficiency experts of the early 20th century found their way into the kitchen. The kitchen now became a "system"; for example, Hoosier Kitchens of Indianapolis, Indiana advertised in 1915 the "Hoosier System" — a "pantry-cupboard-worktable combined" that "groups everything needed in preparing a meal at your fingers' ends — every utensil and every article has its own special place where it is easily reached without taking a single step." A domestic science study in 1927 found that the average housewife walked more than 100 miles in a year, just to bake cakes. The *New York Times* said, "The old notion that a kitchen had to be a luxuriously large room of the house is passing. A small, compact kitchen, where steps are routed and tools grouped, not only makes kitchen work less fatiguing but pro-

motes health and happiness."

Kitchen components became compact, reflecting largely a shift of fuel source. Gas was now more convenient for cooking than wood or coal. Just turn a valve and light a match. No smoky mess.

The Home's Life Center
In households where the wives cooked, the kitchen remained at the heart of the family. Farm families lived mostly in their back kitchens instead of their parlors. In working-class homes, dining rooms stood empty. The kitchen was the important room of the house. Kitchens provided space for a variety of purposes. In tenements, kitchens were used for cooking, eating, family bathing, washing and socializing. Kitchens could mean comfort. Even boards placed over the tub could create a separate table and a folding bed transformed the kitchen into a boarder's bedroom at night. Whole families gathered around the kitchen table to perform the tasks that would earn them income: cigar rolling, garment assembly, laundering, sewing, ironing and baking.

Be it ever so humble, there's no place like the kitchen.

HM

Good For What Ales You

Nicole Brebner takes a sober look at the history of beer.

"THOSE WHO LIKE IT, like it a lot." The advertising slogan for Alexander Keith's India Pale Ale could very appropriately be applied to all beer. On a hot summer day, many adults claim that nothing quenches their thirst more effectively or more pleasantly than ice-cold beer. While beer is a drink that is consumed around the world and people will argue about which brewers make the best beer, it is unlikely that many people stop to ponder the origins of their favorite beverage.

Imagine a life where beer is your primary source of nourishment. It is brewed at home, consumed with every meal, sometimes used as currency and is highly regarded as a gift from God. Everyone drinks it, including children, and the quality of beer is protected by law. The world of pot-bellied, beer loving cartoon-character Homer Simpson's dreams was in fact reality for our ancestors. It is only in the last 200 years or so that beer ceased to be arguably the most important beverage in the world.

The history of beer closely mirrors the history of civilization. Beer, in some form, has existed almost since the beginning of time. Like many great inventions, beer was created entirely by chance. The production of alcohol begins with the fermentation process. When grains or fruits are added to water under the right conditions, the starches and sugars in the grains and fruits will break down over time and begin to ferment. The end product of this process is alcohol. Around the world ancient people stumbled upon liquids that had experienced this phenomenon and they were pleasantly surprised by the euphoric feeling that drinking this liquid would create. Studies of ancient civilizations show that early humans believed that because it was created naturally

The 1837 Édouard Manet painting *Le Bon Bock* (The Good Pint) captures the contentment of a Dutchman taking pleasure in his beer.

and discovered by chance, beer was a gift from the gods. Many beer drinkers would support that belief even today.

Grapes grow only in areas with

A SERIOUS OFFENSE

Brewing has been subjected to laws and regulations almost from the moment it was discovered.

The Babylonians had royal decrees stipulating the proportion of water and grain to be used in brewing and ruled that brewers producing unfit beer would be drowned in their own drink.

The Egyptians passed strict laws governing the manufacture, sale and consumption of beer.

Hammurabi's Code, the first legal code devised, condemned weak and over-priced beer.

In England brewing bad ale was punishable by fines or by ducking (plunging under water).

a favorable climate, limiting the geography of wine production. Grains, however, are grown around the world. The phenomenon of grains fermenting in water could easily have occurred worldwide, with the type of grain varying from region to region. In Africa, millet and sorghum were, and still are, used to brew beer. The Chinese relied on rice and in South America corn was used. In Egypt and the Middle East, the grain used then is the predominant ingredient in beer today — barley. Some historians theorize that the discovery of beer led to the civilization of humanity. The switch from a nomadic lifestyle to an agrarian settlement may have come about because of the desire to have the ingredients for making beer readily available at all times.

The first written records of beer and brewing date back 5,000 years to the Sumerians who lived in the area between the Tigris and Euphrates rivers in what is now Iraq. Their writings, recorded on clay tablets, include recipes using beer as an ingredient and mention 20 varieties of beer.

Medicinal Value
Beer was an essential component of ancient societies. It was a crucial source of nutrition and was considered a food source as well as a beverage. The alcohol content of ancient beer was fairly low and it contained many vitamins and amino acids that contributed to good health. Medical remedies dating back to 4000BC refer to beer-based mixtures for treating a variety of ailments. Beer was also a very social beverage. An ancient Sumerian would not sit back with his or her own drink. Beer was consumed, through reed straws, from a communal vat. The reed straws would help filter out the debris of barley husks and other

WHAT'S ON TAP?

The Oxford English Dictionary defines beer as "an alcoholic drink made from malt and flavored with hops." Beyond that basic description, the methods used to make beer and the ingredients that flavor beer vary from brewery to brewery.

Water: As beer's major ingredient, water is selected for its purity and typically undergoes additional filtering to make sure it meets brewing standards.

Yeast: Yeast plays a dual role in the brewing process — it helps determine a beer's flavor and is responsible for converting sugar into alcohol and carbon dioxide.

Malt: Malt is screened, crushed and examined by highly skilled brewmasters. While malted barley is used in all beers, many wheat beers supplement the barley malt with a proportion of malted wheat. Along with a unique flavor, wheat produces a longer lasting, creamier head.

Hops: The type of hops used in the brewing process determines a beer's fragrance, flavor and bitterness.

Adjuncts: Adjuncts are added to beers to produce a lighter taste. Common adjuncts include corn and rice.

WHAT WOULD YOU LIKE TO DRINK?

Lager: Made with yeast that ferments slowly at a low temperature to create a smooth, mellow beer.

Ale: Made with yeast that ferments more rapidly and at a higher temperature, resulting in an aromatic and fruity product.

Amber: Malty, hoppy beers with a rich golden color.

Bitter: A British style, highly hopped for a more dry and aromatic beer, pale in color but strong in alcohol content.

Fruit Beer: Fruit may be added either during the primary fermentation or later. Usually made with berries, although other fruits can be used.

India Pale Ale: The name is often shortened to IPA. This ale was originally brewed in England for export to India. The large quantities of hops added were intended as a preservative and to mask potential off-flavors that might develop during the long voyage.

Pilsner: This is the term for the classic lager originally developed in Czechoslovakia, a pale, golden-hued, light beer after which many mass-produced American beers are modeled.

Porter: Very bitter and very dark, this beer was developed in England as a "nourishing" drink for manual laborers such as porters.

Stout: Very dark and heavy, with roasted unmalted barley and, often, caramel malt or sugar. Invented by Guinness as a variation on traditional porter.

Wheat beer (Weizen): Malted wheat, in addition to barley, is used for this German style beer.

The sign outside this English pub shows two brewers carrying a cask of beer. In medieval times, beer was commonly transported over short distances by chaining the barrel to a pole.

contaminants that commonly floated in ancient beer. Wealthy citizens would carry elaborately decorated straws with them. Special, stronger beers would be brewed to honor gods, celebrate festivals and weddings or mark important events. The rapture produced by the consumption of beer was thought to be a spiritual experience. Beer was valuable enough that it was often used to pay workers.

The original breweries would not have been anything like what we have today. Archeological digs in the Middle East and Egypt have uncovered evidence of how ancient beers were brewed. Associated closely with baking, brewing was done domestically, predominantly by women. A maltings, bakehouse and brewhouse were combined. A mud or reed hut with a hole in the floor was used as an oven to bake loaves made from grains. Flat stones were used to mill the grains. The loaves would be crumbled into water to make a brewing mash that was allowed to age (ferment) until ready to be consumed.

As civilizations became more sophisticated, brewing followed suit. Civic breweries were developed in order to provide enough beer to meet the needs of armies, temples and palaces. Excavations at Ur (in modern Iraq) have uncovered a major brewery from the Babylonian era dating from between 2000 and 539BC.

Brewing proliferated and improved around the world with the cultivation of grain. Egypt was once a major brewing center. Manuscripts show that as early as 3000BC beer was being brewed extensively in Egypt. Brewing on a large scale was perfected and the workers who built the pyramids were provided with daily rations of beer. The Egyptians believed that one of their most important gods, Osiris, taught the first brewers how to make beer and that Osiris was the protector of all brewers. In 430BC the historian Herodotus traveled through Egypt. Herodotus came from Greece where wine was common and of Egypt he wrote: "the Egyptians drink a wine which they get from barley, as they have no vines in their country." The kitchen complex in Queen Nefertiti's Sun Temple, excavated in 1990, showed archeologists that Egyptian beer was made from barley and an ancient strain of wheat called emmer.

However, brewing in Egypt declined with the invasion of the Muslims in the 8th century AD. The Muslim holy book, the Koran, forbids the consumption of alcohol and, as a result, the brewing industry foundered.

Europe Bound

Brewing in Europe followed much the same development pattern that preceded it in the Middle East and Egypt. Barley became the primary grain for use in beer for a number of reasons. It is a hardy grain and grows easily in northern climates; it is easily malted and produces more sugar than other grains, which produces more alcohol. Barley was not particularly well suited for making bread, whereas wheat was, and in times of famine all wheat would be designated for use in the production of bread.

The brewing industry continues to be a huge commercial endeavor. Kegs of beer are delivered to drinking establishments around the world on a daily basis.

Beer was an important part of Norse culture and Viking warriors were promised an afterlife in Valhalla where a "brimming Ale Horn" would be waiting for them. Norse burial customs included laying a pail of beer at the feet of the dead to sustain them in the afterlife. This was done for women as well as for men.

Brewing in Europe and Britain was a woman's domain. However, as communities grew and the need for beer increased, brewing became an extremely important commercial industry. As with most aspects of life during the Middle Ages, the church had an extraordinary influence and monasteries ran highly successful brewing operations. Monasteries brewed beer for their own needs but also sold beer to travelers and pilgrims. Although wine was used for celebrating communion, beer was highly regarded by the church and there are several patron saints for brewers.

The introduction of hops to ale caused a revolution in brewing.

A typical ration of beer for monks was eight pints a day while a woman and her maid-servants would brew 200 gallons a month (approximately 50 pints per day) in a modest household. All large institutions had their own breweries and many of the professional brewers were women called "ale-wives".

Ale vs. Beer

Until the 11th century, the production of beer was dictated by climate and the availability of grains and spices. Beer was produced from fall through spring when the temperatures were cool. During the heat of summer, fermentation would occur too quickly and bacteria would ruin the beer. Beer could not be stored very long, even at cool temperatures, and spices were often added to mask the taste of sour beer.

All beer was made by adding yeast, which fermented on the surface of the beer. Through experimentation, Bavarian monks made a discovery that changed their method of brewing. While trying to store beer for long periods in cool cellars they discovered that some yeasts sank to the bottom of the barrel and fermented slowly. Beer created this way could be stored for longer periods of time in cool caves in the Alps. The German word for storage, *lagern*, gave lager beer its name and it became the most popular type of beer in that region. In Britain, where access to snow and ice was limited, top-fermenting ales remained the common type of beer.

The monasteries of central Europe are credited with another discovery that revolutionized the beer industry. They introduced hops to their beers. The hop is a flowering plant and the addition of its flowers or cones to beer aided in the fermentation process and had a valuable preservative effect. Adding hops to beer quickly became standard practice in Europe.

QUALITY CONTROL

According to H.A. Monckton's *A History of Ale and Beer*, in the 14th century, ale-conners or ale-tasters were hired to make sure that brewers were not contaminating their beer. The method of testing was somewhat unique:

"The official ale-taster wore leather breeches and there is a story which tells of his test for the quality of the product. He would draw a tankard of ale, pour it on to a wooden bench and then sit in the pool he had made. He would talk and drink for half an hour being extremely careful not to shift his position. At the end of this time he would make to rise. If his breeches stuck to the place whereon he sat, the ale was not considered to be of the highest quality as it revealed that it had a high sugar content. The object of fermentation is to convert sugar into alcohol, and therefore if the ale-taster's breeches did not stick to the bench he could pronounce the ale as good."

Other versions of this story claim that if the leather breeches did not stick, the ale was bad. Not surprisingly, taste testing became the accepted method of determining the quality of beer.

We now view ale as a type of beer but for centuries the presence or absence of hops marked a distinction between the two. Ale was made from barley, yeast and water, while beer was made by adding hops to ale. In Britain, there was great resistance to hops and controversy raged for hundreds of years over the merits of each drink. In 1436, Henry VI issued a Royal Writ commending beer as "notable, healthy and temperate." But in 1530, Henry VIII ordered the royal brewer not to add hops to his ale. Gradually though, the benefits of hops were recognized. John Gerard's *Herbal*, 1597, states that "The manifold vertues in Hops do manifestly argue the holsomeness of Beere above Ale; for the Hops

rather make it a Phisicall drinke to keepe the body in health, than an ordinarie drinke for the quenching of our thirst."

The advantages of hops made their eventual acceptance inevitable. Ale would have been extremely sweet and had to be spiced with a variety of herbs to temper the flavor. Adding hops helped to clarify and preserve the beer while adding bitterness, aroma and flavor. In an ironic turn of events, the definition of ale shifted from a malt beverage containing no hops, to the present definition of a highly hopped beer.

Because waterborne illnesses and problems preserving food were common, beer continued to be one of the safest sources of nourishment. The boiling process and alcohol content would kill bacteria, but beer was not too strong for even young children to handle. Beer was served with every meal.

As civilizations continued to expand so did the influence of beer. The pilgrims on the *Mayflower* were originally headed for Virginia but made the decision to land at Plymouth because, according to the ship's log their supplies were dwindling, "especially our beere." The early colonists placed advertisements in British newspapers hoping to entice some brewers to join them in the new world. As in previous settlements, home brewing began and was quickly followed by commercial brewing. Both George Washington and Thomas Jefferson, along with most of the other Founding Fathers of the US, were brewers. Native North American tribes had their own independently created beers made from spruce in the north and corn in the south. The first com-

PERFECTION IN BREWING IS REACHED IN AMERICA

THE INVALID,

Those who lack vitality—the languid, those suffering from some accident which has made them almost hopeless of recovery, those with debilitating ailments, those with an unaccountable weakness and lack of physical force, those with health impaired, or those slowly recovering from disease or fever, *are invalids*.

No gift of modern science is to them a greater blessing than

PABST MALT EXTRACT, THE "BEST" TONIC.

It lifts, strengthens, builds, is vivifying, life-giving, gives vim and bounce —it braces. It takes a subtle hold on disease, wrestles with it, eradicates it, fills the system with warm, pulsating blood, and gives the power to do and dare. For the invalid, therefore, be it father, mother, sister, brother, there is nothing to be compared with Pabst Malt Extract, The "Best" Tonic.

Since its discovery, beer has been promoted for its medicinal properties. Today, beer is not generally considered to be an appropriate source of nourishment.

mercial brewery in the new world was built in New York in 1623. The oldest existing brewery in North America is Canada's Molson, founded in Montreal in 1786 by English immigrant John Molson.

The Industrial Revolution and scientific discoveries combined to make improvements in the brewing process. Louis Pasteur's 1867 *Studies on Beer* described the pasteurization process he developed for beer making and which was later adopted by the dairy industry. The development of refrigeration, automatic bottling and improved methods of distribution helped beer evolve into the worldwide commercial industry it is today. Improvements in food preparation and water purification mean that beer is no longer considered a good source of nutrition. However, beer is still, as it has been throughout history, one of the most popular and important beverages in the world. Cheers.

HM

James Lind: Savior of the Navy

Brian Loosmore recounts the story of how science defeated scurvy.

IN 1744 THE FOLLOWING words were written by the chaplain to Lord Anson, whose fleet of six British Royal Naval ships had sailed around the world attacking Spanish ships and settlements:

"We had buried on board *Centurian*, since our leaving St Helens, two hundred and ninety two, and had now remaining on board two hundred and fourteen. This may appear a most extraordinary mortality but yet on board *Gloucester* it had been much greater for, out of a much smaller crew than ours, they had lost the same number and had only eighty-two remaining alive. The *Tryal* escaped more favorably than the rest since she buried only forty two and had now thirty nine remaining alive." Of a total compliment of 961 officers and seamen, 626 died, almost all as a result of scurvy. Yet this shocking mortality had little public impact. It was to be expected on any ship at sea for extended periods. The fleet guarding the English Channel had 2,400 cases over a 10-week period, and the naval hospital at Haslar, on England's south coast, saw 300 to 400 cases a day.

The blighting influence of this disease on naval operations was devastating, especially when fleets were far from home. Scurvy would put 20 percent of the crew out of action.

By the 18th century, sailing ships had reached a high degree of sophistication. Made of wood with a maze of mast and rigging and skillfully handled, they were beautiful to behold, but on board conditions were poor. However well built, ships always leaked, everything was damp and made worse by the obsession for washing the decks twice a day. In English ships gravel was used as ballast and this, mixed with bilge water, became extremely foul, the stench filling the ship. The British buried their dead at sea but in French and Spanish vessels bodies were often placed in the ballast hold and

James Lind

returned home for burial, adding to the emanation.

It was not scurvy alone that affected the health of sailors. Overcrowding, poor diet, lack of fresh water, poor ventilation, homesickness and severe discipline all added to stress.

Even on land public hygiene had not improved since medieval times. Garbage and slops were thrown into the streets so it was almost necessary to hold one's nose in the streets of Edinburgh, Scotland when, in 1731, 15-year old James Lind, son of a merchant, came to the city as apprentice to

Even well-built ships of the 17th century were prone to continuous leaking and unsanitary conditions.

Dr. Langlands, a physician. After further study at the famous medical school there, Lind was able to join the Royal Navy in 1739 as surgeon's mate.

Lind's daily routine on board ship involved visiting the sick at least twice a day and treating them. Sick parade was held on deck, the captain also attending to discourage malingerers. The surgeon reported daily to the captain on the numbers of sick and the general condition of the crew and made recommendations. In battle he treated the wounded.

The number of sick immediately struck Lind and he was soon able to recognize scurvy. He had no idea about bacteria or other germs causing infection, and diseases caused by poor diet had not been understood at the time. Now we know scurvy is caused by a lack of vitamin C found in fresh foods, particularly fresh fruits and leafy vegetables, onions and potatoes. The body can store a reserve of vitamin C, enough to last two to eight weeks. The disease then begins with weakness, lassitude, swelling of the arms and legs, bleeding gums and bruise-like marks on the skin. Teeth fall out, the breath becomes foul and the sufferer is unable to move easily and will die of pneumonia or sudden heart failure.

For over 200 years, it had already been known that the condition was due to lack of fresh food. Even in the 16th century, Queen Elizabeth's physician, Dr. Clowes, had treated cases successfully with ale in which watercress was cooked. Yet in the three centuries between 1500 and 1800 the suffering had been appalling. Sir John Hawkins said that in his 20 years at sea he knew scurvy had killed at least 10,000 men.

A disease causing such devastation had, naturally, been studied closely and although some concept of scurvy's cause was known, the failure in its conquest was remarkable. As long ago as 1605 a squadron of ships under Capt. James Lancaster sailed for the East Indies. The flagship *Dragon* suffered no scurvy while the crews of the other three ships could hardly bring their vessels to port at Cape Town. The secret was lemon juice given by Lancaster to each man showing any signs of the disease. After docking he cured all the other sick by the same treatment. In 1617 John Woodall published his book *The Surgeon's Mate* in which he recommended citrus fruit as a sure cure and prevention of scurvy and described how these fruits could be carried a great distance without refrigeration, so the fact the fruits were not used was the result of indifference, ignorance or economy. By Lind's time, over 80 papers and books had been written on scurvy, many of them recommending acidic fruits.

With this knowledge Lind carried out an experiment. In May 1747, on his ship, the 74-gun *Salisbury*, at sea, he chose 12 cases "in the scurvy". All sufferers showed the same symptoms: bleeding gums, spots, lassitude and "weakness of the knees". The sufferers were placed in the same area and fed the same diet. Lind also gave two pints of cider a day to two of the sufferers. Two others had 25 drops of Elixir of Vitriol three times daily. Two more were given vinegar and two were given a half pint of seawater three times a day. Two had two oranges and a lemon every day and the remaining patients had garlic, mustard seed and horseradish.

In Lind's own words: "The consequence was that the most sudden and visible good effects were perceived from the use of oranges and lemons, one of those who had taken them being at the end of six days fit for duty."

This was enough to convince Lind of the value of oranges in the treatment of scurvy. He noted the experiences of other ships' crews who had been treated with orange juice or with sauerkraut with excellent effect. He developed a method of concentrating the juice by evaporation; when bottled this would last for several years. Other useful

The nickname "limey" is applied to British sailors because large quantities of vitamin-C-rich limes were carried aboard merchant vessels and used to combat scurvy.

foods for prevention were onions, either raw or in soup, dried gooseberries sealed in bottles, fruit wines, and some captains carried boxes of earth on board in which cress or parsley were grown.

Lind recommended these methods to the British Admiralty. He also suggested the use of supply ships to carry fresh provisions of fruit and vegetables to fleets at sea. When this was done for the fleet at the battle of Quiberon Bay in 1759, of 1,400 men aboard ship only 20 were sick on the day of battle although they had been blockading the French coast for months.

Lind did not publish his *Treatise on the Scurvy* until 1753 but many of his recommendations were already being carried out. He pointed out the adverse effects of cold, wet and fatigue in precipitating the disease and urged the pro-

James Lind's *Treatise on the Scurvy* was one of the most important publications of the 18th century.

tection of crews from these influences as much as possible. The ill effects of monotony, anxiety and homesickness were also considered and simple entertainment, such as a singer or fiddler was suggested.

These recommendations were not put into full effect until 1795 after the efforts of Sir Gilbert Blaine, then physician to the fleet. A daily issue of lemon juice was ordered for every seaman. Two years later not a single case of scurvy was seen at Haslar hospital and few surgeons who joined the navy after 1797 saw a case. In 1810, British naval surgeon Robert Finlayson, said: "The blockading system of warfare which annihilated French naval power could not have been carried on unless sea-scurvy had been subdued." Undoubtedly the conquest of scurvy assisted England's navy in conquering Napoleon's forces and changed the course of history.

The merchant marine copied the practice but used the lime, which grew plentifully in the British West Indies. This gave rise to the term "limey" for any British sailor, a title they can carry with pride in memory of James Lind.

Lind left the navy after 10 years and became secretary to the president of the Royal College of Physicians of Edinburgh, but in 1758 he was appointed director of Haslar hospital. There were 1,500 beds and Lind's salary was £800 a year. He continued to write on preserving the general health of sailors at sea and on tropical diseases and how to avoid them. He wrote on the treatment of drowning and described mouth-to-mouth respiration. He recommended the use of lightning conductors on ships and invented a still to provide fresh water from seawater, this alone entitling him to public regard. But his mightiest achievement was the *Treatise on the Scurvy*, a medical classic.

Lind, who died in 1794, was an able, kind and compassionate man, justly described as the "father of nautical medicine" to whom thousands of sailors have owed their lives and health. In later times he might well have earned a Nobel Prize.

HM

The Great Highland Bagpipe

T. Edward Gardiner looks at the powerful instrument of war.

WHEN WE THINK of the bagpipes, most people conjure up images of kilted highlanders marching into battle. But the history of the bagpipes stretches far beyond the borders of Scotland. Ancient Babylonian armies marched to the sound of the pipes as far back as 1800BC, as did the Roman legions almost 2,000 years later. The emperor Nero was said to have been a piper, although there is probably no truth to the accusation that he piped (or fiddled) while Rome burned.

Some people have claimed that the Romans brought the bagpipes to Britain. Others note that the pipes were widespread throughout Europe as recently as the 17th century, including areas that were never part of the Roman Empire, and have thus concluded that the pipes preceded the Romans to Britain. For all we know, it may have been the Celts who gave them to the Babylonians.

However they got there, the pipes have been part of Scottish history as far back as anyone can remember, and the Great Highland Bagpipe has become synonymous with the country.

Bagpipes Widespread
The basic bagpipe is a relatively simple instrument. Its principal components are a chanter with a reed in

The pipe bands that are so prominent in parades today have a rich military history. Highland Games competitions around the world showcase the powerful music of the bagpipes.

it, which plays the music; a bag, which holds a reservoir of air; and a blowpipe, with a valve on the end to stop the air from coming back up into the player's mouth. Drones, which add a steady "droning" noise, of a single note, were added later.

No one knows when the bagpipe was first invented, but we can guess why. The biggest problem with any wind instrument is that the music stops when the musician stops to breathe. In one of those rare flashes of insight that seem obvious after the fact, some ancient genius must have realized that the problem could be solved by adding a bag and blowpipe. The valve may have been part of the original invention, or it may have been added later, with the tongue being used initially. (This works, as any piper whose valve has failed in the middle of a tune can attest, but a valve is preferable.)

While the Scottish bagpipe, more formally known as the Great Highland Bagpipe or the Great Highland War Pipe, is the most common, there are several other types of bagpipes in use today. Some have been in continuous use over the centuries; scholars of folk music have recently revived others. They include: the Breton Bagpipes or Cornemuse; the Northumbrian Bagpipe; and the Irish, or Uillean Bagpipes.

Evidence that the bagpipes were once widespread across Europe can be found in many paintings by the Dutch and Flemish masters of the 17th century. The pipes died out on the continent during the 18th century. Some

While Scottish bagpipes are the most well-known, bagpipes have been used in many other countries over the centuries. In some variations of the pipes, air was propelled to the drones using a bellows instead of a bag.

people suggest that the accordion supplanted them, since it has a wider range and is more "versatile". However, it may simply reflect a shift in people's musical taste. The recent revival of interest in some of these old forms of pipes by various music scholars suggests that at least some people's taste may be shifting back again.

Scottish Heritage

There is also some suggestion that the pipes would have died out in Scotland as well, had the English not tried to ban them from 1746 to 1786. (The argument for this is based on the assumption that the best way to get a Celt to do something is to tell him he's not allowed to.) The one exception to this ban was for pipers in the British army. This policy led many pipers to flock

to the army, which promptly became, and still remains today, one of the major producers of pipers. Other pipers continued to play as well however, handing the knowledge down to sons and nephews, which suggests that the ban wasn't too strictly enforced, since it's pretty hard to hide the sound of the pipes, even in the remote highlands.

Scotland was, until the mid-1700s, very much a clan-based society. As such, many roles were hereditary, and piping was no exception. Some famous piping families were the MacCrimmons, pipers to the MacLeods; the MacArthurs, pipers to the Mac-Donalds, and the Rankins, pipers to the MacLeans. The most famous of these undoubtedly were the MacCrimmons, who ran a school or "college" of piping on the island of Skye from about 1600 to 1770. Much of today's classical pipe music, called *piobaireachd* (and pronounced "pibroch"), flows from the MacCrimmons. There are also more modern piping families who, while not holding hereditary positions, still continue to produce fine pipers generation after generation such as the Findlaters, the Laidlaws and the Rosses.

An Instrument of War

Bagpipes are used for dancing and other forms of entertainment but the Highland Bagpipe is, first and foremost, an instrument of war. Pipers were expected to lead their clan or regiment into battle. In the early days, when manpower was short and battles tended to become a series of hand-to-hand combats,

pipers usually put down their instruments after the battle began and joined in the combat. Often, pipers from opposing clans would seek each other out. Once they joined the British army however, their role as morale boosters and as a communications medium dictated that they continue to pipe throughout the engagement. In the 18th and 19th centuries, when a highland regiment attacked, the first command was always "officers and pipers to the front", and the pipers marched out first. Since they marched, and the rest of the regiment charged, the attack usually swept past them, but they usually caught up, and remained in the thick of battle until the end. This is in marked contrast to other military musicians, who were always ordered to the rear, where they put down their instruments and acted as stretcher-bearers.

The courage of pipers in these circumstances is legendary. Some famous examples include Piper George Clarke of the 79th Highlanders who, at the battle of Vimeiro in 1812, was severely wounded but propped himself up against a rock and continued to play. For his courage, he was awarded a set of silver-mounted bagpipes. Then there was Piper MacLaughlan of the 74th Highlanders at the siege of Badajos. He was one of the first up the scaling ladders and, when he reached the top of the wall, he began playing until a shot through his pipebag stopped him. He then sat, perched on top of a gun carriage and fully exposed to enemy fire, repairing the damage. Once it was fixed, he resumed playing. He was killed the following year at Vittoria.

Also in 1812, at the battle of the Pass of Maya, 400 Gordon Highlanders faced 10,000 French troops. After the initial attack was beaten back, 2,000 French lay dead or wounded, while the Gordons were down to 200. When British reinforcements arrived they were still outnumbered 8,000 to 3,000, so the British general decided to attack quickly. Thinking that the Gordons had done their part, he ordered them to retire but Pipe Major Cameron had other ideas. Without orders, or even permission, he struck up the charging air *The Haughs of Cromdale*. The Gordons then led the charge and the French, already unnerved by their previous failure, broke and fled.

Yet another piper to win a set of silver-mounted pipes, this time from the king himself, was Pipe-Sergeant Kenneth MacKay of the 79th Highlanders (the Camerons) who, at Waterloo, in defiance of French cavalry, stepped outside the British square and marched back and forth, playing *Cogadh no Sith* (War or Peace).

In more modern times, no fewer than three pipers have won the Victoria Cross. Piper (later Pipe Major) George Findlater of the Gordon Highlanders won his on the Heights of Dargai in 1898. The British had already tried twice to dislodge Pathan tribesmen from the heights and the Gordons were their last reserves. Piper Findlater was shot through both ankles early in the attack, but propped himself up against a rock and continued to play until the rest of the regiment had cleared the enemy positions. All of the pipers who took part in that attack were killed or wounded.

Piper (later Pipe Sergeant) Daniel Laidlaw, of the King's Own Scottish Borderers won his VC at Loos in 1915. The battalion had come under heavy artillery fire and the attack was in danger of bogging down. The commanding officer ordered Laidlaw, the first piper he saw, to "Pipe the lads together." Laidlaw stood up, in full view of the enemy, and exposed to machine gun fire, and led the battalion forward to the sounds of "Blue Bonnets Over the Border".

Piper James Richardson, of the Canadian Scottish, won the Victoria Cross at the Somme in 1916. German barbed wire had not been cut by British artillery fire and, as a result, the attack

Pipers were expected to lead their clan or regiment into battle. Once the battle began, the pipers joined the combat.

stalled and men "went to ground" in shell holes. As sergeants and officers cut the wire, Richardson marched back and forth, over a 400-yard front, ignoring enemy fire. When the way was clear, the regiment charged and took their objectives. Piper Richardson was killed later that day.

In the 1915-16 time frame, because so many pipers were killed, and in recognition of the deadly effect of machine gun fire on marching men, pipers were officially banned from assaults. Some estimates say that over 1,000 pipers fell in WWI, and many more were so badly wounded that they could no longer play. However, because they were regular troops, not strictly musicians, pipers remained in the front lines and often found ways to play at key moments.

Pipers also had a way of appearing, seemingly out of nowhere, when needed. There is a story of a Canadian unit in France in WWII whose piper was killed at a critical moment. The attack faltered until a private picked up the dead man's pipes and began to play. Newly inspired, the attack resumed and the objective was taken.

Another story, perhaps apocryphal, involved a Canadian unit in Italy, also in WWII. On this occasion, headquarters received the message "Unit is pinned down. Need reinforcements. Send six tanks or one piper." History does not record which (if either) form of reinforcement was sent, but it illustrates the value of the pipes, even in modern warfare. In fact, pipers were also present in the Falklands and the Gulf

There is something wild and beautiful about pipe music, yet there are some people who dislike them. One can only assume they have heard them when not properly tuned, or when poorly played. A few bad experiences like that, particularly at close range, could, understandably, turn someone off pipe music permanently.

When the pipes are in tune, however, they produce the sweetest music on earth. They are capable of rousing even the most timid to acts of great courage, and yet move the bravest to tears. They represent the very soul of the Celt, and as long as there are Scots, or people of Scottish descent, the pipes will continue to move and inspire them. *Piobaireachd gu bragh*!

Hindsight

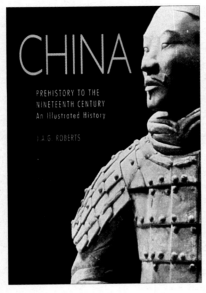

First of a two-volume set, **China: Prehistory to the Nineteenth Century** is an excellent introduction to Chinese history. Much of the early history of China is written with evidence taken from archaeological digs conducted in the country over the last 80 years. Author J.A.G. Roberts covers politics, culture, society and economics of China. The book is divided into chapters by dynasty, and matters unique to each period such as international relations, social or political reform or poetry (with examples) are also covered. From Sutton Publishing, 252 pages, soft cover, with several black and white pictures, maps, notes and an index. At about $20 US or $32 Cdn. Available in bookshops everywhere.

Climate change is not a recent development. Weather fluctuates not only season to season, but also year to year and century to century. **The Little Ice Age: How Climate Made History 1300-1850** examines the effects of lower temperature on nearly six centuries of human history. Author Brian Fagan discusses how harsh winters and cool summers led to devastating famines. The shift in ocean currents in this period led Atlantic fishermen from Europe to

the coast of North America. Fagan argues convincingly that the Industrial Revolution and the Irish Potato Famine were also a result of the cooler climate. A brilliant survey of history founded on an unusual common thread. From Basic Books, 246 pages, hard cover, with black and white maps. Indexed at about $26 US or $40 Cdn. Available in bookshops everywhere.

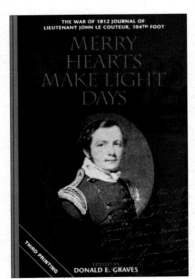

The journals of others are always fascinating and **Merry Hearts Make Light Days: The War of 1812 Journal of Lieutenant John Le Couteur** is no exception. In

1812, Le Couteur arrived in British North America to learn that war had broken between Britain and America. Over the next three years, he traveled vast distances and kept a journal of his experiences, both on the battlefield and in society. Edited by Donald E. Graves, this is an entertaining and informative read. The humor sparkles throughout the book — one excerpt reads: "Three merry young aunts cut out my first dress on my shape. It was so tight that my Mother hardly knew her walking Sausage!" 308 pages, soft cover, with black and white pictures, extensive notes at the end of each chapter, bibliography and index. At about $18 US or $20 Cdn. from bookstores, online retailers and from Robin Brass Studio, fax: 416-698-2120 *www.rbstudiobooks.com*

Offering insight into a life lived more than eight centuries ago; **Saint Hugh of Lincoln** is a delightful book. Hugh was a Carthusian monk who was originally from the Grande Chartreuse near the Alps. In 1186, Henry II of England made Hugh the bishop o[f] Lincoln. Hugh was a beloved ma[n] who was kind to Jews, lepers, the poor and the neglected dead and he also played a background role in the reign of three kings, Henry II and his two sons, Richard I and John. Author David Hugh Farmer also wrote *The Oxford Dictionary of Saints*. Soft cover, 118 pages, with four black and white plates and index. Order directly from Claremont Books, 9/11 Witham Road, Woodhall Spa, Lincs. LN10 6RW UK. 01144-1526-352000. Please enclose £10 sterling with order. Only UK checks made payable to Claremont Books are accepted.

Originally published as 13 installments in the quarterly *U.S. Scots*, **The Scottish Settlers of America: The 17th and 18th Centuries** by Stephen

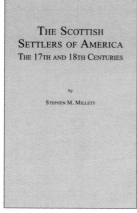

M. Millett examines the Scottish immigrants of colonial America. Each chapter's title describes its focus; for example, chapter six is "Profiles of the Scottish Immigrants", which discusses the socio-economic classes and their respective reasons for emigrating, along with their ages and gender and why these factors played a role in their decisions to come to the new world. An interesting survey of the Scottish experience. 234 pages, soft cover with references at the end of each chapter. At about $25 US from the Genealogical Publishing Co., Inc., 1001 N. Calvert St., Baltimore MD 21202, 1-800-548-1806 or *www.genealogical.com*

First published in conjunction with the television series of the same name, **The Struggle For Democracy** can now stand on its own. Authors Patrick Watson and Benjamin R. Barber present democracy from its birthplace in Athens, through its application in the creation of the US, to its role in governments today. The related demo-

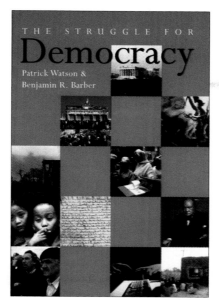

cratic freedoms of citizenship and free speech are also covered. Struggles for democracy in the last decade that led to the collapse of the former Soviet Union and the Tiananmen Square massacre are included in this revised edition. From Key Porter Books, soft cover, 232 pages, with color plates, an index and appendix. Priced at about $20 US or $30 Cdn. Available in bookshops everywhere.

Who's Who in the Classical World covers nearly 500 personalities — real people, not mythical heroes — including some of the more obscure such as Sextus Pompey, Ammianus Mar-

cellinus and Eratosthenes. This reference book gives comprehensive biographies of all entries and longer entries touch upon major events and ideas of the period. Personalities from every walk of life are covered in these thoroughly cross-referenced entries, from leaders to poets to philosophers. Edited by Simon Hornblower and Tony Spawforth, this work is one of the books that should be on your bookshelf. From Oxford University Press, 440 pages, soft cover, with several maps and a chronology. At about $16 US or $26 Cdn. Available in bookshops everywhere.

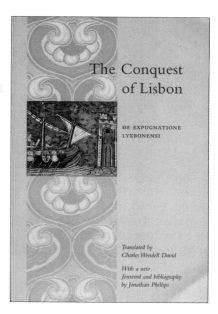

The Crusades were waged not only in the Holy Land, but also throughout Europe. In 1147, Christians involved in the Second Crusade lay siege to the city of Lisbon, held by Muslim Moors. **The Conquest of Lisbon: De Expugnatione Lyxbonesi** is a first-hand account of the episode. Translated by Charles Wendell David, this book offers a wealth of information to those interested in the period's warfare techniques and the ideology of the crusades. The book is printed with the original text of *De Expugnatione Lyxbonesi* on the left side, with notes concerning the text at the end of each page, while the translated text appears on the right with copious footnotes. From Columbia University Press. 206 pages, soft cover, with an index. Available in bookshops everywhere for about $16 US or $24 Cdn.

Knock Me Up in the Morning

Ron Wild explains the industrial origin of the phrase.

Sleeping in cramped, noisy row houses between 12-hour shifts of hard work at the factory was an exhausting way to live.

IN THE FACTORY towns of Northern England in towns with names like Manchester, Bradford, Leeds, Bolton and Sheffield, a unique problem existed. Huge factories had arisen surrounded by thousands of back-to-back, one-room-up and one-down houses with nothing but a narrow alley in between. In such dwellings, factory workers and their families lived among the mixed blessings of the Industrial Age.

Manchester and Bradford grew from being small towns with populations around 30,000 in the early 1800s to become monster factory towns with populations 10 times what they had been a mere 50 years earlier. This factory system dogged the industrial north of England for 150 years and has been written about by writers like Max Engels, J.B. Priestley, Charles Dickens and movies such as *Saturday Night and Sunday Morning*, *Room at the Top* and *Man in the White Suit* show a glamorized version of these hard times.

Factories churned out wool tops and worsted and cotton textile goods at an astounding rate — the factories never closed. Huge high rise chimneys poured out enormous clouds of black smoke and grime that hung above the towns and in the formerly pleasant valleys all year long. Armies of factory workers toiled 12 hours a day for 2/3 shillings a week and the children were so tired at the end of their 12-hour shift that fathers carried them home asleep in their arms. This was the six-day-a-week lot of most factory workers who were soon exhausted by a life of continuous hard work.

Factory Whistles

Factory management insisted on punctuality, docking an hour's pay for even a few minutes of lateness. Non-attendance because of sickness or lateness was rewarded with dismissal. Given that a large percentage of factory workers had recently come from an agricultural background where work moved at the pace that nature set, it is not surprising that workers had difficulty adjusting to factory life. Factory workers paid people to "knock them up" in the morning and the "knocker-ups" would run from gloomy, soot-coated row house to row house banging on doors and getting people up in time to get to the factory before the gates shut and penalties were imposed. In time the "knocker-ups" were replaced with an innovative factory whistle system. Each factory had a distinctive steam-driven whistle, and 30 minutes before shift time three huge blasts warned people that it was time to start getting ready. Two blasts meant 15 minutes to go and one extended blast meant five minutes.

Though I have been away from Bradford for 41 years I cannot imagine mornings without the hundreds of factories in the city sounding off their whistles to sort of "knock people up". **HM**

Fifty Years Ago: The Korean War

History
Magazine

August/September 2001
$4.50 US
$5.50 Cdn.

Life in the 700s

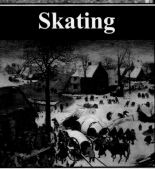

Skating

The Stock Exchange

The Tobacco Trade

Genealogical Publishing

History Magazine

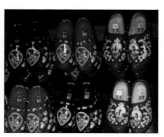

History Notes: Clogs.
Page 4.

The 700s.
Page 7.

Magazines.
Page 17.

Ice Skating.
Page 23.

The Korean War.
Page 27.

OUR COVER: Re-enactors portray life in the 700s. Photograph by Halvor
Moorshead.

Dungeons.
Page 34.

Tobacco.
Page 37.

The Stock Exchange.
Page 47.

News Delivery.
Page 50.

Footbinding.
Page 54.

History Notes

Movable Type

The Arts and Entertainment network chose Johann Gutenburg, the inventor of movable type, as the most influential person of the Second Millennium. Certainly the availability of cheap books had a major impact on people's lives.

Johann Gutenburg

The Chinese made significant contributions to printing. First, they developed paper around the first century AD and later developed inks and wood block printing. Despite these developments, printing had very little impact on Chinese society due to the complexity of Chinese written characters. Over 5,000 different characters were needed, which meant that little time was saved over hand copying. European scripts only used about 26 characters (it varied by language and period), so movable type allowed for huge savings in time and cost.

Gutenburg was a highly skilled craftsman born in Mainz in Germany in 1397, specializing in seal making and as a goldsmith. He conceived the idea of producing molds to make individual characters. His type was formulated from 83 percent lead, five percent tin and 12 percent antimony — virtually the same formula used today (although "hot metal" printing has been largely replaced by modern printing methods).

The first book printed in Europe was Gutenburg's Bible, completed in 1455. Two pages were printed at a time and each had around 2,800 characters. As these pages were being printed, the next two pages were being typeset, so in all about 11,200 characters were required. The process was laborious. Two craftsmen worked for 37 days to typeset a pair of pages and the Bible took over three years to print just 200 copies. —HALVOR MOORSHEAD

Clogs

Although wooden clogs are synonymous with Holland, wooden shoes were in existence for centuries before they became a Dutch fashion.

The Dutch wooden clog called a *klompen* probably originated from the wooden shoes worn in France. These shoes called *sabots* were made out of one piece of wood. Clogs were popular in Lithuania from the 18th to 20th centuries, and were also popular among mill workers in Northern England.

Wooden shoes were most popular with peasants and working people across Europe. Using wood to make shoes had several advantages for working people — wood kept the feet dry and warm, and offered support to the foot and back while one stood working for long hours. Gardeners wore clogs with a flat sole as the

shoes didn't leave footprints. Some workers wore wooden boots because they were safer than softer leather boots that provided no protection if something was dropped on one's foot. Dutch fishermen fitted their wooden shoes with a "nose" that could grip fishing nets during repair.

Clogs were fashioned in several different styles. The Swedish created a wooden clog with an open back. The Dutch version had a closed back. Clogs served as an "outshoe" — the wearer would wear a leather slipper inside of the wooden shoe.

The one-piece wooden shoe was made by cutting a piece of timber into several sections. Each section was cut into the right size for a shoe and then into the general shape of the shoe. The wood was soaked in water and carved by hand. The shoes were dried together in the sun ensuring a perfect fit for each pair. Working shoes were greased or tarred so the wood wouldn't split. Some shoes were varnished and decorated for use at special occasions and ceremonies. In the Netherlands, willow and poplar were the most popular types of wood for making clogs. In Lithuania, aspen was more popular.

In many countries clogs became associated with dancing. The clogs would make clacking sounds on wood or cobblestones. Often pieces of steel were fastened to the bottom of the clog so sparks would be created when the dancer tapped the shoe on the floor. Clog dancing is the forerunner of modern tap dancing and is still practiced in several countries.

Clogs never gained popularity with the middle or upper classes and always remained a working-class fashion. They enjoyed a revival in the 1960s and 70s and remain a popular souvenir in the Netherlands. —SUZANNE RENT

Weathervanes

Rarely used for practical purposes today, weathervanes were once a necessity for most buildings. The ornate roof-toppers were not merely decorative, they were highly informative instruments. The oldest known weather-vane topped the Tower of the Winds in

Athens, built by the astronomer Andronicus around 48BC. Honoring Triton, the Greek god of the sea, the life-sized weathervane was cast in bronze, with the head and body of a man and the tail of a fish. Triton's wand pointed in the direction of the wind. To ancient Greeks and Romans the winds had mystic powers. Many weathervanes were built in honor of their gods and decorated the homes of wealthy citizens.

During the ninth century weathervanes took on religious significance for Christians when a papal edict decreed that every church in Christendom should have the form of a rooster on its steeple. The rooster was to remind the faithful that the disciple Peter denied Christ three times before the cock crowed the morning following the Last Supper and that they should not do the same. Because of its prominent position atop the highest point in every town, the rooster quickly began to serve the dual purpose of religious symbol and weathervane.

Also in the ninth century, it was common for Vikings to use their own style of weathervane on their ships. Decorated with figures from Norse mythology, the quadrant-shaped vanes made their way to Scandinavian churches in the 10th and 11th centuries where some can still be seen in Sweden and Norway.

In the Middle Ages, weathervanes became symbols of power and privilege and began to appear on castles and belfries. As they gained popularity, the vanes came to symbolize more than just status, informing travelers about the inhabitants of a town. The innkeeper, the miller and the ploughman could be easily identified by the figures on their vanes.

Today weathervanes are used for decoration and nostalgia, though as always their primary function is to point in the direction of the wind.
—NICOLE BREBNER

History Magazine

VOLUME 2 NUMBER 6

EDITOR & PUBLISHER . . . . .HALVOR MOORSHEAD
publisher@moorshead.com

EDITOR . . . . .JEFF CHAPMAN
magazine@familychronicle.com

SPECIAL PROJECTS MANAGER . . . . .RON WILD
ronwild@familychronicle.com

EDITORIAL INTERNS . . . . .JODI AVERY, SUZANNE RENT

CONTRIBUTING EDITOR . . . . .BARBARA KRASNER-KHAIT

EDITORIAL ASSISTANTS . . . . .NICOLE BREBNER
gpg@moorshead.com
VICTORIA L. KING
victoria@moorshead.com

CIRCULATION MANAGER . . . . RICK CREE
rick@familychronicle.com

Published by Moorshead Magazines Ltd.
505 Consumers Road, Suite 500,
Toronto, ON, M2J 4V8 Canada
(416) 491-3699 Fax (416) 491-3996
E-Mail: *magazine@moorshead.com*

PRESIDENT . . . . .HALVOR MOORSHEAD

SUBSCRIPTION SERVICES . . . . .JEANNETTE COX
VALERIE CARMICHAEL

POSTAL INFORMATION — CANADA

Canadian Publications Mail Product Sales Agreement No. 40062922. PAP Registration No. 10629. Mailing address for subscription orders, undeliverable copies and change of address notice is: *History Magazine,* 505 Consumers Road, Suite 500, Toronto, Ontario, M2J 4V8 Canada

POSTAL INFORMATION — UNITED STATES

Periodical Postage Paid Lewiston, NY USPS #018-154
Postmaster send address corrections to:
History Magazine, PO Box 1201, Lewiston, NY, 14092-9934
US Office of Publication, 850 Cayuga St., Lewiston, NY, 14092

ISSN 1492-4307

© 2001 Moorshead Magazines Ltd.
Some illustrations copyright www.arttoday.com. We acknowledge the financial assistance of the Government of Canada, through the Publications Assistance Program (PAP), toward our mailing costs in Canada.

SUBSCRIPTIONS

History Magazine is published six times a year (Feb/Mar, Apr/May, Jun/Jul, Aug/Sep, Oct/Nov, Dec/Jan)
Subscription rate for US (US funds):
1 year (6 issues) $24, 2 years (12 issues) $40,
3 years (18 issues) $55
Subscription rate for Canada (Cdn funds):
1 year (6 issues) $28 plus GST/HST
2 years (12 issues) $45 plus GST/HST
3 years (18 issues) $59 plus GST/HST
Quebec residents add 7.5% QST
GST # 139340186 RT

We welcome the submission of articles for publication. Please send a printed copy in addition to the file in electronic format. Please do not send important documents with submissions. We will always contact people who submit articles but the review process may take several weeks. Authors' notes are available on request.

Toll-Free Subscription Line: **1-877-731-4478**
Printed in Canada
WEBSITE: *www.history-magazine.com*

The Guillotine

The namesake of the guillotine, Dr. Joseph Ignace Guillotin (1738-1814), is not the inventor of the decapitation device, but he is responsible for its popularity in France during the French Revolution and beyond. Poets and writers added the 'e' to the doctor's name because they found it was easier to rhyme.

Decapitation machines were used in Europe for hundreds of years before the first guillotine was designed. Evidence has been found that a guillotine-type machine was used as far back as the early 1300s in Ireland. In 1400, a machine called the Halifax Gibbet was built in England for public executions on market-days. The blade of the Halifax Gibbet fell for the last time in 1648. Other countries that used decapitation machines around this time were Scotland, Persia and Germany.

In 1789, Dr. Guillotin proposed the use of a decapitation machine to the French Assembly. He thought that decapitation was more humane and less painful than other methods of execution in use at the time. Dr. Guillotin wanted to have guillotines in every prison to make the death penalty more private. He thought that this would be the first step towards the abolition of executions, which was his true goal. This plan backfired, creating a highly public form of execution in France.

When the Assembly rewrote the penal code in 1789 it included: "Every person condemned to the death penalty shall have his head severed." Not only did this create the demand for a guillotine, it also meant that the wealthy could not buy themselves a "more pleasant" or private kind of execution. The Assembly ignored Dr. Guillotin's suggestion that the decapitations be carried out in prisons rather than in public.

Dr. Guillotin asked harpsichord maker Tobias Schmidt to design France's first guillotine. The guillotine designs were tested on cadavers from hospitals. The first execution performed by the guillotine occurred on 24 April 1792 at Grève. Its victim was convicted murderer Nicolas-Jacques Pelletier.

The guillotine claimed over 13,800 lives during the French Revolution (1787-99) alone. Its notable victims included King Louis XVI and Queen Marie Antoinette in 1793, as well as Georges Danton for conspiracy to restore the monarchy. Ironically the man who once decided who should face the guillotine, public accuser Maximillien Robespierre, also fell victim to the machine in 1794.

Leon Berger, a carpenter, made improvements on the guillotine in 1870 by redesigning the release mechanism for the blade. All guillotines built after this time followed Berger's design.

One hundred and twenty-five years after his death, one of Dr. Guillotin's wishes came true — in 1939, public executions were banned in France. Thirty-eight years later, the guillotine was used for the last time in France. Its final victim was convicted murderer Hamida Djandoubi. —JODI AVERY

Hedge Mazes

The concept and history of hedge mazes is rooted in myth, and flourishes, even today, in Europe.

A legend surrounding hedge mazes can be found in England during the reign of Henry II (1154-89). The story goes that at his palace at Woodstock, Henry II had his gardeners build a hedge maze that is now known as Rosamund's Bower. Legend has it that Henry II placed his mistress, Rosamund, in the center of the complex maze, which only he knew how to solve. This way his wife, Queen Eleanor, was unable to interfere when the King visited Rosamund. According to the legend, Queen Eleanor eventually solved the maze and poisoned Rosamund.

Hedge mazes were not fashionable in the time of this legend, though extravagant gardens enclosed by hedges were popular. During the Renaissance, Europeans reexamined the Rosamund legend. Monarchs, rulers and the wealthy began to hire landscape artists to design and cultivate lavish hedge mazes.

In 1690, William III of England commissioned two landscape artists, George Landon and Henry Wise, to create a hedge maze at Hampton Court. The maze was made of yew, a type of evergreen shrub with purple bark and flat needles, and took six years to complete. The Hampton Court maze is one of the most famous hedge mazes in England and it still survives today. Its design has been copied by many, partly because solving it is not difficult.

In the 19th century, mazes began to appear in public places, such as parks. In the late 19th century, William Waldorf Astor cultivated a maze at Hever Castle, where Anne Boleyn, second Queen of Henry VIII, spent her childhood. Today, the maze is 80-feet high and is known to be more difficult than the maze at Hampton Court, but more picturesque.

During the two world wars, many mazes were neglected and left to ruin. In the 1970s wealthy people all over Europe began to build hedge mazes on their properties and the popularity of these puzzles has been growing ever since.

Today more mazes are being built than in any other time in history. —JODI AVERY

HM

The 700s

Victoria King describes some of the highlights of this momentous century.

THE EIGHTH CENTURY WAS a period of warfare and religious upheaval. Great battles were fought throughout the period. The Muslims were involved in several key battles in Europe, the siege of Constantinople in 717 and the battle of Tours in 732. The Muslims were defeated in both attacks, but remained a threat. Beyond Europe, the Muslims defeated the Chinese at the Battle of Talas in 751. Within the Muslim caliphate (kingdom), internal power struggles waged. Many who became caliph (leader) were not able to maintain power and forfeited their lives. The Umayyad dynasty was defeated and nearly extinguished as a result of the Battle of the Great Zab River in 750 by Abbasid forces who seized control of the caliphate.

The Frankish kingdom was torn by internal wars at the beginning of the century, when the illegitimate son of Pepin II, Charles Martel, took control of the kingdom from Pepin's legitimate heirs. As the Frankish kingdom grew more powerful, the papacy increasingly turned to the nearby Franks for aid and protection.

The shift of papal dependency from Constantinople to the Frankish kingdom in the eighth century strained relations between Rome and Constantinople. Relations were further estranged between the papacy and Constantinople, with the former condemning the Iconoclasm in the Byzantine Empire.

At the beginning of the 700s, present-day Britain was comprised of several kingdoms

During the eighth century, Frankish leader Charles Martel drove back Muslim invaders and gradually consolidated his own rule over much of France and Western Europe.

known as the Anglo-Saxon Heptarcy: East Anglia, Essex, Kent, Mercia, Northumbria, Sussex and Wessex. Towards the end of the eighth century, Mercia under Offa had gained ascendancy and controlled most of the land south of the Humber River.

Religion was an important part of society in the eighth century. Islam grew in popularity as it spread with the Muslim conquests of the period. Conversions to Islam were assisted by a tax system that taxed non-Muslims but exempted Muslims. Taxpayers followed their purses. Toleration of other religions in the Muslim-held Iberian Peninsula also assured the security of the conquest in the eighth century.

Christianity was the dominant religion in eighth-century Europe, and Christian missionaries converted many pagans during this period. Monasteries and cathedral schools became the centers for the Christian faith. Sever-

al secular leaders in the eighth century became monks; Byzantine emperor Anatasius, Pepin the Short's brother Carloman and several Mercian and Northumbrian kings entered monasteries. In the Far East, Buddhism became the state religion of Japan.

There were great cultural advancements in the eighth century. In Japan, two histories were written, the *Nihon shoki* and the *Koyiki*, covering Japanese history from its mythical beginning to 697. Chinese culture was enriched by the works of two great poets writing during this period, Li Po and Tu Fu. In Europe, the Carolingian Renaissance under Charlemagne and Alcuin of York encouraged learning.

Many great buildings of the eighth century survive to this day such as the Umayyad Mosque in Damascus and the Todai Temple in Japan. Offa's Dyke, built in the late 700s, became the traditional boundary between Wales and England.

In the Americas, the Mayan civilization reached its zenith in this period. The Mayans built numerous stone pyramid temples, developed a hieroglyphic writing system and created a highly accurate calendar. On the African continent, the Ghanaian Empire began to flourish from its trade in gold and salt.

The eighth century was a time of great struggles, religious fervor and cultural flowering. The period was a high point in the so-called Dark Ages.

Jonathan Sheppard Books

Box 2020, Plaza Station
Albany, New York 12220

www.jonathansheppardbooks.com

Serving Historians and Genealogists since 1977

Summer Savings Until September 15, 2001 !

Visit our website for descriptions of all available maps and for special prices on featured reprint maps, original antique maps, and out-of-print books.

Check back often!
See what's on special!
◆◆◆◆◆◆◆◆◆◆◆

IMPORTANT - PLEASE READ

ABOUT OUR MAPS: All maps described below are black and white reprints of original maps in our collection and are printed on fine quality parchment stock or heavyweight linen-finish paper. Each group contains one or more maps that are 18" X 24". State and City Groups also contain one or more 8 1/2" X 11" map, and may also contain an 11" X 17" map. See our website or catalogue for details **Prices shown are in US dollars.**

SHIPPING: Map orders can be shipped either folded in a 9" X 12" envelope or unfolded and rolled in a sturdy shipping/storage tube. Please tell us your choice and add a shipping charge of either $3.00 US (folded) or $5.00 US (rolled in tube) to your total order. *Note that the shipping charge is per order, not per map. NYS & MA residents must add appropriate sales tax on total order, including shipping. For shipping to Canada, add an additional $1.50 US.*

TAKE 20% OFF ANY ONE ITEM LISTED BELOW OR ANY ONE REPRINT MAP OR MAP GROUP FROM OUR WEBSITE: Through 9/15/2001 !

Full descriptions of the map groups below are found on our website (see web address above) or in our catalogue (see below).

North American Map Groups

[PNF 1] Map Group for **Vermont & New Hampshire**, 1825-1867; 5 maps. **$17.95**
[PNF 3] Map Group for **Massachusetts**, 1825-1902; 4 maps. **$13.95**
[PNF 5] Map Group for **Connecticut**, 1825-1864; 4 maps. **$16.95**
[PNF 7] Map Group for **Maine**, 1825-1866; 3 maps. **$10.95**

[PNF 9] Map Group for **New York State,** 3 maps; 1825-1866. **$10.95**
[PNF13] Map Group for **19th C. New York City & Brooklyn,** 1848-1891, 3 maps. **$17.95**
[PNF16] Map Group for **New Jersey,** 1853, 1885; 2 maps. **$ 7.95**
[PNF17] Map Group for **Pennsylvania** ,1825-1885, 4 maps on 5 sheets. **$19.95**
[PNF 19] Map Group for **Early Maps of the Philadelphia Area,** 1681, 1750; 2 maps. **$11.95**
[PNF20] Map Group for **19th Century Philadelphia,** 1853-1879; 3 maps. **$12.95**
[PNF21] Map Group for **Virginia and West Virginia,** 1825-1884; 4 maps. **$16.95**
[PNF23] Map Group for **Maryland and Delaware,** 1853-1885; 3 maps. **$ 8.95**
[PNF27] Map Group for **Alabama,** 1825-1878; 4 maps. **$16.95**
[PNF29] Map Group for **Georgia,** 1825-1895; 4 maps. **$16.95**
[PNF39] Map Group for **Ohio,** 1825-1885; 5 maps on 6 sheets. **$23.95**
[PNF41] Map Group for **Indiana,** 1825-1880; 5 maps. **$22.95**
[PNF43] Map Group for **Illinois,** 1825-1885; 5 maps on 6 sheets. **$24.95**
[PNF44] Map Group for **Chicago,** 1853, 1873. 2 maps. **$ 7.95**
[PNF45] Map Group for **Michigan,** 1853-1902; 5 maps. **$22.95**
[PNF49] Map Group for **Wisconsin,** 1853-1902; 5 maps. **$22.95**
[PNF33] Map Group for **Kentucky and Tennessee,** 1825-1890; 5 maps. **$17.95**
[PNF25] Map Group for **North and South Carolina,** 1825-1889; 5 maps. **$17.95**
[PNF51] Map Group for **Missouri,** 1825-1880; 5 maps. **$22.95**
[PNF53] Map Group for **Kansas,** 1865-1880; 3 maps. **$17.95**
[PNF35] Map Group for **Arkansas and Louisiana,** 1825-1866; 4 maps. **$11.95**
[PNF31] Map Group for **Mississippi,** 1825-1878; 4 maps. **$16.95**
[PNF37] Map Group for **Texas,** 1853, 1866. 2 maps. **$ 7.95**
[PNF55] Map Group for **Iowa,** 1853-1880; 4 maps. **$18.95**
[PNF47] Map Group for **Minnesota,** 1853-1902; 3 maps. **$15.95**
[PNF57] Map Group for **Nebraska,** 1864-1888; 3 maps. **$17.95**
[PNF59] Map Group for **North and South Dakota,** 1880/81; 2 maps. **$11.95**
[PNF90] Map Group for **Eastern Canada** (Ontario & Quebec), 1867; 2 maps. **$11.95**

European Map Groups

Except as noted, all maps in the European Group are 18" X 24". Small maps are 8 1/2" X 11".

[PEF 1] Map Group for **Early Germany** 1760, 1766 1780, 1805; 4 maps. **$16.9**
[PEF 3] Map Group for the **Rhine Valley**, 1786 1845; 3 maps. **$17.9**
[PEF 5] Map Group for **Northwest Germany** 1829, 1832; 2 maps. **$11.9**
[PEF 7] Map Group for **Hesse & Environs** 1746-1882; 4 maps. **$21.9**
[PEF 9] Map Group for **Northeast Germany** 1835, 1843; 2 maps. **$11.9**
[PEF11] Map Group for the **Baltic Region**, 184 1845; 3 maps. **$17.9**
[PEF13] Map Group for **Eastern Europe in WW** I, 1914-1916; 3 maps. **$17.9**
[PEF15] Map Group for **Prussia**, 1845; 2 maps **$11.9**
[PEF17] Map Group for **Lithuania, Latvia** Estonia, 1845, 1914; 2 maps. **$11.9**
[PEF19] Map Group for **Poland**, 1799, 1817; maps. **$11.9**
[PEF21] Map Group for **Switzerland**, 179 1875; 2 maps. **$11.9**
[PEF23] Map Group for **Denmark**, 1799, 184 2 maps. **$11.9**
[PEF25] Map Group for **Sweden and Norwa** 1772, 1875; 2 maps. **$11.9**
[PEF27] Map Group for **Holland**, 1772-1860; large, 2 small maps. **$21.9**
[PEF31] Map Group for **Saxony and th Thuringian States**, 1765, 1873; 2 maps. **$11.9**
[PEF33] Map Group for **Czechoslovakia**, 179 1844; 2 maps. **$11.9**
[PEF35] Map Group for **Hungary**, 1774, 1845; maps. **$11.9**
[PEF39] Map Group for **Southern Italy**, 184 1890; 3 maps. **$12.9**
[PEF43] Map Group for **19th Century Irelan** 1820, 1875; 2 maps on 4 sheets. **$19.9**
[PEF47] Map Group for **Wales**, 1869, 1845; large, 12 small maps. **$22.9**

PAYMENT: We accept checks (U. dollars/U.S. Banks), M.O.s, MasterCard a VISA. Please include your card numbe expiration date and signature when ordering. O 24 hour faxline for credit card orders is (518) 76 9181.

OUR SHOP: Our bookshop - MARTLE BOOKS - is located on historic North Street ir Pittsfield, MA. We stock thousands of out of pri local histories and genealogies, along with o map reprints, original antique maps and a sele assortment of unusual books in a variety of subje areas. If you plan to visit, check our website 1 directions and hours or send us a SASE.

CATALOGUE: Can't visit our Pittsfield sho Don't have Internet access? Complete descriptic of all of the hundreds of high-quality reprint ma in our collection are included in our catalog Paper copies are available for 68 cents in stamp

www.jonathansheppardbooks.com
CHECK BACK OFTEN!

700-724

704: Adamnan, abbot of Iona, dies. After visiting Northumbria, Adamnan adopted the Roman date for Easter. Upon his return to Ireland, Adamnan traveled extensively promoting the Roman Easter. A reformer, Adamnan also exempted women from military service.

705: Tervel, leader of the Bulgars and ally of the exiled emperor Justinian II, lays siege to Constantinople. The attack is successful and Justinian returns to the throne.

705: The Empress Wu of China dies. Earlier that year, the Empress Wu had been forced to give the throne to her son, Chung Tsung. The Empress Wu had risen from being a junior concubine to wife of Emperor Kao Tsung, whom she controlled, making her the real ruler of China.

705: 'Abd al-Malik, fifth caliph (civil and religious "successor" of

731: The Venerable Bede completes his five-volume *Historia ecclesiastica gentis Anglorum* (Ecclesiastical History of the English People).

Muhammad) of the Umayyad dynasty dies. Under him, the Umayyad caliphate reaches its zenith. 'Abd al-Malik is succeeded by his son al-Walid.

709: Wilfrid, bishop of York, dies. Wilfrid was responsible for developing close relations between the papacy and the Anglo-Saxon Church, and was an advocate for papal supremacy.

710: Nara is made the capital of Japan.

711: A force of 7,000 Muslims under Tariq ibn Ziyad invades present-day Spain from Gibraltar. The word Gibraltar comes from the Arabic *geleb-al-Tarik* meaning "hill of Tarik".

714: Pepin II, ruler of the Franks, dies. His illegitimate son Charles Martel wages war against Pepin's young legitimate grandsons who inherit the realm.

715: The Umayyad Mosque is completed in Damascus. The Mosque is built on the site of a church dedicated to St. John the Baptist. The Mosque has a shrine believed to contain the saint's head.

715: Byzantine emperor Anastasius II is deposed and Theodosius III, a former tax collector, is placed on the throne by Opsikion troops. Anastasius becomes a monk.

THE BATTLE OF TOURS

IN 711, ISLAMIC FORCES UNDER Tariq ibn Ziyad crossed from Africa into Europe by way of present-day Gibraltar. Taking advantage of the weak Visigoth kingdom that controlled the Iberian Peninsula at the time, the Islamic forces conquered most of the peninsula within two years and called the area al-Andalus.

A Muslim base was established at Narbonne (in present-day France) on the coast of the Mediterranean in 720, from which the Andalusian Muslims attacked the Franks over the next 40 years. From Narbonne, the Muslims in 721 laid siege to Toulouse to the northwest, held by Eudes, Duke of Aquitaine. Muslim leader al-Samh was killed during the siege of the town and the Muslims retreated to Narbonne.

In 732, 50,000 Islamic soldiers advanced along the Garonne River, occupying Bordeaux. From here, the force moved north toward Tours in Aquitaine. Defeated in battle by the Muslims, Eudes appealed to Charles Martel,

At Tours, Frankish leader Charles Martel checked the advance of Muslim forces in Western Europe and secured his own position as ruler.

leader of the Frankish kingdom, for assistance.

In October of that year, a force of 50,000 under Charles Martel met the Muslims somewhere between Tours and Poitiers in northern Aquitaine. The exact location of the battle is not known, and as a result, the Battle of Tours is also known as the Battle of Poitiers.

The Muslims retreated to protect their baggage train, which hampered their movements. The Muslims under emir 'Abd ar-Rahman al-Ghafiqi of Cordoba were defeated by the Franks and 'Abd ar Rahman was killed in battle. It is from this victory that the Frankish ruler earned his name Martel, meaning "the hammer".

The Frankish victory is seen by many scholars as crucial for the preservation of Christian Europe as Islamic expansion from the west was checked. The victory resulted in Eudes, Duke of Aquitaine, swearing allegiance to Charles Martel and the victory also consolidated Martel's leadership of the Franks.

The Muslim defeat at Tours did not end Islamic attacks in the area, however the Battle of Tours marked their furthest penetration into western Europe. In 734, the Muslims captured Avignon and nine years later, Lyons was also attacked. In 759, the Muslim base of Narbonne was attacked and the Muslims were defeated.

717: Muslims lay siege to the Christian city of Constantinople. The siege is unsuccessful due to the superiority of the Byzantine fleet.

717: Byzantine emperor Theodosius III is forced to abdicate by the commander of the Anatolikon troops, Leo the Isaurian who becomes emperor. Theodosius dies in a monastery at Ephesus.

719: After five years of war, Charles Martel becomes mayor of the palace of Austrasia. The term mayor meant an officer of the royal household and later the position of regent or viceroy.

720: Former Byzantine emperor Anastasius II is executed after he abandons monastic life and tries to retake the throne.

720: The *Nihon shoki* (Chronicles of Japan) is published. Together with the *Koyiki* (Records of Ancient Matters) published in 712, the two books cover Japanese history from its mythical beginning to 697. Both histories are originally written in Chinese.

725-749

726: Icons are banned by Byzantine emperor Leo III. His followers become known as Iconoclasts (image breakers). This ban is met with opposition throughout the empire.

731: Pope Gregory II dies and Pope Gregory III is chosen. One of Gregory III's first actions is to denounce the Iconoclasts of the Byzantine Empire.

731: The Venerable Bede completes *Historia ecclesiastica gentis Anglorum* (Ecclesiastical History of the English People). The five books cover the history of Britain from the raids of Julius Caesar in 55BC to St. Augustine's arrival in Kent in 597AD. Bede popularized the method of dating years from the birth of Christ; *Anno Domini* (in the year of the Lord).

732: Charles Martel of the Franks defeats Muslim invaders at the Battle of Tours in France.

715: The Umayyad Mosque is completed in Damascus.

735: York is made an archbishopric independent of Canterbury.

739: Charles Martel succeeds in his six-year campaign against Burgundian chieftains.

741: Byzantine emperor Leo III dies. Leo III's son, Constantine, succeeds to the throne as Constantine V. Constantine, an Iconoclast, begins to persecute monks who are image-worshippers.

741: Charles Martel, ruler of the Franks, dies. Upon his death, his kingdom is divided between his two sons, Carloman and Pepin the Short.

743: Aed Allan mac Fergaile, ruler of the Ui Neill dynasty in the north of Ireland, is killed in battle at Seredmas in County Meath by the king of Meath Domnall Midi.

732: Battle of Tours. Charles Martel defeats advancing Islamic forces.

744: Umayyad caliph Walid II is murdered by his family. Walid was known for his extravagance over buildings and wine — the latter forbidden in the Islamic world. Walid's successor Yazid III dies shortly thereafter and is succeeded by Ibrahim, who is overthrown. Marwan II becomes caliph.

747: Carloman, elder son of Charles Martel and mayor of Alemannia, Austrasia and Thuringia, enters monastic life, making his brother Pepin the Short the sole ruler of the Franks.

750-774

750: The Abbasid caliphate is founded in Baghdad after the fall of the Umayyad dynasty at the Battle of the Great Zab River. The Umayyad dynasty is massacred. The Abbasid dynasty claimed its forefather to be Abbas, uncle of the prophet Muhammad.

751: The Battle of Talas (in present-day Kyrgyzstan) is fought between the Muslims and the Chinese. The Muslims are victorious. The victors learn paper-making technology from their prisoners. The Chinese defeat marks the beginning of the end for the Tang dynasty.

752: The main buildings of the Todai Temple are completed in Nara, Japan. Commissioned by the Emperor Shomu, the buildings signal the adoption of Buddhism as the state religion. The main structure today is the world's largest wooden building.

752: The English missionary Boniface is martyred by pagan Frisians in Dokkum, Frisia (present-day Netherlands). Boniface is known for his conversion of the Germanic people to the Christian faith.

754: Pope Stephen III appeals to Pepin the Short for aid against the Lombards. Within two years, the Lombards are defeated and Pope Stephen III becomes ruler of the Papal States. Papal independence from Constantinople is also secured.

The Carolingian Renaissance

THE CAROLINGIAN RENAISSANCE began in the late eighth century in the town of Aachen (in present-day western Germany). It was here that Charlemagne, king of the Franks, established his palace school. As a devout Christian, Charlemagne had great respect for the Church and saw himself as responsible for protecting and fostering its teachings.

The leading figure of the early Carolingian Renaissance was Alcuin of York. Alcuin had been the head of York Cathedral School, known throughout Europe as a center for learning due to its distinguished library. In 781, Alcuin accepted Charlemagne's invitation to visit Aachen, where scholars from Ireland, Italy, England and Charlemagne's vast kingdom were gathered. Shortly after Alcuin's arrival, he was appointed head of the palace school.

Under Alcuin, the palace school became the center for knowledge and learning in Charlemagne's kingdom. In addition to the pupils who later became monks, Charlemagne, his family,

At Aachen, Charlemagne became a student of his own palace school.

and other members of the royal court were also students of the school. Students were taught the seven liberal arts: the trivium of grammar, logic and rhetoric, and the quadrivium of arithmetic, astronomy, geometry and music. Under Charlemagne's decrees, all clerics were to be able to read, write and have the knowledge necessary for their duties as clerics. In his later years, Charlemagne learned Latin and some Greek

from the palace school.

Alcuin developed a calligraphy known as Carolingian minuscule, which was easier to read than the script in use at that time. Carolingian minuscule is the predecessor of the Roman type used today.

The Carolingian Renaissance spread easily throughout Europe as the learned spoke the universal language of Latin. Alcuin's former students went to monasteries and cathedral schools throughout Christian Europe with the knowledge they had acquired in Aachen. The palace library also allowed its collection to be copied for other libraries.

The Carolingian Renaissance survived the dissolution of Charlemagne's empire in 843. However, the barbarian attacks of the late ninth century heralded the end of the Carolingian Renaissance. The spirit of the Carolingian Renaissance continued within the monasteries into the mediaeval period and the ancient texts copied during this period were again sought in the Renaissance of the 15th century.

754: The first caliph of the Abbasid dynasty, Abu al-'Abbas as-Saffah, dies. His brother al-Mansur succeeds him.

754: Pepin the Short is crowned king of the Franks by Pope Stephen III.

756: Fleeing after the fall of the Umayyad dynasty, 'Abd ar-Rahman I of the Umayyad dynasty makes Cordoba in Spain his capital. The city becomes a center for Islamic culture.

757: Pepin the Short gives Ravenna, the former capital of Byzantine Italy, to the pope as part of his Papal States.

757: Aethelbald, king of Mercia, is murdered by his retainers and his cousin Offa succeeds to the throne.

762: Baghdad is chosen as the capital for the Abbasid dynasty.

752: The main buildings of the Todai Temple are completed in Nara, Japan.

762: Chinese poet Li Po dies. Li Po's poetry, which celebrated romance and the joys of drinking, was very popular during his lifetime.

768: Pepin the Short of the Franks dies. Pepin's eldest son Charles becomes king of the Franks; his younger son, Carloman, inherits Pepin's eastern possessions. Charles becomes so powerful that he is known as Carolus Magnus or Charlemagne in Old French.

770: Koken, empress of Japan, dies. Koken ruled from 749 to 758 and from 764 to 770. She ascended the throne for the first time when her father, Emperor Suomu abdicated and she then abdicated in favor of Prince Oi, known as Emperor Junnin. Junnin was deposed in a civil war and Koken returned to the throne as the Empress Shotoku.

770: Tu Fu, considered by many to be the greatest Chinese poet, dies in Hunan.

771: Carloman, younger brother of Charlemagne, dies. Charlemagne annexes his brother's possessions and becomes sole ruler of the Frankish Empire.

774: Charlemagne's forces lay siege to the Lombard capital of Pavia. When the city falls, Charlemagne crowns himself king of the Lombards.

775-799

775: Caliph al-Mansur dies and is succeeded by Mahdi.

778: Charlemagne lays siege to Zaragoza in northeastern Spain. He fails to take the Muslim-held city as Saxons rebel in the west.

779: Offa of Mercia expands his territory and becomes overlord of most of England south of the Humber River.

780: Byzantine emperor Leo IV dies. His 10-year-old son becomes Emperor Constantine VI under the guardianship of his mother Irene.

781: Charlemagne's second son, Pepin, is made king of Italy.

782: Charlemagne orders the execution of some 4,500 Saxons as punishment for a rebellion.

782: The theologian and scholar Alcuin of York is summoned by Charlemagne to lead the palace school at Aachen. During his time at Aachen, Alcuin of York improves the palace library and the court

794: Kyoto becomes the capital of Japan.

becomes a cultural center.

787: The Second Council of Nicaea is held. The Council is called to deal with the Iconoclasm, which is renting apart the Christian Church.

792: After two years of attempting to retain power after her son Constantine VI comes of age, Irene is arrested and banished from the court. She is later pardoned and

proclaimed co-ruler.

793: The monastic community on the island of Lindisfarne off the coast of England is raided by Vikings.

794: Kyoto becomes the capital city of Japan and remains so for over 1,000 years.

795: Pope Adrian I dies and Leo III is chosen. Adrian I's pontificate of nearly 24 years is the longest until Pope Pius VI's pontificate eight centuries later.

796: Offa of Mercia dies. One of Offa's most enduring legacies is the penny, a coin similar to the *deniers* of the Franks. The word "penny" is derived from the Anglo-Saxon word *penig*.

796: Alcuin of York retires from Charlemagne's Palace School and becomes bishop of Tours.

797: Constantine VI is deposed by his mother Irene, who has her son arrested and blinded. Irene reigns alone as emperor (not empress).

The Iconoclasm

IN 726, THE BYZANTINE emperor Leo III banned the devotional pictures of holy figures known as icons. Leo III was against the perceived idolatry of worshippers towards the devotional pictures, which he felt was against the Second Commandment's prohibition of image worship. Those who followed him in rejecting icons were called Iconoclasts, and their destruction of icons came to be called the Iconoclasm.

Leo III began to persecute the Iconodules (image venerators) and focused on the dissenting monasteries. Iconodules were beaten, imprisoned and exiled.

Pope Gregory II condemned the Iconoclasm, but Leo III and his successors continued the Iconoclastic polices until the regency of Constantine VI began in 780. Constantine's regent was his mother Irene who called the

The Iconoclasts believed that the veneration of religious images violated the Second Commandment's prohibition against image worship. Iconodules felt otherwise.

Council of Nicaea in 787. The council condemned the Iconoclasts and began the restoration of icons.

The second Iconoclasm began in 814 with the reign of Leo V. Leo V was a former general of the

Byzantine army where a strong Iconoclast sentiment remained. Shortly after taking the throne, Leo reinstated the Iconoclastic policies and began persecuting Iconodules.

In 842, three-year-old Michael III came to the Byzantine throne. His mother and regent, Theodora, was an Iconodule and began to reverse the Iconoclastic policies. In 843, icons were used in a religious procession on the first Sunday of Lent and this event is still celebrated as the Feast of Orthodoxy.

Rome's reaction to the Iconoclasm distanced its relations with Constantinople. The Byzantines turned to their own patriarchs who accommodated the concerns of the empire. The Iconoclasm was a key factor in the estrangement between Rome and Constantinople before the Great Schism of 1054.

Lindisfarne

THE CHURCH AND MONASTERY of Lindisfarne, also known as Holy Island, was located in the North Sea off the coast of Northumbria. St. Aiden (d. 642), an Irish monk, established the monastery in 635 to convert the Northumbrians to Christianity. Lindisfarne became a religious center in the late seventh and early eighth centuries.

Lindisfarne's reputation was due in part to St. Cuthbert (c.635-687). St. Cuthbert was bishop of Lindisfarne for the last two years of his life. Eleven years after St. Cuthbert's death, the bones of the former bishop were to be transformed into relics, however, the body was found uncorrupted. This miracle increased St. Cuthbert's reputation for holiness and he became known in death as a "wonder worker". St. Cuthbert's tomb at Lindisfarne attracted many pilgrims.

In this period, Lindisfarne's monks established many churches, especially in Northern England and southern Scotland. Wilfrid, bishop of York (634-709), who was responsible for establishing close ties between the papacy and the Anglo-Saxon Church, began his clerical life at Lindisfarne.

The Church and Monastery of Lindisfarne served as an important religious center during the 700s.

The Venerable Bede (c.672-735), a historian and theologian, considered to be the greatest thinker of his period, visited Lindisfarne several times. Bede also wrote of the life of St. Cuthbert.

The famed Lindisfarne Gospels was also created in the early eighth century. The text of the illuminated manuscript states it was written by Eadfrith (d. 721) before he became bishop of Lindisfarne. The Lindisfarne Gospels was a beautiful manuscript of the four Gospels written to honor the life of St. Cuthbert. Today the manuscript is housed in the British Museum.

In 793, the Viking age in Europe began with a raid on the monastery at Lindisfarne. The Anglo-Saxon Chronicle records for that year "Terrible portents appeared over Northumbria … fiery dragons were seen … a great famine, and after that in the same year the harrying of the heathen miserably destroyed God's church in Lindisfarne by rapine and slaughter." Vikings pillaged the church and slaughtered the monks. Alcuin of York suggested the raid was God's punishment for the lax ways of the monks in recent years, as the monastery had begun to decline.

The Vikings returned to Lindisfarne in 875, however, the monks of Lindisfarne had abandoned the island, taking with them the body of St. Cuthbert, which now rests in Durham Cathedral.

Offa's Dyke

OFFA'S DYKE, the traditional boundary between Wales and England, was built in the late eighth century. Commissioned by Offa, King of Mercia (r. 757-796) after he succeeded to the throne, the earthwork dyke originally extended about 150 miles (240 kilometers) from the River Dee in the north to the River Wye in the south.

The dyke was built up to 60 feet (18 meters) high in some places with a ditch on the Welsh side that was 12 feet (3.5 meters) in depth at some points. Archaeological information suggests that a wall at the top of the dyke may have also existed.

Work on the dyke is believed to have begun late in Offa's reign

Built by thousands of laborers in the late eighth century, Offa's Dyke has since served as the traditional boundary between Wales and England.

as his possessions grew, but it is not known if the dyke was built as a boundary or as a fortification. The dyke's construction required thousands of laborers. A project involving similar numbers was not repeated until a millennium later with the great projects of the Industrial Revolution. That Offa's Dyke runs straight over vast distances is a testament to the skill of the laborers.

Offa's Dyke no longer serves as the political boundary between Wales and England, although the 1,200-year-old dyke still exists today. Breaks have appeared in the earthenwork, with the best-preserved sections of the dyke between Presteign and Montgomery.

A walking path now runs along the dyke.

HM

Colonial Midwives

Christine Inge describes the herbal nurses of the colonial era.

MARTHA BALLARD WAS a highly respected primary care provider in the small town of Hallowell, Maine. Thanks to her outstanding skill, her practice thrived. During her 27-year career, she delivered 996 children and treated hundreds of general patients — a remarkable record for someone working in a sparsely populated area where she often traveled miles to reach her patients. Ballard's career was remarkable in another way as well: she lived in the 18th century. She began keeping a diary chronicling her work in 1787 — a diary that is the best record we have of the vital role midwives played in colonial medicine.

Martha Ballard's practice was fairly typical in colonial America. Throughout the 17th and 18th centuries, people turned to women practitioners for most of their medical needs. According to historians Carol Hymowitz and Michaele Weissman, the authors of *A History of Women in America*, "It seems probable that throughout most of the colonial period more women practiced medicine than men. Women were nurses, apothecaries... physicians, and midwives. Only surgery... was dominated by men." In most rural areas, a woman herbalist was often the only medical practitioner.

How did women come to play such a dominant role in early American medicine? There are several related reasons. For one thing, colonial medicine was highly democratic. Colonies generally lacked licensing laws for physicians, so anyone with medical skills could legally practice medicine. Medical training was likewise open and egalitarian, emphasizing practical skill over

Martha Ballard's life, as recorded in her diary, was the subject of a movie titled *A Midwife's Tale*.

formal, theoretical learning. Until the University of Pennsylvania opened its medical school in 1767, physicians learned their profession by being apprenticed to an older doctor. In this democratic atmosphere, women with a knowledge of traditional medicine could practice freely.

The care of women practitioners was more accessible than that of conventional doctors. Doctors were scarce in the colonies, while women who understood medicinal herbs lived in virtually every village. Women herbalists also tended to charge lower fees than doctors did so poorer patients, who otherwise couldn't afford medical care, turned to midwives when they were ill.

However, perhaps the main reason women had a leading role in medicine is that the care they provided was often superior to other medical care that was available. A midwife's training was essentially the same as a conventional doctor's, and was in many cases more extensive. Midwives, like doctors, learned by observing an experienced practitioner, helping with cases until they gained the skills to start their own practices. However, unlike doctors,

midwives' daily experiences from early on helped prepare them for their work. Women in colonial America were responsible for the day-to-day healthcare of their families. The average woman, whether she lived on a farm or in the city, kept a "physic garden" beside her house where she cultivated a variety of herbs to treat her family's ailments. She would also get together with other women to care for a neighbor during childbirth or illness. Thus, most women developed medical knowledge as part of their everyday skills. Training in such skills started early, so midwives were often better trained than doctors.

Practical training was not the only reason midwives were often better healers. Midwives' treatments were generally safer than those of conventional practitioners. These women relied on proven herbs to cure diseases. For instance, when one of Martha Ballard's patients came to her with an injury, she turned to a safe plant-based treatment: "Mrs Pollard came here with her son Amos who had a lame knee. I bath'd it with Camphor and mellolot oinment, applied a plaster of my salve."

On another occasion, Ballard recorded the case of her neighbor, James Andrews, writing that he "has a swelling on his right side. Applied a Cataplasm [poultice] of the yolk of an Egg, Honey, & Flour." Other treatments she used regularly included chamomile, sage and aloe. Sometimes she did prescribe medicines, such as Anderson's pills, favored by conventional doctors, but only as a last resort. However, she never bled her patients or gave them opiates, as doctors regularly did.

In contrast with the safe treatments employed by midwives, doctors tended to favor hazardous treatments, particularly bleeding, blistering and leeches. They prescribed herbal medicines, the most effective of which were based on traditional remedies, such as sassafras, a cure for malaria early settlers learned from Native Americans. However, doctors also relied heavily on potent narcotics, especially opium. Dr. Zerobabel Endecott, a 17th-century Salem, Massachusetts, physician, wrote a manuscript of medical "recipes" that included the following: "For Ye Tooth-Ache: Take a Little Pece of opium as big as a great pinnes head, & put it in the hollow place of the Akeing Tooth & it will give preseant Ease, often tried by me upon many people & never fayled." At the time, several non-addictive herbal remedies for toothaches were well known.

In Martha Ballard's time, physicians were increasing their reliance on opiates. As more doctors sought university training, they began to reject herbs entirely, branding them unscientific. Unfortunately, science had yet to discover safe alternatives to herbs. So, doctors relied on opium and calomel, a toxic mercury compound. One of Hallowell's conventional practitioners, Dr. Page, regularly sought advice from a nearby university-trained physician, Dr. Vaughan. Vaughan repeatedly advised Page to prescribe opium. "I wish you would apply opium & the digitalis to the patient at Mr. West's," he wrote in 1800, noting that another patient, Miss Hallowell, was already "in the habit of taking [opium]." Vaughan also urged the use of bloodletting for virtually every disease, from infections to injuries, and also urged regular bleedings for healthy people as preventive medicine.

Given the midwives' high degree of training and the dangerous measures used by conventional doctors, it's not surprising

Martha Ballard's grandniece, Clara Barton, founded the American Red Cross. Barton regarded Ballard as an inspiration.

that many people preferred to call a midwife even if they had access to a conventional doctor. In one instance, one of Ballard's patients turned away the local doctor, preferring the midwife: "Dr. Page was call'd," wrote Ballard of a 1793 delivery, "but Mrs. Robbins did not wish to see him when he came & he returned home."

Midwives were regarded so highly by their patients not just because of their skill but also because of their great devotion to their work. A midwife/herbalist's work was arduous, requiring enormous dedication. Mrs. Whitman, a midwife in Marlborough, Massachusetts, walked miles over fields in snowshoes to reach her patients during the winter months. Martha Ballard's diary chronicles many such challenges, too. Throughout the summer of 1787, Ballard's hometown of Hallowell experienced a scarlet fever epidemic. She attended five or six patients on many days. Gathering herbs to use in treating the epidemic added to her work. On 5 August 1787, she sat up with a patient through the night, as she did dozens of times in her career. Two days later, she rushed from home to home seeing her patients, then came home to find her husband ill as well: "I was call'd to Mrs Howards this morning for to see her son. Went from

Mrs Howards to see Mrs Williams. From thence to [Mrs] Joseph Fosters to see her sick children, Came home went to the field & got some Cold water root. Returned home after dark. Mr. Ballard been to Caseby. His throat is very sore. He gargled with my tincture. Find relief & went to bed comfortably."

Even during quieter times, being a country midwife required courage and stamina, as an entry in Ballard's December 1793 diary demonstrates. Called to a woman in labor, Ballard set out on foot at dawn in a snowstorm. "I had two falls," she wrote, "one on my way there, the other on my return. I traveled some Roads in the snow where it was almost as high as my waist." Soon thereafter, she was called again to a patient. This time she went in a carriage: "we were once overset.... Once I got out & helpt push the carriage." On other occasions, she traveled on horseback, and was thrown by her horse several times. Despite all these obstacles, Ballard persevered, reaching her patients even in severe storms. Dedicated and skilled, midwives were the practitioner of choice for many early Americans.

Despite its vital role in earlier years, midwifery was in decline by the early 1800s. As the Industrial Revolution progressed, the public began to view anything labeled scientific as inherently superior to anything perceived as traditional. As conventional medicine improved, so did patients' faith in it. But the legacy of early American women healers was not forgotten. In the mid-19th century, Martha Ballard's sister Dorothy Barton, regaled her granddaughter Clara with stories about the dedicated midwife. Clara viewed Martha Ballard as an inspiration to her in her own work as founder of the American Red Cross. The work of Martha Ballard and her fellow midwives was vital to the health of an emerging nation and remained an inspiring legacy for the next generation of medical women.

HM

The Magazine: Storehouse of News and Views

Barbara Krasner-Khait charts the rise of the modern magazine.

"A successful magazine is exactly like a successful store: it must keep its wares constantly fresh and varied to attract the eye and hold the patronage of its customers." —Edward Bok, Editor, *Ladies' Home Journal*

AS YOU READ THIS ISSUE of *History Magazine*, you'll notice a few things. The cover features headlines and a large photo.

Today, the reading public can select from tens of thousands of magazine titles covering hundreds of subjects and in dozens of languages.

Inside, the masthead identifies the publisher, editor and staff. The articles are written by either staff or freelancers. The paper, thicker and better quality than that of a newspaper, is meant to last a while. And you've come to expect this magazine every other month.

These characteristics are the hallmark of the magazine, the name given to "a collection of articles published at regular intervals," derived from the Arabic *makhzan*, meaning "storehouse". No one knows for sure which publication rightfully lays claim to being the first magazine. One of the earliest magazines was the *Monthly Discussions*, published by German theologian Johann Rist in 1663. *Journal des Savans*, founded in Paris in 1665, carried book abstracts, though it later included original material. *Le Mercure Galant* made its appearance in 1672, containing poetry and court gossip. The *Athenian Gazette* (renamed *Athenian Mercury* after only one issue) debuted in England in 1690. Its publisher, John Dunton, spurred by his own extramarital affair, included a "problem page" —

the first advice column. To accommodate the rising female literacy level, Dunton launched

Edward Carey's *Gentleman's Magazine* enjoyed success in Britain, and served as inspiration for several American publishers.

The Ladies Mercury, the first periodical for women, in 1693. We probably wouldn't recognize any of these as magazines by today's standards.

An early British magazine that served as a prototype for the format we know today was Edward Cave's *Gentleman's Magazine*. It was the first periodical to use the word magazine, because as Cave explained, his periodical was intended to be "a storehouse of wisdom and life of the age". Its publication began in 1731 as a collection of articles from a variety of books and pamphlets. Later, it carried original content, including contributions from Samuel Johnson. Publication ceased in 1914.

The Tatler And The Spectator
Richard Steele began *The Tatler* in 1709, one of 18 papers published that year in London. It came out on Tuesdays, Thursdays and Saturdays, and was more of a "views" paper than a "news" paper. Steele and school chum Joseph Addison were the major contributing writers. When *The Tatler* folded in 1711, Steel and Addison began *The Spectator*. And that, too, only lasted a short while, from March 1711 to December 1712.

Though short-lived, both periodicals influenced public opinion and provided impetus to the growth of journalism and magazine writing. They also continue to serve as valuable sources of social history, based on their commentaries on manners, morals and literature of the day.

Magazines Come To America

The first magazine attempts in the Colonies in 1741 were dismal failures. Andrew Bradford's *American Magazine* ceased publication after only three issues. Benjamin Franklin's *General Magazine and Historical Chronicle* lasted six issues. More than 40 years later, Mathew Carey, a Philadelphia printer and bookseller, started two magazines, *The Columbian* in 1786 (which lasted until 1790) and *The American Museum* in 1787 (which lasted until 1792).

These early American magazines were well intended yet short lived. Lyon Richardson rationalized the situation as it related to *The American Museum* in *A History of Early American Magazines*, "The plan required . . . a wide and generous support by a general public as willing to pay as to receive; this was not forthcoming. Had the subscribers uniformly honored their debts to Carey, the magazine might have prospered, but, as announcements in many of the advertisements show, collections were not easily made. The age of advertising had not yet arrived, and the project was abandoned."

Though they didn't last long, they did have impact as early instruments of mass media. In 1788, George Washington wrote Carey, "I consider such easy vehicles of knowledge, more happily calculated than any other, to preserve the liberty, stimulate the industry and meliorate the morals of an enlightened and free people."

Magazine Explosion

The year 1825 was a turning point in both Europe and America. Change was the order of the day, accompanied by the rise of cities, education and printing. In that year came "the nearly incredible expansion of the magazine business from its modest beginnings to mass-market size, surpassing the simultaneous explosion of the newspaper,"

Graham's Magazine prided itself on carrying well-known writers, like William Cullen Bryant, of whom it carried portraits.

says John Tebbel, author of *The Media in America*.

The New York Mirror, itself a weekly periodical launched in 1823, explained the phenomenon in 1828:

"These United States are fertile in most things, but in periodicals they are extremely luxuriant. They spring up as fast as mushrooms, in every corner, and like all rapid vegetation, bear the seeds of early decay within them.... They put forth their young green leaves in the shape of promises and prospectuses — blossom through a few numbers — and then comes a 'frost, a killing frost,' in the form of bills due and debts unpaid. This is the fate of hundreds, but hundreds more are found to supply their place, to tread in their steps, and share their destiny. The average age of periodicals in this country is found to be six months."

In 1825, there were fewer than 100 magazines in the US. By 1850, there were about 600.

One of the first monthly magazines, *The Casket: Flowers of Literature, Wit and Sentiment*, began publication in 1826 by Samuel C. Atkinson and Charles Alexander, the same men who brought out

The Saturday Evening Post, originally launched in 1821. (The word "casket" in this sense meant repository and was a popular name for magazines.) Atkinson sold the magazine in 1839 to George Graham, who changed the format from "a rather cheap-looking miscellany to a well-printed, entertaining magazine." Graham then bought *Gentleman's Magazine* and he combined the two into *Graham's Magazine*. It became one of the most important and popular magazines in America.

Another popular and innovative magazine was the New York publication, *Knickerbocker*, introduced in 1833. Its editor, Gaylord Clark, introduced a section called "Editor's Table," giving the magazine a more personal voice and Clark a platform for expressing his views. It became the predecessor for similar departments of later magazines like *The New Yorker* and *Harper's*. Clark's publication also boasted an impressive array of contributing writers of the day — Irving, Cooper, Bryant, Longfellow, Hawthorne, Whittier and Holmes.

For The Ladies

Sarah Josepha Hale was the first to produce a popular magazine aimed at women. *Ladies Magazine* was launched in Boston in 1828. Like other editors, Hale used the magazine as a platform for her opinions — in this case, education for women. It caused quite a stir since prevailing attitudes at the time were in favor of women keeping house and raising children. After nine annual volumes and mediocre financial success, the magazine merged with its rival, *Godey's Ladies Book*. Hale, though, stayed on as editor and made *Godey's* the best women's magazine before the Civil War. Like *Graham's*, this high-quality magazine attracted fine writers and paid them well. By 1850, it was selling 40,000 copies a month — the highest of any magazine up to that point.

The success of *Godey's* demonstrated that the women's market was more significant than anyone realized and that by targeting and reaching this market, circulation would surely rise. Graham took immediate action and targeted half his magazine's content to women. Magazines in London did the same.

In 1872, Ebenezer Butterick, of Butterick tissue-paper dress pattern fame, introduced a fashion magazine, the *Delineator*, which ran more than 200 pages per issue. Eventually, its scope broadened to include fiction and home activity. It became known as a "cookie and pattern" magazine, a name given to women's magazines with the belief that these were women's interests. Similarly, another dress pattern maker, James McCall, issued *McCall's* in 1897. It started as *The Queen: Illustrating McCall's Bazar Glove-Fitting Patterns* in 1873.

The *Women's Home Companion* launched in January 1897 following its 1874 start as the *Home* in Cleveland, Ohio. *Ladies' Home Journal* began as a *Tribune and Farmer* newspaper supplement, owned by Cyrus Curtis. The supplement was so successful that Curtis sold the newspaper and kept the supplement in 1883 when it took on the new name. Its editor during the early days, Edward Bok, made the magazine an intimate friend to his readers. By the turn of the century, the *Journal* surpassed every other magazine in circulation. Surprisingly, it was the third most requested magazine by WWI soldiers.

The Literati

The literary weeklies, though, dominated the women's magazines and general monthlies. They were cheap and their mortality rate was high. *The New York Mirror* provided running commentary on the morals and manners of the times. Anne Royall's *Paul Pry* out of Washington, DC

Alice Van Leer Carrick

COLLECTOR'S LUCK

The first of these extremely popular and entertaining volumes on the joys of hunting antiques. Collecting adventures in America, seeking treasures of Colonial days. $3.00

COLLECTOR'S LUCK IN FRANCE

Not only collector's, but traveler's luck as well. Mrs. Carrick had a glorious time with the French in Paris and Tours, and shares it joyously with her readers. $3.00

COLLECTOR'S LUCK IN ENGLAND

This volume has a double spell, the charm of the lovely English countryside, plus the lure of finding old and beautiful things in one of the world's richest treasure-lands. $3.00

SHADES OF OUR ANCESTORS

American Profiles and Profilists

A lavishly illustrated book of great beauty, presenting the fruits of the author's years of research among early masters of the art of the silhouette who flourished in Colonial America. $5.00

ATLANTIC MONTHLY PRESS BOOKS

Published by Little, Brown and Company

For periodicals such as *Atlantic Monthly*, promoting the parent company's book publishing efforts became a priority.

was a forerunner of the gossip and society columns popular in daily newspapers today.

A number of quarterlies appeared that were considered the crème de la crème such as *North American Review* and *The Dial*.

North American Review started in 1815 and was considered to be one of the finest magazines, modeled after the British *Quarterly* and *Edinburgh* reviews. Even a rival said about it: "It is unquestionably true that the *North American* is regarded by more people, in all parts of the country, as at once the highest and most impartial platform upon which current public issue can be discussed, than is any other magazine or review." An agent of the Japanese government bought the magazine as an American front; publication ceased in 1939.

The Dial debuted July 1840 and contained work by some of the best thinkers in New England.

The Magazinists

Nathan Willis, publisher of *Youth's Companion*, was the first professional writer known as a "magazinist". He wrote for *Graham's*, *Godey's* and others. A whole corps of writers emerged in this category. Edgar Allan Poe contributed to more than 30 magazines and served on five editorial staffs, though he didn't earn much money doing so. Certainly, the most prolific was Lydia Sigourney, who over the course of her 50-year career, wrote more than 2,000 articles for more than 300 magazines.

Opportunity For Book Publishers

An incestuous relationship developed between book and magazine publishing. Magazine articles became books, book excerpts appeared in magazines, and sometimes the whole book appeared in the magazine. The Boston publishing firm Phillips, Sampson & Co. launched *Atlantic Monthly* in 1857. The publishing firm of Harper Brothers began *Harper's Monthly* in 1850, still in operation today. *Harper's Weekly* started in 1857 and folded in 1916. During the Civil War, many people turned to *Harper's Weekly* for its drawings of the battlefront. Many considered it to be the forerunner of *Life*. New York's Scribner Brothers developed *Scribner's*, "the great middle class magazine of its day". Lippincott put out *Lippincott's* in 1868 and was the first magazine to incorporate a full novel in a single issue. It ceased publication in 1914.

The post-Civil War period witnessed a second explosion of magazines, spurred by the availability of capital, technological advances in printing, and then in the 1880s, by favorable periodical mailing rates set forth by the Postal Act of 3 March 1879. There were 700 magazines in 1865 and 3,300 in 1885.

In the mid-1800s, a number of important magazines started.

still exist today: *Boy's Life*, started by the Boy Scouts in 1911, and *American Girl*, started by the Girl Scouts in 1917. The venerable *Highlights for Children*, aimed at children between the ages of two and 12, was founded in 1946 and *Humpty Dumpty* in 1952.

Issue Platforms

Because magazines were growing in popularity, they became useful organs for writers and policy leaders to communicate — and debate — their positions. They discussed slavery, tariffs and westward movement.

Just before the turn of the 20th century, a new kind of journalism appeared that exposed business and industry practices, social conditions and politics. It was called the "New Journalism" or "muckraking." Writers became media activists, informing the readership about conditions they thought the public should know. For instance, Lincoln Steffens, writing for *Everybody's Magazine*, addressed city conditions. Ida M. Tarbell, a staff writer for *McClure's*, exposed, among other things, Standard Oil, ultimately leading to its dissolution in 1911.

But by 1911, both the public and the writers tired. Readers wanted to hear good news and the writers moved on to other endeavors. Though short-lived, muckraking did bring about some reform and made magazines the most important medium in the country.

Change Comes With War

In the post-WWI years, many of the magazines that had become icons — including *North American Review*, *Century*, *St. Nicholas* and *Delineator* — fell to the wayside, unable to transform themselves for the new age. But this was also a time of great innovation. During the 1920s and 1930s, Henry Luce brought out *Time*, *Fortune* and *Life*. Harold Ross launched *The New Yorker* and DeWitt Wallace began *Reader's Digest*. They followed in the footsteps of their

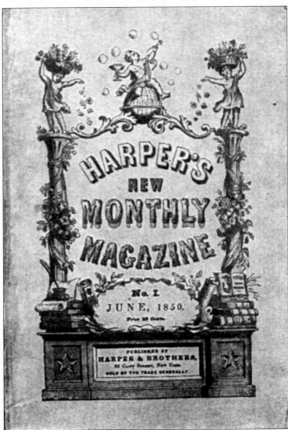

Harper's, which launched in June 1850, is one of the oldest magazines still being regularly published, though the *Harper's* of today has assumed a radically different form.

predecessors and were closely rivaled.

At the same time, specialization increased and still goes on today. Network television could not hope to reach niche markets. Specialized magazines boomed in the 1950s and 1960s as a result.

Niche Markets

On the one hand, there were general magazines aimed at general audiences. But the majority of magazines appealed to specialized groups with very specific interests. In the early days of magazines, a group known as "knowledge" magazines emerged. Offering all kinds of factual information, these penny magazines often contained the title "Cabinet of Instruction".

Trade magazines developed and influenced American business. Four railroad magazines operated before 1850, including *The American Rail-Road Journal* (1831). Six others appeared by 1865.

The use of magazines for mass

communication extended to the religious community. The Congregationalists had at least 25 periodicals during this first expansion period and the Catholics as many as 50. From 1865-85, they grew from 350 to 650 publications, though most were of inferior quality.

Scientific magazines appeared relatively early. *Scientific American* debuted in 1845. The magazine was established by painter Rufus Porter who felt that matters of scientific importance were rarely covered in newspapers and general interest magazines. It focused on applied rather than theoretical research. *Popular Science* launched in 1872.

Interest in sports, humor, travel and more generated even more magazines with very targeted content.

Magazines exploded as a means of mass communication in the early 19th century. Publications for general as well as specific audiences appeared, many introducing innovations as a way to increase circulation. Edward Bok, longtime editor of the *Ladies' Home Journal*, viewed the magazine as a "great clearinghouse for information".

Today, there seems to be a magazine for every nook and cranny of interest. The word "magazine" is living up to its definition. So as you read this issue, think about all the great publishers, editors and writers who preceded. If it weren't for them, this magazine would not have been possible.

Further Reading

• Peterson, Theodore. *Magazines in the Twentieth Century, 2nd Edition.* Urbana: University of Illinois Press, 1964.
• Reed, David. *The Popular Magazine in Britain and the United States 1880-1960.* Toronto: University of Toronto Press, 1997.
• Richardson, Lyon N. *A History of Early American Magazines.* New York: Thomas Nelson and Sons, 1931.
• Tebbel, John. *The Media in America.* New York: Thomas Y. Cromwell Company, 1974.

HM

Ice Skating

Edwin M. Knights relates how skating became more than a way of getting around.

PROBABLY THE FIRST ATTEMPTS at skating on ice occurred as early as the neolithic period, when lake dwellers in the northern climates devised means of sliding themselves, their food and their fuel across frozen surfaces. Before long humans found that bones were superior to wood for gliding over the ice, and runners made from shank or rib bones of elk, reindeer and other large animals have been found in Scandinavia, Switzerland and parts of northern Europe. In some cases the articulating ends have been shaved and tapered and holes drilled so that the bones could be attached by leather thongs. It's also likely that many such devices fashioned from hardwoods have failed to survive the ages. Similar arrangements were fashioned for pulling small sleds or sledges across the ice.

As it wasn't possible to create very sharp edges from these materials, propulsion was achieved by means of a sturdy wooden stick, or a rod tipped with an animal's long bone that had been sharpened to a point. Maybe some skaters already carried spears, which would push you along just fine and were also very useful if you encountered some wild animals or hungry neighbors on the way home. They could also be used to check the ice to see if it was thick enough for safe passage.

Early Records Of Skating

References to skates and skating abound in early northern European records and suggest people experimented with it just about everywhere where the winters

On The Ice At Faarborg by **Peter Hansen**.

were cold and the ice was thick. The low-German word *schake* and the Dutch word *schenkel* each refer to a shank-bone or shank; the English used the word *scatch*. Other terms are found which describe stilt-like devices that raised a person above the ground, such as the Dutch *schaats*, Danish and Norwegian *skoite* and Scots *sketcher*. In Latin the word was *scacia*. Scandinavian sagas contain comments about skating.

Nigel Brown quotes early observations of skating on ice in Fitzstephen's *Description of the most noble City of London*, published in Latin in 1180.

"When the great fenne or Moore (which watereth the walls of the cities on the North side) is frozen, many young men play upon the yce, some stryding as wide as they may, doe slide swiftly...some type bones to their feete, and under their heels, and shoving themselves by a little picked staff, doe slide as swiftly as a birde flyeth in the aire, or an arrow out of a crossbow." He obviously was greatly impressed by the speed attained by the skaters. He also describes jousting with poles and breaking of arms and legs, a tradition which has been perpetuated in today's

professional ice hockey.

Experimenting With Metal Runners

Around the 14th century, the Dutch were among the first to use flat iron strips fastened to the bottoms of wooden blocks. These strips, which served as runners, were curved upward in the front so they could glide over irregular surfaces of the ice. The wood was shaped to conform to the soles and heels of the owner's winter boots and drilled to permit the use of broad leather straps. Often the block could be tightened against the heel of the boot by means of a screw.

The iron strips were at first about 1/8 inch thick, but later evolved into thicker blades that could be sharpened. This led to the development of the "Dutch roll" technique of skating, as skaters leaned slightly outward on each stride, cutting shallow arcs in the ice. Now they could propel themselves by pushing off against the outer edges of the skate blades, eliminating the need for poles (except for jousting). By shifting body weight from the outer edge of one skate to the inner edge of the other, it was possible to skate in circles. And by reversing the procedure, it now became possible to skate backwards, even in circles. The development of steel resulted in far better edges and more improvements in skate design.

Pictorial Portrayals Of Skating

Skating became a popular winter activity in the Netherlands, where the people took advantage of frozen rivers, canals and meres to develop fast means of travel. Of course the Scandinavian countries also had numerous frozen bodies of water, but by mid-winter many of these would be buried in deep snow. Also Holland is not well endowed with mountains, so skating did not have to compete with the thrills of downhill skiing.

The earliest print about skating seems to be one published in Holland in Brugman's *Vita Lijdwine*. It depicts the skating accident of a 16-year-old girl named Liedwi in 1396. She appears in considerable distress and is said to have broken some ribs. She is obviously wearing bladed skates, as is a man in the background hastening across the ice to her aid.

Two early paintings by Dutch artists, both in the Kröller-Müller Museum in The Hoge Veluwe National Park, show how popular ice skating had become as a winter sport. Hendrick Vercamp's (1585-1634) *Winterlandscape with Iceskaters*, shows a frozen Dutch mere teeming with activity, mostly involving men, but including some women and children. Some couples are skating hand-in-hand, and one man carries a bladed stick of a shape similar to that used in hockey. Another oil painting by Aert Van der Neer (1603/04-77), *River View in the Winter*, is also highly detailed. The skaters, mostly males, have broad-brimmed hats and wear knickers and tall boots. A few skaters have short-bladed sticks that resemble golf clubs. Some men are ice fishing and a horse pulls five persons in a small boat fitted with wooden runners. One burgher skates along confidently, with a broad stride, his hands clasped behind his back.

From Ice Brigades To Ice Capades

The Dutch were also aware of the military advantages of footwear designed for combat on

The Bethlehem Census by Peter Bruegel the Elder shows Dutch burghers using skating as a method of transportation.

ice. The use of ice skates and of wooden clogs fitted with spiked nails to grip the ice played a role in saving the frozen Dutch fleet from destruction by Don Frederick's Spaniards in 1572. Skaters also prolonged the resistance of Haarlem to a Spanish siege by delivering food and military supplies over the frozen mere. But the military uses were limited, and it was the sport of skating that captivated all levels of Dutch society. The speed attained by skating is impressive even to the novice, and this led to the organization of races. The long iron blades used by the Dutch were well suited for speed. The nobility were also attracted to the sport, but they were more concerned with the art of skating, emphasizing grace and balance. When the Stuarts were exiled to the Netherlands during Cromwell's Protectorate, they also became fascinated (if a bit shocked) watching the Duke of Monmouth and the Princess of Orange gliding across the ice and performing an English country dance, especially when the young lady's petticoats were all tucked above her waist.

The British embraced ice skating in 1662, as documented by Samuel Pepys, who described the use of iron-bladed skates on the canal in St. James Park. Ice skating enthusiasm peaked in 1683, when the Thames froze from December well into Febru-

ary and even King Charles II and Queen Catherine took part in the frosty festivities.

Skates Become Specialized

The first all steel clamp-on skates are attributed to E.V. Bushnell of Philadelphia in 1848. Hollow grinding of some steel blades was already providing excellent edges for intricate skating. Ice skating evolved into three categories requiring different skate designs. Classic figure skating eventually expanded to include free skating, artistic skating, jumps, spins and dancing, but acceptance of innovations was a slow, tortuous process. The first blades developed by the British were slightly curved, hollow ground, and extended posterior to the heel, all of which made it easier to carve figures. Later they were fastened to custom-fitted boots. An American skater, Jackson Haines, developed a two-plate steel blade fastened to a boot. He added toe picks, or teeth, at the front of the blade, making it possible to perform dance steps, spins and jumps. Numerous improvements were made, especially in America, in fastening skates to boots and in boot design, providing rigidity around the arch and heel of the foot and some play in other areas.

Speed skates are easily recognized by their long, thin blades, measuring up to 18 inches in length. The low cut boots permit freer ankle movement. Hockey skates were designed with short, thicker blades, curved at the ends to facilitate turning. These are attached to sturdy boots.

Skating Becomes Organized

The British formed the first skating clubs, and these clubs set higher and higher standards for performance. By 1784 acceptance

In a photograph from the early 1930s, Adeline Meinert and Earl Myr demonstrate couples' figures.

for Edinburgh Skating Club membership required skating a complete circle on either foot. It was also necessary to jump over first one, two and finally three hats placed on the ice. In 1830, The Skating Club was founded in London, and soon had an exclusive membership of talented skaters culled from the upper strata of society. Members wore a miniature silver skate dangling from their lapels. By the time of Queen Victoria, the British skating hierarchy had completely stifled creativity and established rigid parameters for the performance of each required figure. Artistry had succumbed to compulsory figures. Unfortunately the skating clubs in North America meekly fell into line and mimicked their British cousins.

By 1879 the sport of ice skating was under the control of the National Skating Association of Great Britain; in 1886 and 1888 the National Amateur Skating Associations of the United States and Canada were formed. These organizations joined with others to establish the International Skating Union in 1892, which became the world governing body for speed skating, ice dancing and figure skating. They succeeded in establishing international standards for the sports, with more consistent judging of competitions, but this progress

had some distinct drawbacks. New skate designs permitting much more precise figures allowed many new skating movements, but the authorities frowned upon experimentation or innovation.

In spite of this, new skating styles were devised, along with new ways to enjoy the sport. Canadians, with their long skating season, experimented with covered rinks to protect natural ice from the wind and snow. Gas lighting also helped to improve safety for night skating, leading the way to ice carnivals. The Dutch developed skating with a pole, in tandem against the wind or side-by-side with the wind. While the British contented themselves with squads of skaters performing military-style drills, other nations formed grape-vine chains of skaters or frolicked to band music. Skating had two major needs: improved equipment and creative leadership.

Haines Unfreezes Figure Skating

Jackson Haines was born about 1840 — possibly in Chicago, but nobody really knows where. His parents were Canadian, but his mother was of Dutch descent, his father British. He was destined to have an enormous impact on ice skating.

Jackson Haines

Jackson's father had wanted him to be a cabinetmaker, but he preferred cutting ice to cutting wood. He had studied ballet in Europe and had his own ideas about a career. He set about merging ballet with ice skating. He soon realized that ice skates needed to be improved and designed his solid blade forged on to the toe and heel plates of a skating boot. The blade also featured a turned-up toe. He left the US for England in 1864, but the

John Wilson Skates

John Wilson Skates is one of the most well-known manufacturers of ice skates today. The name Wilson has been synonymous with skate blades since its inception over 300 years ago.

During the Commonwealth, Charles, Prince of Wales, lived in Holland while exiled from his home. It was here that he first saw people gliding over ice on blades. Charles was enthralled by how graceful they looked and he took up skating immediately. When Charles returned to England in 1660, he asked John Wilson, a toolmaker by trade who was known for his high quality work and attention to detail, to manufacture a pair of skates for him. Wilson used various parts of tools he already manufactured to create his first pair of blades.

Wilson formed his own company in Sheffield, England in 1696, intending to manufacture tools. However, by this time ice-skating had become popular among the English aristocracy and Wilson found he was continually asked to make skate blades. In the following years, interest in skating spread to all social classes and soon skating was a popular pastime throughout England. The John Wilson Company soon stopped making tools to concentrate on manufacturing skate blades under the name John Wilson Skates.

As ice skating spread worldwide, so did John Wilson Skates. Today the company is still based in Sheffield, England, and it exports to over 40 countries. More international skating-medal winners have worn John Wilson Skates than all the other manufacturers put together — not bad for a 300-year-old tool-making company. —JODI AVERY

British would have none of his "fancy skating". By contrast, Stockholm was impressed with his artistry. So were the succeeding European capitals, until he triumphantly waltzed his way into the heart of Vienna, leaving behind a lasting legacy of free skating, with new moves such as the arabesque and spread eagle. Haines's career was spectacular but short. Unfortunately he died of pneumonia when traveling by sleigh from Russia to Stockholm when he was only 35 years old. The founder of the "international style" of skating was buried in Finland, and his tombstone is inscribed, "The American Skating King".

Haines opened up opportunities for many other talented skaters to display their artistry as well as their precision; there were jumps, such as the Salchow and the Axel (named after a Swede and a Norwegian), the loop named for the German, Rittberger, and the Lutz, invented by an Austrian in 1913. Two Swiss skaters, Mauch and Groebh, better known as Frick and Frack, would later delight thousands as skating clowns with their masterful spread eagles. These are but a few of the moves used by today's freestyle figure skaters, who employ various spins, lifts and flips, along with the dramatic death spiral. Olympic gold medallist Sonja Henie helped make skating shows popular in America. Dick Button introduced the double Axel and the triple jump. Doing poorly in the compulsory figures inspired Donald Jackson to perform the first triple Lutz. Peggy Fleming, Dorothy Hamill, Jayne Torvill, Christopher Dean and many other fine skaters became household names in the 20th century, as the combination of artificial ice and television brought the sport into the homes of millions. Haines brought new life to the sport of ice skating, but the dominance of inbred tradition and resistance to change was not

Ice pageants, such as the 1950 Ice Follies show, became more popular with the spread of heated indoor arenas and broadcast television.

easily overcome. Compulsory figures were required skating at World Championships for the last time in Halifax, Nova Scotia, in 1990, 150 years after Jackson Haines was born!

Ice Hockey

Ice hockey appears to have evolved from field hockey in France and Britain, where other goal-scoring games on ice included bandy, shinty and ice hurling. A McGill University (Montreal) student, J.G.A. Creighton, is credited with devising most of the rules for modern hockey. Canada had a virtual monopoly on hockey players in North America for many years. The National Hockey League began with the arrival of the Boston Bruins in 1924. For many years the League consisted of six teams, but eventually the availability of spacious ice arenas in densely populated urban areas multiplied the numbers of professional teams and the rosters now feature highly talented skaters from all over Europe and North America. The sport of amateur hockey also grew enormously, with skilled high school graduates being sought by the coaches of college hockey teams. Formerly a sport largely limited to men, ice hockey now attracts many talented female athletes, especially at the college level, and women's ice hockey has become a medal sport at the Winter Olympic Games.

Largely thanks to the wide

availability of artificial ice rinks, skating is now being enjoyed by young and old, and is also amazingly popular as a spectator sport. Over the centuries it always appealed to a broad spectrum of people, but for remarkably different reasons. It graduated from a rapid means of travel and communication to an enjoyable cultural diversion for the wealthy and the poor; it could not be shackled by regimentation because it offered too many possibilities for freedom of expression. In it there is room for athletes, artists, dancers, health enthusiasts, and competitive sportspersons of either sex. It blends well with music, visual arts and theater and is a perfect medium for the choreographer. It can provide the ultimate challenges for the individual, yet provides spectacular opportunities for team efforts. It continues to present opportunities for technical improvements of equipment ranging from improved ice skates to creative costumes to Zamboni machines. It offers exciting possibilities for television. If it keeps its head up and its edges sharp, its future looks as bright as a silver blade. 　HM

The Korean War

Edwin M. Knights describes the origins and events of this war that took place 50 years ago.

WARFARE IS TYPICALLY enveloped in confusion — confusion about the political breakdown that led to war, confusion about the military strategies employed on both sides, and concerns about the permanence of the agreements leading to its cessation. It is left to the historians to unearth enough evidence surrounding the event to enable succeeding generations to learn about the causes of the conflict, military successes and failures, and whether the final settlement was appropriate and conducive to a lasting peace.

Although one might think that the facts would necessarily become blurred with the passage of time, other information, previously classified or censored, sometimes leads to a better understanding of what really happened. In the US, where there is a policy of freedom of speech, information that might be of political damage to an incumbent party usually surfaces at an appropriate time. On the other hand, electronic and printed journalism frequently distorts the truth by presenting it with an editorial bias, and movies deliberately alter the facts to conform to the presentation of a plot.

The Korean War is no exception. What should we think about it? What caused it? What motivated our response? Did we react promptly and efficiently? Did we respond appropriately? Who made the major decisions and was their judgment sound? And why did it conclude as it did? What should the world learn from its accomplishments, and its mistakes?

Why Was There a War?

The causes of the Korean War stem from WWII agreements made at Cairo in 1943 and in Potsdam in 1945. The Allies agreed that prolonged Japanese domination over Korea should cease and that the nation should at last be free. When Japan surrendered, the US and the Soviet Union found the 38th Parallel (of latitude) to be a convenient dividing line for military control. They also agreed that a trusteeship should be established to oversee the Koreans while they organized their new government; the trustees would be the US, the Soviet Union, the United Kingdom and China.

As might have been predicted, the Soviets promptly established a Communist regime in the northern part of Korea under Kim Il Sung, a Soviet-trained military officer. In the south, Syngman Rhee was elected President of a new democratic government. North Korea and South Korea became ideologically divided. A UN commission created to supervise free elections was refused permission by the Soviets to enter North Korea. By the end of 1947 both the Soviets and the Americans had withdrawn most of their troops from their sectors.

1950 proved to be a trying year for President Truman. Republicans were insisting that he had been too soft on Communism. Wisconsin Senator Joseph McCarthy was claiming he had proof that scores of Communists were active in the US State Department. Distorting, twisting and ignoring the truth, McCarthy carried on a campaign of vilification that was one of the more disgraceful episodes in the history of the US Senate. The same year saw the perjury conviction of Alger Hiss. Living in the Blair-Lee House while the White House was being renovated, the Trumans' security proved to be barely adequate to repel an assassination attack by Puerto Rican nationalists later in the year. Between 1947 and 1950, Americans were insisting upon reduction of the size and cost of their huge military establishment created to win WWII. There was

Even as it appeared that UN forces might be driven into the sea, MacArthur was planning a daring move to land a Marine Division and South Korean forces at Inchon, the major port on the west coast of Korea just south of the 38th Parallel, then move inland and recapture nearby Seoul.

would make them economically competitive with other nations. The Chinese army was enormous, seasoned in battle and recently victorious over the Chinese Nationalists. With a population then estimated at 600 million, there was no shortage of manpower to serve in an army that had no retirement pension plans: you served until you were killed or no longer useful to your country.

Under experienced General Lin Piao, whole divisions of Chinese soldiers began to infiltrate the plateaus of North Korea, moving stealthily at night, carefully concealed during the day, and silently waiting for UN troops to advance into their massive trap. It was a technique they had used with great success in their homeland. The American and UN forces advanced steadily without resistance toward their goal, which was the Yalu River, confident that this would complete their mission of occupying North Korea and looking forward to being sent home by Christmas, as MacArthur had promised on Thanksgiving Day. The massive Chinese buildup went completely undetected due to inadequate American surveillance.

As fall turned into winter, the greatest obstacles to occupying North Korea seemed to be the rugged terrain and the bitter cold. They reached the Chosin Reservoir and according to plan, dispersed widely — the 8th Army, plus the 5th and 7th Marine Regiments. It was here that the Chinese sprung their trap.

The Chinese had completely infiltrated the 8th Army, and thousands of them appeared out of nowhere, sending 25,000 combat infantrymen into headlong retreat. Entire divisions of Chinese rapidly penetrated deep into the rear units. The 8th Army, dying and demoralized, was no longer a cohesive fighting force. Another trap had been set for the Marines near a dam on the east side of the Chosin Reservoir. As there had been no contact with enemy forces that day, half of

Gen. Douglas MacArthur (center) watches the shelling of Inchon from the *USS Mt. McKinley*, September 1950.

the Marines were asleep; the others were wrapped in their sleeping bags trying to escape the cold, which was far below zero degrees. This was where the Chinese first attacked, but it was only an inkling of what was to follow. Meanwhile, the Marines had heard nothing of the rout of the 8th Army.

Multiple encounters followed, and it soon became apparent that there were massive numbers of Chinese troops in the area. Farther north, a squadron of FU-4 Corsair fighter-bombers spotted thousands of Chinese infantrymen marching through the snow. Before the planes departed they had emptied their 50-caliber machine guns, dropped their pairs of 500lb. bombs and fired their 5-inch rockets on the troops below. Air superiority, combined with the tactical ground-to-air coordination that had been perfected by the Marine Corps, was to prove invaluable to the Marines as they

fought their way out of seemingly impossible situations. In contrast to the Army, the breakout from the Chosin Reservoir trap and their subsequent retreat south became a strategic withdrawal for which the Chinese forces paid an enormous price in casualties. Many books have been written about the heroic efforts of Marines to rescue their comrades or foil enemy attempts to overrun their positions. Probably not enough credit is given to ROK, British Marines and other UN units who fought bravely and doggedly beside them.

The bitter cold of Korea played a very important role in the conflict. US and UN troops were eventually provided fur-lined parkas with a jacket hood designed to help protect the face from the cold. Clothing was worn in multiple layers. Felt boot liners had to be changed frequently. If they became wet from sweat, frostbite was inevitable. Hands were protected by gloves inside of mittens with a trigger-finger opening. Nevertheless, casualties from frostbite were very common.

The Chinese wore quilted reversible mustard-yellow and white cotton uniforms and a heavy cotton cap with fur-lined earflaps. This was worn over the standard summer uniform plus any other clothing acquired along the way. Many had canvas shoes with rubber crepe soles. Later they received half-leather shoes or leather boots. Most also carried a blanket. They carried old-style American weapons — Springfield rifles, carbines and Thompson sub-machine guns taken from the Chinese Nationalist Army. Often the cold caused their weapons to malfunction. Their soldiers were well accustomed to hardships, walked great distances with ease and were agile climbers. They showed remarkable stamina, especially considering they often were required to "live off the land" when it came to finding food. In North Korea they soon exhausted the food they could take from civilians, and their

The *USS Missouri* firing a 16-inch salvo during the Korean War.

Suggested Reading on the Korean War

● Cagle, Cdr. Malcolm W. & Manson, Cdr. Frank A.: *The Sea War in Korea*. Annapolis, Md., US Naval Institute, 1957.
● Craig, Lt. Gen. Edward A.: *Korea Remembered in Traditions*, Military History Journal of the Pacific. Escondido, Calif., Heritage Press, 1997-98.
● Crawford, C. S.: *The Four Deuces — A Korean War Story*. Novato, Calif., Presidio Press, 1989.
● Giangreco, D. M.: *War in Korea, 1950-1953*. Olathe, Kan., Ringier America, 1990
● Hammel, Eric: *Chosin — Heroic Ordeal of the Korean War*. Novato, Calif., Presidio Press, 1990
● Hastings, Max: *The Korean War*. London, Michael Joseph, 1987.
● Hopkins, William B.: *One Bugle No Drums. The Marines at Chosin*. Chapel Hill, N.C., Algonquin Books, 1986.
● Hoyt, Edwin P.: *On to Yalu*. New York, Jove Publications, 1991.
● Lowe, Peter: *The Origins of the Korean War*. New York, Longman Inc., 1986.
● Luce, Henry R.; Matthews, T. S., et al.,: *Time Capsule/1950*. New York, Time Inc., 1967.
● Russ, Martin: *The Last Parallel. A Marines War Journal*. New York, Rinehart & Co., 1957.
● Russ, Martin: *Breakout. The Chosin Reservoir Campaign, Korea, 1950*. New York, Fromm International Publ., 1999.
● Toland, John: *In Mortal Combat, Korea, 1950-1953*. New York, William Morrow & Co., 1991.

uniforms proved poor protection against the bitter cold.

Turnaround

General Matthew Ridgeway was able to take a disorganized and defeated 8th Army and turn it into an efficient fighting force by the spring of 1951, halting the advance of the Chinese. MacArthur refused to take any blame for the defeats north of the 38th Parallel, and advocated unrestricted use of military force against the Chinese, blockading the Chinese coast and using Chiang Kai-shek's nationalist army (now in Formosa) against the Red Chinese. Many Americans supported his views. He steadily refused to acknowledge the value of tactical air support but he advocated the bombing, even the use of nuclear weapons, against the Chinese in Manchuria. He ignored the fact that there were relatively few targets in Manchuria. He also carried out widespread "strategic" bombing of North Korea, with the resultant killing of large numbers of North Korean civilians.

As the US was to learn again in Vietnam, the strategic bombing did little to stem the flow of arms and supplies to the Chinese armies. Thousands of surviving North Koreans, angered by the indiscriminate bombing, now began to assist the Chinese by forming battalions to repair the roads and railroad tracks and rebuild important bridges.

At the same time, President Truman and his advisors were beginning to conclude that the mission was to police and protect the free world, not attempt to subjugate every living Communist. MacArthur's actions were visibly stiffening Chinese determination to defend their country and prolonging a military action that could only result in massive additional casualties on both sides without a satisfactory resolution. The Chinese were not acting in concert with the Russians to help them regain control of North Korea, but rather responding to their convictions that MacArthur was determined to overthrow their regime. MacArthur never agreed with this policy, and stubbornly persisted independently with his own approach to fighting the war. Finally, he was relieved of command by President Truman. Upon his return to the US he received a hero's welcome.

The End of the Fighting

Fighting continued until a cease-fire agreement was signed at 10 a.m., Monday, 27 July 1953. Major Arthur N. Dadirrian describes how the war concluded in his sector. Dadirrian was stationed in a ramshackle metal building that was the center for providing medical services for the 3rd Infantry Division of the 8th Army. The Division had been realigned to

Men of the US 1st Marine Division capture Chinese Communists during fighting in central Korea.

cover the ROK Capital Division's left flank as the Chinese attempted to secure one last battlefield victory against the South Korean Army — a victory with which they could later claim they forced the "Yankee Imperialists and their lackeys" to sue for peace. For several days over 250 American field pieces, mostly 105mm howitzers, had conducted an incessant barrage against the Chinese. Each salvo shook the entire building. At 9 p.m. that Sunday, there was a sudden, complete silence, "as if someone had thrown a switch." For the troops in that sector, the war had abruptly ceased.

In the end, the same arbitrary line across the 38th Parallel again divided North and South Korea. North Korea remained a Communist state; South Korea struggled to re-establish its democracy. To achieve this, the US suffered 157,530 casualties, including 33,629 deaths. Other UN forces lost over 1.3 million, including over 400,000 dead. North Korean

KOREAN CONFLICT CASUALTY FILES

Fifty years ago the North Korean Army streamed south across the 38th Parallel into South Korea, abruptly starting a war that would claim close to two million lives on both sides, including 33,629 Americans, 415,000 South Koreans, plus over 3,000 British Commonwealth and other UN troops. Estimates of North Korean and Chinese deaths vary between 1.5 and 2.0 million.

People who wish to know more about relatives who died in service to America during the Korean War may now search the Korean Conflict Casualty File (KCCF), 1950-57, posted on the National Archives and Records Administration (NARA) web page at *www.nara.gov/nara/electronic/ korvnsta.html*.

These lists are by state, and include each service member's name, rank or grade, branch of service, home of record, date of casualty and category of casualty. The files include service members from the US Air Force, Army, Coast Guard, Marine Corps and Navy. They were created because so many local communities were seeking to memorialize their deceased Korean War veterans.

Home of Record
Two formats are provided: one is arranged alphabetically by last name of the casualty and the other by "home of record." When you click the service member's state, the state list appears. "Home of Record" means the location provided at the time of enlistment and may not be the service member's place of birth or even the hometown. The US Army lists the county for the home of record, while the US Air Force, Coast Guard, Marine Corps and Navy use a city or town. Casualty types are "killed in action," "died of wounds," "died while captured," or "died while missing." Records of US military casualties from the Korean War are part of the Records of the Office of the Secretary of Defense, Record Group 330, and the KCCF is for persons who died as a result of hostilities in Korea, 1950-57. These online casualty state lists extracts are supplemented by numerous other records available from NARA, including files on WWII and the Vietnam War. Further information is available from:

Center for Electronic Records (NWME)
ATTN: Reference Staff
National Archives at College Park
8601 Adelphi Road
College Park MD 20740-6001
Telephone: 301-713-6645
Fax: 301-713-6911
email: *cer@nara.gov*
Home page: *www.nara.gov/nara/electronic*

Ref: Hull, Theodore J.: *Electronic Records of Korean and Vietnam Conflict Casualties, in Prologue, Quarterly of the National Archives and Records Administration, Vol. 32, No. 1*, College Park, Md., Spring 2000

and Chinese losses are estimated at over two million wounded and dead.

Do We Ever Learn?
The furor that developed over the war in Vietnam tended to obscure the magnitude of the Korean engagement, abetted by the fact that it was still officially regarded as a UN "police action". The casualty figures speak for themselves. The failure of strategic bombing to interdict supply lines or settle political differences is a lesson yet to be learned. The danger of a regional conflict escalating into a major confrontation is generally appreciated, but not always anticipated in time.

Perhaps worst of all, in a world where international communication is now almost instantaneous, we speak but we do not listen. Communication is not synonymous with understanding. Cultural differences between the East and the West make it difficult to appreciate each other's concerns. Communication within a family unit is often difficult; communication between nations even more so. Intense nationalism arouses passions that defy reason and invite conflict. Political leaders who run foreign policy by a knee-jerk reaction to public opinion polls run the risk of making grave errors in judgment.

The Communist Chinese, working through the government of India, made serious attempts to warn the US about their concerns over what they considered the escalation of the Korean conflict and a threat to Manchuria. The American government and the American press wrote this off as a bluff. Recently, the Chinese, in the opinion of American news media, over-reacted when a US spy plane and Chinese fighter were involved in a mid-air collision. They continue to threaten to invade Taiwan and insist it must soon become united with Mainland China. The American press generally dismisses this as a bluff. History's lesson is clear: one day it may not be a bluff. The legacy of Chiang Kai-shek, preserved by the Nationalist Kuomintang Party in Taiwan for 50 years, was ended recently when the Taiwanese electorate selected Chen Shui-bian of the pro-independence Democratic Progressive Party as the next president. This was the candidate Beijing feared most. Attempting to ease tensions across the Taiwan Strait, Chen stated, "We are willing to take the most friendly attitude and determination to carry out full and constructive talks." Westerners would like to see democracy in Mainland China before they annex Taiwan, but this may not be realistic.

Unfortunately it is easier for dictators than for democracies to plan their political actions ahead. Let us hope that lessons learned so painfully just 50 years ago in Korea have not been forgotten, and that a peaceful diplomatic solution will be achieved.

HM

The Complete History

History Magazine

Volume One

October 1999 - September 2000

The First Year of History Magazine

History Magazine Volume One is a reissue of almost all the editorial from the issues dated October 1999 to September 2000.

The colorful, bound volume includes all the editorial material from our first year of publication, including such features as: The Atlantic Cable, The Black Death, The National Road, Cleanliness, Bread, The Code Napoleon, The First Radio Station, The Longbow, 1000AD, The US Cavalry, Custer, Army Wives, Death Customs, Bellevue Hospital, The Impact of the Potato, An 1860s Dinner for Eight, The Rifle, The Oregon Trail, The Handcart Pioneers, Refrigeration, Games People Played, Contraception, The Suez Canal, Midwives, Longitude, The 1910s, Country Store, Connecting the World, Alchemy, Freemasonry, Early Newspapers, Influenza Pandemic, Chicago in 1880, The Privy, The Blacksmith, Saffron, Eli Whitney, Lunatic Asylums, Lighthouses, The 1900 House, Carpetbaggers, The Natchez Trace, Let's Eat!, How Brands Began, The Stirrup, The Shakers, Development of Photography, Insurance, Underground Railroad, Memsahibs of the Raj, California Gold Rush, Poliomyelitis, Wigs, decade profiles, historical trivia — and more!

History Magazine Volume One provides a full year of information about the lives our ancestors led.

Dungeons and Dragons

Nicole Brebner examines the myths and misconceptions about the dreaded dungeon.

DEEP BELOW GROUND, DANK and gloomy, lies the most horrifying accommodation for unwelcome guests of the medieval castle — the dungeon. Any tourist who has visited some of Europe's most famous dwellings has likely encountered a thrilling Dungeon Tour. Tales of gruesome torture and barbaric cruelty create an unforgettable and chilling glimpse into the past. However, much of what is commonly believed about dungeons is legend, based on rumor as much as fact.

The history of dungeons is inextricably tied to the history of the buildings that housed them — castles. The word dungeon is a corruption of the French *donjon* which itself is derived from the Latin *dominium* meaning lordship. Castles were introduced in northern France sometime in the ninth century and were made from timber. Very little evidence of these structures exists today, however, the superiority of stone as a building material quickly replaced the timber structures and remains of the earliest stone castles of Doué-la-Fontaine (c. 900) and Langeais (c. 990) still stand today.

That so many stone castles open their drawbridges to fascinated tourists today is testament to the successful achievement of their primary function as fortified residences. Castle building followed the spread of feudalism across Europe, and extended to the Middle East with the Crusades. Castle life was vastly different from the dramatic and romantic scenes painted by movies and novels. Built from stone and impervious to most attacks, accommodations in a castle were not luxurious. Most likely they were cold, damp, dark and

The popular conception of dungeons as places of continual darkness, starvation and torture is largely mythical.

at times prison-like. Many castle owners lived there only when necessary. In times of peace, they would travel throughout their vast lands, retreating to their fortresses in times of unrest.

Dungeons, as we think of them now, did not come about until the 13th century. Below the keep, or *donjon*, of most castles were storage areas for food and weapons. Some of these hollowed-out areas would, on occasion, be used to house prisoners of the castle.

It suited the purposes of kings, lords and knights to have their subjects live in fear of being tossed in a dungeon. And, while there are stories of such things happening, it was not a common occurrence. The most likely candidate to be held prisoner in a castle would be a rival to those in power. In many cases, these prisoners were men or women of considerable status themselves. As such, they were often held in quite comfortable surroundings and were treated as valuable assets worthy of considerable ransoms. The prisoners may have been held in cold, dark, cell-like rooms but that was the best most castle keeps had to offer.

It is not difficult to understand how dungeons developed such a sinister reputation when you look at them in context. One of the world's most notorious "prisons", the Tower of London, is steeped in tales of horror and blood and dungeons. The original building, the White Tower (actually a castle keep) was constructed by William the Conqueror late in the 11th century. The White Tower was the first stone keep in England and remains one of the largest. As construction of the White Tower began, the people of London were angry. A rumor was widely circulated, and over the centuries became a legend, that the reddish tinge in the mortar was because dragon's blood had been mixed in. That this was widely believed is a testimony to the fear, hatred and lack of knowledge of the people at that time. The reddish

While dungeons such as the one at Cawdor Castle were far from cozy, castles weren't very comfortable generally.

The majority of the prisoners kept in dungeons were not common criminals, but possible rival claimants to a throne, such as Lady Jane Grey.

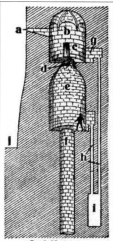

Oubliette.

a, ventilation passage; *b*, dungeon; *c*, entrance; *d*, opening of the entrance to the oubliette; *e*, oubliette proper; *f*, well; *g*, latrine; *h*, drain=pipes; *i*, cesspool; *j*, moat of the castle.

tinge was actually the result of using crushed Roman bricks to make the mortar.

The Tower of London was host to many famous prisoners over time. Most prisoners were deprived only of their liberty. There were no dungeons in the Tower of London and prisoners were held wherever convenient. Captives were expected to make themselves as comfortable as their resources allowed. Some lived with their families within the Tower, while others were free to come and go while escorted by guards. The first official prisoner of the Tower was also the first official escapee. In 1100, Henry I imprisoned Ranulf Flambard, Bishop of Durham. He was lodged in the White Tower and lived like a lord for six months. He was served by his own personal servants and had regular contact with the outside world. On 2 February 1101, with Henry I absent from the castle, Flambard hosted a banquet for his guards and supplied generous amounts of wine. Once his guards were well-lubricated, Flambard lowered a rope from a window and escaped.

According to Russell Chamberlin in *The Tower of London:* "The Tower's reputation as a grisly torture chamber rose largely as a result of the religious struggles of the 16th century, the legends fanned by such lurid propaganda works as Foxe's *Book of Martyrs.*" Of course, the practice of displaying the heads of executed prisoners on spikes around the castle walls certainly enhanced the Tower's bloody reputation.

While the majority of dungeons may not have been as awful as we sometimes imagine, some were. Not all captives were worthy of a large ransom. For those unfortunates, many castles had something called an *oubliette.* The French architectural term comes from *oublier* meaning to forget. Oubliettes were dungeons or cells that were reached by a trap-door in the floor, usually of the guard-room, through which a prisoner would be lowered by a rope or simply dropped. The opening would be too high for the prisoner to reach once inside. Some of these openings led to a small pit where the prisoner would be held and sometimes starved to death. The oubliette was often below ground level and occasionally filled with water that seeped up through the earthen floor drowning the prisoner. Some oubliettes had a concealed passage leading from the dungeon to the moat or river. Prisoners who were to be secretly disposed of would be dropped through to their

deaths. Many so-called oubliettes in medieval castles were probably outlets for the disposal of drainage and refuse, which at times served as makeshift cells.

The earliest known true oubliettes are in the castle at Pierrefords, France and at the Bastille in Paris. The Black Tower at Rumeli Hisari, in present-day Turkey, has a variation. Prisoners were forced to walk down a long, dark passageway that ended above an opening in the floor. The unsuspecting prisoners would tumble though and were promptly forgotten.

The Scottish favored the bottle-dungeon. It was a type of oubliette but was shaped like a bottle so that the prisoner could never lie down. Pit prisons, known as "black holes of Caledonia", were fairly common in Scotland. Prisoners were lowered to a dank, subterranean chamber on a rope and left until their captors returned. Usually, there were no sanitary provisions and no light. Pit prisons were thought to be a powerful deterrent to challenging the ruling classes.

The tales of horror and torture associated with dungeons seem to be largely fictional. Rumors of dragon's blood and other myths spread quickly through unsettled and war-torn lands. By the 17th century, with the rise of responsible governments and the acceptance of formal justice systems, the need for fortified castles declined. Many castles were, for a short time, used as prisons. In the past, the exaggerated and frightening tales of dungeons kept the peasants in line. Today, those same tales encourage tourists to storm the castles. **HM**

Subscribe Now to

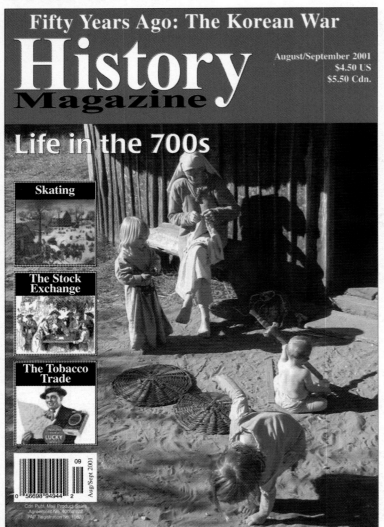
How did our ancestors live?

There is no magazine that covers history like *History Magazine*. We cover military history *only* as it impacted people's lives and we rarely cover personalities or histories of an area. **But** we carry features about the lives of ordinary people that you will find nowhere else like:

The Atlantic Cable, The Black Death, The National Road, Cleanliness, Bread, The Code Napoleon, The First Radio Station, The Longbow, 1000AD, The US Cavalry, Custer, Army Wives, Death Customs, Bellevue Hospital, The Impact of the Potato, An 1860s Dinner for Eight, The Rifle, The Oregon Trail, The Handcart Pioneers, Refrigeration, Games People Played, Contraception, The Suez Canal, Midwives, Longitude, The Country Store, Connecting the World, Alchemy, Freemasonry, Early Newspapers, Influenza Pandemic, Chicago in 1880, The Privy, The Blacksmith, Saffron, Eli Whitney, Lunatic Asylums, Lighthouses, The 1900 House, Carpetbaggers, The Natchez Trace, Let's Eat!, How Brands Began, The Stirrup, The Shakers, Development of Photography, Insurance, The Underground Railroad, Memsahibs of the Raj, California Gold Rush, Poliomyelitis, Wigs, period profiles, historical trivia — and more!

The Tobacco Trade

Jeff Chapman traces one cash crop's impact on world trade.

FOR CENTURIES BEFORE THE European discovery of the New World, Indians from Canada to Brazil had been growing the plant that came to be called tobacco. The use of tobacco varied from tribe to tribe — chewing the leaves or crumbling and smoking them in a pipe was preferred in the north, while those in tropical areas typically wrapped the leaves together inside larger leaves or corn husks to make cigars. Tobacco was widely revered and used as a part of many spiritual ceremonies, and the smoking of the peace pipe, or *calumet*, was an important component of intertribal politics.

The first encounter between Europeans and "smoke drinking" Indians was recorded in Columbus' logs on 15 October 1492. Not wanting to appear impolite, Columbus accepted the Indians' gift of "certain dried leaves which gave off a distinct fragrance"; he later dumped these leaves overboard, not knowing what to do with them. Soon, however, the Indians taught his sailors how to place the leaves in a pipe and smoke them. In a typical miscommunication, Columbus' men named the dried yellow leaf the Indians smoked tobacco, no doubt when the Indians were intending to refer to the y-shaped pipes they employed, *toboco* or *tobaga*. Columbus himself was not impressed with the plant, and reproached his men for sinking to the level of savages by smoking. Tobacco smoking proved addictively popular to the sailors, however, and by 1531, Spaniards living in Hispaniola were smoking cigars and had begun to cultivate their own tobacco.

Tobacco Debuts in the Old World

Tobacco did not begin to make an

Columbus' sailors were the first Europeans to sample tobacco, but tobacco didn't become popular with upper class Europeans until several decades later.

impression in Europe itself until the late 1550s, when it was introduced by Spanish and Portuguese sailors returning from the New World with tobacco leaves and seeds.

While tobacco's popularity remained confined to seaports in Spain and Portugal, in 1561 Jean Nicot, France's ambassador in Lisbon, sent snuff tobacco to French queen Catherine Medici recommending it as a cure for the migraines that plagued her. With Nicot's backing, snuff soon became popular throughout the French court and the upper strata of French society. Tobacco's supporters attested to the healing properties of Nicot's import, claiming it could cure ailments from bad breath to cancer. Tobacco ashes were even used as a dentifrice. Nicot's influence on the popularity of the tobacco plant among the upper classes was so profound that it was named for him: *nicotiana tabacum*.

Italian and Portuguese sailors transported the plant to trading points in Africa, the Levant, Turkey, Arabia, Persia and India. Dutch and Portuguese traders took it further still to the East Indies, China and Japan. In Japan, smoking was swiftly adopted among everyone from geisha girls to workers in the rice fields. The

Japanese term for "tobacco merchant" was used as early as 1578. The Japanese introduced tobacco to Korea, at that time a Japanese colony.

In 1564 or 1565, Sir John Hopkins and his crew first introduced tobacco in England, and in 1586, Sir Francis Drake imported large quantities of plundered Spanish tobacco into London. The practice of smoking tobacco in pipes spread through the English lower classes quickly. Sir Walter Raleigh became greatly enamored of the New World import and promoted its use among the English aristocracy; he is rumored to have persuaded Queen Elizabeth herself to try smoking. In 1598, German traveler Paul Hertzner remarked that "the English are constantly smoking the Nicotian weed, which in America is called Tobaca — others call it Pætum — and generally in this manner: they have pipes on purpose, made of clay, into the farther end of which they put the herb, so dry that it may be rubbed into powder, and lighting it, they draw the smoke into their mouths, which they puff out again through their nostrils, like funnels, along with it plenty of defluxion and phlegm from the head."

By 1600, some English apothecaries who supplied tobacco to the public had realized that one of their products was outselling all the rest, and the first tobacconist shops opened for business.

First Backlash

Many English physicians who had concerns about the supposed health benefits of tobacco became concerned that the drug was being widely used without prescription, and they presented their concerns to King James I. In 1604, James issued his famous *Counterblaste to Tobacco*. The *Counterblaste* denounced tobacco in the strongest terms, on grounds of health and morality, describing smoking as "a custome lothsome to the eye, hatefull to the nose, harmefull to the braine, daungerous to the Lungs, and in the blacke stinking fume thereof, nearest resembling the horrible Stigian smoke of the pit that is bottomelesse." To make certain the English public got his point, James increased the import duty on Spanish tobacco by 4,000 percent.

A similar backlash against tobacco was occurring in many parts of the world. In France, King Louis XIII prohibited the sale of non-prescription tobacco. In 1624, Pope Urban VIII issued a bull of excommunication against anyone found taking snuff in church. The Greek Church followed in 1634 by forbidding its adherents from using tobacco in any form. Russian czars outlawed tobacco and imposed punishments ranging from torture to Siberian exile to execution. In Turkey, where tobacco had become popular despite the Koran's strictures against its use, Sultan Murad IV blamed a fire in Constantinople on careless smoking and issued an edict saying that any subject found smoking tobacco would be beheaded immediately. The Japanese emperor also issued a complete ban on tobacco use.

World leaders maintained a firm anti-tobacco stance only until they realized that the Spanish were growing very rich off the tobacco trade.

Tobacco and Slavery
Tobacco is a very difficult crop to grow. The plants are tall, sticky and highly attractive to insects; a tobacco crop requires hundreds of hours of backbreaking labor to cultivate and harvest a single acre. It is the sort of labor that few people would choose to pursue unless they had no other choice.

Europeans first began to transport African slaves to help

By the late 1500s, tobacco plantations were big business in the Spanish West Indies, but had achieved little success in Britain's North American colonies.

cultivate tobacco in the New World in the 16th century; ironically, the first shipments of slaves were probably purchased with tobacco from local African rulers. Later, merchants purchased slaves in Africa in exchange for European manufactured goods, then resold them in the New World for cash crops such as tobacco and sugar, and then returned to Europe to sell these raw materials in exchange for further manufactured goods. In this manner, tobacco became a key component of a highly profitable triangular trade between three continents.

In 1619, Dutch traders imported the first African slaves into Jamestown, Virginia, where they quickly became the backbone of the local tobacco economy. Aside from buying and selling, slaves were used to do virtually all the work associated with tobacco cultivation: they tilled the ground, planted the seeds, raised the plants, harvested the crop, cured the leaves and bound and transported the finished product to market. By 1750, the slave population in the Chesapeake region had risen to 35 percent of the total population.

Influence on World Trade
Tobacco's influence on trading patterns between the Old World and the New was enormous. Spanish colonists in the West Indies began cultivating tobacco

soon after the founding of the first permanent Spanish settlements in Hispaniola. Before long, the tobacco grown in the West Indies was recognized to be far superior in taste and quality to anything that could be grown in Europe or anywhere else. While gold and silver did more to capture the imagination of potential immigrants to the Spanish Main, tobacco was the first crop that could be counted on to produce a continuous and steady source of income.

Inspired by the vast fortunes being made by tobacco growers and merchants, so many Spaniards were immigrating to the West Indies to begin tobacco plantations that Spain had to pass laws to prevent excessive emigration.

Further north, the stagnant English colony of Virginia wished it had such problems. Though Powhatan Indians had been growing tobacco in Virginia for centuries, the local variety of tobacco, *nicotiana rustica*, was said to be far inferior to the *nicotiana tabacum* grown in the West Indies. Historian George Arents comments that "the same difference in taste exists between these two species, as between a crab apple and an Albemarle pippin." Even tremendous duties against the importation of non-Virginian tobacco could not persuade English smokers to use the inferior tobacco grown in Jamestown. Faced with tremendous difficulties in clearing land, unfavorable farming conditions, constant conflicts with local Indians, and no valuable exports to generate revenue, the Virginia colony appeared to be doomed to failure.

John Rolfe, an Englishman working for the Virginia Company, was determined to see the colony succeed. In 1612, Rolfe imported tobacco seed from Trinidad and began to cross-breed it with native plants until he achieved a variety that was pleasing to European tastes, and in

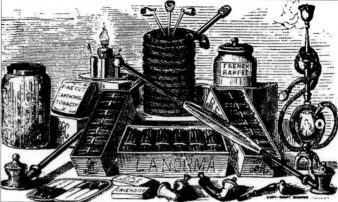

Once John Rolfe cultivated a strain of tobacco that suited European tastes, the market for Virginian tobacco exploded. Soon tobacco was the major source of revenue for Virginia and its neighbors, and the colonies began exporting tobacco to Europe in huge quantities.

1614 Rolfe's new strain of tobacco sold well in London. In 1617, 20,000 pounds of tobacco were exported from Virginia, and by 1618 that figure had doubled. Within a decade tobacco was the colony's chief source of revenue, and had become central to the life of Virginians: wives, servants and slaves were purchased with tobacco, wages were paid with tobacco, and goods were valued in tobacco.

In contrast to the Spanish and English, France never developed its own tobacco plantations in Louisiana and the West Indies, and in consequence became dependent upon tobacco from the English colonies in North America. Even when France was at war with England, its rulers granted English traders a special license to import American tobacco: ships carrying only tobacco were allowed to unload at a French port and return to England empty. It has been suggested that French addiction to Virginian tobacco may have been a factor in persuading the French to take the side of the American colonists in the Revolutionary War. Certainly, tobacco was the main source of collateral used in obtaining loans from France.

Prior to the Virginia colony's successful development of a tobacco export trade, the Dutch had been the world's greatest merchant power. Lacking their own source of cheap, high-quality tobacco, the Dutch became unable to supply Scandinavia, Russia and markets further abroad with all the tobacco they craved, and gradually lost valuable monopolies and favorable

trade concessions to the English. By 1700, tobacco was so important in English trade that it was considered to be the mainstay of English shipping. The English merchant fleet began to expand more rapidly than the Dutch, leading to the English dominance of world trade and the seas that continued into the 20th century. Dutch traders had to content themselves with a smaller role in the tobacco triangle trade, becoming one of the principle exporters of African slaves to Virginia.

Virginia's colonists were eager for all the labor they could get. Seeing that tobacco was leading to quick fortunes and that tobacco generated a higher return per acre than any other crop, Virginians all but abandoned every other crop and endeavor. Colonists began to grow tobacco in every available clearing, including city streets and marketplaces. A contemporary description of Jamestown describes the colony's tobacco-driven delirium: "the palizado's broken, the bridge in pieces, the well of fresh water spoiled; the storehouse used for the church… the colony [is] dispersed all about, planting tobacco." Colonists took out loans from English creditors in order to purchase ever-increasing numbers of slaves to help them cultivate more tobacco, as well new land in the inland Piedmont region, and in the Carolinas, Maryland, Kentucky and Tennessee. While the market for tobacco in England was expanding rapidly, it was still quickly saturated. Supply rapidly outpaced demand and prices dove. Many

Chesapeake colonists suddenly found themselves with vast acreages of unprofitable tobacco and enormous debts to English creditors; by 1776, tobacco farmers owed English mercantile houses millions of pounds. Many residents of the "Tobacco Coast" began to listen with interest to plans some northern colonists had to limit or sever ties with England, which would allow them to avoid paying their debts. The Revolutionary War was not far off.

After the Revolution
Despite the loss of access to English markets immediately following independence, the US continued to increase its production of tobacco, which was now enjoying increased popularity in the rapidly expanding local market. While Spaniards preferred cigars, Frenchmen took snuff, and Englishmen smoked pipes, most Americans preferred to chew their tobacco. One foreign visitor described the young US as "the land of the moving jaw", and suggested Americans adopt the spittoon as their national symbol. Tobacco was grown widely from Maryland to South Carolina. The 1860 Census for Virginia and North Carolina listed 348 tobacco factories, virtually all of which produced chewing tobacco.

The 1861 outbreak of the US Civil War was devastating to tobacco growers in the southern states. Shortly after the outbreak of war, Jefferson Davis forbade southern farmers from planting inedibles, encouraging them to instead grow food to feed the cities and armies of the South. Tobacco factories were converted for use as prisons, hospitals and plants for making military supplies. Soldiers from both sides yearned for the vices they no longer had access to, and some Rebel soldiers found that Yankee soldiers were quite willing to trade coffee for tobacco during breaks in the fighting. After the war, however, the South found it difficult to bring tobacco production back to its old level. Pillaged farms, lack of capital and lack of slave labor combined to set the tobacco industry back considerably.

These turbulent conditions allowed dynamic elements, such as the Virginia-based Reynolds family, to expand their holdings considerably. By the 1890s, Richard Joshua Reynolds had lead his R.J. Reynolds Tobacco Company to a dominant position in the chewing tobacco market. At the same time, James Buchanan "Buck" Duke consolidated a group of chewing tobacco companies, as well as a few producers of a new variety of not-very-profitable miniature cigars called cigarettes, into a new corporation called the American Tobacco Company. Though chewing tobacco was the company's main product, Duke wanted to convert cigarettes from a slow-to-manufacture luxury item into a mass market consumer product. In 1880, 21-year-old inventor James Albert Bonsack patented a new cigarette-rolling machine that revolutionized the cigarette manufacturing industry. The Bonsack machine did the work of 40 hand-rolling workers, turning out 100,000 cigarettes a day, and allowed Duke's American Tobacco Company to lower the price of its packs of 10 cigarettes to a single nickel, squeezing many competitors out of the market. In 1900, Duke's American Tobacco Company swallowed R.J. Reynolds and achieved complete dominance of the American tobacco market. In 1911, the company was cited under the Anti-

P. A. has such a joy'us way of making men glad about jimmy pipes!

R. J. REYNOLDS TOBACCO COMPANY, Winston-Salem, N.C.

Tobacco companies spent lavishly on advertising throughout the 20th century, and had little difficulty in acquiring more new customers than they lost due to concerns about health risks.

Trust Act and broken up into smaller pieces.

By now, however, the American tobacco market was large enough for dozens of companies to make large profits. The 1914 outbreak of war in Europe was a boon to tobacco growers and cigarette manufacturers, as troops overseas had easy access to cigarettes from home and quickly spread the tobacco habit to one another. Understanding how popular smoking was among enlisted men during WWII, Roosevelt declared tobacco to be a strategic wartime commodity.

Advertising vs. Science

Big tobacco companies were among the first companies to recognize the importance of branding and marketing to commercial success, and companies such as Philip Morris and R.J. Reynolds spent huge sums both to capture the business of existing smokers and to encourage non-smokers to try their products.

In 1958, US Surgeon General Dr. Leroy E. Burney concluded that the weight of evidence indicated a causative relationship between excessive smoking and lung cancer. In 1959, Burney went another step, stating that the principal factor in the increased incidence of lung cancer was smoking. Tobacco companies were united in denying that their products were health risks; a 1962 report to Philip Morris stockholders went so far as to claim, "There is growing evidence that smoking has pharmacological... effects that are of real value to the smokers." In 1982, the Surgeon General's office released an even more strongly worded warning, stating that "cigarette smoking is the major single cause of cancer mortality in the United States." The American Cancer Society believes that tobacco is the cause of almost one in five deaths in the US. Though all US states have introduced excise taxes on cigarettes, and many have begun to place some restrictions on tobacco advertising, companies like Philip Morris and R.J. Reynolds are currently enjoying higher sales than at any point in their history.

Further Reading
• Herndon, Melvin. *Tobacco in Colonial Virginia* (Williamsburg, Va.: Virginia 350th Anniversary Celebration Corporation, 1957).
• Kluger, Richard. *Ashes to Ashes* (New York: Alfred A. Knopf, 1996).
• MacInnes, C.M. *The Early English Tobacco Trade* (London: K. Paul, Trench, Trubner & Co., Ltd., 1926).
• Reynolds, Patrick and Tom Shachtman. *The Gilded Leaf* (Boston: Little, Brown and Company, 1989).

HM

A Brand New Special from Family Chronicle

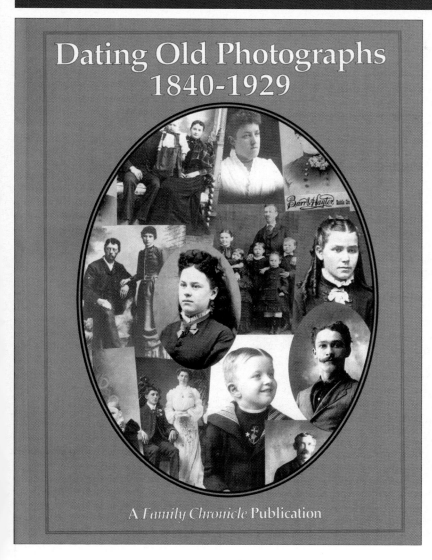

Dating Old Photographs 1840-1929

Barr & Hayter

A *Family Chronicle* Publication

YOU'VE ALMOST CERTAINLY faced the problem: you've got an album or box of old photographs but almost all of them lack any identification. *Family Chronicle's* new special can't help you to identify the subject but it probably can help you with dating when the picture was taken — often within a couple of years.

A number of books have already been published that describe how to date old photographs but they rely almost entirely on descriptions: *Family Chronicle's* book is almost all reproductions of old photographs of known date. There are over 650 pictures covering the period from 1840 to the 1920s. By comparing your undated pictures to those in our book, you will be able to compare clothing and hair fashions, the poses adopted by the subject and the background settings. The book provides convincing evidence that our ancestors were at least as fashion conscious as we are today and that their fashions changed just as frequently.

Some of *Family Chronicle's* most popular issues have been those that have included supplements featuring old photographs of known date.

Our *Dating Old Photographs* book has been compiled from a number of sources but the majority of them are photographs submitted by readers of our magazine.

To Order:

US orders: Send $12 (includes shipping) check, money order, Visa or MasterCard (including expiry date) to Family Chronicle, P.O. Box 1201, Lewiston, NY, 14092.

Canadian orders: Send $15 (includes shipping) plus GST/HST as applicable. Send cheque, money order, Visa or MasterCard (incl. expiry date) to Family Chronicle, 505 Consumers Rd., Suite 500, Toronto, ON, M2J 4V8.

Or call Toll-Free (888) 326-2476 during office hours EST with your credit card. Or order online at *www.familychronicle.com*

$12 (US) including shipping **$15** (Cdn)

Horrors that Thrilled Our Ancestors

Ron Wild looks at some of the human monsters of the past.

THE SENSATIONAL CRIME stories that thrilled our ancestors and were talked about in the taverns are the same type of stories that fascinate us today. Multiple murders and monstrous human acts are not modern phenomena, and the human fascination with these events has been evident in all ages of history.

Scotland 1435

In the medieval era, Scotland was haunted by several instances of human throwbacks who succumbed to some primitive, ferocious instinct to consume their own kind. The most notorious of these was a man named Sawney Beane. For 25 years he and his feral, inbred clan waylaid travelers and feasted on their flesh. They may have preyed upon as many as a thousand victims.

Sawney Beane was born into a farmer's family on the outskirts of Edinburgh but as a young man left with a young female companion for the southwestern coast of Galloway. There, in a cave overlooking the Irish Sea, they raised a brood of 14 children. Travelers began disappearing and it was at first thought that they had fallen prey to packs of wolves that roamed the district. As Beane's family grew and began mating between themselves, the need for food increased and more and more travelers started to disappear. It was only when a group of local residents returning from a county fair came across Beane and his clan butchering a traveler and his wife that they at last knew of the real reason for the disappearance of hundreds of people.

Beane and his clan fled into the hills, but on hearing of this atrocity King James I dispatched 400 troops and bloodhounds to hunt them down. The dogs even-

Gilles de Rais, once Marshal of France, became the country's most hated villain.

tually led the army to an opening at the bottom of a cliff. Huddled in a cavern that Sawney Beane called home were Beane, his wife, their 14 children and their 32 incest-spawned grandchildren. Suspended above them were arms, legs and human torsos. Some of the meat had been pickled for the lean months ahead. Sawney Beane and the other 26 Beane men were dismembered and left to die. The 21 Beane women were burned alive on three great bonfires. King James had ruled that they were wild beasts and did not deserve a trial.

France 1440

Gilles de Rais is known to history as a deranged French aristocrat, guilty of crimes so terrible they are difficult to contemplate. The great irony is that Rais was one of France's greatest heroes before he became its most despicable villain. Raised to be a knight, he was a soldier in the closing phases of France's Hundred Years' War with England and was a great favorite of Joan of Arc. He was Joan's most trusted lieutenant and played a crucial part in her greatest victories. He was

so appreciated by King Charles VII that, at the age of 25, he was named Marshal of France. In 1431, after Joan of Arc's capture and execution, Rais left the battlefield and returned to his estates in Brittany.

Rais now revealed a dark side that led him and his servants to capture, sodomize, mutilate and decapitate hundreds of young children, mostly boys, living on his estates. When low on funds, he was forced to sell off parts of his estate. It was when he arrogantly refused to turn over a castle to the new owner, but instead callously killed him, that he came to the attention of the Bishop of Nantes. Rais was investigated under authority of the Duke of Brittany who had designs on acquiring the Rais lands. The mutilated bodies of over 50 children were found in the tower of his castle and, under threat of torture and excommunication, Rais finally admitted to having killed 140 children — although it was felt that 300 was a more likely number. On 26 October 1440, Rais was executed by being simultaneously hanged and burned. His accomplices were burned alive.

Romania 1456

Dracula, or Vlad III as he is more properly known, was a member of an aristocratic family of Walachia, a Romanian state bordered on the north by Moldavia and the much-mythologized Transylvania. His father, Vlad II, had been nicknamed Dracul, meaning dragon, and Dracula simply means son of Dracul.

Between the ages of 13 and 17, the young Vlad was held as a hostage in a Turkish prison and it is felt that this experience may have twisted his mind and stimulated an existing streak of cruelty.

On his release from captivity, he became an officer in the Turkish army. He was made military leader for Transylvania before assuming the Walachian throne in 1456 and becoming the absolute ruler of his country. Vlad's reign was one of terror and atrocities, and though he was never the blood-drinking vampire that popular fiction has made him out to be, he did earn the nickname Vlad The Impaler. Vlad's preferred means of inflicting agony and death was to impale his victims on stakes driven through their bodies and then leave them as a very visible reminder to his enemies. On one occasion he impaled 500 Walachian noblemen who he felt were not sufficiently impressed with his rule. On other occasions, Vlad impaled the citizenry of entire towns so as not to leave in any doubt the fate of towns that would not submit voluntarily to his rule. Vlad's female subjects often bore the brunt of his sadism, which could include skinning and boiling alive those women he felt had committed indiscretions. It is believed that during his six-year reign he may have been responsible for 100,000 tortuous deaths. In January 1477, Vlad was killed near Budapest in a battle against the Turks.

England 1802

Sweeney Todd was born into a harsh London life in 1748. After being orphaned at a young age, he became a cutler's apprentice and learned the trade of manufacturing and sharpening knives. After spending some time in Newgate Prison for attempting to supplement his income by cutting a few purses, the 19-year-old Todd set up shop as a "flying barber," one of the city's countless gypsy tradesmen who practiced their craft wherever they could find space. Flying barbers guarded their territory jealously, and contemporary newspapers frequently reported episodes of territorial battles ending in

Vlad III was nicknamed The Impaler after his favorite method of executing his opponents.

bloodshed.

It was during Sweeney's time as a flying barber that circumstantial evidence points to the Demon Barber committing his first murder. One day when a drunken cavalier came to him for a shave and reported having experienced the favors of a woman matching the description of Todd's lover, then Todd used his razor as a weapon for the first time. "My first 'un was a young gent at Hyde Park Corner," Todd later confessed. "Slit him from ear to ear, I did."

Several years later, Todd moved into a new shop on Fleet Street. The church next door to Todd's shop had been rebuilt several times prior to 1785, and had once occupied more land on the narrow block. Beneath the church lay forgotten and seldom-used tunnels, some of which served as catacombs for long-dead parishioners. One of these tunnels ran on a 45-degree angle beneath the church, passing under Chancery Lane between Bell Yard and Fleet Street. Somehow Todd had learned of these tunnels, though whether it was before or after he purchased the lease will never be known. Todd

used the skills he had learned as a cutler's apprentice to build an ingenious device that would help him get rid of the evidence of his crimes. Cutting a square hole in the center of the floor of his shop, he attached a pipe to the center of the bottom of the cut out, and fastened the pipe to the ceiling of the basement. He then fashioned a series of levers that would allow him to withdraw a latch holding the square in place. When a customer reclined in the chair, his weight would cause the trap door to rotate, tumbling the unwitting victim into the basement below. Another barber chair, fastened to the bottom of the trapdoor would swing up into place, ready for the next victim. Todd stored the bodies in the abandoned crypts beneath the church — at least at first.

Little is known of Todd's accomplice. Her surname was Lovett, but whether her first name was Margery or Sarah remains a mystery. Lovett was a widow whose first husband had died under mysterious circumstances, and she had become Todd's lover. Lovett's pie shop was one of the most celebrated shops for the sale of veal and pork pies that London had ever produced. At noon every day, when the first batch of pies was sold, there was a tremendous rush to obtain them. The pies had a flavor never surpassed and rarely equaled; the pastry was of the most delicate construction, and impregnated with the aroma of delicious gravy that defied description. The two-story shop had a storefront and sales counter at street level and the basement of the shop was the bakery. A false wall could be opened to reveal the catacombs behind. It was through this false wall that Todd would apparently deliver the ghastly pie fillings — namely, his butchered victims.

The pair were caught after the smell of death and decay wafting into the church became unbearable. The authorities launched an investigation, descending into the bowels of the church and inspecting the vaults.

After a few moments of searching, they stumbled across the crypt of the Weston family, which had been one of the Demon Barber's favorite dumping grounds. What they found there was reported in the newspapers in gruesome detail. "Piled one upon each other and reaching halfway up to the ceiling, lay a decomposing mass of human remains. Heaped one upon another heedlessly tossed into the disgusting heap any

In 1979, the story of Sweeney Todd, The Demon Barber of Fleet Street, was made into a Broadway musical starring Angela Lansbury and Len Cariou.

way, lay pieces of gaunt skeletons with pieces of flesh here and there only adhering to the bones. Heads in a similar state of decay were tumbled about, the whole enough to strike such horror into the heart of any man," wrote the *Courier* in its account of Sweeney Todd's trial.

It was soon realized that Todd was murdering his clients, and disposing of the evidence by

having Lovett serve the flesh in her famous pies. Lovett was narrowly saved from a lynch mob and taken to a cell in Newgate Prison, while on 25 January 1802, Todd was strung up on the gallows before a crowd of thousands, where he apparently "died hard".

After Todd's execution, his body was given over to a handful of learned "barber-surgeons" where it was dissected. Sweeney Todd ended up, like so many of his victims, as a pile of meat and bones. **HM**

The Stock Exchange

Barbara Krasner-Khait traces the development of stock exchanges.

THREE PEOPLE SIT AT A WOODEN table in a dimly lit London coffeehouse, deep in conversation. One of them, a would-be explorer, needs funds to support his adventure to unknown lands and riches. Another is a businessman with an urge to buy into a piece of the action. The third brokers the deal and closes the transaction. The businessman invests his money hoping to get a profitable return. The explorer can now buy the materials he needs to make the journey. Both parties get what they want. And the broker earns a little something for his troubles.

Such was the spirit of the London Stock Exchange in its nascent days. Throughout 17th-century London, people gathered in the city's coffeehouses to either invest or raise money. The government could sell its bonds there. Joint-stock companies and trading companies could sell their shares.

The stock exchange, or bourse as it was known in other parts of Europe, first appeared in the mid-16th century at markets and trade fairs. Transactions consisted mainly of buying and selling shares in trading companies.

Over time, the practice grew and moved indoors to coffeehouses. Some 150 brokers from the Royal Exchange formed a club at Jonathan's Coffee House in London and in 1773, voted to change its name to the Stock Exchange.

More and more people became interested in having their money work harder for them. They saw an opportunity to increase their personal worth based on a paper system of stocks rather than on the time-honored system of land acquisition. Says David Liss, author of *Conspiracy of Paper*, "There was incredible concern about lower-and middle-class people neglecting their labors and instead buying lottery tickets or playing the market. Their desire to rise above their station was described as greed,

After being kicked out of the Royal Exchange for rowdiness, London's brokers moved their business to Jonathan's Coffee House.

something that became detrimental to [England's] financial well-being, because they weren't making shoes or barrels."

Continental Bourses

While the London Stock Exchange was certainly the largest, continental Europe boasted its own bourses. Trading in Amsterdam, for instance, began at the end of the 15th century in the streets and on

The Philadelphia Stock Exchange was the first exchange in the US.

bridges. The beginning of the exchange dates back to 1602 with the start of the "VOC" — *Verenigde Oostindische Compagnie*, or the Dutch East India Company — hailed by the Dutch as the first multinational company in the world and the first to issue shares. Amsterdam led the world's securities market until 1795 when French troops overtook the city. The Paris Bourse, first established in 1720, was a strong contender as a leading exchange during the mid-1800s. It lost steam as a result of the Franco-Prussian War of 1870.

London then emerged as the most powerful exchange until 1914. Not only did the London Exchange deal in greater volumes, it also was considered to be the most international.

The Stock Market in the US

The urge for expansion and growth was clearly not limited to the boundaries of Europe. Philadelphia was young America's financial center. The first US stock exchange, the Philadelphia Stock Exchange, was established there in 1790.

As the American economy grew, so did the securities markets in Baltimore, Boston, New York and Philadelphia.

New York City soon began to challenge Philadelphia's prominence as the national financial center. In 1792, 21 brokers gathered under a buttonwood tree outside 68 Wall Street in New York City and signed what became known as the Buttonwood Agreement: "We, the Subscribers, Brokers, for the Purchase and Sale of Public Stock, do hereby solemnly promise and pledge ourselves to each other, that we will not buy or sell from this day for any person whatsoever any kind of Public Stock, at a less rate than one quarter per cent Commission on the specie value, and that we give preference to each other in our negotiations."

Their first meeting was held at Merchant's Coffee House, continuing the London tradition. But they wanted a place of their own and built the Tontine Coffee House at the corner of Wall and Water Streets. They offered 203 shares at $200 each and only members were able to participate in the auctions there. Thus, the New York Stock Exchange was born, though it would not be called that for some time.

Philadelphia brokerages captured much of the War of 1812's federal bond business. In 1817, their New York counterparts sent broker William Lamb to Philadelphia to examine the Exchange's organizational structure. When he returned, several leading brokers met and composed a constitution much like that of Philadelphia. Twenty-eight people representing seven firms became the original members of the Board of Brokers, soon renamed the New York Stock and Exchange Board. They moved into rented space on the second floor of 40 Wall Street.

In 1800, about nine percent of the US's foreign commerce passed through New York. The opening of the Erie Canal catalyzed the shift of money from Philadelphia to New York and caused New York's explosive growth. By 1860, 62 percent of foreign commerce went through New York. And the growth naturally meant more business for the city's brokers. Foreign investors, particularly from England, looked to cash in on the fast-growing American economy. The demand for new securities for new companies and state bonds was high. By 1837, when the boom came to an end, New York practices and the mania in canal securities helped make this booming city the country's new financial capital.

Money Makes The World Go Around

Stock exchanges didn't just trade

Meeting under a tree on New York's Wall Street, traders formalized the Buttonwood Agreement for the sale and purchase of public stock.

in local markets. A number of "foreign" securities were quoted on stock exchanges elsewhere. For instance, French and American railway stocks were also listed in London. In 1852, a large Austrian loan was issued simultaneously in London and Frankfurt and was traded in Paris as well.

The American economy continued to attract investments from overseas. The influx of gold from California in 1849 created a major boom, expanded the money supply and increased the backing of the dollar. Foreign investors, who shied away from American securities during the depression that began in 1837, now put their money into American railroads and government bonds. The Mining Exchange appeared on Wall Street to handle volume on a formal basis. By 1856, traded securities included 360 railroad stocks, 985 bank stocks, 75 insurance stocks, and hundreds of corporate, municipal, state and federal bonds.

But an efficient world market needed an efficient communications system. Since face-to-face meetings would certainly not be possible, and carrier pigeons didn't seem to work out very well (an experiment that failed on the London-Paris route), something more was needed. Something that would eliminate the delay causing London to quote days-old prices on Austrian bonds from the Ams-

terdam bourse. Something that would eliminate the wide disparity between American and British prices for the same securities.

Undersea cables and the telegraph began to address the situation. Critical telegraph lines developed between London, Paris, Amsterdam and Vienna. As significant as these improvements were to stock exchange transactions, it was the telephone that eventually created the best link. In 1891 the first telephone line linked the London Stock Exchange to the Paris Bourse. Using the foundation of the transatlantic cable laid in 1866, London and New York connected, transmitting an estimated 5,000 cable messages a day by the beginning of WWI.

The London and New York markets were moving closer together. While the US remained an importer of foreign capital for some time, it was beginning to handle foreign bond issues of its own.

A New Generation

Another depression in 1857 caused half of New York's brokers to go out of business. The Mining Exchange was gone, trading on the curb disappeared, and the New York Stock and Exchange Board now had some empty seats, open for the younger, more aggressive brokers.

These new brokers had plenty of opportunity during the Civil War. In 1861, the US went off the gold standard and Wall Street panicked. Trading and speculation in gold began on Wall Street. The price of gold tended to fall after Union victories and rise with Confederate ones. Though the Board banned gold trading in 1862, curb brokers organized Gilpin's News Room in 1863 for the distinct purpose of trading it.

The ability to get and communicate information meant money. Brokers used agents attached to each army to get news from the front. Wall Street knew the outcome of the Battle of Gettysburg before Lincoln did. Though it was criticized as unpatriotic, there was just too much money to be made and it looked like the war was going to take a while. A vast influx of bonds and bondholders transformed Wall Street almost overnight and made Wall Street the second largest exchange in the world, after London.

The trading floor of the New York Stock Exchange, as seen in 1894.

This unprecedented boom led to changes on the Street. The Regular Board, which became the New York Stock Exchange (NYSE) in 1863, couldn't keep up with the volume, creating the opportunity for other exchanges to develop. One of these, the Open Board of Brokers, exceeded the volume of the NYSE and introduced several innovations. For instance, it engaged in continuous auction, where trading took place simultaneously at designated places on the trading floor known as posts. It also necessitated more precise knowledge of current prices and created much higher trading volume. In 1867, the first stock ticker entered the financial world, printing stock prices it received from the trading floor on paper tape.

In 1869, the Open Board of Brokers and the NYSE merged.

Yet another panic occurred in 1873. The NYSE announced for the first time in its history that it would close for an indefinite period, though it was only closed for 10 days. The effect on the economy lasted much longer — six years. And during that time, railroad stocks lost about half their value and 287 brokerage concerns closed.

The Gorgon Of Wall Street
By 1900, "industrials" were rapidly becoming the dominant stock group. Industrialization required massive amounts of capital and industry leaders turned to Wall Street. No one personified Wall Street more than John Pierpont Morgan. A pro at restructuring, he reorganized the railroads, General Electric, International Harvester and US Steel. He brought Wall Street from the Civil War era to the emerging global economy.

In 1893, Morgan personally bailed the US government out of financial trouble following a four-hour meeting with President Grover Cleveland. Cleveland was at his mercy. Theodore Roosevelt had no choice either when the Panic of 1907 hit. With no central bank to pump money into the system, the Roosevelt administration turned to J.P. Morgan, who, according to business history author John Steele, was "the only man with the power and prestige to command the cooperation of all Wall Street." Morgan called upon his circle of colleagues and raised $27 million in five minutes to help brokers meet their obligations. J.P. Morgan and Company was the de facto central bank of America.

A national system was finally put in place in 1913 with the Federal Reserve Act, creating 12 district banks. The Federal Reserve Bank of New York maintained strong ties to Wall Street through its president, Benjamin Strong, who had a close connection to Morgan.

The World Capital Of Capital
An initial panic occurred at the outbreak of WWI. The London Stock Exchange — the greatest security market in the world — dealt with a large volume of international business and became subject to the war. On 31 July 1914, the London Stock Exchange announced it would suspend trading — for the first time ever — until further notice. Bourses in other parts of Europe did the same. Prices fell sharply. Stockbrokers who had purchased stock for foreign clients were not able to get paid.

For America, the war meant unprecedented economic opportunity, just as it had in the past with the Mexican-American and Civil Wars. Other countries moved their gold to the US for safekeeping. Britain, France and Russia needed supplies and materials and turned to American industry, creating a huge bull market. General Motors, for instance, closed 1914 at $81^{1}/_{2}$ and was at 500 a year later. Bethlehem Steel experienced sharp increases, reaching as high as 600 during the war. New York investment banks helped finance the war, heavily relied upon by the Triple Entente for capital.

At the beginning of the war, the US was the world's largest debtor; by the end, it was the world's largest creditor. New York took center stage as the world's financial capital.

Stock Exchanges Around the World

More than 50 stock exchanges exist throughout the world, ranging from Argentina to Indonesia to Panama to Sri Lanka to Turkey. Aside from the major US stock exchanges and those of London, Amsterdam, and Paris, some other well-known world markets include:

Frankfurt Stock Exchange: Established in 1585 and is now part of the Deutsche Börse Group

Hong Kong: Though security trading in Hong Kong dates back to the mid-1800s, a formal market first appeared in 1891 with the Association of Stockbrokers in Hong Kong. It was renamed the Hong Kong Stock Exchange in 1914.

Tokyo Stock Exchange: Established in May 1878, caused by a request for a public trading institution to deal with the country's new securities system and public bond negotiation.

The Walls Come Crashing Down

In 1928 Federal Reserve President Benjamin Strong said, "The problem now is to shape our policy as to avoid a calamitous break in the stock market…and at the same time accomplish if possible" the recovery of Europe. A prophesy, perhaps. During 1928, the US stock market grew nearly 50 percent. On the eve of 1929, many who knew the market well felt a dramatic change was about to occur. Wall Street, aided by the power of Madison Avenue advertising, pitched consumerism and the means — through stock purchases — to pay for it. A young shop girl new to New York could easily make a $15,000 profit and warm herself in a new fur coat. Investors borrowed heavily to finance their stock purchases, and relied on margin loans from their brokers, who then took out bro-

kers' loans from banks and the stock exchange floor. Wild speculation continued. By May, stocks were being traded well beyond their real value. A financial press survey indicated that most brokers became concerned about their margin loans that summer and began to raise margin requirements to 50 percent on most stocks. Richard Whitney, president of the New York Stock Exchange at that time, later testified that "during the period of 1929, spring-summer even, our brokers felt that terrific inflation had taken place and raised their margin requirements from a customary 20 percent."

Charles Merrill, who later founded brokerage firm Merrill Lynch, was the first well-known man of Wall Street to see the crash coming. He futilely pleaded with then President Calvin Coolidge to speak against speculation. Merrill liquidated his firm's stock and advised his clients to do the same early in 1929.

The US stock market continued to rise and peaked at the end of August. Prices dropped in September and early October but speculation continued. On 18 October, the stock market began to fall. Six days later on "Black Thursday," panic set in and nearly 13 million shares traded. The gallery at the New York Stock Exchange was filled with people, screaming and crying. Unmet margin calls and urgent cries of "Sell, sell!" were rampant. By noon on that day, paper losses had reached $9.5 billion. Panic hit again on the following Monday and continued on Tuesday ("Black Tuesday," 29 October) when 16 million shares traded. Unmet margin calls dumped

The New York Stock Exchange can still claim to be the capital of the financial world.

stocks onto the market, causing prices to collapse. The entire stock market collapsed.

There was no easy remedy to this market condition, no Morgan to step in and save the day. The Federal Reserve, weakened by the 1929 death of Benjamin Strong, could not help. And the public now demanded protection that eventually came in the form of 1933's banking and securities regulations.

It was only with WWII that the economy fully recovered. Again, war presented an economic opportunity to be seized.

Over the course of some 500 years, buyers and sellers have continued to come together for the purposes of financial gain. They no longer meet at Jonathan's. They've been replaced by millions of investors trading at dozens of world markets, continuing to expand their world and wallet.

Further Reading

• Geisst, Charles R. *Wall Street: A History.* New York: Oxford University Press, 1997.
• Gordon, John Steele. *The Great Game: The Emergence of Wall Street as a World Power, 1653-2000.* New York: Touchstone, 1999.
• Mitchie, R.C. *The London and New York Stock Exchanges 1850-1914.* London: Allen & Unwin, 1987.
• Morgan, E. Victor and W.A. Thomas. *The London Stock Exchange: Its History and Functions, 2nd Edition.* New York: St. Martin's Press, 1969.
• Thomas, Gordon and Max Morgan-Witts. *The Day the Bubble Burst: A Social History of the Wall Street Crash of 1929.* Garden City, N.Y.: Doubleday, 1979.

HM

STEP INTO HISTORY.
THEN GET OUT OF THE WAY.

Relive an era with Mississippi's Civil War battle re-enactments

and magnificent antebellum homes.

Or catch a casino show, stroll along the beach and trace the origin

of the blues. Call 1-888-669-7662

for your free Mississippi *Travel Planner*.

THE SOUTH'S WARMEST WELCOME

www.visitmississippi.org

Hear Ye! Hear Ye!

Suzanne Rent delivers the history of news transmission.

PEOPLE HAVE ALWAYS wanted to know what was going on in the world around them. News of battles, changing political conditions, natural disasters and, of course, the weather was a concern to everyone. While people receive the news today by radio, television, Internet or a newspaper on the doorstep, receiving news in the past required much more effort and innovation.

Early News
Since spoken language first developed, news traveled by word of mouth. News reports of early people concerned their survival, such as the location of food, the weather and natural disasters.

Some of the early forms of communications required human messengers. One of the most famous, though probably mythical, stories of a human messenger was the story of Phidippides, who in 490BC ran from Marathon to Athens — a distance of 22.5 miles or 36.2 kilometers — to warn the Athenians of an approaching army.

Some forms of human messenger systems were quite effective for their time. Early messaging systems used humans, sometimes on horseback, in a relay system to send messages to other cities or villages. During Cyrus the Great's reign (580-529BC), horses and messengers were stationed at several posts throughout the Persian countryside. When a message was to be delivered, it would pass from one messenger who then rode to the next post to relay the message. The relay continued until the message reached its destination.

The relay system of the Roman Empire was called the

Human messengers like these Egyptian runners were used to transmit news in the ancient world.

cursus publicus. Messengers of the *cursus publicus* traveled 50 miles (80km) a day to deliver a regular message and up to 100 miles (160km) for an urgent message.

Chinese ruler Kublai Khan (1215-94AD) introduced more frequent switch points to prevent horses from becoming tired. When a messenger was about to arrive at the next post, he would blow a horn to announce his arrival. The next messenger would be waiting on horseback to take the message to the next post. This system reached speeds comparable to the Pony Express of the young US in the 1860s, which could carry news from Missouri to California in 10 days.

Town Criers
The position of town crier started in 1066 in England. The crier, who was appointed by the king, was held in great standing in the community. The town crier was often one of few people in a town who could read. Dressed in a brightly-colored uniform and often ringing a bell or playing a drum, the town crier read the news from a

written proclamation. After he finished the reading, the proclamation was posted on the door of a local inn. This is where the common name for newspapers, "Post," originated.

Often town criers were a husband-and-wife team. The law protected town criers and anyone who harmed one was charged with treason. Other countries that used town criers included Holland, France and colonial North America. Town criers still exist today, but their position is usually ceremonial.

Birds as Messengers
Homing pigeons were used as early as 2900BC in Egypt to relay messages. The birds were released from incoming ships to announce the arrival of an important visitor. Pigeons were also used in ancient Greece to spread news of the outcomes of the Olympic Games.

Mesopotamian king Sargon Akkad used a combination of human and pigeon messengers. A messenger always traveled with a pigeon. If the messenger was attacked during his travels, he released the pigeon. The returning bird was a signal that a new messenger should be sent by another route.

Homing pigeons continued to be used by the military up to the 20th century. Over 20,000 pigeons were killed sending messages for the British Air Force during WWI.

Telegraphy
Human messengers were not as quick and reliable as other forms of long-distance communication. Telegraphing signals via smoke, fire, drums, horns and mirrors was often more efficient.

The word telegraphy is of Greek origin — *tele* meaning distant and *graphein* meaning to write. Some of the earliest forms of acoustic telegraphy were simple. The first recorded use of stentors — shouters who passed messages between posts — took place in Persia in 315BC. Stentors were used for high-priority messages and could deliver messages up to 30 times faster than runners. In the Greek city-states, rulers would send messages through several men standing on hilltops shouting messages to each other until the message reached its destination.

Fire signals were used to send messages during the siege of Troy. Some other visual telegraphic systems were more elaborate. In his *Histories*, Polybius described one such system, possibly invented by the Carthaginians. Two identical vases filled with water were placed on two distant hills. In each vase was a pole decorated with various symbols. Water was then emptied or added to the vessels allowing certain symbols on the pole to be visible. The waving of a flag or torch marked the beginning and the ending of the message.

The Greeks used another elaborate method around 500BC. A series of brick walls were built with indents along the top. A watcher would stand on top of each brick wall. Each indent in the wall represented a letter. A message was sent by lighting a fire above the appropriate indent. The watcher on the next wall would decipher and relay the message. A similar system used in Persia around 500BC was so effective that it took only one day for the Persian king to receive news of events taking place in distant Asia Minor.

Visual systems were only as good as the eyesight of the watchmen receiving the messages. French engineer Claude Chappe invented the semaphore visual telegraph during the French Revolution. Chappe thought a line of communication

Town criers read the news aloud to the largely illiterate townsfolk.

between war fronts was necessary. Towers were built on several hills between Paris and Lille, each with two arms or semaphores used to make the signals. These semaphores could make 49 combinations and each was assigned a letter or symbol. Unlike the earlier methods, Chappe's invention used telescopes, thus requiring fewer towers.

Newspaper Forerunners
Perhaps the forerunner to the newspaper was the *Acta Diurna*, which means "daily events". Once kept as a secret record of political events in Rome, Julius Caesar ordered that the *Acta*

Claude Chappe devised a system of telegraphy that used telescopes.

Diurna be published. The text was events of general interest carved in stone or metal.

Early European newsletters began to appear in the late Roman Empire and the Middle Ages. The contents usually included issues of trade, business and some politics. While only a small group of the rich and literate benefited from these early newsletters, they established a routine of regular publication similar to today's newspapers.

The invention of the printing press by Johann Gutenburg in the mid-15th century created the ability to provide news on a mass scale. The ensuing spread of literacy helped create a demand for written information.

By the 16th century, pamphlets or newsbooks had become a popular form of news reporting. These usually dealt with a particular subject, such as great battles or tragedies. During the Renaissance, newsbooks were read in coffeehouses all over London where people could read them and discuss the news of the day.

The first newspaper was a called a *coranto,* which is Dutch for "current news". These papers covered international events and appeared on a regular basis. The first English newspaper was actually a translation of a Dutch coranto called *Corante.* The first US newspaper was called *Public Occurences*. It was published in 1690 by Benjamin Harris, but only lasted for one issue because Harris didn't have a license. The first permanent US newspaper, the *Boston News-Letter*, lasted for 72 years. The first Canadian newspaper, *The Halifax Gazette*, was first published in 1752. It still exists today as a government publication.

The creation of newspapers published on daily basis and the spread of literacy meant that everyone could receive the news quickly and efficiently.

Hindsight

A selection of new books and products we believe may be of interest to *History Magazine* readers.

Beginning in the Industrial Revolution and finishing with the latest technology, **Brand New: How Entrepreneurs Earned Consumers' Trust from Wedgwood to Dell** looks at the history of six major brands. Earning customers' loyalty is intrinsic to brand success and Nancy R. Koehn's book details the history of the six entrepreneurs behind the brands covered in the book; Josiah Wedgwood, H.J. Heinz, Marshall Field, Estée Lauder, Howard Schultz of Starbucks and Michael Dell of Dell Computers. Historical background is included with each story and primary sources are included. From Harvard Business School Press, hard cover, 468 pages, with several black and white pictures, extensive notes and an index. Priced at about $40 US or $64 Cdn. Available in bookshops everywhere.

Now available in paperback, **Everyday Life in the 1800s** by Marc McCutheon offers an in-depth understanding of that fascinating century. The 14 chapters are laid out with a brief introduction, followed by a glossary of objects and terms of the period. Some chapters have short focus boxes covering subjects such as

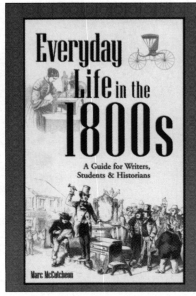

medical treatments and the prices of tailoring for the period. Of interest is the chapter devoted to slang and everyday speech; words such as "dude" and "bodaciously" have been in the lexicon for a lot longer than you might suppose. 310 pages, soft cover, with several timelines, not indexed. Formerly published in hard cover with the title *The Writer's Guide to Everyday Life in the 1800s*. At about $17 US or $27 Cdn from bookstores and from Writer's Digest Books, 1507 Dana Ave., Cincinnati, OH 45207. Tel: 800-289-0396.

Originally published in 1957, **Domestic Life in Virginia in the Seventeenth Century** looks at the society of the early European settlers. Founded in 1607, Jamestown, Virginia, was the first permanent settlement of Europeans in North America. In the first half of her book, author Annie Lash Jester covers the history of the settlement beginning with the first women arriving a

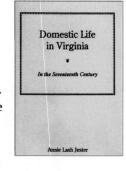

year after the colony's establishment. The second part of the book deals with the homes and lives of the settlers, covering everything from servants to funerals. 91 pages, soft cover with an index and several black and white pictures. At about $12. Reprinted by the Genealogical Publishing Co., Inc., 1001 N. Calvert St., Baltimore MD 21202, *www.Genealogical.com* or 1-800-548-1806.

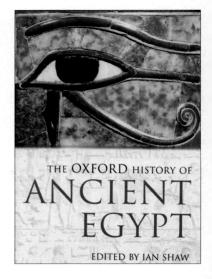

The Oxford History of Ancient Egypt covers Egypt's history from the early Stone Age through to its incorporation into the Roman Empire. A different author covers each period, but consistency is brought to the work by editor Ian Shaw. Understanding one of the world's first great civilizations is made easy by this beautiful and heavy tome featuring many black and white photographs of Egyptian artifacts. From Oxford University Press, 512 pages, hard cover, with 24 color plates, several maps, a chronology and an index. At about $36 US or $72 Cdn. Available in bookshops everywhere.

The US Civil War has shaped the American psyche like no other event. A collection of letters, journal and diary entries and military

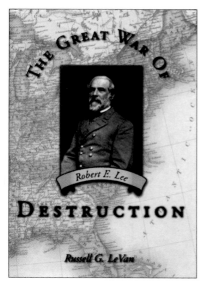

battle records from the Civil War are brought together in **The Great War of Destruction** by Russell G. LeVan, which details the tragic war from a Southern soldier's point of view. The book is divided into two sections: Memories of the Civil War and From Confederate Archives. The sections are full of testimony from first-hand experiences, giving insight into the people behind the war. From Pentland Press, Inc., hard cover, 656 pages, black and white photographs. No index. Priced at about $50 US or $70 Cdn. Available in bookshops everywhere.

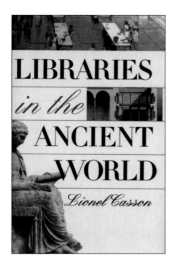

A wonderful book for those who love libraries and the books within, **Libraries in the Ancient World** by Lionel Casson details the early history of the library. Casson's book begins in the fifth

century BC with the private collections of clay tablets amassed by readers in the Middle East. The library at Alexandria, founded by Ptolemy I in the third century BC as the world's first public library, is discussed at length. From Alexandria, libraries spread across the ancient world through the Roman Empire to the first Christian monastic libraries. The change from rolls to codices is also covered. From Yale University Press, hard cover, 177 pages, black and white illustrations, with notes and an index. Priced at about $23 US or $35 Cdn. Available in bookshops everywhere.

Naming Canada: Stories about Canadian Place Names reveals the history behind the names of Canadian places like Ladysmith

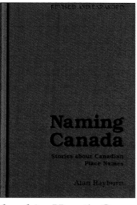

in British Columbia, Heart's Content in Newfoundland and the numerous place names with the word "devil" included. The names covered are not divided geographically, but by origin. Author Alan Rayburn covers the different pronunciations of place names, a phenomenon compounded by Canada having two official languages. The book also mentions some of Canada's misrepresenting names such as the Thousand Islands (Rayburn informs us that there are actually 1,149 islands). Revised and expanded, 360 pages, soft cover, with an index. At about $25 from University of Toronto Press, 5201 Dufferin St., Toronto, ON M3H 5T8 Canada. Tel: 800-565-9523, fax: 800-221-9985.

The Catholics of Ulster: A History details the history of Catholics in the former province of Ulster (now divided between Northern Ireland and Ireland) from 8000BC

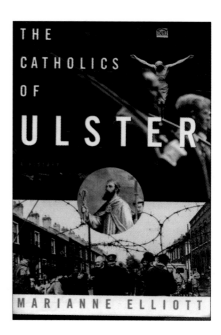

to the Good Friday Agreement of April 1998. Ulster, for both Catholics and Protestants, has a history created in part from misunderstanding, lies and half-truths. After nine years of research, Ulster-born author Marianne Elliott reveals the history of a people set apart. Chapters cover the Cromwellian occupation of the island in the 17th century, the Potato Famine of the early 19th century and the conflicts and uneasy peaces of the 20th century. From Basic Books, 642 pages, hard cover, with maps, extensive notes and index. At about $35 US or $53 Cdn. Available in bookshops everywhere.

Bound by Tradition

Jodi Avery looks at the abandoned Chinese practice of footbinding.

LEGEND SURROUNDS the once popular Chinese tradition of foot binding. The practice of making women's feet as small as possible originated in a story of a Chinese prince with a foot fetish.

It is said that Prince Li Houzhu (936-978AD) was deeply in love with one of his concubines, Yao Niang, because of her elegance and tiny, delicate feet. Houzhu once wrote that she walked with such grace that "she skimmed over the top of golden lilies." Wealthy women of China who wanted to be "lily-footed" like this fabled concubine began to bind their feet to make them small and elegant.

Upper-class Chinese women began binding their feet sometime during the Song (Sung) Dynasty (960-1279AD). The vast majority of women during the Yuan (Mongol) Dynasty (1279-1368), the Ming Dynasty (1368-1644) and the Qing (Ching) Dynasty (1644-1911) had their feet bound, including the lower classes.

The process of foot binding was very painful and time consuming. The initial binding was private, involving only the mother and daughter, although sometimes the maternal grandmother would observe the binding. The daughter would have her feet bound for the first time between the ages of six and 11. To begin the process, the mother would wash and massage the young girl's feet with very hot water and herbs. Next, each toe except the big toe was broken. The broken toes were then turned under and pressed tightly into the sole of the foot. The position was bound in place by wrapping white cloths that were two inches

Most lotus shoes were about four inches long, though three-inch-long shoes were considered better still.

wide and 10 feet long around the feet. The goal was to prevent the foot from growing any longer than four inches. The final step of the initial binding involved making the foot straight with the leg by breaking the arches of the foot.

The bound feet were displayed in tiny, pointed shoes, known as lotus shoes. A young girl would sew herself a collection of these in the months before her feet were bound. The shoes were made of colorful silk and decorated with embroidery.

Young girls in wealthy families were then assigned a servant to help with the daily up-keep, as it could take hours each day to keep the feet at the desired size and free from infection. The feet needed to be cleaned and massaged daily to relieve pain and promote circulation. Often, if the feet were bound too tightly and not massaged daily, skin would rot and fall off. The nails needed to be manicured to prevent them from digging into the skin and causing infection. A saying was created out of the pain women endured to create and maintain their lily-feet: "Every pair of small feet costs a bath of tears."

Women put up with the painful tradition of foot binding for many reasons. If a mother wanted to have her daughter marry into an upper-class family, the daughter's feet must be bound. When choosing a wife, men saw the feet as a sign not only of class, but of femininity, beauty and as a way to prevent infidelity.

Women's movements were so severely restricted by their tiny feet that men thought it made them less likely to wander into the arms of another lover. Lily-feet were often a part of a couple's sex life as well. Many men enjoyed kissing and caressing the foot as a part of foreplay.

Foot binding eventually spread from the upper classes to the lower classes, and made the lily-foot less a symbol of breeding and more a symbol of feminity. For the lower classes, the procedure created more problems than just pain. Bound feet inhibited women from working long hours. However much it hurt physically and financially, the lower classes highly valued foot binding in the same way as the upper classes.

In 1911, the new Chinese Republic banned foot binding, citing the health problems it created. Gangrene, ulceration, pelvic deformity and paralysis were only some of the common ailments the women faced in their quest for lily feet. The new rulers of the Republic estimated that 10 percent of women died due to complications associated with foot binding. Some aristocratic families continued to practice foot binding after the ban, and the practice was not completely abolished in China until the 1930s.

HM